Contents

Preface

◆ For over than three decades, a quiet methodological revolution has been taking place in the social sciences. A blurring of disciplinary boundaries has occurred. The social sciences and humanities have drawn closer together in a mutual focus on an interpretive, qualitative approach to research and theory. Although these trends are not new, the extent to which the "qualitative revolution" has overtaken the social sciences and related professional fields has been nothing short of amazing.

Reflecting this revolution, a host of textbooks, journals, research monographs, and readers have been published in recent years. In 1994 we published the first edition of the *Handbook of Qualitative Research* in an attempt to represent the field in its entirety, to take stock of how far it had come and how far it might yet go. The immediate success of the first edition suggested the need to offer the *Handbook* in terms of three separate volumes. So in 1998 we published a three-volume set, *The Landscape of Qualitative Research: Theories and Issues*; *Strategies of Inquiry*; and *Collecting and Interpreting Qualitative Materials*. In 2003 we offer a new three-volume set, based on the second edition of the handbook.

In 2000 we published the second edition of the *Handbook*. Although it became abundantly clear that the "field" of qualitative research is still defined primarily by tensions, contradictions, and hesitations—and that they exist in a less-than-unified arena—we believed that the handbook could and would be valuable for solidifying, interpreting, and organizing the field in spite of the essential differences that characterize it.

The first edition attempted to define the field of qualtiative research. The second edition went one step further. Building on themes in the first edition, we asked how the practices of qualitative inquiry could be used to address issues of equity and of social justice.

We have been enormously gratified and heartened by the response to the *Handbook* since its publication. Especially gratifying has been that it has been used and adapted by such a wide variety of scholars and graduate students in precisely the way we had hoped: as a starting point, a springboard for new thought and new work.

◆ The Paperback Project

The second edition of the *Landscape Series* of the *Handbook of Qualitative Research* is virtually all new. Over half of the authors from the first edition have been replaced by new contributors. Indeed, there are 33 new chapter authors or co-authors. There are six totally new chapter topics, including contributions on queer theory, performance ethnography, *testimonio*, focus groups in feminist research, applied ethnography, and anthropological poetics. All returning authors have substantially revised their original contributions, in many cases producing totally new chapters.

The second edition of the *Handbook of Qualitative Research* continues where the first edition ended. With Thomas Schwandt (Chapter 7 of this volume), we may observe that qualitative inquiry, among other things, is the name for a "reformist movement that began in the early 1970s in the academy." The interpretive and critical paradigms, in their multiple forms, are central to this movement. Indeed, Schwandt argues that this movement encompasses multiple paradigmatic formulations. It also includes complex epistemological and ethical criticisms of traditional social science research. The movement now has its own journals, scientific associations, conferences, and faculty positions.

The transformations in the field of qualitative research that were taking place in the early 1990s continued to gain momentum as we entered the new century. Today, few in the interpretive community look back with skepticism on the narrative turn. The turn has been taken, and that is all there is to say about it. Many have now told their tales from the field. Further, today we know that men and women write culture differently and that writing itself is not an innocent practice.

Experimental ways of writing first-person ethnographic texts are now commonplace. Sociologists and anthropologists continue to explore new ways of composing ethnography, and many write fiction, drama, performance texts, and ethnographic poetry. Social science journals hold fiction contests. Civic journalism shapes calls for a civic, or public, ethnography.

There is a pressing need to show how the practices of qualitative research can help change the world in positive ways. So, at the beginning of the twenty-first century, it is necessary to re-engage the promise of qualitative research as a generative form of inquiry (Peshkin, 1993) and as a form of radical democratic practice. This is the agenda of the second edition of the *Landscape Series*, as it is for the second edition of the *Handbook:* namely, to show how the discourses of qualitative research can be used to help imagine and create a free, democratic society. Each of the chapters in the three-volume set takes up this project, in one way or another.

A handbook, we were told by our publisher, should ideally represent the distillation of knowledge of a field, a benchmark volume that synthesizes an existing literature, helping to define and shape the present and future of that discipline. This mandate organized the second edition. In metaphoric terms, if you were to take one book on qualitative research with you to a desert island (or for a comprehensive graduate examination), a handbook would be the book.

We decided that the part structure of the *Handbook* could serve as a useful point of departure for the organization of the paperbacks. Thus Volume 1, titled *The Landscape of Qualitative Research: Theories and Issues*, takes a look at the field from a broadly theoretical perspective and is composed of the *Handbook*'s Parts I ("Locating the Field"), II ("Major Paradigms and Perspectives"), and III ("The Future of Qualitative Research"). Volume 2, titled *Strategies of Qualitative Inquiry*, focuses on just that and consists of Part IV of the *Handbook*. Volume 3, titled *Collecting and Interpreting Qualitative Materials*, considers the tasks of collecting, analyzing, and interpreting empirical materials and comprises the *Handbook*'s Parts IV ("Methods of Collecting and Analyzing Empirical Materials") and V ("The Art of Interpretation, Evaluation, and Presentation").

As with the first edition of the *Landscape* series, we decided that nothing should be cut from the original *Handbook*. Nearly everyone we spoke to who used the *Handbook* had his or her own way of using it, leaning heavily on certain chapters and skipping others altogether. But there was consensus that this reorganization made a great deal of sense both pedagogically and economically. We and Sage are committed to making this iteration of the *Handbook* accessible for classroom use. This commitment is reflected in the size, organization, and price of the paperbacks, as well as in the addition of end-of-book bibliographies.

It also became clear in our conversations with colleagues who used the *Handbook* that the single-volume, hard-cover version has a distinct place and value, and Sage will keep the original version available until a revised edition is published.

◆ Organization of This Volume

The Landscape of Qualitative Research attempts to put the field of qualitative research in context. Part I locates the field, starting with history, then action research and the academy, research for whom?, and the politics and ethics of qualitative research. Part II isolates what we regard as the major historical and contemporary paradigms that now structure and influence qualitative research in the human disciplines. The chapters move from competing paradigms (positivist, postpositivist, constructivist, critical theory) to specific interpretive perspectives, feminisms, racialized discourses, cultural studies, sexualities, and queer theory. Part III considers the future of qualitative research.

◆ Acknowledgments

Of course, this book would not exist without its authors or the editorial board members for the *Handbook* on which it is based. These individuals were able to offer both long-term sustained commitments to the project and short-term emergency assistance.

In addition, we would like to thank the following individuals and institutions for their assistance, support, insights, and patience: our respective universities and departments, as well as Jack Bratich, Ben Scott, Ruoyun Bai, and Francyne Huckaby, our respective graduate students. Without them, we could never have kept this project on course. There are also several people to thank at Sage Publications. We thank Margaret Seawell, our new editor; this three-volume version of the *Handbook* would not have been possible without Margaret's wisdom, support, humor, and grasp of the field in all its current diversity.

As always, we appreciate the efforts of Greg Daurelle, the director of books marketing at Sage, along with his staff, for their indefatigable efforts in getting the word out about the *Handbook* to teachers, researchers, and methodologists around the world. Claudia Hoffman was essential in moving the series through production; we are also grateful to the *Handbook's* copy editor, Judy Selhorst, and to those whose proofreading and indexing skills were so central to the publication of the *Handbook* on which these volumes are based. Finally, as ever, we thank our spouses, Katherine Ryan and Egon Guba, for their forbearance and constant support.

The idea for this three-volume paperback version of the *Handbook* did not arise in a vacuum, and we are grateful for the feedback we received from countless teachers and students.

—Norman K. Denzin
University of Illinois at Urbana-Champaign

—Yvonna S. Lincoln
Texas A&M University

1
Introduction

The Discipline and
Practice of Qualitative Research

Norman K. Denzin and Yvonna S. Lincoln

◆ Qualitative research has a long, distinguished, and sometimes anguished history in the human disciplines. In sociology, the work of the "Chicago school" in the 1920s and 1930s established the importance of qualitative inquiry for the study of human group life. In anthropology, during the same time period, the discipline-defining studies of Boas, Mead, Benedict, Bateson, Evans-Pritchard, Radcliffe-Brown, and Malinowski charted the outlines of the fieldwork method (see Gupta & Ferguson, 1997; Stocking, 1986, 1989). The agenda was clear-cut: The observer went to a foreign setting to study the customs and habits of another society and culture (see in this volume Vidich & Lyman, Chapter 2; Tedlock, Volume 2, Chapter 6; see also Rosaldo, 1989, pp. 25-45, for criticisms of this tradition). Soon, qualitative research would be employed in other social and behavioral science disciplines, including education (especially the work of Dewey), history, political science, business, medicine, nursing, social work, and communications.

In the opening chapter in Part I of this volume, Vidich and Lyman chart many key features of this history. In this now classic analysis, they note,

AUTHORS' NOTE: We are grateful to many who have helped with this chapter, including Egon Guba, Mitch Allen, Peter Labella, Jack Bratich, and Katherine E. Ryan. We take our subtitle for this chapter from Guba and Ferguson (1997).

with some irony, that qualitative research in sociology and anthropology was "born out of concern to understand the 'other.' " Furthermore, this other was the exotic other, a primitive, nonwhite person from a foreign culture judged to be less civilized than that of the researcher. Of course, there were colonialists long before there were anthropologists. Nonetheless, there would be no colonial, and now no postcolonial, history were it not for this investigative mentality that turned the dark-skinned other into the object of the ethnographer's gaze.

Thus does bell hooks (1990, pp. 126-128) read the famous photo that appears on the cover of *Writing Culture* (Clifford & Marcus, 1986) as an instance of this mentality (see also Behar, 1995, p. 8; Gordon, 1988). The photo depicts Stephen Tyler doing fieldwork in India. Tyler is seated some distance from three dark-skinned persons. A child is poking his or her head out of a basket. A woman is hidden in the shadows of a hut. A man, a checkered white-and-black shawl across his shoulder, elbow propped on his knee, hand resting along the side of his face, is staring at Tyler. Tyler is writing in a field journal. A piece of white cloth is attached to his glasses, perhaps shielding him from the sun. This patch of whiteness marks Tyler as the white male writer studying these passive brown and black persons. Indeed, the brown male's gaze signals some desire, or some attachment to Tyler. In contrast, the female's gaze is completely hidden by the shadows and by the words of the book's title, which cross her face (hooks, 1990, p. 127). And so this cover photo of perhaps the most influential book on ethnography in the last half of the 20th century reproduces "two ideas that are quite fresh in the racist imagination: the notion of the white male as writer/authority . . . and the idea of the passive brown/black man [and woman and child] who is doing nothing, merely looking on" (hooks, 1990, p. 127).

In this introductory chapter, we will define the field of qualitative research and then navigate, chart, and review the history of qualitative research in the human disciplines. This will allow us to locate this volume and its contents within their historical moments. (These historical moments are somewhat artificial; they are socially constructed, quasi-historical, and overlapping conventions. Nevertheless, they permit a "performance" of developing ideas. They also facilitate an increasing sensitivity to and sophistication about the pitfalls and promises of ethnography and qualitative research.) We will present a conceptual framework for reading the qualitative research act as a multicultural, gendered process, and then provide a brief introduction to the chapters that follow.

2

Returning to the observations of Vidich and Lyman as well as those of hooks, we will conclude with a brief discussion of qualitative research and critical race theory (see also in this volume Ladson-Billings, Chapter 9; and in Volume 3, Denzin, Chapter 13). As we indicate in our preface, we use the metaphor of the bridge to structure what follows. We see this volume as a bridge connecting historical moments, research methods, paradigms, and communities of interpretive scholars.

◆ **Definitional Issues**

Qualitative research is a field of inquiry in its own right. It crosscuts disciplines, fields, and subject matters.[1] A complex, interconnected family of terms, concepts, and assumptions surround the term *qualitative research*. These include the traditions associated with foundationalism, positivism, postfoundationalism, postpositivism, poststructuralism, and the many qualitative research perspectives, and/or methods, connected to cultural and interpretive studies (the chapters in Part II take up these paradigms).[2] There are separate and detailed literatures on the many methods and approaches that fall under the category of qualitative research, such as case study, politics and ethics, participatory inquiry, interviewing, participant observation, visual methods, and interpretive analysis.

In North America, qualitative research operates in a complex historical field that crosscuts seven historical moments (we discuss these moments in detail below). These seven moments overlap and simultaneously operate in the present.[3] We define them as the traditional (1900–1950); the modernist or golden age (1950–1970); blurred genres (1970–1986); the crisis of representation (1986–1990); the postmodern, a period of experimental and new ethnographies (1990–1995); postexperimental inquiry (1995–2000); and the future, which is now (2000–). The future, the seventh moment, is concerned with moral discourse, with the development of sacred textualities. The seventh moment asks that the social sciences and the humanities become sites for critical conversations about democracy, race, gender, class, nation-states, globalization, freedom, and community.

The postmodern moment was defined in part by a concern for literary and rhetorical tropes and the narrative turn, a concern for storytelling, for composing ethnographies in new ways (Ellis & Bochner, 1996). Laurel Richardson (1997) observes that this moment was shaped by a new sensibility, by doubt, by a refusal to privilege any method or theory (p. 173).

3

But now, at the beginning of the 21st century, the narrative turn has been taken. Many have learned how to write differently, including how to locate themselves in their texts. We now struggle to connect qualitative research to the hopes, needs, goals, and promises of a free democratic society.

Successive waves of epistemological theorizing move across these seven moments. The traditional period is associated with the positivist, foundational paradigm. The modernist or golden age and blurred genres moments are connected to the appearance of postpositivist arguments. At the same time, a variety of new interpretive, qualitative perspectives were taken up, including hermeneutics, structuralism, semiotics, phenomenology, cultural studies, and feminism.[4] In the blurred genres phase, the humanities became central resources for critical, interpretive theory, and for the qualitative research project broadly conceived. The researcher became a *bricoleur* (see below), learning how to borrow from many different disciplines.

The blurred genres phase produced the next stage, the crisis of representation. Here researchers struggled with how to locate themselves and their subjects in reflexive texts. A kind of methodological diaspora took place, a two-way exodus. Humanists migrated to the social sciences, searching for new social theory, new ways to study popular culture and its local, ethnographic contexts. Social scientists turned to the humanities, hoping to learn how to do complex structural and poststructural readings of social texts. From the humanities, social scientists also learned how to produce texts that refused to be read in simplistic, linear, incontrovertible terms. The line between text and context blurred. In the postmodern experimental moment researchers continued to move away from foundational and quasi-foundational criteria (see in Volume 3, Smith & Deemer, Chapter 12, and Richardson, Chapter 14; and in this volume, Gergen & Gergen, Chapter 13). Alternative evaluative criteria were sought, criteria that might prove evocative, moral, critical, and rooted in local understandings.

Any definition of qualitative research must work within this complex historical field. *Qualitative research* means different things in each of these moments. Nonetheless, an initial, generic definition can be offered: Qualitative research is a situated activity that locates the observer in the world. It consists of a set of interpretive, material practices that make the world visible. These practices transform the world. They turn the world into a series of representations, including field notes, interviews, conversations, photographs, recordings, and memos to the self. At this level, qualitative research involves an interpretive, naturalistic approach to the world. This means that qualitative researchers study things in their natural settings, attempting to make sense of, or to interpret, phenomena in terms of the meanings people bring to them.[5]

Qualitative research involves the studied use and collection of a variety of empirical materials—case study; personal experience; introspection; life story; interview; artifacts; cultural texts and productions; observational, historical, interactional, and visual texts—that describe routine and problematic moments and meanings in individuals' lives. Accordingly, qualitative researchers deploy a wide range of interconnected interpretive practices, hoping always to get a better understanding of the subject matter at hand. It is understood, however, that each practice makes the world visible in a different way. Hence there is frequently a commitment to using more than one interpretive practice in any study.

The Qualitative Researcher as *Bricoleur* and Quilt Maker

The qualitative researcher may take on multiple and gendered images: scientist, naturalist, field-worker, journalist, social critic, artist, performer, jazz musician, filmmaker, quilt maker, essayist. The many methodological practices of qualitative research may be viewed as soft science, journalism, ethnography, bricolage, quilt making, or montage. The researcher, in turn, may be seen as a *bricoleur*, as a maker of quilts, or, as in filmmaking, a person who assembles images into montages. (On montage, see the discussion below as well as Cook, 1981, pp. 171-177; Monaco, 1981, pp. 322-328. On quilting, see hooks, 1990, pp. 115-122; Wolcott, 1995, pp. 31-33.)

Nelson, Treichler, and Grossberg (1992), Lévi-Strauss (1966), and Weinstein and Weinstein (1991) clarify the meanings of *bricolage* and *bricoleur*.[6] A *bricoleur* is a "Jack of all trades or a kind of professional do-it-yourself person" (Lévi-Strauss, 1966, p. 17). There are many kinds of *bricoleurs*—interpretive, narrative, theoretical, political (see below). The interpretive bricoleur produces a *bricolage*—that is, a pieced-together set of representations that are fitted to the specifics of a complex situation. "The solution [bricolage] which is the result of the *bricoleur's* method is an [emergent] construction" (Weinstein & Weinstein, 1991, p. 161) that changes and takes new forms as different tools, methods, and techniques of representation and interpretation are added to the puzzle. Nelson et al.

5

(1992) describe the methodology of cultural studies "as a bricolage. Its choice of practice, that is, is pragmatic, strategic and self-reflexive" (p. 2). This understanding can be applied, with qualifications, to qualitative research.

The qualitative researcher as *bricoleur* or maker of quilts uses the aesthetic and material tools of his or her craft, deploying whatever strategies, methods, or empirical materials are at hand (Becker, 1998, p. 2). If new tools or techniques have to be invented, or pieced together, then the researcher will do this. The choices as to which interpretive practices to employ are not necessarily set in advance. The "choice of research practices depends upon the questions that are asked, and the questions depend on their context" (Nelson et al., 1992, p. 2), what is available in the context, and what the researcher can do in that setting.

These interpretive practices involve aesthetic issues, an aesthetics of representation that goes beyond the pragmatic, or the practical. Here the concept of *montage* is useful (see Cook, 1981, p. 323; Monaco, 1981, pp. 171-172). Montage is a method of editing cinematic images. In the history of cinematography, montage is associated with the work of Sergei Eisenstein, especially his film *The Battleship Potemkin* (1925). In montage, several different images are superimposed onto one another to create a picture. In a sense, montage is like pentimento, in which something that has been painted out of a picture (an image the painter "repented," or denied) becomes visible again, creating something new. What is new is what had been obscured by a previous image.

Montage and pentimento, like jazz, which is improvisation, create the sense that images, sounds, and understandings are blending together, overlapping, forming a composite, a new creation. The images seem to shape and define one another, and an emotional, gestalt effect is produced. Often these images are combined in a swiftly run filmic sequence that produces a dizzily revolving collection of several images around a central or focused picture or sequence; such effects are often used to signify the passage of time.

Perhaps the most famous instance of montage is the Odessa Steps sequence in *The Battleship Potemkin*.[7] In the climax of the film, the citizens of Odessa are being massacred by czarist troops on the stone steps leading down to the harbor. Eisenstein cuts to a young mother as she pushes her baby in a carriage across the landing in front of the firing troops. Citizens rush past her, jolting the carriage, which she is afraid to push down to the next flight of stairs. The troops are above her firing at the citizens. She is trapped between the troops and the steps. She screams. A line of rifles pointing to the sky erupt in smoke. The mother's head sways back. The wheels of the carriage teeter on the edge of the steps. The mother's hand clutches the silver buckle of her belt. Below her people are being beaten by soldiers. Blood drips over the mother's white gloves. The baby's hand reaches out of the carriage. The mother sways back and forth. The troops advance. The mother falls back against the carriage. A woman watches in horror as the rear wheels of the carriage roll off the edge of the landing. With accelerating speed the carriage bounces down the steps, past the dead citizens. The baby is jostled from side to side inside the carriage. The soldiers fire their rifles into a group of wounded citizens. A student screams as the carriage leaps across the steps, tilts, and overturns (Cook, 1981, p. 167).[8]

Montage uses brief images to create a clearly defined sense of urgency and complexity. Montage invites viewers to construct interpretations that build on one another as the scene unfolds. These interpretations are built on associations based on the contrasting images that blend into one another. The underlying assumption of montage is that viewers perceive and interpret the shots in a "montage sequence not *sequentially*, or one at a time, but rather *simultaneously*" (Cook, 1981, p. 172). The viewer puts the sequences together into a meaningful emotional whole, as if in a glance, all at once.

The qualitative researcher who uses montage is like a quilt maker or a jazz improviser. The quilter stitches, edits, and puts slices of reality together. This process creates and brings psychological and emotional unity to an interpretive experience. There are many examples of montage in current qualitative research (see Diversi, 1998; Jones, 1999; Lather & Smithies, 1997; Ronai, 1998). Using multiple voices, different textual formats, and various typefaces, Lather and Smithies (1997) weave a complex text about women who are HIV positive and women with AIDS. Jones (1999) creates a performance text using lyrics from the blues songs sung by Billie Holiday.

In texts based on the metaphors of montage, quilt making, and jazz improvisation, many different things are going on at the same time— different voices, different perspectives, points of views, angles of vision. Like performance texts, works that use montage simultaneously create and enact moral meaning. They move from the personal to the political, the local to the historical and the cultural. These are dialogical texts. They presume an active audience. They create spaces for give-and-take between reader and writer. They do more than turn the other into the object of the social science gaze (see McCall, Chapter 4, Volume 2).

Qualitative research is inherently multimethod in focus (Flick, 1998, p. 229). However, the use of multiple methods, or triangulation, reflects an attempt to secure an in-depth understanding of the phenomenon in question. Objective reality can never be captured. We can know a thing only through its representations. Triangulation is not a tool or a strategy of validation, but an alternative to validation (Flick, 1998, p. 230). The combination of multiple methodological practices, empirical materials, perspectives, and observers in a single study is best understood, then, as a strategy that adds rigor, breadth, complexity, richness, and depth to any inquiry (see Flick, 1998, p. 231).

In Chapter 14 of Volume 3, Richardson disputes the concept of triangulation, asserting that the central image for qualitative inquiry is the crystal, not the triangle. Mixed-genre texts in the postexperimental moment have more than three sides. Like crystals, Eisenstein's montage, the jazz solo, or the pieces that make up a quilt, the mixed-genre text, as Richardson notes, "combines symmetry and substance with an infinite variety of shapes, substances, transmutations. . . . Crystals grow, change, alter. . . . Crystals are prisms that reflect externalities *and* refract within themselves, creating different colors, patterns, and arrays, casting off in different directions."

In the crystallization process, the writer tells the same tale from different points of view. For example, in *A Thrice-Told Tale* (1992), Margery Wolf uses fiction, field notes, and a scientific article to give an accounting of the same set of experiences in a native village. Similarly, in her play *Fires in the Mirror* (1993), Anna Deavere Smith presents a series of performance pieces based on interviews with people involved in a racial conflict in Crown Heights, Brooklyn, on August, 19, 1991 (see Denzin, Chapter 13, Volume 3). The play has multiple speaking parts, including conversations with gang members, police officers, and anonymous young girls and boys. There is no "correct" telling of this event. Each telling, like light hitting a crystal, reflects a different perspective on this incident.

Viewed as a crystalline form, as a montage, or as a creative performance around a central theme, triangulation as a form of, or alternative to, validity thus can be extended. Triangulation is the display of multiple, refracted realities simultaneously. Each of the metaphors "works" to create simultaneity rather than the sequential or linear. Readers and audiences are then invited to explore competing visions of the context, to become immersed in and merge with new realities to comprehend.

8

The methodological *bricoleur* is adept at performing a large number of diverse tasks, ranging from interviewing to intensive self-reflection and introspection. The theoretical *bricoleur* reads widely and is knowledgeable about the many interpretive paradigms (feminism, Marxism, cultural studies, constructivism, queer theory) that can be brought to any particular problem. He or she may not, however, feel that paradigms can be mingled or synthesized. That is, one cannot easily move between paradigms as overarching philosophical systems denoting particular ontologies, epistemologies, and methodologies. They represent belief systems that attach users to particular worldviews. Perspectives, in contrast, are less well developed systems, and one can more easily move between them. The researcher-as-*bricoleur*-theorist works between and within competing and overlapping perspectives and paradigms.

The interpretive *bricoleur* understands that research is an interactive process shaped by his or her personal history, biography, gender, social class, race, and ethnicity, and by those of the people in the setting. The political *bricoleur* knows that science is power, for all research findings have political implications. There is no value-free science. A civic social science based on a politics of hope is sought (Lincoln, 1999). The gendered, narrative *bricoleur* also knows that researchers all tell stories about the worlds they have studied. Thus the narratives, or stories, scientists tell are accounts couched and framed within specific storytelling traditions, often defined as paradigms (e.g., positivism, postpositivism, constructivism).

The product of the interpretive *bricoleur*'s labor is a complex, quiltlike bricolage, a reflexive collage or montage—a set of fluid, interconnected images and representations. This interpretive structure is like a quilt, a performance text, a sequence of representations connecting the parts to the whole.

Qualitative Research as a
Site of Multiple Interpretive Practices

Qualitative research, as a set of interpretive activities, privileges no single methodological practice over another. As a site of discussion, or discourse, qualitative research is difficult to define clearly. It has no theory or paradigm that is distinctly its own. As the contributions to Part II of this volume reveal, multiple theoretical paradigms claim use of qualitative research methods and strategies, from constructivist to cultural studies, feminism, Marxism, and ethnic models of study. Qualitative research is used in many separate disciplines, as we will discuss below. It does not belong to a single discipline.

Nor does qualitative research have a distinct set of methods or practices that are entirely its own. Qualitative researchers use semiotics, narrative, content, discourse, archival and phonemic analysis, even statistics, tables, graphs, and numbers. They also draw upon and utilize the approaches, methods, and techniques of ethnomethodology, phenomenology, hermeneutics, feminism, rhizomatics, deconstructionism, ethnography, interviews, psychoanalysis, cultural studies, survey research, and participant observation, among others.[9] All of these research practices "can provide important insights and knowledge" (Nelson et al., 1992, p. 2). No specific method or practice can be privileged over any other.

Many of these methods, or research practices, are used in other contexts in the human disciplines. Each bears the traces of its own disciplinary history. Thus there is an extensive history of the uses and meanings of ethnography and ethnology in education (see Fine, Weis, Weseen, & Wong, Chapter 4, this volume); of participant observation and ethnography in anthropology (see Tedlock, Volume 2, Chapter 6; Ryan & Bernard, Volume 3, Chapter 7; Brady, Volume 3, Chapter 15), sociology (see Gubrium & Holstein, Volume 2, Chapter 7; Harper, Volume 3, Chapter 5; Fontana & Frey, Volume 3, Chapter 2; Silverman, Volume 3, Chapter 9), communication (see Ellis & Bochner, Volume 3, Chapter 6), and cultural studies (see Frow & Morris, Chapter 11, this volume); of textual, hermeneutic, feminist, psychoanalytic, semiotic, and narrative analysis in cinema and literary studies (see Olesen, Chapter 8, this volume; Brady, Volume 3, Chapter 15); of archival, material culture, historical, and document analysis in history, biography, and archaeology (see Hodder, Volume 3, Chapter 4; Tierney, Volume 2, Chapter 9); and of discourse and conversational analysis in medicine, communications, and education (see Miller & Crabtree, Volume 2, Chapter 12; Silverman, Volume 3, Chapter 9).

The many histories that surround each method or research strategy reveal how multiple uses and meanings are brought to each practice. Textual analyses in literary studies, for example, often treat texts as self-contained systems. On the other hand, a researcher taking a cultural studies or feminist perspective will read a text in terms of its location within a historical moment marked by a particular gender, race, or class ideology. A cultural studies use of ethnography would bring a set of understandings from feminism, postmodernism, and poststructuralism to the project.

These understandings would not be shared by mainstream postpositivist sociologists. Similarly, postpositivist and poststructuralist historians bring different understandings and uses to the methods and findings of historical research (see Tierney, Volume 2, Chapter 9). These tensions and contradictions are all evident in the chapters in this volume.

These separate and multiple uses and meanings of the methods of qualitative research make it difficult for researchers to agree on any essential definition of the field, for it is never just one thing.[10] Still, we must establish a definition for our purposes here. We borrow from, and paraphrase, Nelson et al.'s (1992, p. 4) attempt to define cultural studies:

> Qualitative research is an interdisciplinary, transdisciplinary, and sometimes counterdisciplinary field. It crosscuts the humanities and the social and physical sciences. Qualitative research is many things at the same time. It is multiparadigmatic in focus. Its practitioners are sensitive to the value of the multimethod approach. They are committed to the naturalistic perspective and to the interpretive understanding of human experience. At the same time, the field is inherently political and shaped by multiple ethical and political positions.
>
> Qualitative research embraces two tensions at the same time. On the one hand, it is drawn to a broad, interpretive, postexperimental, postmodern, feminist, and critical sensibility. On the other hand, it is drawn to more narrowly defined positivist, postpositivist, humanistic, and naturalistic conceptions of human experience and its analysis. Further, these tensions can be combined in the same project, bringing both postmodern and naturalistic or both critical and humanistic perspectives to bear.

This rather complex statement means that qualitative research, as a set of practices, embraces within its own multiple disciplinary histories constant tensions and contradictions over the project itself, including its methods and the forms its findings and interpretations take. The field sprawls between and crosscuts all of the human disciplines, even including, in some cases, the physical sciences. Its practitioners are variously committed to modern, postmodern, and postexperimental sensibilities and the approaches to social research that these sensibilities imply.

Resistances to Qualitative Studies

The academic and disciplinary resistances to qualitative research illustrate the politics embedded in this field of discourse. The challenges

11

to qualitative research are many. Qualitative researchers are called journalists, or soft scientists. Their work is termed unscientific, or only explor-
atory, or subjective. It is called criticism and not theory, or it is interpreted
politically, as a disguised version of Marxism or secular humanism (see
Huber, 1995; see also Denzin, 1997, pp. 258-261).

These resistances reflect an uneasy awareness that the traditions of
qualitative research commit the researcher to a critique of the positivist or
postpositivist project. But the positivist resistance to qualitative research
goes beyond the "ever-present desire to maintain a distinction between
hard science and soft scholarship" (Carey, 1989, p. 99; see also in this volume Schwandt, Chapter 7; in Volume 3, Smith & Deemer, Chapter 12).
The experimental (positivist) sciences (physics, chemistry, economics, and
psychology, for example) are often seen as the crowning achievements of
Western civilization, and in their practices it is assumed that "truth" can
transcend opinion and personal bias (Carey, 1989, p. 99; Schwandt,
1997b, p. 309). Qualitative research is seen as an assault on this tradition,
whose adherents often retreat into a "value-free objectivist science"
(Carey, 1989, p. 104) model to defend their position. They seldom
attempt to make explicit, or to critique, the "moral and political commitments in their own contingent work" (Carey, 1989, p. 104; see also
Lincoln & Guba, Chapter 6, this volume).

Positivists further allege that the so-called new experimental qualitative
researchers write fiction, not science, and that these researchers have no
way of verifying their truth statements. Ethnographic poetry and fiction
signal the death of empirical science, and there is little to be gained by
attempting to engage in moral criticism. These critics presume a stable,
unchanging reality that can be studied using the empirical methods of
objective social science (see Huber, 1995). The province of qualitative research, accordingly, is the world of lived experience, for this is where individual belief and action intersect with culture. Under this model there is no
preoccupation with discourse and method as material interpretive practices that constitute representation and description. Thus is the textual,
narrative turn rejected by the positivists.

The opposition to positive science by the postpositivists (see below)
and the poststructuralists is seen, then, as an attack on reason and truth. At
the same time, the positivist science attack on qualitative research is
regarded as an attempt to legislate one version of truth over another.

This complex political terrain defines the many traditions and strands
of qualitative research: the British tradition and its presence in other

12

national contexts; the American pragmatic, naturalistic, and interpretive traditions in sociology, anthropology, communication, and education; the German and French phenomenological, hermeneutic, semiotic, Marxist, structural, and poststructural perspectives; feminist studies, African American studies, Latino studies, queer studies, studies of indigenous and aboriginal cultures. The politics of qualitative research create a tension that informs each of the above traditions. This tension itself is constantly being reexamined and interrogated, as qualitative research confronts a changing historical world, new intellectual positions, and its own institutional and academic conditions.

To summarize: Qualitative research is many things to many people. Its essence is twofold: a commitment to some version of the naturalistic, interpretive approach to its subject matter and an ongoing critique of the politics and methods of postpositivism. We turn now to a brief discussion of the major differences between qualitative and quantitative approaches to research. We then discuss ongoing differences and tensions within qualitative inquiry.

Qualitative Versus Quantitative Research

The word *qualitative* implies an emphasis on the qualities of entities and on processes and meanings that are not experimentally examined or measured (if measured at all) in terms of quantity, amount, intensity, or frequency. Qualitative researchers stress the socially constructed nature of reality, the intimate relationship between the researcher and what is studied, and the situational constraints that shape inquiry. Such researchers emphasize the value-laden nature of inquiry. They seek answers to questions that stress *how* social experience is created and given meaning. In contrast, quantitative studies emphasize the measurement and analysis of causal relationships between variables, not processes. Proponents of such studies claim that their work is done from within a value-free framework.

Research Styles: Doing the Same Things Differently?

Of course, both qualitative and quantitative researchers "think they know something about society worth telling to others, and they use a variety of forms, media and means to communicate their ideas and findings" (Becker, 1986, p. 122). Qualitative research differs from quantitative research in five significant ways (Becker, 1996). These points of difference

13

turn on different ways of addressing the same set of issues. They return always to the politics of research, and to who has the power to legislate correct solutions to these problems.

Uses of positivism and postpositivism. First, both perspectives are shaped by the positivist and postpositivist traditions in the physical and social sciences (see the discussion below). These two positivist science traditions hold to naïve and critical realist positions concerning reality and its perception. In the positivist version it is contended that there is a reality out there to be studied, captured, and understood, whereas the postpositivists argue that reality can never be fully apprehended, only approximated (Guba, 1990, p. 22). Postpositivism relies on multiple methods as a way of capturing as much of reality as possible. At the same time, emphasis is placed on the discovery and verification of theories. Traditional evaluation criteria, such as internal and external validity, are stressed, as is the use of qualitative procedures that lend themselves to structured (sometimes statistical) analysis. Computer-assisted methods of analysis that permit frequency counts, tabulations, and low-level statistical analyses may also be employed.

The positivist and postpositivist traditions linger like long shadows over the qualitative research project. Historically, qualitative research was defined within the positivist paradigm, where qualitative researchers attempted to do good positivist research with less rigorous methods and procedures. Some mid-20th-century qualitative researchers (e.g., Becker, Geer, Hughes, & Strauss, 1961) reported participant observation findings in terms of quasi-statistics. As recently as 1998, Strauss and Corbin, two leaders of the grounded theory approach to qualitative research, attempted to modify the usual canons of good (positivist) science to fit their own postpositivist conception of rigorous research (but see Charmaz, Chapter 8, Volume 2; see also Glaser, 1992). Some applied researchers, while claiming to be atheoretical, often fit within the positivist or postpositivist framework by default.

Flick (1998, pp. 2-3) usefully summarizes the differences between these two approaches to inquiry. He observes that the quantitative approach has been used for purposes of isolating "causes and effects . . . operationalizing theoretical relations . . . [and] measuring and . . . quantifying phenomena . . . allowing the generalization of findings" (p. 3). But today doubt is cast on such projects, because "Rapid social change and the resulting diversification of life worlds are increasingly confronting social researchers with new social contexts and perspectives. . . . traditional deductive methodologies . . . are failing. . . . thus research is increasingly forced to make use of inductive strategies instead of starting from theories and testing them. . . . knowledge and practice are studied as local knowledge and practice" (p. 2).

Spindler and Spindler (1992) summarize their qualitative approach to quantitative materials: "Instrumentation and quantification are simply procedures employed to extend and reinforce certain kinds of data, interpretations and test hypotheses across samples. Both must be kept in their place. One must avoid their premature or overly extensive use as a security mechanism" (p. 69).

Although many qualitative researchers in the postpositivist tradition will use statistical measures, methods, and documents as a way of locating groups of subjects within larger populations, they will seldom report their findings in terms of the kinds of complex statistical measures or methods to which quantitative researchers are drawn (i.e., path, regression, or log-linear analyses).

Acceptance of postmodern sensibilities. The use of quantitative, positivist methods and assumptions has been rejected by a new generation of qualitative researchers who are attached to poststructural and/or postmodern sensibilities (see below; see also in this volume Vidich & Lyman, Chapter 2, this volume; and in Volume 3, Richardson, Chapter 14). These researchers argue that positivist methods are but one way of telling stories about society or the social world. These methods may be no better or no worse than any other methods; they just tell different kinds of stories.

This tolerant view is not shared by everyone (Huber, 1995). Many members of the critical theory, constructivist, poststructural, and postmodern schools of thought reject positivist and postpositivist criteria when evaluating their own work. They see these criteria as irrelevant to their work and contend that such criteria reproduce only a certain kind of science, a science that silences too many voices. These researchers seek alternative methods for evaluating their work, including verisimilitude, emotionality, personal responsibility, an ethic of caring, political praxis, multivoiced texts, and dialogues with subjects. In response, positivists and postpositivists argue that what they do is good science, free of individual bias and subjectivity. As noted above, they see postmodernism and poststructuralism as attacks on reason and truth.

Capturing the individual's point of view. Both qualitative and quantitative researchers are concerned with the individual's point of view. However, qualitative investigators think they can get closer to the actor's perspective through detailed interviewing and observation. They argue that quantitative researchers are seldom able to capture their subjects' perspectives because they have to rely on more remote, inferential empirical methods and materials. The empirical materials produced by interpretive methods are regarded by many quantitative researchers as unreliable, impressionistic, and not objective.

Examining the constraints of everyday life. Qualitative researchers are more likely to confront and come up against the constraints of the everyday social world. They see this world in action and embed their findings in it. Quantitative researchers abstract from this world and seldom study it directly. They seek a nomothetic or etic science based on probabilities derived from the study of large numbers of randomly selected cases. These kinds of statements stand above and outside the constraints of everyday life. Qualitative researchers, on the other hand, are committed to an emic, idiographic, case-based position, which directs their attention to the specifics of particular cases.

Securing rich descriptions. Qualitative researchers believe that rich descriptions of the social world are valuable, whereas quantitative researchers, with their etic, nomothetic commitments, are less concerned with such detail. Quantitative researchers are deliberately unconcerned with rich descriptions because such detail interrupts the process of developing generalizations.

The five points of difference described above (uses of positivism and postpositivism, postmodernism, capturing the individual's point of view, examining the constraints of everyday life, securing thick descriptions) reflect commitments to different styles of research, different epistemologies, and different forms of representation. Each work tradition is governed by its own set of genres; each has its own classics, its own preferred forms of representation, interpretation, trustworthiness, and textual evaluation (see Becker, 1986, pp. 134-135). Qualitative researchers use ethnographic prose, historical narratives, first-person accounts, still photographs, life histories, fictionalized "facts," and biographical and autobiographical materials, among others. Quantitative researchers use mathematical models, statistical tables, and graphs, and usually write about their research in impersonal, third-person prose.

Tensions Within Qualitative Research

It is erroneous to presume that all qualitative researchers share the same assumptions about the five points of difference described above. As the discussion below will reveal, positivist, postpositivist, and poststructural differences define and shape the discourses of qualitative research. Realists and postpositivists within the interpretive qualitative research tradition criticize poststructuralists for taking the textual, narrative turn. These critics contend that such work is navel gazing. It produces conditions "for a dialogue of the deaf between itself and the community" (Silverman, 1997, p. 240). Those who attempt to capture the point of view of the interacting subject in the world are accused of naive humanism, of reproducing "a Romantic impulse which elevates the experiential to the level of the authentic" (Silverman, 1997, p. 248).

Still others argue that lived experience is ignored by those who take the textual, performance turn. Snow and Morrill (1995) argue that "this performance turn, like the preoccupation with discourse and storytelling, will take us further from the field of social action and the real dramas of everyday life and thus signal the death knell of ethnography as an empirically grounded enterprise" (p. 361). Of course, we disagree.

With these differences within and between the two traditions now in hand, we must now briefly discuss the history of qualitative research. We break this history into seven historical moments, mindful that any history is always somewhat arbitrary and always at least partially a social construction.

◆ The History of Qualitative Research

The history of qualitative research reveals, as Vidich and Lyman remind us in Chapter 2 of this volume, that the modern social science disciplines have taken as their mission "the analysis and understanding of the patterned conduct and social processes of society." The notion that this task could be carried out presupposed that social scientists had the ability to observe this world objectively. Qualitative methods were a major tool of such observations.[11]

Throughout the history of qualitative research, investigators have always defined their work in terms of hopes and values, "religious faiths, occupational and professional ideologies" (Vidich & Lyman, Chapter 2, this volume). Qualitative research (like all research) has always been judged on the "standard of whether the work communicates or 'says' something to us" (Vidich & Lyman, Chapter 2, this volume), based on how we conceptualize our reality and our images of the world. *Epistemology* is the word that has historically defined these standards of evaluation. In the contemporary period, as we have argued above, many received discourses on epistemology are now being reevaluated.

Vidich and Lyman's history covers the following (somewhat) overlapping stages: early ethnography (to the 17th century); colonial ethnography (17th-, 18th-, and 19th-century explorers); the ethnography of the American Indian as "other" (late-19th- and early-20th-century anthropology); the ethnography of the "civic other," or community studies, and ethnographies of American immigrants (early 20th century through the 1960s); studies of ethnicity and assimilation (midcentury through the 1980s); and the present, which we call the *seventh moment*.

In each of these eras, researchers were and have been influenced by their political hopes and ideologies, discovering findings in their research that confirmed prior theories or beliefs. Early ethnographers confirmed the racial and cultural diversity of peoples throughout the globe and attempted to fit this diversity into a theory about the origins of history, the races, and civilizations. Colonial ethnographers, before the professionalization of ethnography in the 20th century, fostered a colonial pluralism that left natives on their own as long as their leaders could be co-opted by the colonial administration.

European ethnographers studied Africans, Asians, and other Third World peoples of color. Early American ethnographers studied the American Indian from the perspective of the conqueror, who saw the life world of the primitive as a window to the prehistoric past. The Calvinist mission to save the Indian was soon transferred to the mission of saving the "hordes" of immigrants who entered the United States with the beginnings of industrialization. Qualitative community studies of the ethnic other proliferated from the early 1900s to the 1960s and included the work of E. Franklin Frazier, Robert Park, and Robert Redfield and their students, as well as William Foote Whyte, the Lynds, August Hollingshead, Herbert Gans, Stanford Lyman, Arthur Vidich, and Joseph Bensman. The post-1960 ethnicity studies challenged the "melting pot" hypothesis of Park and his followers and corresponded to the emergence of ethnic studies programs that saw Native Americans, Latinos, Asian Americans, and African Americans attempting to take control over the study of their own peoples.

The postmodern and poststructural challenge emerged in the mid-1980s. It questioned the assumptions that had organized this earlier history in each of its colonializing moments. Qualitative research that crosses the "postmodern divide" requires one, Vidich and Lyman argue in Chapter 2, this volume, to "abandon all established and preconceived values, theories, perspectives . . . and prejudices as resources for ethnographic study." In this new era, the qualitative researcher does more than observe history; he or she plays a part in it. New tales from the field will now be written, and they will reflect the researcher's direct and personal engagement with this historical period.

Vidich and Lyman's analysis covers the full sweep of ethnographic history. Ours is confined to the 20th century and complements many of their divisions. We begin with the early foundational work of the British and French as well the Chicago, Columbia, Harvard, Berkeley, and British schools of sociology and anthropology. This early foundational period established the norms of classical qualitative and ethnographic research (see Gupta & Ferguson, 1997; Rosaldo, 1989; Stocking, 1989).

◆ The Seven Moments of Qualitative Research

As suggested above, our history of qualitative research in North America in this century divides into seven phases, each of which we describe in turn below.

The Traditional Period

We call the first moment the traditional period (this covers Vidich and Lyman's second and third phases). It begins in the early 1900s and continues until World War II. In this period, qualitative researchers wrote "objective," colonializing accounts of field experiences that were reflective of the positivist scientist paradigm. They were concerned with offering valid, reliable, and objective interpretations in their writings. The "other" who was studied was alien, foreign, and strange.

Here is Malinowski (1967) discussing his field experiences in New Guinea and the Trobriand Islands in the years 1914–1915 and 1917–1918. He is bartering his way into field data:

> Nothing whatever draws me to ethnographic studies. . . . On the whole the village struck me rather unfavorably. There is a certain disorganization . . . the rowdiness and persistence of the people who laugh and stare and lie discouraged me somewhat. . . . Went to the village hoping to photograph a few stages of the bara dance. I handed out half-sticks of tobacco, then watched a few dances; then took pictures—but results were poor. . . . they would not pose long enough for time exposures. At moments I was furious at them, particularly because after I gave them their portions of tobacco they all went away. (quoted in Geertz, 1988, pp. 73-74)

In another work, this lonely, frustrated, isolated field-worker describes his methods in the following words:

> In the field one has to face a chaos of facts. . . . in this crude form they are not scientific facts at all; they are absolutely elusive, and can only be fixed by interpretation. . . . *Only laws and generalizations are scientific facts,* and field work consists only and exclusively in the interpretation of the chaotic social reality, in subordinating it to general rules. (Malinowski, 1916/1948, p. 328; quoted in Geertz, 1988, p. 81)

Malinowski's remarks are provocative. On the one hand they disparage fieldwork, but on the other they speak of it within the glorified language of science, with laws and generalizations fashioned out of this selfsame experience.

The field-worker during this period was lionized, made into a larger-than-life figure who went into and then returned from the field with stories about strange people. Rosaldo (1989, p. 30) describes this as the period of the Lone Ethnographer, the story of the man-scientist who went off in search of his native in a distant land. There this figure "encountered the object of his quest . . . [and] underwent his rite of passage by enduring the ultimate ordeal of 'fieldwork' " (p. 30). Returning home with his data, the Lone Ethnographer wrote up an objective account of the culture studied. These accounts were structured by the norms of classical ethnography. This sacred bundle of terms (Rosaldo, 1989, p. 31) organized ethnographic texts in terms of four beliefs and commitments: a commitment to objectivism, a complicity with imperialism, a belief in monumentalism

(the ethnography would create a museumlike picture of the culture studied), and a belief in timelessness (what was studied would never change).
The other was an "object" to be archived. This model of the researcher,
who could also write complex, dense theories about what was studied,
holds to the present day.

The myth of the Lone Ethnographer depicts the birth of classic ethnography. The texts of Malinowski, Radcliffe-Brown, Margaret Mead, and
Gregory Bateson are still carefully studied for what they can tell the novice
about conducting fieldwork, taking field notes, and writing theory. Today
this image has been shattered. The works of the classic ethnographers are
seen by many as relics from the colonial past (Rosaldo, 1989, p. 44).
Although many feel nostalgia for this past, others celebrate its passing.
Rosaldo (1989) quotes Cora Du Bois, a retired Harvard anthropology
professor, who lamented this passing at a conference in 1980, reflecting
on the crisis in anthropology: "[I feel a distance] from the complexity and
disarray of what I once found a justifiable and challenging discipline. . . . It
has been like moving from a distinguished art museum into a garage sale"
(p. 44).

Du Bois regards the classic ethnographies as pieces of timeless artwork
contained in a museum. She feels uncomfortable in the chaos of the garage
sale. In contrast, Rosaldo (1989) is drawn to this metaphor: "[The garage
sale] provides a precise image of the postcolonial situation where cultural
artifacts flow between unlikely places, and nothing is sacred, permanent,
or sealed off. The image of anthropology as a garage sale depicts our present global situation" (p. 44). Indeed, many valuable treasures may be
found if one is willing to look long and hard, in unexpected places. Old
standards no longer hold. Ethnographies do not produce timeless truths.
The commitment to objectivism is now in doubt. The complicity with
imperialism is openly challenged today, and the belief in monumentalism
is a thing of the past.

The legacies of this first period begin at the end of the 19th century,
when the novel and the social sciences had become distinguished as separate systems of discourse (Clough, 1992, pp. 21-22; see also Clough,
1998). However, the Chicago school, with its emphasis on the life story
and the "slice-of-life" approach to ethnographic materials, sought to
develop an interpretive methodology that maintained the centrality of
the narrated life history approach. This led to the production of texts
that gave the researcher-as-author the power to represent the subject's
story. Written under the mantle of straightforward, sentiment-free social

realism, these texts used the language of ordinary people. They articulated a social science version of literary naturalism, which often produced the sympathetic illusion that a solution to a social problem had been found. Like the Depression-era juvenile delinquent and other "social problems" films (Roffman & Purdy, 1981), these accounts romanticized the subject. They turned the deviant into a sociological version of a screen hero. These sociological stories, like their film counterparts, usually had happy endings, as they followed individuals through the three stages of the classic morality tale: being in a state of grace, being seduced by evil and falling, and finally achieving redemption through suffering.

Modernist Phase

The modernist phase, or second moment, builds on the canonical works from the traditional period. Social realism, naturalism, and slice-of-life ethnographies are still valued. This phase extended through the postwar years to the 1970s and is still present in the work of many (for reviews, see Wolcott, 1990, 1992, 1995; see also Tedlock, Chapter 6, Volume 2). In this period many texts sought to formalize qualitative methods (see, for example, Bogdan & Taylor, 1975; Cicourel, 1964; Filstead, 1970; Glaser & Strauss, 1967; Lofland, 1971, 1995; Lofland & Lofland, 1984, 1995; Taylor & Bogdan, 1998).[12] The modernist ethnographer and sociological participant observer attempted rigorous qualitative studies of important social processes, including deviance and social control in the classroom and society. This was a moment of creative ferment.

A new generation of graduate students across the human disciplines encountered new interpretive theories (ethnomethodology, phenomenology, critical theory, feminism). They were drawn to qualitative research practices that would let them give a voice to society's underclass. Postpositivism functioned as a powerful epistemological paradigm. Researchers attempted to fit Campbell and Stanley's (1963) model of internal and external validity to constructionist and interactionist conceptions of the research act. They returned to the texts of the Chicago school as sources of inspiration (see Denzin, 1970, 1978).

A canonical text from this moment remains *Boys in White* (Becker et al., 1961; see also Becker, 1998). Firmly entrenched in mid-20th-century methodological discourse, this work attempted to make qualitative research as rigorous as its quantitative counterpart. Causal narratives were central to this project. This multimethod work combined open-ended and quasi-structured interviewing with participant observation and the careful analysis of such materials in standardized, statistical form. In a classic article, "Problems of Inference and Proof in Participant Observation," Howard S. Becker (1958/1970) describes the use of quasi-statistics:

> Participant observations have occasionally been gathered in standardized form capable of being transformed into legitimate statistical data. But the exigencies of the field usually prevent the collection of data in such a form to meet the assumptions of statistical tests, so that the observer deals in what have been called "quasi-statistics." His conclusions, while implicitly numerical, do not require precise quantification. (p. 31)

In the analysis of data, Becker notes, the qualitative researcher takes a cue from statistical colleagues. The researcher looks for probabilities or support for arguments concerning the likelihood that, or frequency with which, a conclusion in fact applies in a specific situation (see also Becker, 1998, pp. 166-170). Thus did work in the modernist period clothe itself in the language and rhetoric of positivist and postpositivist discourse.

This was the golden age of rigorous qualitative analysis, bracketed in sociology by *Boys in White* (Becker et al., 1961) at one end and *The Discovery of Grounded Theory* (Glaser & Strauss, 1967) at the other. In education, qualitative research in this period was defined by George and Louise Spindler, Jules Henry, Harry Wolcott, and John Singleton. This form of qualitative research is still present in the work of such persons as Strauss and Corbin (1998) and Ryan and Bernard (see Chapter 7, Volume 3).

The "golden age" reinforced the picture of qualitative researchers as cultural romantics. Imbued with Promethean human powers, they valorized villains and outsiders as heroes to mainstream society. They embodied a belief in the contingency of self and society, and held to emancipatory ideals for "which one lives and dies." They put in place a tragic and often ironic view of society and self, and joined a long line of leftist cultural romantics that included Emerson, Marx, James, Dewey, Gramsci, and Martin Luther King, Jr. (West, 1989, chap. 6).

As this moment came to an end, the Vietnam War was everywhere present in American society. In 1969, alongside these political currents, Herbert Blumer and Everett Hughes met with a group of young sociologists called the "Chicago Irregulars" at the American Sociological

Association meetings held in San Francisco and shared their memories of the "Chicago years." Lyn Lofland (1980) describes the 1969 meetings as a

> moment of creative ferment—scholarly and political. The San Francisco meetings witnessed not simply the Blumer-Hughes event but a "counter-revolution." . . . a group first came to . . . talk about the problems of being a sociologist and a female. . . . the discipline seemed literally to be bursting with new . . . ideas: labelling theory, ethnomethodology, conflict theory, phenomenology, dramaturgical analysis. (p. 253)

Thus did the modernist phase come to an end.

Blurred Genres

By the beginning of the third stage (1970–1986), which we call the moment of blurred genres, qualitative researchers had a full complement of paradigms, methods, and strategies to employ in their research. Theories ranged from symbolic interactionism to constructivism, naturalistic inquiry, positivism and postpositivism, phenomenology, ethnomethodology, critical theory, neo-Marxist theory, semiotics, structuralism, feminism, and various racial/ethnic paradigms. Applied qualitative research was gaining in stature, and the politics and ethics of qualitative research—implicated as they were in various applications of this work—were topics of considerable concern. Research strategies and formats for reporting research ranged from grounded theory to the case study, to methods of historical, biographical, ethnographic, action, and clinical research. Diverse ways of collecting and analyzing empirical materials were also available, including qualitative interviewing (open-ended and quasi-structured) and observational, visual, personal experience, and documentary methods. Computers were entering the situation, to be fully developed as aids in the analysis of qualitative data in the next decade, along with narrative, content, and semiotic methods of reading interviews and cultural texts.

Two books by Geertz, *The Interpretation of Culture* (1973) and *Local Knowledge* (1983), defined the beginning and end of this moment. In these two works, Geertz argued that the old functional, positivist, behavioral, totalizing approaches to the human disciplines were giving way to a more pluralistic, interpretive, open-ended perspective. This new perspective took cultural representations and their meanings as its point of

24

departure. Calling for "thick descriptions" of particular events, rituals, and customs, Geertz suggested that all anthropological writings are interpretations of interpretations.[13] The observer has no privileged voice in the interpretations that are written. The central task of theory is to make sense out of a local situation.

Geertz went on to propose that the boundaries between the social sciences and the humanities had become blurred. Social scientists were now turning to the humanities for models, theories, and methods of analysis (semiotics, hermeneutics). A form of genre diaspora was occurring: documentaries that read like fiction (Mailer), parables posing as ethnographies (Castañeda), theoretical treatises that look like travelogues (Lévi-Strauss). At the same time, other new approaches were emerging: poststructuralism (Barthes), neopositivism (Philips), neo-Marxism (Althusser), micro-macro descriptivism (Geertz), ritual theories of drama and culture (V. Turner), deconstructionism (Derrida), ethnomethodology (Garfinkel). The golden age of the social sciences was over, and a new age of blurred, interpretive genres was upon us. The essay as an art form was replacing the scientific article. At issue now is the author's presence in the interpretive text (Geertz, 1988). How can the researcher speak with authority in an age when there are no longer any firm rules concerning the text, including the author's place in it, its standards of evaluation, and its subject matter?

The naturalistic, postpositivist, and constructionist paradigms gained power in this period, especially in education, in the works of Harry Wolcott, Frederick Erickson, Egon Guba, Yvonna Lincoln, Robert Stake, and Elliot Eisner. By the end of the 1970s, several qualitative journals were in place, including *Urban Life and Culture* (now *Journal of Contemporary Ethnography*), *Cultural Anthropology*, *Anthropology and Education Quarterly*, *Qualitative Sociology*, and *Symbolic Interaction*, as well as the book series *Studies in Symbolic Interaction*.

Crisis of Representation

A profound rupture occurred in the mid-1980s. What we call the fourth moment, or the crisis of representation, appeared with *Anthropology as Cultural Critique* (Marcus & Fischer, 1986), *The Anthropology of Experience* (Turner & Bruner, 1986), *Writing Culture* (Clifford & Marcus, 1986), *Works and Lives* (Geertz, 1988), and *The Predicament of Culture* (Clifford, 1988). These works made research and writing more reflexive and called into question the issues of gender, class, and race. They articulated the consequences of Geertz's "blurred genres" interpretation of the field in the early 1980s.[14]

New models of truth, method, and representation were sought (Rosaldo, 1989). The erosion of classic norms in anthropology (objectivism, complicity with colonialism, social life structured by fixed rituals and customs, ethnographies as monuments to a culture) was complete (Rosaldo, 1989, pp. 44-45; see also Jackson, 1998, pp. 7-8). Critical, feminist, and epistemologies of color now competed for attention in this arena. Issues such as validity, reliability, and objectivity, previously believed settled, were once more problematic. Pattern and interpretive theories, as opposed to causal, linear theories, were now more common, as writers continued to challenge older models of truth and meaning (Rosaldo, 1989).

Stoller and Olkes (1987, pp. 227-229) describe how the crisis of representation was felt in their fieldwork among the Songhay of Niger. Stoller observes: "When I began to write anthropological texts, I followed the conventions of my training. I 'gathered data,' and once the 'data' were arranged in neat piles, I 'wrote them up.' In one case I reduced Songhay insults to a series of neat logical formulas" (p. 227). Stoller became dissatisfied with this form of writing, in part because he learned that "everyone had lied to me and . . . the data I had so painstakingly collected were worthless. I learned a lesson: Informants routinely lie to their anthropologists" (Stoller & Olkes, 1987, p. 9). This discovery led to a second—that he had, in following the conventions of ethnographic realism, edited himself out of his text. This led Stoller to produce a different type of text, a memoir, in which he became a central character in the story he told. This story, an account of his experiences in the Songhay world, became an analysis of the clash between his world and the world of Songhay sorcery. Thus Stoller's journey represents an attempt to confront the crisis of representation in the fourth moment.

Clough (1992) elaborates this crisis and criticizes those who would argue that new forms of writing represent a way out of the crisis. She argues:

> While many sociologists now commenting on the criticism of ethnography view writing as "downright central to the ethnographic enterprise" [Van Maanen, 1988, p. xi], the problems of writing are still viewed as different

26

from the problems of method or fieldwork itself. Thus the solution usually offered is experiments in writing, that is a self-consciousness about writing. (p. 136)

It is this insistence on the difference between writing and fieldwork that must be analyzed. (Richardson is quite articulate about this issue in Chapter 14, Volume 3.)

In writing, the field-worker makes a claim to moral and scientific authority. This claim allows the realist and experimental ethnographic texts to function as sources of validation for an empirical science. They show that the world of real lived experience can still be captured, if only in the writer's memoirs, or fictional experimentations, or dramatic readings. But these works have the danger of directing attention away from the ways in which the text constructs sexually situated individuals in a field of social difference. They also perpetuate "empirical science's hegemony" (Clough, 1992, p. 8), for these new writing technologies of the subject become the site "for the production of knowledge/power . . . [aligned] with . . . the capital/state axis" (Aronowitz, 1988, p. 300; quoted in Clough, 1992, p. 8). Such experiments come up against, and then back away from, the difference between empirical science and social criticism. Too often they fail to engage fully a new politics of textuality that would "refuse the identity of empirical science" (Clough, 1992, p. 135). This new social criticism "would intervene in the relationship of information economics, nation-state politics, and technologies of mass communication, especially in terms of the empirical sciences" (Clough, 1992, p. 16). This, of course, is the terrain occupied by cultural studies.

Richardson (Volume 3, Chapter 14), Tedlock (Volume 2, Chapter 6), Brady (Volume 3, Chapter 15), and Ellis and Bochner (Volume 3, Chapter 6) develop the above arguments, viewing writing as a method of inquiry that moves through successive stages of self-reflection. As a series of written representations, the field-worker's texts flow from the field experience, through intermediate works, to later work, and finally to the research text, which is the public presentation of the ethnographic and narrative experience. Thus fieldwork and writing blur into one another. There is, in the final analysis, no difference between writing and fieldwork. These two perspectives inform one another throughout every chapter in these volumes. In these ways the crisis of representation moves qualitative research in new and critical directions.

A Triple Crisis

The ethnographer's authority remains under assault today (Behar, 1995, p. 3; Gupta & Ferguson, 1997, p. 16; Jackson, 1998; Ortner, 1997, p. 2). A triple crisis of representation, legitimation, and praxis confronts qualitative researchers in the human disciplines. Embedded in the discourses of poststructuralism and postmodernism (see Vidich & Lyman, Chapter 2, this volume; and Richardson, Chapter 14, Volume 3), these three crises are coded in multiple terms, variously called and associated with *the critical, interpretive, linguistic, feminist,* and *rhetorical* turns in social theory. These new turns make problematic two key assumptions of qualitative research. The first is that qualitative researchers can no longer directly capture lived experience. Such experience, it is argued, is created in the social text written by the researcher. This is the representational crisis. It confronts the inescapable problem of representation, but does so within a framework that makes the direct link between experience and text problematic.

The second assumption makes problematic the traditional criteria for evaluating and interpreting qualitative research. This is the legitimation crisis. It involves a serious rethinking of such terms as *validity, generalizability,* and *reliability,* terms already retheorized in postpositivist (Hammersley, 1992), constructionist-naturalistic (Guba & Lincoln, 1989, pp. 163-183), feminist (Olesen, Chapter 8, this volume), interpretive (Denzin, 1997), poststructural (Lather, 1993; Lather & Smithies, 1997), and critical (Kincheloe & McLaren, Chapter 10, this volume) discourses. This crisis asks, How are qualitative studies to be evaluated in the contemporary, poststructural moment? The first two crises shape the third, which asks, Is it possible to effect change in the world if society is only and always a text? Clearly these crises intersect and blur, as do the answers to the questions they generate (see in this volume Schwandt, Chapter 7; Ladson-Billings, Chapter 9; and in Volume 3, Smith & Deemer, Chapter 12).

The fifth moment, the postmodern period of experimental ethnographic writing, struggled to make sense of these crises. New ways of composing ethnography were explored (Ellis & Bochner, 1996). Theories were read as tales from the field. Writers struggled with different ways to represent the "other," although they were now joined by new representational concerns (see Fine et al., Chapter 4, this volume). Epistemologies from previously silenced groups emerged to offer solutions to these problems. The concept of the aloof observer has been abandoned. More action, participatory, and activist-oriented research is on the horizon. The search for grand narratives is being replaced by more local, small-scale theories fitted to specific problems and particular situations.

The sixth (postexperimental) and seventh (the future) moments are upon us. Fictional ethnographies, ethnographic poetry, and multimedia texts are today taken for granted. Postexperimental writers seek to connect their writings to the needs of a free democratic society. The demands of a moral and sacred qualitative social science are actively being explored by a host of new writers from many different disciplines (see Jackson, 1998; Lincoln & Denzin, Chapter 6, this volume).

Reading History

We draw four conclusions from this brief history, noting that it is, like all histories, somewhat arbitrary. First, each of the earlier historical moments is still operating in the present, either as legacy or as a set of practices that researchers continue to follow or argue against. The multiple and fractured histories of qualitative research now make it possible for any given researcher to attach a project to a canonical text from any of the above-described historical moments. Multiple criteria of evaluation compete for attention in this field (Lincoln, in press). Second, an embarrassment of choices now characterizes the field of qualitative research. There have never been so many paradigms, strategies of inquiry, or methods of analysis for researchers to draw upon and utilize. Third, we are in a moment of discovery and rediscovery, as new ways of looking, interpreting, arguing, and writing are debated and discussed. Fourth, the qualitative research act can no longer be viewed from within a neutral or objective positivist perspective. Class, race, gender, and ethnicity shape the process of inquiry, making research a multicultural process. It is to this topic that we now turn.

◆ Qualitative Research as Process

Three interconnected, generic activities define the qualitative research process. They go by a variety of different labels, including *theory, method, analysis, ontology, epistemology,* and *methodology.* Behind these terms stands the personal biography of the researcher, who speaks from a particular class, gender, racial, cultural, and ethnic community perspective. The gendered, multiculturally situated researcher approaches the world with a set of ideas, a framework (theory, ontology) that specifies a set of questions (epistemology) that he or she then examines in specific ways (methodology, analysis). That is, the researcher collects empirical materials bearing on the question and then analyzes and writes about them. Every researcher speaks from within a distinct interpretive community that configures, in its special way, the multicultural, gendered components of the research act.

In this volume we treat these generic activities under five headings, or phases: the researcher and the researched as multicultural subjects, major paradigms and interpretive perspectives, research strategies, methods of collecting and analyzing empirical materials, and the art, practices, and politics of interpretation. Behind and within each of these phases stands the biographically situated researcher. This individual enters the research process from inside an interpretive community. This community has its own historical research traditions, which constitute a distinct point of view. This perspective leads the researcher to adopt particular views of the "other" who is studied. At the same time, the politics and the ethics of research must also be considered, for these concerns permeate every phase of the research process.

◆ The Other as Research Subject

Since its early-20th-century birth in modern, interpretive form, qualitative research has been haunted by a double-faced ghost. On the one hand, qualitative researchers have assumed that qualified, competent observers can, with objectivity, clarity, and precision, report on their own observations of the social world, including the experiences of others. Second, researchers have held to the belief in a real subject, or real individual, who is present in the world and able, in some form, to report on his or her experiences. So armed, researchers could blend their own observations with the self-reports provided by subjects through interviews and life story, personal experience, case study, and other documents.

These two beliefs have led qualitative researchers across disciplines to seek a method that would allow them to record accurately their own observations while also uncovering the meanings their subjects bring to their life experiences. This method would rely upon the subjective verbal and written expressions of meaning given by the individuals studied as windows into the inner lives of these persons. Since Dilthey (1900/1976), this search for a method has led to a perennial focus in the human disciplines on qualitative, interpretive methods.

Recently, as noted above, this position and its beliefs have come under assault. Poststructuralists and postmodernists have contributed to the understanding that there is no clear window into the inner life of an individual. Any gaze is always filtered through the lenses of language, gender, social class, race, and ethnicity. There are no objective observations, only observations socially situated in the worlds of—and between—the observer and the observed. Subjects, or individuals, are seldom able to give full explanations of their actions or intentions; all they can offer are accounts, or stories, about what they did and why. No single method can grasp all of the subtle variations in ongoing human experience. Consequently, qualitative researchers deploy a wide range of interconnected interpretive methods, always seeking better ways to make more understandable the worlds of experience they have studied.

Table 1.1 depicts the relationships we see among the five phases that define the research process. Behind all but one of these phases stands the biographically situated researcher. These five levels of activity, or practice, work their way through the biography of the researcher. We take them up briefly in order here; we discuss these phases more fully in the introductions to the individual parts of this volume.

Phase 1: The Researcher

Our remarks above indicate the depth and complexity of the traditional and applied qualitative research perspectives into which a socially situated researcher enters. These traditions locate the researcher in history, simultaneously guiding and constraining work that will be done in any specific study. This field has been characterized constantly by diversity and conflict, and these are its most enduring traditions (see Greenwood & Levin, Chapter 3, this volume). As a carrier of this complex and contradictory history, the researcher must also confront the ethics and politics of research (see Christians, Chapter 5, this volume). The age of value-free inquiry for the human disciplines is over (see Vidich & Lyman, Chapter 2 and Fine et al., Chapter 4, this volume). Today researchers struggle to develop situational and transsituational ethics that apply to all forms of the research act and its human-to-human relationships.

TABLE 1.1   The Research Process

Phase 1: The Researcher as a Multicultural Subject

   history and research traditions
   conceptions of self and the other
   ethics and politics of research

Phase 2: Theoretical Paradigms and Perspectives

   positivism, postpositivism
   interpretivism, constructivism, hermeneutics
   feminism(s)
   racialized discourses
   critical theory and Marxist models
   cultural studies models
   queer theory

Phase 3: Research Strategies

   study design
   case study
   ethnography, participant observation, performance ethnography
   phenomenology, ethnomethodology
   grounded theory
   life history, *testimonio*
   historical method
   action and applied research
   clinical research

Phase 4: Methods of Collection and Analysis

   interviewing
   observing
   artifacts, documents, and records
   visual methods
   autoethnography
   data management methods
   computer-assisted analysis
   textual analysis
   focus groups
   applied ethnography

Phase 5: The Art, Practices, and Politics of Interpretation and Presentation

   criteria for judging adequacy
   practices and politics of interpretation
   writing as interpretation
   policy analysis
   evaluation traditions
   applied research

Phase 2: Interpretive Paradigms

All qualitative researchers are philosophers in that "universal sense in which all human beings . . . are guided by highly abstract principles" (Bateson, 1972, p. 320). These principles combine beliefs about ontology (What kind of being is the human being? What is the nature of reality?), epistemology (What is the relationship between the inquirer and the known?), and methodology (How do we know the world, or gain knowledge of it?) (see Guba, 1990, p. 18; Lincoln & Guba, 1985, pp. 14-15; see also Lincoln & Guba, Chapter 6, this volume). These beliefs shape how the qualitative researcher sees the world and acts in it. The researcher is "bound within a net of epistemological and ontological premises which—regardless of ultimate truth or falsity—become partially self-validating" (Bateson, 1972, p. 314).

The net that contains the researcher's epistemological, ontological, and methodological premises may be termed a *paradigm*, or an interpretive framework, a "basic set of beliefs that guides action" (Guba, 1990, p. 17). All research is interpretive; it is guided by a set of beliefs and feelings about the world and how it should be understood and studied. Some beliefs may be taken for granted, invisible, only assumed, whereas others are highly problematic and controversial. Each interpretive paradigm makes particular demands on the researcher, including the questions he or she asks and the interpretations the researcher brings to them.

At the most general level, four major interpretive paradigms structure qualitative research: positivist and postpositivist, constructivist-interpretive, critical (Marxist, emancipatory), and feminist-poststructural. These four abstract paradigms become more complicated at the level of concrete specific interpretive communities. At this level it is possible to identify not only the constructivist, but also multiple versions of feminism (Afrocentric and poststructural)[15] as well as specific ethnic, Marxist, and cultural studies paradigms. These perspectives, or paradigms, are examined in Part II of this volume.

The paradigms examined in Part II of this volume work against and alongside (and some within) the positivist and postpositivist models. They all work within relativist ontologies (multiple constructed realities), interpretive epistemologies (the knower and known interact and shape one another), and interpretive, naturalistic methods.

Table 1.2 presents these paradigms and their assumptions, including their criteria for evaluating research, and the typical form that an

TABLE 1.2   Interpretive Paradigms

Paradigm/ Theory	Criteria	Form of Theory	Type of Narration
Positivist/ postpositivist	internal, external validity	logical-deductive, grounded	scientific report
Constructivist	trustworthiness, credibility, transferability, confirmability	substantive-formal	interpretive case studies, ethnographic fiction
Feminist	Afrocentric, lived experience, dialogue, caring, accountability, race, class, gender, reflexivity, praxis, emotion, concrete grounding	critical, standpoint	essays, stories, experimental writing
Ethnic	Afrocentric, lived experience, dialogue, caring, accountability, race, class, gender	standpoint, critical, historical	essays, fables, dramas
Marxist	emancipatory theory, falsifiable, dialogical, race, class, gender	critical, historical, economic	historical, economic, sociocultural analyses
Cultural studies	cultural practices, praxis, social texts, subjectivities	social criticism	cultural theory as criticism
Queer theory	reflexivity, deconstruction	social criticism, historical analysis	theory as criticism, autobiography

interpretive or theoretical statement assumes in each paradigm.[16] These paradigms are explored in considerable detail in Part II by Lincoln and Guba (Chapter 6), Schwandt (Chapter 7), Olesen (Chapter 8), Ladson-Billings (Chapter 9), Kincheloe and McLaren (Chapter 10), Frow and

Morris (Chapter 11), and Gamson (Chapter 12). We have discussed the positivist and postpositivist paradigms above. They work from within a realist and critical realist ontology and objective epistemologies, and rely upon experimental, quasi-experimental, survey, and rigorously defined qualitative methodologies. Ryan and Bernard (Chapter 7, Volume 3) develop elements of this paradigm.

The constructivist paradigm assumes a relativist ontology (there are multiple realities), a subjectivist epistemology (knower and respondent cocreate understandings), and a naturalistic (in the natural world) set of methodological procedures. Findings are usually presented in terms of the criteria of grounded theory or pattern theories (see in this volume Lincoln & Guba, Chapter 6; in Volume 2, Charmaz, Chapter 8; and in Volume 3, Ryan & Bernard, Chapter 7). Terms such as *credibility, transferability, dependability,* and *confirmability* replace the usual positivist criteria of internal and external validity, reliability, and objectivity.

Feminist, ethnic, Marxist, and cultural studies and queer theory models privilege a materialist-realist ontology; that is, the real world makes a material difference in terms of race, class, and gender. Subjectivist epistemologies and naturalistic methodologies (usually ethnographies) are also employed. Empirical materials and theoretical arguments are evaluated in terms of their emancipatory implications. Criteria from gender and racial communities (e.g., African American) may be applied (emotionality and feeling, caring, personal accountability, dialogue).

Poststructural feminist theories emphasize problems with the social text, its logic, and its inability ever to represent the world of lived experience fully. Positivist and postpositivist criteria of evaluation are replaced by other terms, including the reflexive, multivoiced text that is grounded in the experiences of oppressed people.

The cultural studies and queer theory paradigms are multifocused, with many different strands drawing from Marxism, feminism, and the postmodern sensibility (see in this volume, Frow & Morris, Chapter 11; Gamson, Chapter 12; and in Volume 3, Richardson, Chapter 14). There is a tension between a humanistic cultural studies, which stresses lived experiences (meaning), and a more structural cultural studies project, which stresses the structural and material determinants (race, class, gender) and effects of experience. Of course, there are two sides to every coin, and both sides are needed and are indeed critical. The cultural studies and queer theory paradigms use methods strategically—that is, as resources for understanding and for producing resistances to local structures of domination. Scholars may do close textual readings and discourse analyses of cultural texts (see Olesen, Chapter 8, this volume; Frow & Morris, Chapter 11, this volume; and in Volume 3, Silverman, Chapter 9) as well as conducting local ethnographies, open-ended interviewing, and participant observation. The focus is on how race, class, and gender are produced and enacted in historically specific situations.

Paradigm and personal history in hand, focused on a concrete empirical problem to examine, the researcher now moves to the next stage of the research process—namely, working with a specific strategy of inquiry.

Phase 3: Strategies of Inquiry and Interpretive Paradigms

Table 1.1 presents some of the major strategies of inquiry a researcher may use. Phase 3 begins with research design, which, broadly conceived, involves a clear focus on the research question, the purposes of the study, "what information most appropriately will answer specific research questions, and which strategies are most effective for obtaining it" (LeCompte & Preissle, 1993, p. 30; see also in Volume 2, Janesick, Chapter 2; Cheek, Chapter 3). A research design describes a flexible set of guidelines that connect theoretical paradigms first to strategies of inquiry and second to methods for collecting empirical material. A research design situates researchers in the empirical world and connects them to specific sites, persons, groups, institutions, and bodies of relevant interpretive material, including documents and archives. A research design also specifies how the investigator will address the two critical issues of representation and legitimation.

A strategy of inquiry comprises a bundle of skills, assumptions, and practices that the researcher employs as he or she moves from paradigm to the empirical world. Strategies of inquiry put paradigms of interpretation into motion. At the same time, strategies of inquiry also connect the researcher to specific methods of collecting and analyzing empirical materials. For example, the case study relies on interviewing, observing, and document analysis. Research strategies implement and anchor paradigms in specific empirical sites, or in specific methodological practices, such as making a case an object of study. These strategies include the case study, phenomenological and ethnomethodological techniques, and the use of grounded theory, as well as biographical, autoethnographic, historical, action, and clinical methods. Each of these strategies is connected to a complex literature, and each has a separate history, exemplary works, and preferred ways for putting the strategy into motion.

Phase 4: Methods of Collecting and Analyzing Empirical Materials

The researcher has several methods for collecting empirical materials.[17] These methods are taken up in Part I of Volume 3. They range from the interview to direct observation, the analysis of artifacts, documents, and cultural records, and the use of visual materials or personal experience. The researcher may also use a variety of different methods of reading and analyzing interviews or cultural texts, including content, narrative, and semiotic strategies. Faced with large amounts of qualitative materials, the investigator seeks ways of managing and interpreting these documents, and here data management methods and computer-assisted models of analysis may be of use. Ryan and Bernard (Volume 3, Chapter 7) and Weitzman (Volume 3, Chapter 8) discuss these techniques.

Phase 5: The Art and Politics of Interpretation and Evaluation

Qualitative research is endlessly creative and interpretive. The researcher does not just leave the field with mountains of empirical materials and then easily write up his or her findings. Qualitative interpretations are constructed. The researcher first creates a field text consisting of field notes and documents from the field, what Roger Sanjek (1990, p. 386) calls "indexing" and David Plath (1990, p. 374) calls "filework." The writer-as-interpreter moves from this text to a research text: notes and interpretations based on the field text. This text is then re-created as a working interpretive document that contains the writer's initial attempts to make sense of what he or she has learned. Finally the writer produces the public text that comes to the reader. This final tale from the field may assume several forms: confessional, realist, impressionistic, critical, formal, literary, analytic, grounded theory, and so on (see Van Maanen, 1988).

The interpretive practice of making sense of one's findings is both artistic and political. Multiple criteria for evaluating qualitative research now exist, and those that we emphasize stress the situated, relational, and textual structures of the ethnographic experience. There is no single interpretive truth. As we argued earlier, there are multiple interpretive communities, each with its own criteria for evaluating an interpretation.

Program evaluation is a major site of qualitative research, and qualitative researchers can influence social policy in important ways. The contributions by Greenwood and Levin (this volume, Chapter 3), Kemmis and McTaggart (Volume 2, Chapter 11), Miller and Crabtree (Volume 2, Chapter 12), Chambers (Volume 3, Chapter 11), Greene (Volume 3, Chapter 16), and Rist (Volume 3, Chapter 17) trace and discuss the rich history of applied qualitative research in the social sciences. This is the critical site where theory, method, praxis, action, and policy all come together. Qualitative researchers can isolate target populations, show the immediate effects of certain programs on such groups, and isolate the constraints that operate against policy changes in such settings. Action-oriented and clinically oriented qualitative researchers can also create spaces for those who are studied (the other) to speak. The evaluator becomes the conduit through which such voices can be heard. Chambers, Greene, and Rist explicitly develop these topics in their chapters.

◆ Bridging the Historical Moments: What Comes Next?

Ellis and Bochner (Volume 3, Chapter 6), Gergen and Gergen (this volume, Chapter 13), and Richardson (Volume 3, Chapter 14) argue that we are already in the post "post" period—post-poststructuralist, post-postmodernist, post-postexperimental. What this means for interpretive ethnographic practices is still not clear, but it is certain that things will never again be the same. We are in a new age where messy, uncertain, multivoiced texts, cultural criticism, and new experimental works will become more common, as will more reflexive forms of fieldwork, analysis, and intertextual representation. We take as the subject of our final essay in this volume these fifth, sixth, and seventh moments. It is true that, as the poet said, the center no longer holds. We can reflect on what should be at the new center.

Thus we come full circle. Returning to our bridge metaphor, the chapters that follow take the researcher back and forth through every phase of the research act. Like a good bridge, the chapters provide for two-way traffic, coming and going between moments, formations, and interpretive communities. Each chapter examines the relevant histories, controversies, and current practices that are associated with each paradigm, strategy, and method. Each chapter also offers projections for the future, where a specific paradigm, strategy, or method will be 10 years from now, deep into the formative years of the 21st century.

In reading the chapters that follow, it is important to remember that the field of qualitative research is defined by a series of tensions, contradictions, and hesitations. This tension works back and forth between the broad, doubting postmodern sensibility and the more certain, more traditional positivist, postpositivist, and naturalistic conceptions of this project. All of the chapters that follow are caught in and articulate this tension.

◆ Notes

1. Qualitative research has separate and distinguished histories in education, social work, communications, psychology, history, organizational studies, medical science, anthropology, and sociology.

2. Some definitions are in order here. *Positivism* asserts that objective accounts of the real world can be given. *Postpositivism* holds that only partially objective accounts of the world can be produced, because all methods for examining them are flawed. According to *foundationalism*, we can have an ultimate grounding for our knowledge claims about the world, and this involves the use of empiricist and positivist epistemologies (Schwandt, 1997a, p. 103). *Nonfoundationalism* holds that we can make statements about the world without "recourse to ultimate proof or foundations for that knowing" (p. 102). *Quasi-foundationalism* holds that certain knowledge claims can be made about the world based on neorealist criteria, including the correspondence concept of truth; there is an independent reality that can be mapped (see Smith & Deemer, Chapter 12, Volume 3).

3. Jameson (1991, pp. 3-4) reminds us that any periodization hypothesis is always suspect, even one that rejects linear, stagelike models. It is never clear to what reality a stage refers, and what divides one stage from another is always debatable. Our seven moments are meant to mark discernible shifts in style, genre, epistemology, ethics, politics, and aesthetics.

4. Some further definitions are in order. *Structuralism* holds that any system is made up of a set of oppositional categories embedded in language. *Semiotics* is the science of signs or sign systems—a structuralist project. According to *poststructuralism*, language is an unstable system of referents, thus it is impossible ever to capture completely the meaning of an action, text, or intention. *Postmodernism* is a contemporary sensibility, developing since World War II, that privileges no single authority, method, or paradigm. *Hermeneutics* is an approach to the analysis of texts that stresses how prior understandings and prejudices shape the interpretive process. *Phenomenology* is a complex system of ideas associated with the works of Husserl, Heidegger, Sartre, Merleau-Ponty, and Alfred Schutz. *Cultural studies* is a complex, interdisciplinary field that merges critical theory, feminism, and poststructuralism.

5. Of course, all settings are natural—that is, places where everyday experiences take place. Qualitative researchers study people doing things together in the places where these things are done (Becker, 1986). There is no field site or natural place where one goes to do

this kind of work (see also Gupta & Ferguson, 1997, p. 8). The site is constituted through the researcher's interpretive practices. Historically, analysts have distinguished between experimental (laboratory) and field (natural) research settings, hence the argument that qualitative research is naturalistic. Activity theory erases this distinction (Keller & Keller, 1996, p. 20; Vygotsky, 1978).

6. According to Weinstein and Weinstein (1991), "The meaning of *bricoleur* in French popular speech is 'someone who works with his (or her) hands and uses devious means compared to those of the craftsman.' . . . the *bricoleur* is practical and gets the job done" (p. 161). These authors provide a history of the term, connecting it to the works of the German sociologist and social theorist Georg Simmel and, by implication, Baudelaire. Hammersley (in press) disputes our use of this term. Following Lévi-Strauss, he reads the *bricoleur* as a mythmaker. He suggests the term be replaced with the notion of the boatbuilder. Hammersley also quarrels with our "moments" model of qualitative research, contending that it implies some sense of progress.

7. Brian De Palma reproduced this baby carriage scene in his 1987 film *The Untouchables*.

8. In the harbor, the muzzles of the *Potemkin*'s two huge guns swing slowly toward the camera. Words onscreen inform us, "The brutal military power answered by guns of the battleship." A final famous three-shot montage sequence shows first a sculptured sleeping lion, then a lion rising from his sleep, and finally the lion roaring, symbolizing the rage of the Russian people (Cook, 1981, p. 167). In this sequence Eisenstein uses montage to expand time, creating a psychological duration for this horrible event. By drawing out this sequence, by showing the baby in the carriage, the soldiers firing on the citizens, the blood on the mother's glove, the descending carriage on the steps, he suggests a level of destruction of great magnitude.

9. Here it is relevant to make a distinction between techniques that are used across disciplines and methods that are used within disciplines. Ethnomethodologists, for example, employ their approach as a method, whereas others selectively borrow that method as a technique for their own applications. Harry Wolcott (personal communication, 1993) suggests this distinction. It is also relevant to make distinctions among topic, method, and resource. Methods can be studied as topics of inquiry; that is how a case study gets done. In this ironic, ethnomethodological sense, method is both a resource and a topic of inquiry.

10. Indeed, any attempt to give an essential definition of qualitative research requires a qualitative analysis of the circumstances that produce such a definition.

11. In this sense all research is qualitative, because "the observer is at the center of the research process" (Vidich & Lyman, Chapter 2, this volume).

12. See Lincoln and Guba (1985) for an extension and elaboration of this tradition in the mid-1980s, and for more recent extensions see Taylor and Bogdan (1998) and Creswell (1997).

13. Greenblatt (1997, pp. 15-18) offers a useful deconstructive reading of the many meanings and practices Geertz brings to the term *thick description*.

14. These works marginalized and minimized the contributions of standpoint feminist theory and research to this discourse (see Behar, 1995, p. 3; Gordon, 1995, p. 432).

15. Olesen (Chapter 8, this volume) identifies three strands of feminist research: mainstream empirical, standpoint and cultural studies, and poststructural, postmodern. She

places Afrocentric and other models of color under the cultural studies and postmodern categories.

16. These, of course, are our interpretations of these paradigms and interpretive styles.

17. *Empirical materials* is the preferred term for what are traditionally described as data.

◆ References

Aronowitz, S. (1988). *Science as power: Discourse and ideology in modern society.* Minneapolis: University of Minnesota Press.

Bateson, G. (1972). *Steps to an ecology of mind.* New York: Ballantine.

Becker, H. S. (1970). Problems of inference and proof in participant observation. In H. S. Becker, *Sociological work: Method and substance.* Chicago: Aldine. (Reprinted from *American Sociological Review, 1958, 23,* 652-660)

Becker, H. S. (1986). *Doing things together.* Evanston: Northwestern University Press.

Becker, H. S. (1996). The epistemology of qualitative research. In R. Jessor, A. Colby, & R. A. Shweder (Eds.), *Ethnography and human development: Context and meaning in social inquiry* (pp. 53-71). Chicago: University of Chicago Press.

Becker, H. S. (1998). *Tricks of the trade: How to think about your research while you're doing it.* Chicago: University of Chicago Press.

Becker, H. S., Geer, B., Hughes, E. C., & Strauss, A. L. (1961). *Boys in white: Student culture in medical school.* Chicago: University of Chicago Press.

Behar, R. (1995). Introduction: Out of exile. In R. Behar & D. A. Gordon (Eds.), *Women writing culture* (pp. 1-29). Berkeley: University of California Press.

Bogdan, R. C., & Taylor, S. J. (1975). *Introduction to qualitative research methods: A phenomenological approach to the social sciences.* New York: John Wiley.

Campbell, D. T., & Stanley, J. C. (1963). *Experimental and quasi-experimental designs for research.* Chicago: Rand McNally.

Carey, J. W. (1989). *Communication as culture: Essays on media and society.* Boston: Unwin Hyman.

Cicourel, A. V. (1964). *Method and measurement in sociology.* New York: Free Press.

Clifford, J. (1988). *The predicament of culture: Twentieth-century ethnography, literature, and art.* Cambridge, MA: Harvard University Press.

Clifford, J., & Marcus, G. E. (Eds.). (1986). *Writing culture: The poetics and politics of ethnography.* Berkeley: University of California Press.

Clough, P. T. (1992). *The end(s) of ethnography: From realism to social criticism.* Newbury Park, CA: Sage.

Clough, P. T. (1998). *The end(s) of ethnography: From realism to social criticism* (2nd ed.). New York: Peter Lang.

Cook, D. A. (1981). *A history of narrative film.* New York: W. W. Norton.

Creswell, J. W. (1997). *Qualitative inquiry and research design: Choosing among five traditions.* Thousand Oaks, CA: Sage.

Denzin, N. K. (1970). *The research act.* Chicago: Aldine.

Denzin, N. K. (1978). *The research act* (2nd ed.). New York: McGraw-Hill.

Denzin, N. K. (1997). *Interpretive ethnography.* Thousand Oaks, CA: Sage.

Dilthey, W. L. (1976). *Selected writings.* Cambridge: Cambridge University Press. (Original work published 1900)

Diversi, M. (1998). Glimpses of street life: Representing lived experience through short stories. *Qualitative Inquiry, 4,* 131-137.

Ellis, C., & Bochner, A. P. (Eds.). (1996). *Composing ethnography: Alternative forms of qualitative writing.* Walnut Creek, CA: AltaMira.

Filstead, W. J. (Ed.). (1970). *Qualitative methodology.* Chicago: Markham.

Flick, U. (1998). *An introduction to qualitative research: Theory, method and applications.* London: Sage.

Geertz, C. (1973). *The interpretation of cultures: Selected essays.* New York: Basic Books.

Geertz, C. (1983). *Local knowledge: Further essays in interpretive anthropology.* New York: Basic Books.

Geertz, C. (1988). *Works and lives: The anthropologist as author.* Stanford, CA: Stanford University Press.

Glaser, B. G. (1992). *Emergence vs. forcing: Basics of grounded theory.* Mill Valley, CA: Sociology Press.

Glaser, B. G., & Strauss, A. L. (1967). *The discovery of grounded theory: Strategies for qualitative research.* Chicago: Aldine.

Gordon, D. A. (1995). Culture writing women: Inscribing feminist anthropology. In R. Behar & D. A. Gordon (Eds.), *Women writing culture* (pp. 429-441). Berkeley: University of California Press.

Gordon, D. A. (1988). Writing culture, writing feminism: The poetics and politics of experimental ethnography. *Inscriptions, 3/4*(8), 21-31.

Greenblatt, S. (1997). The touch of the real. In S. B. Ortner (Ed.), The fate of "culture": Geertz and beyond [Special issue]. *Representations, 59,* 14-29.

Guba, E. G. (1990). The alternative paradigm dialog. In E. G. Guba (Ed.), *The paradigm dialog* (pp. 17-30). Newbury Park, CA: Sage.

Guba, E. G., & Lincoln, Y. S. (1989). *Fourth generation evaluation.* Newbury Park, CA: Sage.

Gupta, A., & Ferguson, J. (1997). Discipline and practice: "The field" as site, method, and location in anthropology. In A. Gupta & J. Ferguson (Eds.), *Anthropological locations: Boundaries and grounds of a field science* (pp. 1-46). Berkeley: University of California Press.

Hammersley, M. (1992). *What's wrong with ethnography? Methodological explorations.* London: Routledge.

Hammersley, M. (in press). Not bricolage but boatbuilding. *Journal of Contemporary Ethnography.*

hooks, b. (1990). *Yearning: Race, gender, and cultural politics.* Boston: South End.

Huber, J. (1995). Centennial essay: Institutional perspectives on sociology. *American Journal of Sociology, 101,* 194-216.

Jackson, M. (1998). *Minima ethnographica: Intersubjectivity and the anthropological project.* Chicago: University of Chicago Press.

Jameson, F. (1991). *Postmodernism; or, The cultural logic of late capitalism.* Durham, NC: Duke University Press.

Jones, S. H. (1999). Torch. *Qualitative Inquiry, 5,* 235-250.

Keller, C. M., & Keller, J. D. (1996). *Cognition and tool use: The blacksmith at work.* New York: Cambridge University Press.

Lather, P. (1993). Fertile obsession: Validity after poststructuralism. *Sociological Quarterly, 35,* 673-694.

Lather, P., & Smithies, C. (1997). *Troubling the angels: Women living with HIV/AIDS.* Boulder, CO: Westview.

LeCompte, M. D., & Preissle, J. (with Tesch, R.). (1993). *Ethnography and qualitative design in educational research* (2nd ed.). New York: Academic Press.

Lévi-Strauss, C. (1966). *The savage mind* (2nd ed.). Chicago: University of Chicago Press.

Lincoln, Y. S. (1999, June). Courage, vulnerability and truth. Keynote address delivered at the conference "Reclaiming Voice II: Ethnographic Inquiry and Qualitative Research in a Postmodern Age," University of California, Irvine.

Lincoln, Y. S. (in press). Varieties of validity: Quality in qualitative research. In J. S. Smart & C. Ethington (Eds.), *Higher education: Handbook of theory and research.* New York: Agathon Press.

Lincoln, Y. S., & Guba, E. G. (1985). *Naturalistic inquiry.* Beverly Hills, CA: Sage.

Lofland, J. (1971). *Analyzing social settings.* Belmont, CA: Wadsworth.

Lofland, J. (1995). Analytic ethnography: Features, failings, and futures. *Journal of Contemporary Ethnography, 24,* 30-67.

Lofland, J., & Lofland, L. H. (1984). *Analyzing social settings: A guide to qualitative observation and analysis* (2nd ed.). Belmont, CA: Wadsworth.

Lofland, J., & Lofland, L. H. (1995). *Analyzing social settings: A guide to qualitative observation and analysis* (3rd ed.). Belmont, CA: Wadsworth.

Lofland, L. (1980). The 1969 Blumer-Hughes Talk. *Urban Life and Culture, 8,* 248-260.

Malinowski, B. (1948). *Magic, science and religion, and other essays.* New York: Natural History Press. (Original work published 1916)

Malinowski, B. (1967). *A diary in the strict sense of the term* (N. Guterman, Trans.). New York: Harcourt, Brace & World.

Marcus, G. E., & Fischer, M. M. J. (1986). *Anthropology as cultural critique: An experimental moment in the human sciences.* Chicago: University of Chicago Press.

Monaco, J. (1981). *How to read a film: The art, technology, language, history and theory of film* (Rev. ed.). New York: Oxford University Press.

Nelson, C., Treichler, P. A., & Grossberg, L. (1992). Cultural studies: An introduction. In L. Grossberg, C. Nelson, & P. A. Treichler (Eds.), *Cultural studies* (pp. 1-16). New York: Routledge.

Ortner, S. B. (1997). Introduction. In S. B. Ortner (Ed.), The fate of "culture": Geertz and beyond [Special issue]. *Representations, 59,* 1-13.

Plath, D. W. (1990). Fieldnotes, filed notes, and the conferring of note. In R. Sanjek (Ed.), *Fieldnotes: The makings of anthropology* (pp. 371-384). Ithaca, NY: Cornell University Press.

Richardson, L. (1997). *Fields of play: Constructing an academic life.* New Brunswick, NJ: Rutgers University Press.

Roffman, P., & Purdy, J. (1981). *The Hollywood social problem film.* Bloomington: Indiana University Press.

Ronai, C. R. (1998). Sketching with Derrida: An ethnography of a researcher/erotic dancer. *Qualitative Inquiry, 4,* 405-420.

Rosaldo, R. (1989). *Culture and truth: The remaking of social analysis.* Boston: Beacon.

Sanjek, R. (Ed.). (1990). *Fieldnotes: The makings of anthropology.* Ithaca, NY: Cornell University Press.

Schwandt, T. A. (1997a). *Qualitative inquiry: A dictionary of terms.* Thousand Oaks, CA: Sage.

Schwandt, T. A. (1997b). Textual gymnastics, ethics and angst. In W. G. Tierney & Y. S. Lincoln (Eds.), *Representation and the text: Re-framing the narrative voice* (pp. 305-311). Albany: State University of New York Press.

Silverman, D. (1997). Towards an aesthetics of research. In D. Silverman (Ed.), *Qualitative research: Theory, method and practice* (pp. 239-253). London: Sage.

Smith, A. D. (1993). *Fires in the mirror: Crown Heights, Brooklyn, and other identities.* Garden City, NY: Anchor.

Snow, D., & Morrill, C. (1995). Ironies, puzzles, and contradictions in Denzin and Lincoln's vision of qualitative research. *Journal of Contemporary Ethnography, 22,* 358-362.

Spindler, G., & Spindler, L. (1992). Cultural process and ethnography: An anthropological perspective. In M. D. LeCompte, W. L. Millroy, & J. Preissle (Eds.), *The handbook of qualitative research in education* (pp. 53-92). New York: Academic Press.

Stocking, G. W., Jr. (1986). Anthropology and the science of the irrational: Malinowski's encounter with Freudian psychoanalysis. In G. W. Stocking, Jr.

(Ed.), Malinowski, Rivers, Benedict and others: *Essays on culture and personality* (pp. 13-49). Madison: University of Wisconsin Press.

Stocking, G. W., Jr. (1989). The ethnographic sensibility of the 1920s and the dualism of the anthropological tradition. In G. W. Stocking, Jr. (Ed.), *Romantic motives: Essays on anthropological sensibility* (pp. 208-276). Madison: University of Wisconsin Press.

Stoller, P., & Olkes, C. (1987). *In sorcery's shadow: A memoir of apprenticeship among the Songhay of Niger.* Chicago: University of Chicago Press.

Strauss, A. L., & Corbin, J. (1998). *Basics of qualitative research: Techniques and procedures for developing grounded theory* (2nd ed.). Thousand Oaks, CA: Sage.

Taylor, S. J., & Bogdan, R. (1998). *Introduction to qualitative research methods: A guidebook and resource* (3rd ed.). New York: John Wiley.

Turner, V., & Bruner, E. (Eds.). (1986). *The anthropology of experience.* Urbana: University of Illinois Press.

Van Maanen, J. (1988). *Tales of the field: On writing ethnography.* Chicago: University of Chicago Press.

Vygotsky, L. S. (1978). *Mind in society: The development of higher psychological processes* (M. Cole, V. John-Steiner, S. Scribner, & E. Souberman, Eds.). Cambridge, MA: Harvard University Press.

Weinstein, D., & Weinstein, M. A. (1991). Georg Simmel: Sociological flaneur bricoleur. *Theory, Culture & Society, 8,* 151-168.

West, C. (1989). *The American evasion of philosophy: A genealogy of pragmatism.* Madison: University of Wisconsin Press.

Wolcott, H. F. (1990). *Writing up qualitative research.* Newbury Park, CA: Sage.

Wolcott, H. F. (1992). Posturing in qualitative inquiry. In M. D. LeCompte, W. L. Millroy, & J. Preissle (Eds.), *The handbook of qualitative research in education* (pp. 3-52). New York: Academic Press.

Wolcott, H. F. (1995). *The art of fieldwork.* Walnut Creek, CA: AltaMira.

Wolf, M. A. (1992). *A thrice-told tale: Feminism, postmodernism, and ethnographic responsibility.* Stanford, CA: Stanford University Press.

PART I

Locating the Field

This part begins with the history and traditions of qualitative methods in the social and human sciences. It then turns to action research and the relationship between universities and society. It next takes up issues surrounding the social, political, and moral responsibilities of the researcher as well as the ethics and politics of qualitative inquiry.

◆ History and Tradition

Chapter 2, by Arthur Vidich and Stanford Lyman, and Chapter 3, by Davydd Greenwood and Morten Levin, reveal the depth and complexity of the traditional and applied qualitative research perspectives that are consciously and unconsciously inherited by the researcher-as-interpretive-*bricoleur.*[1] These traditions locate the investigator in a system of historical (and organizational) discourse. This system guides and constrains the interpretive work that is done in any specific study.

Vidich and Lyman show how the ethnographic tradition extends from the Greeks through the 15th- and 16th-century interests of Westerners in the origins of primitive cultures; to colonial ethnology connected to the empires of Spain, England, France, and Holland; to several 20th-century transformations in the United States and Europe. Throughout this history, the users of qualitative research have displayed commitments to a small set of beliefs, including objectivism, the desire to contextualize experience, and a willingness to interpret theoretically what they have observed.

These beliefs supplement the positivist tradition of complicity with colonialism, commitment to monumentalism, and the production of timeless texts discussed in Chapter 1. The colonial model located qualitative inquiry in racial and sexual discourses that privileged white patriarchy. Of course, as we have indicated in our introductory chapter, recently these beliefs have come under considerable attack. Vidich and Lyman, as well as Gloria Ladson-Billings (Chapter 9), document the extent to which early qualitative researchers were implicated in these systems of oppression.

Greenwood and Levin expand upon and extend this line of criticism. They are quite explicit that scholars have a responsibility to do work that is socially meaningful and socially responsible. The relationships among researchers, universities, and society in general must change. Politically informed action research, inquiry committed to praxis and social change, is the vehicle for accomplishing this transformation.

Action researchers are committed to a set of disciplined, material practices that produce radical, democratizing transformations in the civic sphere. These practices involve collaborative dialogue, participatory decision making, inclusive democratic deliberation, and the maximal participation and representation of all relevant parties (Ryan & Destefano, 2000, p. 1; see also Stringer, 1996, p. 38). Action researchers literally help transform inquiry into praxis, or action. Research subjects become co-participants and stakeholders in the process of inquiry. Research becomes praxis—practical, reflective, pragmatic action—directed toward solving problems in the world.

These problems originate in the lives of the research co-participants—they do not come down from on high, by way of grand theory. Together, stakeholders and action researchers create knowledge that is pragmatically useful. In the process, they jointly define research objectives and political goals, co-construct research questions, pool knowledge, hone shared research skills, and fashion interpretations and performance texts that implement specific strategies for social change (see Conquergood, 1998).

Academic science in the 20th century was often unable to accomplish goals such as these. According to Greenwood and Levin, there are several reasons for this failure, including the inability of a so-called positivistic, value-free social science to produce useful social research; the increasing tendency of outside corporations to define the needs and values of the university; the loss of research funds to entrepreneurial and private sector research organizations; and bloated, inefficient internal administrative infrastructures.

Greenwood and Levin do not renounce the practices of science; rather, they call for a reformulation of what science is all about. Their model of pragmatically grounded action research is not a retreat from disciplined scientific inquiry.[2] This form of inquiry reconceptualizes science as a collaborative, communicative, communitarian, context-centered, moral project. Greenwood and Levin's chapter is a call for a civic social science, a pragmatic science that will lead to the radical reconstruction of the university's relationships with society, state, and community in the 21st century.

◆ Reflexivity, Social Responsibility, and the Ethics of Inquiry

The contributions of Michelle Fine, Lois Weis, Susan Weseen, and Loonmun Wong (Chapter 4) and Clifford Christians (Chapter 5) extend this call for a committed, moral, civic social science. Fine and her colleagues argue that a great deal of qualitative research has reproduced a colonizing discourse of the "Other"; that is, the Other is interpreted through the eyes and cultural standards of the researcher. They review the traditions that have led researchers to speak on behalf of the Other, especially those connected to the belief systems identified by Vidich and Lyman. They then offer a series of "writing-stories" from their ongoing study of 150 poor and working-class men and women, white, African American, Latino, and Asian American. These stories reveal a set of knotty, emergent ethical and rhetorical dilemmas that the researchers encountered as they attempted to write for, with, and about these poor and working-class stakeholders.

These are the problems of the sixth and seventh moments. They turn on the issues of voice, reflexivity, "race," informed consent, good and bad stories, coming clean at the hyphen. Voice and reflexivity are primary. Fine and her coauthors struggled with how to locate themselves and their stakeholders in the text, including whether or not to tell stories that would reflect negatively on the working poor, especially given that conservatives welcome stories about persons who cheat to receive welfare. They avoided such tales. They struggled, as well, with how to write about "race," a floating, unstable fiction that is also an inerasable aspect of the self and its personal history.

Fine and her colleagues paid their respondents $40 per interview. Who owns an interview once it has been transcribed? Whose story is it, and what does informed consent mean when you pay for the story? Who is consenting to what, and who is being protected? Informed consent can work against the formation of open, sharing, collaborative relationships. At the same time, how does the researcher move to the other side of the hyphen, become an advocate for the stakeholder? What is lost, and what is gained, when this is done? How can one write in a way that answers the needs of the urban poor in time when, to paraphrase Fine and her co-authors, many people of color no longer trust whites or academics to do them or their communities any good?

◆ A Feminist, Communitarian Ethical Framework

Clifford Christians locates the ethics and politics of qualitative inquiry within a broader historical and intellectual framework. He first examines the Enlightenment model of positivism, value-free inquiry, utilitarianism, and utilitarian ethics. In a value-free social science, codes of ethics for professional societies become the conventional format for moral principles. By the 1980s, each of the major social science associations in the United States (contemporaneous with passage of federal laws and promulgation of national guidelines) had developed its own ethical code, with an emphasis on several guidelines: informed consent, nondeception, the absence of psychological or physical harm, privacy and confidentiality, and a commitment to collecting and presenting reliable and valid empirical materials. Institutional review boards (IRBs) implemented these guidelines, including ensuring that informed consent is always obtained in human subject research. However, Christians notes, as do Fine and her colleagues, that in reality IRBs protect institutions and not individuals.

Several events challenged the Enlightenment model, including the Nazi medical experiments, the Tuskegee Syphilis Study, Project Camelot in the 1960s, Milgram's deception of subjects in his psychology experiments, Humphrey's deceptive study of homosexuals, and the complicity of social scientists with military initiatives in Vietnam. In addition, charges of fraud, plagiarism, data tampering, and misrepresentation continue to the present day. Christians details the poverty of this model. It creates the conditions for deception, for the invasion of private spaces, for the duping of subjects, and for challenges to subject's moral worth and dignity (see also

Angrosino & Pérez, Chapter 3, Volume 3; Guba & Lincoln, 1989, pp. 120-141).

Christians calls for the replacement of this model with an ethics based on the values of a feminist communitarianism. This is an evolving, emerging ethical framework that serves as a powerful antidote to the deception-based, utilitarian IRB system. It presumes a community that is ontologically and axiologically prior to the person. This community has common moral values, and research is rooted in a concept of care, shared governance, neighborliness, love, kindness, and the moral good. Accounts of social life should display these values and should be based on interpretive sufficiency. They should have sufficient depth to allow the reader to form a critical understanding about the world studied. These texts should exhibit an absence of race, class, and gender stereotyping. They should generate social criticism and lead to resistance, empowerment, and social action; they should stimulate positive change in the social world.

In the feminist, communitarian model, as with the model of action research advocated by Greenwood and Levin (see also Kemmis & McTaggart, Chapter 11, Volume 2), participants have a coequal say in how research should be conducted, what should be studied, which methods should be used, which findings are valid and acceptable, how the findings are to be implemented, and how the consequences of such action are to be assessed. Spaces for disagreement are recognized at the same time discourse aims for mutual understanding, for the honoring of moral commitments.

A sacred, existential epistemology places us in a noncompetitive, nonhierarchical relationship to the earth, to nature, and to the larger world (Bateson, 1972, p. 335). This sacred epistemology stresses the values of empowerment, shared governance, care, solidarity, love, community, covenant, morally involved observers, and civic transformation. As Christians observes, this ethical epistemology recovers the moral values that were excluded by the rational, Enlightenment science project. This sacred epistemology is based on a philosophical anthropology that declares "all humans are worthy of dignity and sacred status without exception for class or ethnicity" (Christians, 1995, p. 129). A universal human ethic stressing the sacredness of life, human dignity, truth telling, and nonviolence derives from this position (Christians, 1997, pp. 12-15). This ethic is based on locally experienced, culturally prescribed protonorms (Christians, 1995, p. 129). These primal norms provide a defensible "conception of good rooted in universal human solidarity" (Christians, 1995,

p. 129; see also Christians, 1997, 1998). This sacred epistemology recognizes and interrogates the ways in which race, class, and gender operate as important systems of oppression in the world today.

Thus Christians outlines a radical ethical path for the future. In so doing, he transcends the usual middle-of-the-road ethical models that focus on the problems associated with betrayal, deception, and harm in qualitative research. Christians's call for a collaborative social science research model makes the researcher responsible not to a removed discipline (or institution), but to those studied. This implements critical, action, and feminist traditions that forcefully align the ethics of research with a politics of the oppressed. Christians's framework reorganizes existing discourses on ethics and the social sciences.[3]

With Christians, we endorse a feminist, communitarian ethic that calls for collaborative, trusting, nonoppressive relationships between researchers and those studied. Such an ethic presumes that investigators are committed to recognizing personal accountability, the value of individual expressiveness and caring, the capacity for empathy, and the sharing of emotionality (Collins, 1990, p. 216).

◆ Notes

1. Any distinction between applied and nonapplied qualitative research traditions is somewhat arbitrary. Both traditions are scholarly. Each has a long tradition and a long history, and each carries basic implications for theory and social change. Good theoretical research should also have applied relevance and implications. On occasion it is argued that applied and action research are nontheoretical, but even this conclusion can be disputed, as Kemmis and McTaggart demonstrate in Chapter 11 of Volume 2.

2. We will develop a notion of a sacred science below and in Chapter 14.

3. Given Christians's framework, there are primarily two ethical models: utilitarian and nonutilitarian. However, historically, and most recently, researchers have taken one of five ethical stances: absolutist, consequentialist, feminist, relativist, or deception. Often these stances merge with one another. The absolutist position argues that any method that contributes to a society's self-understanding is acceptable, but only conduct in the public sphere should be studied. The deception model says that any method, including the use of lies and misrepresentation, is justified in the name of truth. The relativist stance says that researchers have absolute freedom to study what they want; ethical standards are a matter of individual conscience. Christians's feminist, communitarian framework elaborates a contextual-consequential framework that stresses mutual respect, noncoercion, nonmanipulation, and the support of democratic values (see Guba & Lincoln, 1989, pp. 120-141; House, 1990; Smith, 1990; see also Collins, 1990, p. 216; Mitchell, 1993).

◆ References

Bateson, G. (1972). *Steps to an ecology of mind.* New York: Ballantine.

Christians, C. G. (1995). The naturalistic fallacy in contemporary interactionist-interpretive research. *Studies in Symbolic Interaction: A Research Annual, 19,* 125-130.

Christians, C. G. (1997). The ethics of being in a communications context. In C. G. Christians & M. Traber (Eds.), *Communication ethics and universal values* (pp. 3-23). Thousand Oaks, CA: Sage.

Christians, C. G. (1998). The sacredness of life. *Media Development, 45*(2), 3-7.

Collins, P. H. (1990). *Black feminist thought: Knowledge, consciousness, and the politics of empowerment.* New York: Routledge.

Conquergood, D. (1998). Health theatre in a Hmong refugee camp: Performance, communication and culture. In J. Cohen-Cruz (Ed.), *Radical street performance: An international anthology* (pp. 220-229). New York: Routledge.

Guba, E. G., & Lincoln, Y. S. (1989). *Fourth generation evaluation.* Newbury Park, CA: Sage.

House, E. R. (1990). An ethics of qualitative field studies. In E. G. Guba (Ed.), *The paradigm dialog* (pp. 158-164). Newbury Park, CA: Sage.

Mitchell, R. J., Jr. (1993). *Secrecy and fieldwork.* Newbury Park, CA: Sage.

Ryan, K., & Destefano, L. (2000). Introduction. In K. Ryan & L. Destefano (Eds.), *Evaluation in a democratic society: Deliberation, dialogue and inclusion* (pp. 1-20). San Francisco: Jossey-Bass.

Smith, L. M. (1990). Ethics, field studies, and the paradigm crisis. In E. G. Guba (Ed.), *The paradigm dialog* (pp. 139-157). Newbury Park, CA: Sage.

Stringer, E. T. (1996). *Action research: A handbook for practitioners.* Thousand Oaks, CA: Sage.

2

Qualitative Methods

Their History in

Sociology and Anthropology

Arthur J. Vidich and Stanford M. Lyman

◆ Modern sociology has taken as its mission the analysis and understanding of the patterned conduct and social processes of society,
and of the bases in values and attitudes on which individual and collective
participation in social life rests. It is presupposed that, to carry out the
tasks associated with this mission, the sociologist has the following:

1. The ability to perceive and contextualize the world of his or her own experience as well as the capacity to project a metaempirical conceptualization
   onto those contexts of life and social institutions with which he or she has not
   had direct experience. The sociologist requires a sensitivity to and a curiosity
   about both what is visible and what is not visible to immediate perception—
   and sufficient self-understanding to make possible an empathy with the roles
   and values of others.

2. The ability to detach him- or herself from the particular values and special interests of organized groups in order that he or she may gain a level of understanding that does not rest on a priori commitments. For every individual and
   group, ideologies and faiths define the distinction between good and evil and
   lead to such nonsociological but conventional orientations as are involved in

everyday judging and decision making. The sociologist's task in ethnography is not only to be a part of such thoughts and actions but also to understand them at a higher level of conceptualization.

3. A sufficient degree of social and personal distance from prevailing norms and values to be able to analyze them objectively. Usually, the ability to engage in self-objectification is sufficient to produce the quality of orientation necessary for an individual to be an ethnographic sociologist or anthropologist.

Qualitative ethnographic social research, then, entails an attitude of detachment toward society that permits the sociologist to observe the conduct of self and others, to understand the mechanisms of social processes, and to comprehend and explain why both actors and processes are as they are. The existence of this sociological attitude is presupposed in any meaningful discussion of methods appropriate to ethnographic investigation (see Adler, Adler, & Fontana, 1991; Hammersley, 1992).

Sociology and anthropology are disciplines that, born out of concern to understand the "other," are nevertheless also committed to an understanding of the self. If, following the tenets of symbolic interactionism, we grant that the other can be understood only as part of a relationship with the self, we may suggest a different approach to ethnography and the use of qualitative methods, one that conceives the observer as possessing a self-identity that by definition is re-created in its relationship with the observed—the other, whether in another culture or that of the observer.

In its entirety, the research task requires both the act of observation and the act of communicating the analysis of these observations to others (for works describing how this is accomplished, see Johnson, 1975; Schatzman & Strauss, 1973; see also Pratt, 1986). The relationships that arise between these processes are not only the determinants of the character of the final research product, but also the arena of sociological methods least tractable to conventionalized understanding. The data gathering process can never be described in its totality because these "tales of the field" are themselves part of an ongoing social process that in its minute-by-minute and day-to-day experience defies recapitulation. To take as one's objective the making of a total description of the method of gathering data would shift the frame of ethnological reference, in effect substituting the means for the end. Such a substitution occurs when exactitude in reporting research methods takes priority over the solution to substantive sociological problems.

In fact, a description of a particular method of research usually takes place as a retrospective account, that is, a report written after the research has been completed. This all-too-often unacknowledged fact illustrates the part of the research process wherein the acts of observation are temporally separated from the description of how they were accomplished. Such essays in methodology are reconstructions of ethnographic reality; they take what was experienced originally and shrink it into a set of images that, although purporting to be a description of the actual method of research, exemplify a textbook ideal.

The point may be clarified through a comparison of the world of a supposedly "scientific" sociologist with that of such artists as painters, novelists, composers, poets, dancers, or chess masters. Viewing a painting, listening to music, reading a novel, reciting a poem, watching a chess game, or attending to the performance of a ballerina, one experiences a finished production, the "front region," as Goffman (1959, p. 107) puts it. The method seems to be inherent in the finished form (Goffman, 1949, pp. 48-77). More appropriately, we might say that the method—of composing, writing, painting, performing, or whatever—is an intrinsic part of the creator's craftsmanship, without which the creation could not be made. If the artist were to be asked, "How did you do it? Tell me your method," his or her answer would require an act of ex post facto reconstruction: the method of describing the method. However, the original production would still retain its primordial integrity; that cannot be changed, whatever conclusions are to be drawn from later discussions about how it was accomplished. Speaking of sociological methods, Robert Nisbet (1977) recalls:

> While I was engaged in exploration of some of the sources of modern sociology [it occurred to me] that none of the great themes which have provided continuing challenge and also theoretical foundation for sociologists during the last century was ever reached through anything resembling what we are to-day fond of identifying as "scientific method." I mean the kind of method, replete with appeals to statistical analysis, problem design, hypothesis, verification, replication, and theory construction, that we find described in textbooks and courses on methodology. (p. 3)

From Nisbet's pointed observation we may conclude that the method-in-use for the production of a finished sociological study is unique to that study and can be neither described nor replicated as it actually occurred. That societal investigators may choose to use different kinds of material as their data—documents for the historian, quantified reports for the demographer, or direct perception of a portion of society for the ethnographer—does not alter the fact that social scientists are observers. As observers of the world they also participate in it; therefore, they make their observations within a mediated framework, that is, a framework of symbols and cultural meanings given to them by those aspects of their life histories that they bring to the observational setting. Lurking behind each method of research is the personal equation supplied to the setting by the individual observer (Clifford, 1986). In this fundamental sense all research methods are at bottom qualitative and are, for that matter, equally objective; the use of quantitative data or mathematical procedures does not eliminate the intersubjective element that underlies social research. Objectivity resides not in a method, per se, but in the framing of the research problem and the willingness of the researchers to pursue that problem wherever the data and their hunches may lead (Vidich, 1955; see also Fontana, 1980; Goffman, 1974).[1] If, in this sense, all research is qualitative—because the observer is at the center of the research process—does this mean that the findings produced by the method are no more than the peculiar reality of each observer (Atkinson, 1990)?

One simple answer is that we judge for ourselves on the standard of whether the work communicates or "says" something to us—that is, does it connect with our reality?[2] Does it provide us with insights that help to organize our own observations? Does it resonate with our image of the world? Or does it provide such a powerful incursion on the latter that we feel compelled to reexamine what we have long supposed to be true about our life world?

Or, put another way, if the method used is not the issue, by what standards are we able to judge the worth of sociological research (Gellner, 1979)? Each is free to judge the work of others and to accept it or reject it if it does not communicate something meaningful about the world; and what is meaningful for one person is not necessarily meaningful for another.

In the present and for the foreseeable future, the virtually worldwide disintegration of common values and a deconstruction of consensus-based societies evoke recognition of the fact that there exist many competing realities, and this fact poses problems not previously encountered by sociology. In effect, this situation sets up a condition wherein the number of possible theoretical perspectives from which the world, or any part of it, may be viewed sociologically is conditioned only by the number of extant scientific worldviews. As for the potential subjects of investigation, their outlooks are limited only by the many religious faiths, occupational and professional ideologies, and other *Weltanschauungen* that arise to guide or upset their lives. At the time of this writing, a new outlook on epistemology has come to the fore. It disprivileges all received discourses and makes discourse itself a topic of the sociology of knowledge.[3]

The history of qualitative research suggests that this has not always been the case (Douglas, 1974). In the past, the research problems for many investigators were given to them by their commitment to or against a religious faith or an ethnic creed, or by their identification with or opposition to specific national goals or socioeconomic programs. In the historical account of the use of qualitative methods that follows, we shall show that their use has been occasioned by more than the perspective of the individual observer, but also that the domain assumptions that once guided qualitative research have lost much of their force. However, the faiths, creeds, and hopes that had given focus to the work of our predecessors have not disappeared altogether from the sociologist's mental maps (Luhmann, 1986). Rather, they remain as a less-than-conscious background, the all-too-familiar furniture of the sociological mind. Milan Kundera (1988) has pointed to a central issue in our present dilemma in *The Art of the Novel*: "But if God is gone and man is no longer the master, then who is the master? The planet is moving through the void without any master. There it is, the unbearable lightness of being" (p. 41).

Throughout all of the eras during which social science made use of observational methods, researchers have entered into their studies with problems implicitly and, in some cases, explicitly defined by hopes and faiths. Focusing on the substance of these problems and their ideational adumbrations, we shall confine our discussion of this history to the qualitative methods used by anthropologists and sociologists in ethnographic research, that is, the direct observation of the social realities by the individual observer. Our history proceeds along a continuum that begins with the first encounters of early ethnographers with the New World and ends with the practical and theoretical problems facing the work of our contemporaries.

◆ Early Ethnography: The Discovery of the Other

Ethnos, a Greek term, denotes a people, a race or cultural group (A. D. Smith, 1989, pp. 13-18). When *ethno* as a prefix is combined with *graphic* to form the term *ethnographic,* the reference is to the subdiscipline known as descriptive anthropology—in its broadest sense, the science devoted to describing ways of life of humankind. *Ethnography,* then, refers to a social scientific description of a people and the cultural basis of their peoplehood (Peacock, 1986). Both descriptive anthropology and ethnography are thought to be atheoretical, to be concerned solely with description. However, the observations of the ethnographer are always guided by world images that determine which data are salient and which are not: An act of attention to one rather than another object reveals one dimension of the observer's value commitment, as well as his or her value-laden interests.

Early ethnography grew out of the interests of Westerners in the origins of culture and civilization and in the assumption that contemporary "primitive" peoples, those thought by Westerners to be less civilized than themselves, were, in effect, living replicas of the "great chain of being" that linked the Occident to its prehistoric beginnings (Hodgen, 1964, pp. 386-432). Such a mode of ethnography arose in the 15th and 16th centuries as a result of fundamental problems that had grown out of Columbus's and later explorers' voyages to the Western hemisphere, the so-called New World, and to the island cultures of the South Seas.

The discovery of human beings living in non-Occidental environments evoked previously unimagined cosmological difficulties for European intellectuals, who felt it necessary to integrate the new fact into the canon of received knowledge and understanding.[4] Because the Bible, especially the book of Genesis, was taken to be the only valid source on which to rely for an understanding of the history of geography and processes of creation, and because it placed the origin of humankind in the Garden of Eden—located somewhere in what is today called the Middle East—all human beings were held to be descended from the first pair, and, later, in accordance with flood ethnography (Numbers, 1992), from the descendants of Noah and his family, the only survivors of a worldwide deluge. Linking Columbus's encounter with what we now know as the Taino, Arawak, and Carib (Keegan, 1992; Rouse, 1992) peoples in the New World to the biblical account proved to be difficult. Specifically, the existence of others outside the Christian brotherhood revealed by his "discovery" posed this question: How had the ancestors of these beings reached the Americas in pre-Columbian times? Any thesis that they had not migrated from Eurasia or Africa was held to be heresy and a claim that humankind might have arisen from more than one creative act by God.

In general, the racial and cultural diversity of peoples throughout the globe presented post-Renaissance Europeans with the problem of how to account for the origins, histories, and development of a multiplicity of races, cultures, and civilizations (see Baker, 1974; Barkan, 1992; Trinkhaus & Shipman, 1993). Not only was it necessary for the cosmologist to account for the disconcerting existence of the "other," [5] but such a scholar was obliged to explain how and why such differences in the moral values of Europeans and these "others" had arisen. In effect, such a profusion of values, cultures, and ways of life challenged the monopolistic claim on legitimacy and truth of the doctrines of Christianity. Such practices as infanticide, cannibalism, human sacrifice, and what at first appeared as promiscuity reopened the problem of contradictions among cultural values and the inquiry into how these contradictions might be both explained and resolved (Oakes, 1938).

These issues of value conflicts were conflated with practical questions about the recruitment, organization, and justification for the division of labor in the Spanish settlements in the Americas, and these confusions are to be found in the debates of Bartolome de Las Casas with Juan Gines de Sepulveda at the Council of Valladolid. Sepulveda, "who used Aristotle's doctrine of natural slavery in order to legitimize Spanish behavior against the Indians" (Hosle, 1992, p. 238), in effect won the day against Las Casas, who insisted that the peoples we now call Native Americans were "full fellow human beings, possessing valid traditions, dignity and rights" (Marty, 1992, p. xiii). Today, despite or perhaps because of the new recognition of cultural diversity, the tension between universalistic and relativistic values remains an unresolved conundrum for the Western ethnographer (Hosle, 1992).[6] In practice, it becomes this question: By which values are observations to be guided? The choices seem to be either the values of the ethnographer or the values of the observed—that is, in modern parlance, either the *etic* or the *emic* (Pike, 1967; for an excellent discussion, see Harré, 1980, pp. 135-137). Herein lies a deeper and more fundamental problem: How is it possible to understand the other when the other's values are not one's own? This problem arises to plague ethnography at a time when Western Christian values are no longer a surety of truth and, hence, no longer the benchmark from which self-confidently valid observations can be made.

◆ Colonial Mentalities and the Persistence of the Other

Before the professionalization of ethnography, descriptions and evaluations of the races and cultures of the world were provided by Western
missionaries, explorers, buccaneers, and colonial administrators. Their
reports, found in church, national, and local archives throughout the world
and, for the most part, not known to contemporary ethnologists, were
written from the perspective of, or by the representatives of, a conquering
civilization, confident in its mission to civilize the world (for pertinent discussion of this issue, see Ginsburg, 1991, 1993). Some of the 17th-, 18th-,
and 19th-century explorers, missionaries, and administrators have provided thick descriptions of those practices of the "primitives" made salient
to the observer by his Christian value perspective.[7] For societies studied by
these observers (see, for example, Degerando, 1800/1969), the author's
ethnographic report is a reversed mirror image of his own ethnocultural
ideal. That these early ethnographies reveal as much about the West as
about their objects of study may explain why they have not been recovered
and reanalyzed by contemporary anthropologists: Present-day ethnographers hope to separate themselves from the history of Western conquest
and reject the earlier ethnographies as hopelessly biased (see "Symposium
on Qualitative Methods," 1993). Recently they have begun to take seriously the accounts the natives have given of their Western "discoverers"
and to "decenter" or "disprivilege" the reports presented by the latter
(Abeyesekere, 1992; Salmond, 1991; Todorov, 1984).

A rich resource, through which one can discern the effects that this
early ethnographic literature had on the subjugation of these peoples, is to
be found in the works of latter-day colonial administrators (e.g., Olivier,
1911/1970). Ethnology arose out of the reports written by administrators
of the long-maintained seaborne empires of the Spanish, English, French,
and Dutch (Maunier, 1949). These empires provided opportunities for
amateur and, later, professional ethnologists not only to examine hosts of
"native" cultures,[8] but also to administer the conditions of life affecting
the "cultural advancement" of peoples over whom their metropole exercised domination (Gray, 1911/1970, pp. 79-85). In respect to the seaborne empires, European interest was often confined to exploiting the
labor power of the natives, utilizing their territory for extractive industry
and/or establishing it in terms of the strategic military advantage it provided them in their struggles against imperialist rivals (for some representative examples, see Aldrich, 1990; Boxer, 1965; Duffy, 1968; Gullick,

1956; Suret-Canale, 1988a, 1988b). Hence the anthropology that developed under colonial administrators tended toward disinterest in the acculturation of the natives and encouragement for the culturally preservative effects of indirect rule. Their approach came to be called pluralistic development (M. G. Smith, 1965). Colonial pluralism left the natives more or less under the authority of their own indigenous leaders so long as these leaders could be co-opted in support of the limited interests of the colonial administration (Lugard, 1922/1965). This tendency led to the creation of a market economy at the center of colonial society (Boeke, 1946; Furnivall, 1956) surrounded by a variety of local culture groups (Boeke, 1948), some of whose members were drawn willy-nilly into the market economy and suffered the effects of marginalized identity (Sachs, 1947).

Ethnographers who conducted their field studies in colonialized areas were divided with respect to their attitudes toward cultural and/or political nationalism and self-determination. A few became champions of ethnocultural liberation and anticolonial revolt. Some respected the autonomy of the traditional culture and opposed any tendency among natives in revolt against colonialism to seek further modernization of their lifestyles. The latter, some of whom were Marxists, admired the anticolonial movement but were concerned to see that the natives remained precapitalist. Some of these might have imagined that precapitalist natives would practice some form of primitive communism (see Diamond, 1963, 1972) as described by Friedrich Engels (1884) in *The Origins of the Family, Private Property and the State*. Engels, in fact, had derived his idea of primitive communism from Lewis Henry Morgan's (1877/1964) *Ancient Society,* an original study in the Comtean ethnohistorical tradition of American aborigines that conceived of the latter as "ancestors" to the ancient Greeks (for a critique, see Kuper, 1988). Others, no longer concerned to prove that "mother-right" preceded "father-right" by presenting ethnographic accounts of Melanesians, Tasmanians, Bantus, or Dayaks (for a fine example, see Hartland, 1921/1969), turned their attention to acculturation, and, unsure of how long the process might take and how well the formerly colonized subjects would take to Occidental norms, reinvoked "the doctrine of survivals" (Hodgen, 1936) to account for elements of the natives' culture that persisted (see, e.g., Herskovitz, 1958, 1966) or marveled at how well some native peoples had traded "new lives for old" (Mead, 1956/1975). These diverse value and ideological orientations are pervasive in the work of early professional ethnologists and provided anthropology the grounding for most of its theoretical debates.

◆ The "Evolution" of Culture
and Society: Comte and the Comparative Method

Even before the professionalization of anthropology engulfed the discipline, the enlightened ethnographer had abandoned any attitude that might be associated with that of a merciless conqueror and replaced it with that of an avatar of beneficent evolutionary progress. Value conflicts arising within anthropology from the history of colonialism, and with the moral relativism associated with them were, in part, replaced by theories of social evolution. The application of Darwinian and Spencerian principles to the understanding of how societies and cultures of the world have developed over eons freed the ethnographer from the problems presented by moral relativism; it permitted the assertion that there existed a spatio-temporal hierarchy of values. These values were represented synchronically in the varieties of cultures to be found in the world, but might be classified diachronically according to the theory of developmental advance.

This new approach to comprehending how the lifeways of the Occident related to those of the others had first been formally proposed by Auguste Comte and was soon designated the "comparative method" (Bock, 1948, pp. 11-36). According to Comte and his followers (see Lenzer, 1975), the study of the evolution of culture and civilization would postulate three stages of culture and would hold fast to the idea that the peoples and cultures of the world are arrangeable diachronically, forming "a great chain of being" (Lovejoy, 1936/1960). Moreover, these stages are interpretable as orderly links in that chain, marking the epochs that occurred as human societies moved from conditions of primitive culture to those of modern civilization.[9] By using technological as well as social indicators, ethnographers could discover where a particular people belonged on the "chain" and thus give that people a definite place in the evolution of culture. (For a discussion and critique of Comte as a theorist of history and evolution, see R. Brown, 1984, pp. 187-212.) The seemingly inconvenient fact that all of these different cultures coexisted in time—that is, the time in which the ethnographer conducted his or her field study—was disposed of by applying the theory of "uneven evolution," that is, the assertion, in the guise of an epistemological assumption, that all cultures except that of Western Europe had suffered some form of arrested development (Sanderson, 1990; Sarana, 1975). In this way, and in the absence of documentary historical materials, ethnographers could utilize their on-the-spot field studies to contribute to the construction of the prehistory of civilization and at the same time put forth a genealogy of morals. Following Comte, this diachrony of civilizational development was usually characterized as having three progressive and irreversible stages: savagery, barbarism, and civilization. The peoples assigned to each of these stages corresponded to a color-culture hierarchical diachrony and fitted the ethnocentric bias of the Occident (Nisbet, 1972).

In the 19th century, Comte had formalized this mode of thinking for both anthropologists and sociologists by designating as epochs of moral growth (Comte's terms) three stages that, he averred, occurred in the development of religion. The ethnologists' adaptation of Comte's comparative method to their own efforts provided them with a set of a priori assumptions on the cultures of "primitives"—assumptions that vitiated the need to grant respect to these cultures in their own terms—that is, from the perspective of those who are its participants (for a countervailing perspective, see Hill-Lubin, 1992). The imposition of a preconceived Eurocentric developmental framework made the work of the ethnographer much simpler;[10] the task became that of a classifier of cultural traits in transition, or in arrest. Ultimately, this approach was institutionalized in the Human Relations Area Files (HRAF) housed at Yale University, which became the depository for an anthropological database and the resource for a vast project dedicated to the classification and cross-classification of virtually all the extant ethnographic literature—in the drawers of the HRAF any and all items of culture found a secure classificatory niche (Murdock, 1949/1965). A Yale-produced handbook of categories provided the ethnographer with guidelines to direct his or her observations and provided the basis for the classification of these and other collections of cultural traits.[11] The trait data in the Yale cross-cultural files represent ethnography in a form disembodied from that of a lived social world in which actors still exist. They are a voluminous collection of disparate cultural items that represent the antithesis of the ethnographic method.

◆ 20th-Century Ethnography: Comteanism and the Cold War

Two 20th-century developments have undermined both the various "colonial" anthropological perspectives and evolutionary schemes. Within 30 years of the termination of World War II, the several decolonization movements in Africa and Asia succeeded in ending the direct forms of Western global colonialism. As part of the same movements, an anticolonial assault on Western ethnocentrism led to a critical attack on the idea of "the primitive" and on the entire train of ethnological thought that went with it (Montagu, 1968). In effect, by the 1960s anthropologists had begun not only to run out of "primitive" societies to study but also to abandon the evolutionary epistemology that had justified their very existence in the first place.

A new term, *underdeveloped,* tended to replace *primitive.* The colonial powers and their supporters became defendants in an academic prosecution of those who were responsible for the underdevelopment of the newly designated "Third World" and who had neglected to recognize the integrity of "black culture" and that of other peoples of color in the United States (see Willis, 1972).[12] Ethnologists discovered that their basic orientation was under attack. Insofar as that orientation had led them or their much-respected predecessors to cooperate with imperial governments in the suppression and exploitation of natives, or with the American military and its "pacification" programs in Vietnam, anthropologists began to suffer from the effects of a collective and intradisciplinary guilt complex (see Nader, 1972).[13]

Changes in what appeared to be the direction of world history led anthropologists to retool their approach to ethnography. Because, by definition, there were few, if any, primitives available for study, and because the spokespersons for the newly designated Third World of "underdeveloped" countries often held anthropologists to have contributed to the latter condition, access to tribal societies became more difficult than it had been. As opportunities for fieldwork shrank, recourse was had to the study of linguistics, to the database of the Yale files, or to the discovery of the ethnographic possibilities for anthropological examinations of American society. Anthropology had come full circle, having moved back to a study of its own society, the point of departure—as well as the benchmark—for its investigation of more "primitive" cultures. Linguistics and databases lend themselves to the study of texts, as does the study of Western society, with its rich literary and historical archives. These tendencies opened ethnography to the modernist and, later, the postmodernist approaches to the study of exotic peoples and to the investigation of alien culture bearers residing within industrial societies of the Occident.

However, even as anthropology was convulsed by decolonization movements and constrained by restricted access to its traditional fieldwork sites, the Cold War gave to sociology an opportunity to revive Comte's and Spencer's variants of evolutionary doctrine in modernist form and to combine them with a secular theodicy harking back to America's Puritan beginnings.

Talcott Parsons's (1966, 1971) two-volume study of the development of society restored the Calvinist-Puritan imagery, applying the latter to those "others" not yet included in the Christian brotherhood of the Occident. Written during the decades of the U.S. global contest with the Soviet Union, it arranged selected nations and societies in a schema according to which the United States was said to have arrived at the highest stage of societal development; other peoples, cultures, and civilizations were presumed to be moving in the direction plotted by America, "the first new nation" (Lipset, 1979; for a critique, see Lyman, 1975), or to be suffering from an arrest of advancement that prevented them from doing so. That developmental scheme held to the idea that economic progress was inherent in industrialization and that nation building coincided with capitalism, the gradual extension of democratization, and the orderly provision of individual rights. Despite the pointed criticisms of the comparative method that would continue to be offered by the school of sociohistorical thought associated with Frederick J. Teggart (1941) and his followers (Bock, 1952, 1956, 1963, 1974; Hodgen, 1974; Nisbet, 1969, 1986; for a critical discussion of this school, see Lyman, 1978; see also Kuper, 1988), a Comtean outlook survived within sociology in the work of Talcott Parsons and his macrosociological epigoni.

Social scientific literature during the Cold War included such titles as Robert Heilbroner's *The Great Ascent,* A. F. K. Organski's *The Stages of Political Development,* and W. W. Rostow's *The Stages of Economic Growth.* The American political economy and a democratic social order replaced earlier images of the ultimate stage of cultural evolution. Changes in the rest of the nations of the world that seemed to herald movement toward adoption of an American social, political, and economic institutional structure became the standard by which social scientists could measure the "advance" of humankind. This standard provided the analyst-ethnographer with a new measure for evaluating the "progress" of the "other" (which, after 1947, included the peoples and cultures of the Soviet Union as well as those of the "underdeveloped" world). The matter reached epiphany in the early 1990s, when students and scholars of the cosmological, moral, economic, and military problems faced by claimants of the right to spread a benevolent variant of Christianized Western civilization throughout the world began to rejoice over the collapse of communism, the disintegration of the Soviet Union, and the decomposition of its allies and alliances in Eastern Europe (Gwertzman & Kaufman, 1992). But for some there arose a new apprehension: worry over whether these events signaled the very end of history itself (see Fukuyama, 1992).[14]

The end of the Cold War and the deconstruction of the Soviet Union revived nationalist and ethnic claims in almost every part of the world. In such a newly decentered world, cultural pluralism has become a new watchword, especially for all those who hope to distinguish themselves from ethnonational "others." The dilemmas once posed by cultural relativism have been replaced by the issues arising out of the supposed certainties of primordial descent. Ethnographers now find themselves caught in the cross fire of incommensurable but competing values.

◆ The Ethnography of the American Indian: An Indigenous "Other"

In the United States, the Calvinist variant of the Protestant errand into the wilderness began with the arrival of the Puritans in New England. Convinced of their own righteousness and of their this-worldly mission to bring to fruition God's kingdom on the "new continent," the Puritans initially set out to include the so-called Indians in their covenant of faith. But, having misjudged both the Indians' pliability and their resistance to an alien worldview, the Puritans did not succeed in their attempt (Calloway, 1991, pp. 57-90; A. T. Vaughan, 1965). Nevertheless, they continued their missionary endeavors throughout the 19th and 20th centuries (Coleman, 1985; Keller, 1983; Milner & O'Neil, 1985). American political and jurisprudential policy toward the Indian, as well as the ethnographic work on the cultures of Native Americans, derive from this failure and shape its results. As one consequence, the several tribes of North American aborigines would remain outside the ethnographic, moral, and cultural pale of both European immigrant enclaves and settled white American communities.

From the 17th through the 19th centuries—that is, during the period of westward expansion across the American continent—ethnographic reports on Indian cultures were written from the perspective of the Euro-American conqueror and his missionary allies (Bowden, 1981). Even more than the once-enslaved Africans and their American-born descendants, the Indians have remained in a special kind of "otherness." One salient social indicator of this fact is their confinement to reservations of the mind as well as the body. In the conventional academic curriculum, the study of Native Americans is a part of the cultural anthropology of "primitive" peoples, whereas that of European and Asian immigrants and American blacks is an institutionalized feature of sociology courses on "minorities" and "race and ethnic relations."

In the United States a shift in ethnographic perspective from that written by missionaries and military conquerors to that composed exclusively by anthropologists arose with the establishment of the ethnology section of the Smithsonian Institution (Hinsley, 1981). However, ethnographies of various Indian "tribes" had been written earlier by ethnologists in service to the Bureau of Indian Affairs (BIA) (Bieder, 1989; two representative examples of pre-Smithsonian Amerindian ethnography are found in McKenney & Hall, 1836/1972; Schoolcraft, 1851/1975). In addition to being "problem peoples" for those theorists who wished to explain Indian origins in America and to construct their ancestry in terms consistent with the creation and flood myths of the Bible, the presence of the Indians within the borders of the United States posed still another problem: their anomalous status in law (R. A. Williams, 1990). Politically, the Indian "tribes" regarded themselves as separate sovereign nations and, for a period, were dealt with as such by the colonial powers and the U.S. government. However, in 1831, their legal status was redesignated in a Supreme Court case, *Cherokee Nation v. Georgia* (1831). In his decision, Chief Justice Marshall declared the Indians to occupy a unique status in law. They form, he said, "a domestic dependent nation." As such, he went on, they fall into a special "ward" relationship to the federal government. The latter had already established the Bureau of Indian Affairs to deal with them. Within the confines and constraints of this decision, the BIA administered the affairs of the Indian. From the special brand of anthropology that it fostered, American ethnography developed its peculiar outlook on Native Americans.[15]

The BIA and later the Smithsonian Institution employed ethnographers to staff the various reservation agencies and to study the ways of the Indians. The focus of study for this contingent of observers was not the possible conversion of Indians, but rather the depiction of their cultures—ceremonies recorded, kinship systems mapped, technology described, artifacts collected—all carried out from a secular and administrative point of view.[16] The theoretical underpinning of the BIA's perspective was the civilized/primitive dichotomy that had already designated Indians as preliterates. In effect, the tribal lands and reservation habitats of these "domestic, dependent nationals" became a living anthropological museum from which ethnologists could glean descriptions of the early stages of primitive life. In those parts of the country where Indians lived in large numbers—especially the Southwest[17]—and where archaeological artifacts were numerous, the Comtean evolutionary perspective was used to trace the ancestry of existing tribes back to an origin that might be found by paleontological efforts. From the beginning, however, the Southwest would also be the setting where debates—over how ethnography was to be carried out, and what purpose it ought to serve—would break out and divide anthropologists not only from missionaries and from federal agents, but from one another (Dale, 1949/1984; Dockstader, 1985).

The life world of "the primitive" was thought to be a window through which the prehistoric past could be seen, described, and understood. At its most global representation, this attitude had been given the imprimatur of ethnological science at the St. Louis World's Fair in 1904, when a scientifically minded missionary, Samuel Phillips Verner, allowed Ota Benga, a pygmy from the Belgian Congo, to be put on display as a living specimen of primitivism. A year later, Ota Benga was exhibited at the Monkey House of the Bronx Zoo (Bradford & Blume, 1992). In 1911, the American anthropologist Alfred Kroeber took possession of Ishi, the last surviving member of the Yahi tribe, and placed him in the Museum of Anthropology at the University of California. In the two years before his death, Ishi dwelled in the museum and, like Ota Benga before him, became, in effect, a living artifact, a primitive on display, one to be viewed by the civilized in a manner comparable to their perspective on the presentation of Indians in American museum dioramas (see Kroeber, 1962, 1965; for contemporary accounts in newspapers and other media, see Heizer & Kroeber, 1979).

Although U.S. Indian policy established both the programs and the perspectives under which most ethnographers worked, its orthodoxy was not accepted by all of the early field-workers. Among these heterodoxical ethnologists, perhaps the most important was Frank Hamilton Cushing (1857-1900), who became a Zuni shaman and a war chief while working as an ethnologist for the Smithsonian Institution (see Cushing, 1920/1974, 1979, 1901/1988, 1990; see also Culin, 1922/1967).[18] Cushing's case stands out because, though he was an active participant in Zuni life, he continued to be a professional ethnographer who tried to describe both Zuni culture and the Zuni worldview from an indigenous perspective. Moreover, Cushing joined with R. S. Culin in proposing the heterodoxical thesis that America was the cradle of Asia, that is, that in pre-Columbian times the ancestors of the Zuni had migrated to Asia and contributed significantly to the development of Chinese, Japanese, Korean, and other Asiatic civilizations that in turn had been diffused over the centuries into Africa and Europe (Lyman, 1979, 1982a, 1982b).

Without attempting to become a native himself, Paul Radin (1883-1959) devoted a lifetime to the ethnographic study of the Winnebago Indians (see Radin, 1927, 1927/1957a, 1937/1957b, 1920/1963, 1933/1966, 1953/1971b, 1923/1973, 1956/1976).[19] Maintaining that an inner view of an alien culture could be accomplished only through a deep learning of its language and symbol system, Radin documented the myths, rituals, and poetry in Winnebago and, in his reports, provided English translations of these materials. Taking Cushing's and Radin's works as a standard for Amerindian ethnography, their perspective could be used to reinterpret the works of earlier ethnographers; they might enable future field investigators to comprehend the cultural boundedness of American Indian ethnography and at the same time provide the point of departure for a critical sociology of ethnological knowledge (Vidich, 1966). But, in addition, their work recognizes both the historicity of preliterate cultures and the problems attendant upon understanding the world of the other from the other's point of view. In this, as in the work of Thucydides and in the Weberian conception of a sociology of understanding (*verstehende* sociology), Cushing and Radin transcended the problem of value incommensurability.

♦ **The Ethnography of the Civic Other:**
The Ghetto, the Natural Area, and the Small Town

The Calvinist mission to save and/or include the Indian found its later counterpart in a mission to bring to the urban ghetto communities of blacks and Asian and European immigrants the moral and communitarian values of Protestantism. That these immigrants had carried their Catholic, Judaic, or Buddhist religious cultures to the United States and that the lifestyles of the recently emancipated blacks did not accord with those of the white citizens of the United States were causes for concern among representatives of the older settled groups, who feared for the future integrity of America's Protestant civilization (Contosta, 1980, pp. 121-144; Hartmann, 1948/1967; Jones, 1992, pp. 49-166). Initially, efforts to include these groups focused on Protestant efforts to preach and practice a "social gospel" that found its institutionalization in the settlement houses that came to dot the urban landscape of immigrant and ghetto enclaves (Holden, 1922/1970; Woods & Kennedy, 1922/1990).

About three decades after the Civil War, when it became clear that the sheer number and cultural variety of the new urban inhabitants had become too great to be treated by individual efforts, recourse was had to the statistical survey. It would provide a way to determine how many inhabitants from each denomination, nationality, and race there were in any one place, and to describe each group's respective problems of adjustment (C. A. Chambers, 1971; Cohen, 1981; McClymer, 1980). In this manner, the "other" was transformed into a statistical aggregate and reported in a tabular census of exotic lifestyles. These quantified reports, sponsored in the first years by various churches in eastern cities of the United States, were the forerunners of the corporate-sponsored surveys of immigrants and Negroes and of the massive government-sponsored surveys of European, Asian, Mexican, and other immigrant laborers in 1911 (Immigration Commission, 1911/1970). The church surveys and their corporate and sociological successors were designed to facilitate the "moral reform" and social adjustment of newcomer and ghetto populations. What is now known as qualitative research in sociology had its origins in this Christian mission (see Greek, 1978, 1992).

It was out of such a movement to incorporate the alien elements within the consensual community that the first qualitative community study was carried out. W. E. B. Du Bois's (1899/1967) *The Philadelphia Negro,* a survey of that city's seventh ward, was supported by Susan B. Wharton, a leader of the University of Pennsylvania's college settlement. To Wharton, Du Bois, and their colleagues, the "collection and analysis of social facts were as much a religious as a scientific activity offered as a form of prayer for the redemption of dark-skinned people" (Vidich & Lyman, 1985, p. 128). This study, which included 5,000 interviews conducted by Du Bois, aimed not only at description, but also at the uplift of Philadelphia's Negro population by the Quaker community that surrounded it. The tone of noblesse oblige that inspires the final pages of Du Bois's book are a stark reminder of the paternalistic benevolence underlying this first ethnographic study of a community.

Church- and corporate-sponsored survey methods continued to dominate social research until the early 1920s (see Burgess, 1916), when Helen and Robert Lynd began their study of Middletown. Robert Lynd, a newly ordained Protestant minister, was selected by the Council of Churches, then concerned about the moral state of Christian communities in industrial America, to examine the lifeways of what was thought to be a typical American community. Rather suddenly catapulted into the position of a two-person research team, the Lynds consulted the anthropologist Clark Wissler (1870-1947), then on the staff of the American Museum of Natural History,[20] for advice on how to conduct such a survey and how to report it once the data had been gathered. Wissler provided them with what was then known as the cultural inventory, a list of standard categories used by anthropologists to organize field data (see Wissler, 1923, chaps. 5, 7). Those categories—getting a living, making a home, training the young, using leisure, engaging in religious practices, engaging in community activities—became the organizing principle of Lynd and Lynd's (1929/ 1956) book and provided them with a set of cues for their investigation. Although the Middletown study was designed to provide its church sponsors with information that might be used to set church policy, the Lynds approached the Middletown community in the manner of social anthropologists. As Wissler (1929/1956) states in his foreword to the published volume of the study, "To most people anthropology is a mass of curious information about savages, and this is so far true, in that most of its observations are on the less civilized. . . . The authors of this volume have approached an American community as an anthropologist does a primitive tribe" (p. vi). In Middletown, the "other" of the anthropologist found its way into American sociological practice and purpose. Moreover, from the point of view of the policy makers in the central church bureaucracy, he who had once been assumed to be the civic "brother" had to all intents and purposes become the "other," an ordinary inhabitant of Muncie, Indiana.

Shortly after the publication of *Middletown* in 1929, the Great Depression set in. Soon, the Lynds were commissioned to do a restudy of Muncie. Published in 1937 as *Middletown in Transition: A Study in Cultural Conflicts,* this investigation reflected not only changes in the town, but also a transformation in the outlook of its two ethnographers. During the early years of the Depression, Robert Lynd, a church progressive, had begun to look to the Soviet Union for answers to the glaring contradictions of capitalism that seemed to have manifested themselves so alarmingly in Depression-ridden America. This new political orientation was reflected in both what the Lynds observed and how they reported it. Where the first volume had made no mention of the Ball family's domination of what was a virtual "company town," or of the family's philanthropic sponsorship of Ball State University and the local library and hospital, or its control over the banks, *Middletown in Transition* included a chapter titled "The X Family: A Pattern of Business-Class Control" and an appendix titled "Middletown's Banking Institutions in Boom and Depression." Responding to what they believed to be the utter failure of America's laissez-faire, free market economy, the Lynds abandoned the ethnographic categories they had used in *Middletown*. Choosing instead to employ categories and conceptualizations derived from their own recently acquired Marxist outlook, they shifted the sociological focus from religious to political values.

Middletown in Transition would become a standard and much-praised work of sociological ethnography for the next half century. At Columbia University, where Robert Lynd taught generations of students, explicit Christian values and rhetoric were replaced by those of an ethically inclined political radicalism. With the radicalization of many Columbia-trained youths (as well as of their fellow students at City College, many of whom would later become prominent sociologists), variants of Marxism would provide a counterperspective to that of the anthropologically oriented ethnographic observer of American communities. Ironically, however, Middletown's second restudy, conducted by a team of non-Marxist sociologists nearly 50 years after *Middletown in Transition* was published, returned the focus to the significance of kinship and family that had characterized the early anthropological perspective, combining it with the kind of concern for Protestant religiosity that had been the stock-in-trade of the earlier American sociological orientation (Caplow, Bahr, Chadwick, Hill, & Williamson, 1982, 1983).

Even before the Lynds' original study, ethnography as a method of research had become identified with the University of Chicago's Department of Sociology. The first generation of Chicago sociologists, led by Albion W. Small, supposed that the discipline they professed had pledged itself to reassert America's destiny—the nation that would be "the city upon a hill." America would become a unified Christian brotherhood, committed to a covenant through which the right and proper values would be shared by all (Vidich & Lyman, 1985, p. 179). Small sought a sociological means to impress the values and morals of Protestantism upon the inhabitants of the newer ethnic, racial, and religious ghettos then forming in Chicago. However, this explicitly Christian attitude—in service to which the University of Chicago had been brought into existence by John D. Rockefeller in 1892—did not survive at Chicago. It was discarded after

Robert E. Park, Ernest W. Burgess, W. I. Thomas, and Louis Wirth had become the guiding professoriat of Chicago's sociology, and after Park's son-in-law, Robert Redfield, had become an important figure in that university's anthropology program. Park's secular conceptualization of the "natural area" replaced the Christian locus of the unchurched in the city, while, at the same time, and in contradistinction to Park's point of view, Redfield's formulation of the morally uplifting "little community" introduced a counterimage to that of the metropolis then emerging in Chicago.

Park (1925/1967) conceived the city to be a social laboratory containing a diversity and heterogeneity of peoples, lifestyles, and competing and contrasting worldviews. To Park, for a city to be composed of others, ghettoized or otherwise, was intrinsic to its nature. Under his and Ernest W. Burgess's direction or inspiration, a set of ethnographic studies emerged focusing on singular descriptions of one or another aspect of human life that was to be found in the city. Frequently, these studies examined urban groups whose ways of life were below or outside the purview of the respectable middle classes. In addition to providing descriptions of the myriad and frequently incompatible values by which these groups lived, these ethnographies moved away from the missionary endeavor that had characterized earlier studies. Instead, Park and his colleagues occupied themselves with documenting the various forms of civil otherhood that they perceived to be emerging in the city (see Burgess & Bogue, 1967).

Central to Park's vision of the city was its architectonic as a municipal circumscription of a number of "natural areas," forming a mosaic of minor communities, each strikingly different from the other, but each more or less typical of its kind. Park (1952a) observed, "Every American city has its slums; its ghettos; its immigrant colonies, regions which maintain more or less alien and exotic cultures. Nearly every large city has its bohemias and hobohemias, where life is freer, more adventurous and lonely than it is elsewhere. These are called natural areas of the city" (p. 196). For more than three decades, urban ethnography in Chicago's sociology department focused on describing such "natural areas" as the Jewish ghetto (Wirth, 1928/1956), Little Italy (Nelli, 1970), Polonia (Lopata, 1967; Thomas & Znaniecki, 1958, pp. 1511-1646), Little Germany (Park, 1922/1971), Chinatown (Lee, 1978; Siu, 1987; Wu, 1926), Bronzeville and Harlem (Drake & Cayton, 1962; Frazier, 1931, 1937a, 1937b), the gold coast and the slum (Zorbaugh, 1929), hobo jungles (N. Anderson, 1923/1961), single-room occupants of furnished rooms (Zorbaugh,

1968), enclaves of cultural and social dissidents (Ware, 1935/1965),[21] the urban ecology of gangdom (Thrasher, 1927/1963), and the urban areas that housed the suicidal (Cavan, 1928/1965), the drug addicted (Dai, 1937/1970), and the mentally disturbed (Faris & Dunham, 1939/1965), and on the social and economic dynamics of real estate transactions and the human and metropolitical effects arising out of the occupational interests of realtors as they interfaced with the state of the economy (Hughes, 1928; McCluer, 1928; Schietinger, 1967). Park's (1952b, 1952c) orientation was that of Montesquieu; he emphasized the freedom that the city afforded to those who would partake of the "romance" and "magic" of its sociocultural multiverse.

Some of Park's students, on the other hand, following up an idea developed by Louis Wirth (1938), all too often took to contrasting its forms of liberty in thought and action—that is, its encouragement of "segmented" personalities and role-specific conduct and its fostering of impersonality, secondary relationships, and a blasé attitude (see Roper, 1935, abstracted in Burgess & Bogue, 1967, pp. 231-244)—with what they alleged was the sense of personal security—that is, the gratification that came from conformity to custom, the comfort that arose out of familiar face-to-face contacts, the wholesomeness of whole personalities, and the companionability of primary relationships—to be found among the people who dwelt in rural, ethnoracially homogeneous small towns (see Bender, 1978, pp. 3-27; Redfield & Singer, 1973; see also M. P. Smith, 1979). For those who idealized the "folk society," and who conflated it with concomitant idealizations of the "little community," "primitive" primordialism, pastoral peace, and the small town, the impending urbanization of the countryside—heralded by the building of highways (Dansereau, 1961; McKenzie, 1968), the well-documented trend of young people departing to the city (for early documentation of this phenomenon, see Weber, 1899/1967), and the intrusion of the automobile (Bailey, 1988; Rae, 1965), the telephone (Ball, 1968; Pool, 1981), and the radio (Gist & Halbert, 1947, pp. 128, 505-507) on rural folkways—was a portent not merely of change but of irredeemable tragedy (see Blake, 1990; Gusfield, 1975; Lingeman, 1980; Tinder, 1980). On the other hand, for those ethnographers who concluded on the basis of their own field experiences that the processes as well as the anomalies of America's inequitable class structure had already found their way into and become deeply embedded within the language and customs of the nation's small towns, there was an equally portentous observation: America's Jeffersonian ideals were professed but not practiced in the very communities that had been alleged to be their secure repository. As August B. Hollingshead (1949/1961) would point out on the basis of his ethnographic study of "Elmtown's youth": "The . . . American class system is extra-legal . . . [but] society has other dimensions than those recognized in law. . . . It is the culture which makes men face toward the facts of the class system and away from the ideals of the American creed" (pp. 448, 453).

Ethnographic studies that followed in this tradition were guided by a nostalgia for 19th-century small-town values, an American past that no longer existed, but during the heyday of which—so it was supposed—there had existed a society in which all had been brothers and sisters.

However, neither the civil otherhood conceived by Park nor the class-less brotherhood sought by Hollingshead could account for American society's resistance to the incorporation of blacks. It was to address this point that E. Franklin Frazier (1894-1962) would stress the "otherhood" of the American Negro. Building on the teachings of both Park and Du Bois, Frazier began his sociological studies in Chicago with an analysis of the various lifeways within the black ghetto. In the process, he discovered both the ghetto's separateness and its isolation from the larger social and political economy. In his later evaluation of the rise of the "black bourgeoisie" (1957a) he saw it as a tragic, although perhaps inevitable, outcome of the limited economic and social mobility available to the black middle classes. Based on his observations of largely university-based black middle classes, Frazier presented their lifestyle as an emulation of the lifestyle of the white middle classes: as such, his monograph on the subject should be regarded as much as a study of the white bourgeoisie as of the black. Frazier's ethnographic studies were based on almost a lifetime of observation, not only of this specific class, but also of African American ghetto dwellers in Harlem and Chicago, of black families in the rural South and the urban North, and of Negro youths caught up in the problems of their socioeconomic situation (see Frazier, 1925, 1957b, 1963, 1939/1966, 1940/1967, 1968). Frazier's work stands apart, not only because it points to the exclusion of blacks from both the American ideal of brotherhood and the then-emerging civic otherhood, but also because its research orientation drew on the life histories of Frazier's subjects and on his own experience.

The importance of personal experience in ethnographic description and interpretation is implicit in all of Frazier's work. His methodology and chosen research sites are comparable to those employed by a very different kind of ethnographer—Thorstein Veblen. In such studies of American university ghettos as *The Higher Learning in America: A Memorandum on the Conduct of Universities by Businessmen,* Veblen (1918/1965) drew on his own experiences at the University of Chicago, Stanford University, and the University of Missouri, three sites that provided the raw materials for his highly organized and prescient examination of the bureaucratic transformations then occurring in American universities.[22] Frazier's and Veblen's oeuvres are, in effect, examples of qualitative research based on data acquired over the course of rich and varied life experiences. In these studies it is impossible to disentangle the method of study from either the theory employed or the person employing it. Such a method would appear to be the ultimate desideratum of ethnographic research.

The ethnographic orientation at the University of Chicago was given a new twist by William Foote Whyte. Whyte made what was designed to be formal research into part of his life experience and called it "participant observation." The Chicago sociology department provided Whyte with an opportunity to report, in *Street Corner Society* (1943a, 1955, 1981), his findings about Italian Americans residing in the North End of Boston. That work, initially motivated by a sense of moral responsibility to uplift the slum-dwelling masses, has become the exemplar of the techniques appropriate to participant observation research: Whyte lived in the Italian neighborhood and in many but not all ways became one of the "Cornerville" boys.[23] Although he presents his findings about Cornerville descriptively, Whyte's theoretical stance remains implicit. The book has an enigmatic quality, because Whyte presents his data from the perspective of his relationships with his subjects. That is, Whyte is as much a researcher as he is a subject in his own book; the other had become the brother of Italian ghetto dwellers.

Anthropology at the University of Chicago was also informed by a qualitative orientation. Until 1929, anthropology and ethnology at that university had been subsumed under "historical sociology" in a department called the Department of Social Science and Anthropology. Anthropological and ethnological studies were at first directed by Frederick A. Starr, formerly head of ethnology at the American Museum of Natural History (Diner, 1975). Starr became a Japanophile after his first trip to Japan, while he was on assignment to bring a few of the Ainu people to be displayed, like Ota Benga, at the St. Louis World's Fair in 1904 (Statler, 1983, pp. 237-255). A separate Department of Anthropology was established in 1929, but, unlike Starr's, it reflected the orientation developed by the sociologists W. I. Thomas and Ellsworth Faris (see Faris, 1970, p. 16). One year before the advent of the new department, Robert Redfield presented his dissertation, *A Plan for the Study of Tepoztlan, Mexico* (1928). Borrowing from Tönnies's (1887/1957) dichotomous paradigm, gemeinschaft-gesellschaft, and drawing upon Von Wiese's and Becker's (1950/1962, 1932/1974) sacred-secular continuum, Redfield asserted the virtues of "the folk culture" and what he would later call "the little community" (Redfield, 1962, pp. 143-144; see also Redfield, 1930, 1941, 1960, 1950/1962b; Redfield & Rojas, 1934/1962a).

Regarding the metropolis as a congeries of unhappy and unfulfilled others, Redfield stood opposed to the values associated with urban life and industrial civilization. He extolled the lifestyles of those nonindustrial peoples and small communities that had resisted incorporation into the globally emerging metropolitan world. In his final essay, written in 1958, the year of his death, describing an imaginary conversation with a man from outer space, Redfield (1963) abjured the condition of mutually assured destruction that characterized the Cold War, despaired of halting the march of technocentric progress, conflated the pastoral with the premodern, and concluded by lamenting the rise of noncommunal life in the metropolitan city. Redfield's orientation, Rousseauean in its ethos, would provide a generation of anthropologists with a rustic outlook—a postmissionary attitude that sought to preserve and protect the lifeways of the primitive. His was the antiurban variant of Puritanism, a point of view that held small-scale, face-to-face communities to be superior to all others. To those ethnologists who followed in the ideological footsteps of Redfield, these communal values seemed representative of primordial humanity.[24]

A counterimage to that of ethnography's romance with small-town, communitarian and primordial values of primitivism was offered in 1958 when Arthur J. Vidich and Joseph Bensman published their ethnographic account of "Springdale," a rural community in Upstate New York.[25] As their title forewarned, this was a "small town in mass society." [26] Its situation, moreover, was typical of other American towns. Springdale's much-vaunted localism, its claims to societal, economic, and political autonomy, were illusions of a bygone era. Their "central concern," the authors observed in their introduction to a revised edition released 10 years after the original publication of their monograph, "was with the processes by which the small town (and indirectly all segments of American society) are continuously and increasingly drawn into the central machinery, processes and dynamics of the total society" (Vidich & Bensman, 1968, p. xi).

In so presenting their findings, Vidich and Bensman reversed the direction and exploded what was left of the mythology attendant upon the gemeinschaft-gesellschaft (Parsons, 1937/1949, 1973) and folk-urban continua in American sociological thought (Duncan, 1957; Firey, Loomis, & Beegle, 1950; Miner, 1952). Although the theoretical significance of their study was often neglected in the wake of the controversy that arose over its publication and the charge that they had not done enough to conceal the identities of the town's leading citizens (Vidich & Bensman, 1968, pp. 397-476), their concluding observations—namely, that there had occurred a middle-class revolution in America, that the rise and predominance of the new middle classes had altered the character and culture of both the cities and towns of America, and that "governmental, business, religious and educational super-bureaucracies far distant from the rural town formulate policies to which the rural world can respond only with resentment" (p. 323; see also Bensman & Vidich, 1987)—challenged the older paradigms guiding field research on community life.

By 1963, Roland L. Warren would take note of what he called "the 'great change' in American communities" and point out how a developing division of labor, the increasing differentiation of interests and associations, the growing systemic relations to the larger society, a transfer of local functions to profit enterprises and to state and federal governments, urbanization and suburbanization, and the shifts in values that were both cause and consequences of these changes had been accompanied by a "corresponding decline in community cohesion and autonomy" (see Warren, 1972, pp. 53-94). In effect, community ethnography would not only have to adjust to the encroachment of the city and the suburb on the town, but also enlarge its outlook to embrace the effects of the state and the national political economy on the towns and villages of the Third World as well as of the United States (see, e.g., the ethnographies collected in Toland, 1993; see also Marcus, 1986). ("The point is," Maurice Stein [1964] observed in his reflection on nearly six decades of American community studies, "that both the student of the slum and of the suburb [and, he might have added, the small town] require some sort of total picture of the evolution of American communities and of emerging constellations and converging problems"; p. 230. Had the practitioners of American community studies taken their point of departure from Otto von Gierke's [1868/ 1990] or Friedrich Ratzel's [1876/1988] orientations, they might have been more critical of the "Rousseauean" variant of Tönnies's outlook from the beginning of their research [see McKinney, 1957].)[27]

◆ The Ethnography of Assimilation: The Other Remains an Other

A breakdown in another fundamental paradigm affected the ethnographic study of ethnic and racial minorities. Until the 1960s, much of the sociological outlook on race and ethnic relations had focused on the processes and progress of assimilation, acculturation, and amalgamation among America's multiverse of peoples. Guided by the cluster of ideas and notions surrounding the ideology of the "melting pot," as well as by the prediction of the eventual assimilation of everyone that accompanied the widely held understanding of Robert E. Park's theory of the racial cycle, ethnographers of America's many minority groups at first sought to chart each people's location on a continuum that began with "contact," passed consecutively through stages of "competition and conflict" and "accommodation," and eventually culminated in "assimilation" (for critical evaluations of Park's cycle, see Lyman, 1972, 1990b, 1992b). Although by 1937 Park had come to despair of his earlier assertion that the cycle was progressive and irreversible (see Park, 1937/1969b), his students and followers would not give up their quest for a pattern and process that promised to bring an ultimate and beneficent end to interracial relations and their attendant problems.

When the ethnic histories of particular peoples in the United States seemed to defy the unidirectional movement entailed in Park's projected sequence—for example, when Etzioni's (1959) restudy of the Jewish ghetto showed little evidence that either religion or custom would be obliterated, even after many years of settlement in America; when Lee's (1960) discovery that Chinatowns and their old world-centered institutions persisted despite a decline in Sinophobic prejudices; when Woods's (1972) careful depiction of how 10 generations of settlement in America had failed to erode either the traditions or the ethnoracial identity of a marginalized people, the Letoyant Creoles of Louisiana (see also Woods, 1956); and, more generally, when Kramer (1970) had documented the many variations in minority community adaptation in America—there arose a cacophony of voices lamenting the failure of assimilation and calling for a resurgence of WASP hegemony (Brookhiser, 1991, 1993) or expressing grave apprehension about America's ethnocultural future (Christopher, 1989; Schlesinger, 1991; Schrag, 1973).

Even before popularizers and publicists announced the coming of an era in which there would be a "decline of the WASP" (Schrag, 1970) and a rise of the "unmeltable ethnics" (Novak, 1972), some sociologists had begun to reexamine their assumptions about ethnicity in America and to rethink their own and their predecessors' findings on the matter. In 1952, Nathan Glazer caused Marcus Lee Hansen's (1938/1952) hitherto over-looked work on the "law of third generation return" to be republished,[28] sparking a renewed interest in documenting whether, how, and to what extent the grandchildren of immigrants retained, reintroduced, rediscov-ered, or invented the customs of their old-world forebears in modern America (Kivisto & Blanck, 1990). Stanford M. Lyman (1974, 1986) com-bined participant observation with documentary and historical analyses to show that the solidarity and persistence over time of territorially based Chinatowns was related in great measure to persistent intracommunity conflict and to the web of traditional group affiliations that engendered both loyalty and altercation. Kramer and Leventman (1961) provided a picture of conflict resolution among three generations of American Jews who had retained many but not all aspects of their ethnoreligious tradi-tions despite, or perhaps because of, the fact that the third generation had become "children of the gilded ghetto." Richard Alba (1985, 1989, 1990) reopened the questions of whether and how European ethnic survival had occurred in the United States, pointing to the several dimensions of its presentation, representation, and disintegration, and carrying out, once more, a study of Italian Americans, a group often chosen by sociologists for ethnographic studies seeking to support, oppose, modify, or reformu-late the original assimilation thesis (see, e.g., Covello, 1967; Gans, 1962; Garbaccia, 1984; Landesco, 1968; Lopreato, 1970; Tricarico, 1984; Whyte, 1943a, 1943b).

The reconsideration of assimilation theory in general and Park's race relations cycle in particular produced a methodological critique so telling that it cast doubt on the substance of that hypothesis. In 1950, Seymour Martin Lipset observed that "by their very nature, hypotheses about the inevitability of cycles, whether they be cycles of race relations or the rise and fall of civilization, are not testable at all" (p. 479). Earlier, some ethnographers of racial minority groups in America had attempted to con-struct lengthier or alternative cycles that would be able to accommodate the findings of their field investigations. Bogardus's (1930, 1940; Ross &

Bogardus, 1940) three distinctive cycles for California's diversified Japanese communities and Masuoka's (1946) warning that three generations would be required for the acculturation of Japanese in America and that the third generation would still be victims of "a genuine race problem" evidence the growing disappointment with assimilation's promise. Others, including W. O. Brown (1934), Clarence E. Glick (1955), Stanley Lieberson (1961), and Graham C. Kinloch (1974, pp. 205-209), came to conclusions similar to that of Park's 1937 reformulation—namely, that assimilation was but one possible outcome of sustained interracial contact, and that isolation, subordination, nationalist or nativist movements, and secession ought also to be considered.

Those seeking to rescue the discredited determinism of Park's original cycle from its empirically minded critics turned to policy proposals or hortatory appeals in its behalf. Wirth (1945) urged the adoption of programs that would alleviate the frustration experienced by members of minority groups who had been repeatedly rebuffed in their attempts to be incorporated within a democratic America; Lee (1960, pp. 429-430) converted her uncritical adherence to Park's prophecy into a plaintive plea that Chinese ghetto dwellers live up to it—that is, that they assimilate themselves as rapidly as possible (see also Lyman, 1961-1962, 1963). Still others resolved the ontological and epistemological problems in Park's cycle by treating it as a "logical" rather than "empirical" perspective. Frazier (1953) suggested that, rather than occurring chronologically, the stages in the theory might be spatiotemporally coexistent: "They represent logical steps in a systematic sociological analysis of the subject." Shibutani and Kwan (1965), after examining the many studies of integrative and disintegrative social processes in racial and ethnic communities, concurred, holding that although there were many exceptions to its validity as a descriptive theory, Park's stages provided a "useful way of ordering data on the manner in which immigrants become incorporated into an already-established society" (see pp. 116-135). And Geschwender (1978) went further, holding that Park's race relations cycle was "an abstract model of an 'ideal type' sequence which might develop" (p. 25).

In 1918, Edward Byron Reuter had defined America's race issue as "the problem of arriving at and maintaining mutually satisfactory working relations between members of two nonassimilable groups which occupy the same territory" (Reuter, 1918/1969, p. 18). After a half century of sociological studies had seemed to demonstrate that virtually none of the racial or ethnic groups had traversed the cyclical pathway to complete assimilation, America's race problem seemed not only to be immense, but also to have defied as well as defined the basic problematic of sociological theory. Such, at any rate, was the position taken by the ethnological anthropologist Brewton Berry (1963), whose field investigations would eventually include studies of various peoples in Latin America as well as several communities of previously unabsorbed racial hybrids in the United States (see also Lyman, 1964). Having shown that none of the proposed cycles of race relations could claim universal validity on the basis of available evidence, Berry and Tischler (1978) observed, "Some scholars . . . question the existence of any universal pattern, and incline rather to the belief that so numerous and so various are the components that enter into race relations that each situation is unique, and [that] the making of generalizations is a hazardous procedure" (p. 156). Berry's thesis, although not necessarily intended in this direction, set the tone for the subsequent plethora of ethnographies that offered little in the way of theoretical advancements but much more of the detail of everyday life among minorities and other human groups.

During the two decades after 1970, ethnological studies of African American, Amerindian, Mexican American, and Asian peoples also cast considerable doubt on whether, when, and to whose benefit the much-vaunted process of ethnocultural meltdown in America would occur. Ethnographies and linguistic studies of black enclaves, North and South, slave and free, suggested that the tools employed in earlier community analyses had not been honed sufficiently for sociologists to be able to discern the cultural styles and social practices that set African American life apart from that of other segments of the society (see, e.g., Abrahams, 1964, 1970, 1992; E. Anderson, 1978; Bigham, 1987; Blassingame, 1979; Duneier, 1992; Evans & Lee, 1990; Joyner, 1984; Liebow, 1967; for an overview, see Blackwell, 1991). Other critics observed that sociological studies of the "American dilemma" had paid insufficient attention to politics, civil rights, and history (Boxhill, 1992; Button, 1989; Jackson, 1991; Lyman, 1972; V. J. Williams, 1989). Anthropological studies of the culture-preserving and supposedly isolated Native American nations and tribes had to give way in the face of a rising ethnoracial consciousness (Cornell, 1988; Martin, 1987; Sando, 1992), selective demands for the return of Amerindian museum holdings (Berlo, 1992; Clifford, 1990; Messenger, 1991; Milson, 1991-1992; "A Museum Is Set," 1993), Indian recourse to American courts in quest of redress and treaty rights (see T. L. Anderson, 1992; Jaimes, 1992), and political alliances and the tracing of

84

ethnohistorical descent that would connect Amerindians with Hispanics, African Americans, and Jews (Forbes, 1973, 1988; Gutierrez, 1991; Tobias, 1990; Vigil, 1980). Mexican American studies moved from early historical institutional studies through ethnographies of farm-workers, and in the 1980s became part of the new postmodernist revolution.[29] To the Amerasian peoples conventionally treated by ethnographic sociologists—namely, the Chinese and Japanese—were added more recent arrivals, including Koreans, Thais, Vietnamese, Cambodians, Laotians, and the Hmong (see, e.g., Chan, 1991; Hune et al., 1991; Knoll, 1982; Nomura et al., 1989; Okihiro et al., 1988; Takaki, 1989). And, as in the instance of Mexican American ethnographers, a shift in issues and methods is beginning to emerge—moving away from debates about whether and how to measure assimilation and acculturation and toward such postmodern topics as the character, content, and implications of racial discourse about Asians in America (e.g., K. J. Anderson, 1991; Okihiro, 1988). As East Indians, Burmese, Oceanians, Malaysians, and other peoples of what used to be called "the Orient" began to claim common cause with the earlier-established Asian groups (Espiritu, 1992; Ignacio, 1976; Mangiafico, 1988), but insisted on each people's socio-cultural and historical integrity, as well as the right of each to choose its own path within U.S. society, it became clear that the trend toward ethnographic postmodernism would continue (see, e.g., Hune et al., 1991; Leonard, 1992).

In 1980, Harvard University Press issued its mammoth *Harvard Encyclopedia of American Ethnic Groups* (Thernstrom, 1980), a work that includes not only separate entries for "Africans" and "Afro-Americans" but also individual essays devoted to each of 173 different tribes of American Indians and reports on each of the Asian peoples coming to the United States from virtually all the lands east of Suez. Harold J. Abrahamson's entry, "Assimilation and Pluralism," in effect announces American sociology's awakening not only from its dream of the eventual assimilation of every people in the country, but also from its conflation of assimilation with Americanization: "American society . . . is revealed as a composite not only of many ethnic backgrounds but also of many different ethnic responses. . . . There is no one single response or adaptation. The variety of styles in pluralism and assimilation suggest that ethnicity is as complex as life itself" (p. 160; see also Gleason, 1980; Novak, 1980; Walzer, 1980).

For the moment, pluralism had won its way onto paradigmatic center stage.[30] But even that orientation did not exhaust the possibilities or dispose of the problems arising out of the presence of diverse races and peoples in America. In 1993, together with Rita Jalali, Seymour Martin Lipset, who had criticized Park's formulation of an inevitable cycle leading to assimilation four decades earlier, observed that "race and ethnicity provide the most striking example of a general failure among experts to anticipate social developments in varying types of societies" (Jalali & Lipset, 1992-1993, p. 585). Moreover, the celebration of pluralism that now prevails in social thought obscures recognition of a fundamental problem: the self-restraint to be placed upon the competitive claims put forward by each ethnic and racial group.

◆ Ethnography Now: The Postmodern Challenge

Historically, the ethnographic method has been used by both anthropologists and sociologists. The guiding frameworks for those who have used this method in the past have all but been abandoned by contemporary ethnographers. The social-historical transformations of society and consciousness in the modern world have undermined the theoretical and value foundations of the older ethnography.

With the present abandonment of virtually every facet of what might now be recognized as the interlocked, secular, eschatological legacies of Comte, Tönnies, Wissler, Redfield, Park, and Parsons—that is, the recognition that the "comparative method" and the anthropology of primitivism is inherently flawed by both its Eurocentric bias and its methodological inadequacies; the determination that the gemeinschaft of the little community has been subverted by the overwhelming force of the national political economy of the gesellschaft; the discovery that assimilation is not inevitable; and the realization that ethnic sodalities and the ghettos persist over long periods of time (sometimes combining deeply embedded internal disharmonies with an outward display of sociocultural solidarity, other times existing as "ghost nations," or as hollow shells of claimed ethnocultural distinctiveness masking an acculturation that has already eroded whatever elementary forms of existence gave primordial validity to that claim, or, finally, as semiarticulated assertions of a peoplehood that has moved through and "beyond the melting pot" without having been fully dissolved in its fiery cauldron)—ethnography and ethnology could emerge on their own terms.[31]

No longer would ethnography have to serve the interests of a theory of progress that pointed toward the breakup of every ethnos. No longer would ethnology have to describe the pastoral peacefulness, proclaim the moral superiority, or document the psychic security supposed to be found in the villages of the nonliterate, the folk societies of non-Western peoples, the little communities of the woods and forests, the small towns of America, or the urban ethnic enclaves of U.S. or world metropolises. No longer would ethnography have to chart the exact position of each traditional and ascriptively based status group as it moved down the socioculturally determined pathway that would eventually take it into a mass, class, or civil society, and recompose it in the process.

Liberated from these conceptual and theoretical constraints, ethnography and ethnology are, for the first time as it were, in a position to act out their own versions of the revolution of "life" against "the forms of life"—a cultural revolution of the 20th century that Simmel (1968) foresaw as both imminent and tragic. Just as Simmel predicted that the cultural revolutionaries that he saw emerging in pre-World War I Europe would oppose both marriage and prostitution on the grounds that each was a form of the erotic and that they wished to emancipate the erotic from all forms of itself, so the new ethnographers proclaim themselves to be self-liberated from the weight of historical consciousness, relieved of the anxiety of influence (see Bloom, 1979),[32] and, in effect, content to become witnesses to and reporters of the myriad scenes in the quixotic world that has emerged out of the ruins of both religion and secular social theory (see Kundera, 1988).

The proclamation of ethnography as a self-defining orientation and practice in sociology and anthropology and the importation of the postmodernist outlook into it took place recently, irregularly, and in somewhat disorderly moves. Aleksandr Solzhenitsyn (1993) once pointed out that "no new work of art comes into existence (whether consciously or unconsciously) without an organic link to what was created earlier" (p. 3). Such also remains the case in social science, as will be shown with the new developments in sociological and anthropological ethnography.

One beginning of the emancipatory movement in ethnographic methodology is to be found in Peter Manning's seminal essay "Analytic Induction" (1982/1991). Seeking to set ethnography on an even firmer foundation of the symbolic interactionist perspective and hoping to reinforce its connections to the classical period of the "Chicago school," Manning sought first to warn any practitioners of the sociological enterprise against employing any "concepts and theories developed to deal with the problems of such other disciplines as behavioristic psychology, economics, medicine, or the natural or physical sciences." He identified analytic induction as a procedure derivable from George Herbert Mead's and Florian Znaniecki's writings on scientific method, and he observed that it had been employed with greater or lesser precision by such classical Chicago ethnographers as Thomas and Znaniecki, and, later, by Robert Cooley Angell, Alfred Lindesmith, and Donald Cressey. Distinguishable from deductive, historical-documentary, and statistical approaches, analytic induction was "a nonexperimental qualitative sociological method that employs an exhaustive examination of cases in order to prove universal, causal generalizations." The case method was to be the critical foundation of a revitalized qualitative sociology.

The claim to universality of the causal generalizations is—in the example offered by Manning as exemplary of the method[33]—the weakest, for it is derived from the examination of a single case studied in light of a preformulated hypothesis that might be reformulated if the hypothesis does not fit the facts. And "practical certainty" of the (reformulated) hypothesis is obtained "after a small number of cases has been examined." Discovery of a single negative case is held to disprove the hypothesis and to require its reformulation. After "certainty" has been attained, "for purposes of proof, cases outside the area circumscribed by the definition are examined to determine whether or not the final hypothesis applies to them." If it does, it is implied, there is something wrong with the hypothesis, for "scientific generalizations consist of descriptions of conditions which are always present when the phenomenon is present but which are never present when the phenomenon is absent." The two keys to the entire procedure, Manning points out, are the definition of the phenomenon under investigation and the formulation of the tentative hypothesis. Ultimately, however, as Manning concedes, despite its aim, analytic induction does not live up to the scientific demand that its theories "understand, predict, and control events." After a careful and thoroughgoing critique of the procedure he has chosen over its methodological competitors, Manning asserts, "Analytic induction is not a means of prediction; it does not clearly establish causality; and it probably cannot endure a principled examination of its claims to [be] making universal statements." Indeed, Manning goes further, pointing out that, "according to the most demanding ideal standards of the discipline, analytic induction as a distinctive, philosophical, methodological perspective is less powerful than either enumerative induction or axiomatic-modelling methods." Manning's essay seems about to eject a method intrinsic to ethnography from the scientific community.

Manning's frank appraisal of the weaknesses of analytic induction is "drawn from a positivistic, deductive model of the scientific endeavor, a model seizing on a selected group of concerns." The proponents of that model seek to set the terms and limits of the social sciences according to its criteria. In fact, although few American scholars seem to know much about either the long history or the irresolution of debates over epistemological matters in the social sciences, the very issues of those debates are central to the questions the positivists are raising (see, in this regard, Rorty, 1982, pp. 191-210).

In his defense of analytic induction, Manning invokes an unacknowledged earlier critique by Sorokin (1965), namely, "that what is taken to be [appropriate] methodology at a given time is subject to fads, fashions, and foibles." Manning goes on to credit analytic induction with being a "viable source of data and concepts" and with helping investigators to sort out "the particulars of a given event [and to distinguish them from] those things that are general and theoretical." Erving Goffman, surely a sociological practitioner whose methodological orientation is akin to but not the same as analytic induction, goes even further, however. Opposing, in a defense of his own brand of ethnographic sociology, both system building and enumerative induction, in 1961 he wrote, "At present, if sociological concepts are to be treated with affection, each must be traced back to where it best applies, followed from there wherever it seems to lead, and pressed to disclose the rest of its family. Better, perhaps, different coats to clothe the children well than a single splendid tent in which they all shiver" (p. xiv). A decade later, Goffman (1971) dismissed the scientific claims of positivistic sociologists altogether: "A sort of sympathetic magic seems to be involved, the assumption being that if you go through the motions attributable to science then science will result. But it hasn't" (p. xvi).

With the waning of interest in, support for, or faith in the older purposes for doing ethnology, by the 1970s there had also arisen a concomitant discontent with the epistemological claims as well as the latent or secretive political usages (see Diamond, 1992; Horowitz, 1967) of the mainstream perspectives of both sociology (see Vidich, Lyman, & Goldfarb, 1981) and anthropology (e.g., Clifford & Marcus, 1986; Fox, 1991; Manganaro, 1990). An outlook that could be used to carry out research projects and at the same time to treat the very resources of each discipline as a topic to be investigated critically was needed. Postmodernism appeared and seemed to fill that need.

Toward the end of his essay, Manning hints at the issue that would explode on the pages of almost every effort to come to terms with postwar and post-Cold War America: "In an age of existentialism, self-construction is as much a part of sociological method as theory construction." What he would later perceive as a reason for developing a formalistic and semiotic approach to doing fieldwork (Manning, 1987, pp. 7-24, 66-72) was that each construction would come to be seen as inextricably bound up with the other and that each would be said to provide a distorted mirror image of both the body (Cornwell, 1992; Featherstone, Hepworth, & Turner, 1991; Feher, 1989; Sheets-Johnstone, 1990, pp. 112-133; 1992) and the self (Kotarba & Fontana, 1987; Krieger, 1991; Zaner, 1981), of both one's *Umwelt* and the world of the other (the concept of *Umwelt* is developed by Gurwitsch, 1966). But for those who accepted the critique but rejected neoformalism as a technique for ethnography, there opened up a new field of investigation— representation. Hence some of the best postmodern ethnography has focused on the media that give imagery to real life (Bhabha, 1990b; Early, 1993; Gilman, 1991; Trinh, 1991). Justification for turning from the fields of lived experience to what is represented as such is the assumption that the former is itself perceived holographically, calling for the thematization of representation as a problem in the construction of "persuasive fictions" (Baudrillard, 1988a, pp. 27-106; Norris, 1990).

The postmodern ethnographer takes Simmel's tragedy of culture to be a fait accompli: It is not possible at the present time to emancipate free-floating life from all of its constraining forms (Strathern, 1990). The postmodern sociologist-ethnographer and his or her subjects are situated in a world suspended between illusory memories of a lost innocence and millennial dreams of a utopia unlikely to be realized. From such a position, not only is the standpoint of the investigator problematic (Lemert, 1992; Weinstein & Weinstein, 1991), but also that of the people to be investigated. Each person has in effect been "touched by the mass media, by alienation, by the economy, by the new family and child-care systems, by the unceasing technologizing of the social world, and by the threat of nuclear annihilation" (Denzin, 1989, p. 139). And, if the anthropologist-ethnographer is to proceed in accordance with the postmodern perspective, he or she must, on the one hand, become less fearful about "going primitive" (Torgovnick, 1990) and, on the other, contend with the claim that Eurocentric imagery has attended virtually all previous reports from the "primitive" world (Beverly, 1992; Bhabha, 1990a; Dirlik, 1987; Turner, 1992; West, 1992). For these ethnographers, Helmut Kuzmics (1988) observes, "The claim that the 'evolutionary gradualism' of the theory of civilization renders it incapable of explaining the simultaneous appearance of civilization (in a narrower sense than is presupposed by the highest values of the Enlightenment) and 'barbarism' still needs to be confronted more thoroughly" (p. 161).

As analytic induction advocates propose, let us begin with a definition of the new outlook—the postmodern. Charlene Spretnak (1991), a critic of much of the postmodernism she surveys, provides one that is comprehensive and useful:

> A sense of detachment, displacement, and shallow engagement dominates deconstructive-postmodern aesthetics because groundlessness is the only constant recognized by this sensibility. The world is considered to be a repressive labyrinth of "social production," a construction of pseudoselves who are pushed and pulled by cultural dynamics and subtly diffused "regimes of power." Values and ethics are deemed arbitrary, as is "history," which is viewed by deconstructive postmodernists as one group or another's self-serving selection of facts. Rejecting all "metanarratives," or supposedly universal representations of reality, deconstructive postmodernists insist that the making of every aspect of human existence is culturally created and determined in particular, localized circumstances about which no generalizations can be made. Even particularized meaning, however, is regarded as relative and temporary. (pp. 13-14)

Spretnak's definition permits us to see how the postmodern ethnographer proceeds. The post-modernist ethnographer enters into a world from which he or she is methodologically required to have become detached and displaced. Such an ethnographer is in effect reconstituted as Simmel's (1950) "stranger" (see also Frisby, 1992) and Park's (1929/1969a) and Stonequist's (1937/1961) "marginalized" person (see also Wood, 1934/1969, pp. 245-284). Like those ideal-typical ethnographers-in-spite-of-themselves, this social scientist begins work as a self-defined newcomer to the habitat and life world of his or her subjects (see Agar, 1980; Georges & Jones, 1980; D. Rose, 1989). He or she is a citizen-scholar (Saxton, 1993) as well as a participant observer (Vidich, 1955). Older traditions and aims of ethnography, including especially the quest for valid generalizations and substantive conclusions, are temporarily set aside in behalf of securing "thick descriptions" (Geertz, 1973) that will in turn make possible "thick interpretations"—joining ethnography to both biography and lived experience (Denzin, 1989, pp. 32-34). History is banished from the ethnographic enterprise except when and to the effect that local folk histories enter into the vocabularies of motive and conduct employed by the subjects.[34] Because crossing the postmodern divide (Borgmann, 1992; I. Chambers, 1990) requires one to abandon all established and preconceived values, theories, perspectives, preferences, and prejudices as resources for ethnographic study, the ethnographer must bracket these, treating them as if they are arbitrary and contingent rather then hegemonic and guiding (Rosenau, 1992, pp. 25-76). Hence the postmodernist ethnographer takes seriously the aim of such deconstructionists as Derrida (e.g., 1976, 1981), Lyotard (e.g., 1989), and Baudrillard (e.g., 1981, 1983, 1988b), namely, to disprivilege all received texts and established discourses in behalf of an all-encompassing critical skepticism about knowledge. In so doing, the ethnographer displaces and deconstructs his or her own place on the hierarchy of statuses that all too often disguise their invidious character as dichotomies (see Bendix & Berger, 1959; for a postmodern analysis of a dichotomy, see Lyman, 1992a). To all of these, instead, is given contingency—the contingencies of language, of selfhood, and of community (Rorty, 1989; C. Taylor, 1989).

For anthropologists, the new forms for ethnography begin with a recognition of their irreducible limitation: the very presentation of ethnographic information in a monograph is a "text" and therefore subject to the entire critical apparatus that the postmodern perspective brings to bear on any text.[35] The ethnographic enterprise is to be conceived as a task undertaken all too often by an unacculturated stranger who is guided by whatever the uneasy mix of poetry and politics gives to his or her efforts to comprehend an alien culture. Above all, an ethnography is now to be regarded as a piece of writing—as such, it cannot be said either to present or to represent what the older and newly discredited ideology of former ethnography claimed for itself: an unmodified and unfiltered record of immediate experience and an accurate portrait of the culture of the "other."

The postmodern critique has engendered something of a crisis among present-day anthropologists. As in the responses to other crises, a new self- and-other consciousness has come to the fore, and the imperatives of reflexivity have shifted attention onto the literary, political, and historical features of ethnography as well as onto career imperatives, all of which have hitherto been overlooked. Engaging themselves with these issues, such disciplinary leaders as Clifford Geertz, Mary Douglas, Claude Lévi-Strauss, and the late Victor Turner have blurred the old distinction between art and science and challenged the very basis of the claim to exacting rigor, unblinking truth telling, and unbiased reporting that marked the boundary separating one from the other.

Rereading the works in the classical ethnographic canon has now become a critical task of the highest importance. A new form of structuralist method must be devised if we are to dig beneath the works and uncover both their hidden truths and their limiting blinders. That canon is now to be seen as a product of the age of Occidental colonialism and to have been methodologically constrained by the metropole ideologies and literary conventions that gave voice and quality to them. Yet these ethnographies are not to be relegated to the historical dustbin of a rejectable epoch of disciplinary childhood by today's and tomorrow's anthropologists. Rather, in consideration of the fact that few of the latter will follow career trajectories like those of Malinowski or Powdermaker—that is, either spending decades of their lives in residence with a nonliterate Oceanic people or moving from the ethnographic task of observing at close range a group of South Africans to another, living among blacks in a segregated Mississippi town, and then to still another, closely examining how the Hollywood film industry became a "dream factory,"—the ethnologist of the present age and the immediate future is likely to do but one ethnography—a dissertation that stakes his or her claim to the title of ethnologist and to the perquisites of an academic life spent largely away from the field. Moreover, career considerations are not the only element affecting ethnology. The "field" itself has become constricted by the march of decolonization and the modernization that has overtaken once "primitive" peoples. For these reasons, rereading old ethnographies becomes a vicarious way to experience the original ways of the discipline, whereas criticizing them provides the ethnologist with a way to distance him- or herself from modernist foibles. Except for the dissertation ethnography and for those anthropologists who choose to move in on the turf of the equally postmodern sociological ethnographers of urban and industrial settings, the ethnographic task of anthropology may become one devoted to reading texts and writing critiques. The "field" may be located in one's library or one's study.

Given the postmodern ethnographers' epistemological stance and disprivileged social status, two fundamental problems for the sociological version of the new ethnography are its relationship to social change and social action, and the applicable scope of its representations of reality.

The first problem has been posed as well as answered by Michael Burawoy et al. (1992) in their conception of "ethnography unbound" and the role of the "extended case method." They direct the ethnographer toward the macropolitical, economic, and historical contexts in which directly observed events occur, and perceive in the latter fundamental issues of domination and resistance (see also Feagin, Orum, & Sjoberg, 1991). Norman Denzin (1989), a leader of postmodern approaches to ethnography, approaches the generality issue in two distinct though related ways. His advice to ethnographers is that they first immerse themselves in the lives of their subjects and, after achieving a deep understanding of these through rigorous effort, produce a contextualized reproduction and interpretation of the stories told by the subjects. Ultimately, an ethnographic report will present an integrated synthesis of experience and theory. The "final interpretive theory is multivoiced and dialogical. It builds on native interpretations and in fact simply articulates what is implicit in those interpretations" (p. 120). Denzin's strategic move out of the epistemological cul-de-sac presented by such daunting observations as Berry's specific skepticism about the possibility of making valid generalizations in an ethnoracially pluralist society, or by the growing skepticism about the kind and quality of results that sociologists' adherence to positivistic and natural science models will engender (T. R. Vaughan, 1993, p. 120), is to take the onset of the postmodern condition as the very occasion for presenting a new kind of ethnography. He encourages, in effect, an ethnographic attitude of engagement with a world that is ontologically absurd but always meaningful to those who live in it (see Lyman & Scott, 1989). Thus he concludes his methodological treatise by claiming that the world has now entered its Fourth Epoch (following Antiquity, the Middle Ages, and the Modern Age), and that this latest epoch is in fact the "postmodern period" (Denzin, 1989, p. 138). The ethnographic method appropriate to this period, Denzin goes on, is one that is dedicated "to understanding how this historical moment universalizes itself in the lives of interesting individuals" (p. 189). Method and substance are joined in the common recognition that everyone shares in the same world and responds to it somehow. The study of the common condition and the uncovering of the uncommon response become the warp and woof of the fragile but not threadbare sociological skein of the postmodern era.

The postmodern is a cultural form as well as an era of history. As the former, like all the forms noted by Simmel, it invites and evokes its counteracting and rebellious tendencies. It too, then, is likely to suffer the penultimate tragedy of culture—the inability to emancipate life from all of its forms (Weinstein & Weinstein, 1990). However, in this era, the sociologist-ethnographer will not merely observe that history; he or she will participate in its everlasting quest for freedom, and be a partner in and a reporter on "the pains, the agonies, the emotional experiences, the small and large victories, the traumas, the fears, the anxieties, the dreams, fantasies and the hopes" of the lives of the peoples. These constitute this era's ethnographies—true tales of the field (Van Maanen, 1988).

The methods of ethnography have become highly refined and diverse, and the reasons for doing ethnography have multiplied. No longer linked to the values that had guided and focused the work of earlier ethnographers, the new ethnography ranges over a vastly expanded subject matter, limited only by the varieties of experience in modern life; the points of view from which ethnographic observations may be made are as great as the choices of lifestyles available in modern society. It is our hope that the technological refinement of the ethnographic method will find its vindication in the discovery of new sets of problems that lead to a greater understanding of the modern world.

Although it is true that at some level all research is a uniquely individual enterprise—not part of a sacrosanct body of accumulating knowledge—it is also true that it is always guided by values that are not unique to the investigator: We are all creatures of our own social and cultural pasts. However, in order to be meaningful to others, the uniqueness of our own research experience gains significance when it is related to the theories of our predecessors and the research of our contemporaries. Ethnographers can find social and cultural understanding only if they are aware of the sources of the ideas that motivate them and are willing to confront them—with all that such a confrontation entails.

◆ Notes

1. For a discussion of the fundamental similarities between so-called quantitative and qualitative methods, see Vidich and Bensman (1968, chap. 13).

2. Here we merely gloss a serious problem in the philosophy and epistemology of the social sciences and present one possible approach to it. Some of the issues are discussed and debated in such works as those by C. W. Smith (1979), Rabinow and Sullivan (1979), G. Morgan (1983), Fiske and Shweder (1986), Hare and Blumberg (1988), Ashmore (1989), Minnich (1990), Bohman (1991), Sadri (1992, pp. 3-32, 105-142), and Harré (1984).

3. Many of the issues raised by this new outlook are treated in the essays collected in A. Rose (1988).

4. The following draws on Lyman (1990a).

5. This orientation differs from that used by Thucydides (1972) in *History of the Peloponnesian War*. His observations were made from the perspective of a participant who detached himself from the norms of both warring sides while never making explicit his own values. His book has confounded legions of scholars who have attempted to find his underlying themes, not understanding that the work is replete with ambiguities that do not lend themselves to a single viewpoint. For various perspectives on Thucydides' work, see Kitto (1991, pp. 136-152), Kluckhohn (1961, pp. 4, 34-35, 55, 64-66), Humphreys (1978, pp. 94, 131, 143, 227-232, 300-307), and Grant (1992, pp. 5, 45, 148-149).

6. When discussing the crimes committed by the Spaniards against the Indians, Hosle (1992) states: "It is certainly not easy to answer the following question: Were the priests who accompanied the conquistadors also responsible, even if they condemned the violence committed, insofar as their presence in a certain sense legitimized the enterprise? It is impossible to deny that by their mere presence they contributed to Christianity appearing as an extremely hypocritical religion, which spoke of universal love and nevertheless was the religion of brutal criminals. Yet it is clear that without the missionaries' presence even more cruelties would have been committed. Hypocrisy at least acknowledges in theory certain norms, and by so doing gives the oppressed the possibility to claim certain rights. Open brutality may be more sincere, but sincerity is not the only value. Sincere brutality generates nothing positive; hypocrisy, on the other side, bears in itself the force which can overcome it" (p. 236). If it does anything, Hosle's defense of Christianity reveals the difficulty still remaining in debates over universalistic as opposed to relativistic values and leaves wide open any resolution of the problem. See also Lippy, Choquette, and Poole (1992). For further history and discussion of the de Las Casas-Sepulveda dispute and its implications for ethnohistory and ethnology of the Americas, see Hanke (1949/1965, 1959/1970, 1974).

7. A fine example is the ethnographic study by Bishop Robert Henry Codrington (1891) titled *The Melanesians*. Codrington's study provided the sole source for Yale University anthropologist Loomis Havemeyer's (1929) chapter on the Melanesians (pp. 141-160). See Codrington (1974) for an excerpt from *The Melanesians* titled "Mana." See also the critical discussion in Kuper (1988, pp. 152-170).

8. A good example that also illustrates the anthropologists' despair over the disastrous effects of missionary endeavor on native life and culture is to be found in the last published work of William Hale R. Rivers (1922/1974).

9. Thus if the reader wishes to peruse one well-known exposition of "primitive" culture, George Peter Murdock's (1934) *Our Primitive Contemporaries,* as an example of one aspect of the "comparative method," he or she will discover therein ethnographies of 18 peoples who occupy time and space coincident to that of the author, arranged in terms of geography, but—with the term *primitive* as the descriptive adjective in use throughout—

making the title of the book historically (that is, diachronically) oxymoronic. For a thought-ful critique, see Bock (1966).

10. Two exceptions to this mode of ethnocentric expression are worthy of note: William Graham Sumner (1840-1910), who coined the term *ethnocentrism,* seemed also to suggest that the failure of either Congress or the courts to do anything to halt the lynching of Negroes in the South signaled something less than that nation's rise to perfected civilization that other ethnologists were willing to credit to America and to other republics of the Occident: "It is unseemly that anyone should be burned at the stake in a modern civilized state" (Sumner, 1906/1940, p. 471; see also Sumner, 1905/1969). Thorstein Veblen (1857-1929) used such categories as "savagery" and "barbarism" tongue-in-cheek, often treating the moral codes and pecuniary values of the peoples so labeled as superior to those of the peoples adhering to the Protestant ethic or the spirit of capitalism, and disputing the claims of Aryan superiority so much in vogue in his day (see Veblen, 1899/1959, 1914/1990, 1919/1961a, 1919/1961b; see also A. K. Davis, 1980; Diggins, 1978; Tilman, 1991).

11. The Human Relations Area Files were reproduced, marketed, and distributed to anthropology departments in other universities. This not only added an element of stan-dardization and uniformity to culture studies, but also made it possible for the analyst of eth-nography to forgo a trip to the field. That this approach is still in vogue is illustrated by two researches by the Harvard sociologist Orlando Patterson (1982). Patterson relies on Murdock's "World Sample" of 61 slaveholding societies (out of a total of 186 societies), which are arranged geographically, but rearranges them temporally to make them serve a developmentalist thesis that seeks to uncover the variations in as well as the functional ori-gins of slavery. On the basis of this method, it is not surprising to find that in the sequel to his study Patterson (1991) believes he can show that "the Tupinamba, the ancient Greeks and Romans, and the southerners of the United States, *so markedly different in time, place, and levels of sociocultural development,* nonetheless reveal the remarkable tenacity of this culture-character complex" (p. 15; emphasis added).

12. For the conceptualization of a sector of the world's peoples as belonging to the Third World, as well as for the conceptualization of "developed" and "undeveloped" or "underdeveloped" societies, see Worsley (1964, 1984).

13. That capitalism had contributed to underdevelopment in both the European over-seas empires and America's homegrown "ghetto colonialism" became an assumption and even an article of faith that could shape the perspective of posttraditional ethnography (see Blauner, 1972; Marable, 1983; see also Hechter, 1975).

14. For a historical view on eschatological, millennial, sacred, and secular "end-times" theories, as well as other modes of chronologizing events, see Paolo Rossi (1987).

15. It should be noted that American ethnography up to the beginnings of World War II focused almost exclusively on American Indians and the aboriginal inhabitants of American colonies. Anthropologists' interests in the high cultures of Central and South America were archaeologically oriented and were designed both to fill in the "prehistoric record" and to fill museums. Some ethnographic work was carried out in the U.S.-controlled Pacific Islands (in association with the Bernice P. Bishop Museum in Hawaii). Margaret Mead worked on American Samoa and was one of the earliest of the nonmissionaries to ethnograph a Pacific Island. Her work, aimed in part at criticizing the Puritanical sexual mores of America, over-stated the actual situation in Oceania and eventually led to a counterstatement (see

Freeman, 1983; Holmes, 1987; Mead, 1928/1960a, 1930/1960b, 1949/1960c, 1935/1960d).

16. This was the same perspective used by anthropologists who administered the Japanese relocation centers during World War II and who had had some of their training on the reservation. For accounts by those anthropologists who moved from Amerindian to Japanese American incarceration ethnography and administration, see Leighton (1945), Wax (1971), Spicer, Hansen, Luomala, and Opler (1969), and Myer (1971). For a spirited critique, see Drinnon (1987).

17. For some representative ethnographies of the southwestern Amerindian peoples, see Schwatka (1893/1977), Nordenskiold (1893/1979), McGee (1899/1971), Goddard (1913/1976), White (1933/1974), Spier (1933/1978), and Kluckhohn (1944). See also Eggan (1966, pp. 112-141).

18. A recent ethnography of the Zuni by Tedlock (1992) both reflects upon and critically appraises Cushing's work among that tribe.

19. Radin (1935/1970, 1936/1971a) also did fieldwork among the Italians and Chinese of San Francisco.

20. Clark Wissler (1940/1966a, 1938/1966b) established his credentials on the basis of a lifetime in service to ethnohistorical and ethnographic study of the United States.

21. Although not carried out at the University of Chicago, this study bears the stamp of that school's approach.

22. In that report, he was the first to see the new role of the university president as an administrative "Captain of Erudition," the beginnings of university public relations designed to protect the image of learning, and the business foundations in real estate and fund-raising (endowments) of the university system in the United States.

23. In 1992, when new questions were raised about the ethnocultural and ethical aspects of Whyte's study of "Cornerville," a symposium reviewed the matter extensively (see "*Street Corner Society* Revisited," 1992).

24. A social variant of Redfield's perspective found its way into some of the urban community, ethnic enclave, and small-town studies of America that were conducted or supervised by anthropologists or Chicago sociologists (see Hannerz, 1980; Lyon, 1987; Suttles, 1972, pp. 3-20). (A revival of ecological studies rooted in the idea that the uses of space are socially constructed was begun with the publication of Lyman & Scott, 1967; see also Ericksen, 1980.) As early as 1914, M. C. Elmer, a promising graduate student at the University of Chicago, had written a Ph.D. dissertation on social surveys in urban communities that reflected the shift from the church to the "scientific" survey tradition in both the social gospel movement and the discipline of sociology; seven years later, Raleigh Webster Stone (1921) in effect signaled that the transition to a newer orientation was well under way when he offered *The Origin of the Survey Movement* as his Ph.D. dissertation at Chicago. In 1933, Albert Bailie Blumenthal submitted *A Sociological Study of a Small Town* as his doctoral dissertation at the same university (Faris, 1970, pp. 135-140). However, the central thrust of ethnological studies in Chicago's sociology department after Robert E. Park had joined its faculty concerned community and subcommunity organization within the city (see, e.g., N. Anderson, 1959), and, for some, how the gemeinschaft could be reconstituted in the metropolis (see Fishman, 1977; Quandt, 1970).

25. That ethnographies of small towns and large cities adopted an approach more or less consistent with the macropolitical-economic orientation emphasized by Vidich and

Bensman is evidenced in works by P. Davis (1982), Wallace (1987), Arsenault (1988), Campbell (1992), Moorhouse (1988), and Reid (1992).

26. Earlier, Vidich (1952, 1980) had contributed to the reconsideration of anthropological approaches to so-called primitive societies, reconceiving such studies as requiring an orientation that focused on the effects of global colonialism and its rivalries on the structure and process of colonialized societies. For the connections between his anthropological study of Palau under various colonial administrations and the study of "Springdale," see Vidich (1986).

27. British approaches to the historical sociology of small towns did not adopt Tönnies's theoretical stance (see, e.g., Abrams & Wrigley, 1979).

28. See also Glazer (1954). "Hansen's law" was the basis for work by Kennedy (1944) and Herberg (1960).

29. For monographs illustrating the stages in the evolution of these studies, see Blackman (1891/1976), P. S. Taylor (1930/1970, 1983), Gamio (1930/1969, 1931/1971), Bogardus (1934/1970), and Galarza (1964, 1970, 1977). For community studies in New Mexico, see Gonzalez (1967), Sanchez (1967), and Forrest (1989). For Arizona, see Sheridan (1986); for Texas, see Rubel (1971); for Indiana, see Lane and Escobar (1987); for Chicago, see Padilla (1985). For general and historical studies, see Burma (1985), Officer (1987), and D. J. Weber (1992). For the shift from eth-class to postmodern analysis, see Barrera (1979, 1988).

30. Subsequent works (e.g., Fuchs, 1990; Keyes, 1982; Kivisto, 1984, 1989; Lieberson, 1980; Lieberson & Waters, 1988; Royce, 1982; Steinberg, 1981; Waters, 1990) emphasized pluralism, contingency, and the voluntary and social constructionist aspects of race and ethnicity.

31. In anthropology, the shift toward a new outlook included a critical reevaluation and commentary on virtually every aspect of ethnology and ethnography in what has thus far produced seven volumes of essays edited by George W. Stocking, Jr. (1983, 1984, 1985, 1986, 1988, 1989, 1991). A turn toward the classics of antiquity and their relation to modern and postmodern anthropology was appraised by Redfield's son (see J. Redfield, 1991).

32. One element of intellectual and moral influence has given rise to anxiety, recriminations, and rhetorical attempts to excuse, justify, or escape from the burden it lays on those who believe that postmodernism is a countercultural orientation of the Left, namely, the accusation that its preeminent philosophical founders—Heidegger and de Man—were sympathetic to and supporters of the Hitler regime and Nazism. For debates on this far-from-resolved issue, see Habermas (1983), Farias (1989), Neske and Kettering (1990), Ferry and Renaut (1990), Lyotard (1990), Rockmore (1992), Derrida (1992), Hamacher, Hertz, and Keenan (1989), and Lehman (1992). Another important contributor to postmodernism, Michel Foucault, has aroused apprehension over the extent to which his sexual preferences and promiscuous lifestyle affected his philosophical perspective. For various opinions on the matter, see Poster (1987-1988), Foucault (1992), Eribon (1991), Miller (1993); and Nikolinakos (1990). See also Paglia (1991).

33. The procedural example used by Manning is from Cressey (1953, p. 16).

34. For a discussion of the several issues involved in the relationship of history to ethnography, see Comaroff and Comaroff (1992); compare Natanson (1962).

35. The following draws on the essays and commentaries in Clifford and Marcus (1986).

◆ References

Abeyesekere, G. (1992). *The apotheosis of Captain Cook: European mythmaking in the Pacific.* Princeton, NJ: Princeton University Press.

Abrahams, R. D. (1964). *Deep down in the jungle: Negro narrative folklore from the streets of Philadelphia.* Hatboro, PA: Folklore Associates.

Abrahams, R. D. (1970). *Positively black.* Englewood Cliffs, NJ: Prentice Hall.

Abrahams, R. D. (1992). *Singing the master: The emergence of African American culture in the plantation South.* New York: Pantheon.

Abrahamson, H. J. (1980). Assimilation and pluralism. In S. Thernstrom (Ed.), *Harvard encyclopedia of American ethnic groups.* Cambridge, MA: Harvard University Press.

Abrams, P., & Wrigley, E. A. (Eds.). (1979). *Towns and societies: Essays in economic history and historical sociology.* Cambridge: Cambridge University Press.

Adler, P. A., Adler, P., & Fontana, A. (1987). Everyday life sociology. In K. Plummer (Ed.), *Symbolic interactionism: Vol. 1. Foundations and history* (pp. 436-454). Brookfield, VT: Edward Elgar.

Agar, M. H. (1980). *The professional stranger: An informal introduction to ethnography.* New York: Academic Press.

Alba, R. (1985). *Italian Americans: Into the twilight of ethnicity.* Englewood Cliffs, NJ: Prentice Hall.

Alba, R. (Ed.). (1989). *Ethnicity and race in the U.S.A.: Toward the twenty-first century.* New York: Routledge, Chapman Hall.

Alba, R. (1990). *Ethnic identity: The transformation of white America.* New Haven, CT: Yale University Press.

Aldrich, R. (1990). *The French presence in the South Pacific, 1842-1940.* Honolulu: University of Hawaii Press.

Anderson, E. (1978). *A place on the corner.* Chicago: University of Chicago Press.

Anderson, K. J. (1991). *Vancouver's Chinatown: Racial discourse in Canada, 1875-1980.* Montreal: McGill-Queen's University Press.

Anderson, N. (1959). *The urban community: A world perspective.* New York: Henry Holt.

Anderson, N. (1961). *The hobo: The sociology of the homeless man.* Chicago: University of Chicago Press. (Original work published 1923)

Anderson, T. L. (Ed.). (1992). *Property rights and Indian economics.* Lanham, MD: Rowman & Littlefield.

Arsenault, R. (1988). *St. Petersburg and the Florida dream, 1888-1950.* Norfolk, VA: Donning.

Ashmore, M. (1989). *The reflexive thesis: Writing sociology of scientific knowledge.* Chicago: University of Chicago Press.

Atkinson, P. (1990). *The ethnographic imagination: Textual constructions of reality.* London: Routledge.

Bailey, B. L. (1988). *From front porch to back seat: Courtship in twentieth century America*. Baltimore: Johns Hopkins University Press.

Baker, J. R. (1974). *Race*. New York: Oxford University Press.

Ball, D. W. (1968). Toward a sociology of telephones and telephoners. In M. Truzzi (Ed.), *Sociology and everyday life* (pp. 59-75). Englewood Cliffs, NJ: Prentice Hall.

Barkan, E. (1992). *The retreat of scientific racism: Changing concepts of race in Britain and the United States*. Cambridge: Cambridge University Press.

Barrera, M. (1979). *Race and class in the Southwest: A theory of racial inequality*. Notre Dame, IN: University of Notre Dame Press.

Barrera, M. (1988). *Beyond Aztlan: Ethnic autonomy in comparative perspective*. Notre Dame, IN: University of Notre Dame Press.

Baudrillard, J. (1981). *For a critique of the political economy of the sign* (C. Levin, Trans.). St. Louis, MO: Telos.

Baudrillard, J. (1983). *In the shadow of the silent majorities; Or, the end of the social and other essays* (P. Foss, J. Johnston, & P. Patton, Trans.). New York: Semiotext(e).

Baudrillard, J. (1988a). *America* (C. Turner, Trans.). London: Verso.

Baudrillard, J. (1988b). *The ecstasy of communication* (S. Lotringer, Ed.; B. Schutze & C. Schutze, Trans.). New York: Semiotext(e).

Becker, H. (1962). *Through values to social interpretation: Essays on social contexts, actions, types, and prospects*. New York: Greenwood. (Original work published 1950)

Becker, H. (1974). *Systematic sociology: On the basis of the* Beziehungslehre *and* Begildlehre *of Leopold von Wiese*. New York: Arno. (Original work published 1932)

Bender, T. (1978). *Community and social change in America*. New Brunswick, NJ: Rutgers University Press.

Bendix, R., & Berger, B. (1959). Images of society and problems of concept formation in sociology. In L. Gross (Ed.), *Symposium on sociological theory* (pp. 92-118). Evanston, IL: Row, Peterson.

Bensman, J., & Vidich, A. J. (1987). *American society: The welfare state and beyond* (2nd ed.). Amherst, MA: Bergin & Garvey.

Berlo, J. C. (Ed.). (1992). *The early years of Native American art history: The politics of scholarship and collecting*. Seattle: University of Washington Press.

Berry, B. (1963). *Almost white*. New York: Macmillan.

Berry, B., & Tischler, H. (1978). *Race and ethnic relations* (4th ed.). Boston: Houghton Mifflin.

Beverly, J. (1992). The margin at the center: On *testimonio* (testimonial narrative). In S. Smith & J. Watson (Eds.), *De/colonizing the subject: The politics of gender in women's autobiography*. Minneapolis: University of Minnesota Press.

Bhabha, H. K. (Ed.). (1990a). *Nation and narration*. London: Routledge.

Bhabha, H. K. (1990b). The other question: Differences, discrimination and the discourse of colonialism. In R. Ferguson, M. Gever, Trinh T. M., & C. West (Eds.), *Out there: Marginalization and contemporary cultures* (pp. 71-88). Cambridge: MIT Press.

Bieder, R. E. (1989). *Science encounters the Indian, 1820-1880: The early years of American ethnology.* Norman: University of Oklahoma Press.

Bigham, D. E. (1987). *We ask only a fair trial: A history of the black community of Evansville, Indiana.* Bloomington: Indiana University Press/University of Southern Indiana.

Blackman, F. M. (1976). *Spanish institutions of the Southwest.* Glorieta, NM: Rio Grande. (Original work published 1891)

Blackwell, J. E. (1991). *The black community: Diversity and unity* (3rd ed.). New York: HarperCollins.

Blake, C. N. (1990). *Beloved community: The cultural criticism of Randolph Bourne, Van Wyck Brooks, Waldo Frank, and Lewis Mumford.* Chapel Hill: University of North Carolina Press.

Blassingame, J. W. (1979). *The slave community: Plantation life in the antebellum South* (Rev. ed.). New York: Oxford University Press.

Blauner, R. (1972). *Racial oppression in America.* New York: Harper & Row.

Bloom, H. (1979). *The anxiety of influence: A theory of poetry.* London: Oxford University Press.

Blumenthal, A. B. (1933). *A sociological study of a small town.* Unpublished doctoral dissertation, University of Chicago.

Bock, K. E. (1948). *The comparative method.* Unpublished doctoral dissertation, University of California, Berkeley.

Bock, K. E. (1952). Evolution and historical process. *American Anthropologist, 54,* 486-496.

Bock, K. E. (1956). *The acceptance of histories: Toward a perspective for social science.* Berkeley: University of California Press.

Bock, K. E. (1963). Evolution, function and change. *American Sociological Review, 27,* 229-237.

Bock, K. E. (1966). The comparative method of anthropology. *Comparative Studies in Society and History, 8,* 269-280.

Bock, K. E. (1974). Comparison of histories: The contribution of Henry Maine. *Comparative Studies in Society and History, 16,* 232-262.

Boeke, J. H. (1946). *The evolution of the Netherlands Indies economy.* New York: Institute of Pacific Relations.

Boeke, J. H. (1948). *The interests of the voiceless Far East: Introduction to Oriental economics.* Leiden, Netherlands: Universitaire Pers Leiden.

Bogardus, E. S. (1930). A race relations cycle. *American Journal of Sociology, 35,* 612-617.

Bogardus, E. S. (1940). Current problems of Japanese Americans. *Sociology and Social Research, 25,* 63-66.

Bogardus, E. S. (1970). *The Mexican in the United States.* New York: Arno/New York Times. (Original work published 1934)

Bohman, J. (1991). *New philosophy of social science.* Cambridge: MIT Press.

Borgmann, A. (1992). *Crossing the postmodern divide.* Chicago: University of Chicago Press.

Bowden, H. W. (1981). *American Indians and Christian missions: Studies in cultural conflict.* Chicago: University of Chicago Press.

Boxer, C. R. (1965). *Portuguese society in the tropics: The municipal councils of Goa, Macao, Bahia, and Luanda.* Madison: University of Wisconsin Press.

Boxhill, B. R. (1992). *Blacks and social justice* (Rev. ed.). Lanham, MD: Rowman & Littlefield.

Bradford, P. V., & Blume, H. (1992). *Ota Benga: The Pygmy in the zoo.* New York: St. Martin's.

Brookhiser, R. (1991). *The way of the WASP: How it made America, and how it can save it, so to speak.* New York: Free Press.

Brookhiser, R. (1993, March 1). The melting pot is still simmering. *Time,* p. 72.

Brown, R. (1984). *The nature of social laws: Machiavelli to Mill.* Cambridge: Cambridge University Press.

Brown, W. O. (1934). Culture contact and race conflict. In E. B. Reuter (Ed.), *Race and culture contacts* (pp. 34-47). New York: McGraw-Hill.

Burawoy, M., Burton, A., Ferguson, A. A., Fox, K. J., Gamson, J., Gartrell, N., Hurst, L., Kurzman, C., Salzinger, L., Schiffman, J., & Ui, S. (Eds.) (1992). *Ethnography unbound: Power and resistance in the modern metropolis.* Berkeley: University of California Press.

Burgess, E. W. (1916). The social survey: A field for constructive service by departments of sociology. *American Journal of Sociology, 21,* 492-500.

Burgess, E. W., & Bogue, D. J. (Eds.). (1967). *Contributions to urban sociology.* Chicago: University of Chicago Press.

Burma, J. H. (Ed.). (1985). *Mexican-Americans in comparative perspective.* Washington, DC: Urban Institute.

Button, J. W. (1989). *Blacks and social change: Impact of the civil rights movement in southern communities.* Princeton, NJ: Princeton University Press.

Calloway, C. G. (Ed.). (1991). *Dawnland encounters: Indians and Europeans in northern New England.* Hanover, NH: University Press of New England.

Campbell, W. D. (1992). *Providence.* Atlanta: Longstreet.

Caplow, T., Bahr, H. M., Chadwick, B. A., Hill, R., & Williamson, M. H. (1982). *Middletown families: Fifty years of change and continuity.* Minneapolis: University of Minnesota Press.

Caplow, T., Bahr, H. M., Chadwick, B. A., Hill, R., & Williamson, M. H. (1983). *All faithful people: Change and continuity in Middletown's religion.* Minneapolis: University of Minnesota Press.

Cavan, R. S. (1965). *Suicide.* New York: Russell & Russell. (Original work published 1928)

Chambers, C. A. (1971). *Paul U. Kellogg and the survey: Voices for social welfare and social justice.* Minneapolis: University of Minnesota Press.

Chambers, I. (1990). *Border dialogues: Journeys into postmodernity.* London: Routledge.

Chan, S. (1991). *Asian Americans: An interpretive history.* Boston: Twayne.

Cherokee Nation v. Georgia, 30 U.S. (5 Pet.) 1 (1831).

Christopher, R. C. (1989). *Crashing the gates: The de-WASPing of America's power elite.* New York: Simon & Schuster.

Clifford, J. (1986). On ethnographic self-fashioning: Conrad and Malinowski. In T. C. Heller, M. Sosna, & D. E. Wellbery (Eds.), *Reconstructing individualism: Autonomy, individuality, and the self in Western thought* (pp. 140-162). Stanford, CA: Stanford University Press.

Clifford, J. (1990). On collecting art and culture. In R. Ferguson, M. Gever, Trinh T. M., & C. West (Eds.). *Out there: Marginalization and contemporary cultures* (pp. 1-169). Cambridge: MIT Press.

Clifford, J., & Marcus, G. E. (Eds.). (1986). *Writing culture: The poetics and politics of ethnography.* Berkeley: University of California Press.

Codrington, R. H. (1891). *The Melanesians.* Oxford: Clarendon.

Codrington, R. H. (1974). Mana. In A. Montagu (Ed.), *Frontiers of anthropology* (pp. 255-259). New York: G. P. Putnam's Sons. (Reprinted from *The Melanesians,* Oxford: Clarendon, 1891)

Cohen, S. R. (1981). *Reconciling industrial conflict and democracy: The Pittsburgh survey and the growth of social research in the United States.* Unpublished doctoral dissertation, Columbia University.

Coleman, M. C. (1985). *Presbyterian missionary attitudes toward American Indians, 1837-1893.* Jackson: University Press of Mississippi.

Comaroff, J., & Comaroff, J. (1992). *Ethnography and the historical imagination.* Boulder, CO: Westview.

Contosta, D. R. (1980). *Henry Adams and the American experiment.* Boston: Little, Brown.

Cornell, S. (1988). The transformation of tribe: Organization and self-concept in Native American ethnicities. *Ethnic and Racial Studies, 11,* 27-47.

Cornwell, R. (1992). Interactive art: Touching the "body in the mind." *Discourse: Journal for Theoretical Studies in Media and Culture, 14,* 203-221.

Covello, L. (1967). *The social background of the Italo-American school child: A study of the southern Italian family mores and their effect on the school situation in Italy and America* (F. Cordesco, Ed.). Leiden, Netherlands: E. J. Brill.

Cressey, D. R. (1953). *Other people's money: A study in the social psychology of embezzlement*. Glencoe, IL: Free Press.

Culin, S. (1967). Zuni pictures. In E. C. Parsons (Ed.), *American Indian life* (pp. 175-178). Lincoln: University of Nebraska Press. (Original work published 1922)

Cushing, F. H. (1974). *Zuni breadstuff*. New York: Museum of the American Indian, Keye Foundation. (Original work published 1920)

Cushing, F. H. (1979). *Zuni: Selected writings of Frank Hamilton Cushing* (J. Green, Ed.). Lincoln: University of Nebraska Press.

Cushing, F. H. (1988). *Zuni folk tales*. Tucson: University of Arizona Press. (Original work published 1901)

Cushing, F. H. (1990). *Cushing at Zuni: The correspondence and journals of Frank Hamilton Cushing, 1878-1884* (J. Green, Ed.). Albuquerque: University of New Mexico Press.

Dai, B. (1970). *Opium addiction in Chicago*. Montclair, NJ: Patterson Smith. (Original work published 1937)

Dale, E. E. (1984). *The Indians of the Southwest: A century of development under the United States*. Norman: University of Oklahoma Press. (Original work published 1949)

Dansereau, H. K. (1961). Some implications of modern highways for community ecology. In G. A. Theodorsen (Ed.), *Studies in human ecology* (pp. 175-187). Evanston, IL: Row, Peterson.

Davis, A. K. (1980). *Thorstein Veblen's social theory*. New York: Arno.

Davis, P. (1982). *Hometown: A contemporary American chronicle*. New York: Simon & Schuster.

Degerando, J.-M. (1969). *The observation of savage peoples* (F. C. T. Moore, Trans.). London: Routledge & Kegan Paul. (Original work published 1800)

Denzin, N. K. (1989). *Interpretive interactionism*. Newbury Park, CA: Sage.

Derrida, J. (1976). *Of grammatology* (G. C. Spivak, Trans.). Baltimore: Johns Hopkins University Press.

Derrida, J. (1981). *Positions* (A. Bass, Trans.). Chicago: University of Chicago Press.

Derrida, J. (1992). *The other heading: Reflections on today's Europe* (P.-A. Brault & M. B. Naas, Trans.). Bloomington: Indiana University Press.

Diamond, S. (1963). The search for the primitive. In I. Goldston (Ed.), *Man's image in medicine and anthropology* (pp. 62-115). New York: International University Press.

Diamond, S. (1972). Anthropology in question. In D. Hymes (Ed.), *Reinventing anthropology* (pp. 401-429). New York: Pantheon.

Diamond, S. (1992). *Compromised campus: The collaboration of universities with the intelligence community, 1945-1955*. New York: Oxford University Press.

Diggins, J. P. (1978). *The bard of savagery: Thorstein Veblen and modern social theory*. New York: Seabury.

Diner, S. J. (1975). Department and discipline: The Department of Sociology at the University of Chicago, 1892-1920. *Minerva, 13*, 518-519, 538.

Dirlik, A. (1987). Culturalism as hegemonic ideology and liberating practice. *Cultural Critique, 6*, 13-50.

Dockstader, F. J. (1985). *The Kachina and the white man: The influences of white culture on the Hopi Kachina religion* (Rev. ed.). Albuquerque: University of New Mexico Press.

Douglas, J. (1974). A brief history of sociologists of everyday life. In J. Douglas et al. (Eds.), *Introduction to the sociologies of everyday life* (pp. 182-210). Boston: Allyn & Bacon.

Drake, S. C., & Cayton, H. R. (1962). *Black metropolis: A study of Negro life in a northern city* (Rev. ed., Vols. 1-2). New York: Harper Torchbooks.

Drinnon, R. (1987). *Keeper of concentration camps: Dillon S. Myer and American racism.* Berkeley: University of California Press.

Du Bois, W. E. B. (1967). *The Philadelphia Negro: A social study.* New York: Benjamin Blom. (Original work published 1899)

Duffy, J. (1959). *Portuguese Africa.* Cambridge, MA: Harvard University Press.

Duncan, O. D. (1957). Community size and the rural-urban continuum. In P. K. Hatt & A. J. Reiss, Jr. (Eds.), *Cities and society: The revised reader in urban sociology* (pp. 35-45). Glencoe, IL: Free Press.

Duneier, M. (1992). *Slim's table: Race, respectability, and masculinity.* Chicago: University of Chicago Press.

Early, G. (Ed.). (1993). *Lure and loathing: Essays on race, identity, and the ambivalence of assimilation.* New York: Allen Lane/Penguin.

Eggan, F. (1966). *The American Indian: Perspectives for the study of social change* (The Lewis Henry Morgan Lectures). Cambridge: Cambridge University Press.

Elmer, M. C. (1914). *Social surveys of urban communities.* Unpublished doctoral dissertation, University of Chicago.

Engels, F. (1884). *The origins of the family, private property and the state.* Moscow: Foreign Languages.

Eribon, D. (1991). *Michel Foucault* (B. Wing. Trans.). Cambridge, MA: Harvard University Press.

Ericksen, E. G. (1980). *The territorial experience: Human ecology as symbolic interaction.* Austin: University of Texas Press.

Espiritu, Y. L. (1992). *Asian American panethnicity: Bridging institutions and identities.* Philadelphia: Temple University Press.

Etzioni, A. (1959). The ghetto: A re-evaluation. *Social Forces, 37*, 255-262.

Evans, A. S., & Lee, D. (1990). *Pearl City, Florida: A black community remembers.* Boca Raton: Florida Atlantic University Press.

Farias, V. (1989). *Heidegger and Nazism* (J. Margolis & T. Rickmore, Eds.; P. Burrell & G. Ricci, Trans.). Philadelphia: Temple University Press.

Faris, R. E. L. (1970). *Chicago sociology, 1920-1932.* Chicago: University of Chicago Press.

Faris, R. E. L., & Dunham, H. W. (1965). *Mental disorders in urban areas: An ecological study of schizophrenia and other psychoses.* Chicago: University of Chicago Press. (Original work published 1939)

Feagin, J. R., Orum, A., & Sjoberg, G. (1991). The present crisis in U.S. sociology. In J. R. Feagin, A. M. Orum, & G. Sjoberg, *A case for the case study* (pp. 269-278). Chapel Hill: University of North Carolina Press.

Featherstone, M., Hepworth, M., & Turner, B. S. (Eds.). (1991). *The body: Social process and cultural theory.* London: Sage.

Feher, M. (Ed.). (1989). *Fragments for a history of the human body* (Vols. 1-3). Cambridge: MIT Press/Zone.

Ferry, L., & Renaut, A. (1990). *Heidegger and modernity* (F. Philip, Trans.). Chicago: University of Chicago Press.

Firey, W., Loomis, C. P., & Beegle, J. A. (1950). The fusion of urban and rural. In J. Labatut & W. J. Lane (Eds.), *Highways in our national life: A symposium* (pp. 154-163). Princeton, NJ: Princeton University Press.

Fishman, R. (1977). *Urban utopias in the twentieth century: Ebenezer Howard, Frank Lloyd Wright, and Le Corbusier.* New York: Basic Books.

Fiske, D. W., & Shweder, R. A. (Eds.). (1986). *Metatheory in social science: Pluralisms and subjectivities.* Chicago: University of Chicago Press.

Fontana, A. (1974). Toward a complex universe: Existential sociology. In J. Douglas et al. (Eds.), *Introduction to the sociologies of everyday life* (pp. 155-181). Boston: Allyn & Bacon.

Forbes, J. D. (1973). *Aztecs del norte: The Chicanos of Aztlan.* Greenwich, CT: Fawcett.

Forbes, J. D. (1988). *Black Africans and Native Americans: Color, race and caste in the evolution of red-black peoples.* New York: Blackwell.

Forrest, S. (1989). *The preservation of the village: New Mexico's Hispanics and the New Deal.* Albuquerque: University of New Mexico Press.

Foucault, M. (1992). *Michel Foucault, philosopher* (T. J. Armstrong, Ed. & Trans.). New York: Routledge, Chapman & Hall.

Fox, R. G. (Ed.). (1991). *Recapturing anthropology: Working in the present.* Santa Fe, NM: School of American Research Press.

Frazier, E. F. (1925). Durham: Capital of the black middle class. In A. Locke (Ed.), *The new Negro* (pp. 333-340). New York: Albert & Charles Boni.

Frazier, E. F. (1931). *The Negro family in Chicago.* Unpublished doctoral dissertation, University of Chicago.

Frazier, E. F. (1937a). The impact of urban civilization upon Negro family life. *American Sociological Review, 2,* 609-618.

Frazier, E. F. (1937b). Negro Harlem: An ecological study. *American Journal of Sociology, 43,* 72-88.

Frazier, E. F. (1953). The theoretical structure of sociology and sociological research. *British Journal of Sociology, 4,* 292-311.

Frazier, E. F. (1957a). *Black bourgeoisie: The rise of a new middle class in the United States.* Glencoe, IL: Free Press/Falcon's Wing.

Frazier, E. F. (1957b). *The Negro in the United States* (Rev. ed.). New York: Macmillan.

Frazier, E. F. (1963). *The Negro church in America.* New York: Schocken.

Frazier, E. F. (1966). *The Negro family in the United States* (Rev. ed.). Chicago: University of Chicago Press/Phoenix. (Original work published 1939)

Frazier, E. F. (1967). *Negro youth at the crossways: Their personality development in the middle states.* New York: Schocken. (Original work published 1940)

Frazier, E. F. (1968). *E. Franklin Frazier on race relations: Selected papers* (G. F. Edwards, Ed.). Chicago: University of Chicago Press.

Freeman, D. (1983). *Margaret Mead and Samoa: The making and unmaking of an anthropological myth.* Cambridge, MA: Harvard University Press.

Frisby, D. (1992). *Simmel and since: Essays on Georg Simmel's social theory.* London: Routledge.

Fuchs, L. H. (1990). *The American kaleidoscope: Race, ethnicity, and the civic culture.* Hanover, NH: University Press of New England.

Fukuyama, F. (1992). *The end of history and the last man.* New York: Free Press.

Furnivall, J. S. (1948). *Colonial policy and practice: A comparative study of Burma and Netherlands India.* New York: New York University Press.

Galarza, E. (1964). *Merchants of labor: The Mexican bracero story—an account of the managed migration of Mexican farm workers in California, 1942-1960.* San Jose, CA: Rosicrucian.

Galarza, E. (1970). *Spiders in the house and workers in the field.* Notre Dame, IN: University of Notre Dame Press.

Galarza, E. (1977). *Farm workers and agri-business in California, 1947-1960.* Notre Dame, IN: University of Notre Dame Press.

Gamio, M. (1969). *Mexican immigration to the United States: A study of human migration and adjustment.* New York: Arno/New York Times. (Original work published 1930)

Gamio, M. (1971). *The life story of the Mexican immigrant: Autobiographic documents.* New York: Dover. (Original work published 1931)

Gans, H. J. (1962). *The urban villagers: Group and class in the life of Italian-Americans.* New York: Free Press.

Garbaccia, D. R. (1984). *From Sicily to Elizabeth Street: Housing and social change among Italian immigrants, 1880-1930.* Albany: State University of New York Press.

Geertz, C. (1973). Thick description: Toward an interpretive theory of culture. In C. Geertz, *The interpretation of cultures: Selected essays* (pp. 3-32). New York: Basic Books.

Gellner, E. (1979). Beyond truth and falsehood, or no method in my madness. In E. Gellner, *Spectacles and predicaments: Essays in social theory* (pp. 182-198). Cambridge: Cambridge University Press.

Georges, R. A., & Jones, M. O. (1980). *People studying people: The human element in fieldwork.* Berkeley: University of California Press.

Geschwender, J. A. (1978). *Racial stratification in America.* Dubuque, IA: William C. Brown.

Gilman, S. L. (1991). *Inscribing the other.* Lincoln: University of Nebraska Press.

Ginsburg, C. (1991). *Ecstasies: Deciphering the witches' sabbath* (R. Rosenthal, Trans.). New York: Pantheon.

Ginsburg, C. (1993). The European (re)discovery of the shamans. *London Review of Books, 15,* 2.

Gist, N. P., & Halbert, L. A. (1947). *Urban society* (2nd ed.). New York: Thomas Y. Crowell.

Glazer, N. (1954). Ethnic groups in America: From national culture to ideology. In M. Berger, T. Able, & C. H. Page (Eds.), *Freedom and control in modern society* (pp. 158-173). New York: D. Van Nostrand.

Gleason, P. (1980). American identity and Americanization. In S. Thernstrom (Ed.), *Harvard encyclopedia of American ethnic groups* (pp. 31-58). Cambridge, MA: Harvard University Press.

Glick, C. E. (1955). Social roles and social types in race relations. In W. A. Lind (Ed.), *Race relations in world perspective* (pp. 239-262). Honolulu: University of Hawaii Press.

Goddard, P. E. (1976). *Indians of the Southwest.* Glorieta, NM: Rio Grande. (Original work published 1913)

Goffman, E. (1949). *Some characteristics of response to depicted experience.* Unpublished master's thesis, University of Chicago.

Goffman, E. (1959). *The presentation of self in everyday life.* Garden City, NY: Doubleday.

Goffman, E. (1961). *Asylums: Essays on the social situation of mental patients and other inmates.* Garden City, NY: Doubleday.

Goffman, E. (1971). *Relations in public: Microstudies of the public order.* New York: Basic Books.

Goffman, E. (1974). *Frame analysis: An essay on the organization of experience.* New York: Harper Colophon.

Gonzalez, N. L. (1967). *The Spanish Americans of New Mexico: A heritage of pride.* Albuquerque: University of New Mexico Press.

Grant, M. (1992). *A social history of Greece and Rome.* New York: Charles Scribner's Sons.

Gray, J. (1970). The intellectual standing of different races and their respective opportunities for culture. In G. Spiller (Ed.), *Papers on inter-racial problems communicated to the First Universal Race Congress, University of London,*

July 26-29, 1911 (pp. 79-85). New York: Citadel. (Original work published 1911)

Greek, C. E. (1978). The social gospel movement and early American sociology, 1870-1915. *Graduate Faculty Journal of Sociology, 3*(1), 30-42.

Greek, C. E. (1992). *The religious roots of American sociology.* New York: Garland.

Gullick, J. M. (1956). *The story of early Kuala Lumpur.* Singapore: Donald Moore.

Gurwitsch, A. (1966). The last work of Edmund Husserl. In A. Gurwitsch, *Studies in phenomenology and psychology.* Evanston, IL: Northwestern University Press.

Gusfield, J. R. (1975). *Community: A critical response.* New York: Harper Colophon.

Gutierrez, R. A. (1991). *When Jesus came the corn mothers went away: Marriage, sexuality and power in New Mexico, 1500-1846.* Stanford, CA: Stanford University Press.

Gwertzman, B., & Kaufman, M. T. (Eds.). (1992). *The decline and fall of the Soviet empire.* New York: New York Times.

Habermas, J. (1983). Martin Heidegger: The great influence (1959). In J. Habermas, *Philosophical-political profiles* (F. G. Lawrence, Trans.; pp. 53-60). Cambridge: MIT Press.

Hamacher, W., Hertz, N., & Keenan, T. (Eds.). (1989). *On Paul de Man's wartime journalism.* Lincoln: University of Nebraska Press.

Hammersley, M. (1992). *What's wrong with ethnography? Methodological explorations.* London: Routledge.

Hanke, L. (1965). *The Spanish struggle for justice in the conquest of America.* Boston: Little, Brown. (Original work published 1949)

Hanke, L. (1970). *Aristotle and the American Indians: A study in race prejudice in the modern world.* Bloomington: Indiana University Press. (Original work published 1959)

Hanke, L. (1974). *All mankind is one: A study of the disputation between Bartolome de Las Casas and Juan Gines de Sepulveda on the religious and intellectual capacity of the American Indians.* De Kalb: Northern Illinois University Press.

Hannerz, U. (1980). *Exploring the city: Inquiries toward an urban anthropology.* New York: Columbia University Press.

Hansen, M. L. (1952). The problem of the third generation immigrant. *Commentary, 14,* 492-500. (Original work published 1938)

Hare, A. P., & Blumberg, H. H. (1988). *Dramaturgical analysis of social interaction.* New York: Praeger.

Harré, R. (1980). *Social being: A theory for social psychology.* Totowa, NJ: Rowman & Littlefield.

Harré, R. (1984). *Personal being: A theory for individual psychology.* Cambridge, MA: Harvard University Press.

Hartland, E. S. (1969). *Primitive society: The beginnings of the family and the reck-oning of descent.* New York: Harper & Row. (Original work published 1921)

Hartmann, E. G. (1967). *The movement to Americanize the immigrant.* New York: AMS. (Original work published 1948)

Havemeyer, L. (1929). *Ethnography.* Boston: Ginn.

Hechter, M. (1975). *Internal colonialism: The Celtic fringe in British national development, 1536-1966.* London: Routledge & Kegan Paul.

Heizer, R. F., & Kroeber, T. (Eds.). (1979). *Ishi the last Yahi: A documentary history.* Berkeley: University of California Press.

Herberg, W. (1960). *Protestant-Catholic-Jew: An essay in American religious sociology.* Garden City, NY: Doubleday.

Herskovitz, M. (1958). *The myth of the Negro past.* Boston: Beacon. (Original work published 1941)

Herskovitz, M. (1966). *The new world Negro: Selected papers in Afroamerican studies* (F. S. Herskovitz, Ed.). Bloomington: Indiana University Press.

Hill-Lubin, M. A. (1992). "Presence Africaine": A voice in the wilderness, a record of black kinship. In V. Y. Mudimbe (Ed.), *The surreptitious speech: Presence Africaine and the politics of otherness, 1947-1987* (pp. 157-173). Chicago: University of Chicago Press.

Hinsley, C. M., Jr. (1981). *Savages and scientists: The Smithsonian Institution and the development of American anthropology, 1846-1910.* Washington, DC: Smithsonian Institution Press.

Hodgen, M. T. (1936). *The doctrine of survivals: A chapter in the history of scientific method in the study of man.* London: Allenson.

Hodgen, M. T. (1964). *Early anthropology in the sixteenth and seventeenth centuries.* Philadelphia: University of Pennsylvania.

Hodgen, M. T. (1974). *Anthropology, history and cultural change.* Tucson: University of Arizona Press/Wenner-Gren Foundation for Anthropological Research.

Holden, A. C. (1970). *The settlement idea: A vision of social justice.* New York: Arno/New York Times. (Original work published 1922)

Hollingshead, A. B. (1961). *Elmtown's youth: The impact of social classes on adolescents.* New York: Science Editions. (Original work published 1949)

Holmes, L. D. (1987). *Quest for the real Samoa: The Mead/Freeman controversy and beyond.* South Hadley, MA: Bergin & Garvey.

Horowitz, I. L. (Ed.). (1967). *The rise and fall of Project Camelot: Studies in the relationship between social science and practical politics.* Cambridge: MIT Press.

Hosle, V. (1992). The Third World as a philosophical problem. *Social Research, 59,* 230-262.

Hughes, E. C. (1928). *A study of a secular institution: The Chicago Real Estate Board.* Unpublished doctoral dissertation, University of Chicago.

Humphreys, S. C. (1978). *Anthropology and the Greeks*. London: Routledge & Kegan Paul.

Hune, S., et al. (Eds.). (1991). *Asian Americans: Comparative and global perspectives*. Pullman: Washington State University Press.

Ignacio, L. F. (1976). *Asian Americans and Pacific Islanders (Is there such an ethnic group?)*. San Jose, CA: Pilipino Development Associates.

Immigration Commission (W. P. Dillingham, Chair). (1970). *Immigrants in industry* (25 parts). New York: Arno/New York Times. (Original work published 1911)

Jackson, J. S. (Ed.). (1991). *Life in black America*. Newbury Park, CA: Sage.

Jaimes, M. E. (Ed.). (1992). *The state of Native America: Genocide, colonization and resistance*. Boston: South End.

Jalali, R., & Lipset, S. M. (1992-1993). Racial and ethnic conflicts: A global perspective. *Political Science Quarterly, 107*(4), 585-606.

Johnson, J. M. (1975). *Doing field research*. New York: Free Press.

Jones, J. (1992). *Soldiers of light and love: Northern teachers and Georgia blacks, 1865-1873*. Athens: University of Georgia Press.

Joyner, C. (1984). *Down by the riverside: A South Carolina slave community*. Urbana: University of Illinois Press.

Keegan, W. F. (1992). *The people who discovered Columbus: The prehistory of the Bahamas*. Gainesville: University Press of Florida.

Keller, R. W., Jr. (1983). *American Protestantism and United States Indian policy, 1869-1882*. Lincoln: University of Nebraska Press.

Kennedy, R. J. R. (1944). Single or triple melting pot: Intermarriage trends in New Haven, 1870-1940. *American Journal of Sociology, 44*, 331-339.

Keyes, C. F. (Ed.). (1982). *Ethnic change*. Seattle: University of Washington Press.

Kinloch, G. C. (1974). *The dynamics of race relations*. New York: McGraw-Hill.

Kitto, H. D. F. (1951). *The Greeks*. London: Penguin.

Kivisto, P. (1984). *Immigrant socialists in the United States: The case of Finns and the Left*. Cranbury, NJ: Associates University Presses.

Kivisto, P. (Ed.). (1989). *The ethnic enigma: The salience of ethnicity for European-origin groups*. Philadelphia: Balch Institute Press.

Kivisto, P., & Blanck, D. (Eds.). (1990). *American immigrants and their generations: Studies and commentaries on the Hansen thesis after fifty years*. Urbana: University of Illinois Press.

Kluckhohn, C. (1944). *Navajo witchcraft*. Boston: Beacon.

Kluckhohn, C. (1961). *Anthropology and the classics: The Colver Lectures in Brown University, 1960*. Providence, RI: Brown University Press.

Knoll, T. (1982). *Becoming Americans: Asian sojourners, immigrants and refugees in the western United States*. Portland, OR: Coast to Coast.

Kotarba, J. A., & Fontana, A. (Eds.). (1987). *The existential self in society*. Chicago: University of Chicago Press.

Kramer, J. R. (1970). *The American minority community.* New York: Thomas Y. Crowell.

Kramer, J. R., & Leventman, S. (1961). *Children of the gilded ghetto: Conflict resolutions of three generations of American Jews.* New Haven, CT: Yale University Press.

Krieger, S. (1991). *Social science and the self: Personal essays on an art form.* New Brunswick, NJ: Rutgers University Press.

Kroeber, T. (1962). *Ishi in two worlds: A biography of the last wild Indian in North America.* Berkeley: University of California Press.

Kroeber, T. (1965). *Ishi: Last of his tribe.* New York: Bantam.

Kundera, M. (1988). *The art of the novel* (L. Ascher, Trans.). New York: Grove.

Kuper, A. (1988). *The invention of primitive society: Transformations of an illusion.* London: Routledge.

Kuzmics, H. (1988). The civilizing process (H. G. Zilian, Trans.). In J. Keane (Ed.), *Civil society and the state: New European perspectives.* London: Verso.

Landesco, J. (1968). *Organized crime in Chicago* (Part 3 of the Illinois Crime Survey, 1929). Chicago: University of Chicago Press.

Lane, J. B., & Escobar, E. J. (Eds.). (1987). *Forging a community: The Latino experience in Northwest Indiana, 1919-1975.* Chicago: Cattails.

Lee, R. H. (1960). *The Chinese in the United States of America.* Hong Kong: Hong Kong University Press.

Lee, R. H. (1978). *The growth and decline of Chinese communities in the Rocky Mountain region.* New York: Arno.

Lehman, D. (1992). Signs of the times: Deconstruction and the fall of Paul de Man. *Contention: Debates in Society, Culture and Science, 1*(2), 23-38.

Leighton, A. H. (1945). *The governing of men: General principles and recommendations based on experience at a Japanese relocation camp.* Princeton, NJ: Princeton University Press.

Lemert, C. (1992). Subjectivity's limit: The unsolved riddle of the standpoint. *Sociological Theory, 10,* 63-72.

Lenzer, G. (Ed.). (1975). *Auguste Comte and positivism: The essential writings.* New York: Harper Torchbooks.

Leonard, K. I. (1992). *Making ethnic choices: California's Punjabi Mexican Americans.* Philadelphia: Temple University Press.

Lieberson, S. (1961). A societal theory of race and ethnic relations. *American Sociological Review, 26,* 902-910.

Lieberson, S. (1980). *A piece of the pie: Blacks and white immigrants since 1880.* Berkeley: University of California Press.

Lieberson, S., & Waters, M. C. (1988). *From many strands: Ethnic and racial groups in contemporary America.* New York: Russell Sage Foundation.

Liebow, E. (1967). *Tally's corner: A study of Negro street corner men.* Boston: Little, Brown.

Lingeman, R. (1980). *Small town America: A narrative history, 1620-the present.* New York: G. P. Putnam's Sons.

Lippy, C. H., Choquette, R., & Poole, S. (1992). *Christianity comes to the Americas, 1492-1776.* New York: Paragon.

Lipset, S. M. (1950, May). Changing social status and prejudice: The race theories of a pioneering American sociologist. *Commentary, 9,* 475-479.

Lipset, S. M. (1963). *The first new nation: The United States in historical and comparative perspective.* New York: Basic Books.

Lipset, S. M. (1979). *The first new nation: The United States in historical and comparative perspective* (Rev. ed.). New York: W. W. Norton.

Lopata, H. Z. (1967). The function of voluntary associations in an ethnic community: "Polonia." In E. W. Burgess & D. J. Bogue (Eds.), *Contributions to urban sociology* (pp. 203-223). Chicago: University of Chicago Press.

Lopreato, J. (1970). *Italian Americans.* New York: Random House.

Lovejoy, A. O. (1960). *The great chain of being: A study of the history of an idea.* New York: Harper Torchbooks.

Lugard, L. (1965). *The dual mandate in British tropical Africa.* Hamden, CT: Archon/Shoe String. (Original work published 1922)

Luhmann, N. (1986). The individuality of the individual: Historical meanings and contemporary problems. In T. C. Heller, M. Sosna, & D. E. Wellbery (Eds.), *Reconstructing individualism: Autonomy, individuality, and the self in Western thought* (pp. 313-328). Stanford, CA: Stanford University Press.

Lyman, S. M. (1961-1962). Overseas Chinese in America and Indonesia: A review article. *Pacific Affairs, 34,* 380-389.

Lyman, S. M. (1963). Up from the "hatchet man." *Pacific Affairs, 36,* 160-171.

Lyman, S. M. (1964). The spectrum of color. *Social Research, 31,* 364-373.

Lyman, S. M. (1972). *The black American in sociological thought: A failure of perspective.* New York: G. P. Putnam's Sons.

Lyman, S. M. (1974). Conflict and the web of group affiliation in San Francisco's Chinatown, 1850-1910. *Pacific Historical Review, 43,* 473-499.

Lyman, S. M. (1975). Legitimacy and consensus in Lipset's America: From Washington to Watergate. *Social Research, 42,* 729-759.

Lyman, S. M. (1978). The acceptance, rejection, and reconstruction of histories. In R. H. Brown & S. M. Lyman (Eds.), *Structure, consciousness and history* (pp. 53-105). New York: Cambridge University Press.

Lyman, S. M. (1979). Stuart Culin and the debate over trans-Pacific migration. *Journal for the Theory of Social Behaviour, 9,* 91-115.

Lyman, S. M. (1982a). Stewart Culin: The earliest American Chinatown studies and a hypothesis about pre-Columbian migration. *Annual Bulletin of the Research Institute for Social Science* (Ryukoku University, Kyoto, Japan), 12, 142-162.

Lyman, S. M. (1982b). Two neglected pioneers of civilizational analysis: The cultural perspectives of R. Stewart Culin and Frank Hamilton Cushing. *Social Research, 44,* 690-729.

Lyman, S. M. (1986). *Chinatown and Little Tokyo: Power, conflict and community among Chinese and Japanese immigrants in America.* Millwood, NJ: Associated Faculty.

Lyman, S. M. (1990a). Asian American contacts before Columbus: Alternative understandings for civilization, acculturation, and ethnic minority status in America. In S. M. Lyman, *Civilization: Contents, discontents, malcontents and other essays in social theory.* Fayetteville: University of Arkansas Press.

Lyman, S. M. (1990b). *Civilization: Contents, discontents, malcontents and other essays in social theory.* Fayetteville: University of Arkansas Press.

Lyman, S. M. (1992a). The assimilation-pluralism debate: Toward a postmodern resolution of the American ethnoracial dilemma. *International Journal of Politics, Culture and Society, 6,* 181-210.

Lyman, S. M. (1992b). *Militarism, imperialism and racial accommodation: An analysis and interpretation of the early writings of Robert E. Park.* Fayetteville: University of Arkansas Press.

Lyman, S. M., & Scott, M. B. (1967). Territoriality: A neglected sociological dimension. *Social Problems, 15,* 236-248.

Lyman, S. M., & Scott, M. B. (1989). *A sociology of the absurd* (2nd ed.). Dix Hills, NY: General Hall.

Lynd, R. S., & Lynd, H. M. (1937). *Middletown in transition: A study in cultural conflicts.* New York: Harcourt, Brace.

Lynd, R. S., & Lynd, H. M. (1956). *Middletown: A study in modern American culture.* New York: Harcourt, Brace. (Original work published 1929)

Lyon, L. (1987). *The community in urban society.* Chicago: Dorsey.

Lyotard, J.-F. (1989). The sign of history. In A. Benjamin (Ed.), *The Lyotard reader* (pp. 393-411). Cambridge, MA: Blackwell.

Lyotard, J.-F. (1990). *Heidegger and "the Jews"* (A. Michel & M. Roberts, Trans.). Minneapolis: University of Minnesota Press.

Manganaro, M. (1990). Textual play, power, and cultural critique: An orientation to modernist anthropology. In M. Manganaro (Ed.), *Modern anthropology: From fieldwork to text* (pp. 3-47). Princeton, NJ: Princeton University Press.

Mangiafico, L. (1988). *Contemporary American immigrants: Patterns of Filipino, Korean, and Chinese settlement in the United States.* New York: Praeger.

Manning, P. K. (1987). *Semiotics and fieldwork.* Newbury Park, CA: Sage.

Manning, P. K. (1991). Analytic induction. In K. Plummer (Ed.), *Symbolic interactionism: Vol. 2. Contemporary issues* (pp. 401-430). Brookfield, VT: Edward Elgar. (Reprinted from *Qualitative methods,* by R. Smith & P. K. Manning, Eds., 1982, Cambridge, MA: Ballinger)

Marable, M. (1983). *How capitalism underdeveloped black America: Problems in race, political economy, and society.* Boston: South End.

Marcus, G. E. (1986). Contemporary problems of ethnography in the modern world system. In J. Clifford & G. E. Marcus (Eds.), *Writing culture: The poetics and politics of ethnography* (pp. 165-193). Berkeley: University of California Press.

Martin, C. (Ed.). (1987). *The American Indian and the problem of history.* New York: Oxford University Press.

Marty, M. E. (1992). Foreword. In Bartolome de Las Casas, *In defense of the Indians: The defense of the most reverend Lord, Don Fray Bartolome de Las Casas, of the Order of Preachers, late Bishop of Chiapa, against the persecutors and slanderers of the peoples of the New World discovered across the seas* (C. M. S. Poole, Ed. & Trans.). De Kalb: Northern Illinois University Press. (Original work published 1552)

Masuoka, J. (1946). Race relations and Nisei problems. *Sociology and Social Research, 30,* 452-459.

Maunier, R. (1949). *The sociology of colonies: An introduction to the study of race contact* (E. O. Lorimer, Ed. & Trans.; Vols. 1-2). London: Routledge & Kegan Paul.

McCluer, F. L. (1928). *Living conditions among wage-earning families in forty-one blocks in Chicago.* Unpublished doctoral dissertation, University of Chicago.

McClymer, J. F. (1980). *War and welfare: Social engineering in America, 1890-1925.* Westport, CT: Greenwood.

McGee, W. J. (1971). *The Seri Indians of Bahia Kino and Sonora, Mexico* (Seventeenth Annual Report of the Bureau of American Ethnology to the Secretary of the Smithsonian Institution, 1895-1896, part 1). Glorieta, NM: Rio Grande. (Original work published 1899)

McKenney, T. L., & Hall, J. (1972). *The Indian Tribes of North America—with biographical sketches and anecdotes of the principal chiefs* (Vols. 1-3). Totowa, NJ: Rowman & Littlefield. (Original work published 1836)

McKenzie, R. D. (1968). *On human ecology: Selected writings* (A. H. Hawley, Ed.). Chicago: University of Chicago Press.

McKinney, J. C., in collaboration with Loomis, C. P. (1957). The application of *Gemeinschaft* and *Gesellschaft* as related to other typologies. In F. Tönnies, *Community and society (Gemeinschaft und Gesellschaft)* (C. P. Loomis, Ed. & Trans.; pp. 12-29). East Lansing: Michigan State University Press.

Mead, M. (1960a). *Coming of age in Samoa: A psychological study of primitive youth for Western civilization.* New York: Mentor. (Original work published 1928)

Mead, M. (1960b). *Growing up in New Guinea: A comparative study of primitive education.* New York: Mentor. (Original work published 1930)

Mead, M. (1960c). *Male and female: A study of the sexes in a changing world*. New York: Mentor. (Original work published 1949)

Mead, M. (1960d). *Sex and temperament in three primitive societies*. New York: Mentor. (Original work published 1935)

Mead, M. (1975). *New lives for old: Cultural transformation—Manau, 1928-1953*. New York: William Morrow. (Original work published 1956)

Messenger, P. M. (Ed.). (1991). *The ethics of collecting cultural property: Whose culture? Whose property?* Albuquerque: University of New Mexico Press.

Miller, J. (1993). *The passion of Michel Foucault*. New York: Simon & Schuster.

Milner, C. A., II, & O'Neil, F. A. (Eds.). (1985). *Churchmen and the Western Indians, 1820-1920*. Norman: University of Oklahoma Press.

Milson, K. (1991-1992). (En)countering imperialist nostalgia: The Indian reburial issue. *Discourse: Journal for Theoretical Studies in Media and Culture, 14,* 58-74.

Miner, H. (1952). The folk-urban continuum. *American Sociological Review, 17,* 529-537.

Minnich, E. K. (1990). *Transforming knowledge*. Philadelphia: Temple University Press.

Montagu, A. (Ed.). (1968). The concept of the primitive. New York: Free Press.

Morgan, G. (Ed.). (1983). *Beyond method: Strategies for social research*. Beverly Hills, CA: Sage.

Morgan, L. H. (1964). *Ancient society* (L. White, Ed.). Cambridge, MA: Belknap.

Moorhouse, G. (1988). *Imperial city: New York*. New York: Henry Holt.

Murdock, G. P. (1965). *Social structure*. New York: Free Press. (Original work published 1949)

Murdock, G. P. (1934). *Our primitive contemporaries*. New York: Macmillan.

A museum is set to part with its Indian treasures. (1993, February 19). *New York Times,* p. A12.

Myer, D. S. (1971). *Uprooted Americans: The Japanese Americans and the War Relocation Authority during World War II*. Tucson: University of Arizona Press.

Nader, L. (1972). Up the anthropologist: Perspectives gained from studying up. In D. Hymes (Ed.), *Reinventing anthropology* (pp. 284-311). New York: Pantheon.

Natanson, M. (1962). History as a finite province of meaning. In H. Natanson, *Literature, philosophy and the social sciences: Essays in existentialism and phenomenology* (pp. 172-178). The Hague: Martinus Nijhoff.

Nelli, H. S. (1970). *The Italians in Chicago, 1880-1930*. New York: Oxford University Press.

Neske, G., & Kettering, E. (1990). *Martin Heidegger and National Socialism: Questions and answers* (L. Harries & J. Neugroschel, Trans.). New York: Paragon House.

Nikolinakos, D. D. (1990). Foucault's ethical quandary. *Telos, 23,* 123-140.

Nisbet, R. A. (1969). *Social change and history: Aspects of the Western theory of development.* New York: Oxford University Press.

Nisbet, R. A. (1972). Ethnocentrism and the comparative method. In A. R. Desai (Ed.), *Essays on modernization of underdeveloped societies* (Vol. 1, pp. 95-114). New York: Humanities Press.

Nisbet, R. A. (1977). *Sociology as an art form.* New York: Oxford University Press.

Nisbet, R. A. (1986). Developmentalism: A critical analysis. In R. A. Nisbet, *The making of modern society* (pp. 33-69). New York: New York University Press.

Nomura, G. M., et al. (Eds.). (1989). *Frontiers of Asian American studies: Writing, research and commentary.* Pullman: Washington State University Press.

Nordenskiold, G. (1979). *The cliff dwellers of the Mesa Verde* (O. L. Morgan, Trans.). Glorieta, NM: Rio Grande. (Original work published 1893)

Norris, C. (1990). Lost in the funhouse: Baudrillard and the politics of post-modernism. In R. Boyne & A. Rattansi (Eds.), *Postmodernism and society* (pp. 119-153). New York: St. Martin's.

Novak, M. (1972). *The rise of the unmeltable ethnics: Politics and culture in the seventies.* New York: Macmillan.

Novak, M. (1980). Pluralism: A humanistic perspective. In S. Thernstrom (Ed.), *Harvard encyclopedia of American ethnic groups* (pp. 772-781). Cambridge, MA: Harvard University Press.

Numbers, R. (1992). *The creationists: The evolution of scientific creationism.* New York: Alfred A. Knopf.

Oakes, K. B. (1938). *Social theory in the early literature of voyage and exploration in Africa.* Unpublished doctoral dissertation, University of California, Berkeley.

Officer, J. E. (1987). *Hispanic Arizona, 1536-1856.* Tucson: University of Arizona Press.

Okihiro, G. Y. (1988). The idea of community and a "particular type of history." In G. Y. Okihiro et al. (Eds.), *Reflections on shattered windows: Promises and prospects for Asian American studies* (pp. 175-183). Pullman: Washington State University Press.

Okihiro, G. Y., et al. (Eds.). (1988). *Reflections on shattered windows: Promises and prospects for Asian American studies.* Pullman: Washington State University Press.

Olivier, S. (1970). The government of colonies and dependencies. In G. Spiller (Ed.), *Papers on inter-racial problems communicated to the First Universal Race Congress, University of London, July 26-29, 1911* (pp. 293-312). New York: Citadel. (Original work published 1911)

Padilla, F. M. (1985). *Latino ethnic consciousness: The case of Mexican Americans and Puerto Ricans in Chicago.* Notre Dame, IN: University of Notre Dame Press.

Paglia, C. (1991). Junk bonds and corporate raiders: Academe in the hour of the wolf. *Arion: A Journal of Humanities and the Classics* (third series), *1*(2), 139-212.

Park, R. E. (1952a). *The collected papers of Robert Ezra Park: Vol. 2. Human communities: The city and human ecology* (E. C. Hughes et al., Eds.). Glencoe, IL: Free Press.

Park, R. E. (1952b). Community organization and the romantic temper. In R. E. Park, *The collected papers of Robert Ezra Park: Vol. 2. Human communities: The city and human ecology* (E. C. Hughes et al., Eds.; pp. 64-72). Glencoe, IL: Free Press.

Park, R. E. (1952c). Magic, mentality and city life. In R. E. Park, *The collected papers of Robert Ezra Park: Vol. 2. Human communities: The city and human ecology* (E. C. Hughes et al., Eds.; pp. 102-117). Glencoe, IL: Free Press.

Park, R. E. (1967). The city: Suggestions for the investigation of human behavior in the urban environment. In R. E. Park, E. W. Burgess, & R. D. McKenzie (Eds.), *The city* (pp. 1-46). Chicago: University of Chicago Press. (Original work published 1925)

Park, R. E. (1969a). Human migration and the marginal man. In E. W. Burgess (Ed.), *Personality and the social group* (pp. 64-77). Freeport, NY: Books for Libraries Press. (Original work published 1929)

Park, R. E. (1969b). Introduction. In R. Adams, *Interracial marriage in Hawaii: A study of mutually conditioned responses to acculturation and amalgamation* (pp. xiii-xiv). Montclair, NJ: Patterson Smith. (Original work published 1937)

Park, R. E. (1971). *The immigrant press and its control: The acculturation of immigrant groups into American society.* Montclair, NJ: Patterson Smith. (Original work published 1922)

Parsons, T. (1949). *The structure of social action: A study on social theory with special reference to a group of recent European writers.* Glencoe, IL: Free Press. (Original work published 1937)

Parsons, T. (1966). *Societies: Evolutionary and comparative perspectives.* Englewood Cliffs, NJ: Prentice Hall.

Parsons, T. (1971). *The system of modern societies.* Englewood Cliffs, NJ: Prentice Hall.

Parsons, T. (1973). Some afterthoughts on *Gemeinschaft* and *Gesellschaft*. In W. J. Cahnman (Ed.), *Ferdinand Tönnies: A new evaluation* (pp. 140-150). Leiden, Netherlands: E. J. Brill.

Patterson, O. (1982). *Slavery and social death: A comparative study.* Cambridge, MA: Harvard University Press.

Patterson, O. (1991). *Freedom: Vol. 1. Freedom in the making of Western culture.* New York: Basic Books.

Peacock, J. L. (1986). *The anthropological lens: Harsh lights, soft focus.* Cambridge: Cambridge University Press.

Pike, K. (1967). *Language in relation to a unified theory of the structure of human behaviour.* The Hague: Mouton.

Pool, I. de S. (Ed.). (1981). *The social impact of the telephone.* Cambridge: MIT Press.

Poster, M. (1987-1988). Foucault, the present and history. *Cultural Critique, 8,* 105-121.

Pratt, M. L. (1986). Fieldwork in common places. In J. Clifford & G. E. Marcus (Eds.), *Writing culture: The poetics and politics of ethnography.* Berkeley: University of California Press.

Quandt, J. B. (1970). *From the small town to the great community: The social thought of the progressive intellectuals.* New Brunswick, NJ: Rutgers University Press.

Rabinow, P., & Sullivan, W. M. (Eds.). (1979). *Interpretive social science: A reader.* Berkeley: University of California Press.

Radin, P. (1927). *The story of the American Indian.* New York: Boni & Liveright.

Radin, P. (1957a). *Primitive man as philosopher.* New York: Dover. (Original work published 1927)

Radin, P. (1957b). *Primitive religion: Its nature and origin.* New York: Dover. (Original work published 1937)

Radin, P. (1963). *The autobiography of a Winnebago Indian: Life, ways, acculturation, and the peyote cult.* New York: Dover. (Original work published 1920)

Radin, P. (1966). *The method and theory of ethnology: An essay in criticism.* New York: Basic Books. (Original work published 1933)

Radin, P. (1970). *The Italians of San Francisco: Their adjustment and acculturation.* San Francisco: R&E Research Associates. (Original work published 1935)

Radin, P. (Ed.). (1971a). *The golden mountain: Chinese tales told in California, collected by Jon Lee.* Taipei: Caves. (Original work published 1936)

Radin, P. (1971b). *The world of primitive man.* New York: Dutton. (Original work published 1953)

Radin, P. (1973). *The Winnebago tribe.* Lincoln: University of Nebraska Press. (Original work published 1923)

Radin, P. (1976). *The trickster: A study in American Indian mythology.* New York: Schocken. (Original work published 1956)

Rae, J. B. (1965). *The American automobile: A brief history.* Chicago: University of Chicago Press.

Ratzel, F. (1988). *Sketches of urban and cultural life in North America* (S. A. Stehlin, Ed. & Trans.). New Brunswick, NJ: Rutgers University Press. (Original work published 1876)

Redfield, J. (1991). Classics and anthropology. *Arion: A Journal of Humanities and the Classics* (third series), *1*(2), 5-23.

Redfield, R. (1928). *A plan for the study of Tepoztlan, Mexico*. Unpublished doctoral dissertation, University of Chicago.

Redfield, R. (1930). *Tepoztlan—A Mexican village: A study of folk life*. Chicago: University of Chicago Press.

Redfield, R. (1941). *The folk culture of Yucatan*. Chicago: University of Chicago Press.

Redfield, R. (1960). *The little community and peasant society and culture*. Chicago: University of Chicago Press.

Redfield, R. (1962a). The folk society and civilization. In M. P. Redfield (Ed.), *The papers of Robert Redfield: Vol. 1. Human nature and the study of society*. Chicago: University of Chicago Press.

Redfield, R. (1962b). *A village that chose progress: Chan Kom revisited*. Chicago: University of Chicago Press. (Original work published 1950)

Redfield, R. (1963). Talk with a stranger. In M. P. Redfield (Ed.), *The papers of Robert Redfield: Vol. 2. The social uses of social science* (pp. 270-284). Chicago: University of Chicago Press.

Redfield, R., & Rojas, A. V. (1962). *Chan Kom: A Maya village*. Chicago: University of Chicago Press. (Original work published 1934)

Redfield, R., & Singer, M. B. (1973). The cultural role of the cities: Orthogenetic and heterogenetic change. In G. Germani (Ed.), *Modernization, urbanization, and the urban crisis* (pp. 61-71). Boston: Little, Brown.

Reid, D. (Ed.). (1992). *Sex, death and God in L.A.* New York: Pantheon.

Reuter, E. B. (1969). *The mulatto in the United States: Including a study of the role of mixed-blood races throughout the world*. New York: Negro Universities Press. (Original work published 1918)

Rivers, W. H. R. (1974). The psychological factor. In A. Montagu (Ed.), *Frontiers of anthropology* (pp. 391-409). New York: G. P. Putnam's Sons. (Reprinted from *Essays on the depopulation of Melanesia*, by W. H. R. Rivers, Ed., 1922, Cambridge: Cambridge University Press)

Rockmore, T. (1992). *On Heidegger's Nazism and philosophy*. Berkeley: University of California Press.

Roper, M. W. (1935). *The city and the primary group*. Unpublished doctoral dissertation, University of Chicago.

Rorty, R. (1982). *Consequences of pragmatism: Essays, 1972-1980*. Minneapolis: University of Minnesota Press.

Rorty, R. (1989). *Contingency, irony and solidarity*. Cambridge: Cambridge University Press.

Rose, A. (Ed.). (1988). *Universal abandon? The politics of postmodernism*. Minneapolis: University of Minnesota Press.

Rose, D. (1989). *Patterns of American culture: Ethnography and estrangement*. Philadelphia: University of Pennsylvania Press.

Rosenau, P. M. (1992). *Post-modernism and the social sciences: Insights, inroads, and intrusions.* Princeton, NJ: Princeton University Press.

Ross, R. H., & Bogardus, E. S. (1940). The third generation race relations cycle: A study in Issei-Nisei relationships. *Sociology and Social Research, 24,* 357-363.

Rossi, P. (1987). *The dark abyss of time: The history of the earth and the history of nations from Hooke to Vico* (L. G. Cochrane, Trans.). Chicago: University of Chicago Press.

Rouse, I. (1992). *The Tainos: Rise and decline of the people who greeted Columbus.* New Haven, CT: Yale University Press.

Royce, P. (1982). *Ethnic identity: Strategies of diversity.* Bloomington: Indiana University Press.

Rubel, A. J. (1971). *Across the tracks: Mexican Americans in a Texas city.* Austin: University of Texas Press.

Sachs, W. (1947). *Black anger.* New York: Grove.

Sadri, A. (1992). *Max Weber's sociology of intellectuals.* New York: Oxford University Press.

Salmond, A. (1991). *Two worlds: First meetings between Maori and Europeans, 1642-1772.* Honolulu: University of Hawaii Press.

Sanchez, G. S. (1967). *Forgotten people: A study of New Mexicans.* Albuquerque: Calvin Horn.

Sanderson, S. K. (1990). *Social evolutionism: A critical history.* Cambridge, MA: Blackwell.

Sando, J. S. (1992). *Pueblo nations: Eight centuries of Pueblo Indian history.* Santa Fe, NM: Clear Light.

Sarana, G. (1975). *The methodology of anthropological comparison: An analysis of comparative methods in social and cultural anthropology.* Tucson: University of Arizona Press.

Saxton, S. L. (1993). Sociologist as citizen-scholar: A symbolic interactionist alternative to normal sociology. In T. R. Vaughan, G. Sjoberg, & L. J. Reynolds (Eds.). *A critique of contemporary American sociology* (pp. 232-251). Dix Hills, NY: General Hall.

Schatzman, L., & Strauss, A. L. (1973). *Field research: Strategies for a natural sociology.* Englewood Cliffs, NJ: Prentice Hall.

Schietinger, E. F. (1967). Racial succession and changing property values in residential Chicago. In E. W. Burgess & D. J. Bogue (Eds.), *Contributions to urban sociology* (pp. 86-99). Chicago: University of Chicago Press.

Schlesinger, A. M., Jr. (1991). *The disuniting of America: Reflections on a multicultural society.* Knoxville, TN: Whittle.

Schoolcraft, H. R. (1975). *Personal memoirs of a residence of thirty years with the Indian tribes of the American frontiers, with brief notices of passing events, facts and opinions, A.D. 1812 to A.D. 1842.* New York: Arno. (Original work published 1851)

Schrag, P. (1970). *The decline of the WASP.* New York: Simon & Schuster.

Schrag, P. (1973). *The end of the American future.* New York: Simon & Schuster.

Schwatka, F. (1977). *In the land of cave and cliff dwellers.* Glorieta, NM: Rio Grande. (Original work published 1893)

Sheets-Johnstone, M. (1990). *The roots of thinking.* Philadelphia: Temple University Press.

Sheets-Johnstone, M. (Ed.). (1992). *Giving the body its due.* Albany: State University of New York Press.

Sheridan, T. E. (1986). *Los Tucsonenses: The Mexican community in Tucson, 1854-1941.* Tucson: University of Arizona Press.

Shibutani, T., & Kwan, K. M.(1965). *Ethnic stratification: A comparative approach.* New York: Macmillan.

Simmel, G. (1950). The stranger. In G. Simmel, *The sociology of Georg Simmel* (K. H. Wolff, Ed. & Trans.; pp. 402-408). Glencoe, IL: Free Press.

Simmel, G. (1968). *The conflict in modern culture and other essays* (K. P. Etzkorn, Ed. & Trans.). New York: Teachers College Press.

Siu, P. C. P. (1987). *The Chinese laundrymen: A study of social isolation* (J. K. W. Tchen, Ed.). New York: New York University Press.

Smith, A. D. (1989). *The ethnic origin of nations.* New York: Blackwell.

Smith, C. W. (1979). *A critique of sociological reasoning: An essay in philosophical sociology.* Oxford: Blackwell.

Smith, M. G. (1965). *The plural society in the British West Indies.* Berkeley: University of California.

Smith, M. P. (1979). *The city and social theory.* New York: St. Martin's.

Solzhenitsyn, A. (1993, February 7). The relentless cult of novelty and how it wrecked the century. *New York Times Book Review*, p. 3.

Sorokin, P. (1965). *Fads and foibles in modern sociology and related sciences.* Chicago: Henry Regnery-Gateway.

Spicer, E. A., Hansen, A. T., Luomala, K., & Opler, M. K. (1969). *Impounded people: Japanese-Americans in the relocation centers.* Tucson: University of Arizona Press.

Spier, L. (1978). *Yuman tribes of the Gila River.* New York: Dover. (Original work published 1933)

Spretnak, C. (1991). *States of grace: The recovery of meaning in the postmodern age.* New York: HarperCollins.

Statler, O. (1983). *Japanese pilgrimage.* New York: William Morrow.

Stein, M. (1964). The eclipse of community: Some glances at the education of a sociologist. In A. J. Vidich, J. Bensman, & M. Stein (Eds.), *Reflections on community studies.* New York: John Wiley.

Steinberg, S. (1981). *The ethnic myth: Race, ethnicity, and class in America*. New York: Atheneum.

Stocking, G. W., Jr. (Ed.). (1983). *Observers observed: Essays on ethnographic field work*. Madison: University of Wisconsin Press.

Stocking, G. W., Jr. (Ed.). (1984). *Functionalism historicized: Essays on British social anthropology*. Madison: University of Wisconsin Press.

Stocking, G. W., Jr. (Ed.). (1985). *Objects and others: Essays on museums and material culture*. Madison: University of Wisconsin Press.

Stocking, G. W., Jr. (Ed.). (1986). *Malinowski, Rivers, Benedict and others: Essays on culture and personality*. Madison: University of Wisconsin Press.

Stocking, G. W., Jr. (Ed.). (1988). *Bones, bodies, behavior: Essays on biological anthropology*. Madison: University of Wisconsin Press.

Stocking, G. W., Jr. (Ed.). (1989). *Romantic motives: Essays on anthropological sensibility*. Madison: University of Wisconsin Press.

Stocking, G. W., Jr. (Ed.). (1991). *Colonial situations: Essays on the contextualization of ethnographic knowledge*. Madison: University of Wisconsin Press.

Stone, R. W. (1921). *The origin of the survey movement*. Unpublished doctoral dissertation, University of Chicago.

Stonequist, E. V. (1961). *The marginal man: A study in personality and culture conflict*. New York: Russell & Russell. (Original work published 1937)

Strathern, M. (1990). Out of context: The persuasive fictions of anthropology, with comments by I. C. Jarvie, Stephen A. Tyler and George E. Marcus. In M. Manganaro (Ed.), *Modern anthropology: From fieldwork to text* (pp. 80-130). Princeton, NJ: Princeton University Press.

Street corner society revisited [Special issue]. (1992). *Journal of Contemporary Ethnography, 21*(1), 3-132.

Sumner, W. G. (1940). *Folkways: A study of the sociological importance of usages, manners, customs, mores, and morals*. Boston: Ginn. (Original work published 1906)

Sumner, W. G. (1969). Foreword. In J. E. Cutler, *Lynch-law: An investigation into the history of lynching in the United States* (p. v). Montclair, NJ: Patterson Smith. (Original work published 1905)

Suret-Canale, J. (1988a). The end of chieftancy in Guinea. In J. Suret-Canale, *Essays on African history: From the slave trade to neocolonialism* (C. Hurst, Trans.). Trenton, NJ: Africa World.

Suret-Canale, J. (1988b). Guinea in the colonial system. In J. Suret-Canale, *Essays on African history: From the slave trade to neocolonialism* (C. Hurst, Trans.). Trenton, NJ: Africa World.

Suttles, G. D. (1972). *The social construction of communities*. Chicago: University of Chicago Press.

Symposium on qualitative methods. (1993). *Contemporary Sociology, 22*, 1-15.

Takaki, R. (1989). *Strangers from a different shore: A history of Asian Americans.* New York: Penguin.

Taylor, C. (1989). *Sources of the self: The making of modern identity.* Cambridge, MA: Harvard University Press.

Taylor, P. S. (1970). *Mexican labor in the United States* (Vols. 1-2). New York: Arno/ New York Times. (Original work published 1930)

Taylor, P. S. (1983). *On the ground in the thirties.* Salt Lake City: Peregrine Smith.

Tedlock, B. (1992). *The beautiful and the dangerous: Encounters with the Zuni Indians.* New York: Viking.

Teggart, F. J. (1941). *The theory and processes of history.* Berkeley: University of California Press.

Thernstrom, S. (Ed.). (1980). *Harvard encyclopedia of American ethnic groups.* Cambridge, MA: Harvard University Press.

Thomas, W. I., & Znaniecki, F. (1958). *The Polish peasant in Europe and America.* New York: Dover.

Thrasher, F. M. (1963). *The gang: A study of 1,313 gangs in Chicago.* Chicago: University of Chicago Press. (Original work published 1927)

Thucydides. (1972). *History of the Peloponnesian War* (R. Warner, Trans.). Harmondsworth: Penguin.

Tilman, R. (1991). *Thorstein Veblen and his critics, 1891-1963.* Princeton, NJ: Princeton University Press.

Tinder, G. (1980). *Community: Reflections on a tragic ideal.* Baton Rouge: Louisiana State University Press.

Tobias, H. J. (1990). *A history of the Jews in New Mexico.* Albuquerque: University of New Mexico Press.

Todorov, T. (1984). *The conquest of America* (R. Howard, Trans.). New York: Harper & Row.

Toland, J. D. (Ed.). (1993). *Ethnicity and the state.* New Brunswick, NJ: Transaction.

Tönnies, F. (1957). *Community and society (Gemeinschaft und Gesellschaft)* (C. P. Loomis, Ed. & Trans.). East Lansing: Michigan State University Press. (Original work published 1887)

Torgovnick, M. (1990). *Gone primitive: Savage intellects, modern lives.* Chicago: University of Chicago Press.

Tricarico, D. (1984). *The Italians of Greenwich Village: The social structure and transformation of an ethnic community.* Staten Island, NY: Center for Migration Studies of New York.

Trinh T. M. (1991). *When the moon waxes red: Representation, gender and cultural politics.* New York: Routledge.

Trinkhouse, E., & Shipman, P. (1993). *The Neanderthals: Changing the image of mankind.* New York: Alfred A. Knopf.

Turner, V. (1992). African ritual and Western literature: Is a comparative symbology possible? In V. Turner, *Blazing the trail: Way marks in the exploration of symbols* (E. Turner, Ed.; pp. 66-88). Tucson: University of Arizona Press.

Van Maanen, J. (1988). *Tales of the field: On writing ethnography*. Chicago: University of Chicago Press.

Vaughan, A. T. (1965). *New England frontier: Puritans and Indians, 1620-1675*. Boston: Little, Brown.

Vaughan, T. R. (1993). The crisis in contemporary American sociology: A critique of the discipline's dominant paradigm. In T. R. Vaughan, G. Sjoberg, & L. J. Reynolds (Eds.), *A critique of contemporary American sociology*. Dix Hills, NY: General Hall.

Veblen, T. (1959). *The theory of the leisure class*. New York: Mentor. (Original work published 1899)

Veblen, T. (1961a). The blond race and the Aryan culture. In T. Veblen, *The place of science in modern civilization and other essays*. New York: Russell & Russell. (Original work published 1919)

Veblen, T. (1961b). The mutation theory and the blond race. In T. Veblen, *The place of science in modern civilization and other essays*. New York: Russell & Russell. (Original work published 1919)

Veblen, T. (1965). *The higher learning in America: A memorandum on the conduct of universities by businessmen*. New York: Augustus M. Kelley. (Original work published 1918)

Veblen, T. (1990). *The instinct of workmanship and the state of the industrial arts*. New Brunswick, NJ: Transaction. (Original work published 1914)

Vidich, A. J. (1952). *The political impact of colonial administration*. Unpublished doctoral dissertation, Harvard University, Boston.

Vidich, A. J. (1955). Participant observation and the collection and interpretation of data. *American Journal of Sociology, 60*, 335-360.

Vidich, A. J. (1966). Introduction. In P. Radin, *The method and theory of ethnology: An essay in criticism* (pp. vii-cxv). New York: Basic Books.

Vidich, A. J. (1980). *The political impact of colonial administration*. New York: Arno.

Vidich, A. J. (1986). *Anthropology and truth: Some old problems*. Paper presented at the annual meeting of the American Anthropological Society, Philadelphia.

Vidich, A. J., & Bensman, J. (1968). *Small town in mass society: Class, power and religion in a rural community* (2nd ed.). Princeton, NJ: Princeton University Press.

Vidich, A. J., & Lyman, S. M. (1985). *American sociology: Worldly rejections of religion and their directions*. New Haven, CT: Yale University Press.

Vidich, A. J., Lyman, S. M., & Goldfarb, J. C. (1981). Sociology and society: Disciplinary tensions and professional compromises. *Social Research, 48,* 322-361.

Vigil, J. D. (1980). *From Indians to Chicanos: The dynamics of Mexican American culture.* Prospect Heights, IL: Waveland.

von Gierke, O. (1990). *Community in historical perspective: A translation of selections from Das Deutsche Genossenschaftsrecht (the German law of fellowship)* (A. Black, Ed.; M. Fischer, Trans.). Cambridge: Cambridge University Press. (Original work published 1868)

Wallace, A. F. C. (1987). *St. Clair: A nineteenth-century coal town's experience with a disaster-prone industry.* New York: Alfred A. Knopf.

Walzer, M. (1980). Pluralism: A political perspective. In S. Thernstrom (Ed.), *Harvard encyclopedia of American ethnic groups* (pp. 781-787). Cambridge, MA: Harvard University Press.

Ware, C. (1965). *Greenwich Village, 1920-1930: A comment on American civilization in the post-war years.* New York: Harper Colophon. (Original work published 1935)

Warren, R. L. (1963). *The community in America.* Chicago: Rand McNally.

Warren, R. L. (1972). *The community in America* (2nd ed.). Chicago: Rand McNally.

Waters, M. C. (1990). *Ethnic options: Choosing identities in America.* Berkeley: University of California Press.

Wax, R. H. (1971). *Doing fieldwork: Warnings and advice.* Chicago: University of Chicago Press.

Weber, A. F. (1967). *The growth of cities in the nineteenth century: A study in statistics.* Ithaca, NY: Cornell University Press. (Original work published 1899)

Weber, D. J. (1992). *The Spanish frontier in North America.* New Haven, CT: Yale University Press.

Weinstein, D., & Weinstein, M. A. (1990). Dimensions of conflict: Georg Simmel on modern life. In M. Kaern, B. H. Phillips, & R. S. Cohen (Eds.), *Georg Simmel and contemporary sociology* (pp. 341-356). Dordrecht, Netherlands: Kluwer.

Weinstein, D., & Weinstein, M. A. (1991). Simmel and the theory of postmodern society. In B. S. Turner (Ed.), *Theories of modernity and postmodernity* (pp. 75-87). London: Sage.

West, C. (1992). Diverse new world. In P. Berman (Ed.), *Debating P.C.: The controversy over political correctness on college campuses* (pp. 326-332). New York: Dell.

White, L. A. (1974). *The A'Coma Indians: People of the sky city* (Forty-Seventh Annual Report of the Bureau of American Ethnology to the secretary of the Smithsonian Institution, 1929-1930). Glorieta, NM: Rio Grande. (Original work published 1933)

Williams, R. A., Jr. (1990). *The American Indian in Western legal thought: The discourses of conquest.* New York: Oxford University Press.

Williams, V. J., Jr. (1989). *From a caste to a minority: Changing attitudes of American sociologists toward Afro-Americans, 1896-1945.* Westport, CT: Greenwood.

Willis, W. S., Jr. (1972). Skeletons in the anthropological closet. In D. Hymes (Ed.), *Reinventing anthropology* (pp. 121-152). New York: Pantheon.

Wirth, L. (1938). Urbanism as a way of life. *American Journal of Sociology, 44,* 1-24.

Wirth, L. (1945). The problem of minority groups. In R. Linton (Ed.), *The science of man in the world crisis* (pp. 347-372). New York: Columbia University Press.

Wirth, L. (1956). *The ghetto.* Chicago: University of Chicago Press. (Original work published 1928)

Wissler, C. (1923). *Man and culture.* New York: Thomas Y. Crowell.

Wissler, C. (1956). Foreword. In R. S. Lynd & H. M. Lynd, *Middletown: A study in modern American culture.* New York: Harcourt, Brace. (Original work published 1929)

Wissler, C. (1966a). *Indians of the United States* (Rev. ed.). Garden City, NY: Doubleday. (Original work published 1940)

Wissler, C. (1966b). *Red man reservations.* New York: Collier. (Original work published 1938)

Wood, M. M. (1969). *The stranger: A study in social relationships.* New York: AMS. (Original work published 1934)

Woods, F. J. (1956). *Cultural values of American ethnic groups.* New York: Harper & Brothers.

Woods, F. J. (1972). *Marginality and identity: A colored Creole family through ten generations.* Baton Rouge: Louisiana State University Press.

Woods, R. A., & Kennedy, A. J. (1990). *The settlement horizon.* New Brunswick, NJ: Transaction. (Original work published 1922)

Wu, C. C. (1926). *Chinese immigration in the Pacific area.* Unpublished doctoral dissertation, University of Chicago.

Whyte, W. F. (1943a). *Street corner society: The social structure of an Italian slum.* Chicago: University of Chicago Press.

Whyte, W. F. (1943b). A slum sex code. *American Journal of Sociology, 49,* 24-31.

Whyte, W. F. (1955). *Street corner society: The social structure of an Italian slum* (2nd ed.). Chicago: University of Chicago Press.

Whyte, W. F. (1981). *Street corner society: The social structure of an Italian slum* (3rd ed.). Chicago: University of Chicago Press.

Zaner, R. M. (1981). *The context of self: A phenomenological inquiry using medicine as a clue.* Athens: Ohio University Press.

Zorbaugh, H. W. (1929). *The Gold Coast and the slum.* Chicago: University of Chicago Press.

Zorbaugh, H. W. (1968). The dweller in furnished rooms: An urban type. In E. W. Burgess (Ed.), *The urban community: Selected papers from the Proceedings of the American Sociological Society, 1925* (pp. 98-105). Westport, CT: Greenwood.

3

Reconstructing the Relationships Between Universities and Society Through Action Research

Davydd J. Greenwood and Morten Levin

◆   Two sets of relationships form the core of this essay: those between
theory and praxis in the social sciences and those between the university and society, particularly as they affect the academic social sciences.[1]
To get at these, we argue in favor of action research as a critique of the
premises of conventional academic social science, as a vehicle for changing some of the internal structures of universities, and as a way to enhance
the relationships between academic social researchers and their broader

AUTHORS' NOTE: This chapter is a synthesis and expansion of arguments developed in
three other pieces of our writing: "Action Research, Science, and the Co-optation of Social
Research" (Greenwood & Levin, 1998a), "The Reconstruction of Universities: Seeking a Different Integration Into Knowledge Development Processes" (Greenwood & Levin, 1998c),
and *Introduction to Action Research: Social Research for Social Change* (Greenwood & Levin,
1998b).

constituencies beyond the university. In making these arguments, we dispute a number of standard premises of academic discourse, among them the clarity of the widely used distinctions between applied and pure research and between quantitative and qualitative research in the social sciences. We argue that these dichotomies do not line up with each other and that, despite the value of these conceptual distinctions, they are insufficient as guiding concepts for the practice of social research.[2]

Our critique of academia is blunt and uncompromising. We make it so in the interest of clarity, but we realize that the world is not as simple as the picture of it presented here. Some social scientists do integrate practice and theory effectively, some social scientists link up to extra-university constituencies effectively, some multidisciplinary projects and teams have succeeded in academia, and some social researchers envision a complex combination of quantitative and qualitative research as central to reform in the social sciences. Nevertheless, the bulk of university-based research has a decidedly antipraxis orientation built deeply into the current structure of the academic social sciences, and this influences the mind-sets of university administrators. We believe that, despite the efforts of a growing group of praxis-oriented social researchers, there is little sense of urgency about changing existing arrangements in fundamental ways in most parts of the university system.[3]

Even if a reader agrees with our highly critical portrait of academic institutions and the social sciences, there is still plenty of room for disagreement about the action implications deriving from it. We know there are many good and committed people at work in other institutions who are making a difference with their publications, their teaching, and their pressures for university reform. However, we personally do not believe that this kind of necessary but modestly incremental reform effort alone is going to be sufficient to achieve the necessary transformations. In our view, the current situation is overdetermined by a powerful constellation of forces and will require a more systematic, confrontational, and transnational reform effort. For this reason, we seek to move to a more direct confrontation through our writing and work, even though we also keep working incrementally at our own institutions and through networks with many colleagues around the world. Our uncompromising critique makes ethical and political sense only if we believe that the situation can indeed be changed. We do, and thus we see the following as a contribution to a constructive social process and not a mere jeremiad.

We believe that different, vibrant universities could be built out of existing institutions and that they would have important social functions to play. It is not evident that any new institution could now take the place of universities in educating new cadres of critical, reflected, literate, and socially engaged youth, even if we think they are doing a poor job of it now. We are deeply concerned that critical and socially engaged research efforts are being undermined by autopoetic and self-referential academic activities in universities dominated by career opportunism and by students who are treated as imitators of their teachers rather than as original thinkers in the making. The current educational system privileges imitative students, not creative, critical, and analytic professionals with a broad and independent understanding of society at large. The core challenge for universities is to turn away from conventional lecturing to learning situations based on the search for solutions to real-life, open-ended problems.

Why is it proper for us to hold academic social researchers accountable to higher standards of social responsibility? For generations, academic social scientists have argued for public and private support of their disciplines and activities with the claim that their work is valuable to society at large. We need only look at the mission statements of most of the professional social science societies to see such justifications. In spite of this, the behavior of many academic social scientists reveals the center of their lives to be dialogues with their own disciplinary colleagues. This is how they are socialized professionally from the beginning of their university training in most institutions. As a result, they either show a lack of concern with the application of the results of their work or reject such application outright, arguing either that connections to the world beyond the university invade their intellectual autonomy or, if they are positivists, that such linkages threaten their "objectivity." In criticizing this behavior, we draw attention to the inconsistencies between the justificatory statements for the academic social sciences and the daily practices of members of these disciplines.

While we advocate action research as a promising way of moving the academic social sciences to socially meaningful missions, we do not base our claims for action research only on its putative moral superiority. Central to our argument is the claim that action research creates the valid knowledge, theoretical development, and social improvements that the conventional social sciences have promised. Action research does better what academic social science claims to do. Thus we advocate action research as a fruitful replacement for conventional social science practice in academia. The only alternative seems to be for the academic social sciences to continue on their current path while openly acknowledging that they have no obligation to play a useful social role, either because they simply do not wish to or because they are unable to imagine how their work could be applied. Obviously, such an admission would have both institutional and financial consequences, but at least it would clear up any remaining confusion.

◆ The History of Universities

To understand how the dilemmas of the social sciences in contemporary universities arose, we need to develop some common ground about the history of universities. The following discussion is brief and superficial, but it contains an essential component of our argument.

Our universities have a monastic origin, and they have specialized in being centers of higher learning, functions originally given by the Church to monasteries. Although, initially, universities were Church institutions that provided advanced training to the clergy, over time they became both Church- and state-supported institutions for training doctors, lawyers, notaries, engineers, and other secular professionals. The earliest European universities date from the 13th century (e.g., Bologna, Salamanca).

The form of the university most familiar to us today is mainly a Prussian invention whose architect and champion was Wilhelm von Humboldt (1767-1835). Although not a lonely culture hero, Humboldt articulated the design and logic of the university in an especially clear way. One important operating principle in Humboldt's restructuring of the university was the union of research and teaching. University faculties and students were to be able to both study and conduct research because university teaching was to be based on research rather than on untested doctrines. Humboldt's university curriculum included history, philosophy, classical languages, and political economy, crossing boundaries that were generally not bridgeable in the earlier universities.

In Humboldt's system, freedom of thought and inquiry were the central imperatives in university life, a point that is central to our argument. Free inquiry meant that research was not to be limited by theological and political constraints. To protect this, the Humboldtian university gave the collegial system the final say about what could be or could not be taught or written, rather than leaving those determinations to Church or political authorities. Colleagues, presumed to be well-informed and driven by the quest for knowledge (rather than by Church authorities or political leaders), were empowered to regulate each other's intellectual activities.

This kind of university was enormously successful, and these institutions quickly became Western society's most "advanced" knowledge centers. In a short time, the Humboldtian university model took nearly unlimited control over setting the curriculum, conducting research, and teaching society's elites. These social elites then became supporters of the university, and the university-elite relationship became strongly self-reinforcing (see, e.g., Bourdieu, 1988). The university became a key instrument for the creation of "citizens" (Readings, 1996) to manage and celebrate the nation-state.

The collegial system and its related peer review structures centered on an effort to gain intellectual freedom from the constraints of theological doctrine and political manipulation. Although addressing this problem was obviously important, the solution adopted has subsequently done much to weaken the social articulation of the university to all groups other than powerful elites.

One of the main goals of the collegiate system was to create an environment for free and self-directed research based on the preferences and abilities of individual or groups of researchers. This made the university research process somewhat independent of the Church and state but at the cost of making the construction of research agendas highly self-referential and autopoetic within academia.[4] With the topics of research and the decisions about the appropriate frameworks for research being made within the research community, research was encouraged but the connection between the research agenda and the needs or interests of many parts of society beyond the university was diminished.

Although this division occurred as a by-product of the effort to secure freedom of thought and research, this dynamic created an ongoing tension between universities and the larger society supporting them. Many universities use significant public resources to finance their teaching and research operations, either through direct support or through tax benefits. Not surprisingly, society at large occasionally thinks it should be getting a more useful return for its investment and the freedom it gives to the professoriate. This situation is predictable because the autopoetic research process provides important supports for intellectual freedom but simultaneously opens the door to useless research and academic careerism divorced from attention to important public social issues.

Of course, we know that the university is not nearly as independent from society as the ideal Humboldtian model suggests. The professoriate is drawn from society at large and lives in a specific social context, taking on issues and agendas that emerge from general social life, even if indirectly. And the students who come from beyond the university's boundaries have to be made interested in the subjects being taught within it and must emerge from it able to function in the larger society after graduation. Despite the often feigned indifference of much university research to the extra-academic world, the history of research issues and intellectual topics in universities tracks major social forces closely: wars, immigration, racism, changing gender roles, ethnic conflict, the arms race, information systems, and the like (see Chomsky et al., 1997).

Another influence arises from the sizable investment in universities made by governments and large corporations. These entities have long treated universities as socially valuable research sites and have allocated financial resources to sustain them. It is hardly surprising, then, that they also channel university research activities by using their control of funds to emphasize projects of interest to them. Governments and industry also control the regulatory environment in which universities operate, including auditing university accounts, setting the legal frameworks within which universities operate, and requiring evaluations of both the institutions themselves and the work they do. Various kinds of science foundations and other national funding agencies, as well as large public and private sector corporations and foundations, have the ability to focus research in universities by setting terms of reference for funding research.

None of this is surprising. What is interesting, however, is that one of the features of Western universities that most contemporary academics take for granted is really a peculiar compromise between public and private sector control of universities and the peer review system. In most Western countries, as Richard Lewontin (1997) points out, the powerful funders utilize the very peer review system created to guarantee the independence of university research as a mechanism to evaluate proposals and to allocate funds on a competitive basis among investigators and universities. Thus governments and industry set the research agenda and yet use academic researchers and their universities to compete with and to police each other in the process of acquiring and expending those funds, an odd situation that deserves to be understood better.

The peer review system, important as it is, certainly is not a source of unambiguous liberation. Within each discipline there are dominating paradigms and methods, key actors, and powerful schools (Freidson, 1985; Kuhn, 1962). Research proposals that do not match these paradigms will not receive funding, and so, under current conditions, the peer review system mainly guarantees that research will be kept fully under the control of the elite (and older) members of the academic professions.

This is a fascinating blend of two apparently contradictory organizational principles: external control and internal autonomy. The complexity of the proposal and review processes is one of the labyrinths that all successful academic researchers and university administrators know how to navigate well. A good deal of postgraduate training in universities centers on learning how to operate in this complicated system.

The role of defense-related money in science and engineering research at universities is well-known, but a good deal of non-defense-related money also flows to universities. All told, in the United States, universities now garner "about 60 percent of federal expenditures for basic research . . . 30 percent of applied research and . . . about 7 percent of development [funding]" (Lewontin, 1997, pp. 20-21). These monies are not distributed equally over the entire set of universities. For example, in the United States, the top 10 universities currently control 95% of federal research and development monies (Lewontin, 1997, p. 25).

In addition, most colleges and universities depend on the government and the private sector in other ways. Universities are either directly supported by national and state taxes or receive important tax benefits. In the United States, private sector foundations (also tax advantaged in the way they are created) and private donors receive tax benefits for contributing money to universities. Thus the relationships among universities, governments, and the private sector are close. The autopoetic role of the faculty in setting much of the research agenda is largely a fantasy. Where some freedom of action is created is through the internal redistributions made by university administrations of the overhead funding received by faculty members with large, externally supported research projects. Administrations can support particular disciplines that do not support themselves through the internal reallocation of monies earned by such research operations. However, such reallocation creates all kinds of internal tensions and animosities among highly entrepreneurial researchers and departments.

This obviously is a complex and contradictory situation. On the one hand, universities gain both legitimacy and money by conducting research on subjects emphasized by governments and other extra-university agencies. On the other, the peer review process imposes a competitive dynamic on this process in which researchers from other (often competing) universities and institutes evaluate the research proposals. Rivalries, issues of privacy of information, and the like are constantly in play in these processes. Successful academic research entrepreneurs have to be very savvy politically; they definitely are not the "babes in the woods" that public stereotypes of professors often evoke, nor are their deans, provosts, vice presidents, presidents, rectors, or chancellors.

Despite its complexity, the system generally functions smoothly, but there is evidence that this autopoetic form of academic capitalism is less and less able to satisfy the needs of major social groups. Expressions of dissatisfaction and hostility toward universities from students, their parents, the general public, the private sector, and the government are commonplace, and not just from political conservatives who are offended by the supposed "liberal" ideologies promoted at many universities. In addition to the sheer complexity of the combined entrepreneurial-autopoetic research university, we think that the disconnection of a number of constituencies from universities is a key element in this growing dissatisfaction. Especially disaffected are the less powerful members of society, as well as some of the private sector actors who have been a main source of support for universities in the past.

Community, Small-Scale, Minority, and Other Disempowered Problem Owners

Many groups do not have significant impacts on the focus of university research. Community members, small-scale organizations, minorities, and other powerless or poor people who want assistance with broad social change issues are looking for solutions to everyday problems in particular contexts: poverty, addiction, racism, environmental degradation, and so on. It does not matter to them whether one university has more government grants than another or ranks above another in the annual *Business Week* university ratings; their concern is whether they can get help in producing research that will assist in solving their problems. Significance tests, fat research résumés, and prestige in the eyes of other academics are not central to their interests—results are.

These social groups, belonging to the middle and low end of society's power spectrum, are poorly connected to universities and rarely influence university research agendas. Given the presence of other pressures on the direction of university research from the government and big private sector players, it is no surprise that socially relevant research is marginalized within universities. This means that the majority of people cannot look to universities for assistance with solutions to their most pressing problems. If they are lucky, they can send their children to a university and hope that they will be able to join the elite in this way, but they have learned that they generally cannot expect direct assistance from most academic researchers in solving their own problems.

In the United States, it has occurred to many such people that the protected tax status of universities and the allocation of tax monies to support these institutions is a public investment that does not benefit them enough, and they are increasingly conveying these feelings to their elected representatives in the form of a "value for the dollar" approach to the cost of their children's education. Of course, this kind of change is slow because these voters are not very high on elected legislators' lists of constituents to satisfy. Still, they do vote and they do pay tuition, and what they say is heard to some degree.

Large Businesses

Oddly enough, one of the most powerful supporters and beneficiaries of university work is also now moving into a more contradictory relationship with universities. The troubled link between universities and the corporate world might appear puzzling, given what we have said above. After all, the big funders set the main research agendas, and professional academic associations and publications support those agendas quite unreflectively. The private sector players discussed above further focus the agendas of university researchers, including hiring them as private consultants so that they earn nice salaries in addition to their academic pay.

Despite their still-powerful role in supporting scientific and engineering research in universities, there is evidence that major corporate actors, important national stakeholders in any capitalist society, are becoming disconnected from universities in key ways. Although money still flows into university research from these sources, many corporations are showing dissatisfaction with the kinds of training universities are providing to the people the corporations need to employ. Because gainful employment of graduates is a sine qua non of university success, this is an important issue.

We know that corporations invest great amounts of money in employee training programs. Some of this investment is a consequence of a highly competitive business climate, which demands ongoing learning within corporations as a condition for survival. For a period of time, universities controlled a significant part of the market for corporate training, either through campus programs or through paid consulting in corporate settings. Now larger corporations appear increasingly to seek sources of training on their own, rather than relying on universities to provide it. They either create their own training institutions or use consulting companies that specialize in corporate training.

These training efforts seem to have two quite different components. One involves the training of recent university graduates who have just been hired. Most corporate executives we know do not find the training of recent university graduates to be adequate. Whereas some corporate training is actually socialization into the "corporate cultures" of particular firms, some of it is used to make up for the lack of practical work experience in university curricula. Although the picture is mixed and some in-house corporate training is always likely, it is clear that corporations are also showing dissatisfaction with the training that current graduates have.

The other training component centers on in-service training for corporate personnel. Here it seems that universities are losing out to in-house corporate training centers (Eurich, 1985), consulting companies, and, in the United States, to community colleges. Thus the same major corporations that exercise important influence in the setting of national political priorities—which ultimately include government funding priorities for university research—now increasingly look to their own mechanisms and other organizations to provide the kinds of training that universities once monopolized.

Although none of these conditions by itself is fatal, the combination of forces suggests to us that there is trouble on the horizon for the university-business-government research connection. We must not forget that for businesses and the government, funding university research is mainly a practical proposition, not an act of charity or commitment to the life of the mind. Universities have received research funds primarily because of their infrastructures and cohorts of graduate students who can serve as low-cost researchers. These made universities cheap and efficient sites for research compared with private sector research institutions and government research units. Such research units are a very expensive proposition to create and maintain when they have to provide full-time employment and support to researchers. By contrast, universities have tuition, tax benefits, state and federal allocations, and endowment revenues to keep the doors open and have been able to afford to do private sector and government research at competitive prices as a result.

But in recent years, the increasingly complex administrative apparatus universities have developed to manage research processes and revenues has decreased the responsiveness of the university research system to immediate private sector and government interests. Many universities have created remarkably costly and inefficient administrative infrastructures to manage research. These employ many people and bloat research costs to the point that we think the movement of much private sector and government research money to cheaper and more entrepreneurial extra-university locations is likely, if not already well under way. Not surprisingly, entrepreneurial academic researchers are fully aware of this, and many of the private research organizations that are taking these research monies away from universities are also staffed by current or former university faculty members, who serve them as either paid consultants or full-time employees.[5]

This movement of research away from the core research structures of universities has been occurring for a while in the sciences and engineering. Now it is expanding rapidly into areas of organizational development, leadership training, group dynamics, program evaluation, and so on, subjects that are increasingly in the hands of private, market-driven companies that hire university professors on lucrative private contracts, further diminishing the on-campus research capacity of the universities.

If this sketch is accurate, contemporary universities now satisfy a very specialized set of social interests and do not fully meet the needs of their key supporters. Because universities depend heavily on the goodwill of governments, communities, and parents and students, and on tax advantages for their funding, we doubt this situation is sustainable. It is not clear why major segments of society should continue to support universities. Big business and government may get their research done more cheaply elsewhere. Communities and social change actors whose interests are not heeded and needs are not being met also have a decreasing stake in the future of universities.

Although inertia may keep the current situation going for a while, we do not think it will last much longer. If universities choose not to redirect themselves to be more pluralistic in responding effectively to a wider array of stakeholder groups in society, then we think a significant amount of public and private funding for them not only will but *should* dry up.

As experienced academic researchers ourselves, we know that the complacency and arrogance of many university administrators and faculty members does not enable them to foresee this risky future. We expect universities to begin to feel these competitive pressures very soon, and we do not believe that most currently have the organizational capacity or institutional leadership to respond effectively.[6]

◆ Theory and Praxis in the Social Sciences

Now that we have set the broader historical and political economic context around universities, we can move into a discussion of the overall effect of this complex environment on the social sciences, our central interest here.[7] Our purpose is to describe a role for action research in connecting university social research to some of its primary social constituencies, thereby contributing to a positive restructuring of university-society relationships. How the scientists, engineers, and humanists will address these challenges is a matter for them to consider, although we think that our arguments at least provide them with some useful points upon which to reflect.

What was known at the inception of the social sciences around 1800 and by most social thinkers between Aristotle and the beginning of the 17th century (see Toulmin, 1990) is now more obvious than ever. Social research aimed at social improvement is not an inferior counterpart of "pure" social research. Social change-oriented research, specifically action research, is the form social research must take if it is to achieve valid results, bring about useful social change, and reconnect universities to the larger society.

By contrast, current university-based social research is an armchair activity that claims to embody the scientific study of the structure of society through the argument that being as socially disengaged as possible somehow makes social research more "scientific." It builds explanations of the causes of social processes while disavowing any need to test its speculations in practice.

University social science is the activity of paid groups of full-time academics whose principal social impact is on each other and on the generations of young people in their classrooms. These academics and their disciples show little interest in social change and do not often venture outside the university, except on expeditions to "collect" data. They select their problems according to the intellectual and professional agendas of the most prestigious members of their disciplinary organizations, not in response to needs defined by people outside of academia. As they pursue their studies and refine their methods, there is little chance that their actions will affect most nonuniversity people or that their work will upset the holders of power outside of academia.

Everyone knows that there are wide variances in the kinds of social science practiced in universities: quantitative, qualitative, mixed method, positivist, constructivist, postmodernist, poststructuralist, and so on. One oddity of universities is that, despite the withering critique of positivism over the years, anyone looking at the kind of social research mainly supported by the principal agencies and foundations and privileged by academic administrators will see that it is overwhelmingly positivist (see Scheurich, 1997). That this is the case, and that positivism rests on social disengagement, does not seem to us accidental. It is a product of the systematic removal of academic social research from social change efforts.

Positivism

Positivistically-based quantitative researchers employ the language of objectivity, distance, and control because they believe these are the keys to the conduct of real social science. While we firmly believe in the value of quantitative research that is well carried out under proper conditions for a useful purpose, we also note that the positivist version of quantitative research is socially convenient for those in power who do not want to be the "subjects" of social research and who do not want criticism of their social actions to be brought forward by social researchers. Invoking impartiality and objectivity, positivistic social science absents itself from the controverted social arenas in which the ills produced by bureaucracy, authoritarianism, and inequality are played out, or it washes out this profile through the deployment of numbers rather than words.

The constructivist and postmodernist critiques of recent academic generations have devastated the conceptual and methodological underpinnings of positivism but have had very little effect on displacing the positivist practices and the comfortable "arrangement" among the conventional social sciences, university administrations, and external funders. We are constantly surprised by conventional social scientists' ability to articulate strong criticisms of positivism and yet continue to accept and enact many elements of the positivist approach.[8] And on the other side, there are many (although not all) postmodernists and poststructuralists who argue that all knowledge is so epistemologically compromised that it is impossible to know or do anything about anything, an equally nihilistic self-removal from the field of social engagement.

Qualitative Research

Despite the obvious value of qualitative research, we believe this criticism also applies here. Although it seems that qualitative research could be used very effectively for social change and that some qualitative research includes social criticism, most qualitative work becomes mired in intraprofessional rivalries and ends up chasing the latest trends in the literature, trends that rarely coincide with the felt needs of any particular social group for analysis and support. Although antipositivist in attitude, qualitative research has not as yet succeeded in reconstructing the relationship between the social sciences and society in any fundamental way. And the hostility of many of its adherents to quantification also weakens its credibility, even with the poor and oppressed who know that one must do battle with the powerful by arming oneself with all possible arguments, methods, and data.

While we acknowledge the importance of the qualitative/quantitative distinction and the flourishing productivity of current qualitative research, we are not inclined to give the qualitative/quantitative distinction a major role here because we do not see that this distinction alters our core assertion about the disconnection between social research and social praxis. Without the test of application, no research endeavor can ascertain the utility and validity of its theories, whether its center of gravity be quantitative or qualitative. In addition, action research is inherently multimethod research, including scientific experiments, quantitative social research, and qualitative research methods from as many disciplines as necessary to address the problem at hand. Effective action research cannot accept an a priori limitation to one or another research modality.

Applied Versus Pure Research

A widely used and misleading distinction separates applied and pure research, a distinction that has long been very problematic in the physical and biological sciences. In the United States, the Congress recently has tried to restrict national research funding to "applied" scientific research (which the Congress believes to be more "valuable," for its own confusing reasons). As a result, scientists have had to struggle to figure out how to couch what they do in applied language. Generally, most physical and biological scientists believe this distinction to be unworkable in practice, and they have mostly sought to evade it. Renaming basic research as applied research has not done much to change their patterns of behavior.

If this dichotomy is problematic in the basic sciences, it is much more so in the social sciences, where positivist claims to be "scientific" are made on the basis that positivist social research is not "applied" but "pure."[9] Positivist social scientists are imitating what they imagine to be the model of "real" science, whereas that model does not fit the behavior of "real" scientists in most respects. Given all this, we find the applied/pure distinction useless and misleading in general and devastating to the social sciences.

Social Research Redefined as Action Research

In our view, the answer to the dilemmas we have laid out above is action research. We define action research as research in which the validity and value of research results are tested through collaborative insider-professional researcher knowledge generation and application processes in projects of social change that aim to increase fairness, wellness, and self-determination. For us, action research is the only form of social research that enacts this agenda adequately. In action research, community or organizational stakeholders collaborate with professional researchers in defining the objectives, constructing the research questions, learning research skills, pooling knowledge and efforts, conducting the research, interpreting the results, and applying what is learned to produce positive social change. Action research ignores the boundaries between disciplines when they restrict effective understanding and action and advocates crossing the boundary between academia and society as a basic principle of operation.[10]

Despite defensive reactions to action research from positivist social researchers and disengaged interpretivists, we are hopeful that a fundamental change in the future of social research is on the way. We are realistic enough to know that such changes will not be easy to bring about and that change will not produce an even and smooth outcome in academia or beyond. The academic social sciences have developed strong professional

145

structures with powerful peer review systems, and their current forms are built into the organizational metabolisms of most academic institutions. Shifting the balance of university social research to action research would challenge the hegemony of the professional organizations and the academic division of labor, both notoriously difficult to change. And, of course, social change-oriented social research would be quite upsetting to many power holders in society. They can be counted on to defend themselves against it, especially in this era that Ira Shor (1996) calls the "conservative restoration." So we will press on, but we are not blindly optimistic.

To make our case for action research in the remainder of this chapter, we will do four things in a very short space:

1. Underpin our argument for action research philosophically;

2. Portray the ways the university and its academic research establishment are inimical to the promotion of action research;

3. Examine the larger social forces that make the continued analytic and political passivity of social research the most likely outcome under current conditions; and

4. Give brief examples of university-based action research.

Doing this briefly means that the structure of the argument can be clear, but the demonstration cannot be based on the presentation of much evidence.

◆ Why Action Research?

As we have pointed out above, action researchers reject arguments for separating praxis and theory in social research. Either social research is applied or it is not research. The terms *pure research* and *applied research* imply that a division of labor can exist between the pure and the applied, a division we believe makes social research impossible. For action researchers, social inquiry aims to generate knowledge and action in support of liberating social change. The "test" of social research is whether it provides effective support for the stakeholders' actions, organizations, and/or communities in their processes of self-determining social change. For us, the world divides into action research, which we support and practice, and conventional social research (subdivided into pure and applied social research and organized into professional subgroupings), which we reject on combined epistemological, methodological, and political grounds.

Action Research Is Not a Retreat From Science

Because of the dominance of the positivistic framework in the organization of the conventional social sciences, our view will automatically be heard as a retreat from the scientific method into activism. And for hard-line interpretivists, we will be seen as so naïve as not to understand that it is impossible to commit ourselves to any course of action on the basis of any kind of social research. The operating assumption in the conventional social sciences is that greater relevance and engagement automatically involve a loss of scientific validity or a loss of courage in the face of the yawning abyss of endless subjectivity.

Pragmatist Underpinnings

These arguments are spurious. A different grounding for social research can be found in pragmatic philosophy. Dewey, James, Peirce, and others offer an interesting and fruitful foundation for ontological and epistemological questions inherent in social research that is action relevant (see Diggins, 1994). Pragmatism seeks first of all to link theory and praxis. The core reflection process is connected to action outcomes that involve manipulating material and social factors in a given context. Experience emerges in a continual interaction between people and their environment and, accordingly, this process constitutes both the subjects and the objects of inquiry. The actions taken are purposeful and aim at creating desired outcomes. Hence the knowledge-creation process is based on the inquirer's norms, values, and interests.

Validity claims are identified as "warranted" assertions resulting from an inquiry process in which an indeterminate situation is made determinate through concrete actions in an actual context. The research logic is constituted in the inquiry process itself, and it guides the knowledge-generation process.

As action researchers, we strongly advocate the use of scientific methods and emphasize the importance and possibility of the creation of valid knowledge in social research (see Greenwood & Levin, 1998b). This kind of inquiry is a foundational element in democratic processes in society. John Dewey (1927/1954) especially focused his intellectual energy on

147

issues of participative democracy. In his view, the ethics of participation are a core element in meaningful knowledge-creation processes.

These general characteristics of the pragmatist position ground the action research approach. Two central parameters stand out clearly: knowledge generation through action and experimentation in context and participative democracy as both a method and a goal. Neither of these is met in current university structures. The Cartesian ethos has separated mind from body, praxis from reflection, science from social action. Research questions are formulated according to professional standards and ignore the holistic nature of real-life problem situations.

An Action Research Theory of Science

Everyone is supposed to know by now that social research is different from the study of atoms, molecules, rocks, tigers, and so on. Yet we are amazed by the emphasis so many conventional social scientists still place on the claim that being "scientific" requires researchers to sever all relations with the observed. It is still largely unchallenged, particularly in the fields gaining the bulk of social science research money and dominating in social science publications (economics, sociology, and political science). This positivistic credo is obviously wrong and leads away from the production of reliable information, meaningful interpretations, and social actions in social research. It has been subjected to generations of critique, even from within the conventional social sciences.[11] Yet the credo persists, suggesting that its social embeddedness itself deserves attention.

We believe that broad action research interventions in the organization of universities and the academic professions will be required to root it out. Put more simply, the epistemological ideas underlying action research are not new ideas; they simply have been widely ignored as conventional social researchers on the right and left (and the social interests they serve—consciously or unconsciously) have rejected university engagement in social reform.

How Action Research Integrates Theory and Praxis

Action research aims to solve pertinent problems in given contexts through democratic inquiry in which professional researchers collaborate with local stakeholders to seek and enact solutions to problems of major importance to the stakeholders. We refer to this as *cogenerative inquiry*

148

because it is built on professional researcher-stakeholder collaboration. Action research can be described as follows:

1. Action research is inquiry in which participants and researchers cogenerate knowledge through collaborative communicative processes in which all participants' contributions are taken seriously. The meanings constructed in the inquiry process lead to social action, or these reflections on action lead to the construction of new meanings.
2. Action research treats the diversity of experience and capacities within the local group as an opportunity for the enrichment of the research/action process.
3. Action research produces valid research results.
4. Action research is context centered; it aims to solve real-life problems in context.

We explain each of these elements briefly below.

Cogenerative inquiry. Central to action research are cogenerative inquiry processes in which trained professional researchers and knowledgeable local stakeholders work together to define the problems to be addressed, gather and organize relevant knowledge and data, analyze the resulting information, and design social change interventions. The relationship between the professional researcher and the local stakeholders is based on bringing the diverse bases of all participants' knowledge and their distinctive social locations to bear on a problem collaboratively. The professional researcher often brings knowledge of other relevant cases and of relevant research methods and has experience in organizing research processes. The insiders have extensive and long-term knowledge of the problems at hand and the contexts in which they occur, as well as knowledge about how and from whom to get additional information. They also contribute urgency and focus to the process, because it centers on problems they are anxious to solve. Together these partners create a powerful research team.

Local knowledge/professional knowledge. Action research is built on an interaction between local knowledge and professional knowledge. Whereas conventional social research and consulting privilege professional knowledge over local knowledge, action research does not. Action research is based on the premise that professional knowledge is important and can be valuable, but local knowledge is a necessary ingredient in any research. Only local stakeholders, with their years of experience in a particular situation, have sufficient information and knowledge about the situation to design effective social change processes. Action research does not romanticize local knowledge and denigrate professional knowledge. It is a cogenerative research process precisely because both types of knowledge are essential to it.

Validity/credibility/reliability. Action researchers do not make claims to context-free knowledge, nor are they interested in achieving such knowledge. Credibility, validity, and reliability in action research are measured by the willingness of local stakeholders to act on the results of the action research, thereby risking their welfare on the "validity" of their ideas and the degree to which the outcomes meet their expectations. Thus contextual knowledge, holism, and validity demonstrated in warrants for action are central to action research. The core validity claim centers on the workability of the actual social change activity engaged in, and the test is whether or not the actual solution to a problem arrived at solves the problem.

With Stephen Toulmin, we advocate restarting Western intellectual history just before the wrong turn begun in the 17th century with the emergence of the Cartesian model, in which knowing how (*phronesis*) was separated from the world of reason, abstraction, and distance—the world of *techne*. Action research returns social research to *phronesis*, to "knowing how" by acting on the phenomena, and away from *techne*'s worlds of inaction and putative distance from the subject (Toulmin, 1990; Toulmin & Gustavsen, 1996).

Context-centered knowledge. How can context-centered knowledge be communicated effectively to academics and to other potential recipients? Action research focuses on solving real problems, and so the central inquiry processes of action research are linked to solving practical problems in specific locations. Whether the "problem" is a social/organizational or material one, the results of action research must be tangible in the sense that the participants can figure out whether or not the solution they have developed actually resolves the problem they set themselves. The action research inquiry process is therefore intimately linked to action. By linking inquiry to actions in a given context, action research emphasizes the role of human inquirers as acting subjects in a holistic situation.

The challenges of action research are much more difficult in the realm of communicating and abstracting results of action research in a way that others who did not participate in a particular project (including other stakeholder groups facing comparable but not identical situations) will understand and believe, and that will enable them to generate their own effective courses of action. Precisely because the knowledge is co-generated, includes local knowledge and analyses, and is built deeply into the local context, it is a challenge to compare results across cases and to create generalizations.[12]

We do not think this is sufficient reason to hand over the territory of comparative generalization and abstract theorization to conventional social researchers. The approach of positivistic research to generalization has been to abstract from context, average out cases, lose sight of the world as lived in by human beings, and generally make the knowledge impossible to apply. Despite the vast sums of money and huge numbers of person-hours put into this kind of research, we find the theoretical harvest pretty slim. And the rejection of the possibility of learning and generalizing at all, typical of much interpretivism, constructivism, and vulgar postmodernism, strikes us as an open invitation to vapid intellectual posturing.

The action research view of generalization means that any single case that runs counter to a generalization invalidates it (Lewin, 1948) and requires the generalization to be reformulated. In contrast, positivist research often approaches exceptional cases by attempting to disqualify them in order to preserve the existing generalization. Rather than welcoming the opportunity to revise their generalization, researchers often react by finding a way to ignore it.

Greenwood became particularly well aware of this during his period of action research in the labor-managed cooperatives of Mondragón, the most successful labor-managed industrial cooperatives anywhere (see Greenwood & González Santos, 1992). Because the "official story" is that cooperatives cannot succeed, that Spaniards are not good at working or making money, and so on, the bulk of the literature on Mondragón published in the 1960s and 1970s attempted to explain the case away. Basque cultural predispositions, charismatic leadership, and so on were all tried as ways of making this exception one that could be ignored while the celebration of the supposedly greater competitiveness of the standard capitalist firm went on unaffected by this glaring exception. Positivist theorists did not want to learn from the case, in direct contravention of the requirements of scientific thinking, which views important exceptions as the most potentially valuable sources of new knowledge.

William Foote Whyte (1991) captures the idea of the productivity of exceptions in his concept of "social inventions." He proposes that all forms of business organizations could learn from this Basque case by trying to figure out how the unique social inventions the Basques had made helped explain their success. Having identified these, researchers could then begin the process of figuring out which of these could be generalized and diffused to other contexts where their utility could be tested, again in collaborative action. Of course, the key to this approach is that the validity of the comparison is also tested in action and not treated as a thought experiment.

If we readdress generalizations in light of what we have argued above, we reframe generalizations as including a process of reflection rather than seeing them as a structure of rule-based interpretations. Given our position that knowledge is context-bound, the key to utilizing this knowledge in a different setting is to follow a two-step model. First, it is important to understand the contextual conditions under which the knowledge has been created. This contextualizes the knowledge itself. Second, the transfer of this knowledge to a new setting implies understanding the contextual conditions of the new setting, how these differ from the setting in which the knowledge was produced, and involves reflection on what consequences this has for applying the actual knowledge in the new context. Hence generalization becomes an active process of reflection in which involved actors must make up their minds about whether or not the previous knowledge makes sense in the new context.

It would take much more space to make the full case (see Greenwood & Levin, 1998b), but we believe we have said enough to make it clear that action research is not some kind of a social science dead end. It is a disciplined way of developing valid knowledge and theory while promoting positive social change.

◆ Can Universities Promote the Kind of Knowledge Production Involved in Action Research?

We believe that the proper response to the epistemological, methodological, political economic, and ethical issues we have been raising is to reconstruct the relationships between the universities and the multiple stakeholders in society. We believe that part of the answer is to make action research the central social research strategy. This is because action research, as we have explained above, involves research efforts in which the users (governments, social service agencies, corporations large and small, communities, nongovernmental organizations, and so on) have a definite stake in the problems under study and the research process integrates collaborative teaching/learning with the nonuniversity partners. We know that this kind of university-based action research is possible because there are a number of successful examples. We provide below accounts of two such successes, drawn from a much larger set.

Case 1: Social Science Engineering Research Relationships and University-Industry Cooperation: The Offshore Yard

This project began when the Norwegian Research Council awarded a major research and development contract to SINTEF, a Norwegian research organization located in Trondheim and closely linked to the Norwegian University of Science and Technology. This contract focused on what is called *enterprise modeling,* an information systems-centered technique for developing models of complex organizational processes both to improve efficiency and to restructure organizational behavior. SINTEF received the contract for this work as part of a major national initiative to support applied research and organizational development in manufacturing industries.

A key National Research Council requirement for this program was that engineering research on enterprise modeling had to be linked to social science research on organization and leadership. This required the collaboration of engineers and social scientists within SINTEF of a more intensive sort than usual. The National Research Council argued that enterprise modeling could not be reduced to a technical effort; rather, the enterprise models themselves had to deal with organizational issues as well, because their deployment would depend on the employees' ability to use the models as a "tool" in everyday work.

The research focus of this activity was not very clear at the outset. The instrumental goal for the national research organization was to create a useful enterprise model rather than one that would only be a nice puzzle for information technologists to solve. The research focus emerged in the form of an engineering focus on enterprise models as learning

153

opportunities for all employees and a social science focus on participatory change processes.

The Offshore Yard agreed to be a partner in this effort, and the project was launched in early 1996.[13] The Yard employs approximately 1,000 persons and is located on the Trondheim fjord, about a 90-minute drive north of Trondheim. The Yard has a long history of specializing in the design and construction of the large and complex offshore installations used in North Sea oil exploration.

The project was to be co-managed by a joint group of engineers and social scientists. The key researchers were Ivar Blikø, Terje Skarlo, Johan Elvemo, and Ida Munkeby (two engineers and two social scientists) all employed at SINTEF. The expectation was that cooperation across professional boundaries would somehow arise as an automatic feature of their being engaged in the same project.

The process was by no means so simple. Throughout the initial phase of the project, the only cooperation seen was merely that team members were present at the company site at the same time. In part, this was because the two engineers on the team had a long history with the company. They had many years of contact with the company as consulting researchers and, before that, had worked as engineers on the staff of the Offshore Yard. As a result, the engineers took the lead in the early project activity.[14] They were running the project, and the social scientists seemed fairly passive. The engineers were working concretely on computer-based mock-ups of enterprise models, and, because this was a strong focus of planning interest in the company, they accordingly received a great deal of attention from the senior management of the Yard.

While this was going on, the social scientists were devoting their attention to a general survey of the company and making an ethnographic effort to learn about the organization and social realities of the company. This was considered important to give the social scientists a grasp of what the company was like. This research-based knowledge generation meant little to company people, as the work was neither understood nor valued by the company or by the engineering members of the team.

The first opening for social science knowledge came when the social researchers organized a search conference to address the problems of the organization of work at the shop-floor level.[15] This search conference produced results that captured the attention of both the local union and management and made it clear locally that the social scientists had skills that offered significant opportunities for learning and collaborative planning in the company. This was also the first time the researchers managed to include a fairly large number of employees from different layers of the organization in the same knowledge-production process.

As a consequence of this experience, university-Offshore Yard cooperation began to deepen. At that time, the company was developing a leadership training program. Through the social scientists, company leaders learned about other experiences in running such programs, and this helped them plan locally. They were better able to match their overall organizational development activity in their own training program because knowing about other programs helped them with their design. In addition, they felt it would be an advantage to them if company participants in the training also could get official university credits for their involvement. Thus the resulting program was designed through a university-company dialogue and, in the end, one of the social scientists on the team ran it. The program also gave official university-based credits to those participants who decided to take a formal exam. The leadership program became an effort that enhanced the formal skill levels of the participants, and the university diploma gave them recognition outside the context of the Yard.

The program was very successful, making evident how close collaboration between the company and the university could be mutually rewarding. The university people could experiment professionally and pedagogically in real-life contexts, and the company got access to cutting-edge knowledge from the university and from other companies through the university's contacts. As an interesting side effect, the Yard leadership decided to invite managers from neighboring plants to participate. They recognized that the Yard's own future depended on its having good relations with neighbors and suppliers. They decided that one way to improve this cooperation would be to share their program, as a gesture symbolizing their interdependent relationships and their mutual stake in each other's success.

Over the course of the project, the cooperation between engineers and social scientists began to grow and create new insights. A key first move in this direction was a redesign of the tube manufacturing facility at the Yard. The reorganization of work processes, which was cogeneratively developed through workers' participation, meant that shop-floor workers gained direct access to the computer-based production planning and scheduling used by the company engineers. Instead of having information from the system filtered down to them through the foreman, workers at the shop-floor level could utilize the information system and decide for themselves how to manage the production process. This form of organizational leveling would probably not have come about had it not been for the increased mutual understanding between the SINTEF engineers and social scientists and their company partners that emerged through their working together on the same concrete problems as a team.

Gradually, based on these experiences, a reconceptualization of the whole way to develop enterprise models emerged. The conventional engineering take on enterprise models was that the experts (e.g., the engineers) collected information, made an analysis, and then made expert decisions regarding what the model should look like. A new approach to enterprise modeling in the Offshore Yard was developed in which the involved employees actually have a direct say. Although this is a modest step in the direction of participation, it is potentially a very important one. It is fair to say that this changed focus toward participation would not have occurred if the social scientists had not presented substantive knowledge on issues of organization and leadership that were testable through participatory processes.

As more mutual trust developed between company people and researchers, the marginalized position of the social scientists gradually changed and the company came to count on the social researchers as well. For example, one of the major challenges for the company in the future will be how to manage with a significant reduction in the number of employees humanely and without destroying company morale. These changes originated both from a restructuring of the corporation of which the Yard is a part and new engineering and production processes that are leading to a reduced need for laborers. The Yard has invited the researchers to take part seriously in this process by asking them to draw knowledge and diverse perspectives on this difficult subject from all over the world. In this process, the researchers have been able to support new and often critical knowledge that has changed or extended the company's understanding of its downsizing challenge.

The research team has now also been asked to assist in working on the learning atmosphere in the Yard. This has involved extensive interviewing of a broad spectrum of employees to build a view about how to improve the Yard's capacity for ongoing learning. The results of these interviews were fed back to the involved employees, and the researchers shaped dialogues with them that aimed at both presenting the results and examining the inferences made by the researchers through comparison with the local knowledge of the workers. Again we can see how models of learning with origins in social science circles can be applied to the local learning process, and the results are important factors in the researchers' assessments of the strength and value of their academic findings.

Perhaps the most interesting overall development in this project is how the company-university relationship has developed. The senior executive officer of the Offshore Yard is now a strong supporter of the fruitfulness of the company's relationship with the university. In public presentations, he credits the researchers with bringing relevant and important knowledge to the company and explains that he can see how this relationship can become increasingly important. It took him several years of cooperation to see these possibilities, but now he does and the university is glad to respond. While there is no reason to romanticize the relationship, given that differences of opinion and interest emerge, the relationship seems so robust that further developments are likely.

In the end, only through multidisciplinary action research over a sustained period of time were these results possible. The research values and the action values in the process have both been respected, and all the partners in the process have benefited.

Case 2: Collaborative Research for Organizational Transformation Within the Walls of the University

Here we report on an example of an action research initiative that occurred at Cornell University, resulting in reform of a major required university course: introductory physics. The protagonist of this effort was Michael Reynolds, who wrote this work up as a doctoral dissertation in science education at Cornell (Reynolds, 1994).[16] Universities are, among other things, redoubts of hierarchical and territorial behavior, and thus changes initiated by students or by graduate assistants and lecturers are quite infrequent.

At the time the project began, Reynolds was employed as a teaching assistant in an introductory physics course that is one of the requirements for students wishing to go on to medical school. This makes the course a key gatekeeping mechanism in the very competitive process of access to the medical profession and makes the stake the students have in doing well high and the power of the faculty and university over their lives considerable. It also means that the course has a guaranteed clientele, almost no matter how badly it is taught.

Although there is more than one physics course offered, this particular one is crucial for students' completion of premed requirements. Because of a comprehensive reform undertaken in the late 1960s, this course was and is delivered in an "autotutorial" format. This means that students work through the course materials at their own pace (within limits), doing experiments and studying in a learning center, asking for advice there, and taking examinations on each unit (often many times) until they have achieved mastery of the material and the grades they seek. Despite the inviting and apparently flexible format, the course had become notoriously unpopular among the students. Performance on standardized national exams was poor, morale among the students and staff was relatively low, and the Physics Department was concerned.

The staff structure included a professor in charge, a senior lecturer who was the de facto principal course manager, and some graduate assistants. Among these, Reynolds was working as a teaching assistant in the course to support himself while he worked on his Ph.D. in education. Having heard about action research and finding it consistent with his view of the world, he proposed to the professor and lecturer in charge that they attempt an action research evaluation and reform of the course. With Greenwood's help, they got funding from the office of the vice president for academic programs to support the reform effort.

There followed a long and complex process, which Reynolds guided skillfully. It involved the undergraduate students, teaching assistants, lecturers, professor, and members of Reynolds's Ph.D. committee in a long-term process. It began with an evaluation of the main difficulties students had with the course and then involved the selection of a new text and pilot testing of the revised course. Reynolds guided this process patiently and consistently. Ultimately, the professor, the lecturer, instructors, teaching assistants, and students collaborated in redesigning the course through intensive meetings and debates.

One of the things they discovered was that the course had become unworkable in part because of its very nature. As new concepts and theories were developed in physics, they were added to the course, but there was no overall system for examining what materials should be eliminated or consolidated to make room for the new ones. The result was an increasingly overstuffed course that the students found harder and harder to deal with. In bringing the whole course before all the stakeholders and in examining the choice of a possible new textbook, the group was able to confront these issues.

There were many conflicts on issues of substance and authority during the process, and it was stressful for all involved. Yet they stayed together and kept at the process until they had completely redesigned the course. It was then piloted and the results were a dramatic improvement in student performance on national tests and a considerable increase in student satisfaction with the course.

Reynolds then wrote the process up from his detailed field notes and journals and drafted his dissertation. He submitted the draft to his collaborators for comment and revision and then explained to them the revisions he would make. He also offered them the options of adding their own written comments in a late chapter of the dissertation and of using either their real names or pseudonyms.

This iteration of the process produced some significant changes in the dissertation and solidified the group's own learning process. Eventually, many of the collaborators attended Reynolds's dissertation defense and were engaged in the discussion, the first time we know of that such a "collaborative" defense occurred at Cornell. Subsequently, this kind of defense with collaborators present has been repeated with another Ph.D. candidate (Grudens-Schuck, 1998).

Interestingly, although the process was extremely stressful for the participants, the results were phenomenally good for the students. A proposal was made to extend this approach to curriculum reform to other courses at Cornell, but the university administration was unprepared to underwrite the process, despite its obvious great success in this case.

Perhaps the reform of a single course does not seem like much of a social change, but we think this case has portentous implications. It demonstrates that action research-based reform initiated from a position of little power within a profoundly bureaucratic and hierarchical organization, the university, is possible. The value of the knowledge of each category of stakeholder was patent throughout, and the shared interests of all in a good outcome for the students helped hold the process together. That such reform is possible and successful means that those who write off the possibility of significant university reforms are simply wrong. Of course, it also shows that an isolated success does not add up to ongoing institutional change without a broader strategy to back it up. So it was a success, but an isolated one.

We are aware that the above two accounts constitute a very modest amount of case material to present in support of our contentions, but we believe that these cases at least give the reader a general sense of the direction of our thinking.

◆ Conclusion: How the Role of the University and Academic Intellectuals Would Change If Action Research Became the Centerpiece of University Social Research

Autopoesis Versus Participatory Evaluation

If action research were to become the central research strategy of universities, then universities would be connected to society in very different ways from those currently found. They would become social partners in a wide range of activities, and internal academic autopoesis would not cease, but its play would be drastically curtailed. Performance reviews of both faculty and administrators would necessarily involve evaluation by external stakeholders as well as by professional peers and students. We know from the history of the extension divisions of U.S. universities that stakeholder evaluations of the performance of university personnel are possible. However, we also know that these evaluations are rarely carried out in an action research framework. Developing strategies for the participatory evaluation of university performance would be an essential ingredient in this process.

The counterforces to university autopoesis would be experienced differently in different parts of the university. For many in engineering, the applied sciences, management, social services, and so on, the change would not be very noticeable, because they deal with external stakeholders all the time. For conventional social scientists, the change would be profound. After generations of claiming social relevance, they would be required to demonstrate the value of their work in practice to the satisfaction of extra-university stakeholders. For the extreme interpretivist and postmodernist humanists, this new situation would be a true shock. After claiming intellectual privilege and having taken an overwhelmingly critical posture toward society for decades while taking almost no positive social action, humanists would find the value of their work questioned in fundamental ways.[17] Many important elements of the humanities would be quite important to these changes (e.g., critical theory, discourse analysis, ethics). What would be different is that the value of these perspectives would have to be demonstrated effectively to extra-university stake-

160

holders rather than to a small circle of professional colleagues. Of course, some humanists have already taken on this role effectively, which shows that it is possible (for example, Jürgen Habermas, Hans-Georg Gadamer, Charles Taylor, Richard Rorty).

Democratizing Research

At the center of these changes would be the overall challenge to democratize research, making the external stakeholders an integral part of the knowledge-generation and evaluation processes. Rather than trying to continue the strategy of claiming that the university is the only social location where competent research is possible, academics would take their skills outside the university to collaborate in broader knowledge-generation and evaluation processes as professional researchers and supporters of collaborative research processes. This is not an entirely new role for universities or academics, but, in our ideal scenario, this role would become the principal one, with autopoetic academic activities reserved for a targeted set of internal university initiatives. With the social support universities might gain by reaching out to a broad array of stakeholders, it could be possible for university-based researchers to isolate a few areas in which research without clear social relevance and intellectual capacity building would be seen as essential for the university to support society more effectively. And we can imagine the determination of the areas for this kind of work arising from consistent problems emerging from action research collaborations in which action is inhibited by a lack of key basic knowledge or techniques. Devoting some of the social subsidy to universities to resolving these recurrent problems and then deploying the results through further action research work would be defensible, especially if determined in democratic dialogue both within the universities and with the external stakeholders. For a wonderful recent example of this kind of work, see Patti Lather and Chris Smithies's *Troubling the Angels* (1997).

Co-optation

We imagine that some readers of these last paragraphs will immediately see the specter of "co-optation" here. One of the core ideas behind the autopoetic university supposedly was to free intellectual work from censorship and direct control by powerful social interests. Yet we seem to be recommending that universities co-opt themselves. There is no doubt that the danger of co-optation of universities to the projects of power is ever present. However, in our view, part of the point of making action research central to university-society relationships is to break the current patterns of co-optation in the social sciences. As we have pointed out, universities are now in the employ of government research agencies and big private sector actors. Although they may do work of value to these stakeholders, universities characteristically ignore the interests of a much more diverse and larger group of stakeholders who do not have the power and money of governments and large corporations. Conventional social scientists and humanists do little to break out of this pattern. Thus the university is co-opted now, and the socially passive quality of the conventional social sciences and humanities is a clear indicator of this status. From our perspective, making a commitment to a broad array of action research efforts in support of a purposely diverse set of social stakeholders who are brought into the projects as partners and colearners can break this pattern of co-optation by the few in favor of service to the many.

Will this automatically avoid co-optation? Certainly not, but it will make the negotiation of subjects of research and the debate about projects to support and to avoid more public. In the end, our experience of action research suggests to us that collaboration does not lead so much to co-optation as it does to radical challenges to the ability of universities to generate and communicate relevant knowledge. In our years of practice, we have found the most difficult theoretical, methodological, and empirical challenges as social researchers in the process of conducting action research. Our collaborators constantly demand more and better knowledge from us to help them achieve their goals. So we have found action research more intellectually challenging than autopoetic university research. Retaining the integrity of our research as good-quality research has been less a problem than has been creating the new knowledge required by our projects.

◆ Notes

1. Preparing this chapter has been an extraordinarily fruitful intellectual experience because of the unique commitment to us made by the editors, Yvonna Lincoln and Norman Denzin, and the very helpful and challenging critiques provided by our readers: Orlando Fals Borda and Linda Smircich. All the comments were useful, but the final stages of this

process were particularly rewarding. Yvonna Lincoln would not let the issues go because she deems them so important, and she proceeded to press us with a wonderful combination of critique and encouragement. At her urging, we rethought and clarified parts of our arguments in a three-way e-mail dialogue that embodied an "ideal speech situation" in a powerful way. These debates both clarified our arguments and enhanced our sense that collegial critique is truly a gratifying experience, and we think the readers will be the beneficiaries of this process.

2. This point may strike some readers as too obvious to mention. However, we are constantly surprised by the conflation of applied research with qualitative methods by both academic colleagues and consumers of social research. We think this conflation is an irrational corollary of the assumption that, because applied research supposedly cannot be scientific, it must somehow be qualitative.

3. Readers will note that we argue that social research must be open to change, to diversity of viewpoints, and to complexity of response. Yet, in an apparently authoritarian posture, we view action research as the most valuable kind of social research. Thus it seems that we are not really advocating pluralism because we do not take a "live and let live" posture toward our academic colleagues. Despite the apparent logic of this criticism, we reject it because we are advocating a view of the mission of the social sciences that is completely consistent with the general justifications that social scientists have given for their work since the inception of these disciplines. Our colleagues have consistently argued that the social science should exist and be funded because of the contributions they make to understanding and thereby improving society. We simply point out that the practices of conventional academic social scientists violate these announced principles, whereas action research lives up to them.

4. The term *autopoetic* refers to the self-referential and self-generating character of a social situation in which a narrow group of socially interdependent individuals generate standards for each other and judge each other's performance without regard to their contextualization within the interests of society at large.

5. We were quite surprised to discover how little literature there is on the size, growth, and costs of university administrative structures over the past 20 years. It is as if the academic community has purposely turned a blind eye to the study of its own immediate environment. Because of this, these assertions arise mainly from anecdotal information. We do acknowledge that some administrative increases are the logical consequence of changed societal conditions, such as the explosion of information technology and the desire to provide more comprehensive student services, but we also strongly believe that a significant portion of the increase in administrative structure has to do with the hierarchization of power within universities and the centralization of university research as a "business." And we believe that, in many cases, this research management operation is both inept and directed at short-term profits at the expense of the creation of an enduring and mutually productive relationship between university research and society's needs.

6. Readers aware of the differences between the public universities in Europe and those in the United States will wonder how this argument applies to the European scene. It is different in important ways, but not as different as might be imagined. European public universities, to the extent that they lose social relevance, lose faculty members and money to private sector and government research institutes. Further, they increasingly lose their

students to universities that are managing these relationships better. Although public universities face a different kind of competitive situation, it remains a competitive situation, and their dependence on public funds makes them vulnerable to criticism from a wide variety of political groups. Thus, in the end, universities everywhere have a major stake in satisfying the needs of a broad spectrum of social groups.

7. The arguments we are about to launch are by no means new. The field of adult education, through the work of Paolo Freire (1970) and Budd Hall (1975), and the fields of participatory research through the pathbreaking work of Orlando Fals Borda (see Fals Borda & Rahman, 1991), Rajesh Tandon (1997), and many others, launched this critique long ago. Orlando Fals Borda also recently organized a monumental meeting of action researchers in Cartagena, Colombia *(Convergencia),* attended by more than 1,800 people. A great percentage of the participants came from university environments, and the problematic relationship between universities and liberating social research was explored from many angles. Some of the results of this meeting have been published already in Fals Borda (1998) and more appear in a special issue of *Studies in Cultures, Organizations and Societies* edited by Timothy Pyrch (1998).

8. See Scheurich (1997, chap. 3) for an excellent discussion of this in his critique of Elliot Mishler's work on postpositivist interviewing.

9. Oddly, interpretivist claims to excellence seem to be made on the basis of being so pure as to be "inapplicable"; they thus support the applied/pure distinction from the other side.

10. For an excellent and succinct discussion of action research, see Brown and Tandon (1983).

11. A critique of this kind of blind positivism was central to the ideas of the major social thinkers who gave rise to the social sciences in the first place (Adam Smith, Karl Marx, Max Weber, Emile Durkheim, John Dewey, and so on). A good source of current critiques is Scheurich (1997).

12. For a full discussion of these issues, see Stake (1995).

13. The name "Offshore Yard" is a pseudonym.

14. Levin observed much of this process because he served as a member of the local steering committee for the project. He recollects how little linkage there was across engineering and the social sciences at the outset.

15. A search conference is a democratically organized action research method for bringing a group of problem owners together for an intensive process of reflection, analysis, and action planning. For a more detailed description, see Greenwood and Levin (1998b).

16. Greenwood served as a member of Reynolds's Ph.D. committee and worked with him throughout this research. However, the ideas, processes, and interpretations offered here are those generated by Reynolds, not Greenwood. As Reynolds is now hard at work on secondary school reform, he has not made a further write-up of his work, so we encourage the interested reader to consult his dissertation directly (Reynolds, 1994).

17. Interestingly, the language and writing teachers within the university might well prosper under these conditions. Their work is mainly a service to the students. They have generally suffered from a lack of prestige in comparison to the literary critics and philosophers. Possibly this prestige hierarchy would be reversed or at least undermined by the changes we suggest.

◆ References

Bourdieu, P. (1988). *Homo academicus* (P. Collier, Trans.). Stanford, CA: Stanford University Press.

Brown, L. D., & Tandon, R. (1983). Ideology and political economy in inquiry: Action research and participatory research. *Journal of Applied Behavioral Sciences, 19,* 277-294.

Chomsky, N., Zinn, H., Lewontin, R. C., Montgomery, D., Wallerstein, I., Katznelson, I., Nader, L., Ohmann, R., & Siever, R. (1997). *The Cold War and the university: Toward an intellectual history of the postwar years.* New York: New Press.

Dewey, J. (1954). *The public and its problems.* Athens: Ohio University Press. (Original work published 1927)

Diggins, J. P. (1994). *The promise of pragmatism.* Chicago: University of Chicago Press.

Eurich, N. (1985). *Corporate classrooms: The learning business.* Princeton, NJ: Carnegie Foundation for the Advancement of Teaching/Princeton University Press.

Fals Borda, O. (Ed.). (1998). *People's participation: Challenges ahead.* New York: Apex.

Fals Borda, O., & Rahman, M. A. (Eds.). (1991). *Action and knowledge: Breaking the monopoly with participatory action-research.* New York: Apex.

Freidson, E. (1985). *Professional powers: A study of the institutionalization of formal knowledge.* Chicago: University of Chicago Press.

Freire, P. (1970). *Pedagogy of the oppressed* (M. B. Ramos, Trans.). New York: Herder & Herder.

Greenwood, D. J., & González Santos, J. L. (with Alonso, J. C., Markaide, I. G., Arruza, A. G., Nuin, I. L., & Amesti, K. S.). (1992). *Industrial democracy as process: Participatory action research in the Fagor Cooperative Group of Mondragón.* Assen-Maastricht, Netherlands: Van Gorcum.

Greenwood, D. J., & Levin, M. (1998a). Action research, science, and the co-optation of social research. In T. Pyrch (Ed.), Convergence [Special issue]. *Studies in Cultures, Organizations and Societies, 5*(1).

Greenwood, D. J., & Levin, M. (1998b). *Introduction to action research: Social research for social change.* Thousand Oaks, CA: Sage.

Greenwood, D. J., & Levin, M. (1998c). The reconstruction of universities: Seeking a different integration into knowledge development processes. *Concepts and Transformation, 2*(2), 145-163.

Grudens-Schuck, N. (1998). *When farmers design curricula: Participatory education for sustainable agriculture in Ontario, Canada.* Unpublished doctoral dissertation, Cornell University.

Hall, B. (1975). Participatory research: An approach for change. *Convergence, 8* (2), 24-32.

Kuhn, T. S. (1962). *The structure of scientific revolutions.* Chicago: University of Chicago Press.

Lather, P., & Smithies, C. (1997). *Troubling the angels: Women living with HIV/ AIDS.* Boulder, CO: Westview.

Lewin, K. (1948). *Resolving social conflicts.* New York: Harper & Row.

Lewontin, R. C. (1997). The Cold War and the transformation of the academy. In N. Chomsky, H. Zinn, R. C. Lewontin, D. Montgomery, I. Wallerstein, I. Katznelson, L. Nader, R. Ohmann, & R. Siever, *The Cold War and the university: Toward an intellectual history of the postwar years.* New York: New Press.

Pyrch, T. (Ed.). (1998). Convergence [Special issue]. *Studies in Cultures, Organizations and Societies, 5*(1).

Readings, B. (1996). *The university in ruins.* Cambridge, MA: Harvard University Press.

Reynolds, M. A. (1994). *Democracy in higher education: Participatory action research in the Physics 101-102 Curriculum Revision Project at Cornell University.* Unpublished doctoral dissertation, Cornell University.

Scheurich, J. J. (1997). *Research method in the postmodern.* London: Falmer.

Shor, I. (1996). *When students have power: Negotiating authority in a critical pedagogy.* Chicago: University of Chicago Press.

Stake, R. E. (1995). *The art of case study research.* Thousand Oaks, CA: Sage.

Tandon, R. (1997). *Struggle for knowledge: A personal journey.* Paper presented at the Convergence World Congress, Cartagena, Colombia. Available Internet: http://www. parnet.org

Toulmin, S. (1990). *Cosmopolis: The hidden agenda of modernity.* Chicago, University of Chicago Press.

Toulmin, S., & Gustavsen, B. (Eds.). (1996). *Beyond theory: Changing organizations through participation.* Philadelphia: John Benjamins.

Whyte, W. F. (1991). *Social theory social action: How individuals and organizations learn to change.* Newbury Park, CA: Sage.

4

For Whom?

Qualitative Research,

Representations, and

Social Responsibilities

Michelle Fine, Lois Weis,

Susan Weseen, and Loonmun Wong

I grew up in a world in which talking about somebody's mama was a way of life, an everyday occurrence. For all of us, boys and girls, it was a kind of game or performance. Whether we called it "capping," "snapping," "ranking," "busting," or simply "the dozens," most of it was ridiculous, surreal humor bearing very little resemblance to reality: "Your mom's so fat she broke the food chain"; "Your mama's skin's so ashy she was a stand-in for Casper the Friendly Ghost"; "Your mama's so dumb she thought ring-around-the-collar was a children's game." More than anything, it was an effort to master the absurd metaphor, an art form intended to entertain rather than to damage. . . .

You would think that as a kid growing up in this world I could handle any insult, or at least be prepared for any slander tossed in the direction of my

AUTHORS' NOTE: This chapter expands on an earlier article by the first two authors titled "Writing the 'Wrongs" of Field Work" (Fine & Weis, 1996). The data reported here were collected with the generous support of both the Spencer Foundation and the Carnegie Foundation.

mom—or, for that matter, my whole family, my friends, or my friends' families. But when I entered college and began reading the newspaper, monographs, and textbooks on a regular basis, I realized that many academics,
journalists, policymakers, and politicians had taken the "dozens" to another
level. In all my years of playing the dozens, I have rarely heard vitriol as
vicious as the words spouted by Riverside (California) county welfare director Lawrence Townsend: "Every time I see a bag lady on the street, I wonder, 'Was that an A.F.D.C. mother who hit the menopause wall—who can
no longer reproduce and get money to support herself?' " I have had kids
tell me that my hair was so nappy it looked like a thousand Africans giving
the Black Power salute, but never has anyone said to my face that my whole
family—especially my mama—was a "tangle of pathology." Senator Daniel
Patrick Moynihan has been saying it since 1965 and, like the one about your
mama tying a mattress to her back and offering "roadside service,"
Moynihan's "snap" has been repeated by legions of analysts and politicians,
including Dinesh D'Souza, the boy wonder of the far Right. (Kelly, 1997,
pp. 1-2)

In this essay, we work through the decisions we made about how to represent the consequences of poverty on the lives of poor and working-class
men and women in times of punishing surveillance and scrutiny by the
state. We have discussed some of these issues—alternately called *ethics,
dilemmas,* and simply *research*—with friends and colleagues. Some think
we make "much ado about nothing." Others are relieved that we are "saying aloud" this next generation of troubles. Many wish we would continue
to hide under the somewhat transparent robe of qualitative research. And
yet we are compelled to try to move a public conversation about researchers and responsibilities toward a sense of research for social justice.

Because we write between poor communities and social policy at a time
of Right-wing triumph, and because we seek to be taken seriously by both
audiences, we know it is essential to think through the power, obligations,
and responsibilities of social research. Entering the contemporary montage of perverse representations of poor and working-class men and
women, especially people of color, we write with and for community orga-
nizers, policy makers, local activists, the public, and graduate students.

This chapter represents a concrete analysis—an update, perhaps—of
what Michelle Fine (1994) has called "working the hyphen":

Much of qualitative research has reproduced, if contradiction-filled, a colonizing discourse of the "Other." This essay is an attempt to review how qual-

itative research projects have *Othered* and to examine an emergent set of activist and/or postmodern texts that interrupt *Othering.* First, I examine the hyphen at which Self-Other join in the politics of everyday life, that is, the hyphen that both separates and merges personal identities with our inventions of Others. I then take up how qualitative researchers work this hyphen . . . [through] a messy series of questions about methods, ethics, and epistemologies as we rethink how researchers have spoken "of" and "for" Others while occluding ourselves and our own investments, burying the contradictions that percolate at the Self-Other hyphen. (p. 70)

We seek not necessarily to engage in simple reflexivity about how our many selves (Jewish, Asian, Canadian, woman, man, straight, gay) co-produce the empirical materials on which we report, although clearly that is an important piece of work (see Weis & Fine, in press). Instead, we gather here a set of self-reflective points of critical consciousness around the questions of how to represent responsibility, that is, transform public consciousness and "common sense" about the poor and working classes, write in ways that attach lives to racial structures and economies, and construct stories and analyses that interrupt and reframe the victim-blaming mantras of the 1990s.

Writing against the grain, we thought it would be useful to speak aloud about the politics and scholarship of decisions we have made.

◆ Flexing Our Reflexivities

In the social sciences, both historically and currently, the relationship between researcher and subject has been "obscured in social science texts, protecting privilege, securing distance, and laminating the contradictions" (Fine, 1994, p. 72). There has long been a tendency to view the self of the social science observer as a potential contaminant, something to be separated out, neutralized, minimized, standardized, and controlled. This bracketing of the researcher's world is evident in social science's historically dominant literary style (Madigan, Johnson, & Linton, 1995), which is predicated on a "clarion renunciation" of the subjective or personal aspects of experience (Morawski & Bayer, 1995), particularly those of researchers. As Ruth Behar (1993) explains, "We ask for revelations from others, but we reveal little or nothing of ourselves; we make others vulnerable, but we ourselves remain invulnerable" (p. 273). Our informants are then left carrying the burden of representations as we hide behind the cloak of alleged neutrality.

169

Although it may be true that researchers are never absent from our texts, the problem of just how to "write the self [and, we would add, our political reflexivities] into the text" (Billig, 1994, p. 326) remains. Simply briefly inserting autobiographical or personal information often serves to establish and assert the researcher's authority, and ultimately produces texts "from which the self has been sanitised" (Okely, 1992, p. 5). But flooding the text with ruminations on the researcher's subjectivities also has the potential to silence participants/"subjects" (Lal, 1996).

It should also be pointed out that a call for the inclusion of subjective experience of the researcher into what has traditionally been conceived of as subject matter bears different implications for differently situated researchers. In the hands of relatively privileged researchers studying those whose experiences have been marginalized, the reflexive mode's potential to silence subjects is of particular concern. It is easy for reflexivity to slip into what Patricia Clough (1992) has called a "compulsive extroversion of interiority" (p. 63). In the words of Renato Rosaldo (1989), "If classic ethnography's vice was the slippage from the ideal of detachment to actual indifference, that of present-day reflexivity is the tendency for the self-absorbed Self to lose sight altogether of the culturally different Other" (p. 7). Yet from an entirely different and overlapping perspective, some critical race theorists (e.g., Ladner, 1971; Lawrence, 1995; Matsuda, 1995) have suggested that for people of color whose stories have not been told, "the assertion of our subjective presence as creators and interpreters of text [is a] political act" (Lawrence, 1995, p. 349). According to Donna Haraway (1991), "Vision is always a question of the power to see—and perhaps of the violence implicit in our visualizing practices" (p. 192); who is afforded—or appropriates—this power to see and speak about what is seen as well as what is hidden from scrutiny is a question that is at the heart of our examinations of our social responsibilities to write and re-present in a time of ideological assault on the poor. Thus we seek to narrate a form of reflexivity in our concerns with representation and responsibilities in these very mean times.

◆ The Textual Subject

In the remainder of this chapter, we reflect on the materials drawn for a book written by Michelle Fine and Lois Weis about poor and working-class city dwellers at the end of the 20th century, *The Unknown City* (1998). In this work, Michelle and Lois center the voices, politics, disappointments, and hopes of young urban adults. These men and women—African American, white, and Latino/Latina, poor and working-class—render oral histories of their struggles, victories, and passions, detailing lives filled with work (and its absence), schooling, family life, spirituality, sexuality, violence on the streets and in their homes, and social movements that seem no longer vibrant. Our analyses suggest that these young adults, men and women, constitute an unknown, unheard-from, and negatively represented constituency of the American democracy. Between the ages of 23 and 35, with neither the resources nor the sense of entitlement typically narrated by members of Generation X, they have been displayed and dissected in the media as the cause of national problems. Depicted as being the reason for the rise in urban crime, they are cast as if they embody the necessity for welfare reform, as if they sit at the heart of moral decay. Although much of contemporary social policy is designed to "fix" them, our investigation reveals that they have much to say back to policy makers and the rest of America.

The late 1990s witnessed a flood of books written about and sometimes despite those who have been grouped together as the poor and working class. But the members of this group, particularly the young, are fundamentally unknown, at once quite visible as "moral spectacle" (Roman, 1997) and yet fundamentally invisible (A. J. Franklin, personal communication, October 14, 1997). As our nation walks away from their needs, desires, strengths, and yearnings, we abandon a generation. Millions of poor and working-class children continue to grow up amid the wreckage of global corporate restructuring, in the shadows of once-bustling urban factories, reinvigorated U.S. nationalism and racism, and a wholesale depletion of the public safety net, at the same time witnessing increasing violence in their communities and often in their homes. And mostly, they blame themselves and each other. The state retreat from the social good and corporate flight from urban centers, the North, and the United States are shockingly absent as blame is doled out. As calls to reverse civil rights, affirmative action, welfare, and immigration policies gain momentum, it is noteworthy that the voices of the men and women in the poor and working classes are never heard.

The Unknown City reveals not only common pains among members of the poor and the working class, but a deeply fractured urban America in the late 20th century. In spite of legislation and social politics designed to lessen inequality and promote social cohesion in the 1960s, we stand as a nation in the late 1990s deeply divided along racial, ethnic, social class, and gender lines. Our goals in conducting the research for *The Unknown City*, then, were to examine the commonalities among Americans and the fractured nature of U.S. society, focusing on what we call "communities of difference," as low-income people settle for crumbs in one of the richest nations in the world. We sought, further, to place these voices at the center of national debates about social policy rather than at the margin, where they currently stand. This chapter consciously reflects back on the work of writing that book—the headaches and struggles we experienced as we entered the battle of representations happening on, about, and despite but rarely with poor and working-class urban dwellers at the end of the 20th century. Amid economic dislocation and a contracted public sphere, we seek to re-present men and women navigating lives of joy and disappointment, anger and laughter, despair and prayer.

Much as we sought to escape the narrow confines of demographic, essentialist categories, what we heard from both Jersey City and Buffalo tended to bring us back to these categories. That is, much as we all know, read, teach, and write about race, class, and gender as social constructions (see Fine, Powell, Weis, & Wong, 1997), loaded with power and complexity, always in quotation marks, when we listened to the taped interviews with African American men living in Jersey City or Buffalo, they were strikingly different from those of white men, or Latinas, or African American women. Indeed, both the very distinct material bases and cumulative historical circumstances of each of these groups and the enormous variety "within" categories demanded intellectual and political respect. So we tell the "big story" of people living in poverty as well as the particular stories narrated through gender, race, and ethnicity. Thus we write with and through poststructural understandings of identity and possibility, ever returning to "common" material bases (the economy, state, and the body) as we move through the nuances of "differences."

◆ On Framing the Work

On Community

Perhaps our most vexing theoretical dilemma swirled around the question, So, what constitutes a community? How do we write about real estate, land-bounded communities like Buffalo or Jersey City, geographically valid, zip-code-varied, "real" spaces in which we nevertheless found so little in the way of psychologically or socially shared biographies or visions?

We recognized from our theoretical interests, confirmed by the narratives we collected, that profound fractures, and variation, cut through lives within these communities. Simple demographic nuances, by race/ethnicity, gender, class, generation, and sexuality marked dramatic distinctions in experience. Within local neighborhoods or racial/ethnic groups, gender, sexuality, and generational divisions boldly sever what may appear to be, at first glance, internal continuities (see West, 1993). For instance, within the presumably "same" part of Jersey City, African Americans refer to local police practices with stories of harassment and fear, whereas whites are far more likely to complain about a rise in crime and to brag about a brother-in-law who's a cop. Whereas Jersey City whites described the "good old days" of economic security and pined for the day when they'd be moving to Bayonne, African Americans from the same block harbored few wistful memories of "good old days" and routinely avoided "getting stopped at red lights" in Bayonne, lest their stay be extended beyond what they expected.

At historic moments of job insecurity and economic hard times, the presumed harmony of working-class/poor communities is ravaged by further interior splits, finger-pointing, blame, and suspicion. Coalitions are few, even if moments of interdependence-for-survival are frequent. Within homes, differences and conflicts explode across genders and across generations. A full sense of community is fictional and fragile, ever vulnerable to external threats and internal fissures. Although there is a class-based story to be told, a sense of class-based coherence prevails only if our methods fail to interrogate differences by race/ethnicity, gender, and sexuality. And yet, at the same time, commonalities across cities—by demography and biography—are all the more striking.

We could, therefore, write about life within these two urban communities, Jersey City and Buffalo, as though the notion of community were unproblematic, a geographic space of shared experience. Or we could, with equal ease and discomfort, present a book about African American men and women, white men and women, and Latinos and Latinas as though each group experiences a social world totally insulated from those of the others. Although some of our data press toward the latter, our theoretical and political inclinations make us look toward the former, searching for common ground, shared languages, and parallel experiences. Our text tries to speak, at once, in these two dialects, to issues of the common and the specific, without diluting either. We decided that *The Unknown City* would offer two chapter forms: one that privileges the unique experiences of groups (for example, African American men) and another that explores the ways in which poor and working-class people travel over similar terrain (schooling, motherhood, crime) in their lives. Scripting a story in which we float a semifictional portrait of each community, we layered over an analytic matrix of differences "within." For our analysis—within and between cities—we delicately move between coherence and difference, fixed boundaries and porous borders, neighborhoods of shared values and homes of contentious interpretations.

On "Race"

Robin Kelly (1997) describes his latest book as "a defense of black people's humanity and a condemnation of scholars and policymakers for their inability to see complexity" (p. 4). Some academics have addressed this complexity: Henry Louis Gates (1985) has written beautifully about "race," always using quotes on the word; Michael Dyson (1993) argues against narrow nationalistic or essentialist definitions for either skin color or language; Kimberlé Crenshaw (1995) forces us to theorize at the intersections of race and gender; and Stuart Hall (1981) narrates the contextual instability of racial identities, as do Michael Omi and Howard Winant (1986). Like these theorists, our informants use/employ/conceive of race as both a floating unstable fiction and a fundamental, unerasable aspect of biography and social experience. Indeed, some of our informants, like the one quoted below, suggest that "race" constitutes inherently indefinable territory, offering narratives not so much of denial as complexity.

Mun: Your dad?

Luisa: Yes, my dad was the craziest Puerto Rican you had ever seen in the 70s. Oh my Lord.

Mun: What is your mom's background?

Luisa: Mom, Mom was raised Catholic, but in my mother's days, when an Irish and German woman went with a Chinese guy, in those days that was like, oh no, no that cannot happen. My grandfather had to drop his whole family for my grandmother, so they could be together. Everybody disowned him in his family.

174

Mun: Because he married a—

Luisa: Yeah, he married my grandmother.

Mun: What about your mom's side?

Luisa: That is my mom's side.

Mun: What about your grandfather's side?

Luisa: My grandfather, he was in Vietnam, World War II, oh, I forgot the name. It was a very big war, that I know.

Mun: Korean War?

Luisa: Yeah, something like that, I just can't remember what it was. Yeah, he had honors and everything my mother told me.

Mun: So you looked very different?

Luisa: Yeah, I'm a mixture.

Mun: You have Chinese blood?

Luisa: Right. I got Irish and German, I got Puerto Rican and Italian, I have a lot. I'm a mixed breed.

Mun: I was wondering. The first time I saw you I thought you were from the Middle East.

Luisa: From the Middle East?

Mun: Yeah.

Luisa: Oh, golly gee, no. I'm, like, really mixed. I'm like everything. I got all these different personalities that just come out all the time. I swear to God. No lie. No lie.

When we began our interviews in Jersey City and Buffalo, we too were taken by poststructural thinking on questions of "race." With Stuart Hall (1997) particularly in mind, willing to acknowledge the artificiality, the performances, and, indeed, the racist "roots" of the notion of race (1/32nd drop of blood and the like), we constructed an interview protocol that generously invited our informants to "play" with "race" as we had. So we asked, in many clever ways, for them to describe time- and context-specific racial identifications—when they fill out census forms, when they walk through supermarkets, when alone or among friends. Informants of color tried to be polite and follow us in our "play," but by hour three they grew exasperated with these questions. White interviewees were either sure we were calling them racist or avoided identifying as white—instead speaking about being Irish, Italian, or human. Needless to say, the "play-fulness" of the questions didn't work.

Many argued that race *shouldn't* make much of a difference.[1] And we wanted, too, to write that book, not out of liberal foolishness but out of profound political commitments to class, race, and gender analyses and to "what should be." And yet, as we listened to our data, the life stories as narrated were so thoroughly drenched in racializing discourse that readers couldn't *not* know even an "anonymous" informant's racial group once they read the transcript. Personal stories of violence and family structure, narrative style, people's histories with money, willingness to trash (pub-licly) violent men and marriages, access to material resources, relations with kin and the state, descriptions of interactions with the police—all were talked through "race."

"Race" is a place in which poststructuralism and lived realities need to talk. "Race" is a social construction, indeed. But "race" in a racist society bears profound consequences for daily life, identity, and social movements and for the ways in which most groups "other." But how we write about "race" to a deeply race-bound audience worries us. Do we take the cate-gory for granted, as if it is unproblematic? By so doing, we (re)inscribe its fixed and essentialist positionality. Do we instead problematize it theoreti-cally, knowing full well its full-bodied impact on daily life? Yes, "race" *is* a social construction, but it is so deeply confounded with racism that it bears enormous power in lives and communities. To the informants with whom we spoke, "race" does exist—it saturates every pore of their lives. How can we destabilize the notion theoretically at one and the same time as we recognize the lived presence of "race"?

To give a trivial, but telling, example: Here's a problem that may appear, at face value, to be a "sampling problem" related to "race." We struggled in both cities to find "equally poor" and "equally working-class" African American, Latino/Latina, and white young adults so that compari-sons by race/ethnicity would not be confounded by class. Guess what? The world is lousy with confounds. Although we did find poor and working-class whites, the spread and depth of their poverty was nowhere near as severe as in the African American sample. Our ambitious search for sam-pling comparability, in spite of our meticulous combing of raced neighbor-hoods, lost hands down to the profound "lived realities" of multigener-ational poverty disproportionately affecting poor and working-class families of color. What may appear to be a methodological problem has been revealed as constitutive of the very fabric of society. Neither problematizing nor (re)inscribing "race" in our writing will help us, as a society, to confront the very real costs and privileges of racial categorization.

◆ Inform(ing) and Consent: Who's Informed and Who's Consenting?

With frame more or less clear, we move to the interviews. At this point, we struggle through the ethics of constructing narratives with poor men and women, each paid $40 for an interview. So, we ask, what is consent? And for whom? Mun Wong confronted this dilemma often. The informed consent form for our interviews states:

> We are conducting interviews with young adults on their perceptions of high school experiences and since. We are particularly interested in discussing concerns, attitudes, and aspirations (then and now) developed during your years in high school. . . . I, [respondent's name], agree to participate in this study on the urban experiences of young adults growing up in Jersey City during the 1980s and 1990s. The interviews will be audiotaped, transcribed and written up in a book. No names will be attached to the interviews.

The consent form sits at the contradictory base of the institutionalization of research. Although the aim of informed consent is presumably to protect respondents, informing them of the possibility of harm in advance and inviting them to withdraw if they so desire, it also effectively releases the institution or funding agency from any liability and gives control of the research process to the researcher. Commenting on this standard formulaic piece of the research process, M. Brinton Lykes (1989) writes, "Reflecting on my experiences with the [informed consent] form revealed the complexity of both my role as researcher/activist and the constraints on developing collaboration between subjects in a context of real power imbalances" (p. 177). She continues:

> The informed consent form which I introduced as a mechanism for "protecting the subjects" of the research project, was instead a barrier and forced me to confront the chasm between the needs and demands of research conducted within the boundaries of the university and the systems of trust and mistrust and of sharing and withholding that were already a part of this collaboration. (p. 178)

In our work, we have come to understand how the introduction of an informed consent form requires analysis as much as what are routinely and easily considered as "data"—such as the narratives of our participants. The (apparent) rapport that Mun had with respondents seemed to unravel whenever he presented the consent form. Many of them asked him, "What is this for?" He was always embarrassed when an explanation was required, in many cases simply mumbling an explanation. In some cases, contrary to official research protocol, he presented the consent form in the second part of the interview. Even so, many women simply signed the form as just another procedural matter, without reading the entire document. Their (apparent) nonchalance probably reflected their general attitude toward procedural matters. These respondents—women on welfare—are constantly required to read bureaucratic forms that are convoluted and technical, and are told to sign off on others' responsibilities while signing on to their own.

The informed consent form forced us to confront and contend with the explicitly differential relationships between the respondents and ourselves; it became a crude tool—a conscience—to remind us of our accountability and position. Stripping us of our illusions of friendship and reciprocity, it made "working the hyphen" even more difficult. No matter how hard Mun tried to downplay "differences" and find a common ground from which to proceed, our participants' responses to the informed consent form reminded us to dispel any artificial attempts at displacing differences (Borland, 1991).

Judith Stacey (1991) has argued that (feminist) ethnography depends upon human relationships, engagement, and attachment, with the research process potentially placing research subjects at grave risk of manipulation and betrayal. She writes:

> Situations of inauthenticity, dissimilitude, and potential, perhaps inevitable, betrayal situations are inherent in fieldwork research. For no matter how welcome, even enjoyable, the field worker's presence may appear to locals, social work often represents an intrusion and intervention into a system of relationships, a system of relationships that the researcher is far freer than the researched to leave. The inequality and potential treacherousness of this relationship is inescapable. (p. 113)

Dorcy came up to Mun after he finished his interview with Regina. She told him that she also wanted to be part of the study, and he told her that he would get to her when he completed the interviews with Melissa and Diane. So for the next 3 weeks or so, whenever Mun ran into Dorcy, she would ask, "When is my turn?" Mun would always give his typical reply to women who kept requesting interviews: "You are next, next week, okay?" "You better make sure," Dorcy laughed. Her repeated but friendly gestures, along with her gigglish laughs and timid smiles, were constant reminders: "I thought you said it was my turn."

At the beginning of their first interview, Dorcy and Mun sat facing each other in Room 216. Mun started off with his script: "Thanks for doing this. As you know, I am interviewing women about their experiences on welfare but also try to get a picture of their lives. This is a consent form and you may want to read it first. If you agree to abide by whatever is written there, please sign it. And I am going to tape-record this. Also, if you do not feel comfortable with whatever, just say you are going to skip it, okay?" She signed the form and the taped interview began.

Mun: How was your family . . . when you were growing up?

Dorcy: Oh, I had . . . I had a good growing . . . growing . . . I had it good. My mother, my father. My father died when I was 12. So, he was . . . he was always there for us, ya know. My mother, she's good. She's a strong woman. She love us and she take care of us . . . things we need. . . . and she help us out a lot . . . yeah.

Mun: How many brothers and sisters do you have?

Dorcy: Excuse me?

Mun: Brothers and sisters?

Dorcy: Oh . . . um . . . three sisters, I make three sisters, and five brothers. I have . . . one of my brother died of AIDS, in '91 . . . of November . . . he died of AIDS.

Mun: What number are you?

Dorcy: I'm 25.

Mun: I mean, number in the family.

Dorcy: Oh, I'm . . . I'm in the middle.

Mun: [laughs]

Dorcy: [laughs] . . . I'm the middle . . . middle child.

Mun: Is it good?

Dorcy: It's good.

Mun: I mean . . . what . . .

Dorcy: It has its ups and downs, but it's good.

Mun: What do you mean?

Dorcy: Huh?

Mun: Ups and downs?

Dorcy: Because like, the oldest get things first and the baby get . . . more . . . the most things before the middle child will get. [And the interview continued.]

At first glance, this extract does not seem different from interviews with the other women. But if one looks more closely—and especially if one listens to the tape—Dorcy's hesitations, monosyllabic answers, and reluctance to speak up become noticeable. This is in sharp contrast to her speech outside of the interview process, as well as that of most of the other women interviewed. At the end of the day, Mun recorded this short memo in his field notes:

Interviewed Dorcy today. She has been urging me for the past two weeks to interview her. And when I was talking to her today, she was giving me monosyllabic answers and speaking in such a soft tone that I could hardly make out a word she was speaking. She was driving me nuts with her inarticulations and "I don't know" . . . she refuses to elaborate her stories and discuss about her life. I don't know why I chose her. . . . I should have stuck to my initial choice of either Mary or Annie.

Thinking that their bantering and gestures were a process in developing a friendship, Mun felt a sense of betrayal and wondered whether Dorcy's friendliness had been a kind of staged performance designed to win his confidence.

Judith Stacey (1991) contends that in our fieldwork, the lives, loves, and tragedies that informants share with researchers are ultimately data— "grist for the ethnographic mill, a mill that has a truly grinding power" (p. 113). When the women are informed and they consent, does this mean that their stories (and aspects of their lives they choose—or feel compelled—to share) no longer belong to them? Does, for example, Mun inform the welfare agency of their problems with particular staff members? Does he interrupt or simply collect narration of the women's racial antagonisms, between and among groups? What about the time Rosita told him in the corridor that she saw her batterer ex-boyfriend walking with the program administrator, Deborah, the person who generously opened the program for his research? How best to respond to the information presented in one of the focus groups that Rosita had been sexually harassed by one of the instructors? Mun found himself working between an organization that was generous enough to allow us "access" and the allegiance and hard-earned trust of respondents. In many of these cases, he was the opportunistic "fly on the wall," recording observations without seeming to become entangled in these ethical conundrums (Roman, 1993). But, as Stacey has noted, ethnographic method is more likely to leave subjects exposed to exploitation: The greater the intimacy, according to Stacey, the greater the danger. And yet, contrary to this view, many of the women and men we interviewed both recognized and delightfully exploited the power inequalities in the interview process. They recognized that we could take their stories, their concerns, and their worries to audiences, policy makers, and the public in ways that they themselves could not, because they would not be listened to. They (and we) knew that we traded on class and race privilege to get a counternarrative out. And so they "consented." They were both informed and informing.

◆ Then, the Stories

Moving from worries of consent to worries about "bad stories" we collected:

Mun: Do you feel that your word is not trusted, that you need someone else to say, you need a lawyer or psychiatrist to say everything is okay now?

Tara: Because of DYFS [Division for Youth and Family Services], yes.

Mun: But you can't have . . .

Tara: They won't, yeah. They won't just take you for your word, no. You need to have—

Mun: You need to have somebody else say that for you?

Tara: Yes. DYFS, yes.

Mun: How would DYFS treat your kids, though?

Tara: Because when you get child, they say I put their life in danger, because I did, but I was . . . I was in jail, I was in the psychiatric ward. They had to do the best interest for the children, I couldn't take care of them at the time.

Mun: Oh, so DYFS took your kids?

Tara: Yeah, so DYFS gave them to their father. I'm in court now.

Mun: At least it's not foster care, though.

Tara: That's what I said. They're with family. They might hate it there, they can't stand it. My kids say that they're treated worse.

Mun: They hate their father?

Tara: No, they don't hate their father, they hate their grandmother, they hate the mother-in-law, they hate their grandmother. They don't like their grandmother.

Mun: His mother?

Tara: Yeah, they don't like their aunts, their uncles.

Mun: They are a lot of Puerto Ricans?

Tara: They're all Puerto Ricans, but my kids were always like the outcasts because they didn't like me so my kids, my kids, I mean, George was 7 years old, 7 years of George's life, George had to have seen his grandmother six times. Nicole, in the 3 years of her life, never seen them. You know, my kids got dumped into a family that they know nothing about.

What does it mean to uncover some of what we have uncovered? How do we handle "hot" information, especially in times when poor and working-class women and men are being demonized by the Right and by Congress? How do we connect theoretically, empirically, and politically troubling social/familial patterns with macrostructural shifts when our informants expressly do not make, or even refuse to make, the connections?

The hegemony of autonomous individualism forces a self-conscious, imposed theorizing (by us) of especially "bad stories," well beyond the perspectives expressed by most of our informants. So, for instance, what do we do with information about the ways in which women on welfare virtually have to become welfare cheats—"Sure he comes once a month and gives me some money. I may have to take a beating, but the kids need the money"—in order to survive (Edin & Lein, 1997)? A few use more drugs than we wished to know about; most are wonderful parents, but some underattend to their children well beyond neglect. These are the dramatic consequences, and perhaps also the "facilitators," of hard economic times. To ignore the information is to deny the effects of poverty, racism, and abuse. To report these stories is to risk their more than likely misuse, all the while *not* studying the tax evasion, use of drugs, and neglect of children perpetrated by elites.

In a moment in history when there are few audiences willing to reflect on the complex social roots of community and domestic violence, the economic impossibilities of sole reliance on welfare, or even the willingness to appreciate the complexity of love, hope, and pain that fills the poor and working class, how do we put out for display the voyeuristic dirty laundry that litters our transcripts? Historian Daryl Michael Scott (1997), in his provocative book *Contempt and Pity,* places in historical perspective the perverse historic use of the "damaged black psyche" by both the Left and the Right today. To what extent do we contribute to this perverse legacy? Is it better if white poor and working-class people are also portrayed as "damaged"? At the same time, isn't it unethical to romanticize, and thereby deny, the devastating impact of the current and historic assault on poor and working-class families launched through the state, the economy, neighbors, and sometimes kin? We are left, then, with two questions: First, must we (i.e., social scientists) document damage in order to justify claims about oppression and injustice? Second, what is the role of the public intellectual in rewriting—that is, interrupting—the "commonsense" script of "their" damage (and, of course, our wholeness) and offering up, instead, a discourse of national damage, outrage, and demands for justice?

With interviews over, we continue to struggle with how best to represent the stories that may do more damage than good, depending on who consumes/exploits them—stories that reveal the adult consequences of physical and sexual abuse in childhood; stories that suggest it is almost impossible to live exclusively on welfare payments, which encourages many to "lie" about their incomes so that they self-define as "welfare cheats"; stories in which white respondents, in particular, portray people of color in gross and dehumanizing ways; data on the depth of violence in women's lives, across race/ethnicity. To what extent are we responsible to add, "Warning! Misuse of data can be hazardous to our collective national health"?

There are some academics writing about such concerns (Cross, 1991; hooks, 1990; Lather, 1991), but few who write about and work with activists to reimagine social research for social justice (for wonderful such work, see Austin, 1992; Lykes, 1989; Saegert, 1997). It is up to all of us to figure out how to say what needs to be said without jeopardizing individuals and feeding perverse social representations (McCarthy et al., 1997).

As with bad stories, we worried about our voyeuristic search for "good stories." While engaged in interviewing, the research assistants would gather informally and share stories. We talked about respondents not showing up for their interviews, the lives of interviewees, "funny things that happened along the way," our pain, and our early understanding of the material. The words and phrases thrown around included "interesting," "boring," "nothing out of the ordinary," "you should have heard this," and "this one has great stories." But just what did we mean by "great stories"?

Great stories can be read as allegories that shed light on both the level of content and the implications of that content. Allegory, as James Clifford (1986) reminds us,

> denotes a practice in which a narrative fiction continuously refers to another pattern of ideas or events. It is a representation that "interprets" itself. . . . [It is] a story [that] has a propensity to generate another story in the mind of its reader (or hearer), to repeat and displace some prior story. . . . A recognition of allegory emphasizes the fact that realistic portraits, to the extent that they are "convincing" or "rich," are extended metaphors, patterns of associations that point to coherent (theoretical, esthetic, moral) additional meanings. . . . Allegory draws special attention to the narrative character of cultural representations, to the stories built into the representational process itself. (pp. 99-100)

We worry that what appear to be great stories might, however, feed our collective misunderstandings and renderings of the poor. Like experimenters who are inevitably inflicted with and inflicting "experimenter's bias," qualitative researchers carry misconceptions and "alluring fictions" (Clifford, 1986) of the subject. We enter the scene looking for stories and may, at times, "unintentionally behav[e] in such a way as to make the prophesied event more likely to occur" (Suls & Rosnow, 1988, p. 168). By looking for great stories, we potentially walk into the field with constructions of the "other," however seemingly benevolent or benign, feeding the politics of representation and becoming part of the negative figuration of poor women and men.

For us, the fundamental "good story" is not simply one laced with "social problems" such as homelessness, welfare, and/or sexual harassment—a victim who is harassed, battered, and overwhelmed by problems. In retrospect, we admit that we also searched for agents who "resisted," enacting the role of the critic of the state and/or economic relations. As Mun's interviews with women on welfare proceeded, he always hoped that they would be perfect critics, able to pierce the veil of structured and state hypocrisy. It is interesting to note how so many hegemonic and victim-blaming positions were narrated by these profoundly oppressed men and women; judgments about "others" often resonated with a broad cultural discourse of holding victims of poverty, racism, and sexual violence accountable for their woes. In many of our interviews, poor women on welfare blamed other women, labeling them "welfare queens," "neglectful mothers," and "insensitive bureaucrats." Our own romanticized images of the resistor—one who desires to speak out against injustice and to act with a collective—turned on us.

Once we collect "great (and not so great) stories" from our respondents, the next difficult stage is the interpretation, representation, and analysis of data. We have, at times, consciously and deliberately left out some of these "great stories" that have the potential to become "bad data" to buttress stereotypes, reaffirm the ideology and rhetoric of the Right, and reinscribe dominant representations. As Hurtado and Stewart (1997) have written, the repetition of certain hurtful and vicious opinions and attitudes will inflict pain on those who are the "victims." In such cases, what is required is "minimal documentation, when views are all-too-familiar and oppressive, while holding ourselves and others to a very high standard of analytic depth when work carries such a high risk of causing suffering in those already the objects of daily racism" (p. 308)—and a close focus, as well, on the mundane.

What happens to the dull details of negotiating daily life in poverty that do not capture our attention in the way that "great stories" do?

> Well, I take . . . I get $424 a month, okay? And I get $270 in food stamps, so I take . . . there's four weeks to a month, so I take . . . I take the $270 and I divide it by four. And that's what I spend on food. It's just me and my daughters. And my oldest don't eat that much and I don't eat. . . . I only eat once a day. I only eat dinner. I'm not hungry in the morning and I don't have breakfast. I have a cup of coffee or hot chocolate. My little one is the one that eats a lot. And whatever I don't . . . like I spend $65 a week in food. I go and I buy

meat every day and I buy their breakfast, their lunch, her snacks for school. And whenever I can . . . I work at night . . . I work . . . if I get a call I go and clean somebody's house. I do that. Their father gives me money, you know. So I do whatever I . . . you know, whatever it takes, you know? Shovel your snow . . . [laughs] I don't care. You know, to me money's money, as long as your kids got what they need. But basically their father helps me the most. You know, he'll come in . . . oh, my dad does this, too, and I get really pissed off at him. He'll come in and he'll start looking through my cabinets and in my refrigerator, and my closet. "Well, what do you have here?" And it's like, "I'm fine. Johnny's coming over later." "No! Blah, blah, blah." And he'll go out and he'll come back with food, and their father's always coming in looking through the refrigerator, and things like that, you know? I always . . . my kids have food, so that's good, you know? They never go hungry. You know, I . . . I hate to say this, but if I had . . . I mean, if it came to where my kids were gonna go hungry, I'd sell my body. To hell with that! My kids ain't gonna starve, you know? I'd do what it takes. I would give two shits. People could . . . my friends could tell me whatever they wanted. I have a . . . I have two friends that sell their bodies for money for their kids. And thank God, I have to knock on wood, I never had to take a loan, if I had to, I would. If that's what it took to feed my kids. . . . I mean, if their father . . . a lot of people that are on welfare have husbands worth shit. They don't care. If they had a father, but I guess that's, if that's what it took. . . . I would try every aspect before doing that. But if that's what it really took to feed my kids, that's what I would do. I would do whatever it takes to feed and clothe my kids, you know, and put a roof over their head. I wouldn't care what the hell it was. I guess that's what I would do, you know?

When we listen to and read narratives, researchers (we) tend to be drawn to—in fact, to *code for*—the exotic, the bizarre, the violent. As we reflect on narratives of poverty we nevertheless feel obligated to explore meticulously the very tedious and mundane sections of the transcripts, those huge sections that are not very exciting: the mundane spots, where "they" (the informants) do what "we" (the researchers) admit that "we" do—walk their kids to school, read the newspaper, turn on the television for a break, look for a doctor they can trust, hope their children are safe on the way home from school. These mundane rituals of daily living—obviously made much more difficult in the presence of poverty and discrimination, but mundane nonetheless—are typically left out of ethnographic descriptions of life in poverty. They don't make very good reading, and yet they are the stuff of daily life. We recognize how careful we need to be so that we do not construct life narratives spiked only with the hot spots.

◆ Different Methods, Different Stories

Once the interviews are complete, triangulation surfaces as a critical element in the practice of social science: "adding" one layer of data to another to build a confirmatory edifice. In quantitative data analysis, triangulation occurs when multiple items within the same scale measure the same construct, or when two different scales join to measure the same construct. In psychological research in particular, and sociological research at times, the tendency is to use qualitative methods to supplement quantitative data.

However, in our work, conducted primarily through narratives but also through surveys on political engagement, we were not looking for a simple, coherent synthesis of data or methods. With a firm reliance on multiple methods, we sought to cross over, converse with, and tap into the different kinds of data; we searched for the very contradictions between methods that would most powerfully inform policy. We learned, as Fine and Weis (1996) have written elsewhere:

> Methods are not passive strategies. They differently produce, reveal, and enable the display of different kinds of identities. To be more specific, if individual interviews produce the most despairing stories, evince the most minimal sense of possibility, present identities of victimization, and voice stances of hopelessness, in focus groups with the same people the despair begins to evaporate, a sense of possibility sneaks through, and identities multiply as informants move from worker to mother, to friend, to lover, to sister, to spiritual healer, to son, to fireman, to once-employed, to welfare recipient. In the context of relative safety, trust, comfort, and counter-hegemonic creativity offered by the few free spaces into which we have been invited, a far more textured and less judgmental sense of self is displayed. In these like-minded communities that come together to trade despair and build hope, we see and hear a cacophony of voices filled with spirit, possibility, and a sense of vitality absent in the individual data. (pp. 267-268)

We recognize that different methodologies are likely to illuminate different versions of men's and women's understandings of welfare, jobs, education, and violence. Convergence is unlikely and, perhaps,

187

undesirable. Following a poststructuralist emphasis on contradiction, heterogeneity, and multiplicity, we produced a quilt of stories and a cacophony of voices speaking to each other in dispute, dissonance, support, dialogue, contention, and/or contradiction. Once women's and men's subjectivities are considered and sought after *as if* multiple, varied, conflicting, and contradictory, then the "data elicited" are self-consciously dependent upon the social locations of participants and the epistemological assumptions of the methods. We join Kum Kum Bhavnani (1993), who demands that multiple methods and a deep commitment to engaging with differences (particularly between researcher and researched) form the core of provocative, politically engaged social science, so that we "cannot be complicit with dominant representations which reinscribe inequality. It follows from a concern with power and positioning that the researcher must address the micropolitics of the conduct of research and . . . given the partiality of all knowledges, questions of differences must not be suppressed but built into research" (p. 98). Denzin and Lincoln (1994) suggest:

> Qualitative research is inherently multimethod in focus (Brewer & Hunter, 1989). However, the use of multiple methods, or triangulation, reflects an attempt to secure an in-depth understanding of the phenomenon in question. Objective reality can never be captured. Triangulation is not a tool or a strategy of validation, but an alternative to validation (Denzin, 1989a, 1989b, p. 244; Fielding & Fielding, 1986, p. 33; Flick, 1992, p. 194). The combination of multiple methods, empirical materials, perspectives and observers in a single study is best understood, then, as a strategy that adds rigor, breadth, and depth to any investigation (see Flick, 1992, p. 194). (p. 2)

◆ In Whose Voice?

Mark, a white working-class informant tells us:

> It goes into another subject where blacks, um, I have nothing against blacks. Um, whether you're black, white, you know, yellow, whatever color, whatever race. But I don't like the black movement where, I have black friends. I talk to them and they agree. You know, they consider themselves, you know, there's white trash and there's white, and there's black trash and there's

blacks. And the same in any, you know, race. But as soon as they don't get a job, they right away call, you know, they yell discrimination.

In whose voice do we write? Well, of course, our own. But we also present long narratives, colorful and edited, drawn with/from informants. Some of these narratives, particularly from the sample of working-class and poor white men, contain hostile, sometimes grotesque references to "others"—people of color, women, black men on the corner. As theorists we refrain from the naïve belief that these voices should stand on their own or that voices should (or do) survive without theorizing. However, we also find ourselves differentially theorizing and contextualizing voices. That is, those voices that historically have been smothered—such as the voices of working-class white women, and men and women of color—we typically present on their own terms, perhaps reluctant to surround them with much of "our" theory (Weis, Marusza, & Fine, 1998). And yet when we present the voices of white men who seem eminently expert at fingering African American men for all the white men's pain and plight, we theorize boldly, contextualize wildly, rudely interrupting "them" to reframe "them" (Weis & Fine, 1996; Weis, Proweller, & Centrie, 1997).

Is this an epistemological double standard in need of reform, or is it a form of narrative affirmative action, creating discursive spaces where few have been in the past? Aida Hurtado and Abigail Stewart (1997), in a fascinating essay titled "Through the Looking Glass: Implications of Studying Whiteness for Feminist Methods," argue that feminist scholars should self-consciously underplay (e.g., not quote extensively) hegemonic voices in our essays and as relentlessly create textual room for counterhegemonic narratives. Although we agree, we also think it is vitally important for us to analyze, critically, what it is that white men are saying about us, about "them," about economic and social relations. To do this, we interpret their words, their stories, and their assertions about "others."

This raises what we have come to think of as the "triple representational problem." We ponder how we present (a) ourselves as researchers choreographing the narratives we have collected; (b) the narrators, many of whom are wonderful social critics, whereas some, from our perspective, are talented ventriloquists for a hateful status quo; and (c) the "others" who are graphically bad-mouthed by these narrators, such as caseworkers blamed for stinginess and disrespect by women on welfare, African American men held responsible for all social evils by white men, and police officers held in contempt by communities of color, which have endured much abuse at the hands of the police. Do we have a responsibility to theorize the agency/innocence/collusion of these groups, too? When white men make disparaging comments about women of color, do we need to re-present women of color and denounce and re-place these representations? If not, are we not merely contributing to the archival representations of disdain that the social science literature has already so horrifically chronicled?

Given that all of these participants deserve to be placed within historical and social contexts, and yet power differences and abuses proliferate, how do theorists respect the integrity of informants' consciousness and narratives, place them within social and historical context, and yet not collude in the social scientific gaze, fixation, moral spectacularizing (Roman, 1997) of the poor and working-class? There are no easy answers to these dilemmas. In *The Unknown City* we try to contextualize the narratives as spoken within economic, social, and racial contexts so that no one narrator is left holding the bag for his or her demographic group, but indeed there are moments when, within the narratives, "others"—people of color, caseworkers, men, women, the neighbor next door—are portrayed in very disparaging ways. Then we wage the battle of *representation*. We work hard to figure out how to represent and contextualize our narrators, ourselves, and the people about whom they are ranting. We try, with the tutelage of historians Joan Scott (1992), Michael Katz (1995), Robin Kelly (1997), and Daryl Scott (1997), sociologist Joyce Ladner (1971), literary critic Eve Sedgwick (1990), and psychologist William Cross (1991), to understand how and why these binaries, these categories of analysis, these "others," these splittings, and these accusations are being cast at this moment in history, and who is being protected by this social science focus on blame (Opotow, 1990). Nevertheless, at times audiences have been alarmed at the language in our texts, at the vivid descriptions and the portraits, for instance, of seemingly cold and heartless social workers. We are working on these issues, and we welcome help from others who are also struggling with both theory and empirical data.

◆ What's Safe to Say Aloud—and by Whom?

How hard it is for us to *think* we can choose to become writers, much less *feel* and *believe* that we can. What have we to contribute, to give? Our own expectations condition us. Does not our class, our culture as well as the white man tell us writing is not for women such as us?

The white man speaks: *Perhaps if you scrape the dark off your face.*
Maybe if you bleach your bones. Stop speaking in tongues, stop writing left-
handed. Don't cultivate your colored skins nor tongues of fire if you want to
make it in a right-handed world. (Anzaldúa, 1981, p. 166)

We have collected stories for the past 6 years on communities, economic and racial relationships, and individual lives deeply affected by
public policies and institutions that had been rotten and rotting for many
years before that. And yet these very same public policies and institutions,
the ones about which we have deeply incriminating data, are today being
excised, yanked away from communities as we speak—public schools,
welfare, social services, public housing. Positioning a critique of the public
sphere as it evaporates, or, more aptly, as it is targeted for downsizing and
for demise, seems an academic waste of time. At its worst, it anticipates
collusion with the Right. Nevertheless, the criticisms are stinging:

Tamara: I didn't want to be with the father of my children anymore.
And at that time he really gave me a lot of headaches. "If you don't
stay with me, then I'm not gonna help you with the kids." Which
he really didn't do, which I'm thankful. But I just figured, "Well,
the hell with it. Then I'll work . . . get the welfare." Because I pay
$640 for this apartment. That's a lot of money for a two-bedroom
apartment, you know? And the welfare only gives me $424, so I
have to make up the difference. And plus I have a telephone, you
know. I have cable for my daughters, you know. And it's just a lot
of money. And I figure, you know, I figured, well, I couldn't make
it on my own. I wasn't making enough to make it on my own back
then, so I had to go on welfare. So I did it, and it was . . . I didn't
like it. I didn't like sitting there. I didn't like the waiting. I didn't
like the questions they asked me, you know?

Mun: What kind of questions did—

Tamara: Well, they asked me if I was sexually active, how many times I
went to bed with him, you know? And I told the guy, "I'm sorry,
but that is none of your business," and I refuse to answer the questions. Because to me, well what, they ask you if you, he asked me if
I slept with black men or white men, Puerto Rican men. What was
my preference. And to me that was the questions—

Mun: Was this on a form, or he—

Tamara: No, he was just asking questions, you know? And I refused to answer them, you know. And he kind of like got upset. "We have to ask you this." I was like, "Bullshit." You know, they just wanted to, they asked, he asked me how many times I had sex in a day, and just really, you know, if I douched, if I was clean, if I took a shower. I don't think these are any of your business, you know? I take a shower every night and every day, you know? I think those are stupid questions he asked. I was, he asked me how many men I had in my life that I had, you know, if I have more than one man. And I turned around and told him, "I'm not your mother." I never heard of questions like—[laughs]

Mun: Neither have I. [laughs]

Tamara: They asked the weird questions.

Mun: So, how, what was the procedure like?

Tamara: It was embarrassing. Like, with Medicaid, for kids it's good. For kids, you know, you can go anywhere you want with the Medicaid. You can go to the doctors for kids. You know, they pay for braces. When it comes to an adult, I was going to, I was hemorrhaging. I was going to a doctor. I'd been bleeding since December, okay, and they're telling me, I've been going to a gynecologist through the welfare. "It's normal, it's normal. Don't worry about it. It's normal." So last week I was getting ready, for the past week I was feeling really dizzy and really weak, and I said the hell with it. Let me go see a gynecologist. And I paid her. Thank God, you know, the Medicaid took care of the hospital. But I had to pay her $700 for the procedure that I had to have done. [laughs] I had to do it. It was either that or bleed to death, you know. [laughs] But a lot of doctors, I asked her, because she used to take Medicaid. And I asked her, "Why don't you, you know, take Medicaid anymore?" And a lot of doctors that don't, doctors tell you because they don't pay them. She said she's been waiting for people that were on Medicaid to get paid for 2 years, 3 years, bills—that's how old the bills are and she's still waiting to get paid.

Our responsibility in this work, as we see it, is not to feed the dismantling of the state by posing a critique of the public sector as it has been, but instead to insist on a state that serves its citizenry well and responsibly. That is, social researchers must create vision and imagination for "what could be" and demand the resurrection of an accountable public sphere that has a full and participatory citizenship at its heart. Then we can layer on the critiques of "what has been." That said, it is important to note that it is not so easy when many are just waiting to use our narrative words to do away with welfare; when Brett Schundler, mayor of Jersey City, is desirous of getting voucher legislation passed in a city in which public schools enjoy little to no positive reputation; when Charles Murray (1984) will abduct our phrases as he paints poor women as lazy and irresponsible. Creating a safe space for intellectual, critical, and complicated discussion when the Right has been so able and willing to extract arguments that sustain the assault may be a naïve wish, but it is a worthwhile one.

◆ On "Safe Spaces"

In conducting our research for *The Unknown City*, we heard from young women and men who grew up within the working-class and poor segments of our society how they view economic opportunities; how they spin images of personal and collective futures, especially as related to the power of schooling; how they conceptualize the shrinking public sector, the econ-omy, labor, and the military; and how they reflect upon progressive social movements that have historically and dramatically affected their ancestors' and their own life chances. We heard about a disappearing public sphere but we tripped upon, as well, those urban pockets of counterhegemonic possibility, sites of critique, engagement, and outrage, excavated by these young men and women. Amid their despair lies hope. And hope appears to be cultivated in these "safe" spaces. So how to write on and through these spaces without romanticizing the tiny corners of sanctuary and possibility available to and created by the poor and working-class in the late 1990s? If people are surviving with hope and optimism, is devastation justified or managed?

The spaces into which we have been invited provide recupera-tion, resistance, and the makings of "home." They are not just a set of geographic/spatial arrangements, they are theoretical, analytic, and spa-tial displacements—a crack, a fissure in an organization or a community. Individual dreams, collective work, and critical thoughts are smuggled in and then reimagined. Not rigidly bounded by walls/fences, the spaces often are corralled by a series of (imaginary) borders where community intrusion and state surveillance are not permitted. These are spaces where trite social stereotypes are fiercely contested. That is, these young women and men, in their constant confrontation with harsh public representations of their races, ethnicities, classes, genders, and sexualities, use these spaces to break down these public images for scrutiny, and to invent new ones.

These spaces include the corners of the African American church where young men ponder how to "take back the streets" to "save the young boys"; the lesbian and gay center carved out quietly by working-class late adolescents and young adults seeking identities and networks when their geographic and cultural contexts deny them sexual expression; the Head Start and EPIC (Every Person Influences Children) programs in which poor mothers, and sometimes fathers, come together to talk about the delights and the minefields of raising children in a culture showered in racism and decimated by poverty; the cultural arts programs where men and women join self-consciously across racial and ethnic borders to create what is "not yet," a space, a set of images, a series of aesthetic products that speak of a world that could be (Weis & Fine, in press).

Spaces such as these spring from the passions and concerns of community members; they are rarely structured from "above." They may be one-time fictions, transitory, or quite stable. They can be designed to restore identities devastated by the larger culture, or they may be opportunities to try on identities and communities rejected by both mainstream culture and local ethnic groups. These spaces hold rich and revealing data about the resilience of young adults without denying the oppression that threatens the borders and interiors of community life amid urban poverty.

Legitimately, one may ask (and some have) whether we have any business floating through or writing about these sequestered quarters. Does our presence affect or interrupt the music of life within "free spaces"? Does our social scientific voyeurism shatter the sanctity of that which is presumably (although recognizably not) "free"?

We come down on these questions, for the moment at least, by presenting two different incidents. One occurred in a basement office in which New Jersey community activists met to discuss local politics. We were welcomed for the initial interview, but the notion of our continued presence clearly provoked discomfort. Not asked to return, we left—in good stead and with enormous respect. In contrast, for instance, we have been invited into some spaces (e.g., an EPIC parenting group, a black church, a community center, a lesbian and gay club) in which members, directors, and others indicate they are eager for documentation—anxious for others to know who they "really" are, what functions their programs serve, how deeply spiritual and religious "those teenage mothers" can be, how organized and supportive "those gays and lesbians" are. They have welcomed us into their spaces to "exploit" our capacity—our class and professional positions and networks—and our willingness to write and to testify to those aspects of community life that the media ignore, that stereotypes deny, that mainstream culture rarely gets to see. And yet we seek not to romanticize resilience—for these spaces represent severe critique as well as warm comfort.

◆ On Responsibilities

We have certainly read much, and even written a fair amount, about researchers' subjectivities (Fine, 1994). Our obligation is to come clean "at the hyphen," meaning that we interrogate in our writings who we are as we coproduce the narratives we presume to "collect," and we anticipate how the public and policy makers will receive, distort, and misread our data. It is now acknowledged that critical ethnographers have a responsibility to talk about our identities, why we interrogate what we do, what we choose not to report, how we frame our data, on whom we shed our scholarly gaze, who is protected and not protected as we do our work. What is our participatory responsibility to research with and for a more progressive community life? As part of this discussion, we want to try to explain how we, as researchers, have worked with communities to capture and build upon exciting community and social movements. In other words, we will put forward parts of our ever-evolving political agenda, sharing the kinds of scholarship/action that we are focusing upon and how our work has been reshaped by the activism in the communities studied.

Thus far, in Jersey City and Buffalo we have been able to document how state policies and local economic/social shifts have affected young women's and men's belief systems, worldviews, social consciousness. Through individual interviews we have gathered much of this information. Through focus groups (e.g., in the lesbian and gay club, in the African American and white churches, in the EPIC parenting group, in the Latina homeless shelter, in the Pre-Cap college program for young adolescents), we have been able to create settings in which our interviewees have begun to weave together analyses about their commitments, for instance, to the "next generation of African American boys" or to "practicing the ways of

195

my grandmother" around Latina spiritual rituals. An activist nun and a local director of Head Start have both invited us to work more closely with groups of women and men in their programs, running focus groups that would raise questions, press issues, and help the participants reshape programs. A college preparation program for "at-risk" youths (labels!) asked us for an evaluation to assist with further funding. In the EPIC group, we were told that the engagement of several members was raised due to the kind of individual and group work in which we were involved. For these women the group interviews offered them a way of piecing together the strengths of their lives, encouraging forward movement as they were raising their families in the midst of poverty. Indeed, Lois Weis was asked to facilitate an EPIC group on a long-term basis.

Further, throughout the course of our 5 years of research, we have moved across the researcher-researched hyphen and into a community of activists to apply our work to support local policy and community efforts. Michelle Fine testified at state hearings in Trenton and in Jersey City on the state takeover of the local schools, advocating with community groups that the state remain in control until authentic local participation can be encouraged and sustained; Mun Wong coordinated a project among women on welfare who were eager to document the differential supermarket prices of similar items at different points in the month and in different markets in the community; Lois Weis supplied testimony in support of continual funding for EPIC; and in Jersey City, we have provided census and qualitative data to city council members from the Latino community. Our graduate students have been deeply involved in various communities as they engage in dissertation work in an Irish community center, an African American church, a neighborhood center that serves white working-class youth, a neighborhood arts center, and numerous others. In all such spaces, graduate students are "giving back" to the communities in which they are working. Across communities, numerous conversations have taken place with key policy makers on a number of issues arising from our data.

We take for granted that the purpose of social inquiry in the 1990s is not only to generate new knowledge but to reform "common sense" and inform critically public policies, existent social movements, and daily community life. A commitment to such "application," however, should not be taken for granted. This is a(nother) critical moment in the life of the social sciences, one in which individual scholars are today making decisions about the extent to which our work should aim to be "useful."

We have colleagues who embrace the commitment to "application," as we do, even if some think it is naïve for us to imagine our being able to infiltrate current policy talk on life within poor and working-class communities; other colleagues have long seen their own scholarship as explicitly aimed toward political and social change (see the work of Gittell, 1990, 1994; Lykes, 1994; Mullings, 1984; Piven & Cloward, 1971; Powell, 1994). And yet we hear a growing chorus of colleagues (on the Right and the Left) who presume that if one is interested in, engaged by, or drawn to policy, one's scholarship is less trustworthy, tainted by advocacy, commitments, passion, or responsibilities. This latter position was perhaps in retreat for a moment in time, but it seems to be returning to the academy in well-orchestrated volume. We do, of course, reject this latter position, but would ask again that academics who see y/our work as deeply nested in community life (recognizing that the notion of "community" is up for grabs) come together to argue cogently our responses to the litany: Is this science? Is this advocacy? Is only progressive work biased? Is this politics or policy?

We must probe to find the sites of intellectual leverage, responsibility, and obligation through which our work can begin to fissure public and political discourse, shifting the ideological and material grounds on which poor and working-class men and women are now being tortured. That said, we take our responsibilities to these communities seriously, and Lois and Michelle are educating their graduate students to work with—not on or despite—local community efforts.

It is important to note another "underground debate" within community studies, which concerns the tension between representing historically oppressed groups as "victimized" and "damaged" or as "resilient" and "strong." This may seem an artificial and dangerous dichotomy—we think it is. But we have encountered colleagues within feminism, critical race theory, poverty work, disability studies, and, most recently, queer theory who argue across these intellectual stances, with these two "choices" carved out as the (presumably only) appropriate alternatives. We share the worries, but worry more about the fixed "choices" that are being offered. Simple stories of victimization, with no evidence of resistance, resilience, or agency, are seriously flawed and deceptively partial; they deny the rich subjectivities of persons surviving amid devastating social circumstances. Equally dreary, however, are the increasingly popular stories of individual heroes who thrive despite their difficulties, denying the burdens of surviving amid such circumstances.

We stretch toward writing that spirals around social injustice and resilience, that recognizes the endurance of structures of injustice and the powerful acts of agency, that appreciates the courage and the limits of individual acts of resistance but refuses to perpetuate the fantasy that "victims" are simply powerless. That these women and men are strong is not evidence that they have suffered no oppression. Individual and collective strength cannot be used against poor and working-class people as evidence—"See? It's not been so bad!" We need to invent an intellectual stance in which structural oppression, passion, social movements, and evidence of strength, health, and "damage" can all be recognized and theorized without erasing essential features of the complex story of injustice that constitutes urban life in poverty.

We take solace in the words of many of our African American male informants—drawn from churches and spiritual communities—who testify, as one said, that "only belief and hope will save our communities. We have come a long, long way . . . and we have much further to go. Only belief will get us through." Amid the pain, the despair, survives hope. This, too, is a big part of community life, rarely seen in the light of day.

◆ Conclusion

We end this essay with a set of what might be called ethical invitations or, put more boldly, ethical injunctions. We offer these in the spirit of wedging open and contributing to a conversation about researcher responsibility, recognizing, of course, that questions of responsibility-for- whom will, and should, forever be paramount—because the "whom" is not a coherent whole, no single constituency, no unified community, group, or set of "others," and because the context in which we write today will change tomorrow, and so too will the readings of this text.

We write on the ethics of responsibility because we don't want to write only for and with friends; we hope to write in ways that contribute to a reshaping of the "common sense" about poverty, the economy, and social and human relations. We consider, then, the ethics of writing research in the interest of social justice and the ethics of publishing what Richardson (1995) has called "writing-stories." We offer the ideas below as lenses through which social analyses might be continually reassessed and (re)imagined.

On Reframing What Seems Like Good and Bad News

Our first injunction is that social researchers dare to speak hard truths with theoretical rigor and political savvy. By that, we mean that "bad stories," like "good stories," are always partial but/and deserve a hearing. They reveal as much as they conceal, whether informants seem too close or too far. Having witnessed the Right-wing assault on education, health care, welfare, and immigration in this country, we have become more convinced, not less, that progressive activists and researchers need to interrogate with deliberation—not camouflage with romance—some of the rough spots in our work. To obscure the bad news is to fool no one. Indeed, the suffocation of "bad stories" only tempers the very real stories of oppression we seek to tell. That there are (unevenly distributed) damaging consequences to all living under advanced capitalism, racist social relations, violent gendered relations, and homophobic community life is no great secret. That individuals engage in activities or behaviors deemed illegal, unethical, or immoral in contexts in which justice and fairness have no role is evidence of social injustice—not a reason to blame victims. That many thrive despite the odds is equally well-known. How survival, damage, and oppressive social/economic relations meld together is the task of explanation that lies before us. How to inform and encourage social movements for "what could be" is the task at hand. Thus, indeed, we err on the side of telling many kinds of stories, attached always to history, larger structures, and social forces, offered neither to glamorize nor to pathologize, but to re-view what has been, to re-imagine what could be in communities of poverty and the working class, and to re-visit, with critical speculation, lives, relations, and communities of privilege.

Upon Reflections

We ask, second, that beginning and veteran researchers, and all those in between, pose a set of questions to themselves as they move through the recursive "stages" of social analysis. These question are listed in no particular order, and have few right answers. But, we insist, they should be asked, as we all write what we write in a world not (necessarily) prepared to hear.

1. *Have I connected the "voices" and "stories" of individuals back to the set of historic, structural, and economic relations in which they are situated?* We

mean this in no linear fashion, in no simple determinative progression, but only to recognize that what people say has a relation to the structures and ideologies around them in ways that will almost certainly not be narrated by interviewees themselves. The work of theory is to articulate these relations, excavating how qualitative narratives or even quantitative responses on a 5-point Likert scale are nested within a system of historic and material conditions.

2. *Have I deployed multiple methods so that very different kinds of analyses can be constructed?* In our work on *The Unknown City,* we found that individual and focus group interviews generated very different kinds of narrations—neither more true than the other, but different, particularly when it came to individuals expressing optimism or pessimism about the future and their place in it. We came to understand that it was important to theorize why and how responses took different forms, not seeking simple confirmation, or concluding too easily that there is contradiction, or one narration is more "true" than the other. Instead, we struggled to cultivate a theoretical relation between possibly very different responses, understanding that the issue of "triangulation" is not simple. Different people do, in fact, seem the same but different at times. The same person can do the same. We cannot see this as "contradictory," or worse, useless data, as this can cause us to miss important facets of individual and community life.

3. *Have I described the mundane?* As we have noted, we found it hard to resist the temptation to surf through our transcripts with a coding eye toward the exotic or the violent. Coding tends to lend itself to that. And yet most of our transcriptions reveal the boring details of life on the ground, day-to-day interactions with friends, kin, neighbors, children, and television. These portraits, although rarely stunning, constitute much of life in poverty and should not be relegated to the edited-out files.

4. *Have some informants/constituencies/participants reviewed the material with me and interpreted, dissented, challenged my interpretations? And then how do I report these departures/agreements in perspective?* This is not a call for handing over veto power, but only a call for conversation, negotiated interpretations, texts in which multiple interpretations flourish, in which challenges are integrated into the manuscript. Much of this work can take place in follow-up focus groups to either participant observation work or individual interviews.

5. *How far do I want to go with respect to theorizing the words of informants?* That is, with respect to what Fine and Weis (1996) have called the triple representation problem, have you worked to understand your contribution to the materials/narrations provided and those silenced? Have you

worked to explain to readers the position from which informants speak? Have you worked to recast the person(s) whom the informant chooses to "blame" or credit for social justice or injustice (be it a social worker, the informant's mother, black men)? Again, we do not hold out that all researchers must answer yes to these questions—only that researchers (faculty and graduate students) must ask themselves these questions and understand why it is that some answers must be no.

6. *Have I considered how these data could be used for progressive, conservative, repressive social policies?* How might the data be heard? Misread? Misappropriated? Do you need to add a "warning" about potential misuse?

7. *Where have I backed into the passive voice and decoupled my responsibility for my interpretations?* That is, where have you hidden your own authority behind "their" narrations or "their" participatory interpretations?

8. *Who am I afraid will see these analyses? Who is rendered vulnerable/responsible or exposed by these analyses? Am I willing to show him/her/them the text before publication? If not, why not? Could I publish his/her/their comments as an epilogue? What's the fear?*

9. *What dreams am I having about the material presented?* What issues are pulling at/out of your own biography? Have you over- or underplayed them?

10. *To what extent has my analysis offered an alternative to the "commonsense" or dominant discourse? What challenges might very different audiences pose to the analysis presented?*

None of the above questions is intended to stifle scholarly license or to insist that there is one "right way" to answer them. Rather, these questions are intended to expand our work by helping us to recognize the potential influence of our writings: the pulls, fantasies, projections, and likely responses of very different kinds of audiences and the responsibility we have, therefore, to anticipate the relation between the texts we produce and the "common sense" that awaits/confronts them. By asking ourselves these questions, we push the issues, forcing ourselves to deal with what are serious dilemmas in our research. We repeat: not all of us will answer in the same ways. But we will clarify why we answer in the ways we do.

On Cautions

After reflections, we suggest that particularly those of us who write on questions of structural relations to the micropolitics of life in poverty should draft and publish a "Legend of Cautions: Ways to Misread, Misappropriate, and Misuse Presented Analyses." That is, we imagine such a legend that warns readers how *not* to read our work—for example, how not to use evidence of welfare fraud to cut payments or resurrect a welfare surveillance system, how not to exploit the real fears inside poor communities to generate support for the building of more prisons, how not to appropriate the anger of poor communities at their public schools as a rallying cry for vouchers likely to serve few but the relatively privileged. We recommend many, many drafts of these warnings, but anticipate that without such warnings the likelihood of our analyses being misappropriated is much higher than the likelihood of our analyses being deployed for ends of which we would approve.

On Educating Students in Multiple Genres

We exit this chapter with our fiercest injunction: that we have an ethical responsibility to retreat from the stance of dispassion all too prevalent in the academy and to educate our students toward analyzing, writing, and publishing in multiple genres at one and the same time—in policy talk, in the voices of empiricism, through the murky swamps of self-reflective "writing-stories," and in the more accessible languages of pamphlets, fliers, and community booklets. That is, if we are serious about enabling our students to be fluent across methods, to be engaged with community struggles, and to theorize conditions of social (in)justice, we must recognize that flickers and movements for social change happen in varied sites—courtrooms, legislative offices, the media, community-based organizations, and church groups, as well as the academy—and therefore through varied texts.

We recognize full well that there may be consequences for nontenured faculty who attempt to write across audiences in the way we are suggesting. Tenure review committees and external reviewers associated with these committees may not "count" writing other than traditional research (including qualitative analyses) as evidence that an individual is deserving of tenure or later promotion to full professor. It is important for junior faculty to establish credibility within a traditional research community. As one writes for a scholarly audience, however, it is possible to exercise simultaneously the option for writing in multiple tongues. We are not urging graduate students and junior faculty to write for broad-based audiences at the expense of writing for scholarly journals, authoring monographs, and so forth. Although the academy is changing, we recognize that the moves are slow, and resistance is always high.

With this caveat in mind, reflections on our responsibilities as social researchers must punctuate all texts we produce. Without such reflection, in the name of neutrality or researcher dispassion, we collude in a retreat from social responsibility, and the academy remains yet another institution without a soul in a world increasingly bankrupt of moral authority.

◆ Note

1. Legal scholar Patricia Williams (1997) tells a story of her preschool-age son, who was seemingly unable to identify the colors of objects. Asked what color the grass was, for example, he would respond, "I don't know" or "It makes no difference." Eventually, Williams discovered that "the well-meaning teachers at his predominantly white school had valiantly and repeatedly assured their charges that color makes no difference. . . . Yet upon further investigation, the very reason that the teachers had felt it necessary to impart this lesson in the first place was that it did matter, and in predictably cruel ways: some of the children had been fighting about whether black people could play 'good guys' " (p. 3).

◆ References

Anzaldúa, G. (1981). Speaking in tongues: A letter to Third World women writers. In C. Moraga & G. Anzaldúa (Eds.), *This bridge called my back: Writings by radical women of color* (pp. 165-173). New York: Kitchen Table/Women of Color Press.

Austin, R. (1992). "The black community," its lawbreakers, and a politics of identification. *Southern California Law Review, 65,* 1769-1817.

Behar, R. (1993). *Translated woman: Crossing the border with Esperanza's story.* Boston: Beacon.

Bhavnani, K. K. (1993). Tracing the contours: Feminist research and feminist objectivity. *Women's Studies International Forum, 16,* 95-104.

Billig, M. (1994). Repopulating the depopulated pages of social psychology. *Theory and Psychology, 4,* 307-335.

Borland, K. (1991). That's not what I said: Interpretive conflict in moral narrative research. In S. B. Gluck & D. Patai (Eds.), *Women's words: The feminist practice of oral history* (pp. 63-76). New York: Routledge.

Brewer, J., & Hunter, A. (1989). *Multimethod research: A synthesis of styles.* Newbury Park, CA: Sage.

Clifford, J. (1986). On ethnographic allegory. In J. Clifford & G. E. Marcus (Eds.), *Writing culture: The poetics and politics of ethnography* (pp. 98-121). Berkeley: University of California Press.

Clough, P. T. (1992). *The end(s) of ethnography: From realism to social criticism.* Newbury Park, CA: Sage.

Crenshaw, K. (1995). Mapping the margins: Intersectionality, identity politics, and violence against women of color. In K. Crenshaw, N. Gotanda, G. Peller, & K. Thomas (Eds.), *Critical race theory: The key writings that formed the movement* (pp. 357-383). New York: New Press.

Cross, W. E., Jr. (1991). *Shades of black: Diversity in African-American identity.* Philadelphia: Temple University Press.

Denzin, N. K. (1989a). *Interpretive interactionism.* Newbury Park, CA: Sage.

Denzin, N. K. (1989b). *The research act: A theoretical introduction to sociological methods* (3rd ed.). Englewood Cliffs, NJ: Prentice Hall.

Denzin, N. K., & Lincoln, Y. S. (1994). Introduction: Entering the field of qualitative research. In N. K. Denzin & Y. S. Lincoln (Eds.), *Handbook of qualitative research* (pp. 1-17). Thousand Oaks, CA: Sage.

Dyson, M. E. (1993). *Reflecting black: African-American cultural criticism.* Minneapolis: University of Minnesota Press.

Edin, K., & Lein, L. (1997). *Making ends meet: How single mothers survive welfare and low-wage work.* New York: Russell Sage Foundation.

Fielding, N. G., & Fielding, J. L. (1986). *Linking data.* Beverly Hills, CA: Sage.

Fine, M. (1994). Working the hyphens: Reinventing self and other in qualitative research. In N. R. Denzin & Y. S. Lincoln (Eds.), *Handbook of qualitative research* (pp. 70-82). Thousand Oaks, CA: Sage.

Fine, M., Powell, L. C., Weis, L., & Wong, L. M. (Eds.). (1997). *Off white: Readings on race, power, and society.* New York: Routledge.

Fine, M., & Weis, L. (1996). Writing the "wrongs" of fieldwork: Confronting our own research/writing dilemmas in urban ethnographies. *Qualitative Inquiry, 2,* 251-274.

Fine, M., & Weis, L. (1998). *The unknown city: The lives of poor and working-class young adults.* Boston: Beacon.

Flick, U. (1992). Triangulation revisited: Strategy of validation or alternative? *Journal for the Theory of Social Behaviour, 22,* 175-198.

Gates, H. L., Jr. (Ed.). (1985). *"Race," writing, and difference.* Chicago: University of Chicago Press.

Gittell, M. J. (1990). Women on foundation boards: The illusion of change. *Women and Foundations/Corporate Philanthropy, 1,* 1-2.

Gittell, M. J. (1994). School reform in New York and Chicago: Revisiting the ecology of local games. *Urban Affairs Quarterly, 30,* 136-151.

Hall, S. (1981). Moving right. *Socialist Review, 55,* 113-137.

Hall, S. (1997). Subjects in history: Making diasporic identities. In W. Lubiano (Ed.), *The house that race built: Black Americans, U.S. terrain* (pp. 289-299). New York: Pantheon.

Haraway, D. J. (1991). *Simians, cyborgs, and women: The reinvention of nature.* New York: Routledge.

hooks, b. (1990). *Yearning: Race, gender, and cultural politics.* Boston: South End Press.

Hurtado, A., & Stewart, A. J. (1997). Through the looking glass: Implications of studying whiteness for feminist methods. In M. Fine, L. C. Powell, L. Weis, & L. M. Wong (Eds.), *Off white: Readings on race, power and society* (pp. 297-311). New York: Routledge.

Katz, M. (1995). *Improving poor people.* Princeton, NJ: Princeton University Press.

Kelly, R. D. G. (1997). *Yo' mama's disfunktional! Fighting the culture wars in urban black America.* Boston: Beacon.

Ladner, J. A. (1971). *Tomorrow's tomorrow: The black woman.* Garden City, NY: Doubleday.

Lal, J. (1996). Situating locations. In D. L. Wolf (Ed.), *Feminist dilemmas in fieldwork* (pp. 185-214). Boulder, CO: Westview.

Lather, P. (1991). *Getting smart: Feminist research and pedagogy with/in the postmodern.* New York: Routledge.

Lawrence, C. R., III. (1995). The word and the river: Pedagogy as scholarship as struggle. In K. Crenshaw, N. Gotanda, G. Peller, & K. Thomas (Eds.), *Critical race theory: The key writings that formed the movement* (pp. 336-351). New York: New Press.

Lykes, M. B. (1989). Dialogue with Guatemalan Indian women: Critical perspectives on constructing collaborative research. In R. K. Unger (Ed.), *Representations: Social constructions of gender* (pp. 167-184). Amityville, NY: Baywood.

Lykes, M. B. (1994). Speaking against the silence: One Maya woman's exile and return. In C. E. Franz & A. J. Stewart (Eds.), *Women creating lives: Identities, resilience, and resistance* (pp. 97-114). Boulder, CO: Westview.

Madigan, R., Johnson, S., & Linton, P. (1995). The language of psychology: APA style as epistemology. *American Psychologist, 50,* 428-436.

Matsuda, M. (1995). Looking to the bottom: Critical legal studies and reparations. In K. Crenshaw, N. Gotanda, G. Peller, & K. Thomas (Eds.), *Critical race theory: The key writings that formed the movement* (pp. 63-79). New York: New Press.

McCarthy, C., Rodriguez, A., Meecham, S., David, S., Wilson-Brown, C., Godina, H., Supryia, K. E., & Buendia, E. (1997). Race, suburban resentment, and the representation of the inner city in contemporary film and television. In M. Fine, L. C. Powell, L. Weis, & L. M. Wong (Eds.), *Off white: Readings on race, power, and society* (pp. 229-241). New York: Routledge.

Morawski, J. G., & Bayer, B. M. (1995). Stirring trouble and making theory. In H. Landrine (Ed.), *Bringing cultural diversity to feminist psychology: Theory, research, and practice* (pp. 113-137). Washington, DC: American Psychological Association.

Mullings, L. (1984). Minority women, work and health. In W. Chavkin (Ed.), *Double exposure: Women's health hazards on the job and at home* (pp. 84-106). New York: Monthly Review Press.

Murray, C. (1984). *Losing ground: American social policy 1950-1980.* New York: Basic Books.

Okely, J. (1992). Anthropology and autobiography: Participatory experience and embodied knowledge. In J. Okely & H. Callaway (Eds.), *Anthropology and autobiography* (pp. 1-49). London: Routledge.

Omi, M. & Winant, H. (1986). *Racial formations in the United States: From the 1960s to the 1980s.* New York: Routledge.

Opotow, S. (1990). Moral exclusion and injustice: An introduction. *Journal of Social Issues, 46,* 1-20.

Piven, F. F., & Cloward, R. A. (1971). *Regulating the poor: The functions of public welfare.* New York: Pantheon.

Powell, L. (1994). Interpreting social defenses: Family group in an urban setting. In M. Fine (Ed.), *Chartering urban school reform: Reflections on public high schools in the midst of change* (pp. 112-121). New York: Teacher's College Press.

Richardson, L. (1995). Writing-stories: Co-authoring "The sea monster," a writing-story. *Qualitative Inquiry, 1,* 189-203.

Roman, L. (1993). Double exposure: The politics of feminist materialist ethnography. *Educational Theory, 43,* 279-308.

Roman, L. (1997). Denying (white) racial privilege: Redemption discourses and the uses of fantasy. In M. Fine, L. C. Powell, L. Weis, & L. M. Wong (Eds.), *Off white: Readings on race, power and society* (pp. 270-282). New York: Routledge.

Rosaldo, R. (1989). *Culture and truth: The remaking of social analysis.* Boston: Beacon.

Saegert, S. (1997, May). *Schools and the ecology of gender.* Paper presented at the Schools and the Urban Environment Conference, National Taiwan University, Taipei.

Scott, D. M. (1997). *Contempt and pity: Social policy and the image of the damaged black psyche 1880-1996.* Chapel Hill: University of North Carolina Press.

Scott, J. W. (1992). Experience. In J. Butler & J. W. Scott (Eds.), *Feminists theorize the political* (pp. 22-40). New York: Routledge.

Sedgwick, E. K. (1990). *Epistemology of the closet.* Berkeley: University of California Press.

Stacey, J. (1991). Can there be a feminist ethnography? In S. B. Gluck & D. Patai (Eds.), *Women's words: The feminist practice of oral history* (pp. 111-119). New York: Routledge.

Suls, J. M., & Rosnow, R. L. (1988). Concerns about artifacts in psychological experiments. In J. G. Morawski (Ed.), *The rise of experimentation in American psychology* (pp. 163-187). New Haven, CT: Yale University Press.

Weis, L., & Fine, M. (1996). Narrating the 1980s and 1990s: Voices of poor and working class white and African American men. *Anthropology and Education, 27,* 1-24.

Weis, L., & Fine, M. (Eds.). (in press). *Speedbumps: A student-friendly guide to qualitative work.* New York: Teachers College Press.

Weis, L., Marusza, J., & Fine, M. (1998). Out of the cupboard: Kids, domestic violence and schools. *British Journal of Sociology of Education, 19,* 53-73.

Weis, L., Proweller, A., & Centrie, C. (1997). Re-examining "A moment in history": Loss of privilege inside white working-class masculinity in the 1990's. In M. Fine, L. C. Powell, L. Weis, & L. M. Wong (Eds.), *Off white: Readings on race, power and society* (pp. 210-226). New York: Routledge.

West, C. (1993). *Race matters.* Boston: Beacon.

Williams, P. J. (1997). *Seeing a color-blind future: The paradox of race.* New York: Farrar, Straus & Giroux.

5

Ethics and Politics in Qualitative Research

Clifford G. Christians

◆ The Enlightenment mind clustered around an extraordinary dichotomy. Intellectual historians usually summarize this split in terms of subject/object, fact/value, or material/spiritual dualisms. And all three of these are legitimate interpretations of the cosmology inherited from Galileo, Descartes, and Newton. None of them puts the Enlightenment into its sharpest focus, however. Its deepest root was a pervasive autonomy. The cult of human personality prevailed in all its freedom. Human beings were declared a law unto themselves, set loose from every faith that claimed their allegiance. Proudly self-conscious of human autonomy, the 18th-century mind saw nature as an arena of limitless possibilities in which the sovereignty of human personality was demonstrated by its mastery over the natural order. Release from nature spawned autonomous individuals who considered themselves independent of any authority. The freedom motif was the deepest driving force, first released by the Renaissance and achieving maturity during the Enlightenment.[1]

Obviously, one can reach autonomy by starting with the subject/object dualism. In constructing the Enlightenment worldview, the prestige of natural science played a key role in setting people free. Achievements in mathematics, physics, and astronomy allowed humans to dominate nature, which formerly had dominated them. Science provided unmistakable evidence that by applying reason to nature and human beings in fairly obvious ways, people could live progressively happier lives. Crime and insanity, for example, no longer needed repressive theological explanations, but were deemed capable of mundane empirical solutions.

Likewise, one can get to the autonomous self by casting the question in terms of a radical discontinuity between hard facts and subjective values. The Enlightenment did push values to the fringe through its disjunction between knowledge of what is and what ought to be. And Enlightenment materialism in all its forms isolated reason from faith, knowledge from belief. As Robert Hooke insisted three centuries ago, when he helped found London's Royal Society: "This Society will eschew any discussion of religion, rhetoric, morals, and politics." With factuality gaining a stranglehold on the Enlightenment mind, those regions of human interest that implied oughts, constraints, and imperatives simply ceased to appear. Certainly those who see the Enlightenment as separating facts and values have identified a cardinal difficulty. Likewise, the realm of the spirit can easily dissolve into mystery and intuition. If the spiritual world contains no binding force, it is surrendered to speculation by the divines, many of whom accepted the Enlightenment belief that their pursuit was ephemeral.

But the Enlightenment's autonomy doctrine created the greatest mischief. Individual self-determination stands as the centerpiece, bequeathing to us the universal problem of integrating human freedom with moral order. And in struggling with the complexities and conundrums of this relationship, the Enlightenment, in effect, refused to sacrifice personal freedom. Even though the problem had a particular urgency in the 18th century, its response was not resolution but a categorical insistence on autonomy. Given the despotic political regimes and oppressive ecclesiastical systems of the period, such an uncompromising stance for freedom at this juncture is understandable. The Enlightenment began and ended with the assumption that human liberty ought to be cut away from the moral order, never integrated meaningfully with it.

Jean-Jacques Rousseau was the most outspoken advocate of this radical freedom. He gave intellectual substance to free self-determination of the human personality as the highest good. Rousseau is a complicated figure. He refused to be co-opted by Descartes's rationalism, Newton's mechanistic cosmology, or Locke's egoistic selves. And he was not merely content to isolate and sacralize freedom, either, at least not in his *Discourse on Inequality* or in the *Social Contract,* where he answers Hobbes.

Rousseau represented the romantic wing of the Enlightenment, revolting against its rationalism. He won a wide following well into the 19th century for advocating immanent and emergent values rather than transcendent and given ones. While admitting that humans were finite and limited, he nonetheless promoted a freedom of breathtaking scope—not just disengagement from God or the Church, but freedom from culture and from any authority. Autonomy became the core of the human being and the center of the universe. Rousseau's understanding of equality, social systems, axiology, and language were anchored in it. He recognized the consequences more astutely than those comfortable with a shrunken negative freedom. But the only solution that he found tolerable was a noble human nature that enjoyed freedom beneficently and, therefore, one could presume, lived compatibly in some vague sense with a moral order.

◆ Value-Free Experimentalism

Typically, debates over the character of the social sciences revolve around the theory and methodology of the natural sciences. However, the argument here is not how they resemble natural science, but their inscription into the dominant Enlightenment worldview. In political theory, the liberal state as it emerged in 17th- and 18th-century Europe left citizens free to lead their own lives without obeisance to the Church or the feudal order. Psychology, sociology, and economics—known as the human or moral sciences in the 18th and 19th centuries—were conceived as "liberal arts" that opened minds and freed the imagination. As the social sciences and liberal state emerged and overlapped historically, Enlightenment thinkers in Europe advocated the "facts, skills, and techniques" of experimental reasoning to support the state and citizenry (Root, 1993, pp. 14-15).

Consistent with the presumed priority of individual liberty over the moral order, the basic institutions of society were designed to ensure "neutrality between different conceptions of the good" (Root, 1993, p. 12). The state was prohibited "from requiring or even encouraging citizens to subscribe to one religious tradition, form of family life, or manner of personal or artistic expression over another" (Root, 1993, p. 12). Given the historical circumstances in which shared conceptions of the good were no longer broad and deeply entrenched, taking sides on moral issues and insisting on social ideals were considered counterproductive. Value neutrality appeared to be the logical alternative "for a society whose members practiced many religions, pursued many different occupations, and identified with many different customs and traditions" (Root, 1993, p. 11). The theory and practice of mainstream social science reflect liberal Enlightenment philosophy, as do education, science, and politics. Only a reintegration of autonomy and the moral order provides an alternative paradigm for the social sciences today.[2]

Mill's Philosophy of Social Science

For John Stuart Mill, "neutrality is necessary in order to promote autonomy. . . . A person cannot be forced to be good, and the state should not dictate the kind of life a citizen should lead; it would be better for citizens to choose badly than for them to be forced by the state to choose well" (Root, 1993, pp. 12-13). Planning our lives according to our own ideas and purposes is sine qua non for autonomous beings in Mill's *On Liberty* (1859/1978): "The free development of individuality is one of the principal ingredients of human happiness, and quite the chief ingredient of individual and social progress" (p. 50; see also Copleston, 1966, p. 303, n. 32). This neutrality, based on the supremacy of individual autonomy, is the foundational principle in his *Utilitarianism* (1861/1957) and in *A System of Logic* (1843/1893) as well. For Mill, "the principle of utility demands that the individual should enjoy full liberty, except the liberty to harm others" (Copleston, 1966, p. 54). In addition to bringing classical utilitarianism to its maximum development and establishing with Locke the liberal state, Mill delineated the foundations of inductive inquiry as social scientific method. In terms of the principles of empiricism, he perfected the inductive techniques of Francis Bacon as a problem-solving methodology to replace Aristotelian deductive logic.

According to Mill, syllogisms contribute nothing new to human knowledge. If we conclude that because "all men are mortal" the Duke of Wellington is mortal by virtue of his manhood, then the conclusion does not advance the premise (see Mill, 1843/1893, II, 3, 2, p. 140). The crucial issue is not reordering the conceptual world but discriminating genuine knowledge from superstition. In the pursuit of truth, generalizing and synthesizing are necessary to advance inductively from the known to the unknown. Mill seeks to establish this function of logic as inference from the known, rather than certifying the rules for formal consistency in reasoning (Mill, 1843/1893, bk. 3). Scientific certitude can be approximated when induction is followed rigorously, with propositions empirically derived and the material of all our knowledge provided by experience.[3] For the physical sciences he establishes four modes of experimental inquiry: agreement, disagreement, residues, and the principle of concomitant variations (Mill, 1843/1893, III, 8, pp. 278-288). He considers them the only possible methods of proof for experimentation, as long as one presumes the realist position that nature is structured by uniformities.[4]

In Book 6 of A System of Logic, "On the Logic of the Moral Sciences," Mill (1843/1893) develops an inductive experimentalism as the scientific method for studying "the various phenomena which constitute social life" (VI, 6, 1, p. 606). Although he conceived of social science as explaining human behavior in terms of causal laws, he warned against the fatalism of full predictability. "Social laws are hypothetical, and statistically-based generalizations by their very nature admit of exceptions" (Copleston, 1966, p. 101; see also Mill, 1843/1893, VI, 5, 1, p. 596). Empirically confirmed instrumental knowledge about human behavior has greater predictive power when it deals with collective masses than when we are dealing with individual agents.

Mill's positivism is obvious throughout his work on experimental inquiry.[5] Based on the work of Auguste Comte, he defined matter as the "permanent possibility of sensation" (Mill, 1865b, p. 198) and believed that nothing else can be said about metaphysical substances.[6] With Hume and Comte, Mill insisted that metaphysical substances are not real and only the facts of sense phenomena exist. There are no essences or ultimate reality behind sensations; therefore Mill (1865a, 1865b) and Comte (1848/1910) argued that social scientists should limit themselves to particular data as a factual source out of which experimentally valid laws can be derived. For both, this is the only kind of knowledge that yields practical benefits (Mill, 1865b, p. 242); in fact, society's salvation is contingent upon such scientific knowledge (p. 241).[7]

As with his consequentialist ethics, Mill's philosophy of social science is built on a dualism of means and ends. Citizens and politicians are responsible for articulating ends in a free society, and science for the know-how for achieving them. Science is amoral, speaking to questions of means but with no wherewithal or authority to dictate ends. Methods in the social sciences must be disinterested regarding substance and content, and rigorously limited to the risks and benefits of possible courses of action. Protocols for practicing liberal science "should be prescriptive, but not morally or politically prescriptive and should direct against bad science but not bad conduct" (Root, 1993, p. 129). Research cannot be judged right or wrong, only true or false. "Science is political only in its applications" (Root, 1993, p. 213). Given his democratic liberalism, Mill advocates neutrality "out of concern for the autonomy of the individuals or groups" social science seeks to serve. It should "treat them as thinking, willing, active beings who bear responsibility for their choices and are free to choose" their own conception of the good life by majority rule (Root, 1993, p. 19).

Value Neutrality in Max Weber

When 20th-century mainstream social scientists contend that ethics is not their business, they typically invoke Weber's essays written between 1904 and 1917. Given Weber's importance methodologically and theoretically for sociology and economics, his distinction between political judgments and scientific neutrality is given canonical status.

Weber distinguishes between value freedom and value relevance. He recognizes that in the discovery phase, "personal, cultural, moral, or political values cannot be eliminated; . . . what social scientists choose to investigate . . . they choose on the basis of the values" they expect their research to advance (Root, 1993, p. 33). But he insists that social science be value-free in the presentation phase. Findings ought not to express any judgments of a moral or political character. Professors should hang up their values along with their coats as they enter their lecture halls.

"An attitude of moral indifference," Weber (1904/1949b) writes, "has no connection with scientific objectivity" (p. 60). His meaning is clear from the value-freedom/value-relevance distinction. For the social sciences to be purposeful and rational, they must serve the "values of relevance."

> The problems of the social sciences are selected by the value relevance of the phenomena treated. . . . The expression "relevance to values" refers simply to the philosophical interpretation of that specifically scientific "interest" which determines the selection of a given subject matter and problems of empirical analysis. (Weber, 1917/1949a, pp. 21-22)

> In the social sciences the stimulus to the posing of scientific problems is in actuality always given by practical "questions." Hence, the very recognition of the existence of a scientific problem coincides personally with the possession of specifically oriented motives and values. . . .

Without the investigator's evaluative ideas, there would be no principle of selection of subject matter and no meaningful knowledge of the concrete reality. Without the investigator's conviction regarding the significance of particular cultural facts, every attempt to analyze concrete reality is absolutely meaningless. (Weber, 1904/1949b, pp. 61, 82)

Whereas the natural sciences, in Weber's (1904/1949b, p. 72) view, seek general laws that govern all empirical phenomena, the social sciences study those realities that our values consider significant. Whereas the natural world itself indicates what reality to investigate, the infinite possibilities of the social world are ordered in terms of "the cultural values with which we approach reality" (1904/1949b, p. 78).[8] However, even though value relevance directs the social sciences, as with the natural sciences, Weber considers the former value-free. The subject matter in natural science makes value judgments unnecessary, and social scientists by a conscious decision can exclude judgments of "desirability or undesirability" from their publicationss and lectures (1904/1949b, p. 52). "What is really at issue is the intrinsically simple demand that the investigator and teacher should keep unconditionally separate the establishment of empirical facts . . . and his own political evaluations" (Weber, 1917/1949a, p. 11).

Weber's opposition to value judgments in the social sciences was driven by practical circumstances. Academic freedom for the universities of Prussia was more likely if professors limited their professional work to scientific know-how. With university hiring controlled by political officials, only if the faculty refrained from policy commitments and criticism would officials relinquish their control.

Few of the offices in government or industry in Germany were held by people who were well trained to solve questions of means. Weber thought that the best way to increase the power and economic prosperity of Germany was to train a new managerial class learned about means and silent about ends. The mission of the university, on Weber's view, should be to offer such training. (Root, 1993, p. 41; see also Weber, 1973, pp. 4-8)[9]

Weber's practical argument for value freedom and his apparent limitation of it to the reporting phase have made his version of value neutrality attractive to 20th-century social science. He is not a positivist such as Comte or a thoroughgoing empiricist in the tradition of Mill. He disavowed the positivist's overwrought disjunction between discovery and justification, and developed no systematic epistemology comparable to Mill's. His nationalism was partisan compared to Mill's liberal political philosophy. Nevertheless, Weber's value neutrality reflects Enlightenment autonomy in a fundamentally similar fashion. In the process of maintaining his distinction between value relevance and value freedom, he separates facts from values and means from ends. He appeals to empirical evidence and logical reasoning rooted in human rationality. "The validity of a practical imperative as a norm," he writes, "and the truth-value of an empirical proposition are absolutely heterogeneous in character" (Weber, 1904/1949b, p. 52). "A systematically correct scientific proof in the social sciences" may not be completely attainable, but that is most likely "due to faulty data" not because it is conceptually impossible (1904/1949b, p. 58).[10] For Weber, as with Mill, empirical science deals with questions of means, and his warning against inculcating political and moral values presumes a means-ends dichotomy (see Weber, 1917/1949a, pp. 18-19; 1904/1949b, p. 52).

As Michael Root (1993) concludes, "John Stuart Mill's call for neutrality in the social sciences is based on his belief" that the language of science "takes cognizance of a phenomenon and endeavors to discover its laws." Max Weber likewise "takes it for granted that there can be a language of science—a collection of truths—that excludes all value-judgments, rules, or directions for conduct" (p. 205). In both cases, scientific knowledge exists for its own sake as morally neutral. For both, neutrality is desirable "because questions of value are not rationally resolvable" and neutrality in the social sciences is presumed to contribute "to political and personal autonomy" (p. 229). In Weber's argument for value relevance in social science, he did not contradict the larger Enlightenment ideal of scientific neutrality between competing conceptions of the good.

Utilitarian Ethics

In addition to its this-worldly humanism, utilitarian ethics was attractive for its compatibility with scientific thought. It fit the canons of rational calculation as they were nourished by the Enlightenment's intellectual culture.

In the utilitarian perspective, one validated an ethical position by hard evidence. You count the consequences for human happiness of one or another course, and you go with the one with the highest favorable total. What

215

counts as human happiness was thought to be something conceptually unproblematic, a scientifically establishable domain of facts. One could abandon all the metaphysical or theological factors which made ethical questions scientifically undecidable. (Taylor, 1982, p. 129)

Utilitarian ethics replaces metaphysical distinctions with the calculation of empirical quantities. It follows the procedural demand that if "the happiness of each agent counts for one . . . the right course of action should be what satisfies all, or the largest number possible" (Taylor, 1982, p. 131). Autonomous reason is the arbiter of moral disputes.

With moral reasoning equivalent to calculating consequences for human happiness, utilitarianism presumes there is "a single consistent domain of the moral, that there is one set of considerations which determines what we ought morally to do." This "epistemologically-motivated reduction and homogenization of the moral" marginalizes the qualitative languages of admiration and contempt—integrity, healing, liberation, conviction, dishonesty, and self-indulgence, for example (Taylor, 1982, pp. 132-133). In utilitarian terms, these languages designate subjective factors that "correspond to nothing in reality. . . . They express the way we feel, not the way things are" (Taylor, 1982, p. 141). This single-consideration theory not only demands that we maximize general happiness, but considers irrelevant other moral imperatives that conflict with it, such as equal distribution. One-factor models appeal to the "epistemological squeamishness" of value-neutral social science, which "dislikes contrastive languages." Moreover, utilitarianism appealingly offers "the prospect of exact calculation of policy through . . . rational choice theory" (Taylor, 1982, p. 143). "It portrays all moral issues as discrete problems amenable to largely technical solutions" (Euben, 1981, p. 117). However, to its critics, this kind of exactness represents "a semblance of validity" by leaving out whatever cannot be calculated (Taylor, 1982, p. 143).[11]

Given its dualism of means and ends, the domain of the good in utilitarian theory is extrinsic. All that is worth valuing is a function of their consequences. Prima facie duties are literally inconceivable. "The degree to which my actions and statements" truly express what is important to someone does not count. Ethical and political thinking in consequentialist terms legislate intrinsic valuing out of existence (Taylor, 1982, p. 144). The exteriority of ethics is seen to guarantee the value neutrality of experimental procedures.[12]

216

Codes of Ethics

In value-free social science, codes of ethics for professional and academic associations are the conventional format for moral principles. By the 1980s, each of the major scholarly associations had adopted its own code, with an overlapping emphasis on four guidelines for directing an inductive science of means toward majoritarian ends.

1. Informed consent. Consistent with its commitment to individual autonomy, social science in the Mill and Weber tradition insists that research subjects have the right to be informed about the nature and consequences of experiments in which they are involved. Proper respect for human freedom generally includes two necessary conditions. Subjects must agree voluntarily to participate—that is, without physical or psychological coercion. In addition, their agreement must be based on full and open information. "The Articles of the Nuremberg Tribunal and the Declaration of Helsinki both state that subjects must be told the duration, methods, possible risks, and the purpose or aim of the experiment" (Soble, 1978, p. 40; see also Veatch, 1996).

The self-evident character of this principle is not disputed in rationalist ethics. Meaningful application, however, generates ongoing disputes. As Punch (1994) observes, "In much fieldwork there seems to be no way around the predicament that informed consent—divulging one's identity and research purpose to all and sundry—will kill many a project stone dead" (p. 90). True to the privileging of means in a means-ends model, Punch reflects the general conclusion that codes of ethics should serve as a guideline prior to fieldwork, but not intrude on full participation. "A strict application of codes" may "restrain and restrict" a great deal of "innocuous" and "unproblematic" research (p. 90).

2. Deception. In emphasizing informed consent, social science codes of ethics uniformly oppose deception. Even paternalistic arguments for possible deception of criminals, children in elementary schools, or the mentally incapacitated are no longer credible. The ongoing exposé of deceptive practices since Stanley Milgram's experiments have given this moral principle special status—deliberate misrepresentation is forbidden. Bulmer (1982) is typical of hard-liners who conclude with the codes that deception is "neither ethically justified nor practically necessary, nor in the best interest of sociology as an academic pursuit" (p. 217; see also Punch, 1994, p. 92).

The straightforward application of this principle suggests that researchers design different experiments free of active deception. But with ethical constructions exterior to the scientific enterprise, no unambiguous application is possible. Given that the search for knowledge is obligatory and deception is codified as morally unacceptable, in some situations both criteria cannot be satisfied. Within both psychology and medicine some information cannot be obtained without at least deception by omission. The standard resolution for this dilemma is to permit a modicum of deception when there are explicit utilitarian reasons for doing so. Opposition to deception in the codes is de facto redefined in these terms: If "the knowledge to be gained from deceptive experiments" is clearly valuable to society, it is "only a minor defect that persons must be deceived in the process" (Soble, 1978, p. 40).

3. Privacy and confidentiality. Codes of ethics insist on safeguards to protect people's identities and those of the research locations. Confidentiality must be assured as the primary safeguard against unwanted exposure. All personal data ought to be secured or concealed and made public only behind a shield of anonymity. Professional etiquette uniformly concurs that no one deserves harm or embarrassment as a result of insensitive research practices. "The single most likely source of harm in social science inquiry is" the disclosure of private knowledge considered damaging by experimental subjects (Reiss, 1979, p. 73; see also Punch, 1994, p. 93).

As Enlightenment autonomy was developed in philosophical anthropology, a sacred innermost self became essential to the construction of unique personhood. Already in John Locke, this private domain received nonnegotiable status. Democratic life was articulated outside these atomistic units, a secondary domain of negotiated contracts and problematic communication. In the logic of social science inquiry revolving around the same autonomy inscribed in being, invading persons' fragile but distinctive privacy is intolerable.

Despite the signature status of privacy protection, watertight confidentiality has proved to be impossible. Pseudonyms and disguised locations are often recognized by insiders. What researchers consider innocent is perceived by participants as misleading or even betrayal. What appears neutral on paper is often conflictual in practice. When government agencies or educational institutions or health organizations are studied, what private parts ought not be exposed? And who is blameworthy if aggressive media carry the research further? Encoding privacy protection is meaningless when "there is no consensus or unanimity on what is public and private" (Punch, 1994, p. 94).

4. *Accuracy.* Ensuring that data are accurate is a cardinal principle in social science codes as well. Fabrications, fraudulent materials, omissions, and contrivances are both nonscientific and unethical. Data that are internally and externally valid are the coin of the realm, experimentally and morally. In an instrumentalist, value-neutral social science, the definitions entailed by the procedures themselves establish the ends by which they are evaluated as moral.

Institutional Review Boards

As a condition of funding, government agencies in various countries have insisted that review and monitoring bodies be established by institutions engaged in research involving human subjects. Institutional review boards (IRBs) embody the utilitarian agenda in terms of scope, assumptions, and procedural guidelines.

In 1978, the U.S. National Commission for the Protection of Human Subjects in Biomedical and Behavioral Research was established. It developed broad ethical principles to serve as the basis upon which specific rules could be established. Three principles, published in what became known as the Belmont Report, were said to constitute the moral standards for research involving human subjects: respect for persons, beneficence, and justice.

1. The section on respect for persons reiterates the codes' demands that subjects enter the research voluntarily and with adequate information about the experiment's procedures and possible consequences. On a deeper level, respect for persons incorporates two basic ethical tenets: "First, that individuals should be treated as autonomous agents, and second, that persons with diminished autonomy [the immature and incapacitated] are entitled to protection" (University of Illinois, 1995).

2. Under the principle of beneficence, researchers are enjoined to secure the well-being of their subjects. Beneficent actions are understood in a double

sense as avoiding harm altogether, and if risks are involved for achieving substantial benefits, minimizing as much harm as possible: "In the case of particular projects, investigators and members of their institutions are obliged to give forethought to the maximization of benefits and the reduction of risks that might occur from the research investigation. In the case of scientific research in general, members of the larger society are obliged to recognize the longer term benefits and risks that may result from the improvement of knowledge and from the development of novel medical, psychotherapeutic, and social procedures" (University of Illinois, 1995).

3. The principle of justice insists on fair distribution of both the benefits and burdens of research. An injustice occurs when some groups (e.g., welfare recipients, the institutionalized, or particular ethnic minorities) are overused as research subjects because of easy manipulation or their availability. And when research supported by public funds leads to "therapeutic devices and procedures, justice demands that these not provide advantages only to those who can afford them" (University of Illinois, 1995).

These principles reiterate the basic themes of value-neutral experimentalism—individual autonomy, maximum benefits and minimal risks, and ethical ends exterior to scientific means. The policy procedures based on them reflect the same guidelines as dominate the codes of ethics: informed consent, protection of privacy, and nondeception. The authority of IRBs was enhanced in 1989 when Congress passed the NIH Revitalization Act and formed the Commission on Research Integrity. The emphasis at that point was on the invention, fudging, and distortion of data. Falsification, fabrication, and plagiarism continue as federal categories of misconduct, with a new report in 1996 adding warnings against unauthorized use of confidential information, omission of important data, and interference (that is, physical damage to the materials of others).

With IRBs the legacy of Mill, Comte, and Weber comes into its own. Value-neutral science is accountable to ethical standards through rational procedures controlled by value-neutral academic institutions in the service of an impartial government. In its conceptual structure, IRB policy is designed to produce the best ratio of benefits to costs. IRBs ostensibly protect the subjects who fall under the protocols they approve. However, given the interlocking utilitarian functions of social science, the academy, and the state that Mill identified and promoted, IRBs in reality protect their own institutions rather than subject populations in society at large (see Vanderpool, 1996, chaps. 2-6).

Current Crisis

Mill and Comte, each in his own way, presumed that experimental social science benefited society by uncovering facts about the human condition. Durkheim and Weber believed that a scientific study of society could help people come to grips with "the development of capitalism and the industrial revolution" (Jennings & Callahan, 1983, p. 3). The American Social Science Association was created in 1865 to link "real elements of the truth" with "the great social problems of the day" (Lazarsfeld & Reitz, 1975, p. 1). This myth of beneficence was destroyed with "the revelations at the Nuremberg trials (recounting the Nazis' 'medical experiments' on concentration camp inmates) and with the role of leading scientists in the Manhattan Project" (Punch, 1994, p. 88).

The crisis of confidence multiplied with the exposure of actual physical harm in the Tuskegee Syphilis Study and the Willowbrook Hepatitis Experiment. In the 1960s, Project Camelot, a U.S. Army attempt to use social science to measure and forecast revolutions and insurgency, was bitterly opposed around the world and had to be canceled. Stanley Milgram's (1974) deception of unwitting subjects and Laud Humphreys's (1970, 1972) deceptive research on homosexuals in a public toilet, and later in their homes, were considered scandalous for psychologically abusing research subjects. Noam Chomsky exposed the complicity of social scientists with military initiatives in Vietnam.

Vigorous concern for research ethics during the 1980s and 1990s, support from foundations, and the development of ethics codes and the IRB apparatus are credited by their advocates with curbing outrageous abuses. However, the charges of fraud, plagiarism, and misrepresentation continue on a lesser scale, with dilemmas, conundrums, and controversies unabated over the meaning and application of ethical guidelines. Entrepreneurial faculty competing for scarce research dollars are generally compliant with institutional control, but the vastness of social science activity in universities and research entities makes full supervision impossible.

Underneath the pros and cons of administering a responsible social science, the structural deficiencies in its epistemology have become transparent (Jennings, 1983, pp. 4-7). A positivistic philosophy of social inquiry insists on neutrality regarding definitions of the good, and this worldview has been discredited. The Enlightenment model setting human freedom at odds with the moral order is bankrupt. Even Weber's weaker version of contrastive languages rather than oppositional entities is not up to the task. Reworking the ethics codes so that they are more explicit and less hortatory will make no fundamental difference. Requiring ethics workshops for graduate students, redefining the mission of IRBs, and strengthening government policy are desirable but of marginal significance.

In utilitarianism, moral thinking and experimental procedures are homogenized into a unidimensional model of rational validation. Autonomous human beings are clairvoyant about aligning means and goals, presuming that they can objectify the mechanisms for understanding themselves and the social world surrounding them (see Taylor, 1982, p. 133). This restrictive definition of ethics accounts for some of the goods we seek, such as minimal harm, but those outside a utility calculus are excluded. "Emotionality and intuition" are relegated "to a secondary position" in the decision-making process, for example, and no attention is paid to an "ethics of caring" grounded in "concrete particularities" (Denzin, 1997, p. 273; see also Ryan, 1995, p. 147). The way power and ideology influence social and political institutions is largely ignored. Under a rhetorical patina of deliberate choice and the illusion of autonomous creativity, a means-ends system operates in fundamentally its own terms.

This constricted environment no longer addresses adequately the complicated issues we face in studying the social world. Celebrity social scientists generate status and prestige—McGeorge Bundy in the Kennedy years, political scientist Henry Kissinger, Daniel Moynihan in the Senate. But failure in the War on Poverty, contradictions over welfare, and ill-fated studies of urban housing have dramatized the limitations of a utility calculus that occupies the entire moral domain.[13]

Certainly, levels of success and failure are open to dispute even within the social science disciplines themselves. More unsettling and threatening to the empirical mainstream than disappointing performance is the recognition that neutrality is not pluralistic but imperialistic. Reflecting on past experience, disinterested research under presumed conditions of value freedom is increasingly seen as de facto reinscribing the agenda in its own terms. Empiricism is procedurally committed to equal reckoning, regardless of how research subjects may constitute the substantive ends of life. But experimentalism is not a neutral meeting ground for all ideas; rather, it is a "fighting creed" that imposes its own ideas on others while uncritically assuming the very "superiority that powers this imposition."[14] In Foucault's (1979, pp. 170-195) more decisive terms, social science is a regime of power that helps maintain social order by normalizing subjects into categories designed by political authorities (see Root, 1993, chap. 7). A liberalism of equality is not neutral but represents only one range of ideals, and is itself incompatible with other goods.

This noncontextual, nonsituational model that assumes "a morally neutral, objective observer will get the facts right" ignores "the situatedness of power relations associated with gender, sexual orientation, class, ethnicity, race, and nationality." It is hierarchical (scientist-subject) and biased toward patriarchy. "It glosses the ways in which the observer-ethnographer is implicated and embedded in the 'ruling apparatus' of the society and the culture." Scientists "carry the mantle" of university-based authority as they venture out into "local community to do research" (Denzin, 1997, p. 272; see also Ryan, 1995, pp. 144-145).[15] There is no sustained questioning of expertise itself in democratic societies that belong in principle to citizens who do not share this specialized knowledge (see Euben, 1981, p. 120).

◆ Feminist Communitarianism

Social Ethics

Over the past decade, social and feminist ethics have made a radical break with the individual autonomy and rationalist presumption of canonical ethics (see Koehn, 1998). The social ethics of Agnes Heller (1988, 1990, 1996), Charles Taylor (1989, 1991; Taylor et al., 1994), Carole Pateman (1985, 1988, 1989), Edith Wyschogrod (1974, 1985, 1990, 1998), and Cornel West (1989, 1991) and the feminist ethics of Carol Gilligan (1982, 1983; Gilligan, Ward, & Taylor, 1988), Nel Noddings (1984, 1989, 1990), Virginia Held (1993), and Seyla Benhabib (1992) are fundamentally reconstructing ethical theory (see Code, 1991). Rather than searching for neutral principles to which all parties can appeal, social ethics rests on a complex view of moral judgments as integrating into an organic whole, everyday experience, beliefs about the good, and feelings of approval and shame, in terms of human relations and social structures. This is a philosophical approach that situates the moral domain within the general purposes of human life that people share contextually and across cultural, racial, and historical boundaries. Ideally, it engenders a new occupational role and normative core for social science research (White, 1995).

Carol Gilligan (1982, 1983; Gilligan et al., 1988) characterizes the female moral voice as an ethic of care. This dimension of moral development is rooted in the primacy of human relationships. Compassion and nurturance resolve conflicting responsibilities among people, standards totally opposite of merely avoiding harm.[16] In *Caring,* Nel Noddings (1984) rejects outright the "ethics of principle as ambiguous and unstable" (p. 5), insisting that human care should play the central role in moral decision making. For Julia Wood (1994), "an interdependent sense of self" undergirds the ethic of care, wherein we are comfortable acting independently while "acting cooperatively . . . in relationship with others" (pp. 108, 110). Feminism in Linda Steiner's work critiques the conventions of impartiality and formality in ethics while giving precision to affection, intimacy, nurturing, egalitarian and collaborative processes, and empathy. Feminists' ethical self-consciousness also identifies subtle forms of oppression and imbalance, and teaches us to "address questions about whose interests are regarded as worthy of debate" (Steiner, 1991, p. 158; see also Steiner, 1997).

While sharing in the turn away from an abstract ethics of calculation, Charlene Seigfried (1996) argues against the Gilligan-Noddings tradition. Linking feminism to pragmatism, in which gender is socially constructed, she contradicts "the simplistic equation of women with care and nurturance and men with justice and autonomy" (p. 206). Gender-based moralities de facto make one gender subservient to another. In her social ethics, gender is replaced with engendering: "To be female or male is not to instantiate an unchangeable nature but to participate in an ongoing process of negotiating cultural expectations of femininity and masculinity" (p. 206). Seigfried challenges us to a social morality in which caring values are central but contextualized in webs of relationships and constructed toward communities with "more autonomy for women and more connectedness for men" (p. 219). Agnes Heller and Edith Wyschogrod are two promising examples of proponents of social ethics that meet Seigfried's challenge while confronting forthrightly today's contingency, mass murder, conceptual upheavals in ethics, and hyperreality.

Heller, a former student of Georg Lukács and a dissident in Hungary, is the Hannah Arendt Professor of Philosophy at the New School for Social Research. Her trilogy developing a contemporary theory of social ethics (Heller, 1988, 1990, 1996) revolves around what she calls the one decisive question: "Good persons exist—how are they possible?" (1988, p. 7). She disavows an ethics of norms, rules, and ideals external to human beings.

Only exceptional acts of responsibility under duress and predicaments, each in their own way, are "worthy of theoretical interest" (1996, p. 3). Accumulated wisdom, moral meaning from our own choices of decency, and the ongoing summons of the Other together reintroduce love, happiness, sympathy, and beauty into a modern, nonabsolutist, but principled theory of morals.

In *Saints and Postmodernism,* Edith Wyschogrod (1990) asserts that antiauthority struggles are possible without assuming that our choices are voluntary. She represents a social ethics of self and Other in the tradition of Emmanuel Levinas (see Wyschogrod, 1974).[17] "The other person opens the venue of ethics, the place where ethical existence occurs." The Other, "the touchstone of moral existence, is not a conceptual anchorage but a living force." Others function "as a critical solvent." Their existence carries "compelling moral weight" (Wyschogrod, 1990, p. xxi). As a professor of philosophy and religious thought at Rice University, with a commitment to moral narrative, Wyschogrod believes that one venue for Otherness is the saintly life, defined as one in "which compassion for the Other, irrespective of cost to the saint, is the primary trait." Saints put their own "bodies and material goods at the disposal of the Other. . . . Not only do saints contest the practices and beliefs of institutions, but in a more subtle way they contest the order of narrativity itself" (1990, pp. xxii-xxiii).

In addition to the Other-directed across a broad spectrum of belief systems who have "lived, suffered, and worked in actuality," Wyschogrod (1990, p. 7) examines historical narratives for illustrations of how the Other's self-manifestation is depicted. Her primary concern is the way communities shape shared experience in the face of cataclysms and calamities, arguing for historians who situate themselves "in dynamic relationship to them" (1998, p. 218). The overriding challenge for ethics, in Wyschogrod's view, is how historians enter into communities that create and sustain hope in terms of immediacy—"a presence here and now" but "a presence that must be deferred" to the future (1998, p. 248). Unless it is tangible and actionable, hope serves those in control. Hope that merely projects a future redemption obscures abuses of power and human need in the present.

Martin Buber (1958) calls the human relation a primal notion in his famous lines, "in the beginning is the relation" and "the relation is the cradle of life" (pp. 69, 60, 3). Social relationships are preeminent. "The one primary word is the combination I-Thou." This irreducible phenomenon—the relational reality, the in-between, the reciprocal bond, the interpersonal—cannot be decomposed into simpler elements without destroying it. Given the primacy of relationships, unless we use our freedom to help others flourish, we deny our own well-being.

Rather than privileging an abstract rationalism, the moral order is positioned close to the bone, in the creaturely and corporeal rather than the conceptual. "In this way, ethics . . . is as old as creation. Being ethical is a primordial movement in the beckoning force of life itself" (Olthuis, 1997, p. 141). The ethics of Levinas is one example:

> The human face is the epiphany of the nakedness of the Other, a visitation, a meeting, a saying which comes in the passivity of the face, not threatening, but obligating. My world is ruptured, my contentment interrupted. I am already obligated. Here is an appeal from which there is no escape, a responsibility, a state of being hostage. It is looking into the face of the Other that reveals the call to a responsibility that is before any beginning, decision or initiative on my part. (Olthuis, 1997, p. 139)

Humans are defined as communicative beings within the fabric of everyday life. Through dialogic encounter, subjects create life together and nurture one another's moral obligation to it. Levinas's ethics presumes and articulates a radical ontology of social beings in relation (see, e.g., Levinas, 1981).

Moreover, in Levinasian terms, when I turn to the face of the Other, I not only see flesh and blood, but a third party arrives—the whole of humanity. In responding to the Other's need, a baseline is established across the human race. For Benhabib (1992), this is interactive universalism.[18] Our universal solidarity is rooted in the principle that "we have inescapable claims on one another which cannot be renounced except at the cost of our humanity" (Peukert, 1981, p. 11). Our obligation to sustain one another defines our existence. The primal sacredness for all without exception is the heart of the moral order (Christians, 1997a, 1998).

A Feminist Communitarian Model

Feminist communitarianism is Denzin's (1997, pp. 274-287) label for the ethical theory to lead us forward at this juncture.[19] This is a normative model that serves as an antidote to individualist utilitarianism. It presumes that the community is ontologically and axiologically prior to persons.

Human identity is constituted through the social realm. We are born into a sociocultural universe where values, moral commitments, and existential meanings are negotiated dialogically. Fulfillment is never achieved in isolation, but only through human bonding at the epicenter of social formation.

For communitarians, the liberalism of Locke and Mill confuses an aggregate of individual pursuits with the common good. Moral agents need a context of social commitments and community ties for assessing what is valuable. What is worth preserving as a good cannot be self-determined in isolation, but can be ascertained only within specific social situations where human identity is nurtured. The public sphere is conceived as a mosaic of particular communities, a pluralism of ethnic identities and worldviews intersecting to form a social bond but each seriously held and competitive as well. Rather than pay lip service to the social nature of the self while presuming a dualism of two orders, communitarianism interlocks personal autonomy with communal well-being. Morally appropriate action intends community. Common moral values are intrinsic to a community's ongoing existence and identity.

Therefore, the mission of social science research is enabling community life to prosper—enabling people to come to mutually held conclusions. The aim is not fulsome data per se, but community transformation. The received view assumes that research advances society's interests by feeding our individual capacity to reason and make calculated decisions. Research is intended to be collaborative in its design and participatory in its execution. Rather than ethics codes in the files of academic offices and research reports prepared for clients, the participants themselves are given a forum to activate the polis mutually. In contrast to utilitarian experimentalism, the substantive conceptions of the good that drive the problems reflect the conceptions of the community rather than the expertise of researchers or funding agencies.

In the feminist communitarian model, participants have a say in how the research should be conducted and a hand in actually conducting it, "including a voice or hand in deciding which problems should be studied, what methods should be used to study them, whether the findings are valid or acceptable, and how the findings are to be used or implemented" (Root, 1993, p. 245). This research is rooted in "community, shared governance . . . and neighborliness." Given its cooperative mutuality, it serves "the community in which it is carried out, rather than the community of knowledge producers and policymakers" (Lincoln, 1995, pp. 280, 287;

see also Denzin, 1997, p. 275). It finds its genius in the maxim that "persons are arbitrators of their own presence in the world" (Denzin, 1989, p. 81).

For feminist communitarians, humans have the discursive power "to articulate situated moral rules that are grounded in local community and group understanding." Moral reasoning goes forward because people are "able to share one another's point of view in the social situation." Reciprocal care and understanding, rooted in emotional experience and not in formal consensus, are the basis on which moral discourse is possible (Denzin, 1997, p. 277; see also Denzin, 1984, p. 145; Reinharz, 1993).

Multiple moral and social spaces exist within the local community, and "every moral act is a contingent accomplishment" measured against the ideals of a universal respect for the dignity of every human being regardless of gender, age, race, or religion (Denzin, 1997, p. 274; see also Benhabib, 1992, p. 6). Through a moral order we resist those social values that are divisive and exclusivist.

◆ Interpretive Sufficiency

Within a feminist communitarian model, the mission of social science research is interpretive sufficiency. In contrast to an experimentalism of instrumental efficiency, this paradigm seeks to open up the social world in all its dynamic dimensions. The thick notion of sufficiency supplants the thinness of the technical, exterior, and statistically precise received view. Rather than reducing social issues to financial and administrative problems for politicians, social science research enables people to come to terms with their everyday experience themselves.

Interpretive sufficiency means taking seriously lives that are loaded with multiple interpretations and grounded in cultural complexity (Denzin, 1989, pp. 81, 77). Ethnographic accounts "should possess that amount of depth, detail, emotionality, nuance, and coherence that will permit a critical consciousness to be formed by the reader. Such texts should also exhibit representational adequacy, including the absence of racial, class, and gender stereotyping" (Denzin, 1997, p. 283; see also Christians, Ferre, & Fackler, 1993, pp. 120-122).

From the perspective of a feminist communitarian ethics, interpretive discourse is authentically sufficient when it fulfills three conditions: represents multiple voices, enhances moral discernment, and promotes social transformation. Consistent with the community-based norms advocated here, the focus is not on professional ethics per se but on the general morality.

Multivocal and Cross-Cultural Representation

Within social and political entities are multiple spaces that exist as ongoing constructions of everyday life. The dialogical self is situated and articulated within these decisive contexts of gender, race, class, and religion. In contrast to contractarianism, where tacit consent or obligation is given to the state, promises are made and sustained to one another. Research narratives reflect a community's multiple voices through which promise keeping takes place.

In Carole Pateman's communitarian philosophy, sociopolitical entities are not to be understood first of all in terms of contracts. Making promises is one of the basic ways in which consenting human beings "freely create their own social relationships" (Pateman, 1989, p. 61; see also Pateman, 1985, pp. 26-29). We assume an obligation by making a promise. When individuals promise, they are obliged to act accordingly. But promises are made not primarily to authorities through political contracts, but to fellow citizens. If obligations are rooted in promises, obligations are owed to other colleagues in institutions and to participants in community practices. Therefore, only under conditions of participatory democracy can there be self-assumed moral obligation.

Pateman understands the nature of moral agency. We know ourselves primarily in relation, and derivatively as thinkers withdrawn from action. Only by overcoming the traditional dualisms between thinker and agent, mind and body, reason and will, can we conceive of being as "the mutuality of personal relationships" (MacMurray, 1961a, p. 38). Moral commitments arise out of action and return to action for their incarnation and verification. From a dialogical perspective, promise keeping through action and everyday language is not a supercilious pursuit, because our way of being is not inwardly generated but socially derived.

> We become full human agents, capable of understanding ourselves, and hence of defining our identity, through . . . rich modes of expression we learn through exchange with others. . . .
>
> My discovering my own identity doesn't mean that I work it out in isolation, but that I negotiate it through dialogue, partly overt, partly internal,

with others. My own identity crucially depends on my dialogical relations with others. . . .

In the culture of authenticity, relationships are seen as the key loci of self discovery and self-affirmation. (Taylor et al., 1994, pp. 32, 34, 36)

If moral bondedness flows horizontally and obligation is reciprocal in character, the affirming and sustaining of promises occur cross-culturally. But the contemporary challenge of cultural diversity has raised the stakes and made easy solutions impossible. One of the most urgent and vexing issues on the democratic agenda at present is how to recognize explicit cultural groups politically. "Nonrecognition or misrecognition can inflict harm, can be a form of oppression, imprisoning someone in a false, distorted and reduced mode of being" (Taylor et al., 1994, p. 26).

However, liberal proceduralism cannot meet this vital human need. Emphasizing equal rights with no particular substantive view of the good life "gives only a very restricted acknowledgement of distinct cultural identities" (Taylor et al., 1994, p. 52). Insisting on neutrality, and without collective goals, produces at best personal freedom, safety, and economic security understood homogeneously. As Bunge (1996) puts it: "Contractualism is a code of behavior for the powerful and the hard—those who write contracts, not those who sign on the dotted line" (p. 230). However, in promise-based communal formation the flourishing of particular cultures, religions, and citizen groups is the substantive goal to which we are morally committed as human beings. With the starting hypothesis that all human cultures have something important to say, social science research recognizes particular cultural values consistent with universal human dignity (Christians, 1997b, pp. 197-202).

Moral Discernment

Societies are embodiments of institutions, practices, and structures recognized internally as legitimate. Without allegiance to a web of ordering relations, society becomes, as a matter of fact, inconceivable. Communities are not only linguistic entities, but require at least a minimal moral commitment to the common good. Because social entities are moral orders and not merely functional arrangements, moral commitment constitutes the self-in-relation. Our identity is defined by what we consider good or worth opposing. According to Taylor, only through the moral dimension can we make sense of human agency. As Mulhall and Swift (1996) write:

> Developing, maintaining and articulating [our moral intuitions and reactions] is not something humans could easily or even conceivably dispense with. . . . We can no more imagine a human life that fails to address the matter of its bearings in moral space than we can imagine one in which developing a sense of up and down, right and left is regarded as an optional human task. . . .
>
> . . . A moral orientation is inescapable because the questions to which the framework provides answers are themselves inescapable. (pp. 106-108; see also Taylor, 1989, pp. 27-29)

A self exists only within "webs of interlocution," and all self-interpretation implicitly or explicitly "acknowledges the necessarily social origin of any and all their conceptions of the good and so of themselves." Moral frameworks are as fundamental for orienting us in social space as the need to "establish our bearings in physical space" (Mulhall & Swift, 1996, pp. 112-113; see also Taylor, 1989, pp. 27-29).

Moral duty is nurtured by the demands of social linkage and not produced by abstract theory. The core of a society's common morality is pretheoretical agreement. However, "what counts as common morality is not only imprecise but variable . . . and a difficult practical problem" (Bok, 1995, p. 99). Moral obligation must be articulated within the fallible and irresolute voices of everyday life. Among disagreements and uncertainty, we look for criteria and wisdom in settling disputes and clarifying confusions, and normative theories of an interactive sort can invigorate our common moral discourse. But generally accepted theories are not necessary for the common good to prosper. The common good is not "the complete morality of every participant . . . but a set of agreements among people who typically hold other, less widely shared ethical beliefs" (Bok, 1995, p. 99). Instead of expecting more theoretical coherence than history warrants, Reinhold Niebuhr inspires us to work through inevitable social conflicts while maintaining "an untheoretical jumble of agreements" called here the common good (Barry, 1967, pp. 190-191). Through a common morality we can approximate consensus on issues and settle disputes interactively. In Jürgen Habermas's (1993) terms, discourse in the public sphere must be oriented "toward mutual understanding" while allowing participants "the communicative freedom to take positions" on claims to final validity (p. 66; see also Habermas, 1990).

Communitarians challenge researchers to participate in a community's ongoing process of moral articulation. In fact, culture's continued existence depends on the identification and defense of its normative base. Therefore, ethnographic texts must enable us "to discover moral truths about ourselves"; narratives ought to "bring a moral compass into readers' lives" by accounting for things that matter to them (Denzin, 1997, p. 284). Feminist communitarianism seeks to engender moral reasoning (Benhabib, 1992, p. 10). Communities are woven together by narratives that invigorate their common understanding of good and evil, happiness and reward, the meaning of life and death. Recovering and refashioning religious word forms help to amplify our deepest humanness.

As a result, for social science research the moral task cannot be reduced to professional ethics. How the moral order works itself out in community formation is the issue, not first of all what practitioners consider virtuous. The challenge for those writing culture is not to limit their moral perspectives to their own codes of ethics, but to understand ethics and values in terms of everyday life.

Resistance and Empowerment

Ethics in the feminist communitarian mode generates social criticism, leads to resistance, and empowers the interactive self and others to action (see Habermas, 1971, pp. 301-317). Thus a basic norm for interpretive research is enabling the humane transformation of the multiple spheres of community life—religion, politics, ethnicity, gender, and so forth.

From his own dialogic perspective, Paulo Freire speaks of the need to reinvent the meaning of power:

> For me the principal, real transformation, the radical transformation of society in this part of the century demands not getting power from those who have it today, or merely to make some reforms, some changes in it. . . . The question, from my point of view, is not just to take power but to reinvent it. That is, to create a different kind of power, to deny the need power has as if it were metaphysics, bureaucratized, anti-democratic. (quoted in Evans, Evans, & Kennedy, 1987, p. 229)

232

Certainly oppressive power blocs and monopolies—economic, technological, and political—need the scrutiny of researchers. Given Freire's political-institutional bearing, power for him is a central notion in social analysis. But, in concert with him, feminist communitarian research refuses to deal with power in cognitive terms only. The issue is how we can empower people instead.

The dominant understanding of power is grounded in nonmutuality; it is interventionist power, exercised competitively and seeking control. In the communitarian alternative, power is relational, characterized by mutuality rather than sovereignty. Power from this perspective is reciprocity between two subjects, a relationship not of domination, but of intimacy and vulnerability—power akin to that of Alcoholics Anonymous, in which surrender to the community enables the individual to gain mastery. Dialogue is the key element in an emancipatory strategy that liberates rather than imprisons us in manipulation or antagonistic relationships. Although the control version of power considers mutuality weakness, the empowerment mode maximizes our humanity and thereby banishes powerlessness. In the research process, power is unmasked and engaged through solidarity. Rather than play semantic games with power, researchers themselves are willing to march against the barricades. As Freire insists, only with everyone filling his or her own political space, to the point of civil disobedience as necessary, will empowerment mean anything revolutionary (see, e.g., Freire, 1970b, p. 129).

What is nonnegotiable in Freire's theory of power is participation of the oppressed in directing cultural formation. If an important social issue needs resolution, the most vulnerable will have to lead the way: "Revolutionary praxis cannot tolerate an absurd dichotomy in which the praxis of the people is merely that of following the [dominant elite's] decisions" (Freire, 1970a, p. 120; see also Freire, 1978, pp. 17ff.).[20] Arrogant politicians—supported by a bevy of accountants, lawyers, economists, and social science researchers—trivialize the nonexpert's voice as irrelevant to the problem or its solution. On the contrary, transformative action from the inside out is impossible unless the oppressed are active participants rather than a leader's object. "Only power that springs from the weakness of the oppressed will be sufficiently strong to free both" (Freire, 1970b, p. 28).

In Freire's (1973) terms, the goal is conscientization, that is, a critical consciousness that directs the ongoing flow of praxis and reflection in everyday life. In a culture of silence, the oppressor's language and way of being are fatalistically accepted without contradiction. But a critical consciousness enables us to exercise the uniquely human capacity of "speaking a true word" (Freire, 1970b, p. 75). Under conditions of sociopolitical control, "the vanquished are dispossessed of their word, their expressiveness, their culture" (1970b, p. 134). Through conscientization the oppressed gain their own voice and collaborate in transforming their culture (1970a, pp. 212-213). Therefore, research is not the transmission of specialized data but, in style and content, a catalyst for critical consciousness. Without what Freire (1970b, p. 47) calls "a critical comprehension of reality" (that is, the oppressed "grasping with their minds the truth of their reality"), there is only acquiescence in the status quo.

Fulfilling the mission of interpretive sufficiency through the three moral principles described above creates for social science research a new set of ethical demands. It still lives with IRBs as a necessity of life and is relentlessly accurate. However, because the research-subject relation is reciprocal, invasion of privacy, informed consent, and deception are non-issues. In communitarianism, conceptions of the good are shared by the research subjects, and researchers collaborate in bringing these definitions into their own.

◆ Conclusion

As Guba and Lincoln (1994) argue, the issues in social science ultimately must be engaged at the worldview level. "Questions of method are secondary to questions of paradigm, which we define as the basic belief system or worldview that guides the investigator, not only in choices of method but in ontologically and epistemologically fundamental ways" (p. 105). The conventional view, with its extrinsic ethics, gives us a truncated and unsophisticated paradigm that needs to be ontologically transformed. This historical overview of theory and practice points to the need for an entirely new model of research ethics in which human action and conceptions of the good are interactive.

"Since the relation of persons constitutes their existence as persons, . . . morally right action is [one] which intends community" (MacMurray, 1961b, p. 119). In feminist communitarianism, personal being is cut into the very heart of the social universe. The common good is accessible to us only in personal form; it has its ground and inspiration in a social ontology of the human.[21] "Ontology must be rescued from submersion in things by

234

being thought out entirely from the viewpoint of person and thus of Being" (Lotz, 1963, p. 294). "Ontology is truly itself only when it is personal and persons are truly themselves only as ontological" (Lotz, 1963, p. 297).

When rooted in a positivist worldview, explanations of social life are considered incompatible with the renderings offered by the participants themselves. In problematics, lingual form, and content, research production presumes greater mastery and clearer illumination than the non-experts who are the targeted beneficiaries. Protecting and promoting individual autonomy have been the philosophical rationale for value neutrality since its origins in Mill. But the incoherence in that view of social science is now transparent. By limiting the active involvement of rational beings or judging their self-understanding to be false, empiricist models contradict the ideal of rational beings who "choose between competing conceptions of the good" and make choices "deserving of respect." The verification standards of an instrumentalist system "take away what neutrality aims to protect: a community of free and equal rational beings legislating their own principles of conduct" (Root, 1993, p. 198). The social ontology of feminist communitarianism escapes this contradiction by reintegrating human life with the moral order.

◆ Notes

1. For greater detail regarding this argument than I can provide in the summary below, see Christians et al. (1993, pp. 18-32, 41-44).

2. Michael Root (1993) is unique among philosophers of the social sciences in linking social science to the ideals and practices of the liberal state on the grounds that both institutions "attempt to be neutral between competing conceptions of the good" (p. xv). As he elaborates: "Though liberalism is primarily a theory of the state, its principles can be applied to any of the basic institutions of a society; for one can argue that the role of the clinic, the corporation, the scholarly associations, or professions is not to dictate or even recommend the kind of life a person should aim at. Neutrality can serve as an ideal for the operations of these institutions as much as it can for the state. Their role, one can argue, should be to facilitate whatever kind of life a student, patient, client, customer, or member is aiming at and not promote one kind of life over another" (p. 13). Root's interpretations of Mill and Weber are crucial to my own formulation.

3. Although committed to what he called "the logic of the moral sciences" in delineating the canons or methods for induction, Mill shared with natural science a belief in the uniformity of nature and the presumption that all phenomena are subject to cause-and-effect relationships. His five principles of induction reflect a Newtonian cosmology.

4. Utilitarianism in John Stuart Mill was essentially an amalgamation of Bentham's greatest happiness principle, David Hume's empirical philosophy and concept of utility as a moral good, and Comte's positivist tenets that things-in-themselves cannot be known and knowledge is restricted to sensations. In his influential *A System of Logic*, Mill (1843/1893) is typically characterized as combining the principles of French positivism (as developed by August Comte) and British empiricism into a single system.

5. For an elaboration of the complexities in positivism—including reference to its Millian connections—see Lincoln and Guba (1985, pp. 19-28).

6. Mill's realism is most explicitly developed in his *Examination of Sir William Hamilton's Philosophy* (1865b). Our belief in a common external world, in his view, is rooted in the fact that our sensations of physical reality "belong as much to other human or sentient beings as to ourselves" (p. 196; see also Copleston, 1966, p. 306, n. 97).

7. Mill (1969) specifically credits to Comte his use of the inverse deductive or historical method: "This was an idea entirely new to me when I found it in Comte; and but for him I might not soon (if ever) have arrived at it" (p. 126). Mill explicitly follows Comte in distinguishing social statics and social dynamics. He published two essays on Comte's influence in the *Westminster Review*, which were reprinted as *Auguste Comte and Positivism* (Mill, 1865a; see also Mill, 1969, p. 165).

8. Emile Durkheim is more explicit and direct about causality in both the natural and the social worlds. While he argues for sociological over psychological causes of behavior and did not believe intention could cause action, he unequivocally sees the task of social science as discovering the causal links between social facts and personal behavior (see, e.g., Durkheim, 1966, pp. 44, 297-306).

9. As one example of the abuse Weber resisted, Root (1993, pp. 41-42) refers to the appointment of Ludwig Bernhard to a professorship of economics at the University of Berlin. Though he had no academic credentials, the Ministry of Education gave Bernhard this position without a faculty vote (see Weber, 1973, pp. 4-30). In Shils's (1949) terms, "A mass of particular, concrete concerns underlies [his 1917] essay—his recurrent effort to penetrate to the postulates of economic theory, his ethical passion for academic freedom, his fervent nationalist political convictions and his own perpetual demand for intellectual integrity" (p. v).

10. The rationale for the Social Science Research Council in 1923 is multilayered, but in its attempt to link academic expertise with policy research, and in its preference for rigorous social scientific methodology, the SSRC reflects and implements Weber.

11. Often in professional ethics at present, we isolate consequentialism from a full-scale utilitarianism. We give up on the idea of maximizing happiness, but "still try to evaluate different courses of action purely in terms of their consequences, hoping to state everything worth considering in our consequence-descriptions." However, even this broad version of utilitarianism, in Taylor's terms, "still legislates certain goods out of existence." It is likewise a restrictive definition of the good that favors the mode of reasoned calculation and prevents us from taking seriously all facets of moral and normative political thinking (Taylor, 1982, p. 144). As Yvonna Lincoln observes, utilitarianism's inescapable problem is that "in advocating the greatest good for the greatest number, small groups of people (all minority groups, for example) experience the political regime of the 'tyranny of the majority.'" She refers correctly to "liberalism's tendency to reinscribe oppression by virtue of the utilitarian principle" (personal communication, February 16, 1999).

12. Given the nature of positivist inquiry, Jennings and Callahan (1983) conclude that only a short list of ethical questions are considered and they "tend to merge with the canons of professional scientific methodology. . . . Intellectual honesty, the suppression of personal bias, careful collection and accurate reporting of data, and candid admission of the limits of the scientific reliability of empirical studies—these were essentially the only questions that could arise. And, since these ethical responsibilities are not particularly controversial (at least in principle), it is not surprising that during this period [the 1960s] neither those concerned with ethics nor social scientists devoted much time to analyzing or discussing them" (p. 6).

13. As Taylor (1982) puts it, "The modern dispute about utilitarianism is not about whether it occupies some of the space of moral reason, but whether it fills the whole space." "Comfort the dying" is a moral imperative in contemporary Calcutta, even though "the dying are in an extremity that makes [utilitarian] calculation irrelevant" (p. 134).

14. This restates the well-known objection to a democratic liberalism of individual rights: "Liberalism is not a possible meeting ground for all cultures, but is the political expression of one range of cultures, and quite incompatible with other ranges. Liberalism can't and shouldn't claim complete cultural neutrality. Liberalism is also a fighting creed. Multiculturalism as it is often debated today has a lot to do with the imposition of some cultures on others, and with the assumed superiority that powers this imposition. Western liberal societies are thought to be supremely guilty in this regard, partly because of their colonial past, and partly because of their marginalization of segments of their populations that stem from other cultures" (Taylor et al., 1994, pp. 62-63).

15. Denzin in this passage credits Smith (1987, p. 107) with the concept of a "ruling apparatus."

16. Gilligan's research methods and conclusions have been debated by a diverse range of scholars. For this debate and related issues, see Brabeck (1990), Card (1991), Tong (1989, pp. 161-168; 1993, pp. 80-157), Wood (1994), and Seigfried (1996).

17. Levinas (b. 1905) was a professor of philosophy at the University of Paris (Nanterre) and head of the Israelite Normal School in Paris. In Wyschogrod's (1974) terms, "He continues the tradition of Martin Buber and Franz Rosenweig" and was "the first to introduce Husserl's work into . . . the French phenomenological school" (pp. vii-viii). Although Wyschogrod is a student of Heidegger, Hegel, and Husserl (see, e.g., Wyschogrod, 1985)— and engaged with Derrida, Lyotard, Foucault, and Deleuze—her work on ethics appeals not to traditional philosophical discourse but to concrete expressions of self-Other transactions in the visual arts, literary narrative, historiography, and the normalization of death in the news.

18. Martha Nussbaum (1993) argues for a version of virtue ethics in these terms, contending for a model rooted in Aristotle that has cross-cultural application without being detached from particular forms of social life. In her model, various spheres of human experience that are found in all cultures represent questions to answer and choices to make— attitudes toward the ill or good fortune of others, how to treat strangers, management of property, control over bodily appetites, and so forth. Our experiences in these areas "fix a subject for further inquiry" (p. 247). And our reflection on each sphere will give us a "thin or nominal definition" of a virtue relevant to this sphere. On this basis we can talk across cultures about behavior appropriate in each sphere (see Nussbaum, 1999).

19. Root (1993, chap. 10) also chooses a communitarian alternative to the dominant paradigm. In his version, critical theory, participatory research, and feminist social science are three examples of the communitarian approach. This chapter offers a more complex view of communitarianism developed in political philosophy and intellectual history, rather than limiting it to social theory and practical politics. Among the philosophical communitarians (Sandel, 1982; Taylor, 1989; Walzer, 1983, 1987), Carole Pateman (1985, 1989) is explicitly feminist, and her promise motif forms the axis for the principle of multivocal representation outlined below. In this chapter's feminist communitarian model, critical theory is integrated into the third ethical imperative—empowerment and resistance. In spite of that difference in emphasis, I agree with Root's (1993) conclusion: "Critical theories are always critical for a particular community, and the values they seek to advance are the values of that community. In that respect, critical theories are communitarian. . . . For critical theorists, the standard for choosing or accepting a social theory is the reflective acceptability of the theory by members of the community for whom the theory is critical" (pp. 233-234).

20. Mutuality is a cardinal feature of the feminist communitarian model generally, and therefore crucial to the principle of empowerment. For this reason, critical theory is inscribed into the third principle here, rather than following Root (see note 18, above), allowing it to stand by itself as an illustration of communitarianism. Root (1993, p. 238) himself observes that critical theorists often fail to transfer the "ideals of expertise" to their research subjects or give them little say in the research design and interpretation. Without a fundamental shift to communitarian interactivity, research in all modes is prone to the distributive fallacy.

21. Michael Theunissen (1984) argues that Buber's relational self (and therefore its legacy in Levinas, Freire, Heller, Wyschogrod, and Taylor) is distinct from the subjectivity of Continental existentialism. The subjective sphere of Husserl and Sartre, for example, "stands in no relation to a Thou and is not a member of a We" (p. 20; see also p. 276). "According to Heidegger the self can only come to itself in a voluntary separation from other selves; according to Buber, it has its being solely in the relation" (p. 284).

◆ References

Barry, B. (1967). Justice and the common good. In A. Quinton (Ed.), *Political philosophy* (pp. 190-191). Oxford: Oxford University Press.

Benhabib, S. (1992). *Situating the self: Gender, community and postmodernism in contemporary ethics*. Cambridge: Polity.

Bok, S. (1995). *Common values*. Columbia: University of Missouri Press.

Brabeck, M. M. (Ed.). (1990). *Who cares? Theory, research, and educational implications of the ethic of care*. New York: Praeger.

Buber, M. (1958). *I and thou* (2nd ed.; R. G. Smith, Trans.). New York: Scribner's.

Bulmer, M. (1982). The merits and demerits of covert participant observation. In M. Bulmer (Ed.), *Social research ethics* (pp. 217-251). London: Macmillan.

Bunge, M. (1996). *Finding philosophy in social science*. New Haven, CT: Yale University Press.

Card, C. (Ed.). (1991). *Feminist ethics*. Lawrence: University of Kansas Press.

Christians, C. G. (1997a). Social ethics and mass media practice. In J. M. Makau & R. C. Arnett (Eds.), *Communication ethics in an age of diversity* (pp. 187-205). Urbana: University of Illinois Press.

Christians, C. G. (1997b). The ethics of being. In C. G. Christians & M. Traber (Eds.), *Communication ethics and universal values* (pp. 3-23). Thousand Oaks, CA: Sage.

Christians, C. G. (1998). The sacredness of life. *Media Development, 45*(2), 3-7.

Christians, C. G., Ferre, J. P., & Fackler, P. M. (1993). *Good news: Social ethics and the press*. New York: Oxford University Press.

Code, L. (1991). *What can she know? Feminist theory and the construction of knowledge*. Ithaca, NY: Cornell University Press.

Comte, A. (1910). *A general view of positivism* (J. H. Bridges, Trans.). London: Routledge. (Original work published 1848; subsequently published as the first volume of *Positive philosophy*, 2 vols., H. Martineau, Trans., London: Trübner, 1853)

Copleston, F. (1966). *A history of philosophy: Vol. 8. Modern philosophy: Bentham to Russell*. Garden City, NY: Doubleday.

Denzin, N. K. (1984). *On understanding emotion*. San Francisco: Jossey-Bass.

Denzin, N. K. (1989). *Interpretive biography*. Newbury Park, CA: Sage.

Denzin, N. K. (1997). *Interpretive ethnography: Ethnographic practices for the 21st century*. Thousand Oaks, CA: Sage.

Durkheim, E. (1966). *Suicide: A study of sociology*. New York: Free Press.

Euben, J. P. (1981). Philosophy and the professions. *Democracy, 1*(2), 112-127.

Evans, A. F., Evans, R. A., & Kennedy, W. B. (1987). *Pedagogies for the non-poor*. Maryknoll, NY: Orbis.

Foucault, M. (1979). *Discipline and punish: The birth of the prison* (A. Sheridan, Trans.). New York: Random House.

Freire, P. (1970a). *Education as the practice of freedom: Cultural action for freedom*. Cambridge, MA: Harvard Educational Review/Center for the Study of Development.

Freire, P. (1970b). *Pedagogy of the oppressed*. New York: Seabury.

Freire, P. (1973). *Education for critical consciousness*. New York: Seabury.

Freire, P. (1978). *Pedagogy in process: The letters of Guinea-Bissau*. New York: Seabury.

Gilligan, C. (1982). *In a different voice: Psychological theory and women's development*. Cambridge, MA: Harvard University Press.

Gilligan, C. (1983). Do the social sciences have an adequate theory of moral development? In N. Haan, R. N. Bellah, P. Rabinow, & W. M. Sullivan (Eds.),

Social science as moral inquiry (pp. 33-51). New York: Columbia University Press.

Gilligan, C., Ward, J. V., & Taylor, J. M. (1988). *Mapping the moral domain.* Cambridge, MA: Harvard University, Graduate School of Education.

Guba, E. G., & Lincoln, Y. S. (1994). Competing paradigms in qualitative research. In N. K. Denzin & Y. S. Lincoln (Eds.), *Handbook of qualitative research* (pp. 105-117). Thousand Oaks, CA: Sage.

Habermas, J. (1971). *Knowledge and human interests* (J. J. Shapiro, Trans.). Boston: Beacon.

Habermas, J. (1990). *Moral consciousness and communicative action* (C. Lenhardt & S. W. Nicholson, Trans.). Cambridge: MIT Press.

Habermas, J. (1993). *Justification and application: Remarks on discourse ethics* (C. Cronin, Trans.). Cambridge: MIT Press.

Held, V. (1993). *Feminist morality: Transforming culture, society, and politics.* Chicago: University of Chicago Press.

Heller, A. (1988). *General ethics.* Oxford: Blackwell.

Heller, A. (1990). *A philosophy of morals.* Oxford: Blackwell.

Heller, A. (1996). *An ethics of personality.* Oxford: Blackwell.

Humphreys, L. (1970). *Tearoom trade: Impersonal sex in public places.* Chicago: Aldine.

Humphreys, L. (1972). *Out of the closet.* Englewood Cliffs, NJ: Prentice Hall.

Jennings, B. (1983). Interpretive social science and policy analysis. In D. Callahan & B. Jennings (Eds.), *Ethics, the social sciences, and policy analysis* (pp. 3-35). New York: Plenum.

Jennings, B., & Callahan, D. (1983, February). Social sciences and the policy-making process. *Hastings Center Report,* pp. 3-8.

Koehn, D. (1998). *Rethinking feminist ethics: Care, trust and empathy.* New York: Routledge.

Lazarsfeld, P., & Reitz, J. G. (1975). *An introduction to applied sociology.* New York: Elsevier.

Levinas, E. (1981). *Otherwise than being or essence.* The Hague: Martinus Nijhoff.

Lincoln, Y. S. (1995). Emerging criteria for quality in qualitative and interpretive inquiry. *Qualitative Inquiry, 1,* 275-289.

Lincoln, Y. S., & Guba, E. G. (1985). *Naturalistic inquiry.* Beverly Hills, CA: Sage.

Lotz, J. B. (1963). Person and ontology. *Philosophy Today, 7,* 294-297.

MacMurray, J. (1961a). *The form of the personal: Vol. 1. The self as agent.* London: Faber & Faber.

MacMurray, J. (1961b). *The form of the personal: Vol. 2. Persons in relation.* London: Faber & Faber.

Milgram, S. (1974). *Obedience to authority.* New York: Harper & Row.

Mill, J. S. (1865a). *Auguste Comte and positivism.* London.

Mill, J. S. (1865b). *Examination of Sir William Hamilton's philosophy and of the principal philosophical questions discussed in his writings.* London: Longman, Green, Roberts & Green.

Mill, J. S. (1893). *A system of logic, ratiocinative and inductive: Being a connected view of the principles of evidence and the methods of scientific investigation* (8th ed.). New York: Harper & Brothers. (Original work published 1843)

Mill, J. S. (1957). *Utilitarianism.* Indianapolis: Bobbs-Merrill. (Original work published 1861)

Mill, J. S. (1969). *Autobiography.* Boston: Houghton Mifflin. (Original work published posthumously 1873)

Mill, J. S. (1978). *On liberty.* Indianapolis: Hackett. (Original work published 1859)

Mulhall, S., & Swift, A. (1996). *Liberals and communitarians* (2nd ed.). Oxford: Blackwell.

Noddings, N. (1984). *Caring: A feminine approach to ethics and moral education.* Berkeley: University of California Press.

Noddings, N. (1989). *Women and evil.* Berkeley: University of California Press.

Noddings, N. (1990). Ethics from the standpoint of women. In D. L. Rhode (Ed.), *Theoretical perspectives on sexual difference* (pp. 160-173). New Haven, CT: Yale University Press.

Nussbaum, M. (1993). Non-relative virtues: An Aristotelian approach. In M. Nussbaum & A. Sen, *The quality of life* (pp. 242-269). Oxford: Clarendon.

Nussbaum, M. (1999). *Sex and social justice.* New York: Oxford University Press.

Olthuis, J. (1997). Face-to-face: Ethical asymmetry or the symmetry of mutuality? In J. Olthuis (Ed.), *Knowing other-wise* (pp. 134-164). New York: Fordham University Press.

Pateman, C. (1985). *The problem of political obligation: A critique of liberal theory.* Cambridge: Polity.

Pateman, C. (1988). *The sexual contract.* Stanford, CA: Stanford University Press.

Pateman, C. (1989). *The disorder of women: Democracy, feminism and political theory.* Stanford, CA: Stanford University Press.

Peukert, H. (1981). Universal solidarity as the goal of ethics. *Media Development, 28*(4), 10-12.

Punch, M. (1994). Politics and ethics in qualitative research. In N. K. Denzin & Y. S. Lincoln (Eds.), *Handbook of qualitative research* (pp. 83-97). Thousand Oaks, CA: Sage.

Reinharz, S. (1993). *Social research methods: Feminist perspectives.* New York: Elsevier.

Reiss, A. J., Jr. (1979). Governmental regulation of scientific inquiry: Some paradoxical consequences. In C. B. Klockars & F. W. O'Connor (Eds.), *Deviance and decency: The ethics of research with human subjects* (pp. 61-95). Beverly Hills, CA: Sage.

Root, M. (1993). *Philosophy of social science: The methods, ideals, and politics of social inquiry.* Oxford: Blackwell.

Ryan, K. E. (1995). Evaluation ethics and issues of social justice: Contributions from female moral thinking. In N. K. Denzin (Ed.), *Studies in symbolic interaction: A research annual* (Vol. 19, pp. 143-151). Greenwich, CT: JAI.

Sandel, M. J. (1982). *Liberalism and the limits of justice.* Cambridge: Cambridge University Press.

Seigfried, C. H. (1996). *Pragmatism and feminism: Reweaving the social fabric.* Chicago: University of Chicago Press.

Shils, E. A. (1949). Foreword. In M. Weber, *The methodology of the social sciences* (pp. iii-x). New York: Free Press.

Smith, D. E. (1987). *The everyday world as problematic: A feminist sociology.* Boston: Northeastern University Press.

Soble, A. (1978, October). Deception in social science research: Is informed consent possible? *Hastings Center Report,* pp. 40-46.

Steiner, L. (1991). Feminist theorizing and communication ethics. *Communication, 12*(3), 157-174.

Steiner, L. (1997). A feminist schema for analysis of ethical dilemmas. In F. L. Casmir (Ed.), *Ethics in intercultural and international communication* (pp. 59-88). Mahwah, NJ: Lawrence Erlbaum.

Taylor, C. (1982). The diversity of goods. In A. Sen & B. Williams (Eds.), *Utilitarianism and beyond* (pp. 129-144). Cambridge: Cambridge University Press.

Taylor, C. (1989). *Sources of the self: The making of the modern identity.* Cambridge, MA: Harvard University Press.

Taylor, C. (1991). *The ethics of authenticity.* Cambridge, MA: Harvard University Press.

Taylor, C., Appiah, K. A., Habermas, J., Rockefeller, S. C., Walzer, M., & Wolf, S. (1994). *Multiculturalism: Examining the politics of recognition* (A. Gutmann, Ed.). Princeton, NJ: Princeton University Press.

Theunissen, M. (1984). *The other: Studies in the social ontology of Husserl, Heidegger, Sartre, and Buber* (C. Macann, Trans.). Cambridge: MIT Press.

Tong, R. (1989). *Feminist thought.* Boulder, CO: Westview.

Tong, R. (1993). *Feminine and feminist ethics.* Belmont, CA: Wadsworth.

University of Illinois at Urbana-Champaign, Institutional Review Board. (1995, May). Part I: Fundamental principles for the use of human subjects in research. In *Handbook for investigators: For the protection of human subjects in research.* Urbana: Author. Available Internet: http://www.uiuc.edu/unit/vcres/irb/handbook/sec1)

Vanderpool, H. Y. (Ed.). (1996). *The ethics of research involving human subjects: Facing the 21st century.* Frederick, MD: University Publishing Group.

Veatch, R. M. (1996). From Nuremberg through the 1990s: The priority of autonomy. In H. Y. Vanderpool (Ed.), *The ethics of research involving human subjects: Facing the 21st century* (pp. 45-58). Frederick, MD: University
Publishing Group.

Walzer, M. (1983). *Spheres of justice: A defense of pluralism and equality.* New
York: Basic Books.

Walzer, M. (1987). *Interpretation and social criticism.* Cambridge, MA: Harvard
University Press.

Weber, M. (1949a). The meaning of ethical neutrality in sociology and economics.
In M. Weber, *The methodology of the social sciences* (E. A. Shils & H. A.
Finch, Eds. & Trans.). New York: Free Press. (Original work published 1917)

Weber, M. (1949b). Objectivity in social science and social policy. In M. Weber, *The
methodology of the social sciences* (E. A. Shils & H. A. Finch, Eds. & Trans.).
New York: Free Press. (Original work published 1904)

Weber, M. (1973). *Max Weber on universities* (E. A. Shils, Ed. & Trans.). Chicago:
University of Chicago Press.

West, C. (1989). *The American evasion of philosophy: A genealogy of pragmatism.*
Madison: University of Wisconsin Press.

West, C. (1991). *The ethical dimensions of Marxist thought.* New York: Monthly
Review Books.

White, R. (1995). From codes of ethics to public cultural truth. *European Journal of
Communication, 10,* 441-460.

Wood, J. (1994). *Who cares? Women, care, and culture.* Carbondale: Southern Illinois University Press.

Wyschogrod, E. (1974). *Emmanuel Levinas: The problem of ethical metaphysics.*
The Hague: Martinus Nijhoff.

Wyschogrod, E. (1985). *Spirit in ashes: Hegel, Heidegger, and man-made death.*
Chicago: University of Chicago Press.

Wyschogrod, E. (1990). *Saints and postmodernism: Revisioning moral philosophy.*
Chicago: University of Chicago Press.

Wyschogrod, E. (1998). *An ethics of remembering: History, heterology, and the
nameless others.* Chicago: University of Chicago Press.

PART II

Paradigms and Perspectives in Transition

In our introductory chapter, following Guba (1990, p. 17), we defined a paradigm as a basic set of beliefs that guide action. Paradigms deal with first principles, or ultimates. They are human constructions. They define the worldview of the researcher-as-interpretive *bricoleur*. These beliefs can never be established in terms of their ultimate truthfulness. Perspectives, in contrast, are not as solidified, or as well unified, as paradigms, although a perspective may share many elements with a paradigm, such as a common set of methodological assumptions or a particular epistemology.

A paradigm encompasses four concepts: ethics (axiology), epistemology, ontology, and methodology. *Ethics* asks, How will I be as a moral person in the world? *Epistemology* asks, How do I know the world? What is the relationship between the inquirer and the known? Every epistemology, as Christians indicates in Chapter 5 of this volume, implies an ethical-moral stance toward the world and the self of the researcher. *Ontology* raises basic questions about the nature of reality and the nature of the human being in the world. *Methodology* focuses on the best means for gaining knowledge about the world.

Part II of this volume examines the major paradigms and perspectives that now structure and organize qualitative research: positivism, postpositivism, constructivism, and participatory action frameworks. Alongside these paradigms are the perspectives of feminism (in its multiple forms), critical race theory, queer theory, and cultural studies. Each of these perspectives has developed its own criteria, assumptions, and methodological practices, which are then applied to disciplined inquiry within that framework. (Tables 6.1 and 6.2 in Chapter 6, by Lincoln and Guba, outline the major differences among the positivist, postpositivist, critical theory, constructivist, and participatory paradigms.)

We have provided a brief discussion of each paradigm and perspective in Chapter 1; here we elaborate them in somewhat more detail. However, before turning to this discussion, it is important to note that within the past decade, the borders and boundary lines separating these paradigms and perspectives have begun to blur. As Yvonna Lincoln and Egon Guba observe in Chapter 6, the various paradigms are beginning to "interbreed." Hence the title of this section, "Paradigms and Perspectives in Transition."

◆ Major Issues Confronting All Paradigms

Lincoln and Guba suggest in Chapter 6 that in the present moment all paradigms must confront seven basic, critical issues: axiology (ethics and values), accommodation and commensurability (can paradigms be fitted into one another?), action (what the researcher does in the world), control (who initiates inquiry, who asks questions), foundations of truth (foundationalism versus anti- and nonfoundationalism), validity (traditional positivist models versus poststructuralist-constructionist criteria), and voice, reflexivity, and postmodern representation (single-voice versus multivoiced representation).

Each paradigm takes a different stance on these topics. Of course the positivist and postpositivist paradigms provide the backdrop against which these other paradigms and perspectives operate. Lincoln and Guba analyze these two traditions in considerable detail, including their reliance on naïve realism, their dualistic epistemologies, their verificational approach to inquiry, and their emphasis on reliability, validity, prediction, control, and a building-block approach to knowledge. Lincoln and Guba discuss the inability of these paradigms to address adequately issues surrounding voice, empowerment, and praxis. They also allude to the failure of these paradigms to address satisfactorily the theory- and value-laden nature of facts, the interactive nature of inquiry, and the fact that the same sets of "facts" can support more than one theory.

◆ Constructivism, Interpretivism, and Hermeneutics

According to Lincoln and Guba, *constructivism* adopts a relativist ontology (relativism), a transactional epistemology, and a hermeneutic, dialectical methodology. Users of this paradigm are oriented to the production of reconstructed understandings of the social world. The traditional positivist criteria of internal and external validity are replaced by such terms as *trustworthiness* and *authenticity*. Constructivists value transactional knowledge. Their work overlaps with the several different participatory action approaches discussed by Kemmis and McTaggart in Chapter 11 of Volume 2. Constructivism connects action to praxis and builds on antifoundational arguments while encouraging experimental and multivoiced texts.

In Chapter 7, Thomas Schwandt offers a carefully nuanced, complex, and subtle analysis of the interpretivist, hermeneutic, and constructionist perspectives. He identifies major differences and strands of thought within each approach while indicating how they are unified by their opposition to positivism and their commitment to study the world from the point of view of the interacting individual. Yet these perspectives, as Schwandt argues, are distinguished more by their commitment to questions of knowing and being than by their specific methodologies, which basically enact an emic, idiographic approach to inquiry. Schwandt traces the theoretical and philosophical foundations of the constructivist and interpretivist traditions, connecting them back to the works of Schutz, Weber, Mead, Blumer, Winch, Heidegger, Gadamer, Geertz, Ricoeur, Gergen, Goodman, Guba, and Lincoln. The constructivist tradition, as Schwandt notes, is rich, deep, and complex. This complexity is evidenced in the ethical and political implications of these perspectives. The interpreter must always ask, How shall I be toward these people I am studying?

◆ The Feminisms

In Chapter 8, Virginia Olesen observes that feminist qualitative research is a highly diversified and contested site. Competing models blur together, but beneath the fray and the debate there is agreement that feminist inquiry is always dialectical and always committed to action in the world. Olesen's is an impassioned feminism. She contends that "rage is not enough"; we need "incisive scholarship to frame, direct, and harness passion in the interests of redressing grievous problems in many areas of women's health."

In her contribution to the first edition of this *Handbook*, Olesen (1994) identified three major strands of feminist inquiry: standpoint epistemology, empiricism, and postmodernism-cultural studies. Six years later, these strands have multiplied (see her Table 8.1) as the field has become much more complex and theoretically diverse. There are today separate feminisms associated with the writings of women of color, women problematizing whiteness, postcolonial discourse, lesbian research and queer theory, disabled women, standpoint theory, and postmodern and deconstructive theory. This complexity has problematized the researcher-participant relationship. It has destabilized the insider-outsider model of inquiry. It has produced a deconstruction of such traditional terms as *experience, difference,* and *gender* while simultaneously seeking a feminist solidarity in the service of the overthrow of oppression. Five newly framed issues have emerged from this discourse, focusing on the concepts of bias and objectivity, validity and trustworthiness, voice, and feminist ethics. On this last point, Olesen's masterful chapter elaborates the framework presented by Clifford Christians in Chapter 5.

◆ Racialized Discourses and Ethnic Epistemologies

In Chapter 9, Gloria Ladson-Billings moves critical race theory directly into the field of qualitative inquiry. Critical race theory "seeks to decloak the seemingly race-neutral, and color-blind ways . . . of constructing and administering race-based appraisals . . . of the law, administrative policy, electoral politics . . . political discourse [and education] in the USA" (Parker, Deyhle, Villenas, & Nebeker, 1998, p. 5). Critical race theory enacts an ethnic epistemology, arguing that ways of knowing and being are shaped by the individual's standpoint, or position in the world. This standpoint undoes the cultural, ethical, and epistemological logic (and racism) of the Eurocentric, Enlightenment paradigm.

Drawing on recent work by African American, Asian Pacific Islander, Asian American, Latino, and Native American scholars, Ladson-Billings introduces the concepts of multiple or double consciousness, *mestiza* consciousness, and tribal secrets. The analysis of these ideas allows her to show how the dominant cultural paradigms have produced fractured, racialized identities and experiences of exclusion for minority scholars. Critical race theorists experiment with multiple interpretive strategies, ranging from storytelling to autoethnography, case studies, textual and narrative analyses, traditional fieldwork, and, most important, collaborative, action-based inquiries and studies of race, gender, law, education, and ethnic oppression in daily life.

◆ Critical Theory

Multiple critical theories and Marxist and neo-Marxist models now circulate within the discourses of qualitative research. In Lincoln and Guba's framework this paradigm, in its many formulations, articulates an ontology based on historical realism, an epistemology that is transactional and a methodology that is both dialogic and dialectical. In Chapter 10, Joe Kincheloe and Peter McLaren trace the history of critical research (and Marxist theory) from the Frankfurt school through more recent transformations in poststructural, postmodern, feminist, critical pedagogy, and cultural studies theory. They outline a critical theory for the new millennium, beginning with the assumption that the societies of the West are not unproblematically democratic and free. Their version of critical theory rejects economic determinism and focuses on the media, culture, language, power, desire, critical enlightenment, and critical emancipation. Their framework (like Schwandt's) embraces a critical hermeneutics. Building on Dewey and Gramsci, Kincheloe and McLaren present a critical, pragmatic approach to texts and their relationships to lived experience. This leads to a "resistance" version of critical theory, a version connected to critical ethnography, and partisan, critical inquiry committed to social criticism and the empowerment of individuals. Critical theorists seek to produce practical, pragmatic knowledge that is cultural and structural, judged by its degree of historical situatedness and its ability to produce praxis, or action.

◆ Cultural Studies

Cultural studies cannot be contained within a single framework. There are multiple cultural studies projects, including those connected to the Birmingham school and the work of Stuart Hall and his associates (see

Hall, 1996). Cultural studies research is historically self-reflective, critical, interdisciplinary, conversant with high theory, and focused on the global and the local, taking into account historical, political, economic, cultural, and everyday discourses. It focuses on "questions of community, identity, agency and change" (Grossberg & Pollock, 1998).

In its generic form, cultural studies involves an examination of how the history people live is produced by structures that have been handed down from the past. Each version of cultural studies is joined by a threefold concern with cultural texts, lived experience, and the articulated relationship between texts and everyday life. Within the cultural text tradition, some scholars examine the mass media and popular culture as sites where history, ideology, and subjective experiences come together. These scholars produce critical ethnographies of the audience in relation to particular historical moments. Other scholars read texts as sites where hegemonic meanings are produced, distributed, and consumed. Within the ethnographic tradition, there is a postmodern concern for the social text and its production.

The open-ended nature of the cultural studies project leads to a perpetual resistance against attempts to impose a single definition over the entire project. There are critical-Marxist, constructionist, and postpositivist paradigmatic strands within the formation, as well as emergent feminist and ethnic models. Scholars within the cultural studies project are drawn to historical realism and relativism as their ontology, to transactional epistemologies, and to dialogic methodologies, while remaining committed to a historical and structural framework that is action oriented.

In Chapter 11, John Frow and Meaghan Morris outline a critical materialist cultural studies project, noting that contemporary versions of cultural studies have been shaped by encounters among diverse feminisms; ethnic and critical race studies; gay, lesbian, and queer studies; postcolonial and diasporic research; and indigenous peoples' scholarship. These interactions have produced a sensitivity to culture in its multiple forms, including the aesthetic, the political, the anthropological, the performative, the historical, and the spatial. Thus there are collections and essays in Australian-Asian cultural studies; Asian Pacific cultural studies; Latin American, Mexican, and Chicana/o cultural studies; black British cultural studies; and Irish, British, Spanish, Italian, Nordic, and African cultural studies.

At the same time, students of cultural studies wrestle with the multiple meanings of such key terms as *identity, place, globalization, the local, nationhood,* and *difference.* These terms are constantly debated in the media and are played out in arenas defined and shaped by the new information and communication technologies. Cultural studies scholars examine how meanings move between and within various media formations. This has yielded studies of Madonna, Elvis, the Gulf War, and Anita Hill, as well as studies of the "memory-work" of museums, tourism, and shopping malls. In such work it becomes clear that culture is a contested, conflictual set of practices bound up with the meanings of identity and community.

The disciplinary boundaries that define cultural studies keep shifting, and there is no agreed-upon standard genealogy of the field's emergence as a serious academic discipline. Nonetheless, there are certain prevailing tendencies, including feminist understandings of the politics of the everyday and the personal; disputes among proponents of textualism, ethnography, and autoethnography; and continued debates surrounding the dreams of modern citizenship.

◆ Sexualities and Queer Theory

Critical race theory brought race and the concept of a complex racial subject squarely into qualitative inquiry. Next it remained for queer theory to do the same—namely, to question and deconstruct the concept of an unreflexive, unified sexual (and racialized) subject. In Chapter 12, Joshua Gamson documents the story of how mainstream social science was forced to confront the politics of sexuality along with the politics of race. He shows how the study of sexualities has long been intertwined with qualitative research (life stories, ethnographies). By troubling the place of the homo/heterosexual binary in everyday life, queer theory has created spaces for multiple discourses on gay, bisexual, transgendered, and lesbian subjects. This means that researchers must examine how any social arena is structured, in part, by this homo/hetero dichotomy. They must ask how the epistemology of the closet is central to the sexual and material practices of everyday life. Queer theory challenges this epistemology, just as it deconstructs the notion of unified subjects. Queerness becomes a topic and a resource for investigating the way group boundaries are created, negotiated, and changed. Institutional and historical analyses are central to this project, for they shed light on how the self and its identities are embedded in institutional and cultural practices.

251

◆ In Conclusion

The researcher-as-interpretive *bricoleur* cannot afford to be a stranger to any of the paradigms and perspectives discussed in Part II of this *Handbook*. The researcher must understand the basic ethical, ontological, epistemological, and methodological assumptions of each and be able to engage them in dialogue. The differences among paradigms and perspectives have significant and important implications at the practical, material, everyday level. The blurring of paradigm differences is likely to continue as long as proponents continue to come together to discuss their differences while seeking to build on those areas where they are in agreement.

It is also clear that there is no single "truth." All truths are partial and incomplete. As Lincoln and Guba argue in Chapter 6, there will be no single conventional paradigm to which all social scientists might ascribe. We occupy a historical moment marked by multivocality, contested meanings, paradigmatic controversies, and new textual forms. This is an age of emancipation; we have been freed from the confines of a single regime of truth and from the habit of seeing the world in one color.

◆ References

Grossberg, L., & Pollock, D. (1998). Editorial statement. *Cultural Studies, 12*(2), 114.

Guba, E. G. (1990). The alternative paradigm dialog. In E. G. Guba (Ed.), *The paradigm dialog* (pp. 17-30). Newbury Park, CA: Sage.

Hall, S. (1996). Gramsci's relevance for the study of race and ethnicity. In D. Morley & K.-H. Chen (Eds.), *Stuart Hall: Critical dialogues in cultural studies* (pp. 411-444). London: Routledge.

Olesen, V. (1994). Feminisms and models of qualitative research. In N. K. Denzin & Y. S. Lincoln (Eds.), *Handbook of qualitative research* (pp. 158-174). Thousand Oaks, CA: Sage.

Parker, L., Deyhle, D., Villenas, S., & Nebeker, K. C. (1998). Guest editors' introduction: Critical race theory and qualitative studies in education. *International Journal of Qualitative Studies in Education, 11*, 5-6.

6

Paradigmatic Controversies, Contradictions, and Emerging Confluences

Yvonna S. Lincoln and Egon G. Guba

◆ In our chapter for the first edition of the *Handbook of Qualitative Research*, we focused on the contention among various research paradigms for legitimacy and intellectual and paradigmatic hegemony (Guba & Lincoln, 1994). The postmodern paradigms that we discussed (postmodernist critical theory and constructivism)[1] were in contention with the received positivist and postpositivist paradigms for legitimacy, and with one another for intellectual legitimacy. In the half dozen years that have elapsed since that chapter was published, substantial change has occurred in the landscape of social scientific inquiry.

On the matter of legitimacy, we observe that readers familiar with the literature on methods and paradigms reflect a high interest in ontologies and epistemologies that differ sharply from those undergirding conventional social science. Second, even those established professionals trained in quantitative social science (including the two of us) want to learn more about qualitative approaches, because new young professionals being

mentored in graduate schools are asking serious questions about and looking for guidance in qualitatively oriented studies and dissertations. Third,
the number of qualitative texts, research papers, workshops, and training
materials has exploded. Indeed, it would be difficult to miss the distinct
turn of the social sciences toward more interpretive, postmodern, and
criticalist practices and theorizing (Bloland, 1989, 1995). This nonpositivist orientation has created a context (surround) in which virtually
no study can go unchallenged by proponents of contending paradigms.
Further, it is obvious that the number of practitioners of new-paradigm
inquiry is growing daily. There can be no question that the legitimacy of
postmodern paradigms is well established and at least equal to the legitimacy of received and conventional paradigms (Denzin & Lincoln, 1994).

On the matter of hegemony, or supremacy, among postmodern paradigms, it is clear that Geertz's (1988, 1993) prophecy about the "blurring
of genres" is rapidly being fulfilled. Inquiry methodology can no longer be
treated as a set of universally applicable rules or abstractions. Methodology is inevitably interwoven with and emerges from the nature of particular disciplines (such as sociology and psychology) and particular perspectives (such as Marxism, feminist theory, and queer theory). So, for
instance, we can read feminist critical theorists such as Olesen (Chapter 8,
this volume) or queer theorists such as Gamson (Chapter 12, this volume),
or we can follow arguments about teachers as researchers (Kincheloe,
1991) while we understand the secondary text to be teacher empowerment and democratization of schooling practices. Indeed, the various paradigms are beginning to "interbreed" such that two theorists previously
thought to be in irreconcilable conflict may now appear, under a different
theoretical rubric, to be informing one another's arguments. A personal
example is our own work, which has been heavily influenced by action research practitioners and postmodern critical theorists. Consequently, to
argue that it is paradigms that are in contention is probably less useful than
to probe where and how paradigms exhibit confluence and where and
how they exhibit differences, controversies, and contradictions.

◆ Major Issues Confronting All Paradigms

In our chapter in the first edition of this *Handbook,* we presented two
tables that summarized our positions, first, on the axiomatic nature of
paradigms (the paradigms we considered at that time were positivism,

postpositivism, critical theory, and constructivism; Guba & Lincoln, 1994, p. 109, Table 6.1); and second, on the issues we believed were most fundamental to differentiating the four paradigms (p. 112, Table 6.2). These tables are reproduced here as a way of reminding our readers of our previous statement. The axioms defined the ontological, epistemological, and methodological bases for both established and emergent paradigms; these are shown in Table 6.1. The issues most often in contention that we examined were inquiry aim, nature of knowledge, the way knowledge is accumulated, goodness (rigor and validity) or quality criteria, values, ethics, voice, training, accommodation, and hegemony; these are shown in Table 6.2. An examination of these two tables will reacquaint the reader with our original *Handbook* treatment; more detailed information is, of course, available in our original chapter.

Since publication of that chapter, at least one set of authors, John Heron and Peter Reason, have elaborated upon our tables to include the *participatory/cooperative* paradigm (Heron, 1996; Heron & Reason, 1997, pp. 289-290). Thus, in addition to the paradigms of positivism, postpositivism, critical theory, and constructivism, we add the participatory paradigm in the present chapter (this is an excellent example, we might add, of the hermeneutic elaboration so embedded in our own view, constructivism).

Our aim here is to extend the analysis further by building on Heron and Reason's additions and by rearranging the issues to reflect current thought. The issues we have chosen include our original formulations and the additions, revisions, and amplifications made by Heron and Reason (1997), and we have also chosen what we believe to be the issues most important today. We should note that *important* means several things to us. An important topic may be one that is widely debated (or even hotly contested)—validity is one such issue. An important issue may be one that bespeaks a new awareness (an issue such as recognition of the role of values). An important issue may be one that illustrates the influence of one paradigm upon another (such as the influence of feminist, action research, critical theory, and participatory models on researcher conceptions of action within and for the community in which research is carried out). Or issues may be important because new or extended theoretical and/or field-oriented treatments for them are newly available—voice and reflexivity are two such issues.

Table 6.3 reprises the original Table 6.1 but adds the axioms of the participatory paradigm proposed by Heron and Reason (1997). Table 6.4

TABLE 6.1   Basic Belief (Metaphysics) of Alternative Inquiry Paradigms

Item	Positivism	Postpostivism	Critical Theory et al.	Constructivism
Ontology	naïve realism— "real" reality but apprehendable	critical realism— "real" reality but only imperfectly and probabilistically apprehendable	historical realism—virtual reality shaped by social, political, cultural, economic, ethnic, and gender values; crystallized over time	relativism—local and specific constructed realities
Epistemology	dualist/ objectivist; findings true	modified dualist/ objectivist;critical tradition/ community; findings probably true	transactional/ subjectivist; value-mediated findings	transactional/ subjectivist; created findings
Methodology	experimental/ manipulative; verification of hypotheses; chiefly quantitative methods	modified experimental/ manipulative; critical multiplism; falsification of hypotheses; may include qualitative methods	dialogic/ dialectical	hermeneutical/ dialectical

deals with seven issues and represents an update of selected issues first presented in the old Table 6.2. "Voice" in the 1994 version of Table 6.2 has been renamed "inquirer posture," and a redefined "voice" has been inserted in the current Table 6.5. In all cases except "inquirer posture," the entries for the participatory paradigm are those proposed by Heron and Reason; in the one case not covered by them, we have added a notation that we believe captures their intention.

We make no attempt here to reprise the material well discussed in our earlier *Handbook* chapter. Instead, we focus solely on the issues in Table 6.5: axiology; accommodation and commensurability; action; control; foundations of truth and knowledge; validity; and voice, reflexivity, and postmodern textual representation. We believe these seven issues to be the most important at this time.

TABLE 6.2   Paradigm Positions on Selected Practical Issues

Item	Positivism	Postpositivism	Critical Theory et al.	Constructivism
Inquiry aim	explanation: prediction and control		critique and transformation; restitution and emancipation	understanding; reconstruction
Nature of knowledge	verified hypotheses established as facts or laws	nonfalsified hypotheses that are probable facts or laws	structural/historical insights	individual reconstructions coalescing around consensus
Knowledge accumulation	accretion—"building blocks" adding to "edifice of knowledge"; generalizations and cause-effect linkages		historical revisionism; generalization by similarity	more informed and sophisticated reconstructions; vicarious experience
Goodness or quality criteria	conventional benchmarks of "rigor": internal and external validity, reliability, and objectivity		historical situatedness; erosion of ignorance and misapprehension; action stimulus	trustworthiness and authenticity
Values	excluded-influence denied		included-formative	
Ethics	extrinsic: tilt toward deception		intrinsic: moral tilt toward revelation	intrinsic: process tilt toward revelation; special problems
Voice	"disinterested scientist" as informer of decision makers, policy makers, and change agents		"transformative intellectual" as advocate and activist	"passionate participant" as facilitator of multivoice reconstruction
Training	technical and quantitative; substantive theories	technical; quantitative and qualitative; substantive theories	resocialization; qualitative and quantitative; history; values of altruism and empowerment	
Accommodation	commensurable		incommensurable	
Hegemony	in control of publication, funding, promotion, and tenure		seeking recognition and input	

TABLE 6.3 Basic Beliefs of Alternative Inquiry Paradigms-Updated

Issue	Positivism	Postpositivism	Critical Theory et al.	Constructivism	Participatory[a]
Ontology	naive realism—"real" reality but apprehendable	critical realism—"real" reality but only imperfectly and probabilistically apprehendable	historical realism—virtual reality shaped by social political, cultural, economic, ethnic, and gender values crystallized over time	relativism—local and specific constructed realities	participative reality-subjective-objective reality, cocreated by mind and given cosmos
Epistemology	dualist/objectivist; findings true	modified dualist/objectivist; critical tradition/community; findings probably true	Transactional/subjectivist; value-mediated findings	Transactional/subjectivist; created findings	critical subjectivity in participatory transaction with cosmos; extended epistemology of experiential, propositional, and practical knowing; cocreated findings
Methodology	experimental/manipulative; verification of hypotheses; chiefly quantitative methods	modified experimental/manipulative; critical multiplism; falsification of hypotheses; may include qualitative methods	dialogic/dialectic	hermeneutic/dialectic	political participation in collaborative action inquiry; primacy of the practical; use of language grounded in shared experiential context

a. Entries in this column are based on Heron and Reason (1997).

TABLE 6.4 Paradigm Positions on Selected Issues-Updated

Issue	Positivism	Postpositivism	Critical Theory et al.	Constructivism	Participatory[a]
Nature of knowledge	verified hypotheses established as facts or laws	nonfalsified hypotheses that are probable facts or laws	structural/historical insights	individual reconstructions coalescing around consensus	extended epistemology: primacy of practical knowing; critical subjectivity; living knowledge
Knowledge accumulation	accretion-"building blocks" adding to "edifice of knowledge"; generalizations and cause-effect linkages		historical revisionism; generalization by similarity	more informed and sophisticated reconstructions; vicarious experience	in communities of inquiry embedded in communities of practice
Goodness or quality criteria	conventional benchmarks of "rigor": internal and external validity, reliability, and objectivity		historical situatedness; erosion of ignorance and misapprehensions; action stimulus	trustworthiness and authenticity	congruence of experiential, presentational, propositional, and practical knowing; leads to action to transform the world in the service of human flourishing
Ethics	Extrinsic-tilt toward deception		intrinsic-moral tilt toward revelation	intrinsic-process tilt toward revelation	

(Continued)

259

TABLE 6.4 (Continued)

Issue	Positivism	Postpositivism	Critical Theory et al.	Constructivism	Participatory[a]
Inquirer posture	"disinterested scientist" as informer of decision makers, policy makers, and change agents	"transformative intellectual" as advocate and activist		"passionate participant" as facilitator of multivoice reconstruction	primary voice manifest through aware self-reflective action; secondary voices in illuminating theory, narrative, movement, song, dance, and other presentational forms
Training	technical and quantitative; substantive theories	technical, quantitative, and qualitative; substantive theories	resocialization; qualitative and quantitative; history; values of altruism and empowerment		coresearchers are initiated into the inquiry process by facilitator/researcher and learn through active engagement in the process; facilitator/researcher requires emotional competence, democratic personality and skills

a. Entries in this column are based on Heron and Reason (1997), except for "ethics" and "values."

TABLE 6.5 Critical Issues of the Time

Issue	Positivism	Postpositivism	Critical Theory et al.	Constructivism	Participatory
Axiology	Propositional knowing about the world is an end in itself, is intrinsically valuable.		Propositional, transactional knowing is instrumentally valuable as a means to social emancipation, which as an end in itself, is intrinsically valuable.		Practical knowing about how to flourish with a balance of autonomy, co-operation, and hierarchy in a culture is an end in itself, is intrinsically valuable.
Accommodation and commensurability	commensurable for all positivist forms		incommensurable with positivist forms; some commensurability with constructivist, criticalist, and participatory approaches, especially as they merge in liberationist approaches outside the West		

(Continued)

261

TABLE 6.5 (Continued)

Issue	Positivism	Postpositivism	Critical Theory et al.	Constructivism	Participatory
Action	not the responsibility of the researcher; viewed as "advocacy" or subjectivity, and therefore a threat to validity and objectivity		found especially in the form of empowerment; emancipation anticipated and hoped for; social transformation, particularly toward more equity and justice, is end goal	intertwined with validity; inquiry often incomplete without action on the part of participants; constructivist formulation mandates training in political action if participants do not understand political systems	
Control	resides solely in researcher		often resides in "transformative intellectual"; in new constructions, control returns to community	shared between inquirer and participants	shared to varying degrees
Relationship to foundations of truth and knowledge	foundational	foundational	foundational within social critique	antifoundational	nonfoundational

Issue	Positivism	Postpositivism	Critical Theory et al.	Constructivism	Participatory
Extended considerations of validity (goodness criteria)	traditional positivist constructions of validity; rigor, internal validity, external validity, reliability, objectivity		action stimulus(see above); social transformation, equity, social justice	extended constructions of validity: (a) crystalline validity (Richardson); (b) authenticity criteria (Guba & Lincoln); (c) catalytic, rhizomatic, voluptuous validities (Lather); (d) relational and ethics-centered criteria (Lincoln); (e) community-centered determinations of validity	see "action" above
Voice, reflexivity, postmodern textual representations	voice of the researcher, principally; reflexivity may be considered a problem in objectivity; textual representation unproblematic and somewhat formulaic		voices mixed between researcher and participants	voices mixed, with participants' voices sometimes dominant; reflexivity serious and problematic; textual representation an extended issue	voices mixed; textual representation rarely discussed, but problematic; reflexivity relies on critical subjectivity and self-awareness

Textual representation practices may be problematic—i.e., "fiction formulas," or unexamined "regimes of truth"

While we believe these issues to be the most contentious, we also believe they create the intellectual, theoretical, and practical space for dialogue, consensus, and confluence to occur. There is great potential for interweaving of viewpoints, for the incorporation of multiple perspectives, and for borrowing or *bricolage,* where borrowing seems useful, richness enhancing, or theoretically heuristic. For instance, even though we are ourselves social constructivists/contructionists, our call to action embedded in the authenticity criteria we elaborated in *Fourth Generation Evaluation* (Guba & Lincoln, 1989) reflects strongly the bent to action embodied in critical theorists' perspectives. And although Heron and Reason have elaborated a model they call the *cooperative paradigm,* careful reading of their proposal reveals a form of inquiry that is post-postpositive, postmodern, and criticalist in orientation. As a result, the reader familiar with several theoretical and paradigmatic strands of research will find that echoes of many streams of thought come together in the extended table. What this means is that the categories, as Laurel Richardson (personal communication, September 12, 1998) has pointed out, "are fluid, indeed what should be a category keeps altering, enlarging." She notes that "even as [we] write, the boundaries between the paradigms are shifting." This is the paradigmatic equivalent of the Geertzian "blurring of genres" to which we referred earlier.

Our own position is that of the constructionist camp, loosely defined. We do not believe that criteria for judging either "reality" or validity are absolutist (Bradley & Schaefer, 1998), but rather are derived from community consensus regarding what is "real," what is useful, and what has meaning (especially meaning for action and further steps). We believe that a goodly portion of social phenomena consists of the meaning-making activities of groups and individuals around those phenomena. The meaning-making activities themselves are of central interest to social constructionists/constructivists, simply because it is the meaning-making/ sense-making/attributional activities that shape action (or inaction). The meaning-making activities themselves can be changed when they are found to be incomplete, faulty (e.g., discriminatory, oppressive, or nonliberatory), or malformed (created from data that can be shown to be false).

We have tried, however, to incorporate perspectives from other major nonpositivist paradigms. This is not a complete summation; space constraints prevent that. What we hope to do in this chapter is to acquaint readers with the larger currents, arguments, dialogues, and provocative writings and theorizing, the better to see perhaps what we ourselves do not even yet see: where and when confluence is possible, where constructive rapprochement might be negotiated, where voices are beginning to achieve some harmony.

◆ Axiology

Earlier, we placed values on the table as an "issue" on which positivists or phenomenologists might have a "posture" (Guba & Lincoln, 1989, 1994; Lincoln & Guba, 1985). Fortunately, we reserved for ourselves the right to either get smarter or just change our minds. We did both. Now, we suspect (although Table 6.3 does not yet reflect it) that "axiology" should be grouped with "basic beliefs." In *Naturalistic Inquiry* (Lincoln & Guba, 1985), we covered some of the ways in which values feed into the inquiry process: choice of the problem, choice of paradigm to guide the problem, choice of theoretical framework, choice of major data-gathering and data-analytic methods, choice of context, treatment of values already resident within the context, and choice of format(s) for presenting findings. We believed those were strong enough reasons to argue for the inclusion of values as a major point of departure between positivist, conventional modes of inquiry and interpretive forms of inquiry.

A second "reading" of the burgeoning literature and subsequent rethinking of our own rationale have led us to conclude that the issue is much larger than we first conceived. If we had it to do all over again, we would make values or, more correctly, axiology (the branch of philosophy dealing with ethics, aesthetics, and religion) a part of the basic foundational philosophical dimensions of paradigm proposal. Doing so would, in our opinion, begin to help us see the embeddedness of ethics within, not external to, paradigms (see, for instance, Christians, Chapter 5, this volume) and would contribute to the consideration of and dialogue about the role of spirituality in human inquiry. Arguably, axiology has been "defined out of" scientific inquiry for no larger a reason than that it also concerns "religion." But defining "religion" broadly to encompass spirituality would move constructivists closer to participative inquirers and would move critical theorists closer to both (owing to their concern with liberation from oppression and freeing of the human spirit, both profoundly spiritual concerns). The expansion of basic issues to include axiology, then, is one way to achieving greater confluence among the various interpretivist inquiry models. This is the place, for example, where Peter Reason's profound concerns with "sacred science" and human functioning find legitimacy; it is a place where Laurel Richardson's "sacred spaces" become authoritative sites for human inquiry; it is a place—or *the* place—where the spiritual meets social inquiry, as Reason (1993), and later Lincoln and Denzin (1994), proposed some years earlier.

◆ Accommodation and Commensurability

Positivists and postpositivists alike still occasionally argue that paradigms are, in some ways, commensurable; that is, they can be retrofitted to each other in ways that make the simultaneous practice of both possible. We have argued that at the paradigmatic, or philosophical, level, commensurability between positivist and postpositivist worldviews is not possible, but that within each paradigm, mixed methodologies (strategies) may make perfectly good sense (Guba & Lincoln, 1981, 1982, 1989, 1994; Lincoln & Guba, 1985). So, for instance, in *Effective Evaluation* we argued:

> The guiding inquiry paradigm most appropriate to responsive evaluation is . . . the naturalistic, phenomenological, or ethnographic paradigm. It will be seen that qualitative techniques are typically most appropriate to support this approach. There are times, however, when the issues and concerns voiced by audiences require information that is best generated by more conventional methods, especially quantitative methods. . . . In such cases, the responsive conventional evaluator will not shrink from the appropriate application. (Guba & Lincoln, 1981, p. 36)

As we tried to make clear, the "argument" arising in the social sciences was *not about method,* although many critics of the new naturalistic, ethnographic, phenomenological, and/or case study approaches assumed it was.[2] As late as 1998, Weiss could be found to claim that "Some evaluation theorists, notably Guba and Lincoln (1989), hold that it is impossible to combine qualitative and quantitative approaches responsibly within an evaluation" (p. 268), even though we stated early on in *Fourth Generation Evaluation* (1989) that

> those claims, concerns and issues that have *not* been resolved become the advance organizers for information collection by the evaluator. . . . *The*

information may be quantitative or qualitative. Responsive evaluation does not rule out quantitative modes, as is mistakenly believed by many, but deals with whatever information is responsive to the unresolved claim, concern, or issue. (p. 43)

We had also strongly asserted earlier, in *Naturalistic Inquiry* (1985), that

qualitative methods are stressed within the naturalistic paradigm not because the paradigm is antiquantitative but because qualitative methods come more easily to the human-as-instrument. *The reader should particularly note the absence of an antiquantitative stance,* precisely because the naturalistic and conventional paradigms are so often—mistakenly— equated with the qualitative and quantitative paradigms, respectively. Indeed, *there are many opportunities for the naturalistic investigator to utilize quantitative data—probably more than are appreciated.* (pp. 198-199; emphasis added)

Having demonstrated that we were not then (and are not now) talking about an antiquantitative posture or the exclusivity of *methods,* but rather the philosophies of which paradigms are constructed, we can ask the question again regarding commensurability: Are paradigms commensurable? Is it possible to blend elements of one paradigm into another, so that one is engaging in research that represents the best of both worldviews? The answer, from our perspective, has to be a cautious *yes.* This is especially so if the models (paradigms) share axiomatic elements that are similar, or that resonate strongly between them. So, for instance, *positivism and postpositivism* are clearly commensurable. In the same vein, elements of interpretivist/postmodern critical theory, constructivist and participative inquiry fit comfortably together. Commensurability is an issue only when researchers want to "pick and choose" among the axioms of positivist and interpretivist models, because the axioms are contradictory and mutually exclusive.

◆ The Call to Action

One of the clearest ways in which the paradigmatic controversies can be demonstrated is to compare the positivist and postpositivist adherents, who view action as a form of contamination of research results and processes, and the interpretivists, who see action on research results as a meaningful and important outcome of inquiry processes. Positivist adherents believe action to be either a form of advocacy or a form of subjectivity, either or both of which undermine the aim of objectivity. Critical theorists, on the other hand, have always advocated varying degrees of social action, from the overturning of specific unjust practices to radical transformation of entire societies. The call for action—whether in terms of internal transformation, such as ridding oneself of false consciousness, or of external social transformation—differentiates between positivist and postmodern criticalist theorists (including feminist and queer theorists).

The sharpest shift, however, has been in the constructivist and participatory phenomenological models, where a step beyond interpretation and *Verstehen,* or understanding, toward social action is probably one of the most conceptually interesting of the shifts (Lincoln, 1997, 1998a, 1998b). For some theorists, the shift toward action came in response to widespread nonutilization of evaluation findings and the desire to create forms of evaluation that would attract champions who might follow through on recommendations with meaningful action plans (Guba & Lincoln, 1981, 1989). For others, embracing action came as both a political and an ethical commitment (see, for instance, in this volume, Greenwood & Levin, Chapter 3; Christians, Chapter 5; Tierney, Volume 2, Chapter 9; see also Carr & Kemmis, 1986; Schratz & Walker, 1995).

Whatever the source of the problem to which inquirers were responding, the shift toward connecting research, policy analysis, evaluation, and/or social deconstruction (e.g., deconstruction of the patriarchal forms of oppression in social structures, which is the project informing much feminist theorizing, or deconstruction of the homophobia embedded in public policies) with action has come to characterize much new-paradigm inquiry work, both at the theoretical and at the practice and *praxis-*oriented levels. Action has become a major controversy that limns the ongoing debates among practitioners of the various paradigms. The mandate for social action, especially action designed and created by and for research participants with the aid and cooperation of researchers, can be most sharply delineated between positivist/postpositivist and new-paradigm inquirers. Many positivist and postpositivist inquirers still consider "action" the domain of communities other than researchers and research participants: those of policy personnel, legislators, and civic and political officials. Hard-line foundationalists presume that the taint of action will interfere with, or even negate, the objectivity that is a (presumed) characteristic of rigorous scientific method inquiry.

◆ Control

Another controversy that has tended to become problematic centers on *control* of the study: Who initiates? Who determines salient questions? Who determines what constitutes findings? Who determines how data will be collected? Who determines in what forms the findings will be made public, if at all? Who determines what representations will be made of participants in the research? Let us be very clear: The issue of control is deeply embedded in the questions of voice, reflexivity, and issues of postmodern textual representation, which we shall take up later, *but only for new-paradigm inquirers.* For more conventional inquirers, the issue of control is effectively walled off from voice, reflexivity, and issues of textual representation, because each of those issues in some way threatens claims to rigor (particularly objectivity and validity). For new-paradigm inquirers who have seen the preeminent paradigm issues of ontology and epistemology effectively folded into one another, and who have watched as methodology and axiology logically folded into one another (Lincoln, 1995, 1997), control of an inquiry seems far less problematic, except insofar as inquirers seek to obtain participants' genuine participation (see, for instance, Guba & Lincoln, 1981, on contracting and attempts to get some stakeholding groups to do more than stand by while an evaluation is in progress).

Critical theorists, especially those who work in community organizing programs, are painfully aware of the necessity for members of the community, or research participants, to take control of their futures. Constructivists desire participants to take an increasingly active role in nominating questions of interest for any inquiry and in designing outlets for findings to be shared more widely within and outside the community. Participatory inquirers understand action controlled by the local context members to be the aim of inquiry within a community. For none of these paradigmatic adherents is control an issue of advocacy, a somewhat deceptive term usually used as a code within a larger metanarrative to attack an inquiry's rigor, objectivity, or fairness. Rather, for new-paradigm researchers control is a means of fostering emancipation, democracy, and community empowerment, and of redressing power imbalances such that those who were previously marginalized now achieve voice (Mertens, 1998) or "human flourishing" (Heron & Reason, 1997).

Control as a controversy is an excellent place to observe the phenomenon that we have always termed "Catholic questions directed to a Methodist audience." We use this description—given to us by a workshop participant in the early 1980s—to refer to the ongoing problem of illegitimate questions: questions that have no meaning because the frames of reference are those for which they were never intended. (We could as well call these "Hindu questions to a Muslim," to give another sense of how paradigms, or overarching philosophies—or theologies—are incommensurable, and how questions in one framework make little, if any, sense in another.) Paradigmatic formulations interact such that control becomes inextricably intertwined with mandates for objectivity. Objectivity derives from the Enlightenment prescription for knowledge of the physical world, which is postulated to be separate and distinct from those who would know (Polkinghorne, 1989). But if knowledge of the social (as opposed to the physical) world resides in meaning-making mechanisms of the social, mental, and linguistic worlds that individuals inhabit, then knowledge cannot be separate from the knower, but rather is rooted in his or her mental or linguistic designations of that world (Polkinghorne, 1989; Salner, 1989).

◆ Foundations of Truth and Knowledge in Paradigms

Whether or not the world has a "real" existence outside of human experience of that world is an open question. For modernist (i.e., Enlightenment, scientific method, conventional, positivist) researchers, most assuredly there is a "real" reality "out there," apart from the flawed human apprehension of it. Further, that reality can be approached (approximated) only through the utilization of methods that prevent human contamination of its apprehension or comprehension. For foundationalists in the empiricist tradition, the foundations of scientific truth and knowledge about reality reside in rigorous application of testing phenomena against a template as much devoid of human bias, misperception, and other "idols" (Francis Bacon, cited in Polkinghorne, 1989) as instrumentally possible. As Polkinghorne (1989) makes clear:

The idea that the objective realm is independent of the knower's subjective experiences of it can be found in Descartes's dual substance theory, with its distinction between the objective and subjective realms. . . . In the splitting of reality into subject and object realms, what can be known "objectively" is only the objective realm. True knowledge is limited to the objects and the relationships between them that exist in the realm of time and space. Human consciousness, which is subjective, is not accessible to science, and thus not truly knowable. (p. 23)

Now, templates of truth and knowledge can be defined in a variety of ways—as the end product of rational processes, as the result of experiential sensing, as the result of empirical observation, and others. In all cases, however, the referent is the physical or empirical world: rational engagement with it, experience of it, empirical observation of it. Realists, who work on the assumption that there is a "real" world "out there," may in individual cases also be foundationalists, taking the view that all of these ways of defining are rooted in phenomena existing outside the human mind. Although we can think about them, experience them, or observe them, they are nevertheless transcendent, referred to but beyond direct apprehension. Realism is an ontological question, whereas foundationalism is a criterial question. Some foundationalists argue that real phenomena necessarily imply certain final, ultimate criteria for testing them as truthful (although we may have great difficulty in determining what those criteria are); nonfoundationalists tend to argue that there are no such ultimate criteria, only those that we can agree upon at a certain time and under certain conditions. Foundational criteria are discovered; nonfoundational criteria are negotiated. It is the case, however, that most realists are also foundationalists, and many nonfoundationalists or antifoundationalists are relativists.

An ontological formulation that connects realism and foundationalism within the same "collapse" of categories that characterizes the ontological-epistemological collapse is one that exhibits good fit with the other assumptions of constructivism. That state of affairs suits new-paradigm inquirers well. Critical theorists, constructivists, and participatory/cooperative inquirers take their primary field of interest to be precisely that subjective and intersubjective social knowledge and the active construction and cocreation of such knowledge by human agents that is produced by human consciousness. Further, new-paradigm inquirers take to the social knowledge field with zest, informed by a variety of social, intellectual, and theoretical explorations. These theoretical excursions include Saussurian linguistic theory, which views all relationships between words and what those words signify as the function of an internal relationship within some linguistic system; literary theory's deconstructive contributions, which seek to disconnect texts from any *essentialist* or transcendental meaning and resituate them within both author and reader historical and social contexts (Hutcheon, 1989; Leitch, 1996); feminist (Addelson, 1993; Alpern, Antler, Perry, & Scobie, 1992; Babbitt, 1993; Harding, 1993), race and ethnic (Kondo, 1990, 1997; Trinh, 1991), and queer theorizing (Gamson, Chapter 12, this volume), which seek to uncover and explore varieties of oppression and historical colonizing between dominant and subaltern genders, identities, races, and social worlds; the postmodern historical moment (Michael, 1996), which problematizes truth as partial, identity as fluid, language as an unclear referent system, and method and criteria as potentially coercive (Ellis & Bochner, 1996); and criticalist theories of social change (Carspecken, 1996; Schratz & Walker, 1995). The realization of the richness of the mental, social, psychological, and linguistic worlds that individuals and social groups create and constantly re-create and cocreate gives rise, in the minds of new-paradigm postmodern and poststructural inquirers, to endlessly fertile fields of inquiry rigidly walled off from conventional inquirers. Unfettered from the pursuit of transcendental scientific truth, inquirers are now free to resituate themselves within texts, to reconstruct their relationships with research participants in less constricted fashions, and to create re-presentations (Tierney & Lincoln, 1997) that grapple openly with problems of inscription, reinscription, metanarratives, and other rhetorical devices that obscure the extent to which human action is locally and temporally shaped. The processes of uncovering forms of inscription and the rhetoric of metanarratives is *genealogical*—"expos[ing] the origins of the view that have become *sedimented and accepted as truths*" (Polkinghorne, 1989, p. 42; emphasis added)—or *archaeological* (Foucault, 1971; Scheurich, 1997).

New-paradigm inquirers engage the foundational controversy in quite different ways. Critical theorists, particularly critical theorists more positivist in orientation, who lean toward Marxian interpretations, tend toward foundational perspectives, with an important difference. Rather than locating foundational truth and knowledge in some external reality "out there," such critical theorists tend to locate the foundations of truth in specific historical, economic, racial, and social infrastructures of oppression, injustice, and marginalization. Knowers are not portrayed as *separate from* some objective reality, but may be cast as unaware actors in such historical realities ("false consciousness") or aware of historical forms of oppression, but unable or unwilling, because of conflicts, to act on those historical forms to alter specific conditions in this historical moment ("divided consciousness"). Thus the "foundation" for critical theorists is a duality: social critique tied in turn to raised consciousness of the possibility of positive and liberating social change. Social critique may exist apart from social change, but both are necessary for criticalist perspectives.

Constructivists, on the other hand, tend toward the antifoundational (Lincoln, 1995, 1998b; Schwandt, 1996). *Antifoundational* is the term used to denote a refusal to adopt any permanent, unvarying (or "foundational") standards by which truth can be universally known. As one of us has argued, truth—and any agreement regarding what is valid knowledge—arises from the relationship between members of some stakeholding community (Lincoln, 1995). Agreements about truth may be the subject of community *negotiations* regarding what will be accepted as truth (although there are difficulties with that formulation as well; Guba & Lincoln, 1989). Or agreements may eventuate as the result of a *dialogue* that moves arguments about truth claims or validity past the warring camps of objectivity and relativity toward "a communal test of validity through the argumentation of the participants in a discourse" (Bernstein, 1983; Polkinghorne, 1989; Schwandt, 1996). This "communicative and pragmatic concept" of validity (Rorty, 1979) is never fixed or unvarying. Rather, it is created by means of a community narrative, itself subject to the temporal and historical conditions that gave rise to the community. Schwandt (1989) has also argued that these discourses, or community narratives, can and should be bounded by moral considerations, a premise grounded in the emancipatory narratives of the critical theorists, the philosophical pragmatism of Rorty, the democratic focus of constructivist inquiry, and the "human flourishing" goals of participatory and cooperative inquiry.

The controversies around foundationalism (and, to a lesser extent, essentialism) are not likely to be resolved through dialogue between paradigm adherents. The likelier event is that the "postmodern turn" (Best & Kellner, 1997), with its emphasis on the social construction of social reality, fluid as opposed to fixed identities of the self, and the partiality of all truths, will simply overtake modernist assumptions of an objective reality, as indeed, to some extent, it has already done in the physical sciences. We might predict that, if not in our lifetimes, at some later time the dualist idea of an objective reality suborned by limited human subjective realities will seem as quaint as flat-earth theories do to us today.

◆ Validity: An Extended Agenda

Nowhere can the conversation about paradigm differences be more fertile than in the extended controversy about validity (Howe & Eisenhart, 1990; Kvale, 1989, 1994; Ryan, Greene, Lincoln, Mathison, & Mertens, 1998; Scheurich, 1994, 1996). Validity is not like objectivity. There are fairly strong theoretical, philosophical, and pragmatic rationales for examining the concept of objectivity and finding it wanting. Even within positivist frameworks it is viewed as conceptually flawed. But validity is a more irritating construct, one neither easily dismissed nor readily configured by new-paradigm practitioners (Enerstvedt, 1989; Tschudi, 1989). Validity cannot be dismissed simply because it points to a question that has to be answered in one way or another: Are these findings sufficiently authentic (isomorphic to some reality, trustworthy, related to the way others construct their social worlds) that I may trust myself in acting on their implications? More to the point, would I feel sufficiently secure about these findings to construct social policy or legislation based on them? At the same time, radical reconfigurations of validity leave researchers with multiple, sometimes conflicting, mandates for what constitutes rigorous research.

One of the issues around validity is the conflation between method and interpretation. The postmodern turn suggests that no method can deliver on ultimate truth, and in fact "suspects all methods," the more so the larger their claims to delivering on truth (Richardson, 1994). Thus, although one might argue that some methods are more suited than others for conducting research on human construction of social realities (Lincoln & Guba, 1985), no one would argue that a single method—or collection of methods—is the royal road to ultimate knowledge. In new-paradigm inquiry, however, it is not merely method that promises to deliver on some set of local or context-grounded truths, it is also the processes of interpretation. Thus we have two arguments proceeding simultaneously. The first, borrowed from positivism, argues for a kind of rigor in the application of method, whereas the second argues for both a community consent and a form of rigor—defensible reasoning, plausible alongside some other reality that is known to author and reader—in ascribing salience to one interpretation over another and for framing and bounding an interpretive study itself. Prior to our understanding that there were, indeed, two forms of rigor, we assembled a set of methodological criteria, largely borrowed from an earlier generation of thoughtful anthropological and sociological methodological theorists. Those methodological criteria are still useful for a variety of reasons, not the least of which is that they ensure that such issues as prolonged engagement and persistent observation are attended to with some seriousness.

It is the second kind of rigor, however, that has received the most attention in recent writings: Are we *interpretively* rigorous? Can our cocreated constructions be trusted to provide some purchase on some important human phenomenon?

Human phenomena are themselves the subject of controversy. Classical social scientists would like to see "human phenomena" limited to those social experiences from which (scientific) generalizations may be drawn. New-paradigm inquirers, however, are increasingly concerned with the single experience, the individual crisis, the epiphany or moment of discovery, with that most powerful of all threats to conventional objectivity, feeling and emotion. Social scientists concerned with the expansion of what count as social data rely increasingly on the experiential, the embodied, the emotive qualities of human experience that contribute the narrative quality to a life. Sociologists such as Ellis and Bochner (see Chapter 6, Volume 3) and Richardson (Chapter 14, Volume 3) and psychologists such as Michelle Fine (see Fine, Weis, Weseen, & Wong, Chapter 4, this volume) concern themselves with various forms of autoethnography and personal experience methods, both to overcome the abstractions of a social science far gone with quantitative descriptions of human life and to capture those elements that make life conflictual, moving, problematic.

For purposes of this discussion, we believe the adoption of the most radical definitions of social science are appropriate, because the paradigmatic controversies are often taking place at the edges of those conversations. Those edges are where the border work is occurring, and, accordingly, they are the places that show the most promise for projecting where qualitative methods will be in the near and far future.

Whither and Whether Criteria

At those edges, several conversations are occurring around validity. The first—and most radical—is a conversation opened by Schwandt (1996), who suggests that we say "farewell to criteriology," or the "regulative norms for removing doubt and settling disputes about what is correct or incorrect, true or false" (p. 59), which have created a virtual cult around criteria. Schwandt does not, however, himself say farewell to criteria forever; rather, he resituates social inquiry, with other contemporary philosophical pragmatists, within a framework that transforms professional social inquiry into a form of practical philosophy, characterized by "aesthetic, prudential and moral considerations as well as more conventionally scientific ones" (p. 68). When social inquiry becomes the practice of a form of practical philosophy—a deep questioning about how we shall get on in the world, and what we conceive to be the potentials and limits of human knowledge and functioning—then we have some preliminary understanding of what entirely different criteria might be for judging social inquiry.

Schwandt (1996) proposes three such criteria. First, he argues, we should search for a social inquiry that "generate[s] knowledge that complements or supplements rather than displac[ing] lay probing of social problems," a form of knowledge for which we do not yet have the *content*, but from which we might seek to understand the aims of practice from a variety of perspectives, or with different lenses. Second, he proposes a "social inquiry as practical philosophy" that has as its aim "enhancing or cultivating *critical* intelligence in parties to the research encounter," critical intelligence being defined as "the capacity to engage in moral critique." And finally, he proposes a third way in which we might judge social inquiry as practical philosophy: We might make judgments about the social inquirer-as-practical-philosopher. He or she might be "evaluated on the success to which his or her reports of the inquiry enable the training or calibration of human judgment" (p. 69) or "the capacity for practical wisdom" (p. 70).

Schwandt is not alone, however, in wishing to say "farewell to criteriology," at least as it has been previously conceived. Scheurich (1997) makes a similar plea, and in the same vein, Smith (1993) also argues that validity, if it is to survive at all, must be radically reformulated if it is ever to serve phenomenological research well (see also Smith & Deemer, Chapter 12, Volume 3).

At issue here is not whether we shall have criteria, or whose criteria we as a scientific community might adopt, but rather what the nature of social inquiry ought to be, whether it ought to undergo a transformation, and what might be the basis for criteria within a projected transformation. Schwandt (1989; also personal communication, August 21, 1998) is quite clear that both the transformation and the criteria are rooted in dialogic efforts. These dialogic efforts are quite clearly themselves forms of "moral discourse." Through the specific connections of the dialogic, the idea of practical wisdom, and moral discourses, much of Schwandt's work can be seen to be related to, and reflective of, critical theorist and participatory paradigms, as well as constructivism, although he specifically denies the relativity of truth. (For a more sophisticated explication and critique of forms of constructivism, hermeneutics, and interpretivism, see Schwandt, Chapter 7, this volume. In that chapter, Schwandt spells out distinctions between realists and nonrealists, and between foundationalists and non-foundationalists, far more clearly than it is possible for us to do in this chapter.)

To return to the central question embedded in validity: How do we know when we have specific social inquiries that are faithful enough to some human construction that we may feel safe in acting on them, or, more important, that members of the community in which the research is conducted may act on them? To that question, there is no final answer. There are, however, several discussions of what we might use to make both professional and lay judgments regarding any piece of work. It is to those versions of validity that we now turn.

Validity as Authenticity

Perhaps the first nonfoundational criteria were those we developed in response to a challenge by John K. Smith (see Smith & Deemer, Chapter 12, Volume 3). In those criteria, we attempted to locate criteria for judging the *processes* and *outcomes* of naturalistic or constructivist inquiries (rather than the application of methods; see Guba & Lincoln, 1989). We described five potential outcomes of a social constructionist inquiry (evaluation is one form of disciplined inquiry; see Guba & Lincoln, 1981), each grounded in concerns specific to the paradigm we had tried to describe and construct, and apart from any concerns carried over from the positivist legacy. The criteria were instead rooted in the axioms and assumptions of the constructivist paradigm, insofar as we could extrapolate and infer them.

Those authenticity criteria—so called because we believed them to be hallmarks of authentic, trustworthy, rigorous, or "valid" constructivist or phenomenological inquiry—were fairness, ontological authenticity, educative authenticity, catalytic authenticity, and tactical authenticity (Guba & Lincoln, 1989, pp. 245-251). *Fairness* was thought to be a quality of balance; that is, all stakeholder views, perspectives, claims, concerns, and voices should be apparent in the text. Omission of stakeholder or participant voices reflects, we believe, a form of bias. This bias, however, was and is not related directly to the concerns of objectivity that flow from positivist inquiry and that are reflective of inquirer blindness or subjectivity. Rather, this fairness was defined by deliberate attempts to prevent marginalization, to act affirmatively with respect to inclusion, and to act with energy to ensure that all voices in the inquiry effort had a chance to be represented in any texts and to have their stories treated fairly and with balance.

Ontological and educative authenticity were designated as criteria for determining a raised level of awareness, in the first instance, by individual research participants and, in the second, by individuals about those who surround them or with whom they come into contact for some social or organizational purpose. Although we failed to see it at that particular historical moment (1989), there is no reason these criteria cannot be—at this point in time, with many miles under our theoretic and practice feet—reflective also of Schwandt's (1996) "critical intelligence," or capacity to engage in moral critique. In fact, the authenticity criteria we originally proposed had strong moral and ethical overtones, a point to which we later returned (see, for instance, Lincoln, 1995, 1998a, 1998b). It was a point to which our critics strongly objected before we were sufficiently self-aware to realize the implications of what we had proposed (see, for instance, Sechrest, 1993).

Catalytic and tactical authenticities refer to the ability of a given inquiry to prompt, first, action on the part of research participants, and second, the involvement of the researcher/evaluator in training participants in specific forms of social and political action if participants desire such training. It is here that constructivist inquiry practice begins to resemble forms of critical theorist action, action research, or participative or cooperative inquiry, each of which is predicated on creating the capacity in research participants for positive social change and forms of emancipatory community action. It is also at this specific point that practitioners of positivist and postpositivist social inquiry are the most critical, because any action on the part of the inquirer is thought to destabilize objectivity and introduce subjectivity, resulting in bias.

The problem of subjectivity and bias has a long theoretical history, and this chapter is simply too brief for us to enter into the various formulations that either take account of subjectivity or posit it as a positive learning experience, practical, embodied, gendered, and emotive. For purposes of this discussion, it is enough to say that we are persuaded that objectivity is a chimera: a mythological creature that never existed, save in the imaginations of those who believe that knowing can be separated from the knower.

Validity as Resistance, Validity as Poststructural Transgression

Laurel Richardson (1994, 1997) has proposed another form of validity, a deliberately "transgressive" form, the *crystalline*. In writing experimental (i.e., nonauthoritative, nonpositivist) texts, particularly poems and plays, Richardson (1997) has sought to "problematize reliability, validity and truth" (p. 165), in an effort to create new relationships: to her research participants, to her work, to other women, to herself. She says that transgressive forms permit a social scientist to "conjure a different kind of social science . . . [which] means changing one's relationship to one's work, *how* one knows and tells about the sociological" (p. 166). In order to see "how transgression looks and how it feels," it is necessary to "find and deploy methods that allow us to uncover the hidden assumptions and life-denying repressions of sociology; resee/refeel sociology. Reseeing and retelling are inseparable" (p. 167).

The way to achieve such validity is by examining the properties of a crystal in a metaphoric sense. Here we present an extended quotation to give some flavor of how such validity might be described and deployed:

I propose that the central imaginary for "validity" for postmodernist texts is not the triangle—a rigid, fixed, two-dimensional object. Rather the central imaginary is the crystal, which combines symmetry and substance with an infinite variety of shapes, substances, transmutations, multidimensionalities, and angles of approach. Crystals grow, change, alter, but are not amorphous. Crystals are prisms that reflect externalities *and* refract within themselves, creating different colors, patterns, arrays, casting off in different directions. What we see depends upon our angle of repose. Not triangulation, crystallization. In postmodernist mixed-genre texts, we have moved from plane geometry to light theory, where light can be *both* waves *and* particles. Crystallization, without losing structure, deconstructs the traditional idea of "validity" (we feel how there is no single truth, we see how texts validate themselves); and crystallization provides us with a deepened, complex, thoroughly partial understanding of the topic. Paradoxically, we know more and doubt what we know. (Richardson, 1997, p. 92)

The metaphoric "solid object" (crystal/text), which can be turned many ways, which reflects and refracts light (light/multiple layers of meaning), through which we can see both "wave" (light wave/human currents) and "particle" (light as "chunks" of energy/elements of truth, feeling, connection, processes of the research that "flow" together) is an attractive metaphor for validity. The properties of the crystal-as-metaphor help writers and readers alike see the interweaving of processes in the research: discovery, seeing, telling, storying, re-presentation.

Other "Transgressive" Validities

Laurel Richardson is not alone in calling for forms of validity that are "transgressive" and disruptive of the status quo. Patti Lather (1993) seeks "an incitement to discourse," the purpose of which is "to rupture validity as a regime of truth, to displace its historical inscription . . . via a dispersion, circulation and proliferation of counter-practices of authority that take the crisis of representation into account" (p. 674). In addition to catalytic validity (Lather, 1986), Lather (1993) poses *validity as simulacra/ironic validity; Lyotardian paralogy/neopragmatic validity,* a form of validity that "foster[s] heterogeneity, refusing disclosure" (p. 679); *Derridean rigor/rhizomatic validity,* a form of behaving "via relay, circuit, multiple openings" (p. 680); and *voluptuous/situated validity,* which "embodies a situated, partial tentativeness" and "brings ethics and epistemology together . . . via practices of engagement and self-reflexivity" (p. 686). Together, these form a way of interrupting, disrupting, and transforming "pure" presence into a disturbing, fluid, partial, and problematic presence—a poststructural and decidedly postmodern form of discourse theory, hence textual revelation.

Validity as an Ethical Relationship

As Lather (1993) points out, poststructural forms for validities "bring ethics and epistemology together" (p. 686); indeed, as Parker Palmer (1987) also notes, "every way of knowing contains its own moral trajectory" (p. 24). Peshkin reflects on Noddings's (1984) observation that "the search for justification often carries us farther and farther from the heart of morality" (p. 105; quoted in Peshkin, 1993, p. 24). The *way* in which we know is most assuredly tied up with both *what* we know and our *relationships with our research participants*. Accordingly, one of us (Lincoln, 1995) worked on trying to understand the ways in which the ethical intersected both the interpersonal and the epistemological (as a form of authentic or valid knowing). The result was the first set of understandings about emerging criteria for quality that were also rooted in the epistemology/ethics nexus. Seven new standards were derived from that search: positionality, or standpoint, judgments; specific discourse communities and research sites as arbiters of quality; voice, or the extent to which a text has the quality of polyvocality; critical subjectivity (or what might be termed intense self-reflexivity); reciprocity, or the extent to which the research relationship becomes reciprocal rather than hierarchical; sacredness, or the profound regard for how science can (and does) contribute to human flourishing; and sharing the perquisites of privilege that accrue to our positions as academics with university positions. Each of these standards was extracted from a body of research, often from disciplines as disparate as management, philosophy, and women's studies (Lincoln, 1995).

◆ Voice, Reflexivity, and Postmodern Textual Representation

Texts have to do a lot more work these days than they used to. Even as they are charged by poststructuralists and postmodernists to reflect upon their representational practices, representational practices themselves become more problematic. Three of the most engaging, but painful, issues are the problem of voice, the status of reflexivity, and the problematics of postmodern/poststructural textual representation, especially as those problematics are displayed in the shift toward narrative and literary forms that directly and openly deal with human emotion.

Voice

Voice is a multilayered problem, simply because it has come to mean many things to different researchers. In former eras, the only appropriate "voice" was the "voice from nowhere"—the "pure presence" of representation, as Lather terms it. As researchers became more conscious of the abstracted realities their texts created, they became simultaneously more conscious of having readers "hear" their informants—permitting readers to hear the exact words (and, occasionally, the paralinguistic cues, the lapses, pauses, stops, starts, reformulations) of the informants. Today voice can mean, especially in more participatory forms of research, not only having a real researcher—and a researcher's voice—in the text, but also letting research participants speak for themselves, either in text form or through plays, forums, "town meetings," or other oral and performance-oriented media or communication forms designed by research participants themselves. Performance texts, in particular, give an emotional immediacy to the voices of researchers and research participants far beyond their own sites and locales (see McCall, Chapter 4, Volume 2).

Rosanna Hertz (1997) describes voice as

> a struggle to figure out how to present the author's self while simultaneously writing the respondents' accounts and representing their selves. Voice has multiple dimensions: First, there is the voice of the author. Second, there is the presentation of the voices of one's respondents within the text. A third dimension appears when the self is the subject of the inquiry.... Voice is how authors express themselves within an ethnography. (pp. xi-xii)

But knowing how to express ourselves goes far beyond the commonsense understanding of "expressing ourselves." Generations of ethnographers trained in the "cooled-out, stripped-down rhetoric" of positivist inquiry (Firestone, 1987) find it difficult, if not nearly impossible, to "locate" themselves deliberately and squarely within their texts (even though, as Geertz [1988] has demonstrated finally and without doubt, the authorial voice is rarely genuinely absent, or even hidden).[3] Specific textual experimentation can help; that is, composing ethnographic work into various literary forms—the poetry or plays of Laurel Richardson are good examples—can help a researcher to overcome the tendency to write in the distanced and abstracted voice of the disembodied "I." But such writing exercises are hard work. This is also work that is embedded in the practices of reflexivity and narrativity, without which achieving a voice of (partial) truth is impossible.

Reflexivity

Reflexivity is the process of reflecting critically on the self as researcher, the "human as instrument" (Guba & Lincoln, 1981). It is, we would assert, the critical subjectivity discussed early on in Reason and Rowan's edited volume *Human Inquiry* (1981). It is a conscious experiencing of the self as both inquirer and respondent, as teacher and learner, as the one coming to know the self within the processes of research itself.

Reflexivity forces us to come to terms not only with our choice of research problem and with those with whom we engage in the research process, but with our selves and with the multiple identities that represent the fluid self in the research setting (Alcoff & Potter, 1993). Shulamit Reinharz (1997), for example, argues that we not only *"bring* the self to the field . . . [we also] *create* the self in the field" (p. 3). She suggests that although we all have many selves we bring with us, those selves fall into three categories: research-based selves, brought selves (the selves that historically, socially, and personally create our standpoints), and situationally created selves (p. 5). Each of those selves comes into play in the research setting and consequently has a distinctive voice. Reflexivity—as well as the poststructural and postmodern sensibilities concerning quality in qualitative research—demands that we interrogate each of our selves regarding the ways in which research efforts are shaped and staged around the binaries, contradictions, and paradoxes that form our own lives. We must question our selves, too, regarding how those binaries and paradoxes shape not only the identities called forth in the field and later in the discovery processes of writing, but also our interactions with respondents, in who we become to them in the process of *becoming* to ourselves.

Someone once characterized qualitative research as the twin processes of "writing up" (field notes) and "writing down" (the narrative). But Clandinin and Connelly (1994) have made clear that this bitextual reading of the processes of qualitative research is far too simplistic. In fact, many texts are created in the process of engaging in fieldwork. As Richardson

(1994, 1997; see also Chapter 14, Volume 3) makes clear, writing is not merely the transcribing of some reality. Rather, writing—of all the texts, notes, presentations, and possibilities—is also a process of discovery: discovery of the subject (and sometimes of the problem itself) and discovery of the self.

There is good news and bad news with the most contemporary of formulations. The good news is that the multiple selves—ourselves and our respondents—of postmodern inquiries may give rise to more dynamic, problematic, open-ended, and complex forms of writing and representation. The bad news is that the multiple selves we create and encounter give rise to more dynamic, problematic, open-ended, and complex forms of writing and representation.

Postmodern Textual Representations

There are two dangers inherent in the conventional texts of scientific method: that they may lead us to believe the world is rather simpler than it is, and that they may reinscribe enduring forms of historical oppression. Put another way, we are confronted with a crisis of authority (which tells us the world is "this way" when perhaps it is some other way, or many other ways) and a crisis of representation (which serves to silence those whose lives we appropriate for our social sciences, and which may also serve subtly to re-create *this* world, rather than some other, perhaps more complex, but just one). Catherine Stimpson (1988) has observed:

> Like every great word, "representation/s" is a stew. A scrambled menu, it serves up several meanings at once. For a representation can be an image—visual, verbal, or aural. . . . A representation can also be a narrative, a sequence of images and ideas. . . . Or, a representation can be the product of ideology, that vast scheme for showing forth the world and justifying its dealings. (p. 223)

One way to confront the dangerous illusions (and their underlying ideologies) that texts may foster is through the creation of new texts that break boundaries; that move from the center to the margins to comment upon and decenter the center; that forgo closed, bounded worlds for those more open-ended and less conveniently encompassed; that transgress the boundaries of conventional social science; and that seek to create a social science about human life rather than *on* subjects.

Experiments with how to do this have produced "messy texts" (Marcus & Fischer, 1986). Messy texts are not typographic nightmares (although they may be typographically nonlinear); rather, they are texts that seek to break the binary between science and literature, to portray the contradiction and truth of human experience, to break the rules in the service of showing, even partially, how real human beings cope with both the eternal verities of human existence and the daily irritations and tragedies of living that existence. Postmodern representations search out and experiment with narratives that expand the range of understanding, voice, and the storied variations in human experience. As much as they are social scientists, inquirers also become storytellers, poets, and playwrights, experimenting with personal narratives, first-person accounts, reflexive interrogations, and deconstruction of the forms of tyranny embedded in representational practices (see Richardson, Chapter 14, Volume 3; Tierney & Lincoln, 1997).

Representation may be arguably the most open-ended of the controversies surrounding phenomenological research today, for no other reasons than that the ideas of what constitutes legitimate inquiry are expanding and, at the same time, the forms of narrative, dramatic, and rhetorical structure are far from being either explored or exploited fully. Because, too, each inquiry, each inquirer, brings a unique perspective to our understanding, the possibilities for variation and exploration are limited only by the number of those engaged in inquiry and the realms of social and intrapersonal life that become interesting to researchers.

The only thing that can be said for certain about postmodern representational practices is that they will proliferate as forms and they will seek, and demand much of, audiences, many of whom may be outside the scholarly and academic world. In fact, some forms of inquiry may never show up in the academic world, because their purpose will be use in the immediate context, for the consumption, reflection, and use of indigenous audiences. Those that are produced for scholarly audiences will, however, continue to be untidy, experimental, and driven by the need to communicate social worlds that have remained private and "nonscientific" until now.

◆ A Glimpse of the Future

The issues raised in this chapter are by no means the only ones under discussion for the near and far future. But they are some of the critical ones, and discussion, dialogue, and even controversies are bound to continue as practitioners of the various new and emergent paradigms continue either to look for common ground or to find ways in which to distinguish their forms of inquiry from others.

Some time ago, we expressed our hope that practitioners of both positivist and new-paradigm forms of inquiry might find some way of resolving their differences, such that all social scientists could work within a common discourse—and perhaps even several traditions—once again. In retrospect, such a resolution appears highly unlikely and would probably even be less than useful. This is not, however, because neither positivists nor phenomenologists will budge an inch (although that, too, is unlikely). Rather, it is because, in the postmodern moment, and in the wake of poststructuralism, the assumption that there is no single "truth"—that all truths are but partial truths; that the slippage between signifier and signified in linguistic and textual terms creates re-presentations that are only and always shadows of the actual people, events, and places; that identities are fluid rather than fixed—leads us ineluctably toward the insight that there will be no single "conventional" paradigm to which all social scientists might ascribe in some common terms and with mutual understanding. Rather, we stand at the threshold of a history marked by multivocality, contested meanings, paradigmatic controversies, and new textual forms. At some distance down this conjectural path, when its history is written, we will find that this has been the era of emancipation: emancipation from what Hannah Arendt calls "the coerciveness of Truth," emancipation from hearing only the voices of Western Europe, emancipation from generations of silence, and emancipation from seeing the world in one color.

We may also be entering an age of greater spirituality within research efforts. The emphasis on inquiry that reflects ecological values, on inquiry that respects communal forms of living that are not Western, on inquiry involving intense reflexivity regarding how our inquiries are shaped by our own historical and gendered locations, and on inquiry into "human flourishing," as Heron and Reason (1997) call it, may yet reintegrate the sacred with the secular in ways that promote freedom and self-determination. Egon Brunswik, the organizational theorist, wrote of "tied" and "untied" variables—variables that were linked, or clearly not linked, with other variables—when studying human forms of organization. We may be in a period of exploring the ways in which our inquiries are both tied and untied, as a means of finding where our interests cross and where we can both be and promote others' being, as whole human beings.

◆ Notes

1. There are several versions of critical theory, including classical critical theory, which is most closely related to neo-Marxist theory; postpositivist formulations, which divorce themselves from Marxist theory but are positivist in their insistence on conventional rigor criteria; and postmodernist, poststructuralist, or constructivist-oriented varieties. See, for instance, Fay (1987), Carr and Kemmis (1986), and Lather (1991). See also Kemmis and McTaggart (Volume 2, Chapter 11) and Kincheloe and McLaren (Chapter 10, this volume).

2. For a clearer understanding of how methods came to stand in for paradigms, or how our initial (and, we thought, quite clear) positions came to be misconstrued, see Lancy (1993) or, even more currently, Weiss (1998, esp. p. 268).

3. For example, compare this chapter with, say, Richardson's (Volume 3, Chapter 14) and Ellis and Bochner's (Volume 3, Chapter 6), where the authorial voices are clear, personal, vocal, and interior, interacting subjectivities. Although some colleagues have surprised us by correctly identifying which chapters each of us has written in given books, nevertheless, the style of this chapter more closely approximates the more distanced forms of "realist" writing than it does the intimate, personal "feeling tone" (to borrow a phrase from Studs Terkel) of other chapters. Voices also arise as a function of the material being covered. The material we chose as most important for this chapter seemed to demand a less personal tone, probably because there appears to be much more "contention" than calm dialogue concerning these issues. The "cool" tone likely stems from our psychological response to trying to create a quieter space for discussion around controversial issues. What can we say?

◆ References

Addelson, K. P. (1993). Knowers/doers and their moral problems. In L. Alcoff & E. Potter (Eds.), *Feminist epistemologies* (pp. 265-294). New York: Routledge.

Alcoff, L., & Potter, E. (Eds.). (1993). *Feminist epistemologies*. New York: Routledge.

Alpern, S., Antler, J., Perry, E. I., & Scobie, I. W. (Eds.). (1992). *The challenge of feminist biography: Writing the lives of modern American women*. Urbana: University of Illinois Press.

Babbitt, S. (1993). Feminism and objective interests: The role of transformation experiences in rational deliberation. In L. Alcoff & E. Potter (Eds.), *Feminist epistemologies* (pp. 245-264). New York: Routledge.

Bernstein, R. J. (1983). *Beyond objectivism and relativism: Science, hermeneutics, and praxis.* Oxford: Blackwell.

Best, S., & Kellner, D. (1997). *The postmodern turn.* New York: Guilford.

Bloland, H. (1989). Higher education and high anxiety: Objectivism, relativism, and irony. *Journal of Higher Education, 60,* 519-543.

Bloland, H. (1995). Postmodernism and higher education. *Journal of Higher Education, 66,* 521-559.

Bradley, J., & Schaefer, K. (1998). *The uses and misuses of data and models.* Thousand Oaks, CA: Sage.

Carr, W. L., & Kemmis, S. (1986). *Becoming critical: Education, knowledge and action research.* London: Falmer.

Carspecken, P. F. (1996). *Critical ethnography in educational research: A theoretical and practical guide.* New York: Routledge.

Clandinin, D. J., & Connelly, F. M. (1994). Personal experience methods. In N. K. Denzin & Y. S. Lincoln (Eds.), *Handbook of qualitative research* (pp. 413-427). Thousand Oaks, CA: Sage.

Denzin, N. K., & Lincoln, Y. S. (Eds.). (1994). *Handbook of qualitative research.* Thousand Oaks, CA: Sage.

Ellis, C., & Bochner, A. P. (Eds.). (1996). *Composing ethnography: Alternative forms of qualitative writing.* Walnut Creek, CA: AltaMira.

Enerstvedt, R. (1989). The problem of validity in social science. In S. Kvale (Ed.), *Issues of validity in qualitative research* (pp. 135-173). Lund, Sweden: Studentlitteratur.

Fay, B. (1987). *Critical social science.* Ithaca, NY: Cornell University Press.

Firestone, W. (1987). Meaning in method: The rhetoric of quantitative and qualitative research. *Educational Researcher, 16*(7), 16-21.

Foucault, M. (1971). *The order of things: An archeology of the human sciences.* New York: Pantheon.

Geertz, C. (1988). *Works and lives: The anthropologist as author.* Cambridge: Polity.

Geertz, C. (1993). *Local knowledge: Further essays in interpretive anthropology.* London: Fontana.

Guba, E. G., & Lincoln, Y. S. (1981). *Effective evaluation: Improving the usefulness of evaluation results through responsive and naturalistic approaches.* San Francisco: Jossey-Bass.

Guba, E. G., & Lincoln, Y. S. (1982). Epistemological and methodological bases for naturalistic inquiry. *Educational Communications and Technology Journal, 31,* 233-252.

Guba, E. G., & Lincoln, Y. S. (1989). *Fourth generation evaluation.* Newbury Park, CA: Sage.

Guba, E. G., & Lincoln, Y. S. (1994). Competing paradigms in qualitative research. In N. K. Denzin & Y. S. Lincoln (Eds.), *Handbook of qualitative research* (pp. 105-117). Thousand Oaks, CA: Sage.

Harding, S. (1993). Rethinking standpoint epistemology: What is "strong objectivity"? In L. Alcoff & E. Potter (Eds.), *Feminist epistemologies* (pp. 49-82). New York: Routledge.

Heron, J. (1996). *Cooperative inquiry: Research into the human condition.* London: Sage.

Heron, J., & Reason, P. (1997). A participatory inquiry paradigm. *Qualitative Inquiry, 3,* 274-294.

Hertz, R. (1997). Introduction: Reflexivity and voice. In R. Hertz (Ed.), *Reflexivity and voice.* Thousand Oaks, CA: Sage.

Howe, K., & Eisenhart, M. (1990). Standards for qualitative (and quantitative) research: A prolegomenon. *Educational Researcher, 19*(4), 2-9.

Hutcheon, L. (1989). *The politics of postmodernism.* New York: Routledge.

Kincheloe, J. L. (1991). *Teachers as researchers: Qualitative inquiry as a path to empowerment.* London: Falmer.

Kondo, D. K. (1990). *Crafting selves: Power, gender, and discourses of identity in a Japanese workplace.* Chicago: University of Chicago Press.

Kondo, D. K. (1997). *About face: Performing race in fashion and theater.* New York: Routledge.

Kvale, S. (Ed.). (1989). *Issues of validity in qualitative research.* Lund, Sweden: Studentlitteratur.

Kvale, S. (1994, April). *Validation as communication and action.* Paper presented at the annual meeting of the American Educational Research Association, New Orleans.

Lancy, D. F. (1993). *Qualitative research in education: An introduction to the major traditions.* New York: Longman.

Lather, P. (1986). Issues of validity in openly ideological research: Between a rock and a soft place. *Interchange, 17*(4), 63-84.

Lather, P. (1991). *Getting smart: Feminist research and pedagogy with/in the postmodern.* New York: Routledge.

Lather, P. (1993). Fertile obsession: Validity after poststructuralism. *Sociological Quarterly, 34,* 673-693.

Leitch, V. B. (1996). *Postmodern: Local effects, global flows.* Albany: State University of New York Press.

Lincoln, Y. S. (1995). Emerging criteria for quality in qualitative and interpretive research. *Qualitative Inquiry, 1,* 275-289.

Lincoln, Y. S. (1997). What constitutes quality in interpretive research? In C. K. Kinzer, K. A. Hinchman, & D. J. Leu (Eds.), *Inquiries in literacy: Theory and practice* (pp. 54-68). Chicago: National Reading Conference.

Lincoln, Y. S. (1998a). *The ethics of teaching qualitative research.* Manuscript submitted for publication.

Lincoln, Y. S. (1998b). From understanding to action: New imperatives, new criteria, new methods for interpretive researchers. *Theory and Research in Social Education, 26*(1), 12-29.

Lincoln, Y. S., & Denzin, N. K. (1994). The fifth moment. In N. K. Denzin & Y. S. Lincoln (Eds.), *Handbook of qualitative research* (pp. 575-586). Thousand Oaks, CA: Sage.

Lincoln, Y. S., & Guba, E. G. (1985). *Naturalistic inquiry.* Beverly Hills, CA: Sage.

Marcus, G. E., & Fischer, M. M. J. (1986). *Anthropology as cultural critique: An experimental moment in the human sciences.* Chicago: University of Chicago Press.

Mertens, D. (1998). *Research methods in education and psychology: Integrating diversity with quantitative and qualitative methods.* Thousand Oaks, CA: Sage.

Michael, M. C. (1996). *Feminism and the postmodern impulse: Post-World War II fiction.* Albany: State University of New York Press.

Noddings, N. (1984). *Caring: A feminine approach to ethics and moral education.* Berkeley: University of California Press.

Palmer, P. J. (1987, September-October). Community, conflict, and ways of knowing. *Change, 19,* 20-25.

Peshkin, A. (1993). The goodness of qualitative research. *Educational Researcher, 22*(2), 24-30.

Polkinghorne, D. E. (1989). Changing conversations about human science. In S. Kvale (Ed.), *Issues of validity in qualitative research* (pp. 13-46). Lund, Sweden: Studentlitteratur.

Reason, P. (1993). Sacred experience and sacred science. *Journal of Management Inquiry, 2,* 10-27.

Reason, P., & Rowan, J. (Eds.). (1981). *Human inquiry.* London: John Wiley.

Reinharz, S. (1997). Who am I? The need for a variety of selves in the field. In R. Hertz (Ed.), *Reflexivity and voice* (pp. 3-20). Thousand Oaks, CA: Sage.

Richardson, Laurel (1994). Writing: A method of inquiry. In N. K. Denzin & Y. S. Lincoln (Eds.), *Handbook of qualitative research* (pp. 516-529). Thousand Oaks, CA: Sage.

Richardson, L. (1997). *Fields of play: Constructing an academic life.* New Brunswick, NJ: Rutgers University Press.

Rorty, R. (1979). *Philosophy and the mirror of nature.* Princeton, NJ: Princeton University Press.

Ryan, K. E., Greene, J. C., Lincoln, Y. S., Mathison, S., & Mertens, D. (1998). Advantages and challenges of using inclusive evaluation approaches in evaluation practice. *American Journal of Evaluation, 19,* 101-122.

Salner, M. (1989). Validity in human science research. In S. Kvale (Ed.), *Issues of validity in qualitative research* (pp. 47-72). Lund, Sweden: Studentlitteratur.

Scheurich, J. J. (1994). Policy archaeology. *Journal of Educational Policy, 9,* 297-316.

Scheurich, J. J. (1996). Validity. *International Journal of Qualitative Studies in Education, 9,* 49-60.

Scheurich, J. J. (1997). *Research method in the postmodern.* London: Falmer.

Schratz, M., & Walker, R. (1995). *Research as social change: New opportunities for qualitative research.* New York: Routledge.

Schwandt, T. A. (1989). Recapturing moral discourse in evaluation. *Educational Researcher, 18*(8), 11-16, 34.

Schwandt, T. A. (1996). Farewell to criteriology. *Qualitative Inquiry, 2,* 58-72.

Sechrest, L. (1993). *Program evaluation: A pluralistic enterprise.* San Francisco: Jossey-Bass.

Smith, J. K. (1993). *After the demise of empiricism: The problem of judging social and educational inquiry.* Norwood, NJ: Ablex.

Stimpson, C. R. (1988). Nancy Reagan wears a hat: Feminism and its cultural consensus. *Critical Inquiry, 14,* 223-243.

Tierney, W. G., & Lincoln, Y. S. (Eds.). (1997). *Representation and the text: Reframing the narrative voice.* Albany: State University of New York Press.

Trinh, T. M. (1991). *When the moon waxes red: Representation, gender and cultural politics.* New York: Routledge.

Tschudi, F. (1989). Do qualitative and quantitative methods require different approaches to validity? In S. Kvale (Ed.), *Issues of validity in qualitative research* (pp. 109-134). Lund, Sweden: Studentlitteratur.

Weiss, C. H. (1998). *Evaluation* (2nd ed.). Upper Saddle River, NJ: Prentice Hall.

7

Three Epistemological Stances for Qualitative Inquiry

Interpretivism, Hermeneutics, and Social Constructionism

Thomas A. Schwandt

Labels in philosophy and cultural discourse have the character that Derrida ascribes to Plato's *pharmakon:* they can poison and kill, and they can remedy and cure. We *need* them to help identify a style, a temperament, a set of common concerns and emphases, or a vision that has determinate shape. But we must also be wary of the ways in which they can blind us or can reify what is fluid and changing.

—Richard J. Bernstein, "What Is the Difference That Makes a Difference?" 1986

AUTHOR'S NOTE: Special thanks to Barry Bull, Jeffrey Davis, Norman Denzin, Davydd Greenwood, Peter Labella, Yvonna Lincoln, and David Silverman for their suggestions on previous drafts of this chapter. Errors and confusions that remain here are probably the result of my not taking all of their good advice.

◆   Qualitative inquiry is the name for a reformist movement that began
in the early 1970s in the academy.[1] The movement encompassed
multiple epistemological, methodological, political, and ethical criticisms
of social scientific research in fields and disciplines that favored experimental, quasi-experimental, correlational, and survey research strategies.
Immanent criticism of these methodologies within these disciplines and
fields as well as insights from external debates in philosophy of science and
social science fueled the opposition.[2] Over the years, the movement has
acquired a political as well as an intellectual place in the academy. It has its
own journals, academic associations, conferences, and university positions, as well as the support of publishers, all of which have both sustained
and, to some extent, created the movement. Moreover, it is not unreason-
able to claim, given the influence that publishers exercise through the promotion and sales of ever more allegedly new and improved accounts of
what qualitative inquiry is, that the movement at times looks more like an
"industry."

Not surprisingly, considerable academic and professional politics are
also entailed in the movement, particularly as it has drawn on intellectual
developments in feminism, postmodernism, and poststructuralism. Current struggles over departmental organization, interdisciplinary alliances,
what constitutes "legitimate" research, who controls the editorship of key
journals, and so forth (compare, for example, Denzin, 1997, and Prus,
1996; see also Shea, 1998), in part, reflect the turmoil over what constitute the appropriate goals and means of human inquiry. Quarrels in university departments over the meaning and value of qualitative inquiry
often reflect broader controversies in the disciplines of psychology, sociology, anthropology, feminist studies, history, and literature about the purpose, values, and ethics of intellectual labor.

Thus qualitative inquiry is more comprehensible as a site or arena for
social scientific criticism than as any particular kind of social theory, methodology, or philosophy. That site is a "home" for a wide variety of scholars
who often are seriously at odds with one another but who share a general
rejection of the blend of scientism, foundationalist epistemology, instrumental reasoning, and the philosophical anthropology of disengagement
that has marked "mainstream" social science. Yet how one further characterizes the site depends, in part, on what one finds of interest there.[3] For
some researchers, the site is a place where a particular set of laudable virtues for social research are championed, such as fidelity to phenomena,

respect for the life world, and attention to the fine-grained details of daily life. They are thus attracted to the fact that long-standing traditions of fieldwork research in sociology and anthropology have been revitalized and appropriated under the banner of "qualitative inquiry" while at the same time immanent criticism of those traditions has inspired new ways of thinking about the field-worker's interests, motivations, aims, obligations, and texts. Others are attracted to the site as a place where debates about aims of the human sciences unfold and where issues of what it means to know the social world are explored. Still others may find social theory of greatest interest and hence look to the site for knowledge of the debate over the merits of symbolic interactionism, social systems theory, critical theory of society, feminist theory, and so forth. Finally, many current researchers seem to view the site as a place for experimentation with empirical methodologies and textual strategies inspired by postmodernist and poststructuralist thinking.

In this chapter, I focus on the site as an arena in which different epistemologies vie for attention as potential justifications for doing qualitative inquiry. I examine three of the philosophies that in various forms are assumed in the many books that explain the aims and methods of qualitative inquiry. Interpretivism, hermeneutics, and social constructionism embrace different perspectives on the aim and practice of understanding human action, different ethical commitments, and different stances on methodological and epistemological issues of representation, validity, objectivity, and so forth.[4] The chapter begins with an overview of each philosophy, and I indicate ways in which they are related to and at odds with one another. I then discuss several epistemological and ethical-political issues that arise from these philosophies and that characterize contemporary concerns about the purpose and justification of qualitative inquiry.

There is no denying that what follows is a Cook's tour of complicated philosophies that demand more detailed attention in their own right as well as in interaction. I apologize in advance for leaving the philosophically minded aghast at the incompleteness of the treatment and for encouraging the methodologically inclined to scurry to later chapters on tools. But I would be remiss were I not to add that the practice of social inquiry cannot be adequately defined as an atheoretical making that requires only methodological prowess. Social inquiry is a distinctive praxis, a kind of activity (like teaching) that in the doing transforms the very theory and aims that guide it. In other words, as one engages in the "practical" activities of generating and interpreting data to answer questions about the meaning of what others are doing and saying and then transforming that understanding into public knowledge, one inevitably takes up "theoretical" concerns about what constitutes knowledge and how it is to be justified, about the nature and aim of social theorizing, and so forth. In sum, acting and thinking, practice and theory, are linked in a continuous process of critical reflection and transformation.

◆ Background: Part 1

Interpretivism and hermeneutics, generally characterized as the *Geisteswissenschaftlichte* or *Verstehen* tradition in the human sciences, arose in the reactions of neo-Kantian German historians and sociologists (i.e., Dilthey, Rickert, Windleband, Simmel, Weber) in the late 19th and early 20th centuries to the then-dominant philosophy of positivism (and later, logical positivism). At the heart of the dispute was the claim that the human sciences (Geisteswissenchaften) were fundamentally different in nature and purpose from the natural sciences (*Naturwissenschaften*). Defenders of interpretivism argued that the human sciences aim to understand human action. Defenders of positivism and proponents of the unity of the sciences held the view that the purpose of any science (if it is indeed to be called a science) is to offer causal explanations of social, behavioral, and physical phenomena.

There was, of course, considerable debate among the neo-Kantians about the precise nature of the difference between the sciences. And to the present day, the issue of whether there is a critical distinction to be drawn between the natural and the human sciences on the basis of different aims—explanation (*Erklären*) versus understanding (*Verstehen*)—remains more or less unsettled.[5] Although it is important to understand how apologists for the uniqueness of the human sciences link their respective philosophies to this issue, in the interest of space, I will forgo that examination here and focus directly on key features of the philosophies themselves. I begin with a sketch of the interpretivist theory of human action and meaning and then show how philosophical hermeneutics offers a critique of this view and a different understanding of human inquiry.

◆ Interpretivist Philosophies

From an interpretivist point of view, what distinguishes human (social) action from the movement of physical objects is that the former is inherently meaningful. Thus, to understand a particular social action (e.g., friendship, voting, marrying, teaching), the inquirer must grasp the meanings that constitute that action. To say that human action is meaningful is to claim either that it has a certain intentional content that indicates the kind of action it is and/or that what an action means can be grasped only in terms of the system of meanings to which it belongs (Fay, 1996; Outhwaite, 1975). Because human action is understood in this way, one can determine that a wink is not a wink (to use Ryle's example popularized by Geertz), or that a smile can be interpreted as wry or loving, or that very different physical movements can all be interpreted as acts of supplication, or that the same physical movement of raising one's arm can be variously interpreted as voting, hailing a taxi, or asking for permission to speak, depending on the context and intentions of the actor.

To find meaning in an action, or to say one understands what a particular action means, requires that one interpret in a particular way what the actors are doing. This process of interpreting or understanding (of achieving *Verstehen*) is differentially represented, and therein lie some important differences in philosophies of interpretivism and between interpretivism and philosophical hermeneutics. These differences can perhaps be most easily grasped through a consideration of four ways of defining (theorizing) the notion of interpretive understanding (*Verstehen*), three that constitute the interpretive tradition and a fourth that marks the distinction of philosophical hermeneutics from that tradition.

Empathic Identification

One way of defining the notion first appears in the earlier work of Wilhelm Dilthey and the *Lebensphilosophers*. Dilthey argued that to understand the meaning of human action requires grasping the subjective consciousness or intent of the actor from the inside.[6] *Verstehen* thus entails a kind of empathic identification with the actor. It is an act of psychological reenactment—getting inside the head of an actor to understand what he or she is up to in terms of motives, beliefs, desires, thoughts, and so on. This interpretivist stance (also called intentionalism) is explained in Collingwood's (1946/1961) account of what constitutes historical knowledge, and it lies at the heart of what is known as objectivist or conservative hermeneutics (e.g., Hirsch, 1976). Both approaches share the general idea that it is possible for the interpreter to transcend or break out of her or his historical circumstances in order to reproduce the meaning or intention of the actor. (I realize that introducing the term *hermeneutics* here is a bit confusing, given that I stated above that I wish to draw a distinction *between* interpretivist and hermeneutic philosophies. But *objectivist* hermeneutics shares the same epistemology as interpretivism, whereas *philosophical* hermeneutics, as I explain below, rejects this epistemology.)[7]

Whether it is possible to achieve interpretive understanding through a process of grasping an actors' intent is widely debated. Geertz (1976/1979), for example, argues that understanding comes more from the act of looking over the shoulders of actors and trying to figure out (both by observing and by conversing) what the actors think they are up to. Nonetheless, the idea of acquiring an "inside" understanding—the actors' definitions of the situation—is a powerful central concept for understanding the purpose of qualitative inquiry.

Phenomenological Sociology

A second way of making sense of the notion of interpretive understanding is found in the work of phenomenological sociologists and ethnomethodologists, including Cicourel and Garfinkel (I will address more recent developments in conversation analysis later). Influenced by the work of Alfred Schutz (1962, 1932/1967), phenomenological analysis is principally concerned with understanding how the everyday, intersubjective world (the life world, or *Lebenswelt*) is constituted. The aim is to grasp how we come to interpret our own and others' action as meaningful and to "reconstruct the genesis of the objective meanings of action in the intersubjective communication of individuals in the social life-world" (Outhwaite, 1975, p. 91). Two conceptual tools often used in that reconstruction are indexicality and reflexivity (Potter, 1996). The former signifies that the meaning of a word or utterance is dependent on its context of use. The latter directs our attention to the fact that utterances are not just about something but are also doing something; an utterance is in part constitutive of a speech act. These two notions are part of the means whereby phenomenological sociologists and ethnomethodologists come to understand how social reality, everyday life, is constituted in conversation and interaction. (For a fuller discussion of this perspective, see Gubrium & Holstein, Chapter 7, Volume 2.)

Language Games

A third definition of interpretive understanding is represented in analysis of language approaches that take their inspiration from Wittgenstein's *Philosophical Investigations,* especially the work of Peter Winch (1958). From Wittgenstein, Winch borrowed the notion that there are many games played with language (testing hypotheses, giving orders, greeting, and so on), and he extended this idea to language games as constituted in different cultures. Each of these games has its own rules or criteria that make the game meaningful to its participants. Reasoning by analogy, we can say that human action, like speech, is an element in communication governed by rules. More simply, human action is meaningful by virtue of the system of meanings (in Wittgenstein's terms, the "language game") to which it belongs. Understanding those systems of meanings (institutional and cultural norms, action-constituting rules, and so on) is the goal of *Verstehen* (Giddens, 1993; Habermas, 1967/1988; Outhwaite, 1975).

Shared Features

These first three ways of conceiving of the notion of interpretive understanding constitute the tradition of interpretivism. All three share the following features: (a) They view human action as meaningful; (b) they evince an ethical commitment in the form of respect for and fidelity to the life world; and (c) from an epistemological point of view, they share the neo-Kantian desire to emphasize the contribution of human subjectivity (i.e., intention) to knowledge without thereby sacrificing the objectivity of knowledge. In other words, interpretivists argue that it is possible to understand the subjective meaning of action (grasping the actor's beliefs, desires, and so on) yet do so in an objective manner. The meaning that the interpreter reproduces or reconstructs is considered the original meaning of the action. So as not to misinterpret the original meaning, interpreters must employ some kind of method that allows them to step outside their historical frames of reference. Method, correctly employed, is a means that enables interpreters to claim a purely theoretical attitude as observers (Outhwaite, 1975). The theoretical attitude or the act of scientific contemplation at a distance requires the cognitive style of the disinterested observer (Schutz, 1962). This, of course, does not necessarily deny the fact that in order to understand the intersubjective meanings of human action, the inquirer may have to, as a methodological requirement, "participate" in the life worlds of others.

Interpretivism generally embraces two dimensions of *Verstehen* as explicated by Schutz (1962, 1932/1967). *Verstehen* is, on a primary level, "the name of a complex process by which all of us in our everyday life interpret the meaning of our own actions and those of others with whom we interact" (Bernstein, 1976, p. 139). Yet *Verstehen* is also "a method peculiar to the social sciences" (Schutz, 1962, p. 57), a process by which the social scientist seeks to understand the primary process. Hence interpretivists aim to reconstruct the self-understandings of actors engaged in particular actions. And in so doing, they assume that the inquirer cannot claim that the ways actors make sense of their experience are irrelevant to social scientific understanding because actors' ways of making sense of their actions are constitutive of that action (Giddens, 1993; Outhwaite, 1975).

Interpretivist epistemologies can in one sense be characterized as hermeneutic because they emphasize that one must grasp the situation in which human actions make (or acquire) meaning in order to say one has an understanding of the particular action (Outhwaite, 1975). This view draws upon the familiar notion of the hermeneutic circle as a method or procedure unique to the human sciences: In order to understand the part (the specific sentence, utterance, or act), the inquirer must grasp the whole (the complex of intentions, beliefs, and desires or the text, institutional context, practice, form of life, language game, and so on), and vice versa. Geertz's (1976/1979) oft-cited description of the process of ethnographic understanding portrays this conception of the hermeneutic circle as

> a continuous dialectical tacking between the most local of local detail and the most global of global structure in such a way as to bring both into view simultaneously. . . . Hopping back and forth between the whole conceived through the parts that actualize it and the parts conceived through the whole which motivates them, we seek to turn them, by a sort of intellectual perpetual motion, into explications of one another. (p. 239)

Garfinkel's (1967) claim about understanding how people make sense of their worlds is similar: "Not only is the underlying pattern derived from its individual documentary evidences, but the individual documentary evidences, in their turn, are interpreted on the basis of 'what is known' about the underlying pattern. Each is used to elaborate the other" (p. 78).

Finally, interpretivism assumes an epistemological understanding of understanding (*Verstehen*). That is, it considers understanding to be an intellectual process whereby a knower (the inquirer as subject) gains knowledge about an object (the meaning of human action). Accordingly, the notion of a hermeneutic circle of understanding is, as Bernstein (1983) explains,

> "object" oriented, in the sense that it directs us to the texts, institutions, practices, or forms of life that we are seeking to understand. . . . No essential reference is made to the interpreter, to the individual who is engaged in the process of understanding and questioning, except insofar as he or she must have the insight, imagination, openness, and patience to acquire this art— an art achieved through practice. (p. 135)[8]

Thus, in interpretive traditions, the interpreter objectifies (i.e., stands over and against) that which is to be interpreted. And, in that sense, the interpreter remains unaffected by and external to the interpretive process.

◆ Philosophical Hermeneutics

A fourth, and radically different, way of representing the notion of interpretive understanding is found in the philosophical hermeneutics of Gadamer (1975, 1977, 1981, 1996) and Taylor (1985a, 1985b, 1995) inspired by the work of Heidegger.[9] Let us begin with the premise that interpretivist philosophies, in general, define the role of the interpreter on the model of the exegete, that is, one who is engaged in a critical analysis or explanation of a text (or some human action) using the method of the hermeneutic circle.[10] Echoing the point made by Bernstein, Kerdeman (1998) explains that

> exegetical methodology plays the strange parts of a narrative [or some social action] off against the integrity of the narrative as whole until its strange passages are worked out or accounted for. An interpreter's self-understanding neither affects nor is affected by the negotiation of understanding. Indeed, insofar as interpreters and linguistic objects are presumed to be distinct, self-understanding is believed to bias and distort successful interpretation. (p. 251; see also Gadamer, 1981, pp. 98-101)

Both the phenomenological observer and the linguistic analyst generally claim this role of uninvolved observer.[11] The understanding that they acquire of some particular social action (or text) is exclusively reproductive and ought to be judged on the grounds of whether or not it is an accurate, correct, valid representation of that action and its meaning.

In several ways, philosophical hermeneutics challenges this classic epistemological (or, more generally, Cartesian) picture of the interpreter's task and the kind of understanding that he or she "produces." First, broadly conceived as a philosophical program, the hermeneutics of Gadamer and Taylor rejects the interpretivist view "that hermeneutics is an art or technique of understanding, the purpose of which is to construct a methodological foundation for the human sciences" (Grondin, 1994, p. 109). Philosophical hermeneutics argues that understanding is not, in the first instance, a procedure- or rule-governed undertaking; rather, it is a very condition of being human. Understanding *is* interpretation. As Gadamer (1970) explains, understanding is not "an isolated activity of human beings but a basic structure of our experience of life. We are always taking something *as* something. That is the primordial givenness of our world orientation, and we cannot reduce it to anything simpler or more immediate" (p. 87).

Second, in the act of interpreting (of "taking something *as* something"), sociohistorically inherited bias or prejudice is not regarded as a characteristic or attribute that an interpreter must strive to get rid of or manage in order to come to a "clear" understanding. To believe this is possible is to assume that the traditions and associated prejudgments that shape our efforts to understand are easily under our control and can be set aside at will. But philosophical hermeneutics argues that tradition is not something that is external, objective, and past—something from which we can free and distance ourselves (Gadamer, 1975). Rather, as Gallagher (1992) explains, tradition is "a living force that enters into all understanding" (p. 87), and, "despite the fact that traditions operate for the most part 'behind our backs,' they are already there, ahead of us, conditioning our interpretations" (p. 91). Furthermore, because traditions "shape what we are and how we understand the world, the attempt to step outside of the process of tradition would be like trying to step outside of our own skins" (p. 87).

Thus reaching an understanding is not a matter of setting aside, escaping, managing, or tracking one's own standpoint, prejudgments, biases, or prejudices. On the contrary, understanding requires the *engagement* of one's biases.[12] As Garrison (1996) explains, prejudices are the very kinds of prejudgments "necessary to make our way, however tentatively, in everyday thought, conversation, and action. . . . The point is not to free ourselves of all prejudice, but to examine our historically inherited and unreflectively held prejudices and alter those that disable our efforts to understand others, and ourselves" (p. 434). The fact that we "belong" to tradition and that tradition in some sense governs interpretation does not mean that we merely reenact the biases of tradition in our interpretation. Although preconceptions, prejudices, or prejudgments suggest the initial conceptions that an interpreter brings to the interpretation of an object or another person, the interpreter risks those prejudices in the encounter with what is to be interpreted.

Third, only in a dialogical encounter with what is not understood, with what is alien, with what makes a claim upon us, can we open ourselves to risking and testing our preconceptions and prejudices (Bernstein, 1983). Understanding is participative, conversational, and dialogic. It is always bound up with language and is achieved only through a logic of question and answer (Bernstein, 1983; Grondin, 1994; Taylor, 1991).[13] Moreover, understanding is something that is *produced* in that dialogue, not something *reproduced* by an interpreter through an analysis of that which he or she seeks to understand. The meaning one seeks in "making sense" of a social action or text is temporal and processive and always coming into being in the specific occasion of understanding (Aylesworth, 1991; Bernstein, 1983; Gadamer, 1975, p. 419).

This different conception of meaning signifies a radical departure from the interpretivist idea that human action *has* meaning and that that meaning is in principle determinable or decidable by the interpreter. Philosophical hermeneutics has a nonobjectivist view of meaning: "The text [or human action] is not an 'object out there' independent of its interpretations and capable of serving as an arbiter of their correctness" (Connolly & Keutner, 1998, p. 17). Grondin (1994) notes that "in terms of its form, understanding is less like grasping a content, a noetic meaning, than like engaging in a dialogue" (p. 117).[14] In other words, meaning is negotiated mutually in the act of interpretation; it is not simply discovered.

In this sense, philosophical hermeneutics opposes a naïve realism or objectivism with respect to meaning and can be said to endorse the conclusion that there is never a finally correct interpretation. This is a view held by some constructivists as well, yet philosophical hermeneutics sees meaning not necessarily as constructed (i.e., created, assembled) but as negotiated (i.e., a matter of coming to terms). Bernstein (1983) summarizes Gadamer's notion of the processive, open, anticipatory character of the coming into being of meaning:

> We are always understanding and interpreting in light of our anticipatory prejudgments and prejudices, which are themselves changing in the course of history. That is why Gadamer tells us that to understand is always to understand differently. But this does not mean that our interpretations are arbitrary and distortive. We should always aim at a correct understanding of what the "things themselves" [the objects of our interpretation] say. But what the "things themselves" say will be different in light of our changing horizons and the different questions we learn to ask. Such analysis of the ongoing and open character of all understanding and interpretation can be construed as distortive only if we assume that a text possesses some meaning in itself that can be isolated from our prejudgments. (p. 139)

Finally, as is suggested in what has been said above, the kind of understanding that results from the encounter is always at once a kind of "application." In other words, in the act of understanding there are not two separate steps—first, acquiring understanding; second, applying that understanding. Rather, understanding is itself a kind of practical experience in and of the world that, in part, constitutes the kinds of persons that we are in the world. Understanding is "lived" or existential. Gadamer (1981) explains this in the following way:

> Understanding, like action, always remains a risk and never leaves room for the simple application of a general knowledge of rules to the statements or texts to be understood. Furthermore where it is successful, understanding means a growth in inner awareness, which as a new experience enters into the texture of our own mental experience. Understanding is an adventure and, like any other adventure is dangerous. . . . But . . . [i]t is capable of contributing in a special way to the broadening of our human experiences, our self-knowledge, and our horizon, for everything understanding mediates is mediated along with ourselves. (pp. 109-110)

A focus on understanding as a kind of moral-political knowledge that is at once embodied, engaged (and hence "interested"), and concerned with practical choice is a central element in the hermeneutic philosophies that draw, at least in part, on Gadamer and Heidegger (e.g., Dunne, Gallagher, Smith, and Taylor).[15]

Philosophical hermeneutics is not a methodology for "solving prob-lems" of misunderstanding or problems concerned with the correct mean-ing of human action. Gadamer (1975) has repeatedly emphasized that the work of hermeneutics "is not to develop a procedure of understand-ing but to clarify the conditions in which understanding takes place. But these conditions are not of the nature of a 'procedure' or a method which the interpreter must of himself bring to bear on the text" (p. 263). The goal of philosophical hermeneutics is philosophical—that is, to under-stand what is involved in the process of understanding itself (Madison, 1991).

◆ Background: Part 2

Philosophical hermeneutics and social constructionist philosophies (like deconstructionist, critical theory, some feminist, and neopragmatic ap-proaches) have their antecedents in the broad movement away from an em-piricist, logical atomistic, designative, representational account of meaning and knowledge.[16] The philosophies of logical positivism and logical empir-icism were principally concerned with the rational reconstruction of scien-tific knowledge by means of the semantic and syntactic analysis of two kinds of scientific statements (statements that explain, i.e., theories and hypotheses, and statements that describe, i.e., observations). In this analy-sis, social, cultural, and historical dimensions of understanding were regarded as extrascientific and hence irrelevant to any valid epistemo-logical account of what constitutes genuine scientific knowledge and its justification. Logical empiricism worked from a conception of knowledge as correct representation of an independent reality and was (is) almost exclusively interested in the issue of establishing the validity of scientific knowledge claims.

In his essay "Overcoming Epistemology," Taylor (1987) argues that logical empiricism (or, more generally, any foundationalist epistemology) draws its strength from an interlocking set of assumptions about meaning, knowledge, language, and self. It embraces a philosophy of language that can be characterized broadly as empiricist and atomistic in that it assumes (a) that the meanings of words or sentences are explained by their relations to things or states of affairs in the world (in short, a designative view of language), (b) that language must exhibit a logical structure (syntax) that prescribes permissible relations among terms and sentences, and (c) that we ought not conflate or confuse the descriptive and evaluative functions of language, lest we "allow language that is really just the expression of a particular cultural or moral code to gain the appearance of objectively describing the world" (Smith, 1997, pp. 11-12).

The epistemology supported by this philosophy of language is that of pictorial description or conceptual representation of an external reality. Language and reason are understood as instruments of control in discovering and ordering the reality of the world (Taylor, 1985a). Further, the locus of representation is the autonomous, disengaged, cognizing agent, or what Bernstein (1983) characterizes as the Cartesian knower.[17] To be sure, there is considerable variation in the ways theories of inquiry and theories of knowledge draw on this concatenation of an empiricist theory of language, an atomistic theory of self, and a representational epistemology. Yet much contemporary social science practice, at least implicitly, continues to be informed by the idea that meaning and knowledge are best explicated by means of some kind of epistemology of representation (Shapiro, 1981; Taylor, 1995), although few social scientists are wedded to a crude correspondence theory of representation or naïvely accept that representation is mimesis.

◆ Social Constructionism

Social constructionist epistemologies aim to "overcome" representationalist epistemologies in a variety of ways.[18] They typically begin by drawing on an everyday, uncontroversial, garden-variety constructivism that might be described in the following way: In a fairly unremarkable sense, we are all constructivists if we believe that the mind is active in the construction of knowledge. Most of us would agree that knowing is not passive—a simple imprinting of sense data on the mind—but active; that is, mind does something with these impressions, at the very least forming abstractions or concepts. In this sense, constructivism means that human beings do not find or discover knowledge so much as we construct or make it. We invent concepts, models, and schemes to make sense of experience, and we continually test and modify these constructions in the light of new experience. Furthermore, there is an inevitable historical and sociocultural dimension to this construction. We do not construct our interpretations in isolation but against a backdrop of shared understandings, practices, language, and so forth.

This ordinary sense of constructionism is also called *perspectivism* in contemporary epistemology (e.g., Fay, 1996). It is the view that all knowledge claims and their evaluation take place within a conceptual framework through which the world is described and explained. Perspectivism opposes a naïve realist and empiricist epistemology that holds that there can be some kind of unmediated, direct grasp of the empirical world and that knowledge (i.e., the mind) simply reflects or mirrors what is "out there."

Philosophies of social constructionism also reject this naïve realist view of representation. But they often go much further in denying any interest whatsoever in an ontology of the real. Consider, for example, Potter's (1996) recent work explicating constructionism in the tradition of ethnomethodology and conversation analysis. He grounds his view in a critique of a representational theory of language and knowledge. He argues that "the world . . . is constituted in one way or another as people talk it, write it and argue it" (p. 98), yet he holds that social constructionism is not an ontological doctrine at all and thus takes no position on what sorts of things exist and what their status is. His primary concern is with how it is that a descriptive utterance is socially (i.e., interactionally) made to appear stable, factual, neutral, independent of the speaker, and merely mirroring some aspect of the world. For example, Potter states that "like money on the international markets, truth can be treated as a commodity which is worked up, can fluctuate, and can be strengthened or weakened by various procedures of representation" (p. 5). For Potter, social construction is interested in how utterances "work," and how they work is neither a matter of the cognitive analysis of how mental versions of the world are built nor a matter of the empirical analysis of semantic content and logical analysis of syntactical relations of words and sentences. Rather, how utterances work is a matter of understanding social practices and analyzing the rhetorical strategies in play in particular kinds of discourse.[19]

Like Potter, Denzin (1997) argues that discourse is the material practice that constitutes representation and description. He cites approvingly Stuart Hall's claim that "there is no way of experiencing the 'real relations' of a particular society outside of its cultural and ideological categories" (p. 245). Gergen (1985, 1994a, 1994b, 1995) is equally skeptical of the "real." He claims that social constructionism is mute or agnostic on matters of ontology: Social constructionism neither affirms nor denies the "world out there." For Gergen (1994a), constructionism is nothing more or less than a "form of intelligibility—an array of propositions, arguments, metaphors, narratives, and the like—that welcome inhabitation" (p. 78). Gergen subscribes to a relational theory of social meaning—"It is human interchange that gives language its capacity to mean, and it must stand as the critical locus of concern" (1994a, pp. 263-264)—and claims that social constructionism simply invites one to play with the possibilities and practices that are made coherent by various forms of relations.

All of these views take issue with what might be called *meaning realism*—the view that meanings are fixed entities that can be discovered and that exist independent of the interpreter. In this respect, these social constructionist views share with philosophical hermeneutics the broad critique of meaning as an object, and they display an affinity with the notion of the coming into being of meaning. Both philosophies endorse an expressivist-constructivist theory of language, in which, broadly conceived, language is understood as a range of activities in which we express and realize a certain way of being in the world. Language is seen neither as primarily a tool for gaining knowledge of the world as an objective process nor "as an instrument whereby we order the things in our world, but as what allows us to have the world we have. Language makes possible the disclosure of the human world" (Taylor, 1995, p. ix). Hence advocates for social constructionism and philosophical hermeneutics might agree on the claim that we are self-interpreting beings and that language constitutes this being (or that we dwell in language, as Gadamer and Heidegger have explained).

However, the similarity ends there. Although "constructionist" in its disavowal of an objectivist theory of meaning, philosophical hermeneutics trusts in the potential of language (conversation, dialogue) to disclose meaning and truth (Gallagher, 1992; Smith, 1997). For both Gadamer and Taylor, there is a "truth to the matter" of interpretation, but it is conceived in terms of disclosure that transpires in actual interpretive practices "rather than as a relation of correspondence between an object and some external means of representation" as conceived in traditional epistemology (Smith, 1997, p. 22). In sharp contrast to the views of Gadamer and Taylor, many (but not all) constructionist accounts hold that there is no truth to the matter of interpretation.

"Weak" and "Strong" Constructionism

A general assumption of social constructionism is that knowledge is not disinterested, apolitical, and exclusive of affective and embodied aspects of human experience, but is in some sense ideological, political, and permeated with values (Rouse, 1996). This assumption is amenable to both weak and strong interpretations. A weak or moderate interpretation of the role that social factors play in what constitutes legitimate, warranted, or true interpretation may well reject definitions of such notions as knowledge, justification, objectivity, and evidence as developed within the representationalist-empiricist-foundationalist nexus. But the perspective will attempt to recast these notions in a different epistemological framework and thereby preserve some way of distinguishing better or worse interpretations. A strong or radical interpretation of the role that social factors play in what constitutes legitimate knowledge results in a more radically skeptical and even nihilistic stance.

"Weak" Constructionism: An Illustration

A moderate version of social constructionism, developed in the context of feminist philosophy of science, is provided by Longino (1990, 1993a, 1993b, 1996). Her aim is to develop "a theory of inquiry that reveals the ideological dimension of knowledge construction while at the same time offering criteria for the comparative evaluation of scientific theories and research programs" (1993a, p. 257). Longino argues that many feminist critiques of science, including both standpoint epistemologies and psychodynamic perspectives, rightly criticize traditional epistemology for focusing exclusively on the logic of justification of scientific claims while ignoring methods of discovery or heuristic biases. She provides examples of how heuristics (e.g., androcentrism, sexism, and gender ideology) "limit the hypotheses in play in specific areas of inquiry" and how different heuristics put different hypotheses into play (1993b, p. 102). Although they are successful critiques of empiricism to the extent that they help "redescribe the process of knowledge acquisition" (by introducing different heuristics), these feminist epistemologies stop short of offering an adequate account of how we are to decide or to justify decisions between what seem to be conflicting knowledge claims. In sum, Longino claims that many feminist epistemologies are descriptively adequate but normatively (or prescriptively) inadequate.

Longino's (1993a) solution to the problem of uniting the descriptive and the normative is something she calls "contextual empiricism." She defends a modest empiricism—one in which the real world constrains our knowledge construction—by claiming that experiential or observational data are the least easily dismissed bases of hypothesis and theory validation. At the same time, she argues that the methods employed to generate, analyze, and organize data and to link evidence to hypotheses are not under the control of an autonomous, disengaged, disembodied subject, knower, or ideal epistemic agent. Rather, such matters are "contextual" in that they are constituted by a context of intersubjectively determined background assumptions that are "the vehicles by which social values and ideology are expressed in inquiry and become subtly inscribed in theories, hypotheses, and models defining research programs" (1993a, p. 263).

Consequently, these background assumptions must be submitted to conceptual and evidential criticism that is not possible as long as we cling to the view that knowledge is a production of an individual cognitive process. But, according to Longino (1993b), if we conceive of the practices of inquiry and knowledge production as *social* and accept the thesis that objectivity is a function of social interactions, then we can begin to explore how to criticize background assumptions effectively. Longino goes on to explain that "effective criticism of background assumptions requires the presence and expression of alternative points of view . . . [which] allows us to see how social values and interests can become enshrined in otherwise acceptable research programs" (p. 112). She offers a set of criteria necessary for a given scientific community to "achieve the transformative dimension of critical discourse" that include recognized avenues/forums for criticism; community response to criticism, not merely tolerance of it; shared standards of evaluation; and equality of intellectual authority (p. 112).

Longino argues for a social epistemology in which ideological and value issues tied to sociocultural practices are interwoven with empirical ones in scientific inquiry.[20] She appears to steer a middle ground by acknowledging that scientific knowledge is in part the product of processes of social negotiation without claiming that such knowledge is *only* a matter of social negotiation. And, in endorsing objectivity and strongly defending the normative aspects of a theory of inquiry, she clearly avoids the relativist view that any interpretation is as good as another. Finally, as is characteristic of many feminist epistemologists, Longino both assumes and builds on an ontology of knowing that is concretely situated and more interactive, relational, and dialogic than representational (Rouse, 1996).

"Strong" Constructionism

One way in which this stance develops is as follows: Taking their cue from Wittgenstein's notion of language games (as elaborated by Winch, 1958), some radical social constructionists begin with the premise that language is embedded in social practices or forms of life.[21] Moreover, the rules that govern a form of life circumscribe and close that form of life off to others. Hence it is only within and with reference to a particular form of life that the meaning of an action can be described and deciphered (Giddens, 1993). Standards for rationally evaluating beliefs are completely dependent on the language games or forms of life in which those beliefs arise. Thus the meanings of different language games or different forms of life are incommensurable. When this view is coupled with an insistence on radical conceptual difference, as it often is in many standpoint epistemologies, it readily leads to epistemological relativism. As Fay (1996) explains, in epistemological relativism, "no cross-framework judgments are permissible [for] the content, meaning, truth, rightness, and reasonableness of cognitive, ethical, or aesthetic beliefs, claims, experiences or actions can only be determined from within a particular conceptual scheme" (p. 77).[22]

Curiously, radical social constructionists such as Gergen and Denzin apparently endorse this idea of the incommensurability of language games or forms of life yet simultaneously claim that social constructionist philosophy somehow leads to an improvement of the human condition. Gergen (1994a) argues that knowledge is the product of social processes and that all statements of the true, the rational, and the good are the products of various particular communities of interpreters and thus to be regarded with suspicion. Yet he links his social constructionist philosophy to an agenda of democratization, possibility, and reconstruction. Above all else, Gergen looks to social constructionism as a means of broadening and democratizing the conversation about human practices and of submitting these practices to a continuous process of reflection.

Likewise, in his defense of a postmodernist interpretive ethnography, Denzin (1997) adamantly rejects what he calls a realist epistemology, one that "asserts that accurate representations of the world can be produced, and [that] these representations truthfully map the worlds of real experience" (p. 265). He defends standpoint epistemologies that study the world

310

of experience from the point of view of the historically and culturally situated individual. But he simultaneously endorses an ethnographic practice given to writing moral and allegorical tales that are not mere records of human experience intended simply to celebrate cultural differences or bring other cultures to our awareness. In Denzin's view, these moral tales are a method of empowerment for readers and a means for readers to discover moral truths about themselves.

A similar paradox is evident in each of these two strong constructionist views. Of Gergen we might ask, Absent any criteria for deciding across various frameworks which is the better (the more just, more democratic, and so on) practice and if there is no epistemic gain or loss resulting from this comparison, why would we bother to engage in the conversation?23 And of Denzin we might inquire, Does not the creation of moral tales assume that there is a (moral) truth to the matter of interpretation that arises from the comparison of historically and culturally situated experience? Does not such a move speak to the need for some criteria whereby we clarify and justify genuine moral truths, thereby distinguishing them from mere illusion or belief?

◆ Summary: Enduring Issues

The qualitative inquiry movement is built on a profound concern with understanding what other human beings are doing or saying. The philosophies of interpretivism, philosophical hermeneutics, and social constructionism provide different ways of addressing this concern. Yet cutting across these three philosophies are several perdurable issues that every qualitative inquirer must come to terms with using the resources of these (and other) philosophies. Three of the most salient issues are (a) how to define what "understanding" actually means and how to justify claims "to understand"; (b) how to frame the interpretive project, broadly conceived; and (c) how to envision and occupy the ethical space where researchers and researched (subjects, informants, respondents, participants, coresearchers) relate to one another on the sociotemporal occasion or event that is "research," and, consequently, how to determine the role, status, responsibility, and obligations the researcher has in and to the society he or she researches. These cognitive, social, and moral issues are obviously intertwined, but I distinguish them here for analytic purposes.

Understanding and Justifying Understanding[24]

All qualitative inquirers who have made the interpretive turn (Hiley et al., 1991; Rabinow & Sullivan, 1979) share a set of commitments.[25] They are highly critical of scientism and reject an anthropology of a disengaged, controlling, instrumental self (Smith, 1997; Taylor, 1995). They hold that the cognitive requirements involved in understanding others cannot be met through the use of foundationalist epistemological assumptions characteristic of logical empiricism (e.g., neutrality of observation, primordial "givenness" of experience, independence of empirical data from theoretical frameworks). Interpretivism, all varieties of social constructionism (including Nietzschean perspectivism, neopragmatism, and deconstructionism), and Gadamerian philosophical hermeneutics all "insist on rejecting the very idea of any foundational, mind-independent, and permanently fixed reality that could be grasped or even sensibly thought of without the mediation of human structuring" (Shusterman, 1991, p. 103), at least in the realm of human studies. Stated somewhat differently, knowledge of what others are doing and saying always depends upon some background or context of other meanings, beliefs, values, practices, and so forth. Hence, for virtually all postempiricist philosophies of the human sciences, understanding is interpretation all the way down.

But the cognitive requirements of understanding in qualitative methodologies are not exhausted by this claim of the inevitability of interpretation. It is necessary to spell out the consequences of this interpretive turn for our efforts to understand.[26] Broadly speaking, two different sets of consequences characterize the contemporary debate.

Strong Holism

On the one hand, there are strong holists who argue that from the fact that we always *see* (make sense of, know) everything through interpretation, we must conclude that everything in fact *is constituted* by interpretation. From the fact that knowledge is perspectival and contextual, they draw the strong skeptical conclusion that it is impossible to distinguish any particular interpretation as more correct, or better or worse, than any other.

In this scenario, the question of justifying an interpretation of what others are doing or saying is irrelevant. How or why justification is irrelevant depends on the particular kind of strong holism in question. Justification may be irrelevant because interpretations are always regarded as "our" interpretations and hence ethnocentric (Hoy, 1991). Justification may not matter because interpretations are thought to be always nothing more than an expression of personal or political subjectivity. Or justification may be a nonissue because it is assumed that an interpretation never goes beyond itself; it is not about justification, disclosure, or clarification of meaning, but "textualistic," caught up in the larger game called the play of signifiers.[27] A good deal of contemporary writing about qualitative inquiry (e.g., Clough, 1998; Denzin, 1994, 1997; Lather, 1993; Richardson, 1997), influenced by postmodern ethnography and other related intellectual currents, appears to be committed to some version of strong holism. Likewise, the radical social constructionists engaged in the social studies of science—Latour, Woolgar, Knorr-Cetina, Barnes, and Bloor—develop strong holistic theses about scientific knowledge.

The issue of evaluating and choosing among competing (different, contradictory, and so on) interpretations raises the question of what constitutes rational behavior. What does it mean to make a reasonable choice from among alternative interpretations? Often a common assumption in strong or skeptical holism is that "if we cannot come up with universal fixed criteria to measure the plausibility of competing interpretations, then this means that we have no *rational* basis for distinguishing better and worse, more plausible or less plausible interpretations, whether these be interpretations of texts, actions, or historical epochs" (Bernstein, 1986, p. 358). Given the impossibility of *foundational* criteria, strong holists, typically, reach one of several conclusions: (a) They hold that the very idea of being rational requires deconstruction; (b) they endorse a noncritical pluralism of views (i.e., "multiple realities," many equally acceptable interpretations, and so on) that requires no comparative evaluation; or (c) they claim that rhetorical criteria—whether an interpretation invites, persuades, compels, entertains, evokes, or delights—are the only proper ones for judging whether one interpretation is better than another.[28]

Weak Holism

Weak or nonskeptical holism argues that it is neither necessary nor desirable to draw such relativistic, suspicious (or, worse, nihilistic) conclusions from the fact that knowledge of others is always dependent on a background of understanding. Weak holists claim that the background (the "mediation" of all understanding) is "not strong enough to act as a

fixed limit or to make it impossible to decide normatively between interpretations on the basis of evidence. Indeed such evaluation will always be
comparative, fallibilistic, and revisable, in that yet a better interpretation
could come along, encompassing the strengths and overcoming the weaknesses of previous interpretations" (Bohman, 1991a, p. 146).

Weak holism seeks to explicate a rational basis for deciding whether an
interpretation is "valid" or justified. But there are a variety of ways in
which justification is attempted. For example, Bohman (1991b), Fay
(1996), and to some extent Longino, as explained above, appear committed to the view that justification of an interpretation is subject to epistemic
norms of internal coherence as well as correctness based on empirical constraints. Other weak holists look to redefine rationality on the basis of
practical reasoning, that is, how "we can and do make comparative judgments and seek to support them with arguments and the appeal to good
reasons" (Bernstein, 1986, p. 358). For example, Bernstein's (1983, 1986,
1991) "nonfoundational pragmatic humanism" (which he also finds as a
common theme in Rorty, Habermas, and Gadamer) illustrates a case for
weak holism built on themes of praxis, practice, discourse, and practical
truth. Gadamer (1975) argues that although the act of understanding
cannot be modeled as a determinate analysis of an object yielding a final,
complete, or definitive interpretation, nonetheless understanding has a
normative dimension manifest in the fact that understanding is a kind of
practical-moral knowledge. In his explanation of choosing between competing interpretations, Taylor (1985a, 1989) denies that there can be any
appeal to empirical evidence or any fixed criterion that would *decisively*
determine the correctness of an interpretation. Yet he develops an argument for the comparative superiority of interpretations grounded in a narrative form of practical reason and linked to his particular explication of
how it is that we are human beings for whom things matter. For Taylor,
what counts as better interpretation is understood as the justified movement from one interpretation to another.[29]

Locating the Interpretive Project

There is little agreement among qualitative inquirers on the social and
scientific goals or purposes of their shared interpretive project. Many
qualitative inquirers locate the project squarely within an emancipatory and transformative agenda. Some neopragmatists, critical theorists,
and feminists are committed to the task of interpretation for purposes of

criticizing and dismantling unjust and undemocratic educational and social practices and transforming them (Howe, 1998).

Other neopragmatists and some defenders of philosophical hermeneutics share this general Enlightenment belief in the power of critical reflection to improve our lot, but connect the interpretive project less directly to political transformation and more closely to dialogue, conversation, and education understood as an interpretational interchange that is self-transformative. They see understanding that results from interpretation less as something that is at our disposal for us subsequently to do something with by "applying" it and more as participation in meaning, in a tradition, and ultimately in a dialogue (Grondin, 1994). In their view, critical emancipation—release (or escape) from reproductive, hegemonic, authoritarian structures—never quite fully happens. Critical reflection is always characterized by both autonomy and authority. As Gallagher (1992) explains, this way of conceiving of the interpretive project does not deny the possibility of emancipation and subsequent transformation, but only the possibility of absolute emancipation: "Emancipation is an on-going process within educational experience, rather than the end result of critical reflection" (p. 272).

Many postmodernists are deeply suspicious of either the emancipatory or the conversational framing of the interpretive project. They opt instead for interpretation as a kind of spontaneous play or an incessant deciphering that unravels the multiple meanings of such notions as self, identity, objectivity, subjectivity, presence, truth, and being.

These different ways of framing the interpretive project reveal that, internally at least, qualitative inquiry is a broadly contentious movement. It is a loose coalition of inquirers seemingly united only in their general opposition to what was earlier called the foundationalist-empiricist-representationalist nexus of beliefs.

Ethical and Political Considerations

Social inquiry is a practice, not simply a way of knowing. Understanding what others are doing or saying and transforming that knowledge into public form involves moral-political commitments. Moral issues arise from the fact that a theory of knowledge is supported by a particular view of human agency. For example, Taylor, Dunne, and others argue that the foundationalist-empiricist-representationalist nexus is built upon a stance of disengagement and objectification: The subject (knower) stands over and against the object of understanding. Moreover, the political dimension of the practice of social inquiry is wedded to the growth of what Bauman (1992) describes as the politics of legislative reason central to the rise of the modern state. Hence the practice of social research (including, but not limited to, qualitative inquiry) is not immune to effects of the central forces of the culture of modernity—technologization, institutionalization, bureaucratization, and professionalization.[30]

A good deal of current criticism of ethnographic realism, or what is more generally called the crisis of representation in ethnography, is directed at the moral and political requirements of social research practices, not just (or even) their cognitive demands. At issue is how to answer the fundamental question, How should I *be* toward these people I am studying? There are at least two sharply different answers to this question. Firmly in line with the interpretivist tradition of disengagement, Prus (1996) defends what some qualitative researchers would perhaps criticize as a conventional, modernist, and dangerous view of the inquirer as one who "attempts to minimize the obtrusiveness of the researcher in the field and in the text eventually produced . . . an image of a researcher who is more chameleon-like . . . who fits into the situation with a minimum of disruption, and whose work allows the life-worlds of the other to surface in as complete and unencumbered a manner as possible" (p. 196). In sharp contrast, Denzin (1994) aims

> to create a form of gazing and understanding fitted to the contemporary, mass-mediated, cinematic societies called postmodern. Such a gaze would undermine from within the cold, analytic, abstract, voyeuristic, disciplinary gaze of Foucault's panopticon. This will be a newer, gentler, compassionate gaze which looks, and desires, not technical instrumental knowledge, but in-depth existential understandings. (p. 64)

How one understands the differences in the ethical-political stances of the researcher illustrated by Prus and Denzin, and how one decides what to do about one's own ethical-political commitments as a researcher depend in part on the ethical framework one draws on to make sense of these kinds of situations.[31] This observation takes us into the realm of ethics and moral philosophy, a topic beyond the scope of this chapter. For present purposes, it will have to suffice simply to point out that at present there is a rather lively ongoing dialogue and debate surrounding the standard framework for moral epistemology.

316

Very briefly, the standard framework embraces a common core of ideas: (a) that morality is deontological (primarily concerned with moral obligations and commitments), (b) that the moral point of view is marked by its impartiality and universalizability, and (c) that conflicts of rights and obligations are open to argumentative resolution. Taken collectively, these ideas constitute a largely formalistic understanding of morality. *Formalistic* here does not mean the well-known quarrel over which is the superior formal theory of ethics. Rather, it means that within the standard framework the moral point of view is defined in terms of formal criteria. Form is privileged over content, as Vetlesen (1997) explains:

> Universalizability, impartiality, and impersonality—the formal criteria instrumental in defining the "moral point of view"—now function as the features a given item must possess in order to qualify as actually having moral content. In other words, only issues, questions, problems, and dilemmas lending themselves to adjudication and consensual resolution by means of [these] formal criteria . . . are allowed to qualify as "moral" in content. (p. 4)

Although they display considerable differences in their views, thinkers such as Kierkegaard, Sartre, Buber, Gabriel Marcel, Levinas, Løgstrup, Nussbaum, Bauman, and Noddings oppose the way morality is defined in the standard framework. They all argue for an ethic of closeness, of care, of proximity, or of relatedness, and hold that morality must be theorized from an *experiential* basis, specifically in the experience of the I-thou relationship. Benhabib contrasts this orientation with the orientation of the standard way of theorizing morality in the following way: "The moral issues which preoccupy us most and which touch us most deeply derive not from problems of justice in the economy and the polity, but precisely from the quality of our relations with others in the 'spheres of kinship, love, friendship, and sex'" (quoted in Vetlesen, 1997, p. 4). These relations demand what Nussbaum (1990) characterizes as attentiveness—"an openness to being moved by the plight of others," the willingness "to be touched by another's life" (p. 162). Normative attention, in turn, requires a way of knowing that is contextual and narrative rather than formal and abstract. *Context* refers both to each individual's specific history, identity, and affective-emotional constitution and to the relationship between parties in the encounter with *its* history, identity, and affective definition. These two elements are linked by narrative.

317

Moreover, because these relations are highly contingent and contextual, the moral act itself, as Bauman (1993) observes, "is endemically ambivalent, forever threading precariously the thin lines dividing care from domination and tolerance from indifference" (p. 181). The inherent fragility, precariousness, and incurable ambivalence of morality means that the moral life is not about decision making, calculation, or procedures. Rather, it is "that unfounded, non-rational, unarguable, no excuses given and non-calculable urge to stretch towards the other, to caress, to be for, to live for, happen what may" (p. 247). Bauman (1995) adds that what the moral life amounts to in this view is a "never-ending string of settlements between mildly attractive or unattractive eventualities" (p. 66). Here, the notion of settlement differs from a calculating decision; it is not a conclusion one reaches based on applying principles; it has no fixed procedure.

Completely absent in this way of thinking of the moral life is the notion that morality is about argumentative resolution of competing moral claims. The moral encounter does not mean rule following but expression and communication. Furthermore, in this framework, there is no teleological, liberalist idea of moral progress driven by a vision, albeit imperfect, of social utopia, or a belief that our values and our moral abilities are evolving to some better form.

In this alternative framework, ethical relationship is grounded in the notion of being-for the Other. The relationship of being-for is prior to intentionality, prior to choice. Morality in this alternative framework is not voluntary. Moral orientation comes prior to any calculating action on the part of the moral agent; it is prior to purposefulness, reciprocity, and contractuality. Morality, in the first instance, is not about a kind of moral decision making that precedes moral action. Morality is not optional. Noddings refers to this notion of morality as caring. But caring is not a method for doing ethics or a particular principle on which to form a professional service ethic. It is an ethical orientation, a particular ground of meaning and value with its own internal logic of relational work (Thompson, 1997).

Caring or being-for is a kind of responsibility that is prevoluntary, unremovable, noncontractual, nonreciprocal, and asymmetrical. As Vetlesen (1997) explains, "The core of being-for is neither right nor rights, neither the happiness nor the good of those concerned. Its core is responsibility. Responsibility not as freely assumed, not as socially or politically or legally sanctioned; and yet as coming from outside rather than inside, as originating from what is exterior not interior to the agent" (p. 9). He adds that matters of justice, goodness, happiness all matter, but come later, and they do not "taken together or singly, define morality the phenomenon, responsibility the task" (p. 9).

It would be both incorrect and naïve to argue that a formalistic theory of ethics and morality as sketched above maps directly onto some set of "quantitative" methodologies, whereas the alternative maps onto some set of "qualitative" methodologies. Linking this work in moral phenomenology and moral epistemology to thinking about the ethics and politics of qualitative (and, more generally, all social) research is a complex matter. Yet this work does suggest that how a researcher ought to relate to and consequently represent others can be framed in at least two ways. On the one hand, ethical-moral relations can be defined as a kind of "problem" that must be solved by adopting the right kind of research ethics for "gazing," or by using the right kind of textual form, or by employing the right kind of methodology. The problem-solving approach assumes that we can draw on some resources for criticism and direction of our choices that somehow lie outside the particular occasion that demands a practical choice. It reduces the dilemmas of human existence to objective problems in need of solutions. On the other hand, the question of relations and representation can also be understood as a mystery about the union of knowing and being to be faced anew in each situation in which the researcher finds her- or himself. This approach understands the situation of "How shall I be toward these people I am studying?" as one that demands a particular kind of understanding noted above as practical-moral knowledge.

◆ Final Note

In outlining these philosophies it has not been my intention to offer a template or typology with which to sort current expressions of qualitative inquiry. (Moreover, the topics discussed here go well beyond any conception of qualitative studies to a concern with all current social inquiry.) It seems to be a uniquely American tendency to categorize and label complicated theoretical perspectives as either this or that.[32] Such labeling is dangerous, for it blinds us to enduring issues, shared concerns, and points of tension that cut across the landscape of the movement, issues that each inquirer must come to terms with in developing an identity as a social inquirer. In wrestling with the ways in which these philosophies forestructure our efforts to understand what it means to "do" qualitative inquiry, what we face is not a choice of which label—interpretivist, constructivist, hermeneuticist, or something else—best suits us. Rather, we are confronted with choices about how each of us wants to live the life of a social inquirer.

◆ Notes

1. Of course, anthropologists and fieldwork sociologists had been doing "qualitative inquiry" for decades earlier. But methods for generating and interpreting qualitative data acquired a particular currency in a variety of other human science fields in the 1970s. This is not the place to develop this historical account, but it seems reasonable to say that several developments in the disciplines converged in the 1970s, thereby providing fertile ground for the recovery of interest in fieldwork methodologies. These developments included the critique of statistical hypothesis testing and experimentation and the growing interest in "naturalistic" methods that was unfolding in psychology, the emergence of humanistic psychology, the renewed attention paid by some sociologists to explaining fieldwork methods, the critique of structural-functionalism and the concomitant development of interpretivist anthropology, and the widening awareness outside the community of philosophers of science of criticisms of the received view.

2. It is not coincidental that the movement in the United States began to flourish as more and more of the European philosophers' broad attack on scientism (Cooper, 1996) became available in English. For example, the first book-length treatment of *Verstehen* appeared in English in 1975 (Outhwaite, 1975); Schutz's *Der sinn hafte Aufbau der sozialen Welt* (*The Phenomenology of the Social World*), first published in German in 1932, appeared in an English translation in 1967; Habermas's monograph *Zur logik der Sozialwissenschaften* (*On the Logic of the Social Sciences*), first published in German in 1967, did not appear in English until 1988; and so on.

3. Sadly, some researchers seem drawn to qualitative inquiry for the simple fact that they do not wish to "deal with numbers." This is doubly tragic. First, it is based on faulty reasoning—there is nothing inherent in the epistemologies of qualitative inquiry that prohibits the use of numbers as data. Second, such a stance can be based in the illusion that so-called qualitative inquiry is somehow "easier" to do than so-called quantitative inquiry. But it is hard to imagine what criteria might be employed to determine that the level of effort and thought required for writing field notes, conducting and transcribing interviews, interpreting different kinds of qualitative data, and so on is somehow lower (or higher, for that matter) than that required for designing and executing a careful and meaningful test of a statistical hypothesis. These inquiry tasks simply require different kinds of awareness, knowledge, and skills.

4. These are by no means the only philosophies that attract the attention of qualitative inquirers. For example, much contemporary "qualitative" work is firmly built on a postempiricist philosophy of science. That is, its methodology takes seriously the implications of the underdetermination of theory by data, the theory-ladenness of observation, the fallibil-

ity of all claims to know, and so on, without being drawn into the Continental philosophers' critique of instrumental reason and scientism, Heideggerian concerns about "being," deconstructionism (whether that of Gadamer or Derrida), feminist critiques of objectivity, and so forth. Feminist, neopragmatic, ethnic, and critical theory philosophies are discussed elsewhere in this handbook. Some claim phenomenology as a founding epistemology for qualitative inquiry, but it is virtually impossible to discuss the relevance for qualitative inquiry of this complex, multifaceted philosophy in general terms without reducing the notion of phenomenology to a caricature. Phenomenology means something far more complicated than a romanticized notion of seeing the world of actors "as it really is." Moreover, simple formulations in introductory methods books (e.g., "Researchers in the phenomenological mode attempt to understand the meaning of events and interactions to ordinary people in particular situations"; Bogdan & Biklen, 1992, p. 34) are misleading because such definitions gloss the crucial difference for epistemologies of qualitative inquiry, namely, defining what *meaning* is. The complexity of the influence of phenomenology on qualitative inquiry is evident when we consider that the phenomenology of Heidegger, for example, figures prominently but in very different ways in both philosophical hermeneutics and deconstructionist approaches; Husserl's phenomenology considerably influenced the work of Alfred Schutz, who, in turn, served as a source of ideas for ethnomethodologists and other sociologists. Gubrium and Holstein take up issues in the tradition of phenomenological sociology in Chapter 7 of Volume 2.

5. However, this issue appears to be more of a concern among defenders of interpretivist/hermeneutic approaches to social science than it is between this group and the logical empiricists (Hiley, Bohman, & Shusterman, 1991). See, for example, the exchange between Geertz and Taylor on this issue in Tully (1994); see also Rouse (1991).

6. Dilthey (1958) emphasized the importance of the psychological reenactment (*Nacherleben*) of the experience of the other. Weber (1949) endorsed a similar notion of *Verstehen* as a "rational understanding of motivation" (p. 95). In his later writings, Dilthey de-emphasized the notion of empathic identification and spoke more of hermeneutic interpretation of cultural products.

7. See Bleicher (1980) and Gallagher (1992) for overviews of these distinctions in types of hermeneutics.

8. Bernstein (1983) adds that "there is no determinate method for acquiring or pursuing this art [of understanding], in the sense of explicit rules that are to be followed" (p. 135). Yet, within the interpretivist tradition, the epistemic status of rules, procedures, or methods is controversial. The work of Geertz, Wolcott, and Stake, I would argue, exemplifies a more artistic interpretation of how one achieves understanding. On the other hand, the work of Hammersley, Goffman, Lofland and Lofland, Miles and Huberman, Prus, Silverman, and Strauss and Corbin illustrates a more social scientific approach to the method of understanding. These scholars emphasize ways of generating and interpreting "understanding" that place a premium on the validity, relevance, and importance of both question and findings. Their methodologies are concerned with asking questions about the type, frequency, magnitude, structure, processes, causes, consequences, and meanings of sociopolitical phenomena and developing defensible answers to those questions. Answers typically take the form of substantive or middle-range theory that explains or accounts for the phenomena. Yet a "third way" of understanding the significance of method in achieving understanding is offered by Garfinkel and other ethnomethodologists who claim that both actors and

observers (i.e., social scientists) are to be treated as "members" who produce and manage (i.e., accomplish) the social activity of organized everyday life. Thus sociological methods, for example, are nothing more or less than evidence of the practical sociological reasoning of sociologists.

9. I focus almost exclusively on philosophical or ontological hermeneutics here because the contours of both critical hermeneutics and radical hermeneutics are discussed elsewhere in this series.

10. I use text and human action interchangeably here, following Ricoeur's (1981) argument for their analogous relationship in hermeneutic interpretation.

11. Again, it must be emphasized that *uninvolved observer* here does not mean that the interpretivist observes literally at a distance or from behind some kind of one-way mirror. What the term signifies is an epistemological relationship between subject (interpreter) and object of interpretation (text, human action) in which the interpreter is unaffected by (and, in this sense, external to) the act of interpretation. At issue here is the theoretical attitude noted above: the idea that the knower is not (or must not be) somehow bound up with the domain of the object he or she seeks to understand. Concerns for managing and tracking bias, inventorying subjectivities, keeping a reflexive journal, peer debriefing, and so forth (familiar procedures in the qualitative methodological literature) are all related to this bid to maintain the theoretical attitude.

12. Not to put too fine a point on it, but this notion of engagement entails more than a confession of positionality or simply inventorying "where one stands" relative to that which is being interpreted. Engagement means risking one's stance and acknowledging the ongoing liminal experience of living between familiarity and strangeness (see Kerdeman, 1998).

13. Grondin (1994) defends Gadamer's hermeneutics against the charge that it is a kind of linguistic idealism. According to Grondin, Gadamer maintains that understanding is *in principle* linguistic "because language embodies the sole means for carrying out the conversation that we are and that we hope to convey to each other. It is for this reason that hermeneutics permits itself an aphorism such as 'Being that can be understood is language.' The emphasis should be on the 'can.' Understanding, itself always linguistically formed and dealing with things verbal, must be capable of engaging the whole content of language in order to arrive at the being that language helps to bring to expression. The essential linguisticality of understanding expresses itself less in our statements than in our search for the language to say what we have on our minds and hearts. For hermeneutics, it is less constitutive that understanding is expressed in language—which is true but trivial—than that it lives in the unending process of 'summoning the word' and the search for a sharable language. Indeed, understanding is to be conceived *as* this process" (p. 120). See also the exchange between Davey (1991) and Smith (1991) on whether Gadamer's critique of the statement, propositional language, and logic is justified.

14. See also Hekman's (1986, pp. 145ff.) argument that a fixed meaning of human action is the fundamental unit of social scientific analysis in Wittgensteinian social science (e.g., Winch, 1958), Schutz's phenomenology, and ethnomethodology.

15. In the philosophical hermeneutics of Gadamer and Taylor, understanding is linked both to the Aristotelian notion of *praxis* and to its distinct form of personal, experiential knowledge and reasoning called *phronesis* or practical wisdom. The latter (*allo eidos gnoseos,* that "other form of cognition") requires "responsiveness, flexibility, and perceptiveness in discerning what is needed" and sharply contrasts to the form of practical

knowledge called *techne* (Dunne, 1993, p. 56). Gadamer connects understanding, interpretation, and application by modeling the activity of understanding on the notion of *phronesis* and by modeling the theory of understanding (hermeneutics) on practical philosophy (Bernstein, 1983, pp. 114-150; Dunne, 1993, pp. 154ff.; Gadamer, 1981).

16. This "movement" takes up an incredible variety of related developments in pragmatism (e.g., Mead's theory of the social self and the sociality of language, Dewey's epistemological behaviorism), theory of science (e.g., the Quine-Duhem thesis, Hanson, Kuhn), philosophy of language (e.g., Wittgenstein's *Philosophical Investigations*, the work of Austin and Louch in ordinary language philosophy), philosophy of social science (e.g., Winch), sociology of knowledge (e.g., Berger and Luckmann), phenomenology (e.g., Heidegger's ideas about language in *Being and Time*), ethnomethodology's concern for situated actions as publicly interpreted linguistic forms (e.g., Garfinkel), and so on. Bernstein (1991, pp. 326ff.) identifies a set of substantive pragmatic themes that characterize in a very general way many different postempiricist philosophies: antifoundationalism, thoroughgoing fallibilism, primary emphasis on the social character of the self, the need to cultivate a community of inquirers, awareness and sensitivity to radical contingency, and recognition that there is no escape from the plurality of traditions.

17. Taylor (1995) refers to this as the "first-person-singular self"; "the human agent as primarily a subject of representations, first, about the world outside; [and] second, about depictions of ends desired or feared. This subject is a monological one. We are in contact with an 'outside' world, including other agents, the objects we and they deal with, our own and others' bodies, but this contact is through representations we have 'within.' The subject is first of all an inner space, a 'mind' to use the old terminology, or a mechanism capable of processing representations, if we follow the more fashionable computer-inspired models of today" (p. 169).

18. Given limited space, I have chosen to focus on social versus psychological forms of constructionism. My primary concern here is with those philosophies that wrestle with joining social-political factors with epistemic concerns in their account of what constitutes a public body of knowledge. Of course, psychological constructionists also wrestle with the significance of social factors in knowledge construction, but their primary interest is in understanding how these play a role in individual acts of cognition. There is considerable within-group as well as between-group difference in psychological constructivist and social constructivist perspectives in social science, psychology, and education (Gergen, 1994a, 1994b; Phillips, 1995, 1997a, 1997b; Potter, 1996) that simply cannot be surveyed here. Moreover, there is a difference in terminology that can get rather confusing. Phillips, for example, divides social constructivists from psychological constructivists; Gergen calls the former group social constructionists and the latter constructivists. I use the terms *constructionist* and *constructionism* here in discussing the "social" end of the continuum.

19. In this emphasis on how language is used to accomplish something, we can find some parallels to issues taken up in informal logic, such as describing and evaluating reasoning and argumentation not in terms of deductive logic but in terms of criteria appropriate to different argument schemes or types of dialogue (Van Eemeren, Grootendorst, Blair, & Willard, 1987; Walton, 1989). Of course, for social constructionists persuaded of radical perspectivalism or the infinite play of signifiers, there would not be much point to studying argumentation.

20. Dorothy Smith (1996) offers another example of this effort to interweave the social and the empirical that preserves the notion that our knowledge claims refer or are "about" something and not merely the infinite play of signifiers.

21. My concern here is with strong interpretations that continue to accord primacy to the role of social factors in knowledge construction, not with views that see the social as something to be undone. For example, references to Nietzsche's radical perspectivalism and Derrida's deconstructionism often appear in texts championing a radical social constructionist view. Yet they offer little support for *social* constructionism. Nietzsche (1979) holds that meaning (truth, knowledge) is nothing more than the product of processes of social negotiation: "What therefore is true? A mobile army of metaphors, metonymies, anthropomorphisms, . . . which after long use seem firm, canonical, and obligatory to a people; truths are illusions of which one has forgotten that they are illusions" (p. 174). But for him, the *social* construction of value has to be acknowledged and carefully criticized in order to make way for and justify the *individual* construction of value. These so-called social truths are, as Smith (1997) explains, "antagonistic to life, where 'life' connotes a vital force of creative energy, a flux of sensuous particularity which resists the conceptual categorization conditioning claims to truth" (p. 17). *Self*-creation and *self*-transformation are Nietzsche's goals. Derrida (1976, 1978) appears to hold a similar view, although of this I am not completely certain. On the one hand, Derrida is highly critical (and suspicious) of any interpretation that appeals to or seeks to reproduce some larger, more encompassing framework. He argues that the *individual* reader has a responsibility to open up or activate the textuality of the text, but this means the reader must open him- or herself to the text because any new reading of the text is not simply the reader's own doing. Meaning is constructed in the play of signifiers within the field of textuality that encompasses text and interpreter. Yet Derrida claims that there is no subjective and reflective control over this interpretation process. Hence he seems to endorse individual construction of meaning, but simultaneously holds that there is no subjective locus of meaning or interpretation (Derrida, 1976, 1978). To be sure, there is an affinity in the view I describe here with Nietzsche's and Derrida's views. All three assume more or less that everything we encounter is an interpretation in terms of our own subjective values and perspectives (or the values and perspectives of our group, community, culture, and the like). Hence the epistemological stance for all three views can be summarized as follows: "All knowledge is interpretation; interpretations are always value-laden; values are ultimately expressions of some heterogeneous non-cognitive faculty, process or event (such as the mechanics of desire, history, or the will to power); therefore truth claims are ultimately expressions of that non-cognitive faculty, process or event" (Smith, 1997, p. 16).

22. It is but a short step from epistemological relativism to ontological relativism: If all we can know about reality depends on our particular conceptual scheme, is it not the case that reality itself can only be how it seems in our conceptual scheme (Fay, 1996; Smith, 1997)?

23. In an exchange with Taylor (1988), Gergen (1988) disputes the idea of strong evaluation or the possibility of sorting out whether some interpretations are better than others. Moreover, Gergen (1994a) (wrongly) interprets the philosophical hermeneutics of Gadamer as endorsing some kind of "essence" of meaning. In my view, Gergen does not adequately come to terms with either Gadamer's or Taylor's view that interpretation as practical reason (*phronesis*) is not exhausted by tradition.

24. See Smith and Deemer (Chapter 12, Volume 3) for more extensive discussion of criteria and cognitive requirements for judging whether understanding has been accomplished.

25. Admittedly, what constitutes having made the "turn," so to speak, is not particularly easy to discern. In general, it means rejecting an epistemology of representation. But that can be wrongly interpreted as abandoning all interest in "traditional" social scientific concerns about validity, objectivity, and generalizability.

26. The argument developed here draws heavily on Bohman (1991a, 1991b), who develops this distinction between strong and weak holism and defends the latter. I do not necessarily agree with the way in which he labels the various positions of Gadamer, Rorty, Derrida, Habermas, and so on in terms of these two kinds of holism, but that sorting and classifying is largely irrelevant to the point I am making here.

27. Gallagher (1992) explains Derrida's view as follows: "Interpretation occurs only within the diacritical system of signifiers and without recourse to a metaphysical reality of the referent. . . . Derrida's radical principle of play is an attempt (from the inside) to unravel the metaphysical belief in the reality and the identity of the referent—objectivity, subjectivity, presence, being, truth, or any other metaphysical concept operative in the Western tradition" (p. 283).

28. Deconstructionism or radical social constructionism (and Rortyian pragmatism) does not regard the absence of foundational criteria as a problem in need of correction. Smith (1997) explains: "On the contrary, the demand for foundations drives the ambition of the philosophical tradition weak hermeneutics [deconstructionism] aspires to overcome. The foundationalism of previous philosophy, it is alleged, encourages an intolerance of 'otherness' and the 'incommensurable.' Weak hermeneutics can take the form of strategies for circumventing or subverting that demand for answerability to reason through which, it is believed, power and control are exercised. The goal of these postmodern strategies is to make space in thought for that which is allegedly non-assimilable to reason: diversity, heterogeneity and difference" (p. 18).

29. Smith (1997) summarizes Taylor's notion of evaluation: "The correctness of a particular practical deliberation is determined by the comparative superiority of the interpretive positions on either side of a move. To be favored by reason is therefore not to be judged positively according to some fixed *criterion,* one that is applicable to *any* practical deliberation independent of context or horizon of self-interpretation. . . . practical reasoning works well when it perspicuously displays epistemic gains or loses in particular concrete cases. Typical ways of achieving this goal are through identifying and resolving a contradiction in the original interpretation, pointing to a confusion that interpretation relied on, or by acknowledging the importance of some factor which it screened out" (p. 61). Note that these *ways* in which perspicuous articulation can occur are not *criteria* for judging whether the interpretation per se is a good or bad one. What counts as an "epistemic gain" cannot be determined independently or in advance of the actual occasion of interpretation. I have drawn on this idea of a criterionless weak holism to elaborate evaluative judgment (see Schwandt, 1996, 1997).

30. See Carr's (1997) discussion of how the 20th-century transformation of education into schooling was accompanied by a modern "methodical" approach to educational inquiry.

31. Understanding how to face the situation of knowing others also has a great deal to do with how researcher role and responsibility are shaped by discourses that dominate universities (Derrida, 1983). That topic is taken up by Greenwood and Levin in Chapter 3 of this volume.

32. The very idea of qualitative inquiry as a category distinct from quantitative inquiry is, of course, part of the origin of the movement portrayed in various ways in this *Handbook*. In the view of many, myself and many of my students included, it is highly questionable whether such a distinction is any longer meaningful for helping us understand the purpose and means of human inquiry. One of my students recently commented that we think we become researchers by learning methodologies, by developing some kind of allegiance to qualitative or quantitative approaches to inquiry. But, she continued, *all* research is interpretive, and we face a multiplicity of methods that are suitable for different kinds of understandings. So the traditional means of coming to grips with one's identity as a researcher by aligning oneself with a particular set of methods (or by being defined in one's department as a student of "qualitative" or "quantitative" methods) is no longer very useful. If we are to go forward, we need to get rid of that distinction.

◆ References

Aylesworth, G. E. (1991). Dialogue, text, narrative: Confronting Gadamer and Ricoeur. In H. Silverman (Ed.), *Gadamer and hermeneutics* (pp. 63-81). New York: Routledge.

Bauman, Z. (1992). *Intimations of postmodernity.* London: Routledge.

Bauman, Z. (1993). *Postmodern ethics.* Oxford: Blackwell.

Bauman, Z. (1995). *Life in fragments: Essays in postmodern morality.* Oxford: Blackwell.

Bernstein, R. J. (1976). *The restructuring of social and political theory.* Philadelphia: University of Pennsylvania Press.

Bernstein, R. J. (1983). *Beyond objectivism and relativism: Science, hermeneutics, and praxis.* Philadelphia: University of Pennsylvania Press.

Bernstein, R. J. (1986). What is the difference that makes a difference? Gadamer, Habermas, and Rorty. In B. R. Wachterhauser (Ed.), *Hermeneutics and modern philosophy* (pp. 343-376). Albany: State University of New York Press.

Bernstein, R. J. (1991). *The new constellation: The ethical-political horizons of modernity/postmodernity.* Cambridge: MIT Press.

Bleicher, J. (1980). *Contemporary hermeneutics: Hermeneutics as method, philosophy, and critique.* London: Routledge & Kegan Paul.

Bogdan, R. C., & Biklen, S. K. (1992). *Qualitative research for education: An introduction to theory and methods* (2nd ed.). Boston: Allyn & Bacon.

Bohman, J. F. (1991a). Holism without skepticism: Contextualism and the limits of interpretation. In D. R. Hiley, J. F. Bohman, & R. Shusterman (Eds.), *The interpretive turn* (pp. 129-154). Ithaca, NY: Cornell University Press.

Bohman, J. F. (1991b). *New philosophy of social science: Problems of indeterminacy*. Cambridge: MIT Press.

Carr, W. (1997). Philosophy and method in educational research. *Cambridge Journal of Education, 27,* 203-209.

Clough, P. (1998). *The end(s) of ethnography:* Now and then. *Qualitative Inquiry, 4,* 3-14.

Collingwood, R. G. (1961). *The idea of history.* Oxford: Clarendon. (Original work published 1946)

Connolly, J. M., & Keutner, T. (1988). Introduction: Interpretation, decidability, and meaning. In J. M. Connolly & T. Keutner (Eds.), *Hermeneutics and science: Three German views* (pp. 1-66). Notre Dame, IN: University of Notre Dame Press.

Cooper, D. E. (1996). Modern European philosophy. In N. Bunnin & E. P. Tsui-James (Eds)., *The Blackwell companion to philosophy* (pp. 702-721). Oxford: Blackwell.

Davey, R. N. (1991). A response to Christopher Smith. In H. Silverman (Ed.), *Gadamer and hermeneutics* (pp. 42-59). New York: Routledge.

Denzin, N. K. (1994). *Chan is missing:* The Asian eye examines cultural studies. *Symbolic Interaction, 17,* 63-89.

Denzin, N. K. (1997). *Interpretive ethnography: Ethnographic practices for the 21st century.* Thousand Oaks, CA: Sage.

Derrida, J. (1976). *Of grammatology* (G. C. Spivak, Trans.). Baltimore: Johns Hopkins University Press.

Derrida, J. (1978). *Writing and difference* (A. Bass, Trans.). Chicago: University of Chicago Press.

Derrida, J. (1983). The principle of reason: The university in the eyes of its pupils. *Diacritics, 13,* 3-20.

Dilthey, W. (1958). *Gesammelte Schriften.* Leipzig: B. G. Teubner.

Dunne, J. (1993). *Back to the rough ground: "Phronesis" and "techne" in modern philosophy and Aristotle.* Notre Dame, IN: University of Notre Dame Press.

Fay, B. (1996). *Contemporary philosophy of social science.* Oxford: Blackwell.

Gadamer, H.-G. (1970). On the scope and function of hermeneutical reflection (G. B. Hess & R. E. Palmer, Trans.). *Continuum, 8,* 77-95.

Gadamer, H.-G. (1975). *Truth and method* (2nd rev. ed.; J. Weinsheimer & D. G. Marshall, Eds. & Trans.). New York: Crossroad.

Gadamer, H.-G. (1977). Theory, technology, practice: The task of the science of man. *Social Research, 44,* 529-561.

Gadamer, H.-G. (1981). *Reason in the age of science* (F. G. Lawrence, Trans.). Cambridge: MIT Press.

Gadamer, H.-G. (1996). *The enigma of health.* Stanford, CA; Stanford University Press.

Gallagher, S. (1992). *Hermeneutics and education.* Albany: State University of New York Press.

Garfinkel, H. (1967). *Studies in ethnomethodology.* Englewood Cliffs, NJ: Prentice Hall.

Garrison, J. (1996). A Deweyan theory of democratic listening. *Educational Theory, 46,* 429-451.

Geertz, C. (1979). From the native's point of view: On the nature of anthropological understanding. In P. Rabinow & W. M. Sullivan (Eds.), *Interpretive social science: A reader* (pp. 225-241). Berkeley: University of California Press. (Reprinted from *Meaning in anthropology,* pp. 221-237, by K. H. Basso & H. A. Selby, Eds., 1976, Albuquerque: University of New Mexico Press)

Gergen, K. J. (1985). The social constructionist movement in modern psychology. *American Psychologist, 40,* 266-275.

Gergen, K. J. (1988). If person are texts. In S. Messer, L. A. Sass, & R. L. Woolfolk (Eds.), *Hermeneutics and psychological theory* (pp. 28-51). New Brunswick, NJ: Rutgers University Press.

Gergen, K. J. (1994a). *Realities and relationships: Soundings in social construction.* Cambridge, MA: Harvard University Press.

Gergen, K. J. (1994b). *Toward transformation in social knowledge* (2nd ed.). Thousand Oaks, CA: Sage.

Gergen, K. J. (1995). Social construction and the educational process. In L. P. Steffe & J. Gale (Eds.), *Constructionism in education* (pp. 17-39). Mahwah, NJ: Lawrence Erlbaum.

Giddens, A. (1993). *New rules of sociological method* (2nd ed.). Stanford, CA: Stanford University Press.

Grondin, J. (1994). *Introduction to philosophical hermeneutics* (J. Weinsheimer, Trans.). New Haven, CT: Yale University Press.

Habermas, J. (1988). *On the logic of the social sciences* (S. W. Nicholsen & J. A. Strak, Trans.). Cambridge: MIT Press.

Hekman, S. J. (1986). *Hermeneutics and the sociology of knowledge.* Notre Dame, IN: University of Notre Dame Press.

Hiley, D. R., Bohman, J. F., & Shusterman, R. (Eds.). (1991). *The interpretive turn.* Ithaca, NY: Cornell University Press.

Hirsch, E. D. (1976). *The aims of interpretation.* Chicago: University of Chicago Press.

Howe, K. (1998). The interpretive turn and the new debate in education. *Educational Researcher, 27*(8), 13-20.

Hoy, D. C. (1991). Is hermeneutics ethnocentric? In D. R. Hiley, J. F. Bohman, & R. Shusterman (Eds.), *The interpretive turn* (pp. 155-178). Ithaca, NY: Cornell University Press.

Kerdeman, D. (1998). Hermeneutics and education: Understanding, control, and agency. *Educational Theory, 48,* 241-266.

Lather, P. (1993). Fertile obsession: Validity after poststructuralism. *Sociological Quarterly, 34,* 673-693.

Longino, H. (1990). *Science as social knowledge.* Princeton, NJ: Princeton University Press.

Longino, H. (1993a). Essential tensions—phase two: Feminist, philosophical, and social studies of science. In L. M. Antony & C. Witt (Eds.), *A mind of one's own: Feminist essays on reason and objectivity* (pp. 257-272). Boulder, CO: Westview.

Longino, H. (1993b). Subjects, power, and knowledge: Description and prescription in feminist philosophies of science. In L. Alcoff & E. Potter (Eds.), *Feminist epistemologies* (pp. 101-120). New York: Routledge.

Longino, H. (1996). Cognitive and noncognitive values in science: Rethinking the dichotomy. In L. H. Nelson & J. Nelson (Eds.), *Feminism, science, and the philosophy of science* (pp. 39-58). Dordrecht, Netherlands: Kluwer.

Madison, G. B. (1991). Beyond seriousness and frivolity: A Gadamerian response to deconstruction. In H. Silverman (Ed.), *Gadamer and hermeneutics* (pp. 119-134). New York: Routledge.

Nietzsche, F. (1979). *The complete works of Friedrich Nietzsche* (O. Levy, Ed.). New York: Russell & Russell.

Nussbaum, M. C. (1990). *Love's knowledge: Essays on philosophy and literature.* New York: Oxford University Press.

Outhwaite, W. (1975). *Understanding social life: The method called Verstehen.* London: George Allen & Unwin.

Phillips, D. C. (1995). The good, the bad, and the ugly: The many faces of constructivism. *Educational Researcher, 24*(7), 5-12.

Phillips, D. C. (1997a). Coming to grips with radical social constructivism. *Science and Education, 6,* 85-104.

Phillips, D. C. (1997b). How, why, what, when, and where: Perspectives on constructivism in psychology and education. *Issues in Education, 3*(2), 151-194.

Potter, J. (1996). *Representing reality: Discourse, rhetoric and social construction.* London: Sage.

Prus, R. (1996). *Symbolic interaction and ethnographic research.* Albany: State University of New York Press.

Rabinow, P., & Sullivan, W. M. (Eds.). (1979). *Interpretive social science: A reader.* Berkeley: University of California Press.

Richardson, L. (1997). *Fields of play: Constructing an academic life.* New Brunswick, NJ: Rutgers University Press.

Ricoeur, P. (1981). The model of the text: Meaningful action considered as text. In P. Ricoeur, *Hermeneutics and the human sciences* (J. B. Thompson, Ed. & Trans.). Cambridge: Cambridge University Press.

Rouse, J. (1991). Interpretation in natural and human science. In D. R. Hiley, J. F. Bohman, & R. Shusterman (Eds.), *The interpretive turn* (pp. 42-57). Ithaca, NY: Cornell University Press.

Rouse, J. (1996). Feminism and the social construction of scientific knowledge. In L. H. Nelson & J. Nelson (Eds.), *Feminism, science, and the philosophy of science* (pp. 195-215). Dordrecht, Netherlands: Kluwer.

Schutz, A. (1962). *Collected papers* (Vol. 1; M. Natanson, Ed.). The Hague: Martinus Nijhoff.

Schutz, A. (1967). *The phenomenology of the social world* (G. Walsh & F. Lehnert, Trans.). Evanston, IL: Northwestern University Press.

Schwandt, T. A. (1996). Farewell to criteriology. *Qualitative Inquiry, 2,* 58-72.

Schwandt, T. A. (1997). Evaluation as practical hermeneutics. *Evaluation, 3,* 69-83.

Shapiro, M. J. (1981). *Language and political understanding.* New Haven, CT: Yale University Press.

Shea, C. (1998, September 11). Tribal skirmishes in anthropology. *Chronicle of Higher Education,* pp. A17, A20.

Shusterman, R. (1991). Beneath interpretation. In D. R. Hiley, J. F. Bohman, & R. Shusterman (Eds.), *The interpretive turn* (pp. 102-128). Ithaca, NY: Cornell University Press.

Smith, D. (1996). Telling the truth after postmodernism. *Symbolic Interaction, 19,* 171-202.

Smith, N. H. (1997). *Strong hermeneutics: Contingency and moral identity.* New York: Routledge.

Smith, P. C. (1991). Plato as an impulse and obstacle in Gadamer's development of a hermeneutical theory. In H. Silverman (Ed.), *Gadamer and hermeneutics* (pp. 23-41). New York: Routledge.

Taylor, C. (1985a). *Philosophical papers: Vol. 1. Human agency and language.* Cambridge: Cambridge University Press.

Taylor, C. (1985b). *Philosophical papers: Vol. 2. Philosophy and the human sciences.* Cambridge: Cambridge University Press.

Taylor, C. (1987). Overcoming epistemology. In K. Baynes, J. Bohman, & T. McCarthy (Eds.), *After philosophy: End or transformation?* (pp. 464-488). Cambridge: MIT Press.

Taylor, C. (1988). Wittgenstein, empiricism, and the question of the "inner": Commentary on Kenneth Gergen. In S. Messer, L. A. Sass, & R. L. Woolfolk (Eds.), *Hermeneutics and psychological theory* (pp. 52-58). New Brunswick, NJ: Rutgers University Press.

Taylor, C. (1989). *Sources of the self: The making of the modern identity.* Cambridge: Cambridge University Press.

Taylor, C. (1991). The dialogical self. In D. R. Hiley, J. F. Bohman, & R. Shusterman (Eds.), *The interpretive turn* (pp. 304-314). Ithaca, NY: Cornell University Press.

Taylor, C. (1995). *Philosophical arguments.* Cambridge, MA: Harvard University Press.

Thompson, A. (1997). Surrogate family values: The refeminization of teaching. *Educational Theory, 47,* 315-339.

Tully, J. (Ed.). (1994). *Philosophy in an age of pluralism.* Cambridge: Cambridge University Press.

Van Eemeren, F. H., Grootendorst, R., Blair, J. A., & Willard, C. A. (Eds.). (1987). *Argumentation: Across the lines of discipline* (Proceedings of the 1986 Conference on Argumentation). Dordrecht, Netherlands: Foris.

Vetlesen, A. J. (1997). Introducing an ethics of proximity. In H. Jodalen & A. J. Vetlesen (Eds.), *Closeness: An ethics* (pp. 1-19). Oslo: Scandinavian University Press.

Walton, D. (1989). *Informal logic: A handbook for critical argumentation.* Cambridge: Cambridge University Press.

Weber, M. (1949). *The methodology of the social sciences* (E. A. Shils & H. A. Finch, Trans.). Glencoe, IL: Free Press.

Winch, P. (1958). *The idea of a social science.* London: Routledge & Kegan Paul.

8

Feminisms
and Qualitative
Research at and
Into the Millennium

Virginia L. Olesen

◆   At the approach of the new millennium, feminist qualitative research
is highly diversified, enormously dynamic, and thoroughly challenging to its practitioners, its followers, and its critics. Competing models of
thought jostle, divergent methodological and analytic approaches compete, once-clear theoretical differences (Fee, 1983) blur. Debates over the
efficacy of such work abound. Feminist qualitative research is variegated
and emergent, characteristics that I will explore in this chapter.

This chapter has its origins in an early feminist declaration I wrote for a
1975 conference on women's health, in which I argued that "rage is not
enough" and called for incisive scholarship to frame, direct, and harness
passion in the interests of redressing grievous problems in many areas of

AUTHOR'S NOTE: Incisive criticisms from Norman Denzin, Yvonna Lincoln, Patricia
Clough, Michelle Fine, and Meaghan Morris and continuing intellectual dialogue with Adele
Clarke added to the quality of this chapter. I'm grateful to them all.

women's health (Olesen, 1975, pp. 1-2). As a symbolic interactionist working primarily within the interactionist-social constructionist tradition (Denzin, 1992, pp. 1-21), I am sympathetic with deconstructive currents in interactionism and feminism that encourage provocative and productive unpacking of taken-for-granted ideas about women in specific material, historical, and cultural contexts. This avoids a "fatal uncluttedness" (Mukherjee, 1994, p. 6). I believe that research for rather than merely about women is possible through theoretical essays and a variety of qualitative modes using combinations of both experimental and text-oriented styles. Feminist work sets the stage for other research, other actions, and policy that transcend and transform (Olesen, 1993). For me, feminist inquiry is dialectical, with different views fusing to produce new syntheses that in turn become the grounds for further research, praxis, and policy (Nielsen, 1990b, p. 29; Westkott, 1979, p. 430).[1]

I will locate this exploration in changing currents of feminist thought (Benhabib, Butler, Cornell, & Fraser, 1995; Tong, 1989) and altering and sometimes controversial themes within qualitative research (Denzin, 1997; Gubrium & Holstein, 1997; Gupta & Ferguson, 1997; Miller & Dingwall, 1997; Scheurich, 1997). To position feminist qualitative research thus does not say it is merely a passive recipient of transitory intellectual themes and controversies. To the contrary, it has had influence, even if sometimes irksome in some people's views, on many aspects of qualitative research (Charmaz & Olesen, 1997; DeVault, 1996; Smith, 1996; Stacey & Thorne, 1996; Taylor, 1998).

Feminisms partake of different theoretical and pragmatic orientations and reflect national contexts among which feminist agendas differ widely. (For an analysis of this in psychology, see Morawski, 1997.) Nevertheless, without in any way positing a global, homogeneous, unified feminism, qualitative feminist research in its many variants, whether or not self-consciously defined as feminist, centers and makes problematic women's diverse situations as well as the institutions that frame those situations. It can refer the examination of that problematic to theoretical, policy, or action frameworks to realize social justice for women in specific contexts (Eichler, 1986, p. 68; 1997, pp. 12-13), or it can present new ideas generated in the research for destabilizing knowledges about oppressive situations for women, or for action or further research (Olesen & Clarke, 1999).[2] Many issues to be reviewed here have also been foregrounded in critical race studies and critical legal studies—for instance, Patricia Williams's (1991) application of literary theory to analysis of legal discourse to reveal the intersubjectivity of legal constructions and Mari Matsuda's (1996) interrogation of race, gender, and the law.

To provide some background, I will briefly outline the scope and types of feminist qualitative research, recognizing that this is only a partial glimpse of a substantial literature in many disciplines. This will lay the groundwork for a discussion of emergent complexities in feminist qualitative work and set the stage for a review of issues that feminist scholars currently debate. These include the obdurate worries (for some) of bias and believability, objectivity and subjectivity, and the demands (for others) posed by new experimental approaches in the realm of representation, voice, text, and ethical issues. I close the chapter with some questions about accomplishments of, shortfalls in, and the future of feminist qualitative research at the outset of the millennium.

It is well to remember that feminist research is highly diverse—experimental work with new complexities engages numerous investigators at the same time that many others remain oriented to views of gendered universals and more traditional approaches. Moreover, even within the same wings of feminist research (experimental or traditional) there are disagreements on issues ranging from treatment of voices to how to prepare research for policy use.

◆ Scope and Topics of Feminist Qualitative Research

Some (including feminists in an early period) may have assumed that qualitative research is most useful for and therefore limited to inquiries into subjective or interpersonal realms wherever found. This reflects early feminist interests in women's subjectivity as well as the erroneous assumption that qualitative research cannot handle large-scale issues. Feminist work has gone far beyond these limited views using a wide range of methods (see Reinharz, 1992, for descriptions of these) and for reasons found in new intellectual themes to be discussed shortly. Extensive feminist work in many disciplines ranges from assessments of women's lives and experiences that foreground the subjective to analyses of relationships through investigation of social movements and large-scale issues of policy and organization. (On qualitative feminist research on social movements, see Taylor, 1998; Taylor & Whittier, 1998, 1999.)

It is well-nigh impossible to cite even part of this work in these brief pages, but feminist qualitative research in two fields, education and health, merits mention. Within the educational realm, studies range widely, from Sandra Acker's (1994) acute observations of classroom experiences to Deborah Britzman's (1991) poststructuralist analysis of the "socialization" of student teachers, Diane Reay's (1998) research on social class in mothers' involvement in their children's schooling, Susan Chase's (1995) narrative analysis of women school superintendents struggling with inhibiting structures, and a study of how women "become gentlemen" in law school (Guinier, Fine, & Balin, 1997).

In the field of health and healing, Lora Bex Lempert's (1994) research links accounts of battered women's experiences to constructions of battering and structural issues. Lempert's clearly subjective approach contrasts with Dorothy Broom's (1991) account of how the emergence of state-sponsored women's health clinics in Australia created contradictions with feminist principles that feminists had to handle as they worked within the health care system.[3]

The arena of policy analysis, being largely quantitative and male dominated, has not been a receptive locus for feminist qualitative research whatever the field, and much remains to be done in two general areas: (a) the substance, construction, and emergence of specific policy issues; and (b) processes through which policy is accomplished.[4] However, there has been some noteworthy qualitative research on construction of policy issues for women: Through content analysis of scientific and lay publications, Patricia Kaufert and Sonja McKinlay (1985) have shown different concerns of clinicians, medical researchers, and feminists about estrogen replacement therapy. Accomplishing policy is a complex topic that feminists have scrutinized at a number of levels. In her theoretical critique of Barbara Ehrenreich and Frances Fox Piven's (1983) positive view of the state for women, Wendy Brown (1992) argues that they do not recognize issues of control. Rosalind Petchesky's (1985) analysis reveals how women's health is framed in the abortion debate. Nancy Fraser's (1989) discourse analysis of women's needs and the state raises questions of emancipatory or controlling definitions. Theresa Montini's (1997) research on the breast cancer informed consent movement found that physicians deflected activists away from the policy goals the activists wanted.

Adele Clarke (1998) has called these latter studies "meso analysis," which refers to how societal and institutional forces mesh with human activity (Maines, 1982). Clarke's own feminist sociohistorical analysis shows how these processes play out around such issues as production of contraceptives. Such studies elevate the question of research for women to an important critique of contemporary and historically male-dominated science and policy making and control, not just of women but also of the policy processes. Linda Gordon's (1994) sociohistorical analysis of welfare mothers, which shows how outmoded ideas about women's place carry into new eras and misplaced policies, is a prime example of work in this category.

◆ Emergent Complexities

If any attribute could be said to characterize qualitative feminist research since the 1960s and the start of the so-called second phase (at least in the United States) of the women's movement, it would be increasing complexity in the feminist research enterprise: the nature of research, the definition of and relationship with those with whom research is done, the characteristics and location of the researcher, and the very creation and presentation of knowledges created in the research. And, indeed, if there is a dominant theme in this growing complexity, it is the question of knowledges. Whose knowledges? Where and how obtained and by whom, from whom, and for what purposes? As Liz Stanley and Sue Wise (1990) reflect, "Succinctly, feminist theorists have moved away from 'the reactive' stance of the feminist critiques of social science and into the realms of exploring what 'feminist knowledge' could look like" (p. 37). This undergirds influential feminist writing such as Lorraine Code's (1991) question, "Who can know?" (p. ix), Donna Haraway's (1991) conceptualization of situated knowledges, Dorothy Smith's (1987) articulation of the everyday world as problematic, and a host of texts on feminist qualitative methods and methodology (Behar, 1996; Behar & Gordon, 1995; Butler, 1986; DeVault, 1999a; Fine, 1992a; Fonow & Cook, 1991; Hekman, 1990b; Lather, 1991; Lewin & Leap, 1996; Maynard & Purvis, 1994; Morawski, 1994; Nielsen, 1990a; Ribbens & Edwards, 1998; Roberts, 1981; Stanley, 1990; Stanley & Wise, 1983; Tom, 1989; Visweswaran, 1994; D. L. Wolf, 1996a). (For an exchange on the politics of feminist knowledge, see Hawkesworth, 1989, 1990a, 1990b; Hekman, 1990a; Shogan, 1990.)

This growing emphasis departed from two important themes of the early years of feminist research. First, Catharine MacKinnon's (1982, p. 353; 1983) assertion that "consciousness-raising" is the basis of feminist methodology gave way as more structural stances were foregrounded. Recognition that there are multiple knowledges grew, a point dramatically made by Patricia Hill Collins (1990) in her explica-

TABLE 8.1 The Growing Complexity of Feminist Qualitative Research and Representative Texts

Strands in emergent complexities

Writings by women of color	Anzaldúa (1990), Collins (1986), Davis (1981), Dill (1979), Garcia (1989), Green (1990), hooks (1990), Hurtado (1989), Zavella (1987)
Problematizing unremitting whiteness	Frankenberg (1993), Hurtado and Stewart (1997)
Postcolonial feminist thought	Alexander and Mohanty (1997), Heng (1997), Mohanty (1988), Spivak (1988), Trinh (1989, 1992)
Lesbian research and queer theory	Anzaldúa (1990), Butler (1993), Kennedy and Davis (1993), Krieger (1983), Lewin (1993), Stevens and Hall (1991), Terry (1994), Weston (1991)
Disabled women	Asch and Fine (1992)
Standpoint theory	Collins (1990), Haraway (1991), Harding (1987), Hartsock (1983), Smith (1987)
Postmodern and deconstructive theory	Clough (1998), Collins (1998b), Flax (1987), Haraway (1991, 1997), Hekman (1990b), Nicholson (1990)

Consequences of complexity

Problematizing research and participant	Behar (1993), Ellis (1995), Frankenberg and Mani (1993), Lather and Smithies (1997), Lincoln (1993, 1997), Reay (1996a)
Destabilizing insider-outsider	Kondo (1990), Lewin (1993), Naples (1996), Narayan (1997a), Ong (1995), Weston (1996), Zavella (1996)

(continued)

TABLE 8.1   (Continued)

Deconstructing traditional concepts

Experience	O'Leary (1997), Scott (1991)
Difference	Felski (1997), hooks (1990)
Gender	Butler (1990, 1993), Lorber (1994), West and Zimmerman (1987)

Newly framed issues

"Bias" and objectivity	Fine (1992a), Haraway (1997), Harding (1996, 1998), Holland and Ramazanoglu (1994), Phoenix (1994), Scheper-Hughes (1992)
"Validity" and trustworthiness	Lather (1993), Manning (1997), Richardson (1993)
Participants' voices	Fine (1992a), Kincheloe (1997), Lincoln (1993, 1997), Mascia-Lees et al. (1989), Opie (1992), Reay (1996), Ribbens and Edwards (1998)
Presenting the account	Behar and Gordon (1995), Ellis (1995), Kondo (1995), Lather and Smithies (1997), McWilliam (1997), Richardson (1997)

tion of black feminist thought, an influential work that—with the writings of Angela Davis (1981), Bonnie Thornton Dill (1979), Effie Chow (1987), bell hooks (1990), Rayna Green (1990), and Gloria Anzaldúa (1987, 1990)—began to dissolve an unremitting whiteness in feminist research. Further, awareness emerged that women are located structurally and in changing organizational and personal contexts that intertwine with subjective assessment to produce knowledge, as Sheryl Ruzek (1978) had earlier demonstrated in her analysis of the women's health movement. Second, important observations about women missing and invisible in certain arenas of social life, such as Judith Lorber's (1975) research on women and medicine and Cynthia Epstein's (1981) work on women in law, led to more complex analyses, such as Darlene Clark Hine's (1989) exploration of the structural, interactional, and knowledge-producing elements in the exclusion of and treatment of African American women in American nursing.

Parallel to these developments were research projects that initially conceptualized women as ubiquitous and invisible workers in the domestic sphere (Abel & Nelson, 1990; Finch & Groves, 1983; Graham, 1984, 1985; Nelson, 1990). Later, through Evelyn Nakano Glenn's (1990) work on Japanese domestic workers, Judith Rollins's (1985) participant observation study of doing housecleaning, and Mary Romero's (1992) interview study of Latina domestic workers, the race, class, and gender issues in domestic service and household work and concomitant contexts of knowledge, seemingly banal but ultimately critical to everyday life, were laid bare. Other work, such as Marjorie DeVault's (1991) research on domestic food preparation, Anne Murcott's (1993) analysis of conceptions of food, and Arlie Hochschild's (1989) findings that household labor is embedded in the political economy of household emotions, further demonstrated the dynamics of knowledge production within gendered relationships in the domestic sphere.

Thus the emergent complexities moved feminist research from justly deserved criticisms of academic disciplines (Stacey & Thorne, 1985, 1996) and social institutions, and of the lack of or flawed attention to women's lives and experiences, to debate and discussion of critical epistemological issues.[5] Paramount among these has been a growing recognition of the differentiation of persons with whom the research is done, the concomitant fading of the concept of a universalized "woman" or "women," and concerns about the researchers' own characteristics. Major strands within contemporary feminist research have fueled these growing and now mostly accepted awarenesses.

◆ Strands Contributing to Growing Complexities

Writing by Women of Color

Beyond the eye-opening work cited earlier in these pages, other work by women of color significantly shaped the new understandings that displaced taken-for-granted views of women of color and revealed the extent to which whiteness can be a factor in creating "otherness"—Asianness in Britain, for example (Puar, 1996). Aside from the critical task of differentiation, writings by Patricia Hill Collins (1986) and Aida Hurtado (1989) moved feminist research to greater recognition of the interplay of race, class, and gender in shaping women's oppression, as did empirical investigations by researchers such as Patricia Zavella (1987) on Mexican American cannery workers and Elaine Bell Kaplan (1997) in her myth-breaking study of black teenage mothers. At the same time these research projects, done in traditional qualitative style, were taking understanding of the lives of women of color in the United States to new levels, Gloria Anzaldúa's (1987) experimental writing and work injected the conceptualization of borders and crossing borders and fluidities in women's lives—familial, national, sexual, international—adding further dimensions and complexities. Recognition of the importance of borders and fluidities, albeit in a very different form, has emerged in the work of feminist researchers concerned with women and immigration (Espin, 1995; Hondagneu-Sotelo, 1992). In spite of this work, feminist scholars Vanessa Bing and P. T. Reid (1996) warn against misapplication of white feminist knowledge, a warning echoed by legal scholar Kimberly Crenshaw (1992) in her discussion of white feminists' appropriation of the 1991 Clarence Thomas hearings.

Parallel to these developments have been critical investigations that problematize not only the construction of women of color in relationship to whiteness but whiteness itself. Ruth Frankenberg's (1993) interview study shifts that category from a privileged, unnamed taken-for-grantedness in research to a questionable issue that must be raised in thinking about all participants in the research process. Noting that "whiteness" is the "natural" state of affairs, Aida Hurtado and Abigail J. Stewart (1997, pp. 309-310) call for studies of whiteness from the standpoint of people of color to find what they call a critical, counterhegemonic presence in the research (see also Wyche & Crosby, 1996). These writings are not simple reminders of diversity among women. They emphasize that multiple identities (and subjectivities) are tentatively constructed in particular historical epochs and social contexts (Ferguson, 1993).

Postcolonial Feminist Thought

If the criticisms of an unremitting whiteness in feminist research in Western industrialized societies began to unsettle feminist research frames, powerful and sophisticated research and feminist thought from postcolonial theorists further shifted the very grounds of feminist research with regard to "woman" and "women" and, indeed, the very definitions of feminism itself. Feminism, they argued, takes many different forms depending on the context of contemporary nationalism (Alexander & Mohanty, 1997; Heng, 1997). Concerned about the invidious effects of "othering" (applying oppressive definitions to the persons with whom research is done), they argued that Western feminist models were inappropriate for thinking of research with women in postcolonial sites (Kirby, 1991, p. 398; see also Mascia-Lees, Sharpe, & Cohen, 1991). Questions such as Gayatri Chakravorti Spivak's (1988) cutting query as to whether subordinates can speak or are forever silenced by virtue of representation within elite thought, a question also raised by Chandra Mohanty (1988), arose. But beyond these issues, they raised questions about whether Third World women or indeed all women could be conceptualized as unified subjectivities easily located in the category of woman. Drawing on her expertise as a filmmaker, Trinh T. Minh-ha (1989, 1992) articulated a fluid framing of woman as other (and not other) and undermined the very doing of ethnographic research by undercutting the concept of woman, the assumptions of subjectivity and objectivity, and the utility of the interview. This literature also pointed to issues in globalization, such as unsafe and exploitative working conditions in offshore manufacturing and the international sex trade, as topics for feminist research.

Lesbian Research

In research that quickly laid to rest Stanley and Wise's (1990, pp. 29-34) criticism that little attention had been paid to lesbians, feminist scholars upended theoretical and research frames saturated with stigma that had essentially rendered lesbians invisible or, where visible, despicable. The new scholarship, such as Susan Krieger's (1983) ethnography of a lesbian community, Patricia Stevens and Joanne Hall's (1991) historical analysis of how medicine has invidiously defined lesbianism, Kath Weston's (1991) study of lesbian familial relationships, Ellen Lewin's (1993) research on lesbian mothers (which shows the surpassing importance of the maternal rather the sexual identity), and Jennifer Terry's (1994) writing on theorizing "deviant" historiography, dissolved a homogeneous view of lesbians. Historical research such as Elizabeth Kennedy and Madeleine Davis's (1993) account of the Buffalo, New York, lesbian community, Gloria Anzaldúa's work noted earlier, and Ellen Lewin's (1996b) edited collection of cultural analyses of lesbian communities further differenti-ated these views by revealing race and class issues within lesbian circles and the multiple bases of lesbian identity.

The very meaning of gender also came in for incisive critical review by Judith Butler (1990, 1993), whose philosophical analysis for some femi-nists evoked themes in an earlier sociological statement by Candace West and Don Zimmerman (1987). In both cases, but for different theoretical reasons, these scholars pointed to sexual identity as performative rather than given or socially ascribed and thus undercut a dualistic conception of gender that had informed feminist thought for decades.

The emergence of the term *queer theory*, referring to those gay men and women who refuse assimilation into either gay culture or oppressive het-erosexual culture, has been loosely used as a cover term for gay and lesbian studies, but it also refers to a more precise political stance (Lewin, 1996a, pp. 6-9). Ellen Lewin's (1998) research on gay and lesbian marriages shows how those ceremonies simultaneously reflect accommodation and subversion. This stance of resistance carries conceptual implications that bear directly on feminist research and that requires recognition of the complex contributions of race and class (Butler, 1994) to diverse expres-sions of identity(ies), always in formation and always labile.

Disabled Women

Recognition of differences among women also emerged with the dis-ability rights movement and publication by feminist women who were themselves disabled. "Socially devalued, excluded from the playing field as women and invisible" (Gill, 1997, p. 96), disabled women were essen-tially depersonalized and degendered, sometimes even, regrettably, within feminist circles (Lubelska & Mathews, 1997, p. 135). Carol Gill (1997) recalled that a prominent Canadian feminist, Bonnie Klein, was treated as an outsider at feminist gatherings after she suffered a disabling stroke (p. 97). She also noted that disabled women are regarded as not capable of or interested in having children, and hence are not part of reproductive health agendas (p. 102). Asch and Fine (1992), reviewing the emergence of disabled women as a problematic issue for feminists, pointed out that even sympathetic research on women with disabilities tended to view them solely in terms of their disabilities and to overlook disabled women as workers, lovers, mothers, friends, sportswomen, and activists.

Standpoint Research

Building on a loosely related set of theoretical positions by feminist scholars from several disciplines, standpoint research (and much of that noted earlier can be so categorized) took up the feminist criticism of the absence of women from or marginalized women in research accounts and foregrounded women's knowledge as emergent from women's situated experiences (Harding, 1987, p. 184). Aptly summarized by Donna Haraway (1997), whose influential work in history of science has been foundational and influential for standpoint thinking, "standpoints are cognitive-emotional-political achievements, crafted out of located social-historical-bodily experience—itself always constituted through fraught, noninnocent, discursive, material, collective practices" (p. 304, n. 32).[6] In the work of sociologist Dorothy Smith, sociologist Patricia Hill Collins, political scientist Nancy Hartsock, and philosopher Sandra Harding, the concept of essentialized, universalized woman disappeared in the lens of standpoint thinking to reappear as a situated woman with experiences and knowledge specific to her in the material division of labor and the racial stratification system. This carries with it the view that all knowledge claims are socially located and that some social locations, especially those at the bottom of social and economic hierarchies, are better than others as starting points for seeking knowledge not only about those particular women but others as well. (This does *not* assume that the researcher's own life or group is the best starting point, nor does it assert the relativist position that all social locations are equally valuable for knowledge projects.)

Although they have been grouped under the rubric of *standpoint,* standpoint theorists are by no means identical, and in their differing versions they offer divergent approaches for qualitative researchers (Harding, 1997, p. 389). It is worthwhile, therefore, to discuss these theorists here, while recognizing the inevitable violence done to subtle thought in such a necessarily brief review.

Dorothy Smith focuses on women's standpoint and conceptualizes the everyday world as a problematic, that is, continually created, shaped, and known by women within it and its organization, which is shaped by external material factors or textually mediated relations (see Smith, 1987, p. 91). Thus the "everyday everynight activities" of women's lives are at the center. To understand that world, the researcher must not objectify the woman as would traditionally be done in sociology, which divides subject and object, researcher and participant. The researcher must be able to "work very differently than she is able to do with established sociological strategies of thinking and inquiry" (Smith, 1992, p. 96) that are not outside the relations of ruling. This requires a high degree of reflexivity from the researcher and a recognition of how feminist sociologists "participate as subjects in the relations of ruling" (p. 96). Smith's own work with Alison Griffith on mothers' work with children's schooling discloses how she and her colleague found in their own discussions the effects of the North American discourse on mothering of the 1920s and 1930s (Griffith & Smith, 1987; see also Smith, 1992, p. 97). A number of researchers have begun self-consciously and with awareness of one another's work to develop and use Smith's ideas of institutional ethnography (Campbell & Manicom, 1995) to discover how textually mediated relationships occur and are sustained in institutional settings, thus knitting an important link between the classic problem of micro and macro issues (Smith, 1990b, p. 10). (For criticisms of Smith, see Collins, 1992; Connell, 1992.)

Patricia Hill Collins's (1990) articulation of black women's standpoint is grounded in black women's material circumstances and political situation. Methodologically, this requires "an alternative epistemology whose 'criteria for substantiated knowledge' and 'methodological adequacy' will be compatible with the experiences and consciousness of Black women" (O'Leary, 1997, p. 62). Collins's writings and those of bell hooks (1984, 1990) shifted feminist thinking and research in the direction of more particularized knowledge and away from any sense of the universal. Collins (1998a) refuses to abandon situated standpoints and articulates a framework for black feminist thought in which she links the standpoint of black women with intersectionality, "the ability of social phenomena, race, class, and gender to mutually construct one another" (p. 205), but *always* within keen consideration for power and structural relations (pp. 201-228). This substantially amplifies standpoint theory. Thinking through this complexity is, as Collins recognizes, a "daunting task" (p. 225), and doing qualitative research within such a frame is equally daunting. Nevertheless, embracing new understandings of social complexity—and the locales of power relationships—is vital to the task of developing black feminist thought as critical social theory and new forms of visionary pragmatism (p. 228).

Sandra Harding, a philosopher, early recognized three types of feminist inquiry, which she termed "transitional epistemologies" (see Harding, 1987, p. 186). In keeping with Harding's concerns about modernity and science in general and science questions in feminism, these types are predicated on how those modes of inquiry relate to traditional science and the problem of objectivity:

1. *Feminist empiricism*, which is of two types: (a) "spontaneous feminist empiricism" (rigorous adherence to existing research norms and standards) and (b) following Helen Longino (1990), "contextual empiricism" (recognition of the influence of social values and interests in science; Harding, 1993, p. 53)

2. *Standpoint theory*, which "claims that all knowledge attempts are socially situated and that some of these objective social locations are better than others for knowledge projects" (Harding, 1993, p. 56; 1998, p. 163).

3. *Postmodern theories*, which void the possibility of a feminist science in favor of the many and multiple stories women tell about the knowledge they have (Harding, 1987, p. 188)

These are still useful ways to look at different styles of feminist qualitative work, but many projects display elements of several or all three as feminist researchers creatively borrow and innovate from multiple styles in their search "to escape damaging limitations of the dominant social relations and their schemes" (Harding, 1990, p. 101).

At issue here is the very form of science and whether "all possible science and epistemology . . . must be containable within modern, androcentric, Western, bourgeois forms" (Harding, 1990, p. 99). Harding argues that other forms of science are quite possible and likely. Her concerns with feminist research as a scientific activity and the attempt to generate "less false stories" prompted her to reject reliance on processes strictly governed by methodological rules and to argue that researchers should examine critically their own personal and historical commitments with which they construct their work (Harding, 1993, pp. 70-71). She points to the critical difference between sociological, cultural, and historical relativism (listening carefully to others' views) and judgmental relativism (abandoning any claims for adjudicating between different systems of beliefs and their social origins). Her solution is a posture of "strong objectivity" (Harding, 1991).[7] Strong objectivity contrasts sharply with value-free objectivity and posits the interplay of the researcher and participant. I discuss her contribution on "strong objectivity" in greater detail later in this chapter.

Nancy Hartsock's Marxist formulation of standpoint theory holds that women's circumstances in the material order provide them with experiences that generate particular and privileged knowledge that reflects both oppression and women's resistance (see Hartsock, 1983, 1985, 1998). Like the lives of the proletariat in Marxist theory, their knowledges provide an opening for a criticism of domination and for political action (Hartsock, 1997b, p. 98). This does not assume that such knowledge is innately essential, or that all women have the same experiences or indeed the same knowledge. Rather, in her recent formulations, Hartsock (1990) articulates the possibility of a "concrete multiplicity" of perspectives (p. 171). Each of these constitutes a different world, and each represents differential influence of power, a consideration that distinguishes standpoint theory from feminist empiricism (Hundleby, 1997, p. 41). Such knowledge is not merely individual, but derives from "interaction of people and groups with each other" and is always transitional (Hundleby, 1997, p. 36). As Hartsock (1997a) has observed, "The subjects who matter are not individual subjects, but collective subjects, or groups" (p. 371).

Standpoint theories and their implications for feminist qualitative research have not gone uncriticized. Some have fretted that standpoint theories contain risks of relativism (Harding, 1987, p. 187), are overly simplistic (Hawkesworth, 1989, p. 347), and raise issues around validity (Ramazanoglu, 1989). Criticisms have arisen about the potential for essentialism (Campbell, 1994; Lemert, 1992, p. 69), neglect of traditions of knowledge among women of color (Collins, 1992, p. 77), problems of evaluating accounts from different perspectives (Hekman, 1997b, p. 355; Longino, 1993, p. 104; Maynard, 1994b; Welton, 1997, p. 21), questions about understanding fragmented identities (Lemert, 1992, p. 68), and the potentially untenable use of experience as a basis for investigation if it is continually mediated and constructed from unconscious desire (Clough, 1993a). Others have argued that queer theory, with its destabilizing elements, undercuts the possibility for standpoint thinking, which, in this view, presumes the replication of heterosexual categories (Clough, 1994, p. 144).

For their part, standpoint theorists have not been silent. Dorothy Smith's (1993) robust exchange with Patricia Clough (1993a, p. 169; 1993b) highlights the centrality of experience, the place of desire, and the primacy of text. In this exchange, Clough argues that Smith has not gone far enough in deconstructing sociology as a dominant discourse of experience, a point Smith rejects, claiming that Clough's view is overly oriented to text and neglects experience. Susan Hekman's (1997a, 1997b) critical review of standpoint theory addresses questions of whether women's knowledge is privileged and how truth claims can be settled. Responses from Smith (1997), Patricia Hill Collins (1997), Nancy Hartsock (1997a), and Sandra Harding (1997) show clearly that standpoint theories have been and are continually being revised (see Harding, 1997, p. 389). Feminist qualitative researchers thinking of using standpoint theories in their work must read these theorists carefully and in their latest versions if they are to avoid misinterpretation and if they are to explore new connections between standpoint theories and postmodernism (Hirschmann, 1997). Indeed, Sandra Harding (1996) has observed that "poststructural approaches have been especially helpful in enabling standpoint theories systematically to examine critically pluralities of power relations, of the sort indicated in the earlier discussion of gender as shaped by class, race and other historical cultural forces and how these are disseminated through 'discourses' that are both structural and symbolic" (p. 451). Patricia Hill Collins (1998b), while warning about the corrosive effects of postmodern and deconstructive thought for black women's group authority and hence social action, also points to postmodernism's powerful analytic tools as useful in challenging not only dominant discourses, but the very rules of the game (pp. 143, 154).[8]

Postmodern and Deconstructive Thought

Complexities would probably have emerged in feminist qualitative research thanks to any of the themes discussed here, but the multiple and seductive intellectual sources of postmodern and deconstructive thought sharpened and enhanced the emerging complexities.[9] Indeed, in varying degrees postmodernism and deconstructionism are present in many of the themes noted above, sometimes constituting the central stance (as in Judith Butler or Trinh T. Minh-ha's analyses), sometimes anticipating future complexities (as in Frankenberg's deconstruction of whiteness), and sometimes reflecting trends and themes firmly set out by feminists not oriented to these modes of thought (as in Collins's analysis of black feminist thought or Lewin's research on lesbian cultures).

Concerned with the difficulties of ever producing more than a partial story of women's lives in oppressive contexts, postmodern feminists regard "truth" as a destructive illusion. Their view of the world is of a series of stories or texts that sustain the integration of power and oppression and actually "constitute us as subjects in a determinant order"

(Hawkesworth, 1989, p. 349). These themes have emerged among feminist researchers working in anthropology, sociology, history, political science, cultural studies, and social studies of science as well as experimental wings in educational and nursing research (see the Australian journal *Nursing Inquiry*).

Carrying the imprint of feminist forebears from deconstruction and postmodernism (French feminists such as Irigaray and Cixous, and Foucault, Deleuze, Lyotard, and Baudrillard), feminist research in cultural studies stresses representation and text. This area is particularly complex for feminist researchers because some scholars also utilize Marxist theory from Althusser, French feminist theory, literary criticism (Abel, Christian, & Moglen, 1997), historical analysis, and psychoanalytic views (Lacan—though by no means do all feminists agree on Lacan's utility for feminist research; see Ferguson, 1993, p. 212, n. 3). In contrast to classical Marxist feminist studies of women, work, and social class, such as Karen Sacks's (1988) investigation of hospital workers and Nona Glazer's (1991) analysis of race and class issues in the profession of nursing, materialist feminist research in an Althusserian mode looks at ideology and its place in the shaping of subjectivity, desire, and authority (Clough, 1994, p. 75). Here enters the elusive question of how desire is expressed in or inferred from cultural products ranging from ethnographic accounts through films to confront the feminist qualitative researcher with difficult questions that go far beyond the easy recognition of intersubjectivity and invoke deeper cultural forms and questions.[10] (For a feminist materialist analysis of narrative, see Roman, 1992.)

These inquiries typically take the form of the analysis of cultural objects (such as films) and their meanings (Balsamo, 1993; Clough, in press; de Lauretis, 1987; Denzin, 1992, p. 80; Morris, 1988) or the analysis of places and contexts (Morris, 1998). This includes textual analysis of these objects and the discourses surrounding them, and the "study of lived cultures and experiences which are shaped by the cultural meanings that circulate in everyday life" (Denzin, 1992, p. 81). This anticipates Valerie Walkerdine's (1995) important call for the analysis of understanding the media as the site of production of subjectivity.

Here will be found the voluminous and growing feminist work in gender and science, wherein science, the sacred cow of the Enlightenment, modernity, and the contemporary moment, is dismembered as a culture to reveal its practices, discourses, and implications for control of women's lives (Haraway, 1991, 1997; Martin, 1987, 1999), including their health (Clarke & Olesen, 1999b), and to provide avenues for resistance and or intervention. Research about women's reproductive status, an issue central to feminist qualitative research from the very start and long productive of influential work (Ginsburg, 1998; Gordon, 1976; Joffe, 1995; Luker, 1984, 1996), is moving into the gender and science area (Balsamo, 1993, 1999; Casper, 1998; Hartouni, 1997). Because this work utilizes interdisciplinary borrowing, it is not easily classified. Studies often appear as hybrids and radical in terms of form, substance, and content, as, for instance, in Donna Haraway's (1997) deft interweaving of fiction, biology, history, humor, religion, and visual imagery in her feminist unpacking of technosciences. These productions for some may be at the least uncomfortable or threatening and subversive, not only for male-dominated institutions such as science, but for feminism itself.

These styles of thought sharpened and enhanced the emerging complexities: the sites (gender, race, and class) of where and how "women" are controlled, how the multiple, shifting identities and selves that supplant earlier notions of a stable identity (self) are produced (Clough, 1992, 1998; Ferguson, 1993; Flax, 1990; Fraser, 1997, p. 381). They emphasized the shift away from binary frameworks to fluid conceptualizations of women's experiences, places, and spaces (Anzaldúa, 1987; Trinh, 1989, 1992). This shift accompanied an emphasis on discourse, narrative, and text, a move to experimental writing away from standard forms of presenting the research account, an issue I will discuss more fully in a moment. Postmodernism and deconstructionism also called into question, as had standpoint theorists, feminist qualitative researchers' unexamined embrace of and adherence to traditional positivist qualitative approaches (known as feminist empiricism) that were thought to forward the feminist agenda, but that, the critics averred, merely repeated structures of oppression. The postmodern position produced an uneasy and sometimes anxious concern that the shifting sands of meaning, text, locale, and the continual proliferation of identities left no grounds for reform-oriented research, reinforced the status quo, erased structural power as well as failed to address problems or to represent a cultural system (Benhabib, 1995; Collins, 1998b; Hawkesworth, 1989; Johannsen, 1992; Mascia-Lees, Sharpe, & Cohen, 1989; Maynard, 1994b; Ramazanoglu, 1989). I will discuss some specific issues raised by this impact more fully below, in the section on issues in feminist qualitative research.

◆ Consequences of Growing Complexities

Thus writings from women of color, gay/lesbian/queer theorists, post-colonial researchers, disabled women, standpoint theorists, and analysts persuaded to a postmodern stance opened and up-ended taken-for-granted conceptualizations of the very grounds and process of doing feminist research as well as critical key concepts such as experience, difference, and gender. Nowhere has this been more and incisively pursued than in the rethinking of the topic of woman as research participant, a point discussed above, and in the destabilization of the conception of the feminist researcher as an all-knowing, unified, distanced, and context-free seeker of objectified knowledge whose very gender guarantees access to women's lives and knowledges. Dissolution of this assumption pushed feminist research to greater awareness of researcher attributes and the impact of the research on the researcher.

Researcher Attributes

The researcher, too, has attributes, characteristics, a history, and gender, class, race, and social attributes that enter the research interaction. Yvonna Lincoln (1997) captures this in her comment, "If we are not just a single person, but rather a multitude of possibilities . . . as ethnographers we could be about utilizing these multiple selves to create multiple texts" (p. 42). However, these possibilities are not static elements; they are, rather, reflections of the intersections of structures and practices. In this vein, borrowing from cultural studies, Ruth Frankenberg and Lata Mani (1993) articulate a conjecturalist approach that "firmly centers the analysis of subject formation and cultural practice within matrices of domination and subordination" and that "asserts that there is an effective but not determining relationship between subjects and their histories, a relationship that is complex, shifting and not 'free' " (p. 306). Although they are writing in a postcolonial, deconstructionist vein, their conceptualization of a conjecturalist approach still has applicability to the dynamics of feminist research wherever found, because it recognizes that both researcher and participant are positioned and are being positioned by virtue of history and context.

A number of feminist researchers have described the dynamics of conjecturalism in their work. Foregrounding her own trajectory from the working class to middle-class researcher, Diane Reay (1998) reflects on class in her analysis of mothers' involvement in their children's primary schooling; Ann Phoenix's (1994) work on young people's social identities demonstrates that the assumption that matching race and gender of interviewers is too simplistic; Catherine Kohler Riessman (1987) points out how ethnic and class differences override gender in achieving understandings in interviews; D. Millen (1997) examines potential problems when feminist researchers work with women who are not sympathetic to feminism.

Impact of the Research on the Feminist Researcher

In light of the multiple positions, selves, and identities at play in the research process, the subjectivity of the researcher, as much as that of the researched, became foregrounded, an indication of the blurring phenomenological and epistemological boundaries between the researcher and the researched. This development did not go unmarked among more traditional researchers, who worried that the emphasis on subjectivity comes "too close . . . to a total elimination of intersubjective validation of description and explanation" (Komarovsky, 1988, p. 592; see also Komarovsky, 1991). This issue led directly into the questions about objectivity, "validity and reliability," and the nature of the text and the voices in it, which will be discussed shortly. In spite of these misgivings, feminists began to publish provocative and even influential work that reflected the blurring of these boundaries: Ruth Behar's (1993) analysis of her Mexican respondent's life and her own crosses multiple national, disciplinary, and personal borders, as do Carolyn Ellis's (1995) poignant account of a terminal illness and Patti Lather and Chris Smithies's (1997) work with HIV-positive women.

These newer views of the researcher's part in the research also bred a host of influential research reflections that rethought the important issue of whether being an "insider" gave feminist researchers access to inside knowledge, a view that partook of Patricia Hill Collins's (1986) important conceptualization of "insider/outsider": Patricia Zavella (1996) discovered that her Mexican background did not suffice in her study of Mexican women doing factory work; Ellen Lewin's (1993) analysis of lesbian mothers showed the surpassing importance of motherhood over sexual orientation; Kirin Narayan (1997) asked, "How native is a 'native' anthropologist?"; Dorinne Kondo (1990) reported unexpected and sometimes unsettling experiences during her fieldwork in Japan around her Japanese identity. These works and others, such as Aihwa Ong's (1995) account of work with immigrant Chinese women and Nancy Naples's (1996) research with women in Iowa, problematized the idea that a feminist researcher who shares some attributes of a cultural background would, by virtue of that background, have full access to women's knowledge in that culture. They also troubled the hidden assumption that insider knowledge is unified, stable, and unchanging. Kath Weston's (1996) report of her struggles with these issues summarizes the problems: "A single body cannot bridge that mythical divide between insider and outsider, researcher and researched. I am neither, in any simple way, and yet I am both" (p. 275).

If the play of increasing complexities has destabilized once-secure views of the researcher and those with whom research is done, it has equally led to a critical examination of once taken-for-granted concepts with which feminist researchers have worked: experience and difference.

Experience

Although feminist qualitative researchers working in the empiricist and standpoint frames still foreground women's experience as key, there has been a growing recognition that merely focusing on experience does not take into account how that experience emerged (Morawski, 1990; Scott, 1991) and what the characteristics of the material, historical, and social circumstances were. One of the problems with taking experience in an unproblematic way is that the research, even standpoint research, although less prone to this problem, replicates rather than criticizes the oppressive system. Personal experience is not a self-authenticating claim to knowledge (O'Leary, 1997, p. 47), a point postmodernists raise in directing attention to the risk of essentialism in unthinking reliance on experience. Historian Joan Scott (1991) comments, "Experience is at once already an interpretation and in need of interpretation" (p. 779).

Feminist research in sociology and anthropology analyzes women's experience and the material, social, economic, and gendered conditions that articulate the experience: Arlie Hochschild's (1983) research on how flight attendants manage emotions, Nona Glazer's (1991) examination of racism and classism in professional nursing, Nancy Scheper-Hughes's

(1992) exploration of motherhood and poverty in northeastern Brazil, Jennifer Pierce's (1995) ethnographic study of how legal assistants play a part in the production of their oppression in law firms. Historian Linda Kerber's (1998) analysis of women's legal obligations as well as their rights also falls into this category.

Difference

The recognition of difference, a conceptual move that pulled feminist thinkers and researchers away from the view of a shared gynocentric identity, surfaced in the dynamics of the trends just discussed, but very quickly gave way to concerns about the almost unassailable nature of the concept and whether its use would lead to an androcentric or imperialistic "othering" (Felski, 1997; hooks, 1990, p. 22). Arguing for the use of such concepts as hybridity, creolization, and metissage, Rita Felski (1997) claimed that these metaphors "not only recognize differences within the subject, fracturing and complicating holistic notions of identity, but also address connections between subjects by recognizing affiliations, cross-pollinations, echoes, and repetitions, thereby unseating difference from a position of absolute privilege" (p. 12).

Theorist Nancy Tuana (1993) enunciated a balance of possible common interests and observable differences in a way that would allow feminist qualitative researchers to grapple with these issues in their work:

> It is more realistic to expect pluralities of experiences that are related through various intersections or resemblances of some of the experiences of various women to some of the experiences of others. In other words, we are less likely to find a common core of shared experiences that are immune to economic conditions, cultural imperatives, etc., than a family of resemblances with a continuum of similarities, which allows for significant differences between the experience of, for example, an upper-class white American woman and an Indian woman from the lowest caste. (p. 283)

While echoing much of this thinking, bell hooks (1990) and Patricia Hill Collins (1990) nevertheless remind feminist researchers that identity cannot be dropped entirely. Rather, they see differences as autonomous, not fragmented, producing knowledge that accepts "the existence of and possible solidarity with, knowledges from other standpoints" (O'Leary, 1997,

p. 63). These views reflect Gadamer's little-recognized concept of the "fusion of horizons," "which carries double or dual vision and dialectical notions a step further than do standpoint epistemologies because it indicates a transcendent third and new view or synthesis" (Nielsen, 1990b, p. 29).

Gender

Like the concepts of experience and difference, gender, the workhorse concept of feminist theory and research, has undergone sea changes that make contemporary use of this concept much more complex and differentiated than at the outset of the "second wave." Theoretical insights going as far back as Suzanne Kessler and Wendy McKenna's (1978) classic ethnomethodological framing of gender, including Judith Butler's (1990) philosophical outline of gender as performative and Judith Lorber's (1994, p. 5) argument that gender is wholly constructed, have shifted research possibilities. Whereas in an earlier time work on gender differences looked for explanations or characteristic of autonomous individuals (Gilligan, 1982), now production and realization of gender in a complex matrix of material, racial, and historical circumstances become the research foci, and differences among women as well as similarities between men and women are acknowledged (Brabeck, 1996; Lykes, 1994). (Gender as causal explanation and as analytic category and the implications for research are examined by Hawkesworth, 1997a, and in responses to Hawkesworth by Connell, 1997; McKenna & Kessler, 1997; Scott, 1997; Smith, 1997. See also the reply to those responses from Hawkesworth, 1997b.)

◆ Issues and Tensions

The shifting currents depicted in the foregoing sections have emphasized and altered tensions within feminist qualitative research and produced new issues relevant to the conduct of the research itself. Whereas in an earlier era, concerns about the research enterprise tended to reflect traditional worries about the qualitative research enterprise (how to manage "bias," what about validity, and so on), the newer worries take the form of uneasiness about voice, the text, and ethical conduct, which I will discuss shortly. Feminist empiricists and those working within one of the standpoint frameworks are apt to share all of these concerns, whereas those who pursue a deconstructionist path are less likely to worry about bias and validity and more likely to be concerned with voice and text, key issues in representation, although there are important exceptions here (e.g., Lather & Smithies, 1997). Because there is a good deal of borrowing across these lines, many feminist researchers grapple simultaneously with these issues, sometimes muting, sometimes emphasizing, because much remains to be articulated, particularly in work that experiments with writing, narrative, voice, and form.

Bias

The dissolving of the distance between the researcher and those with whom the research is done and the recognition that both are labile, nonunitary subjects (Britzman, 1998, p. ix) steps beyond traditional criticisms about researcher bias (Denzin, 1992, pp. 49-52; Huber, 1973) and leads to strong arguments for "strongly reflexive" accounts about the researcher's own part in the research (Fine, 1992b; Holland & Ramazanoglu, 1994; Phoenix, 1994; Warren, 1988) and even reflections from the participants (Appleby, 1997). What Nancy Scheper-Hughes (1992) calls "the cultural self" that every researcher takes into her or his work is no longer a troublesome element to be eradicated or controlled, but rather a set of resources. Indeed, Susan Krieger (1991) early argued that utilization of the self is fundamental to qualitative work. If researchers are sufficiently reflexive about their projects, they can evoke these resources to guide the gathering, creation, and interpretation of data as well as their own behavior (Casper, 1997; Daniels, 1983; Stacey, 1998). Leslie Rebecca Bloom (1998, p. 41) goes further, urging that feminist researchers and their participants work out how they will communicate and that this be part of the research account. Nevertheless, researcher reflexivity needs to be tempered with an acuity as to what elements in the researchers' backgrounds, hidden or those of which they are unaware, contribute. Sherry Gorelick (1991) identifies potential problems when inductivist feminist researchers who espouse a Marxist framework "fail to take account of the hidden structure of oppression (the research participant is not omniscient) and the hidden relations of oppression (the participant may be ignorant of her relative privilege over and difference from other women)" (p. 461). Nancy Scheper-Hughes (1983) has also warned about feminists' unwitting replication of androcentric perspectives in their work.

Objectivity

Bias is related to the issue of subjectivity in feminist research and raises the problem of objectivity, which lurks in even the most liberated accounts (Cannon, Higginbotham, & Leung, 1991). Forgoing traditional and rigid ideas about objectivity, feminist researchers and scholars have opened new spaces in consideration of this enduring question. Arguing that observers' experiences can be useful, Sandra Harding (1993, p. 71) suggests a strategy of "strong objectivity" that takes the researchers as well as those researched as the focus of critical, causal, scientific explanations (Hirsh & Olson, 1995) and calls for critical examination of the researcher's social location (see Harding, 1996, 1998). Harding (1991) notes, "Strong objectivity requires that we investigate the relation between subject and object rather than deny the existence of, or seek unilateral control over this relation" (p. 152). She asks that feminist researchers see the participants in the inquiry as "gazing back" and that the researchers take the participants' view in looking at their own socially situated projects.[11] This goes beyond mere reflection on the conduct of the research and demands a steady, uncomfortable assessment of the interpersonal and interstitial knowledge-producing dynamics of qualitative research. As Janet Holland and Caroline Ramazanoglu (1994) illustrate in their research on young women's sexuality, there is no way to neutralize the social nature of interpretation. They argue:

> Feminist researchers can only try to explain the grounds on which selective interpretation has been made by making explicit the processes of decision making which produces the interpretation and the logic of the method on which these decisions are based. This entails acknowledging complexity and contradiction which may be beyond the researchers' experience, and recognizing the possibility of silences and absences in their data. (p. 133)[12]

Donna Haraway (1997, p. 16) urges researchers to go beyond even strong objectivity to the exercise of diffracting, which turns the lenses with which researchers view phenomena to show multiple fresh combinations and possibilities.

356

Rescuing feminist objectivity from being in thrall to classical positivist definitions and from being lost in an inchoate relativism (all views are equal), Haraway (1988) recognizes the merging of researcher and participant to foreground a position of situated knowledges, accountability (the necessity to avoid reproducing oppressive views of women), and partial truths. In Haraway's apt and oft-quoted phrase, "the view from nowhere" becomes "the view from somewhere," that of connected embodied, situated participants. (For an example of Haraway's conceptualization of objectivity in use, see the research on young, working-class people in Britain conducted by Kum Kum Bhavnani, 1994.)

"Validity" and Trustworthiness

Related to the question of objectivity is the old question of the degree to which the account reflects or depicts what the researcher is looking at. Feminist qualitative researchers address or worry about validity, also known in more recent incarnations as "trustworthiness," in different ways depending on how they frame their approaches (Denzin, 1997, pp. 1-14). For those who work in a traditional vein reflecting the positivist origins of social science (reality is there to be discovered), the search for validity will involve well-established techniques. Those who disdain the positivistic origins of such techniques but nevertheless believe that there are ways of achieving validity that reflect the nature of qualitative work will seek out ways to establish credibility through such strategies as audit trails and member "validation," techniques that reflect their postpositivist views but that do not involve hard-and-fast criteria for according "authenticity" (Lincoln & Guba, 1985; Manning, 1997). Feminist qualitative researchers who worry about whether their research will respect or appreciate those with whom they work and whether, indeed, it may transform those others into another version of themselves, reach for something new, as in Laurel Richardson's (1993) manifesto:

> I challenge different kinds of validity and call for different kinds of science practices. The science practice I model is a feminist-postmodernist one. It blurs genres, probes lived experiences, enacts science, creates a female imagery, breaks down dualisms, inscribes female labor and emotional response as valid, deconstructs the myth of an emotion-free social science, and makes a space for partiality, self-reflexivity, tension and difference. (p. 695)

Among new ways of imagining validity (Denzin, 1997, pp. 9-14; Scheurich, 1997, pp. 88-92), Patti Lather's (1993) transgressive validity is the most completely worked-out feminist model, one that calls for a subversive move ("retaining the term to circulate and break with the signs that code it"; p. 674) in a feminist deconstructionist mode. To assure capturing differences but within a transformative space that can lead to a critical political agenda, Lather rests transgressive validity on four subtypes, here highly condensed: (a) ironic validity, which attends to the problems in representation; (b) paralogical validity, which seeks out differences, oppositions, uncertainties; (c) rhizomatic validity, which counters authority with multiple sites; and (d) voluptuous validity, which deliberately seeks excess and authority through self-engagement and reflexivity (pp. 685-686). Whether even in these bold steps Lather has gone far enough to overcome what some see as the almost obdurate problem in legitimation (the inevitable replication of researcher within the analyzed views of the researched; Scheurich, 1997, p. 90), this formulation nevertheless retains a feminist emancipatory stance while providing leads for feminist qualitative researchers to work out and work on the inherent problems in validity. Lather's own research with Chris Smithies on women with AIDS illustrates these strategies for achieving validity and challenges feminist qualitative researchers (Lather & Smithies, 1997).

◆ Problems of Voice, Reflexivity, and Text

A continuing and worrisome problem for all feminist qualitative researchers, irrespective of which approach they take, is the question of voice and, by implication, the nature of the account, which, as William Tierney and Yvonna Lincoln argue in their introduction to *Representation and the Text* (1997), now "comes under renewed scrutiny" (p. viii), a position echoed by the contributors to Rosanna Hertz's edited volume *Reflexivity and Voice* (1997). This issue goes back to the earliest beginnings of feminist research and the attempts, noted earlier in this chapter, to find and express women's voices. When women of color and postcolonial critics raised concerns about how participants' voices are to be heard, with what authority and in what form, they sharpened and extended this issue. Within this question lie anxiety-provoking matters of whether the account will only replicate hierarchical conditions found in parent disciplines, such as sociology (Smith, 1989, p. 43), and the difficult problems of translating private matters from women's lives into the potentially oppressive and distorting frames of social science (Ribbens & Edwards, 1998). Addressing this latter concern, some feminist researchers have articulated strategies involving voice-centered relational methods (Mauthner & Doucet, 1998), reconstructing research narratives (Birch, 1998), and writing the voices of the less powerful (Standing, 1998).

Voices

How to make women's voices heard without exploiting or distorting those voices is an equally vexatious question. There may be hidden problems of control when literary devices are borrowed to express voice (Mascia-Lees et al., 1989, p. 30). Even though researchers and participants may both shape the flow of silences and comments in the interview situation, the researcher who writes up the account remains in the more powerful position (Phoenix, 1994; Stacey, 1998). Merely letting the tape recorder run and presenting the respondent's voice does not overcome the problem of representation, because the respondent's comments are already mediated when they are made in the interview (Lewin, 1991) and the researcher usually has the final responsibility for the text (Lincoln, 1997). Even taking the account back for comment or as simple courtesy or shaping the account with respondents may not work, as Joan Acker, Kate Barry, and Johanna Esseveld (1991) found in their participatory project; the women wanted them to do the interpreting. Moreover, the choice of audience shapes how voice is found and fashioned (Kincheloe, 1997; Lincoln, 1993, 1997).[13] Michelle Fine (1992b) explores worrisome issues about use of voices (use of pieces of narrative, taking individual voices to reflect group ideas, assuming that voices are free of power relations, researchers' failure to make clear their own positions in relationship to the voices or becoming "ventriloquists") and forcefully urges feminist researchers to "articulate how, how not, and within what limits" voices are framed and used (pp. 217-219).[14] Fine (personal communication, March 2, 1998) has also pointed to the critical tension between treating voices in the raw (as if they were untouched by ideology, hegemony, or interpretation) and critically analyzing those voices by understanding the contexts in which they arise and the hegemonic pressures out of which they are squeezed. J. Miller's (1997) respondents' resistance to her interpretations led her to question whose knowledge and whose interpretations prevail.

Nature of the Account

The issue of voice leads into questions of the form, nature, and content of the account, as well as theoretical issues in the production of ethnographic narratives (Britzman, 1995). There is by now a growing and substantial body of experimental writing, some of which is based on research work and some of which reflects highly reflexive and insightful interpretations of feminist researchers doing their work. Some writers manipulate or work within the printed text, whereas others opt for performances of the account.

Experimentation has bloomed in a number of fields.[15] Margery Wolf (1992) presents three versions of voices from an event in her anthropological field work in Taiwan: a piece of fiction, her anthropological field notes, and a social science article. Ruth Behar (1993) explodes the traditional anthropological form of life history to intertwine her own voice with that of her cocreator in an extended double-voiced text. Patti Lather and Chris Smithies (1997) use a split-page textual format to present the account of their research, their respondents' views, and their own reflections on themselves and the course and outcomes of their research. Richardson (1992, 1997) has pioneered writing and presenting sociological poetry and tales. (For greater detail on textual practice, see Richardson, Chapter 14, Volume 3.) Carolyn Ellis's (1995) accounts, both presented and written, deal with emotionally difficult topics, such as abortion, death in the family, an experience with black-white relations, and the death of her partner; this work has helped to give research in the sociology of emotions a decidedly experimental and feminist tone. *Autoethnography,* Ellis's term for this form, locates the deeply personal and emotional experiences of the researcher as subject in a context that relates to larger social issues (Ellis & Bochner, 1992, 1996). Here, the personal, biographical, political, and social are interwoven with the autoethnography, which in turn illuminates them (Denzin, 1997, p. 200), as Laura Ellingson (1998) does in her reflexive account of communications within a medical setting. These stances link the personal and political and undercut criticisms of personal reflections as mere solipsism (Patai, 1994).

At the same time, some feminists have created performance pieces—dramatic readings and plays. Michal McCall and Howard Becker's (1990) work on the art world and the late Marianne Paget's (1990) poignant play about a woman with an incorrect cancer diagnosis (based on her own research) are early examples. More recently, anthropologist Dorinne

Kondo's play *Dis(Graceful)l Conduct,* about sexual and racial harassment in the academy, embraces a paradigm that shifts "away from the purely textural to the performative, the evanescent, the nondiscursive, the collaborative" and attempts to intervene in another register in what Kondo (1995) calls "powerfully engaging modes quite different from conventional academic prose" (p. 51). For more than a decade, some sessions featuring performance pieces have found a place on the programs of feminist and social science meetings, drawing appreciative, if not always comprehending, audiences. The critical question of how to evaluate such work has only begun to be examined by thoughtful practitioners of performance and dramatic work (McWilliam, 1997) and in questions raised by sympathetic reviewers of experimental writing (Brown, 1998).

◆ Ethics in Feminist Qualitative Research

Feminist qualitative research shares the many ethical concerns regarding privacy, consent, confidentiality, deceit, and deception that trouble the larger field, concerns that call for decent and fair conduct of the research to avoid harm of whatever sort (undue stress, unwanted publicity, loss of reputation) either in the course of data gathering and analysis or in the subsequent text. In research accounts such as Michelle Fine and Lois Weis's (1996) worries about their research with poor working-class respondents, Monica Casper's (1997) anxieties in her ethnographic work on fetal surgery, and Judith Stacey's (1998) candid revelations about relationships with her respondents and writings on research ethics (Ribbens & Edwards, 1998; M. A. Wolf, 1996), feminists have examined and foregrounded ethical issues. As is true with qualitative research in general, concerns for ethical issues in feminist work have become more complex and differentiated. Few researchers face the threat of having their data subpoenaed (Scarce, 1994), but in the face of federal regulations offering anyone access to data gathered in funded studies, for many there are renewed worries about assurances of privacy and confidentiality. Feminist researchers who work in the areas of women's reproductive health (especially abortion), sexual orientation, and homeless women are particularly sensitive to these issues.

These newer worries exist uneasily with older concerns about avoiding deceit and deception and fully informing participants of research goals, strategies, and styles. Contributors to the older qualitative or feminist literature tended to treat informed consent as somewhat problematic, but nevertheless mostly stable and durable during the full course of the research, including publication of findings. Rather rarely has it been noted that informed consent, freely given at one time, may fade or alter so that participants express curiosity or even skepticism about and resistance to the research at a later stage (May, 1980). Although little feminist research has been conducted covertly, there remains a gray area in which personal information about the researcher's life or experiences may be deliberately withheld or blurred (D. L. Wolf, 1996b, pp. 11-12) or other personal information, including views on sex, politics, money, social class, and race, is lost in the complexities of interactions characterized by mobile subjectivities and multiple realities of both participants and researcher. The former case is a research strategy; the latter is characteristic of everyday social life. In both cases the lack of information may influence the mutual construction of data by researcher and participants.

Thoughtful researchers now grapple with older issues and with newly problematic questions such as the intellectual and social processes discussed earlier in these pages that have shifted taken-for-granted feminist assumptions. As Yvonna Lincoln (1995, p. 287) has insightfully noted, standards for quality are now seen to be intertwined with issues of ethics—for example, the demand that the researcher conduct and make explicitly open and honest negotiations around data gathering, analysis, and presentation. These are closely tied to issues of how and where knowledge is created.

Although at the outset in feminist research, some believed that friendly relationships could grow out of research with women (Oakley, 1981), this quickly gave way to a somewhat more distanced view. Feminist qualitative researchers became sensitive to ethical issues arising from the theme that characterizes feminist qualitative work, namely, concern for and even involvement with participating individuals. Janet Finch's (1984) early concern about researchers' unwitting manipulation of participants hungry for social contact anticipated Judith Stacey's (1988) widely cited paper and one by Lila Abu-Lughod (1990) on contradictions in feminist qualitative methodology. Stacey called attention to the uncomfortable question of getting data from respondents as a means to an end and the difficult compromises that may be involved in promising respondents control over the report. These issues, however, as Elizabeth Wheatley (1994) later noted, are characteristic of qualitative work, which can never resolve all ethical dilemmas that arise.

Other ethical dilemmas lie in the potential for "stealing women's words" (Opie, 1992; Reay, 1996b). In a study that involved respondents in the meaning-making process, Sandra Jones (1997) encountered ethical dilemmas. The difficult question of validating or challenging women's taken-for-granted views when they do not accord with feminist perspectives presents another ethical quandary (Kitzinger & Wilson, 1997). Feminist nurse researchers have also pointed out that additional ethical dilemmas may arise when doing research in one's own professional field, where the professional and research roles may conflict (Field, 1991).

The view, long held in feminist research, that researchers occupy a more powerful position than research participants because the researchers are the writers of the accounts has occasioned ethical worries. However, as feminist qualitative researchers have looked more closely at the relations between researchers and participants, the image of the powerless respondent has altered with the recognition that researchers' "power" is often only partial (Ong, 1995), illusory (Visweswaran, 1997; M. A. Wolf, 1996), tenuous (D. L. Wolf, 1996b, p. 36), and confused with researcher responsibility (Bloom, 1998, p. 35), even though the researchers may be more powerfully positioned when out of the field, because they will write the accounts.

Ethics in Participatory Research

These ethical issues and those of voice and account emerge even more vividly in activist studies, where researchers and participants collaborate to enable women to do research for themselves and on topics of concern in their lives and worlds. Participatory research (fully discussed by Kemmis & McTaggart, Chapter 11, Volume 2) confronts both researchers and participants-who-are-also-researchers with challenges about women's knowledge; representations of women; modes of data gathering, analysis, interpretation, and writing of the account; and relationships between and among the collaborating parties. Although this kind of research is not done as widely as might be hoped, nevertheless there is a growing body of literature on such projects and thoughtful discussion of such issues as othering and dissemination (Lykes, 1997). Linda Light and Nancy Kleiber's (1981) early study of a Vancouver women's health collective describes their conversion from traditional field-workers to coresearchers with the members of the women's health collective and the difficulties of closing the distance between researchers and participants both fully engaged in the research. Questions of the ownership of the data also arise (Renzetti, 1997). Issues of power remain, as collaborative research does not dissolve competing interests (Lykes, 1989, p. 179). Alice McIntyre and M. Brinton Lykes (1998) urge that feminist participatory action researchers exercise reflexivity to interrogate power, privilege, and multiple hierarchies.

In a certain sense, participants are always "doing" research, for they, along with researchers, construct the meanings that become "data" for interpretation. Whereas in customary research the researcher frames interpretations, in participatory action research researchers and participants undertake this task (Cancian, 1992, 1996; Craddock & Reid, 1993). This raises issues of evaluation (Lykes, 1997) and management of distortion. Based on her collaborative work, Maria Mies's (1993) conceptualization of "conscious partiality," achieved through partial identification with research participants (p. 68), creates a critical conceptual distance between the researcher and participants to facilitate dialectically correction of distortions on both sides (see also Skeggs, 1994).

Feminist Research on Ethics

Feminist research on ethics has been done in two areas: (a) questions referential to larger issues of moral beingness and (b) practices and situations in health care. Research on moral beingness has a long history reaching back to Carol Gilligan's (1982) well-known and controversial study of young girls' moral development (Benhabib, 1987; Brabeck, 1996; Koehn, 1998; Larrabee, 1993). This history overlaps complex arguments around the question of care (Larrabee, 1993; Manning, 1992; Tronto, 1993) and the substantial conceptual and empirical feminist literature on caregiving (Olesen, 1997, p. 398). Recently, theorists and researchers have shifted away from the view that ethical or moral behavior is inherent in gender (the essentialist view that women are "natural" carers) to one sensitive to the social construction of gender, which recognizes that a trait such as caring emerges from an interaction between the individual and the milieu (Seigfried, 1996, p. 205). These newer positions on an ethic of care also go beyond a focus on personal relationships in the private sphere to concerns with the just community (Seigfried, 1996, p. 210) and the potential for transforming society in the public sphere (Tronto, 1993, pp. 96-97; see also Christians, Chapter 5, this volume).

Feminist researchers' long-standing concerns about and work on ethical (or nonethical) treatment of women in health care systems have carried into inquiries on aspects of new technologies, such as assisted reproduction, genetic screening, and the regrettably enduring problems of equitable care for elderly, poor women of all ethnic groups (Holmes & Purdy, 1992; Sherwin, 1992; Tong, 1997).

◆ Unrealized Agendas

Feminist qualitative research, as glimpsed in these pages, would appear to be at the beginning of the millennium a complex, diverse, and highly energized enterprise of which it can be said there is no single voice and no single voice can claim dominance or a privileged position. Given the substantive range, theoretical complexity, and empirical difficulties represented in the many topics on which feminist qualitative researchers are working, the multiplicity of voices is apt. This is not to argue that these approaches are beyond criticism that could sharpen and improve them for future work on these selfsame difficult topics; rather, the diversity and multiplicity of feminist qualitative research are causes for celebration, not approbation. Having abandoned the strained binary that posed rigid adherence to traditional methods against the view that all competing knowledge claims are valid, feminist researchers in general have moved, as theorist Joan Alway (1995) has argued, "to try to produce less false, less partial and less perverse representations without making any claims about what is absolutely and always true" (p. 225). This posture rests on the important assumptions that women in specific contexts are best suited to help develop presentations of their lives and that contexts are located in specific structures and historical and material moments. The latter point is particularly critical as feminists work to understand—through texts, discourses, and encounters with women—how women's lives are contextualized and framed.

Yet there remain a number of unrealized agendas within the feminist qualitative research realm. Foremost among these is the deeper exploration of how meanings of race, class, and gender emerge and interlock, as well as their various effects, as Patricia Hill Collins (1999) has done in her analysis of "real mothers" and as Sheila Allen (1994) has proposed in her discussion of race, ethnicity, and nationality. Complicating this agenda is the still-unfinished job of problematizing whiteness, discussed earlier, and the realization of different agendas, contexts, and dynamics for women of

365

color and varying social status. In this regard, Dorothy Smith's (1996) proposal to utilize the metaphor of the map to discover the ongoing ways in which people coordinate their activities, particularly "those forms of social organization and relations that connect up multiple and various sites of experience" (p. 194). offers a promising start. Olivia Espin's (1995) analysis of racism and sexuality in immigrant women's narratives does so as well.

Much remains to be done to open traditional feminist research approaches of data gathering, analysis, and representation to experimental moves, but some feminist researchers are appreciative of, if not sympathetic to, the new moves.[16] However, this poses two issues for all feminist qualitative researchers, irrespective of where they locate themselves in various research streams. First is the obdurate necessity to attend to representation, voice, and text in ways that avoid replication of the researcher and instead display representation of the participants. This is an issue that is not resolved through the simple presentation of research materials or findings in new or shocking ways. Rather, it speaks to the ethical and analytic difficulties inherent in the intertwining of researcher and participant and the mutual creation of data, which are brought to the fore usually by the researcher. There can be no dodging the researcher's responsibility for the account, the text, and the voices, as the research texts cited earlier make clear.

Further complicating this issue is the fact that, as Patricia Clough (1993a) notes, "the textuality never refers to a text, but to the processes of desire elicited and repressed, projected and interjected in the activity of reading and writing" (p. 175). Apt though this observation is, resolving this issue is a much more elusive prospect than choosing and positioning voices, texts, and so on. However, like the more traditional questions to be considered next, it merits much more work than has been done thus far.

A second and parallel task that would take different forms depending on the nature of the research is the question of the overarching issues of credibility and believability, or, put another way, how to indicate that the claims produced are less false, less perverse, and less partial without falling back into positivist standards that measure acceptability of knowledge in terms of some ideal, unchanging body of knowledge. The way forward on this problem, in the views of the authors reviewed here, involves scrupulous and open interrogation of the feminist researchers' own postures, views, and practices, turning back on themselves the very lenses with which they scrutinize the lives of the women with whom they work and always looking for tensions, contradictions, and complicities (Humphries, 1997, p. 7). Uncomfortable as this gaze may be, it is as much a strategy for feminist qualitative researchers reaching for new and experimental approaches as it is for those who take more familiar paths. Such unremitting reflexivity is not without difficulties: Rahel Wasserfall (1997) describes deep and tension-laden differences between herself and her participants; Rebecca Lawthom (1997) reveals problems in her work as a feminist researcher in nonfeminist research; Kathy Davis and Ine Gremmen (1998) found that feminist ideals can sometimes stand in the way of doing feminist research.

◆ Contexts and Consequences

In this chapter I have emphasized recognition and awareness of the critical importance of context in women's lives, the situated knowledges that partake of local frames and overarching historical and material trends. It is therefore appropriate to try to locate feminist qualitative research in the many contexts that shape this enterprise and that it in turn shapes.

Academic Life

The traditional structure of academic life—at least in the United States—has influenced feminist qualitative research. Whereas much of the early impetus to reform and transformation emerged outside the academy, in recent decades the major intellectual energies in feminist qualitative research have been found in traditional departments, most usually anthropology, sociology, psychology, political science, philosophy, and history; in interdisciplinary women's studies and cultural studies programs; and in such professional programs as education, nursing, and social work, where it is not surprising to find published research essays focused on problems of quality, the utility of standpoint theory, and so on. Dispersal of feminist qualitative research as well as the feminisms that support it means highly variegated approaches and levels of maturity. It also points to differential reception of qualitative feminist work, which can range from dismissal or hostility to admiration if well, truly, and brilliantly done (depending on evaluators' predilection for traditional or experimental approaches).

How these responses translate into job recruitment, tenure review, and acceptance of publications is a crucial question.

A parallel and intriguing issue is the extent to which strategies in qualitative feminist research, some borrowed from traditional approaches and then modified, are then reborrowed in other disciplines, creating a problem of differentiating feminist work from projects in these other realms. Many feminist qualitative researchers would argue that the criteria for feminist work noted early in these pages will continue to differentiate methodologically similar qualitative projects from feminist research.

The question of whether feminist qualitative research can transform traditional disciplines thus is lodged in the complexities of types of feminist research and the structural nature of the site. Sectors of sociology and psychology tenaciously hold positivistic outlooks, and there are diverse theoretical views within these disciplines that blunt or facilitate feminist transformation (Stacey & Thorne, 1985). Nevertheless, it remains to be seen whether such transformative research stances as Dorothy Smith's (1974, 1987, 1989, 1990a, 1990b) radical critique of sociology and Patricia Hill Collins's (1986, 1990) concerns about the impact of dualistic thought in sociology and the tendency to perpetuate racism will reshape sociology. Or will more deconstructive approaches of abandoning ethnography and focusing on "re-readings of representations in every form of information processing," which Patricia Clough (1992, p. 137) urges, or Ann Game's (1991, p. 47) embrace of discourses rather than a focus on "the social," reconfigure sociology? Within anthropology, Ruth Behar (1993) and Lila Abu-Lughod (1990) argue that many of the influential themes discussed earlier in this chapter (dissolution of self/other, subject/object boundaries) that are fundamental to traditional ethnographic approaches may liberate the discipline from its colonial and colonizing past (Behar, 1993, p. 302; for a different view, see Strathern, 1987). In psychology, Michelle Fine and Susan Merle Gordon (1992, p. 23) urge that feminist psychologists work in the space between the personal and the political to reconstitute psychology, and they urge activist research,[17] whereas Mary Gergen (in press) formulates a constructionist, postmodern agenda for revisioning psychology. Noting that feminists in psychology have made local and partial alterations to established methods rather than a programmatic metatheory, Jill Morawski (1994) foresees an emergent groundwork for radically new forms of psychological inquiry even though feminist psychology remains in transition.

The transformative potential of feminist cultural studies and the vital multidisciplined social studies of science remains to be seen. Here, as in other disciplinary sites, the plight of the fiscally strained academic department will shape feminist qualitative research. Downsized departments or programs relying on part-time faculty are not fertile arenas for experimental or even traditional transformative work. Counterbalancing this is the strong presence of established feminist researchers who take mentoring seriously and who connect politically to other scholars, feminist or not.

Parochialism and Publishing Practices

For at least the past decade and with no apparent end in sight, publishers have brought out hundreds of titles of feminist work—some theoretical, some empirical, some experimental, some methodological. Scholarly essays and books abound, an abundance that has had a beneficial effect on the emergence and growing complexity of qualitative feminist research. Much as this is a cause for rejoicing, given the relatively limited number of offerings three decades ago, it nevertheless presents a worrisome side concerning the quality and future of feminist research and, indeed, even the evaluation of that of the recent past. More specifically, much of this abundant and often very sophisticated literature, which includes some work by feminist scholars from non-English-speaking countries, has been published in English by publishing firms in the United States and Great Britain. Marketing pressures apparently make English-language publication necessary.[18] This means that feminist research that achieves publication is produced primarily in the United States or the United Kingdom. It is not surprising that this has resulted in undifferentiated views and limited or nonexistent understandings of feminist research done beyond Westernized, bureaucratized societies.

Fortunately, different perspectives such as those of postcolonial, Marxist feminists come through these publications to undercut Westernizing and homogenizing assumptions about "women" anywhere and everywhere. The leading English-language feminist journals publish essays by researchers from Asia, Africa, Latin America, the Arab Middle East, and Eastern Europe, although these publications are in the minority. Leading university and trade presses that feature feminist books frequently have publications by non-U.S. feminists on their lists.[19] Yet, as Meaghan Morris (personal communication, April 15, 1999) has pointed out, there is only a small flow of research publications from non-Western feminists because of translation and marketing problems, a criticism also made by Mary Maynard (1996) and Andre Schiffrin (1998). Even when published in English outside the United States or Great Britain, a feminist research-oriented monograph such as Cynthia Nelson and Soraya Altorki's *Arab Regional Women's Studies Workshop* (1997) may not easily reach interested Western feminists. International feminist conferences, such as that sponsored by Zentrum für Interdisziplinäre Frauenforschung at Humboldt Universität zu Berlin, have begun to discuss these issues.

Some, but not enough, of that work is heard at international conferences such as the International Congresses on Women's Health Issues, which meet biannually in such venues as New Zealand, Denmark, Botswana, Thailand, Egypt, and South Korea and draw substantial numbers of international participants from these regions.[20] In sum, there are some trickles of feminist research from international researchers that provide countervailing themes to dilute the weight of English-language publications and the dominance of English-language feminism. Given the economics of publishing, that probably will continue. However, given the increasing complexity in feminist qualitative research, some of which, as noted earlier, derives from postcolonial feminist thinking, new approaches and tactics from international scholars will attract attention not only among open-minded English-language feminist researchers, but among publishers with an eye to profitable publication.

◆ Conclusion

Feminist qualitative research enters the new millennium in a stronger position than it began the "second wave" because both theorists and researchers have critically examined the foundations even as they have tried new research approaches, experimental and traditional. Above all, it appears that feminist qualitative researchers are much more self-conscious and much more aware of and sensitive to issues in the formulation and conduct of the research than was the case earlier. However, there is room for yet further sensitivity, as many of the essays cited in this chapter make clear. Happily, there are more sophisticated approaches and more incisive understandings with which to grapple with the innumerable problems in women's lives, contexts, and situations in the hope of, if not emancipation, at least some modest intervention and transformation. Given the diversity and complexity of feminist qualitative research, it is not likely that any orthodoxy—

experimental or traditional—will prevail, nor in my opinion should it. All feminist qualitative researchers, in making women's lives and contexts problematic, should openly render their own practices problematic, as many researchers cited in this chapter urge.

Elsewhere, I have commented:

> It is important to recognize that knowledge production is continually dynamic—new frames open which give way to others which in turn open again and again. Moreover, knowledges are only partial. Some may find these views discomfiting and see in them a slippery slope of ceaseless constructions with no sure footing for action of whatever sort. It is not that there is no platform for action, reform, transformation or emancipation, but that the platforms are transitory. If one's work is overturned or altered by another researcher with a different, more effective approach, then one should rejoice and move on. . . . What is important for concerned feminists is that new topics, issues of concerns and matters for feminist inquiry are continually produced and given attention to yield more nuanced understandings of action on critical issues. (Olesen & Clarke, 1999, p. 356)[21]

The range of problems is too great, and the issues are too urgent, for feminist researchers to do otherwise.

◆ Notes

1. For a feminist view of public health that takes a similar position, see Lupton (1995).

2. Even though feminist qualitative research may not directly relieve women's suffering in certain contexts, the research can nevertheless contribute to legislation, policy, or agencies' actions (Maynard, 1994a). Beyond the relevance of the findings, the very conduct of the research provides grounds for evaluating the degree to which it is feminist: Does it depict the researched as abnormal, powerless, or without agency? Does it include details of the micropolitics of the research? How is difference handled in the study? Does it avoid replicating oppression (Bhavnani, 1994, p. 30)? Francesca Cancian (1992) enunciates a similar list of criteria for regarding research as feminist.

3. A classic interview study of women's health experiences that undercut medical taken-for-grantedness about female patients was conducted by Linda Hunt, Brigitte Jordan, Susan Irwin, and Carole Browner (1989); these researchers found that women did not comply with medical regimes for reasons that made sense in their own lives, and that the women were not "cranks," a finding similar to Anne Kasper's (1994) in her study of women with breast cancer. Alexandra Dundas Todd (1989) documented cultural conflicts between patients and female patients. At a different level, Sue Fisher's (1995) analysis showed that nurse practitioners provide more attentive care than do physicians, but still exert

considerable control over patients. Addressing large-scale issues, Susan Yadlon's (1997) analysis of discourses around causes for breast cancer revealed that women are blamed for being poor mothers or for being too skinny and that environmental and other extracorporal causes are overlooked. Sarah Nettleton's (1991) deconstructive analysis of discursive practices in dentistry showed how ideal mothers are created, and Kathy Davis's (1995) research on cosmetic surgery highlighted women's dilemmas. Building on her pioneering work on women's preparation of food (1991), Marjorie DeVault (1999b) questioned the "ownership of food and health."

4. Policy research raises the issue of "studying up" and invokes the oft-repeated comment that feminist researchers, like many other qualitative (and quantitative) investigators, find it easy to access respondents in social groups open to them rather than high-status lawmakers or elected officials, an important exception being Margaret Stacey's (1992) analysis of the British Medical Council. A second reason, however, may lie in a failure to explore policy made at local levels, where access may be easier (city governments, school boards, community activist organizations). In this regard the work developing Dorothy Smith's theories of institutional ethnography (Campbell & Manicom, 1995) and particularly Marie Campbell's (1998) analysis of how texts are enacted as policy in a Canadian nursing home offer new and promising leads in the area of feminist policy analysis. Carroll Estes and Beverly Edmonds's (1981) symbolic interactionist model on how emergent policy issues become framed remains a valuable approach for feminists interested in policy analysis. In the area of policy analysis qualitative feminist researchers, like feminist researchers in general, have more to contribute than they have been able to in the past. As Janet Finch (1986) has argued, qualitative research can make an important contribution to our understanding of the framing and making of policy.

5. This shift has evoked worried comments that feminist researchers have moved away from the political agendas of an earlier time concerned with understanding and alleviating women's oppression to descriptions of women's lives or arcane epistemological questions (Glucksman, 1994; Kelly, Burton, & Regan, 1994, p. 29). Clearly, widespread interest in epistemological issues flourishes among those seeking to understand, improve, or de-stabilize feminist approaches, but there is abundant work oriented toward intervention and change on numerous fronts. Patti Lather and Chris Smithies's (1997) participatory study with HIV-positive women combines poststructural approaches with a clear reform agenda, Rachel Pfeffer's (1997) ethnographic inquiry into lives of young homeless women points to programmatic possibilities, and Diana Taylor and Katherine Dower's (1995) policy-oriented focus group research with community women in San Francisco details women's concerns. Olesen, Taylor, Ruzek, and Clarke (1997) extensively review feminist research oriented toward ameliorating women's health, and qualitative feminist researchers discuss difficult issues in researching sexual violence against women, such as sexual harassment of the researcher (Huff, 1997), cross-race research (Huisman, 1997), managing one's own and others' emotions (Mattley, 1997), and negotiating the territory between being an activist and being a researcher (Hippensteele, 1997). Adele Clarke and I argue that "discursive constructions and signifying practices can be handled as constitutive rather than determinative" (Clarke & Olesen, 1999a, p. 13). Sally Kenney and Helen Kinsella's (1997) edited volume details the political and reform implications of standpoint theory. Moreover, a number of

journals (*Qualitative Research in Health Care, International Journal of Qualitative Studies in Education, Feminism and Psychology, Western Journal of Nursing Research, Journal of Social Issues, Sociology of Health and Illness, Qualitative Inquiry, Qualitative Sociology, Journal of Contemporary Ethnography, Feminist Studies, Feminist Review, Gender & Society*, and *Social Problems*) publish feminist qualitative reform-oriented research. However, there, as elsewhere, space limits on the size of essays (usually 25 pages double-spaced) make constructing both an argument and a reform stance difficult, given the necessity for detail in qualitative reporting. (On academy-community connections, see also *Feminist Collections: A Quarterly of Women's Studies Resources,* Vol. 20, No. 3, 1999, which includes a section titled "The Energizing Tension Between Scholars and Activists.")

6. Work by feminist legal scholars also falls within this genre (e.g., Ashe, 1988; Bartlett, 1990; Fry, 1992; MacKinnon, 1983; Matsuda, 1992, 1996; Williams, 1991).

7. Yvonna Lincoln (personal communication, March 4, 1999) has reminded me that relativism "spreads over a continuum" ranging from radical relativists who believe that "anything goes" to those who disavow absolute standards for evaluating accounts but hold that standards should be developed in specific contexts that incorporate participants' ideas of which account represents useful knowledge. This latter view does not jettison any notion of quality, but rather serves as a way to avoid utilizing "scientific standards" in contexts where "they act in oppressing, disabling or power-freighted ways."

8. Beyond the original texts of standpoint theorists cited here, useful interpretive reviews can be found in Denzin (1997), Clough (1998), and Kenney and Kinsella (1997). Harding's (1997, p. 387) summary of standpoint theories' chronology is also instructive.

9. The extensive literature on deconstructionism, postmodernism, and feminism is not always as accessible as it should be for those who are starting to explore or wish to deepen their understanding. Some useful works are the spring 1988 issue of *Feminist Studies,* Nicholson (1990, 1997), Hekman (1990b), Flax (1987, 1990), Rosenau (1992), Lemert (1997), Charmaz's (1995) insightful and evenly balanced analysis of positivism and postmodernism in qualitative research, and Collins's (1998b) incisive discussion of what postmodernism means for black feminists.

10. Feminist researchers who look to deconstruction or psychoanalytic feminist semiotics disavow attention to experience (Clough, 1993a, p. 179). They argue that, irrespective of how close the researcher, experience is always created in discourse and textuality. Text is central to incisive analysis as a fundamental mode of social criticism. In this work the emphasis on desire seems to refer to (a) passion, (b) the mysterious and mischievous contributions of the unconscious, (c) libidinal resources not squeezed out of us by childhood and adult socialization, and (d) the sexuality and politics of cultural life and its representations.

11. Kamela Visweswaran (1994) makes a useful differentiation between reflexive ethnography, which questions its own authority, confronts the researcher's processes of interpretation, and emphasizes how the researcher thinks she knows, and deconstructive ethnography, which abandons authority, confronts power in the interpretive process, and emphasizes how we think we know what we know is not innocent.

12. Other feminist accounts that have explicated how decisions were made include Janet Finch and Jennifer Mason's (1990) detailed report on how they sought "negative cases" and Catherine Kohler Riessman's (1990) worries about her analysis of divorced

persons' reports and the sociologist's interpretive voice. Jennifer Ring (1987, p. 771), following Hegel, avers that dialectical thought prevents stabilizing the border between objectivity and subjectivity.

13. Considerations of voice and preparation of text or alternative presentation raise the question of type of publication. Presenting research materials in popular magazines may reach audiences who would be unlikely to have access to or see more traditional or even experimental accounts in academic sources. At present few of the academic review processes leading to tenure, promotion, or even merit pay increases acknowledge these lay publications as important. Patti Lather and Chris Smithies (1997), in their research with HIV-positive women, in which they consulted with women throughout, initially took their manuscript directly to publication for the mass audience reachable through supermarkets and the like.

14. Earlier feminist accounts developed innovative ways to reflect and present voice, although not all would be free of the problems Fine (1992b) discusses. (For an extensive list of such accounts, see Mascia-Lees et al., 1989, pp. 7-8, n. 1.) Two contrasting examples: Marjorie Shostak (1981) gave a verbatim dialogic account of her voice and that of her !Kung respondent, Nisa, whereas Susan Krieger (1983) used the device of a polyphonic chorus to represent voices of women in a Midwest lesbian community. Krieger's voice is absent, although she clearly selected the materials for the account.

15. Under the editorship of Barbara and Dennis Tedlock, the flagship journal *American Anthropologist* adopted a policy of publishing experimental texts, as have several sociological journals long sympathetic to the new modes (*Qualitative Inquiry, Journal of Contemporary Ethnography, Midwest Sociological Quarterly, Qualitative Sociology*).

16. In a review essay discussing Laurel Richardson's *Fields of Play* (1997) cowritten by a group of women at the University of Michigan's Institute for Research on Women and Gender, Lora Bex Lempert argues that scholars who have moved into the experimental spaces have created intellectual and representation spaces for others in the work of social transformation, an agenda shared with the traditionalists (Dutton, Groat, Hassinger, Lempert, & Ruehl, 1998).

17. Activist-oriented research agendas in women's health are outlined by Narrigan, Zones, Worcester, and Grad (1997) and by Ruzek, Olesen, and Clarke (1997).

18. I am indebted here to a lively exchange on these issues with Meaghan Morris, Norman Denzin, Patricia Clough, and Yvonna Lincoln. In a helpful critical reading of this section, Annie George of the Department of Social and Behavioral Sciences Graduate Program in Sociology, University of California, San Francisco, raised an additional problem: Many English-language publications in non-Western countries are not listed or cited in major databases such as SocAbstracts and ERIC.

19. Notable recent issues of English-language feminist journals with space devoted to international feminist research include a special issue of *Feminist Review* (Mohammed, 1998) and a special section in *Signs* ("Gender, Politics and Islam," 1998). Research by Chinese and Japanese feminists on women office workers (Ogasawara, 1998) and on women factory workers in Hong Kong and south China (Lee, 1998) exemplify international work published by university and trade presses, as do writings by international scholars on their relationship to feminism and scholarship in their home and adopted societies (John, 1996; Narayan, 1997).

20. For those feminist qualitative researchers with computer resources and access to the Internet, a growing number of talk lists and Web sites among feminist organizations publicize international congresses held outside the United States. Computer and Internet resources, however, may not be readily available to less well supported feminist qualitative researchers, wherever they are located.

21. As Deborah Lupton (1995) has noted, "The point is not to seek a certain 'truth,' but to uncover varieties of truth that operate, to highlight the nature of truth as transitory and political and the position of subjects as fragmentary and contradictory" (pp. 160-161).

◆ References

Abel, E., Christian, B., & Moglen, H. (Eds.). (1997). *Female subjects in black and white: Race, psychoanalysis, feminism.* Berkeley: University of California Press.

Abel, E. K., & Nelson, M. K. (Eds.). (1990). *Circles of care: Work and identity in women's lives.* Albany: State University of New York.

Abu-Lughod, L. (1990). Can there be a feminist ethnography? *Women and Performance, 5*(1), 7-27.

Acker, J., Barry, K., & Esseveld, J. (1991). Objectivity and truth: Problems in doing feminist research. In M. M. Fonow & J. A. Cook (Eds.), *Beyond methodology: Feminist scholarship as lived research* (pp. 133-153). Bloomington: Indiana University Press.

Acker, S. (1994). *Gendered education: Sociological reflections on women, teaching and feminism.* Milton Keynes, England: Open University Press.

Alexander, M. J., & Mohanty, C. T. (Eds.). (1997). *Feminist genealogies, colonial legacies, democratic futures.* New York: Routledge.

Allen, S. (1994). Race, ethnicity and nationality: Some questions of identity. In H. Afshar & M. Maynard (Eds.), *The dynamics of "race" and gender: Some feminist interventions* (pp. 85-105). London: Taylor & Francis.

Alway, J. (1995). The trouble with gender: Tales of the still missing feminist revolution in sociological theory. *Sociological Theory, 13,* 209-228.

Anzaldúa, G. (1987). *Borderlands/la frontera: The new mestiza.* San Francisco: Aunt Lute.

Anzaldúa, G. (Ed.). (1990). *Making face, making soul/haciendo caras: Creative and critical perspectives by feminists of color.* San Francisco: Aunt Lute.

Appleby, Y. (1997). How was it for you? Intimate exchanges in feminist research. In M. Ang-Lyngate, C. Corrin, & H. S. Millson (Eds.), *Desperately seeking sisterhood: Still challenging and building* (pp. 127-147). London: Taylor & Francis.

Asch, A., & Fine, M. (1992). Beyond the pedestals: Revisiting the lives of women with disabilities. In M. Fine (Ed.), *Disruptive voices: The possibilities of feminist research* (pp. 139-174). Ann Arbor: University of Michigan Press.

Ashe, M. (1988). Law-language of maternity: Discourse holding nature in contempt. *New England Law Review, 521,* 44-70.

Balsamo, A. (1993). On the cutting edge: Cosmetic surgery and the technological production of the gendered body. *Camera Obscura, 28,* 207-237.

Balsamo, A. (1999). Technologies of surveillance: Constructing cases of maternal neglect. In A. E. Clarke & V. L. Olesen (Eds.), *Revisioning women, health and healing: Feminist, cultural and technoscience perspectives* (pp. 231-253). New York: Routledge.

Bartlett, K. (1990). Feminist legal methods. *Harvard Law Review, 103,* 45-50.

Behar, R. (1993). *Translated woman: Crossing the border with Esperanza's story.* Boston: Beacon.

Behar, R. (1996). *The vulnerable observer: Anthropology that breaks your heart.* Boston: Beacon.

Behar, R., & Gordon, D. A. (Eds.). (1995). *Women writing culture.* Berkeley: University of California Press.

Benhabib, S. (1987). The generalized and the concrete other: The Kohlberg-Gilligan controversy and feminist theory. In S. Benhabib & D. Cornell (Eds.), *Feminism as critique* (pp. 77-95). Minneapolis: University of Minnesota Press.

Benhabib. S. (1995). Feminism and postmodernism: An uneasy alliance. In S. Benhabib, J. Butler, D. Cornell, & N. Fraser, *Feminist contentions: A philosophical exchange* (pp. 17-34). New York: Routledge.

Benhabib, S., Butler, J., Cornell, D., & Fraser, N. (1995). *Feminist contentions: A philosophical exchange.* London: Routledge.

Bhavnani, K.-K. (1994). Tracing the contours: Feminist research and feminist objectivity. In H. Afshar & M. Maynard (Eds.), *The dynamics of "race" and gender: Some feminist interventions* (pp. 26-40). London: Taylor & Francis.

Bing, V. M., & Reid, P. T. (1996). Unknown women and unknowing research: Consequences of color and class in feminist psychology. In N. Goldberger, J. Tarule, B. Clinchy, & M. Belenky (Eds.), *Knowledge, difference, and power: Essays inspired by* Women's ways of knowing (pp. 175-205). New York: Basic Books.

Birch, M. (1998). Reconstructing research narratives: Self and sociological identity in alternative settings. In J. Ribbens & R. Edwards (Eds.), *Feminist dilemmas in qualitative research: Public knowledge and private lives* (pp. 171-185). Thousand Oaks, CA: Sage.

Bloom, L. R. (1998). *Under the sign of hope: Feminist methodology and narrative interpretation.* Albany: State University of New York Press.

Brabeck, M. M. (1996). The moral self, values and circles of belonging. In K. F. Wyche & F. J. Crosby (Eds.), *Women's ethnicities: Journeys through psychology* (pp. 145-165). Boulder, CO: Westview.

Britzman, D. P. (1991). *Practice makes practice: A critical study of learning to teach.* Albany: State University of New York Press.

Britzman, D. P. (1995). The question of belief: Writing poststructural anthropology. *Qualitative Studies in Education, 8*, 229-238.

Britzman, D. P. (1998). Foreword. In L. R. Bloom, *Under the sign of hope, Feminist methodology and narrative interpretation* (pp. ix-xi). Albany: State University of New York Press.

Broom, D. (1991). *Damned if we do: Contradictions in women's health care.* Sydney: Allen & Unwin.

Brown, R. H. (1998). Review of *Fields of play: Constructing an academic life* by Laurel Richardson. *Contemporary Sociology, 27*, 380-383.

Brown, W. (1992). Finding the man in the state. *Feminist Studies, 18*, 7-34.

Butler, J. (1990). *Gender trouble: Feminism and the subversion of identity.* London: Routledge.

Butler, J. (1993). *Bodies that matter: On the discursive limits of "sex."* New York: Routledge.

Butler, J. (1994). Against proper objects. *Differences, 6*, 1-16.

Butler, O. (1986). *Feminist experiences in feminist research.* Manchester: University of Manchester Press.

Campbell, M. (1998). Institutional ethnography and experience as data. *Qualitative Sociology, 21*, 55-74.

Campbell, M., & Manicom, A. (Eds.). (1995). *Knowledge, experience and ruling relations.* Toronto: University of Toronto Press.

Campbell, R. (1984). The virtues of feminist empiricism. *Hypatia, 9*, 90-115.

Cancian, F. M. (1992). Feminist science: Methodologies that challenge inequality. *Gender & Society, 6*, 623-642.

Cancian, F. M. (1996). Participatory research and alternative strategies for activist sociology. In H. Gottfried (Ed.), *Feminism and social change* (pp. 187-205). Urbana: University of Illinois Press.

Cannon, L. W., Higginbotham, E., & Leung, M. L. A. (1991). Race and class bias in qualitative research on women. In M. M. Fonow & J. A. Cook (Eds.), *Beyond methodology: Feminist scholarship as lived research* (pp. 107-118). Bloomington: Indiana University Press.

Casper, M. J. (1997). Feminist politics and fetal surgery: Adventures of a research cowgirl on the reproductive frontier. *Feminist Studies, 23*, 233-262.

Casper, M. J. (1998). *The making of the unborn patient: Medical work and the politics of reproduction in experimental fetal surgery.* New Brunswick, NJ: Rutgers University Press.

Charmaz, K. (1995). Between positivism and postmodernism: Implications for methods. In N. K. Denzin (Ed.), *Studies in symbolic interaction* (Vol. 17, pp. 43-72). Greenwich, CT: JAI.

Charmaz, K., & Olesen, V. L. (1997). Ethnographic research in medical sociology: Its foci and distinctive contributions. *Sociological Methods & Research, 25,* 452-494.

Chase, S. E. (1995). *Ambiguous empowerment: The work narratives of women school superintendents.* Amherst: University of Massachusetts Press.

Chow, E. N. (1987). The development of feminist consciousness among Asian American women. *Gender & Society, 1,* 284-299.

Clarke, A. E. (1998). *Disciplining reproduction: Modernity, American life sciences, and the problems of sex.* Berkeley: University of California Press.

Clarke, A. E., & Olesen, V. L. (1999a). Revising, diffracting, acting. In A. E. Clarke & V. L. Olesen (Eds.), *Revisioning women, health and healing: Feminist, cultural and technoscience perspectives* (pp. 3-38). New York: Routledge.

Clarke, A. E., & Olesen, V. L. (Eds.). (1999b). *Revisioning women, health and healing: Feminist, cultural and technoscience perspectives.* New York: Routledge.

Clough, P. T. (1992). *The end(s) of ethnography: From realism to social criticism.* Newbury Park, CA: Sage.

Clough, P. T. (1993a). On the brink of deconstructing sociology: A critical reading of Dorothy Smith's standpoint epistemology. *Sociological Quarterly, 34,* 169-182.

Clough, P. T. (1993b). Response to Smith. *Sociological Quarterly, 34,* 193-194.

Clough, P. T. (1994). *Feminist thought: Desire, power and academic discourse.* Cambridge, MA: Blackwell.

Clough, P. T. (1998). *The end(s) of ethnography: From realism to social criticism* (2nd ed.). New York: Peter Lang.

Clough, P. T. (in press). *Autoaffection: The unconscious in the age of teletechnology.* Minneapolis: University of Minnesota Press.

Code, L. (1991). *What can she know? Feminist theory and the construction of knowledge.* Ithaca, NY: Cornell University Press.

Collins, P. H. (1986). Learning from the outsider within: The sociological significance of black feminist thought. *Social Problems, 33,* 14-32.

Collins, P. H. (1990). *Black feminist thought: Knowledge, consciousness, and the politics of empowerment.* New York: Routledge, Chapman & Hall.

Collins, P. H. (1992). Transforming the inner circle: Dorothy Smith's challenge to sociological theory. *Sociological Theory, 10,* 73-80.

Collins, P. H. (1997). Comment on Hekman's "Truth and method: Feminist standpoint theory revisited." *Signs, 22,* 375-381.

Collins, P. H. (1998a). *Fighting words: Black women and the search for justice.* Minneapolis: University of Minnesota Press.

Collins, P. H. (1998b). What's going on? Black feminist thought and the politics of postmodernism. In P. H. Collins, *Fighting words: Black women and the search for justice* (pp. 124-154). Minneapolis: University of Minnesota Press.

Collins, P. H. (1999). Will the "real" mother please stand up? The logic of eugenics and American national family planning. In A. E. Clarke & V. L. Olesen (Eds.), *Revisioning women, health and healing: Feminist, cultural and technoscience perspectives* (pp. 266-282). New York: Routledge.

Connell, R. W. (1992). A sober anarchism. *Sociological Theory, 10,* 81-87.

Connell, R. W. (1997). Comment on Hawkesworth's "Confounding gender." *Signs, 22,* 702-706.

Craddock, E., & Reid, M. (1993). Structure and struggle: Implementing a social model of a well woman clinic in Glasgow. *Social Science and Medicine, 19,* 35-45.

Crenshaw, K. (1992). Whose story is it, anyway? Feminist and antiracist appropriations of Anita Hill. In T. Morrison (Ed.), *Race-ing justice, en-gendering power: Essays on Anita Hill, Clarence Thomas, and the construction of social reality* (pp. 402-436). New York: Pantheon.

Daniels, A. K. (1983). Self-deception and self-discovery in field work. *Qualitative Sociology, 6,* 295-214.

Davis, A. Y. (1981). *Women, race and class.* London: Women's Press.

Davis, K. (1995). *Reshaping the female body: The dilemma of cosmetic surgery.* New York: Routledge.

Davis, K., & Gremmen, I. (1998). In search of heroines: Some reflections on normativity in feminist research. *Feminism and Psychology, 8,* 133-153.

de Lauretis, T. (1987). *Technologies of gender: Essays on theory, film, and fiction.* Bloomington: Indiana University Press.

Denzin, N. K. (1992). *Symbolic interactionism and cultural studies.* Newbury Park, CA: Sage.

Denzin, N. K. (1997). *Interpretive ethnography: Ethnographic practices for the 21st century.* Thousand Oaks, CA: Sage.

DeVault, M. L. (1991). *Feeding the family: The social organization of caring as gendered work.* Chicago: University of Chicago Press.

DeVault, M. L. (1996). Talking back to sociology: Distinctive contributions of feminist methodology. *Annual Review of Sociology, 22,* 29-50.

DeVault, M. L. (1999a). *Liberating method: Feminism and social research.* Philadelphia: Temple University Press.

DeVault, M. L. (1999b). Whose science of food and health? Narratives of profession and activism from public health nutrition. In A. E. Clarke & V. L. Olesen (Eds.), *Revisioning women, health and healing: Feminist, cultural and technoscience perspectives* (pp. 166-186). New York: Routledge.

Dill, B. T. (1979). The dialectics of black womanhood. *Signs, 4,* 543-555.

Dutton, J., Groat, L., Hassinger, J., Lempert, L. B., & Ruehl, C. (1998). [Review of the book *Fields of play: Constructing an academic life,* by Laurel Richardson]. *Qualitative Sociology, 21,* 195-204.

Ehrenreich, B., & Piven, F. F. (1983). Women and the welfare state. In I. Howe (Ed.), *Alternatives: Proposals for America from the democratic left* (pp. 30-45). New York: Pantheon.

Eichler, M. (1986). The relationship between sexist, non-sexist, woman-centered and feminist research. *Studies in Communication, 3,* 37-74.

Eichler, M. (1997). Feminist methodology. *Current Sociology, 45,* 9-36.

Ellingson, L. L. (1998). "Then you know how I feel": Empathy, identity, and reflexivity in fieldwork. *Qualitative Inquiry, 4,* 492-514.

Ellis, C. (1995). *Final negotiations: A story of love, loss, and chronic illness.* Philadelphia: Temple University Press.

Ellis, C., & Bochner, A. P. (1992). Telling and performing personal stories. In C. Ellis & M. G. Flaherty (Eds.), *Investigating subjectivity: Research on lived experience* (pp. 79-101). Newbury Park, CA: Sage.

Ellis, C., & Bochner, A. P. (Eds.). (1996). *Composing ethnography: Alternative forms of qualitative writing.* Walnut Creek, CA: AltaMira.

Epstein, C. F. (1981). *Women in law.* New York: Basic Books.

Espin, O. M. (1995). "Race," racism and sexuality in the life narratives of immigrant women. *Feminism and Psychology, 5,* 223-228.

Estes, C. L., & Edmonds, B. C. (1981). Symbolic interaction and social policy analysis. *Symbolic Interaction, 4,* 75-86.

Fee, E. (1983). Women and health care: A comparison of theories. In E. Fee (Ed.), *Women and health: The politics of sex in medicine* (pp. 10-25). Englewood Cliffs, NJ: Baywood.

Felski, R. (1997). The doxa of difference. *Signs, 23,* 1-22.

Ferguson, K. (1993). *The man question: Visions of subjectivity in feminist theory.* Berkeley: University of California Press.

Field, P. A. (1991). Doing fieldwork in your own culture. In J. M. Morse (Ed.), *Qualitative nursing research: A contemporary dialogue* (pp. 91-104). Newbury Park, CA: Sage.

Finch, J. (1984). "It's great to have someone to talk to": The ethics and politics of interviewing women. In C. Bell & H. Roberts (Eds.), *Social researching: Politics, problems, practice* (pp. 70-87). London: Routledge & Kegan Paul.

Finch, J. (1986). *Research and policy: The uses of qualitative research in social and educational research.* London: Falmer.

Finch, J., & Groves, D. (1983). *A labour of love: Women, work and caring.* London: Routledge & Kegan Paul.

Finch, J., & Mason, J. (1990). Decision taking in the fieldwork process: Theoretical sampling and collaborative working. In R. G. Burgess (Ed.), *Studies in qualitative methodology: Vol. 2. Reflections on field experience* (pp. 25-50). Greenwich, CT: JAI.

Fine, M. (Ed.). (1992a). *Disruptive voices: The possibilities of feminist research.* Ann Arbor: University of Michigan Press.

Fine, M. (1992b). Passions, politics and power: Feminist research possibilities. In M. Fine (Ed.), *Disruptive voices: The possibilities of feminist research* (pp. 205-232). Ann Arbor: University of Michigan Press.

Fine, M., & Gordon, S. M. (1992). Feminist transformations of/despite psychology. In M. Fine (Ed.), *Disruptive voices: The possibilities of feminist research* (pp. 1-25). Ann Arbor: University of Michigan Press.

Fine, M., & Weis, L. (1996). Writing the "wrongs" of fieldwork: Confronting our own research/writing dilemma in urban ethnographies. *Qualitative Inquiry, 2,* 151-174.

Fisher, S. (1995). *Nursing wounds: Nurse practitioners, doctors, women patients, and the negotiation of meaning.* New Brunswick, NJ: Rutgers University Press.

Flax, J. (1987). Postmodernism and gender relations in feminist theory. *Signs, 14,* 621-643.

Flax, J. (1990). *Thinking fragments: Psychoanalysis, feminism, and postmodernism in the contemporary West.* Berkeley: University of California Press.

Fonow, M. M., & Cook, J. A. (Eds.). (1991). *Beyond methodology: Feminist scholarship as lived research.* Bloomington: Indiana University Press.

Frankenberg, R. (1993). *White women, race matters: The social construction of whiteness.* Minneapolis: University of Minnesota Press.

Frankenberg, R., & Mani, L. (1993). Cross currents, cross talk: Race, postcoloniality and the politics of location. *Cultural Studies, 7,* 292-310.

Fraser, N. (1989). Struggle over needs: Outline of a socialist-feminist critical theory of late capitalist political culture. In N. Fraser, *Unruly practices: Power, discourse, and gender in contemporary social theory* (pp. 161-187). Minneapolis: University of Minnesota Press.

Fraser, N. (1997). *Justice interruptus: Critical reflections on the post-socialist condition.* New York: Routledge.

Fry, M. J. (1992). *Postmodern legal feminism.* London: Routledge.

Game, A. (1991). *Undoing the social: Towards a deconstructive sociology.* Milton Keynes, UK: Open University Press.

Garcia, A. M. (1989). The development of Chicana feminist discourse, 1970-1980. *Gender & Society, 3,* 217-238.

Gender, politics and Islam [Special section]. (1998, Winter). *Signs.*

Gergen, M. M. (in press). *Psychology and gender.* Thousand Oaks, CA: Sage.

Gill, C. J. (1997). The last sisters: Health issues of women with disabilities. In S. B. Ruzek, V. L. Olesen, & A. E. Clarke (Eds.), *Women's health: Complexities and differences* (pp. 96-112). Columbus: Ohio State University Press.

Gilligan, C. (1982). *In a different voice: Psychological theory and women's development*. Cambridge, MA: Harvard University Press.

Ginsburg, F. D. (1998). *Contested lives: The abortion debate in an American community* (Rev. ed.). Berkeley: University of California Press.

Glazer, N. Y. (1991). "Between a rock and a hard place": Women's professional organizations in nursing and class, racial, and ethnic inequalities. *Gender & Society, 5*, 351-372.

Glenn, E. N. (1990). The dialectics of wage work: Japanese-American women and domestic service, 1905-1940. In E. C. DuBois & V. L. Ruiz (Eds.), *Unequal sisters: A multi-cultural reader in U.S. women's history* (pp. 345-372). London: Routledge.

Glucksman, M. (1994). The work of knowledge and the knowledge of women's work. In M. Maynard & J. Purvis (Eds.), *Researching women's lives from a feminist perspective* (pp. 149-165). London: Taylor & Francis.

Gordon, L. (1976). *Women's body, women's right*. New York: Grossman.

Gordon, L. (1994). *Pitied but not entitled: Single mothers and the history of welfare*. New York: Free Press.

Gorelick, S. (1991). Contradictions of feminist methodology. *Gender & Society, 5*, 459-477.

Graham, H. (1984). *Women, health and the family*. Brighton: Wheatsheaf Harvester.

Graham, H. (1985). Providers, negotiators and mediators: Women as the hidden carers. In E. Lewin & V. L. Olesen (Eds.), *Women, health and healing: Toward a new perspective* (pp. 25-52). London: Tavistock.

Green, R. (1990). The Pocahontas perplex: The image of Indian women in American culture. In E. C. DuBois & V. L. Ruiz (Eds.), *Unequal sisters: A multi-cultural reader in U.S. women's history* (pp. 15-21). London: Routledge.

Griffith, A., & Smith, D. E. (1987). Constructing knowledge: Mothering as discourse. In J. Gaskell & A. McLaren (Eds.), *Women and education* (pp. 87-103). Calgary: Detselig.

Gubrium, J. F., & Holstein, J. A. (1997). *The new language of qualitative method*. New York: Oxford University Press.

Guinier, L., Fine, M., & Balin, J. (1997). *Becoming gentlemen: Women, law school and institutional change*. Boston: Beacon.

Gupta, A., & Ferguson, J. (Eds.). (1997). *Anthropological locations: Boundaries and grounds of a field science*. Berkeley: University of California Press.

Haraway, D. J. (1988). Situated knowledges: The science question in feminism and the privilege of partial perspective. *Feminist Studies, 14*, 575-599.

Haraway, D. J. (1991). *Simians, cyborgs, and women: The reinvention of nature*. New York: Routledge.

Haraway, D. J. (1997). *Modest_witness@second_millennium: Femaleman meets Oncomouse*. New York: Routledge.

Harding, S. (1987). Conclusion: Epistemological questions. In S. Harding (Ed.), *Feminism and methodology: Social science issues* (pp. 181-190). Bloomington: Indiana University Press.

Harding, S. (1990). Feminism, science and the anti-Enlightenment critiques. In L. J. Nicholson (Ed.), *Feminism/postmodernism* (pp. 83-105). New York: Routledge.

Harding, S. (1991). "Strong objectivity" and socially situated knowledge. In S. Harding, *Whose science? Whose knowledge? Thinking from women's lives* (pp. 138-163). Ithaca, NY: Cornell University Press.

Harding, S. (1993). Rethinking standpoint epistemology: What is "strong objectivity"? In L. Alcoff & E. Potter (Eds.), *Feminist epistemologies* (pp. 49-82). New York: Routledge.

Harding, S. (1996). Gendered ways of knowing and the "epistemological crisis" of the West. In N. Goldberger, J. Tarule, B. Clinchy, & M. Belenky (Eds.), *Knowledge, difference, and power: Essays inspired by* Women's ways of knowing (pp. 431-454). New York: Basic Books.

Harding, S. (1997). Comment on Hekman's "Truth and method: Feminist standpoint theory revisited." *Signs, 22,* 382-391.

Harding, S. (1998). *Is science multicultural? Postcolonialisms, feminisms, and epistemologies.* Bloomington: Indiana University Press.

Hartouni, V. (1997). *Cultural conceptions: On reproductive technologies and the remaking of life.* Minneapolis: University of Minnesota Press.

Hartsock, N. C. M. (1983). The feminist standpoint: Developing the ground for a specifically feminist historical materialism. In S. Harding & M. B. Hintikka (Eds.), *Discovering reality* (pp. 283-310). Amsterdam: D. Reidel.

Hartsock, N. C. M. (1985). *Money, sex and power: Towards a feminist historical materialism.* Boston: Northeastern University Press.

Hartsock, N. C. M. (1990). Foucault on power: A theory for women? In L. J. Nicholson (Ed.), *Feminism/postmodernism* (pp. 157-175). New York: Routledge.

Hartsock, N. C. M. (1997a). Comment on Hekman's "Truth and method: Feminist standpoint theory revisited": Truth or justice? *Signs, 22,* 367-374.

Hartsock, N. C. M. (1997b). Standpoint theories for the next century. In S. J. Kenney & H. Kinsella (Eds.), *Politics and feminist standpoint theories* (pp. 93-101). New York: Haworth.

Hartsock, N. C. M. (1998). *The feminist standpoint revisited and other essays.* Boulder, CO: Westview.

Hawkesworth, M. E. (1989). Knowers, knowing, known: Feminist theory and claims of truth. In M. R. Malson, J. F. O'Barr, S. Westphal Wihl, & M. Wyer (Eds.), *Feminist theory in practice and process* (pp. 327-351). Chicago: University of Chicago Press. (Reprinted from *Signs,* 1989, *14,* 533-557)

Hawkesworth, M. E. (1990a). Reply to Hekman. *Signs, 15,* 420-423.

Hawkesworth, M. E. (1990b). Reply to Shogan. *Signs, 15,* 426-428.

Hawkesworth, M. E. (1997a). Confounding gender. *Signs, 22,* 649-686.

Hawkesworth, M. E. (1997b). Reply to McKenna and Kessler, Smith, Scott and Connell: Interrogating gender. *Signs, 22,* 707-713.

Hekman, S. (1990a). Comment on Hawkesworth's "Knowers, knowing, known: Feminist theory and claims of truth." *Signs, 15,* 417-419.

Hekman, S. (1990b). *Gender and knowledge: Elements of a post-modern feminism.* Boston: Northeastern University Press.

Hekman, S. (1997a). Reply to Hartsock, Collins, Harding and Smith. *Signs, 22,* 399-402.

Hekman, S. (1997b). Truth and method: Feminist standpoint theory revisited. *Signs, 22,* 341-365.

Heng, G. (1997). "A great way to fly": Nationalism, the state and varieties of Third World feminism. In M. J. Alexander & C. T. Mohanty (Eds.), *Feminist genealogies, colonial legacies, democratic futures* (pp. 30-45). New York: Routledge.

Hertz, R. (Ed.). (1997). *Reflexivity and voice.* Thousand Oaks, CA: Sage.

Hine, D. C. (1989). *Black women in white: Racial conflict and cooperation in the nursing profession, 1890-1950.* Bloomington: Indiana University Press.

Hippensteele, S. K. (1997). Activist research and social narratives: Dialectics of power, privilege, and institutional change. In M. D. Schwartz (Ed.), *Researching sexual violence against women: Methodological and personal perspectives* (pp. 74-85). Thousand Oaks, CA: Sage.

Hirschmann, N. J. (1997). Feminist standpoint as postmodern strategy. In S. J. Kenney & H. Kinsella (Eds.), *Politics and feminist standpoint theories* (pp. 73-92). New York: Haworth.

Hirsh, E., & Olson, G. A. (1995). Starting from marginalized lives: A conversation with Sandra Harding. In G. A. Olson & E. Hirsh (Eds.), *Women writing culture* (pp. 3-42). Albany: State University of New York Press.

Hochschild, A. R. (1983). *The managed heart: Commercialization of human feeling.* Berkeley: University of California Press.

Hochschild, A. R. (with MacHung, A.). (1989). *The second shift: Working parents and the revolution at home.* New York: Viking.

Holland, J., & Ramazanoglu, C. (1994). Coming to conclusions: Power and interpretation in researching young women's sexuality. In M. Maynard & J. Purvis (Eds.), *Researching women's lives from a feminist perspective* (pp. 125-148). London: Taylor & Francis.

Holmes, H. B., & Purdy, L. M. (Eds.). (1992). *Feminist perspectives in medical ethics.* Bloomington: Indiana University Press.

Hondagneu-Sotelo, P. (1992). Overcoming patriarchal constraints: The reconstruction of gender relations among Mexican immigrant women and men. *Gender & Society, 6,* 393-415.

hooks, b. (1984). *Feminist theory: From margin to center.* Boston: South End.

hooks, b. (1990). The politics of radical black subjectivity. In b. hooks, *Yearning: Race, gender, and cultural politics* (pp. 15-22). Boston: South End.

Huber, J. (1973). Symbolic interaction as a pragmatic perspective: The bias of emergent theory. *American Sociological Review, 38,* 274-284.

Huff, J. K. (1997). The sexual harassment of researchers by research subjects: Lessons from the field. In M. D. Schwartz (Ed.), *Researching sexual violence against women: Methodological and personal perspectives* (pp. 115-128). Thousand Oaks, CA: Sage.

Huisman, K. A. (1997). Studying violence against women of color: Problems faced by white women. In M. D. Schwartz (Ed.), *Researching sexual violence against women: Methodological and personal perspectives* (pp. 179-192). Thousand Oaks, CA: Sage.

Humphries, B. (1997). From critical thought to emancipatory action: Contradictory research goals. *Sociological Research Online, 2,* 1-9.

Hundleby, C. (1997). Where standpoint stands now. In S. J. Kenney & H. Kinsella (Eds.), *Politics and feminist standpoint theories* (pp. 25-44). New York: Haworth.

Hunt, L. M., Jordan, B., Irwin, S., & Browner, C. H. (1989). Compliance and the patient's perspective: Controlling symptoms in everyday life. *Culture, Medicine and Psychiatry, 13,* 315-334.

Hurtado, A. (1989). Relating to privilege: Seduction and rejection in the subordination of white women and women of color. *Signs, 14,* 833-855.

Hurtado, A., & Stewart, A. J. (1997). Through the looking glass: Implications of studying whiteness for feminist methods. In M. Fine, L. C. Powell, L. Weis, & L. M. Wong (Eds.), *Off white: Readings on race, power and society* (pp. 297-311). New York: Routledge.

Joffe, C. (1995). *Doctors of conscience: The struggle to provide abortion before and after Roe v. Wade.* Boston: Beacon.

Johannsen, A. M. (1992). Applied anthropology and post-modernist ethnography. *Human Organization, 51,* 71-81.

John, M. E. (1996). *Discrepant dislocations: Feminism, theory, and postcolonial histories.* Berkeley: University of California Press.

Jones, S. J. (1997). Reflexivity and feminist practice: Ethical dilemmas in negotiating meaning. *Feminism and Psychology, 7,* 348-353.

Kaplan, E. B. (1997). *Not our kind of girl: Unraveling the myths of black teenage motherhood.* Berkeley: University of California Press.

Kasper, A. (1994). A feminist qualitative methodology: A study of women with breast cancer. *Qualitative Sociology, 17,* 263-281.

Kaufert, P. A., & McKinlay, S. M. (1985). Estrogen-replacement therapy: The production of medical knowledge and the emergence of policy. In E. Lewin

& V. L. Olesen (Eds.), *Women, health and healing: Toward a new perspective* (pp. 113-138). London: Tavistock.

Kelly, L., Burton, S., & Regan, L. (1994). Researching women's lives or studying women's oppression? Reflections on what constitutes feminist research. In M. Maynard & J. Purvis (Eds.), *Researching women's lives from a feminist perspective* (pp. 27-48). London: Taylor & Francis.

Kennedy, E. L., & Davis, M. D. (1993). *Boots of leather, slippers of gold: The history of a lesbian community.* New York: Routledge.

Kenney, S. J., & Kinsella, H. (Eds.). (1997). *Politics and feminist standpoint theories.* New York: Haworth.

Kerber, L. (1998). *No constitutional right to be ladies: Women and the obligation of citizenship.* New York: Hill & Wang.

Kessler, S., & McKenna, W. (1978). *Gender: An ethnomethodological approach.* New York: John Wiley.

Kincheloe, J. L. (1997). Fiction formulas: Critical constructivism and the representation of reality. In W. G. Tierney & Y. S. Lincoln (Eds.), *Representation and the text: Re-framing the narrative voice* (pp. 57-80). Albany: State University of New York Press.

Kirby, V. (1991). Comment on Mascia-Lees, Sharpe, and Cohen's "The postmodernist turn in anthropology: Cautions from a feminist perspective." *Signs, 16,* 394-400.

Kitzinger, C., & Wilkinson, S. (1997). Validating women's experiences? Dilemmas in feminist research. *Feminism and Psychology, 7,* 566-574.

Koehn, D. (1998). *Rethinking feminist ethics: Care, trust and empathy.* New York: Routledge.

Komarovsky, M. (1988). The new feminist scholarship: Some precursors and polemics. *Journal of Marriage and the Family, 50,* 585-593.

Komarovsky, M. (1991). Some reflections on the feminist scholarship in sociology. *Annual Review of Sociology, 17,* 1-25.

Kondo, D. K. (1990). *Crafting selves: Power, gender, and discourses of identity in a Japanese workplace.* Chicago: University of Chicago Press.

Kondo, D. K. (1995). Bad girls: Theater, women of color, and the politics of representation. In R. Behar & D. A. Gordon (Eds.), *Women writing culture* (pp. 49-64). Berkeley: University of California Press.

Krieger, S. (1983). *The mirror dance: Identity in a women's community.* Philadelphia: Temple University Press.

Krieger, S. (1991). *Social science and the self: Personal essays on an art form.* New Brunswick, NJ: Rutgers University Press.

Larrabee, M. J. (Ed.). (1993). *An ethic of care: Feminist and interdisciplinary perspectives.* New York: Routledge.

Lather, P. (1991). *Getting smart: Feminist research and pedagogy with/in the postmodern.* New York: Routledge.

Lather, P. (1993). Fertile obsession: Validity after poststructuralism. *Sociological Quarterly, 34,* 673-693.

Lather, P., & Smithies, C. (1997). *Troubling the angels: Women living with HIV/AIDS.* Boulder, CO: Westview.

Lawthom, R. (1997). What can I do? A feminist researcher in non-feminist research. *Feminism and Psychology, 7,* 533-538.

Lee, C. K. (1998). *Gender and the south China miracle: Two worlds of factory women.* Berkeley: University of California Press.

Lemert, C. (1992). Subjectivity's limit: The unsolved riddle of the standpoint. *Sociological Theory, 10,* 63-72.

Lemert, C. (1997). *Postmodernism is not what you think.* Malden, MA: Blackwell.

Lempert, L. B. (1994). Narrative analysis of abuse: Connecting the personal, the rhetorical, and the structural. *Journal of Contemporary Ethnography, 22,* 411-441.

Lewin, E. (1991). Writing gay and lesbian culture: What the natives have to say for themselves. *American Ethnologist, 18,* 786-792.

Lewin, E. (1993). *Lesbian mothers: Accounts of gender in American culture.* Ithaca, NY: Cornell University Press.

Lewin, E. (1996a). Introduction. In E. Lewin (Ed.), *Inventing lesbian cultures in America* (pp. 1-11). Boston: Beacon.

Lewin, E. (Ed.). (1996b). *Inventing lesbian cultures in America.* Boston: Beacon.

Lewin, E. (1998). *Recognizing ourselves: Ceremonies of lesbian and gay commitment.* New York: Columbia University Press.

Lewin, E., & Leap, W. L. (Eds.). (1996). *Out in the field: Reflections of lesbian and gay anthropologists.* Urbana: University of Illinois Press.

Light, L., & Kleiber, N. (1981). Interactive research in a feminist setting. In D. A. Messerschmidt (Ed.), *Anthropologists at home in North America: Methods and issues in the study of one's own society* (pp. 167-184). Cambridge: Cambridge University Press.

Lincoln, Y. S. (1993). I and thou: Method, voice, and roles in research with the silenced. In D. McLaughlin & W. G. Tierney (Eds.), *Naming silenced lives: Personal narratives and processes of educational change* (pp. 20-27). New York: Routledge.

Lincoln, Y. S. (1995). Emerging criteria for quality in qualitative and interpretive inquiry. *Qualitative Inquiry, 1,* 275-289.

Lincoln, Y. S. (1997). Self, subject, audience, text: Living at the edge, writing in the margins. In W. G. Tierney & Y. S. Lincoln (Eds.), *Representation and the text: Re-framing the narrative voice* (pp. 37-56). Albany: State University of New York Press.

Lincoln, Y. S., & Guba, E. G. (1985). *Naturalistic inquiry.* Beverly Hills, CA: Sage.

Longino, H. (1990). *Science as social knowledge.* Princeton, NJ: Princeton University Press.

Longino, H. (1993). Subjects, power, and knowledge: Description and prescription in feminist philosophies of science. In L. Alcoff & E. Potter (Eds.), *Feminist epistemologies* (pp. 101-120). New York: Routledge.

Lorber, J. (1975). Women and medical sociology: Invisible professionals and ubiquitous patients. In M. M. Millman & R. M. Kanter (Eds.), *Another voice: Feminist perspectives on social life and social science* (pp. 75-105). Garden City, NY: Anchor.

Lorber, J. (1994). *Paradoxes of gender.* New Haven, CT: Yale University Press.

Lubelska, C., & Mathews, J. (1997). Disability issues in the politics and processes of feminist studies. In M. Ang-Lygate, C. Corrin, & M. S. Henry (Eds.), *Desperately seeking sisterhood: Still challenging and building* (pp. 117-137). London: Taylor & Francis.

Luker, K. (1984). *Abortion and the politics of motherhood.* Berkeley: University of California Press.

Luker, K. (1996). *Dubious conceptions: The politics of teenage pregnancy.* Cambridge: Harvard University Press.

Lupton, D. (1995). *The imperative of health: Public health and the regulated body.* Thousand Oaks, CA: Sage.

Lykes, M. B. (1989). Dialogue with Guatemalan Indian women: Critical perspectives on constructing collaborative research. In R. K. Unger (Ed.), *Representations: Social constructions of gender* (pp. 167-184). Amityville, NY: Baywood.

Lykes, M. B. (1994). Whose meeting at which crossroads? A response to Brown and Gilligan. *Feminism and Psychology, 4,* 345-349.

Lykes, M. B. (1997). Activist participatory research among the Maya of Guatemala: Constructing meanings from situated knowledge. *Journal of Social Issues, 53,* 725-746.

MacKinnon, C. (1982). Feminism, Marxism, method and the state: An agenda for theory. *Signs, 7,* 515-544.

MacKinnon, C. (1983). Feminism, Marxism and the state: Toward feminist jurisprudence. *Signs, 8,* 635-658.

Maines, D. (1982). In search of the mesostructure: Studies in the negotiated order. *Urban Life, 11,* 267-279.

Manning, K. (1997). Authenticity in constructivist inquiry: Methodological considerations without prescription. *Qualitative Inquiry, 3,* 93-116.

Manning, R. C. (1992). *Speaking from the heart: A feminist perspective on ethics.* Boston: Rowan & Littlefield.

Martin, E. (1987). *The woman in the body: A cultural analysis of reproduction.* Boston: Beacon.

Martin, E. (1999). The woman in the flexible body. In A. E. Clarke & V. L. Olesen (Eds.), *Revisioning women, health and healing: Feminist, cultural and technoscience perspectives* (pp. 97-118). New York: Routledge.

Mascia-Lees, F. E., Sharpe, P., & Cohen, C. B. (1989). The postmodernist turn in anthropology: Cautions from a feminist perspective. *Signs, 15,* 7-33.

Mascia-Lees, F. E., Sharpe, P., & Cohen, C. B. (1991). Reply to Kirby. *Signs, 16,* 401-408.

Matsuda, M. (1992). *Called from within: Early women lawyers of Hawaii.* Honolulu: University of Hawaii Press.

Matsuda, M. (1996). *Where is your body? And other essays on race, gender and the law.* Boston: Beacon.

Mattley, C. (1997). Field research with phone sex workers: Managing the researcher's emotions. In M. D. Schwartz (Ed.), *Researching sexual violence against women: Methodological and personal perspectives* (pp. 101-114). Thousand Oaks, CA: Sage.

Mauthner, N., & Doucet, A. (1998). Reflections on a voice-centered relational method: Analyzing maternal and domestic voices. In J. Ribbens & R. Edwards (Eds.), *Feminist dilemmas in qualitative research: Public knowledge and private lives* (pp. 119-146). Thousand Oaks, CA: Sage.

May, K. A. (1980). Informed consent and role conflict. In A. J. Davis & J. C. Krueger (Eds.), *Patients, nurses, ethics* (pp. 109-118). New York: American Journal of Nursing.

Maynard, M. (1994a). Race, gender and the concept of "difference" in feminist thought. In H. Afshar & M. Maynard (Eds.), *The dynamics of "race" and gender: Some feminist interventions* (pp. 9-25). London: Taylor & Francis.

Maynard, M. (1994b). Methods, practice and epistemology: The debate about feminism and research. In M. Maynard & J. Purvis (Eds.), *Researching women's lives from a feminist perspective* (pp. 10-26). London: Taylor & Francis.

Maynard, M. (1996). Challenging the boundaries: Towards an anti-racist women's studies. In M. Maynard & J. Purvis (Eds.), *New frontiers in women's studies: Knowledge, identity and nationalism* (pp. 11-29). London: Taylor & Francis.

Maynard, M., & Purvis, J. (Eds.). (1994). *Researching women's lives from a feminist perspective.* London: Taylor & Francis.

McCall, M. M., & Becker, H. S. (1990). Performance science. *Social Problems, 37,* 116-132.

McIntyre, A., & Lykes, M. B. (1998). Who's the boss? Confronting whiteness and power differences within a feminist mentoring relationship in participatory action research. *Feminism and Psychology, 8,* 427-444.

McKenna, W., & Kessler, S. (1997). Comment on Hawkesworth's "Confounding gender": Who needs gender theory? *Signs, 22,* 687-691.

McWilliam, E. (1997). Performing between the posts: Authority, posture and contemporary feminist scholarship. In W. G. Tierney & Y. S. Lincoln (Eds.), *Representation and the text: Re-framing the narrative voice* (pp. 219-232). Albany: State University of New York Press.

Mies, M. (1993). Towards a methodology for feminist research. In M. Hammersley (Ed.), *Social research: Philosophy, politics and practice* (pp. 64-82). London: Sage.

Millen, D. (1997). Some methodological and epistemological issues raised by doing feminist research on non-feminist women. *Sociological Research Online, 2,* 2-18.

Miller, G., & Dingwall, R. (Eds.). (1997). *Context and method in qualitative research.* Thousand Oaks, CA: Sage.

Miller, J. (1997). Researching violence against street prostitutes: Issues of epistemology, methodology, and ethics. In M. D. Schwartz (Ed.), *Researching sexual violence against women: Methodological and personal perspectives* (pp. 144-156). Thousand Oaks, CA: Sage.

Mohammed, P. (1998, Summer). Rethinking Caribbean difference [Special issue]. *Feminist Review.*

Mohanty, C. T. (1988). Under Western eyes: Feminist scholarship and colonial discourses. *Feminist Review, 30,* 60-88.

Montini, T. (1997). Resist and redirect: Physicians respond to breast cancer informed consent legislation. *Women and Health, 12,* 85-105.

Morawski, J. (1990). Toward the unimagined: Feminism and epistemology in psychology. In R. Hare-Mustin & J. Marecek (Eds.), *Making a difference: Psychology and the construction of gender* (pp. 159-183). New Haven, CT: Yale University Press.

Morawski, J. (1994). *Practicing feminisms, reconstructing psychology: Notes on a liminal science.* Ann Arbor: University of Michigan Press.

Morawski, J. (1997). The science behind feminist research methods. *Journal of Social Issues, 53,* 667-681.

Morris, M. (1988). *The pirate's fiancée: Feminism, reading, postmodernism.* London: Verso.

Morris, M. (1998). *Too soon, too late: History in popular culture.* Bloomington: Indiana University Press.

Mukherjee, B. (1994). *The holder of the world.* London: Virago.

Murcott, A. (1993). On conceptions of good food; Or, anthropology between the laity and professionals. *Anthropology in Action, 14,* 11-13.

Naples, N. (1996). A feminist revisiting of the insider/outsider debate: The "outsider phenomenon" in rural Iowa. *Qualitative Sociology, 19,* 83-106.

Narayan, K. (1997). How native is a "native" anthropologist? In L. Lamphere, H. Ragone, & P. Zavella (Eds.), *Situated lives: Gender and culture in everyday life* (pp. 23-41). New York: Routledge.

Narayan, U. (1997). *Dislocating cultures: Identities, traditions, and Third World feminism.* New York: Routledge.

Narrigan, D., Zones, J. S., Worcester, N., & Grad, M. J. (1997). Research to improve women's health: An agenda for equity. In S. B. Ruzek, V. L. Olesen,

& A. E. Clarke (Eds.), *Women's health: Complexities and differences* (pp. 551-579). Columbus: Ohio State University Press.

Nelson, C., & Altorki, S. (Eds.). (1997). Arab Regional Women's Studies Workshop [Special issue]. *Cairo Papers in Social Science, 20*(3).

Nelson, M. K. (1990). *Negotiated care: The experience of family day care givers.* Philadelphia: Temple University Press.

Nettleton, S. (1991). Wisdom, diligence and teeth: Discursive practices and the creation of mothers. *Sociology of Health and Illness, 13,* 98-111.

Nicholson, L. J. (Ed.). (1990). *Feminism/postmodernism.* New York: Routledge.

Nicholson, L. J. (Ed.). (1997). *The second wave: A reader in feminist theory.* New York: Routledge.

Nielsen, J. M. (Ed.). (1990a). *Feminist research methods: Exemplary readings in the social sciences.* Boulder, CO: Westview.

Nielsen, J. M. (1990b). Introduction. In J. M. Nielsen (Ed.), *Feminist research methods: Exemplary readings in the social sciences* (pp. 1-37). Boulder, CO: Westview.

Oakley, A. (1981). Interviewing women: A contradiction in terms. In H. Roberts (Ed.), *Doing feminist research* (pp. 30-61). London: Routledge.

Ogasawara, Y. (1998). *Office ladies and salaried men: Power, gender, and work in Japanese companies.* Berkeley: University of California Press.

O'Leary, C. M. (1997). Counteridentification or counterhegemony? Transforming feminist standpoint theory. In S. J. Kenney & H. Kinsella (Eds.), *Politics and feminist standpoint theories* (pp. 45-72). New York: Haworth.

Olesen, V. L. (1975). Rage is not enough: Scholarly feminism and research in women's health. In V. L. Olesen (Ed.), *Women and their health: Research implications for a new era* (DHEW Publication No. HRA-3138; pp. 1-2). Washington, DC: National Center for Health Services Research.

Olesen, V. L. (1993). Unfinished business: The problematics of women, health and healing. *Science of Caring, 5,* 27-32.

Olesen, V. L. (1997). Who cares? Women as informal and formal caregivers. In S. B. Ruzek, V. L. Olesen, & A. E. Clarke (Eds.), *Women's health: Complexities and differences* (pp. 397-424). Columbus: Ohio State University Press.

Olesen, V. L., Taylor, D., Ruzek, S. B., & Clarke, A. E. (1997). Strengths and strongholds in women's health research. In S. B. Ruzek, V. L. Olesen, & A. E. Clarke (Eds.), *Women's health: Complexities and differences* (pp. 580-606). Columbus: Ohio State University Press.

Olesen, V. L., & Clarke, A. E. (1999). Resisting closure, embracing uncertainties, creating agendas. In A. E. Clarke & V. L. Olesen (Eds.), *Revisioning women, health and healing: Feminist, cultural and technoscience perspectives* (pp. 355-357). New York: Routledge.

Ong, A. (1995). Women out of China: Traveling tales and traveling theories in postcolonial feminism. In R. Behar & D. A. Gordon (Eds.), *Women writing culture* (pp. 350-372). Berkeley: University of California Press.

Opie, A. (1992). Qualitative research, appropriation of the "other" and empowerment. *Feminist Review, 40,* 52-69.

Paget, M. (1990). Performing the text. *Journal of Contemporary Ethnography, 19,* 136-155.

Patai, D. (1994, February 23). Sick and tired of nouveau solipsism. *Chronicle of Higher Education,* p. A52.

Petchesky, R. P. (1985). Abortion in the 1980's: Feminist morality and women's health. In E. Lewin & V. L. Olesen (Eds.), *Women, health and healing: Toward a new perspective* (pp. 139-173). London: Tavistock.

Pfeffer, R. (1997). *Children of poverty: Studies on the effect of single parenthood, the feminization of poverty and homelessness.* New York: Garland.

Phoenix, A. (1994). Practicing feminist research: The intersection of gender and "race" in the research process. In M. Maynard & J. Purvis (Eds.), *Researching women's lives from a feminist perspective* (pp. 35-45). London: Taylor & Francis.

Pierce, J. L. (1995). *Gender trials: Emotional lives in contemporary law firms.* Berkeley: University of California Press.

Puar, J. K. (1996). Resituating discourses of "whiteness" and "Asianness" in northern England: Second-generation Sikh women and constructions of identity. In M. Maynard & J. Purvis (Eds.), *New frontiers in women's studies: Knowledge, identity and nationalism* (pp. 125-150). London: Taylor & Francis.

Ramazanoglu, C. (1989). Improving on sociology: The problems of taking a feminist standpoint. *Sociology, 23,* 427-442.

Reay, D. (1996a). Dealing with difficult differences. *Feminism and Psychology, 6,* 443-456.

Reay, D. (1996b). Insider perspectives or stealing the words out of women's mouths: Interpretation in the research process. *Feminist Review, 53,* 57-73.

Reay, D. (1998). Classifying feminist research: Exploring the psychological impact of social class on mothers' involvement in children's schooling. *Feminism and Psychology, 8,* 155-171.

Reinharz, S. (1992). *Feminist methods in social research.* Oxford: Oxford University Press.

Renzetti, C. M. (1997). Confessions of a reformed positivist: Feminist participatory research as good social science. In M. D. Schwartz (Ed.), *Researching sexual violence against women: Methodological and personal perspectives* (pp. 131-143). Thousand Oaks, CA: Sage.

Ribbens, J., & Edwards, R. (Eds.). (1998). *Feminist dilemmas in qualitative research: Public knowledge and private lives.* Thousand Oaks, CA: Sage.

Richardson, L. (1992). The consequences of poetic representation: Writing the other, rewriting the self. In C. Ellis & M. G. Flaherty (Eds.), *Investigating subjectivity: Research on lived experience* (pp. 125-140). Newbury Park, CA: Sage.

Richardson, L. (1993). The case of the skipped line: Poetics, dramatics and transgressive validity. *Sociological Quarterly, 34,* 695-710.

Richardson, L. (1997). *Fields of play: Constructing an academic life.* New Brunswick, NJ: Rutgers University Press.

Riessman, C. K. (1987). When gender is not enough: Women interviewing women. *Gender & Society, 2,* 172-207.

Riessman, C. K. (1990). *Divorce talk: Women and men make sense of personal relationships.* New Brunswick, NJ: Rutgers University Press.

Ring, J. (1987). Toward a feminist epistemology. *American Journal of Political Science, 31,* 753-772.

Roberts, H. (Ed.). (1981). *Doing feminist research.* London: Routledge.

Rollins, J. (1985). *Between women: Domestics and their employers.* Philadelphia: Temple University Press.

Roman, L. G. (1992). The political significance of other ways of narrating ethnography: A feminist materialist approach. In M. D. LeCompte, W. L. Millroy, & J. Preissle (Eds.), *The handbook of qualitative research in education* (pp. 555-594). New York: Academic Press.

Romero, M. (1992). *Maid in the U.S.A.* London: Routledge.

Rosenau, P. M. (1992). *Post-modernism and the social sciences: Insights, inroads, and intrusions.* Princeton, NJ: Princeton University Press.

Ruzek, S. B. (1978). *The women's health movement: Feminist alternatives to medical care.* New York: Praeger.

Ruzek, S. B., Olesen, V. L., & Clarke, A. E. (Eds.). (1997). *Women's health: Complexities and differences.* Columbus: Ohio State University Press.

Sacks, K. B. (1988). *Caring by the hour: Women, work and organizing at Duke University Medical Center.* Urbana: University of Illinois Press.

Scarce, R. (1994). (No) trial (but) tribulations: When courts and ethnography conflict. *Journal of Contemporary Ethnography, 34,* 123-149.

Scheper-Hughes, N. (1983). Introduction: The problem of bias in androcentric and feminist anthropology. *Women's Studies, 19,* 109-116.

Scheper-Hughes, N. (1992). *Death without weeping: The violence of everyday life in Brazil.* Berkeley: University of California Press.

Scheurich, J. J. (1997). The masks of validity: A deconstructive investigation. In J. J. Scheurich, *Research method in the postmodern* (pp. 80-93). London: Falmer.

Schiffrin, A. (1998, November 20). Transnational publishing in microcosm: The Frankfurt Book Fair. *Chronicle of Higher Education,* pp. B6-B7.

Scott, J. (1991). The evidence of experience. *Critical Inquiry, 17,* 773-779.

Scott, J. (1997). Comment on Hawkesworth's "Confounding gender." *Signs, 22,* 697-702.

Seigfried, C. H. (1996). *Pragmatism and feminism: Reweaving the social fabric.* Chicago: University of Chicago Press.

Sherwin, S. (1992). *No longer patient: Feminist ethics and health care.* Philadelphia: Temple University Press.

Shogan, D. (1990). Comment on Hawkesworth's "Knowers, knowing, known: Feminist theory and claims of truth." *Signs, 15,* 424-425.

Shostak, M. (1981). *Nisa: The life and words of a !Kung woman.* Cambridge, MA: Harvard University Press.

Skeggs, B. (1994). Situating the production of feminist ethnography. In M. Maynard & J. Purvis (Eds.), *Researching women's lives from a feminist perspective* (pp. 72-92). London: Taylor & Francis.

Smith, D. E. (1974). Women's perspective as a radical critique of sociology. *Sociological Inquiry, 4,* 1-13.

Smith, D. E. (1987). *The everyday world as problematic.* Boston: Northeastern University Press.

Smith, D. E. (1989). Sociological theory: Methods of writing patriarchy. In R. A. Wallace (Ed.), *Feminism and sociological theory* (pp. 34-64). Newbury Park, CA: Sage.

Smith, D. E. (1990a). *The conceptual practices of power: A feminist sociology of knowledge.* Boston: Northeastern University Press.

Smith, D. E. (1990b). *Texts, facts and femininity: Exploring the relations of ruling.* London: Routledge.

Smith, D. E. (1992). Sociology from women's experience: A reaffirmation. *Sociological Theory, 10,* 88-98.

Smith, D. E. (1993). High noon in Textland: A critique of Clough. *Sociological Quarterly, 34,* 183-192.

Smith, D. E. (1996). Telling the truth after postmodernism. *Symbolic Interaction, 19,* 171-202.

Smith, S. G. (1997). Comment on Hawkesworth's "Confounding gender." *Signs, 22,* 691-697.

Spivak, G. C. (1988). Subaltern studies: Deconstructing historiography. In G. C. Spivak, *In other worlds: Essays in cultural politics* (pp. 201-221). London: Routledge.

Stacey, J. (1988). Can there be a feminist ethnography? *Women's Studies International Forum, 11,* 21-27.

Stacey, J. (1998). *Brave new families: Stories of domestic upheaval in late-twentieth-century America.* Berkeley: University of California Press.

Stacey, J., & Thorne, B. (1985). The missing feminist revolution in sociology. *Social Problems, 32,* 301-316.

Stacey, J., & Thorne, B. (1996). Is sociology still missing its feminist revolution? *Perspectives: The ASA Theory Section Newsletter, 18,* 1-3.

Stacey, M. (1992). *Regulating British medicine: The General Medical Council.* New York: John Wiley.

Standing, K. (1998). Writing the voices of the less powerful. In J. Ribbens & R. Edwards (Eds.), *Feminist dilemmas in qualitative research: Public knowledge and private lives* (pp. 186-202). Thousand Oaks, CA: Sage.

Stanley, L., & Wise, S. (1983). *Breaking out: Feminist consciousness and feminist research.* London: Routledge & Kegan Paul.

Stanley, L., & Wise, S. (1990). Method, methodology and epistemology in feminist research processes. In L. Stanley (Ed.), *Feminist praxis: Research, theory and epistemology in feminist sociology* (pp. 20-60). London: Routledge.

Stanley, L. (Ed.). (1990). *Feminist praxis: Research, theory and epistemology in feminist sociology.* London: Routledge.

Stevens, P. E., & Hall, J. H. (1991). A critical historical analysis of the medical construction of lesbianism. *International Journal of Health Services, 21,* 271-307.

Strathern, M. (1987). An awkward relationship: The case of feminism and anthropology. *Signs, 12,* 684-790.

Taylor, D., & Dower, K. (1995). Toward a women centered health care system: Women's experiences, women's voices, women's needs. *Health Care for Women International, 18,* 407-422.

Taylor, V. (1998). Feminist methodology in social movements research. *Qualitative Sociology, 21,* 357-379.

Taylor, V., & Whittier, N. (Eds.). (1998). Gender and social movements: Part 1 [Special issue]. *Gender & Society, 12*(6).

Taylor, V., & Whittier, N. (Eds.). (1999). Gender and social movements: Part 2 [Special issue]. *Gender & Society, 13*(1).

Terry, J. (1994). Theorizing deviant historiography. In A. L. Shapiro (Ed.), *Feminists revision history* (pp 20-30). New Brunswick, NJ: Rutgers University Press.

Tierney, W. G., & Lincoln, Y. S. (1997). Introduction: Explorations and discoveries. In W. G. Tierney & Y. S. Lincoln (Eds.), *Representation and the text: Reframing the narrative voice.* Albany: State University of New York Press.

Todd, A. D. (1989). *Intimate adversaries: Cultural conflict between doctors and women patients.* Philadelphia: University of Pennsylvania Press.

Tom, W. (1989). *Effects of feminist research on research methods.* Toronto: Wilfred Laurier.

Tong, R. (1989). *Feminist thought: A comprehensive introduction.* Boulder, CO: Westview.

Tong, R. (1997). *Feminist approaches to bioethics: Theoretical reflections and practical applications.* Boulder, CO: Westview.

Trinh T. M. (1989). *Woman, native, other: Writing postcoloniality and feminism.* Bloomington: Indiana University Press.

Trinh T. M. (1992). *Framer framed.* New York: Routledge.

Tronto, J. C. (1993). *Moral boundaries: A political argument for an ethic of care.* New York: Routledge.

Tuana, N. (1993). With many voices: Feminism and theoretical pluralism. In P. England (Ed.), *Theory on gender/feminism on theory* (pp. 281-289). New York: Aldine de Gruyter.

Visweswaran, K. (1994). *Fictions of feminist ethnography.* Minneapolis: University of Minnesota Press.

Walkerdine, V. (1995). Postmodernity, subjectivity and the media. In T. Ibanez & L. Iniguez (Eds.), *Critical social psychology* (pp. 169-177). London: Sage.

Warren, C. A. B. (1988). *Gender issues in field research.* Newbury Park, CA: Sage.

Wasserfall, R. R. (1997). Reflexivity, feminism, and difference. In R. Hertz (Ed.), *Reflexivity and voice* (pp. 150-168). Thousand Oaks, CA: Sage.

Welton, K. (1997). Nancy Hartsock's standpoint theory: From content to "concrete multiplicity." In S. J. Kenney & H. Kinsella (Eds.), *Politics and feminist standpoint theories* (pp. 7-24). New York: Haworth.

West, C., & Zimmerman, D. (1987). Doing gender. *Gender & Society, 1,* 125-151.

Westkott, M. (1979). Feminist criticism of the social sciences. *Harvard Educational Review, 4,* 422-430.

Weston, K. (1991). *Families we chose: Lesbians, gays, kinship.* New York: Columbia University Press.

Weston, K. (1996). Requiem for a street fighter. In E. Lewin & W. L. Leap (Eds.), *Out in the field: Reflections of lesbian and gay anthropologists* (pp. 274-286). Urbana: University of Illinois Press.

Wheatley, E. (1994). How can we engender ethnography with a feminist imagination? A rejoinder to Judith Stacey. *Women's Studies International Forum, 17,* 403-416.

Williams, P. J. (1991). *The alchemy of race and rights.* Cambridge, MA: Harvard University Press.

Wolf, D. L. (Ed.). (1996a). *Feminist dilemmas in fieldwork.* Boulder, CO: Westview.

Wolf, D. L. (1996b). Situating feminist dilemmas in fieldwork. In D. L. Wolf (Ed.), *Feminist dilemmas in fieldwork* (pp. 1-55). Boulder, CO: Westview.

Wolf, M. A. (1992). *A thrice-told tale: Feminism, postmodernism, and ethnographic responsibility.* Stanford, CA: Stanford University Press.

Wolf, M. A. (1996). Afterword: Musings from an old gray wolf. In D. L. Wolf (Ed.), *Feminist dilemmas in fieldwork* (pp. 215-222). Boulder, CO: Westview.

Wyche, K. F., & Crosby, F. J. (Eds.). (1996). *Women's ethnicities: Journeys through psychology.* Boulder, CO: Westview.

Yadlon, S. (1997). Skinny women and good mothers: The rhetoric of risk, control and culpability in the production of knowledge about breast cancer. *Feminist Studies, 23,* 645-677.

Zavella, P. (1987). *Women's work and Chicano families: Cannery workers of the Santa Clara Valley.* Ithaca, NY: Cornell University Press.

Zavella, P. (1996). Feminist insider dilemmas: Constructing ethnic identity with Chicana informants. In D. L. Wolf (Ed.), *Feminist dilemmas in fieldwork* (pp. 138-159). Boulder, CO: Westview.

9

Racialized
Discourses and
Ethnic Epistemologies

Gloria Ladson-Billings

I think, therefore I am.
    —René Descartes, Le Discours de la Méthode, 1637

Ubuntu [I am because we are].

    —African saying

◆ When René Descartes proclaimed that he thought himself into
    being, he articulated a central premise upon which European (and
Euro-American) worldviews and epistemology rest—that the individual
mind is the source of knowledge and existence. In contrast, the African
saying "*Ubuntu*," translated "I am because we are," asserts that the individual's existence (and knowledge) is contingent upon relationships with
others. These two divergent perspectives represent two distinct and often
conflicting epistemological stances with which the academy has grappled
since the mid- to late 1960s. The two traditions are not merely matters of
"alternatives" or "preferences," but rather represent a deliberate choice
between hegemony (Gramsci, 1971) and liberation. This strongly worded

statement is not meant to be polemical; it is meant to be urgent. I have chosen to explore this dichotomy to demonstrate the "effectively aggressive manner" (Ani, 1994) of the Euro-American epistemological tradition. And I will trace how different discourses and epistemologies serve as both counterknowledge and liberating tools for people who have suffered (and continue to suffer) from the Euro-American "regime of truth" (Foucault, 1973).

It is important to reinforce that the concept of epistemology is more than a "way of knowing." An epistemology is a "system of knowing" that has both an internal logic and external validity. This distinction between an epistemology and "ways of knowing" is not a trivial one. For example, literary scholars have created distinctions between literary genres such that some works are called *literature* whereas other works are termed *folklore*. Not surprisingly, the literature of peoples of color is more likely to fall into the folklore category. As a consequence, folklore is seen as less rigorous, less scholarly, and, perhaps, less culturally valuable than literature. The claim of an epistemological ground is a crucial legitimating force.

Epistemology is linked intimately to worldview. Shujaa (1997) argues that worldviews and systems of knowledge are symbiotic—that is, how one views the world is influenced by what knowledge one possesses, and what knowledge one is capable of possessing is influenced deeply by one's worldview. Thus the conditions under which people live and learn shape both their knowledge and their worldviews. The process of developing a worldview that differs from the dominant worldview requires active intellectual work on the part of the knower, because schools, society, and the structure and production of knowledge are designed to create individuals who internalize the dominant worldview and knowledge production and acquisition processes. The hegemony of the dominant paradigm makes it more than just another way to view the world—it claims to be the only legitimate way to view the world. In this chapter I argue that there are well-developed systems of knowledge, or epistemologies, that stand in contrast to the dominant Euro-American epistemology.

I look briefly at the ideological underpinnings of the Euro-American epistemological tradition through its construction of race, and then describe how the Euro-American tradition conflicts with those traditions established by people who have been subordinated in U.S. society and the world. Next, I investigate the notions of double consciousness (Du Bois, 1903/1953), *mestiza* consciousness (Anzaldúa, 1987), and "tribal secrets" (Warrior, 1995) discovered and uncovered by scholars of color to explicate the ways that discursive, social, and institutional structures have created a sense of "otherness" for those who are outside of the dominant culture paradigm. Then I explore two theoretical notions, "alterity" (Wynter, 1992) and "critical race theory" (Delgado, 1995a), as rubrics for considering the scholarship of racial and ethnic "others." Finally, I conclude the chapter with an examination of what these alternate paradigms mean for qualitative research methods.

◆ The Cultural Logic of the Eurocentric Paradigm

> Traditional scientific method can't tell you where you ought to go, unless where you ought to go is a continuation of where you were going in the past.
>
> —Robert M. Pirsig,
> Zen and the Art of Motorcycle Maintenance, 1972

Ani (1994) says, "Rob the universe of its richness, deny the significance of the symbolic, simplify phenomena until it becomes mere object, and you have a knowable quantity. Here begins and ends the European epistemological mode" (p. 29). One such example of this epistemological stance is the way the construct of race has been formulated in the West (Omi & Winant, 1994). New languages and a new regime of truth (Foucault, 1973) were constituted around race. These new languages became "public" languages that are systems of knowledge whose object of inquiry is the social order in which the knower and inquirer are always already subjects.

Wynter (1992) argues that "such systems of knowledge, as 'acts of communication' which influence the behaviors of those being studied, are always generated from the 'paradigm of value and authority' on whose basis the order is instituted" (p. 21). The idea that "there exist three races, and that these races are 'Caucasoid,' 'Negroid,' and 'Mongoloid' is rooted in the European imagination of the Middle Ages, which encompassed only Europe, Africa, and the Near East" (Haney López, 1995, p. 194). The codification of this three-races theory occurred in the treatise of Count Arthur de Gobineau's *Essays on the Inequality of Races,* published in France in 1853-1855. That Gobineau excluded the peoples of the Americas, the Indian subcontinent, East and Southeast Asia, and Oceania (those living

400

outside of the European imagination) reflects social and political decisions, not scientific ones.

Appleby, Hunt, and Jacob (1994) argue that by the 18th century, a small group of reformers established science as the "new foundation for truth" (p. 15). This new truth was much like the older truth established by the Christian church in that it transferred "a habit of mind associated with religiosity—the conviction that transcendent and absolute truth could be known—to the new mechanical understanding of the natural world" (p. 15). Eventually, this mode of thought and conviction was taken up by other forms of inquiry.

This new mode of thought, coming out of a period termed the Enlightenment, suggested that scientific knowledge was pure, elegant, and simple. Natural science could be summarized by its laws and employed an experimental method to seek truth. This mode of thought reasoned that everything from human biology to the art of governing could and should imitate science. Appleby et al. (1994) call this model of science heroic, "because it made scientific geniuses into cultural heroes" (p. 15). They note:

> Until quite recently, heroic science reigned supreme. The heroic model equated science with reason: disinterested, impartial, and, if followed closely, a guarantee of progress in this world. Science took its character from nature itself, which was presumed to be composed solely of matter in motion and hence to be "neutral." . . . The neutral, value-free, objective image of science inherited from the Enlightenment had wide influence in every discipline until well into the postwar era. (pp. 15-16)

This Enlightenment thinking permeated the thinking of the leaders of the American Revolution. However, these men—Washington, Jefferson, Madison, and others—had to rationalize their commitment to liberty, justice, and equality with the fact that they endorsed slavery (Zinn, 1980). Rather than being bound by a religious code that insisted on the dignity and worth of all people (however, a case for master-servant relationships was often made about Christianity), these leaders of the revolution relied on science to justify the injustice of slavery. Jefferson, in his *Notes on the State of Virginia* (1784/1954), insisted that Blacks and Whites could never live together because there were "real distinctions" that "nature" had made between the two races. But we know that there is no biological basis to this concept of race. There are no genetic characteristics possessed by all the members of any group (Lewontin, Rose, & Kamin, 1984). Indeed, even the Enlightenment science demonstrates that there are more intragroup differences than intergroup ones. Current thinking about race argues that it is a social construction, and the process by which racial meanings arise is termed *racial formation* (Haney López, 1995).

Consider how this racial formation operates. According to Haney López (1995), "In the early 1800s, people in the United States ascribed to Latin American nationalities and, separate from these, races. Thus, a Mexican might also be White, Indian, Black, or Asian" (pp. 196-197). However, by the mid-1800s, when animosity developed in the U.S. Southwest between Anglos and Mexicans, social prejudices developed. These social prejudices soon became legal ones, with laws designed to reflect and reify racial prejudices. Enlightenment notions of science (and later, law) did not work independent of prevailing discourses of racial and class superiority. This discourse of Enlightenment science allowed the dominant culture to define, distance, and objectify the other.

Scheurich and Young (1997) identify epistemological racism that exists in the research paradigms that dominate academic and scholarly products. The epistemological challenge that is being mounted by some scholars of color is not solely about racism, however; it is also about the nature of truth and reality. Rosaldo (1993) argues that, in what he terms the classic period (from about 1921 to 1971), "norms of distanced normalizing description gained a monopoly on objectivity. Their authority appeared so self-evident that they became the one and only legitimate form for telling the literal truth about other cultures. . . . All other modes of composition were marginalized or suppressed altogether" (p. 106). As classic norms gain exclusive rights to objective truth, ethnography (as well as other social science methods) becomes "as likely to reveal where objectivity lies as where it tells the truth" (p. 115).

◆ Multiple Consciousness, Multiple Jeopardy

> The Idea of a single civilization for everyone, implicit in the
> cult of progress and technique, impoverishes and mutilates us.
> —Octavio Paz,
> The Labyrinth of Solitude, 1961

Although some scholars of color have attempted to find legitimacy in the dominant paradigm (see, e.g., Williams, 1882-1883) other scholars have looked to a different epistemological frame to describe the experiences and knowledge systems of peoples outside of the dominant paradigm.[1] In 1903, W. E. B. Du Bois wrote in *The Souls of Black Folk* that the African American "ever feels his two-ness . . . two souls, two thoughts, two unreconciled strivings" (1903/1953, p. 5). Historian David Levering Lewis (1993) lauds this conception, stating:

> It was a revolutionary concept. It was not just revolutionary; the concept of the divided self was profoundly mystical, for Du Bois invested this double consciousness with a capacity to see incomparably farther and deeper. The African American . . . possessed the gift of "second sight in this American world," an intuitive faculty enabling him/her to see and say things about American society that possessed heightened moral validity. (p. 281)

Du Bois's notion of double consciousness is being read here not as a pathetic state of marginalization and exclusion, but rather as a transcendent position allowing one to see and understand positions of inclusion and exclusion—margins and mainstreams.

An important synchronic aspect of Du Bois's work is that both he and African American scholar Carter G. Woodson (1933) mounted challenges to the dominant Euro-American scholarly paradigm at about the same time as the formation of the Frankfurt school, out of which critical theories emerged. Max Horkheimer, Theodor Adorno, and Herbert Marcuse were the three primary scholars known for their engagement with the theoretical perspectives of Marx, Hegel, Kant, and Weber and their challenge to the "taken-for-granted empirical practices of American social science researchers" (Kincheloe & McLaren, 1998, p. 261). However, Du Bois and Woodson remain invisible in the scholarly canon except as "Negro" intellectuals concerned with the "Negro" problem. Their forthright and insightful critique of Euro-American scholarship was every bit as "critical" as that of the members of the Frankfurt school, but they would never be mentioned in the same breath as Horkheimer, Weber, Adorno, and Marcuse.

Du Bois's notion of double consciousness applies not only to African Americans but to any people who are constructed outside of the dominant paradigm. It is important to read this entire discussion of multiple consciousness as a description of complex phenomena. It is not an attempt to impose essentialized concepts of "Blackness," "Latina/oness," "Asian Americanness" or "Native Americanness" onto specific individuals or groups.[2] Rather, this discussion is about the multiple ways in which epistemological perspectives are developed. Indeed, the authors cited are not placed here to operate as proxies for what it means to be of a particular race, ethnicity, or cultural group. They are a few examples of the ways *particular* scholars have developed *specific* epistemological stances informed by their own cultural and identity positions.

Anzaldúa describes identities fractured not only by her gender, class, race, religion, and sexuality, but also by the reality of life along the U.S.-Mexico border. In one chapter of *Borderlands/La Frontera*, Anzaldúa (1987) explains the complexity of her life as a Mexican American living along the border:

> My "home" tongues are the languages I speak with my sister and brothers, with my friends. They are [*Pachuco* (called *calo*), Tex-Mex, Chicano Spanish, North Mexican Spanish dialect, and Standard Mexican Spanish, with Chicano Spanish] being closest to my heart. From school, the media and job situations, I've picked up standard and working class English. From Mamagrande Locha and from reading Spanish and Mexican literature, I've picked up Standard Spanish and Standard Mexican Spanish. From *los recien llegados,* Mexican immigrants and *braceros,* I learned Northern Mexican dialect. (pp. 55-56)

Anzaldúa's work, which reflects a long intellectual history of Chicanas/os (see Acuña, 1972; Almaguer, 1974; Balderrama, 1982; Gomez-Quinones, 1977; Mirande & Enriquez, 1979; Padilla, 1987; Paz, 1961), has become a part of what Delgado Bernal (1998) calls a Chicana feminist epistemology. Chicana writers such as Alarcón (1990), Castillo (1995), and the contributors to de la Torre and Pesquera's (1993) edited collection exemplify these intersections of race, class, and gender.

But it is important not to assume a unified Latino/a (or even Chicano/a) subject. Oboler (1995) challenges the amalgamation of Spanish speakers in the Western Hemisphere under the rubric *Hispanic:* The Hispanic label belies the problematic inherent in attempts to create a unitary consciousness from one that is much more complex and multiple than imagined or constructed. According to Oboler:

Insofar as the ethnic label Hispanic homogenizes the varied social and political experiences of 23 million people of different races, classes, languages, and national origins, genders, and religions, it is perhaps not so surprising that the meanings and uses of the term have become the subject of debate in the social sciences, government agencies, and much of the society at large. (p. 3)

Similarly, American Indians have had to grapple with what it means to be Indian. Despite a movement toward "Pan-Indianism" (Hertzberg, 1971), the cultures of American Indians are very diverse. Broad generalizations about American Indians can be essentializing. However, the U.S. federal government movement to "civilize" and detribalize Indian children through boarding schools helped various groups of Indians realize that the experiences of their tribes were not unique and that American Indians share any number of common problems and experiences (Snipp, 1995). Lomawaima (1995) argues that "since the federal government turned its attention to the 'problem' of civilizing Indians, its overt goal has been to educate Indians to be non-Indians" (p. 332). Much of the "double consciousness" Indians face revolves around issues of tribal sovereignty. A loss of sovereignty is amplified by four methods of disenfranchisement experienced by many American Indians (Lomawaima, 1995): relocation by colonial authorities (e.g., mission, reservations), systematic eradication of the native language, religious conversion (to Christianity), and restructured economies toward sedentary agriculture, small-scale craft industry, and gendered labor.

Warrior (1995) asks whether or not an investigation of early American Indian writers can have a significant impact on the way contemporary Native American intellectuals develop critical studies. He urges caution in understanding the scholarship of Fourth World formulations such as that of Ward Churchill and M. Annette Jaimes because it tends to be essentializing in its call for understanding American Indian culture as part of a global consciousness shared by all indigenous peoples in all periods of history. Warrior's work is a call for "intellectual sovereignty" (p. 87)—a position free from the tyranny and oppression of the dominant discourse.

Among Asian Pacific Islanders there are notions of multiple consciousness. Lowe (1996) expresses this in terms of "heterogeneity, hybridity, and multiplicity" (p. 60). She points out:

The articulation of an "Asian American identity" as an organizing tool has provided unity that enables diverse Asian groups to understand unequal circumstances and histories as being related. The building of "Asian American culture" is crucial to this effort, for it articulates and empowers the diverse Asian-origin community vis-à-vis the institutions and apparatuses that exclude and marginalize it. Yet to the extent that Asian American culture fixes Asian American identity and suppresses differences—of national origin, generation, gender, sexuality, class—it risks particular dangers: not only does it underestimate the differences and hybridities among Asians, but it may inadvertently support the racist discourse that constructs Asians as a homogeneous group. (pp. 70-71)

Espiritu (1992) also reminds us that "Asian American" as an identity category came into being within the past 30 years. Prior to that time, most members of the Asian-descent immigrant population "considered themselves culturally and politically distinct" from other Asian-descent groups (p. 19). Indeed, the historical enmity that existed between and among various Asian groups made it difficult for them to transcend their national allegiances to see themselves as one unified group. And the growing anti-Asian sentiments with which the various Asian immigrant groups were faced in the United States caused specific groups to "disassociate themselves from the targeted group so as not to be mistaken for members of it and suffer any possible negative consequences" (p. 20).

Trinh (1989) and Mohanty (1991) offer postmodern analyses of Asian Americanness that challenge any unitary definitions of *Asian American.* Rather than construct a mythical solidarity, these authors examine the ways that Asianness is represented in the dominant imagination. One of the most vivid examples of the distorted, imagined Asian shows up in the work of David Henry Hwang, whose play *M. Butterfly* demonstrates how a constellation of characteristics—size, temperament, submissiveness— allowed a French armed services officer to mistake a man for a woman even in intimate situations.

Lowe (1996) reminds us that "the grouping 'Asian American' is not a natural or static category; it is a socially constructed unity, a situationally specific position assumed for political reasons" (p. 82), but it coexists with the "dynamic fluctuation and heterogeneity of Asian American culture" (p. 68).

What all of these groups (i.e., African Americans, Native Americans, Latino/as, and Asian Americans) have in common is the experience of a racialized identity. Each group is constituted of myriad national and ancestral origins, but the dominant ideology of the Euro-American epistemology has forced each into an essentialized and totalized unit that is perceived to have little or no internal variation. However, at the same moment, members of these groups have used these unitary racialized labels for political and cultural purposes. Identification with the racialized labels means acknowledgment of some of the common experiences group members have had as outsiders and others.

◆ Life on the Margins

Anthropologist Jacob Pandian (1985) points out that in the Judeo-Christian local culture of the West (Geertz, 1983), the *True Christian* was the medieval metaphor of the *Self. Alterity* refers to the alter ego category of otherness that is specific to each culture's "metaphor of the self." Wynter (1992) argues that those constructed as other have a perspective advantage. This advantage does not speak to the economic, social, and political disadvantage that subordinated groups may experience, but rather to the way that not being positioned in the center allows for "wide-angle" vision. This advantage is not due to an inherent racial/cultural difference but is the result of the dialectical nature of constructed otherness that prescribes the liminal status of people of color as beyond the normative boundary of the conception of Self/Other (King, 1995).

King (1995) further argues that this epistemic project is more than simply adding on multiple perspectives or "pivoting" the center. Rather, this liminal position or point of alterity attempts to transcend an "either/or" epistemology. Alterity is not a dualistic position that there are multiple and equally partial standpoints that are either valid or inexorably ranked hierarchically. Recognizing the alterity perspective does not essentialize other perspectives, such as Blackness, Indianness, Asianness, Latino/aness, as homogenizing reverse epistemics (West, 1990).

Those occupying the liminal position do not seek to move from the margins to the mainstream because they understand the corrupting influences of the mainstream—its pull to maintain status quo relations of power and inequities. This liminal view is not unlike the view from the bottom that poor and working-class people have on the middle class. The poor and working classes have a perspective on their own experiences while simultaneously grasping the fundamentals of the workings of the dominant class. Because most poor and working-class people rely on the dominant class for food, clothing, shelter, and work, they are forced to learn dominant practices, at least minimally. The undocumented child-care workers or African American domestics find themselves inside the homes of dominant group members. There they have intimate access to sanctioned beliefs and patterns of behavior.[3]

Legesse (1973) suggests that the liminal group is that which is forcibly constrained to play the role of alter ego to the ideal self prescribed by the dominant cultural model. This dominant cultural model sets up prescriptive rules and canons for regulating thought and action in the society. Thus the "issue is about the 'nature of human knowing' of the social reality in a model of which the knower is already a socialized subject" (Wynter, 1992, p. 26).

> The system-conserving mainstream perspectives of each order (or well-established scholarship) therefore clash with the challenges made from the perspectives of alterity. . . . For it is the task of established scholarship to rigorously maintain those prescriptions which are critical to the order's existence. (Wynter, 1992, p. 27)

Thus the work of the liminal perspective is to reveal the ways that dominant perspectives distort the realities of the other in an effort to maintain power relations that continue to disadvantage those who are locked out of the mainstream. This liminal perspective is the condition of the dominant order's self-definition that "can empower us to free ourselves from the 'categories and prescriptions' of our specific order and from its 'generalized horizon of understanding' " (Wynter, 1992, p. 27).

◆ Critical Race Theory: Challenging Mainstream Orthodoxy

One research paradigm in which racialized discourses and ethnic epistemologies or the liminal perspective may be deployed is critical race theory (CRT).[4] According to Delgado (1995b):

> Critical Race Theory sprang up in the mid-1970s with the early work of Derrick Bell and Alan Freeman, both of whom were deeply concerned over

the slow pace of racial reform in the U.S. They argued that traditional approaches of filing *amicus* briefs, conducting protests and marches, and appealing to moral sensibilities of decent citizens produced smaller and fewer gains than in previous times. Before long, Bell and Freeman were joined by other legal scholars who shared their frustration with traditional civil rights strategies. (p. xiii)

Critical race theory is both an outgrowth of and a separate entity from an earlier legal movement called critical legal studies (CLS). Critical legal studies is a leftist legal movement that challenges the traditional legal scholarship that focuses on doctrinal and policy analysis (Gordon, 1990) in favor of a form of law that speaks to the specificity of individuals and groups in social and cultural contexts. CLS scholars also challenge the notion that "the civil rights struggle represents a long, steady march toward social transformation" (Crenshaw, 1988, p. 1334).

According to Crenshaw (1988), "Critical [legal] scholars have attempted to analyze legal ideology and discourse as a social artifact which operates to recreate and legitimate American society" (p. 1350). Scholars in the CLS movement decipher legal doctrine to expose both its internal and external inconsistencies and reveal the ways that "legal ideology has helped create, support, and legitimate America's present class structure" (p. 1350). The contribution of CLS to legal discourse is in its analysis of legitimating structures in society. Much of the CLS ideology emanates from the work of Gramsci (1971) and depends on the Gramscian notion of "hegemony" to describe the continued legitimacy of oppressive structures in American society (Unger, 1983). However, CLS fails to provide pragmatic strategies for material and social transformation. Cornel West (1993) asserts:

Critical legal theorists fundamentally question the dominant liberal paradigms prevalent and pervasive in American culture and society. This thorough questioning is not primarily a constructive attempt to put forward a conception of a new legal and social order. Rather, it is a pronounced disclosure of inconsistencies, incoherences, silences, and blindness of legal formalists, legal positivists, and legal realists in the liberal tradition. Critical legal studies is more a concerted attack and assault on the legitimacy and authority of pedagogical strategies in law school than a comprehensive announcement of what a credible and realizable new society and legal system would look like. (p. 196)

CLS scholars have critiqued mainstream legal ideology for its portrayal of the United States as a meritocracy, but they have failed to include racism in their critique. Thus CRT became a logical outgrowth of the discontent of legal scholars of color.

CRT begins with the notion that racism is "normal, not aberrant, in American society" (Delgado, 1995b, p. xiv), and because it is so en-meshed in the fabric of the U.S. social order, it appears both normal and natural to people in this society. Indeed, Derrick Bell's major premise in *Faces at the Bottom of the Well* (1992) is that racism is a permanent fix-ture of American life. Therefore, the strategy of those who fight for racial social justice is to unmask and expose racism in all of its various permutations.

Second, CRT departs from mainstream legal scholarship by sometimes employing storytelling to "analyze the myths, presuppositions, and re-ceived wisdoms that make up the common culture about race and that invariably render blacks and other minorities one-down" (Delgado, 1995b, p. xiv). According to Barnes (1990), "Critical race theorists . . . integrate their *experiential knowledge,* drawn from a shared history as 'other,' with their ongoing struggles to transform a world deteriorat-ing under the albatross of racial hegemony" (pp. 1864-1865; emphasis added). Thus the experience of oppressions such as racism and sexism has important components for the development of a CRT perspective.

A third feature of CRT is its insistence on a critique of liberalism. Crenshaw (1988) argues that the liberal perspective of the "civil rights crusade as a long, slow, but always upward pull" (p. 1334) is flawed because it fails to understand the limits of the current legal paradigm to serve as a catalyst for social change because of its emphasis on incre-mentalism. CRT argues that racism requires sweeping changes, but liberalism has no mechanism for such change. Instead, liberal legal prac-tices support the painstakingly slow process of arguing legal precedents to gain citizen rights for people of color.

Fourth, CRT argues that Whites have been the primary beneficiaries of civil rights legislation. For example, although the policy of affirmative action is under attack throughout the nation, it is a policy that also has benefited Whites. A close look at the numbers reveals that the major bene-ficiaries of affirmative action hiring policies have been White women (Guy-Sheftall, 1993). The logic of this argument is that many of these women earn incomes that support households in which other Whites

410

live—men, women, and children. Thus White women's ability to secure employment ultimately benefits Whites in general.

In a recent compilation of key writings in critical race theory, the editors point out that there is no "canonical set of doctrines or methodologies to which [CRT scholars] all subscribe" (Crenshaw, Gotanda, Peller, & Thomas, 1995, p. xiii). But these scholars are unified by two common interests—understanding how a "regime of white supremacy and its subordination of people of color have been created and maintained in America" (p. xiii) and changing the bond that exists between law and racial power.

In the pursuit of these interests, legal scholars such as Patricia Williams (1991) and Derrick Bell (1980, 1992) were among the early critical race theorists whose ideas reached the general public. Some might argue that their wide appeal was the result of their abilities to tell compelling stories into which they embedded legal issues. This use of story is of particular interest to social science scholars because of the growing popularity of narrative inquiry (Connelly & Clandinin, 1990). But merely because the research community is more receptive to story as a part of scholarly inquiry does not mean that all stories are judged as legitimate in knowledge construction and the advancement of a discipline.

Lawrence (1995) asserts that there is a tradition of storytelling in law and that litigation is highly formalized storytelling, although the stories of ordinary people, in general, have not been told or recorded in the literature of law (or any other discipline). But this failure to make it into the canons of literature or research does not make stories of ordinary people less important. The ahistorical and acontextual nature of much law and other "science" renders the voices of the dispossessed and marginalized group members mute. In response, much of the scholarship of CRT focuses on the role of "voice" in bringing additional power to the legal discourses of racial justice. Critical race theorists attempt to inject the cultural viewpoints of people of color, derived from a common history of oppression, into their efforts to reconstruct a society crumbling under the burden of racial hegemony (Barnes, 1990).

Until recently, little of CRT found its way into the literature outside of law. In my own work with Tate, we broached the subject as a challenge to traditional multicultural education paradigms (Ladson-Billings & Tate, 1995). We argued that race continues to be salient in U.S. society; that the nation was premised on property rights, not human rights; and that the

411

intersection of race and property could serve as a powerful analytic tool for explaining social and educational inequities. Later, Tate (1997) provided a comprehensive description of critical race theory and its antecedents as a way to inform the educational research community more fully of CRT's meanings and possible uses in education. In his discussion he cites Calmore (1992), who identified CRT as

> a form of opposition scholarship . . . that challenges the universality of white experience/judgement as the authoritative standard that binds people of color and normatively measures, directs, controls, and regulates the terms of proper thought, expression, presentation, and behavior. As represented by legal scholars, critical race theory challenges the dominant discourses on race and racism as they relate to law. The task is to identify values and norms that have been disguised and subordinated in the law. . . . critical race scholars . . . seek to demonstrate that [their] experiences as people of color are legitimate, appropriate, and effective bases for analyzing the legal system and racial subordination. This process is vital to . . . transformative vision. This theory-practice approach, a praxis, if you will, finds a variety of emphases among those who follow it. . . . From this vantage, consider for a moment how law, society, and culture are texts—not so much like a literary work, but rather like a traditional black minister's citation of a text as a verse or scripture that would lend authoritative support to the sermon he is about to deliver. Here, texts are not merely random stories; like scripture, they are expressions of authority, preemption, and sanction. People of color increasingly claim that these large texts of law, society, and culture must be subjected to fundamental criticisms and reinterpretation. (pp. 2161-2162)

Although CRT has been used as an analytic tool for understanding the law (particularly civil rights law), as previously noted, it has not been deployed successfully in the practical world of courts and legal cases or schools. In fact, the first public exposure CRT received proved disastrous for presidential civil rights commission nominee Lani Guinier. CRT's radical theoretical arguments were seen as a challenge to "the American way." Guinier's (1994) writings about proportional representation were seen as antithetical to the U.S. constitutional notion of one "man," one vote. She had argued that in a postapartheid South Africa it would be necessary to ensure that the White minority had a political voice despite the fact that they were grossly outnumbered within the electorate. Similarly, she argued, people of color in the United States might have to seek new ways to be represented beyond that of majority rule through one person, one

412

vote. Guinier's ideas meant that she could not be confirmed, and the president did nothing to support her nomination.

◆ CRT, the Knower, and the Known

> The power and pull of a paradigm is more than simply a methodological orientation. It is a means by which to grasp reality and give it meaning and predictability.
>
> —Ray Rist, "On the Relations Among
> Educational Research Paradigms," 1990

What are the relationships among liminality, alterity, CRT, and new forms of qualitative research that incorporate racialized discourses and ethnic epistemologies? To answer this question we need to examine the relationship between the knower (the researcher) and the known (the subject, participant, informant, collaborator). Lorraine Code (1991) poses the question, Does the gender of the knower matter in the construction of knowledge? She contends that it does. I assert that along with the gender of the knower, the race, ethnicity, language, class, sexuality, and other forms of difference work to inform his or her relationship to knowledge and its production. However, Narayan (1993) argues that it is dangerous to presume that because the researcher (in her case as an anthropologist) is a member of a particular racial or ethnic group, she or he has emic knowledge of that particular group or community:

"Native" anthropologists, then, are perceived as insiders regardless of their complex backgrounds. The differences between kinds of "native" anthropologists are also obviously passed over. Can a person from an impoverished American minority background who, despite all prejudices, manages to get an education and study her own community be equated with a member of a Third World elite group who, backed by excellent schooling and parental funds, studies anthropology abroad yet returns home for fieldwork among the less privileged? Is it not insensitive to suppress the issue of location, acknowledging that a scholar who chooses an institutional base in the Third World might have a different engagement with Western-based theories, books, political stances, and technologies of written production? Is a middle-class white professional researching aspects of his own society also a "native" anthropologist? (p. 677)

413

Narayan's points are well-taken if we accept an essentialized view of what group membership means. We know that the categories we use to describe also delimit. Who and what constitutes group membership is always at play. However, the search for an approach to research that better represents indigenous and community knowledge remains a worthwhile one.

Asante (1987) builds upon the work of Woodson and Du Bois to craft an Afrocentric or "African-centered" approach to education. Although some other Black scholars have challenged his approach as essentialist and a form of ethnic "cheerleading" (e.g., Appiah, 1992), Asante's (1991) own words suggest that his search for an alternate paradigm is more directed at getting out from under the oppression of dominant perspectives:

> Afrocentricity is *not* a black version of Eurocentricity. Eurocentricity is based on white-supremacist notions whose purposes are to protect white privilege and advantage in education, economics, politics, and so forth. Unlike Eurocentricity, Afrocentricity does not condone ethnocentric valorization at the expense of degrading other groups' perspectives. Moreover, Eurocentricity presents the particular historical reality of Europeans as the sum total of the human experience. It imposes Eurocentric realities as universal; i.e., that which is white is presented as applying to the human condition in general, while that which is nonwhite is viewed as group-specific and therefore not human. (p. 172)

Asante's (1987) major argument, as I see it, is that scholars of color have been searching for a "place to stand . . . in relation to Western standards, imposed as interpretative measures on other cultures" (p. 11). He argues for a "flexible frame of reference" (p. 11) that will allow a more dynamic and transformational interaction between the knower and the known.

Similarly, Anzaldúa (1987) reminds us that dominant culture is defined by the powerful and often operates as a kind of tyranny against those defined as other. Her response against the inequitable relationship between the knower and the known is to press toward a new *mestiza* consciousness that is a consciousness of the borderlands. Her work represents the complexity of identity, representation, and scholarship in the more dynamic way proposed by Asante. Her work moves in a fluid yet exciting way between exposition and art, prose and poetry, Spanish and English, displaying the borders in multiple ways. For instance, she writes in "*Una Lucha de Fronteras*/A Struggle of Borders" (p. 77):

Because I, a *mestiza,*
continually walk out of one culture,
and into another,
because I am in all cultures at the same time,
alma entre dos mundos, tres, cuatro,
me zumba la cabeza con lo contradictorio.
Estoy norteada por todas las voces que me hablan
simultaneamente.

She writes in an unapologetic, multivocal style to reinforce the multiple epistemological positions in which all human beings find themselves, even those who have assumed unitary voices.

Highwater (1981) raises similar issues when he argues that "the greatest distance between people is not space, but culture" (p. 3). He further asserts the importance of representation as a "complex and infinitely varied relationship between reality and the symbols used to depict it" (p. 70). The concept of representation can (and should) be extended to scholarship. Scholars must be challenged to ask not only *about* whom is the research, but also *for* whom is the research. The question of *for whom* is not merely about advocacy, but rather about who is capable to act and demonstrate agency. This agency is enacted through both epistemological and discursive forms.

Fanon (1968) argues that although the oppressed resort to the language of the oppressor for their liberation, ultimately liberation will come from a new person with a new discourse. This new discourse represents the primary argument of Black feminist Audre Lorde (1984), who notes in her oft-quoted essay that "the master's tools will never dismantle the master's house." However, other scholars suggest that "the master's house will only be dismantled with the master's tools."5 This epistemological limbo—between the old discourse and the new—is the place where many scholars of color find themselves. The mechanisms for scholarly recognition, promotion, tenure, and publication are controlled primarily by the dominant ideology. Scholars of color find themselves simultaneously having been trained in this dominant tradition and needing to break free of it.

This ambivalence about the research that scholars of color are trained to do and the research they ultimately do creates the condition that Delgado-Gaitan (1993) describes as "insider/outsider status." One initially begins as an outsider and gradually gains enough trust to be granted insider status. But the move from "outside" to "inside" can be a form of oppression and colonization. As Villenas (1966) notes, "By objectifying the subjectivities of the researched, by assuming authority, and by not questioning their own privileged positions, ethnographers have participated as colonizers of the researched" (p. 713). Rosaldo (1989) has also warned of the dangers the dominant discourse may have for ethnographers by describing the "Lone Ethnographer," who "rode off into the sunset in search of his 'natives'" (p. 30). After spending time among these "natives," this same Lone Ethnographer returned to the comfort and convenience of his (or her) office to write a "true" account of the culture. But scholars born of "new studies" have begun to ask different questions of themselves and their research.[6] Siddle-Walker (1996) raises the question of data versus "real" data. The insider status that scholars of color may have can alert them to the way oppressed peoples both protect themselves and subvert the dominant paradigm by withholding and "distorting" data. These actions may reflect the suspicions of the researched community rather than malice.

In my own research I have attempted to tell a story about myself as well as about my work (Ladson-Billings, 1997). This discursive turn is not merely a new narcissism; rather, it is a concern for situating myself as a researcher—who I am, what I believe, what experiences I have had—because it affects what, how, and why I research. My decision to research the exemplary practices of teachers who are successful with African American children was a decidedly political (not partisan) decision (Ladson-Billings, 1994). It also was a decision to demystify the research process in communities of color, the members of which are often the objects but rarely the beneficiaries of research.[7]

In my work I broke several canons of traditional research. I relied on low-income African American parents to help me locate excellent teachers. I allowed the teachers to assume responsibility for the theoretical leadership of the project, and I created a research collaborative in which I served as one of nine members along with the teachers, not as the expert/ researcher. This changed relationship between researcher and researched forced me to participate in a more self-revealing, vulnerable way. Throughout the process, I sent the other members of the study copies of everything I wrote. They scolded me when I misrepresented their thoughts and ideas, and they affirmed me when I got it right. Over the course of 3 years we became a group of friends with a common concern about the education of African American children. This long-term, intensive form of research made it difficult for members to lie or hide their feelings. It also

416

meant that the end of the funding could not mean the end of the relationship. So, 7 years later, we continue to consult each other and send each other greeting cards. I know who has suffered bereavement, who has coped with illness, whose children have entered college, who has become a grandparent. My research is a part of my life and my life is a part of my research.

The needs to know and to be known are powerful aspects of the human condition. Unfortunately, knowledge of and by people of color has been repressed, distorted, and denied by a Euro-American cultural logic that represents an "aggressive seizure of intellectual space [that,] like the seizure of land, amounts to the aggressor occupying someone else's territory while claiming it as his own" (Asante, 1987, p. 9).

Critical race theory offers the researcher an opportunity to stand in a different relationship to the research (and researched). Some of the key features of CRT are storytelling, counterstorytelling, and "naming one's own reality" (see Delgado, 1995a). The value of storytelling in qualitative research is that it can be used to demonstrate how the same phenomenon can be told in different and multiple ways depending on the storytellers. For instance, where an anthropologist might describe the ritual scarification of a male infant's genitalia, Bertha Rosenfeld may tell of the wonderful bris performed on her new nephew as a part of her family's Jewish religious tradition (Ladson-Billings, 1993). Which story is true? Whose story is deemed legitimate? Who has the power to shape the public perception about the logic and worth of the event? One might argue that the example presented here is an exaggeration, much like that of Horace Miner's classic, "Body Ritual Among the Nacirema" (*Nacirema* is *American* spelled backward), but it is representative of the power of different storytellers. As Robert Williams (1995) notes:

To be a Storyteller . . . is to assume the awesome burden of remembrance for a people, and to perform this paramount role with laughter and tears, joy and sadness, melancholy and passion, as the occasion demands. The Storyteller never wholly belongs to himself or herself. The Storyteller is the one who sacrifices everything in the tellings and retellings of the stories belonging to the tribe.

. . . Whether the story gets the "facts" right is really not all that important. An Indian Storyteller is much more interested in the "truth" contained in a story. And a great Storyteller always makes that "truth" in the story fit the needs of the moment. (pp. xi-xii)[8]

No story was so widely disputed as that told at the murder trial of O.J. Simpson. The prosecutors told a story of a crazed and controlling man who after years of battering his ex-wife snapped when he learned of her romantic interests. They presented it as an open-and-shut case. They asserted that Simpson had motive and they had evidence of opportunity. But the defense attorneys told a different story. They talked about the implausibility of the prosecution's scenario and the deep-seated racism that is a part of the Los Angeles Police Department. They changed the focus of the case from one murder case to the general experiences of men of color (particularly Black and Latino men) with police departments in the United States. Although the telling of vastly differing stories is part of most legal cases, criminal or civil, the response of the jury to these two stories stunned White and/or middle-class Americans.

The posttrial analysis suggested that a "Black" jury failed to convict a Black celebrity defendant, even though the jury had at least one White and one Latino juror. Other analyses asserted that the jury was not intelligent enough to make the "right" decision. The O.J. Simpson murder trial came on the heels of the trials of four Los Angeles police officers for the beating of Rodney King. A predominantly White jury in the suburb of Simi Valley had acquitted the officers of a beating that the entire nation (including the jurors) had witnessed via videotape. In that trial, the defense attorneys told a story of how frame-by-frame analysis of the videotape could lead to an interpretation different from that evoked by real-time viewing. In the context of King's background and driving record, the defense's story was credible to the jurors.

Similarly, "stories" told in the research literature are received differently by different people. In the educational and social science research literature of the 1960s, the stories about children of color were stories of "cultural deprivation" and "cultural disadvantage" (see, e.g., Bettelheim, 1965; Bloom, Davis, & Hess, 1965; Ornstein & Vairo, 1968; Riessman, 1962). These were stories of the substandard, abnormal child of color and poverty, and they positioned White middle-class cultural expression as the normative and correct way of being in school and society. Policy at federal and local levels flowed out of these stories in an attempt to "compensate" for the perceived inadequacies of children of color and their families.

Siddle-Walker's (1996) counterstory of the "good" segregated school presents a decidedly different picture of a working-class community of color. Indeed, throughout the southern United States there are counterstories of poor people working together to secure a better education for their children despite the neglect and antipathy of the dominant culture. The Historically Black Colleges and Universities, tribal colleges, and early ethnic studies programs are examples of some of the ways in which people of color have attempted to create educational structures and discourses that challenge the notion of exclusivity as the only route to excellence.

In 1969, the Asian American Studies Program at San Francisco State College (now San Francisco State University) operated an independent program of study that was conceived on democratic and inclusive principles (Hirabayashi & Alquizola, 1994). The program (in concert with the college's Ethnic Studies Program) grew out of the demands from a student strike staged by the Third World Liberation Front. The program goals were open admissions and the immediate admission of all "non-White" applicants, community control of the curriculum and hiring practices, and self-governance. This model of education represented a radical departure from the top-down, hierarchical, and bureaucratic forms that characterize much of higher education. The Asian American Studies Program dared to tell a counterstory, and it proved to be disruptive and destabilizing to the dominant paradigm.

◆ The Children of Field Hands Return to Do Fieldwork

> My master used to read prayers in public to the ship's crew every Sabbath day; and when I first saw him read, I was never so surprised in my life, as when I saw the book talk to my master, for I thought it did, as I observed him to look upon it, and move his lips. I wished it would do so with me. As soon as my master had done reading, I followed him to the place where he put the book . . . and when nobody saw me, I opened it, and put my ear down close upon it, in great hope that it would say something to me.
>
> —James Gronniosaw,
> *A Narrative of the Most Remarkable*
> *Particulars in the Life of James Albert Ukawsaw Gronniosaw, 1770*

When I was a young child growing up in Philadelphia, there were groups of African American men (some from my family) who waited on street corners during the summer months for the farm labor bus. This broken-down yellow school bus arrived in the Black community looking for willing workers to go to the fields to do the harsh stoop labor of picking tomatoes, strawberries, or any other fruit or vegetable that was in season. Anyone who did not have a steady job could hope to be among those selected to go to the fields. This backbreaking labor did not yield much financial reward, but it was an honest day's work available to people who rarely could find work.

When I moved to California, I saw people with brown faces standing on street corners. This time, instead of a school bus, open-bed trucks would pull up to the curb and the men inside would select a few of those waiting on the corner to do a day's labor at a construction site. Not far from one of the nation's most prestigious universities was a strawberry ranch owned by the university, where a group of itinerant farmworkers lived and worked in inhumane and squalid conditions. Within a few years I began to see people with yellow faces scrubbing dishes and mopping floors in the kitchens of a growing number of restaurants in a community that boasted of a median home price of almost $300,000. The "real" fieldwork being done by people of color and poor people is rarely represented fully in the literature of the academy.

Today, as I attempt to do my own work I am struck by the growing number of scholars of color who have chosen to go back into those fields, construction sites, and kitchens to give voices to their own people—their perspectives, worldviews, and epistemologies. These scholars, like James Gronniosaw (quoted above), are attempting to have the lives of subordinated people "talk to them." Tired of bending their ears to hear the master's book talk, scholars of color are writing new texts from the lives and experiences of people much like themselves. The work of scholars such as Gwaltney (1980), Torres-Guzman (1992), Nieto (1992), Takaki (1989, 1993), Ellison (1986), Churchill (1992, 1993), Silko (1977, 1981), Spivak (1988), hooks (1984, 1989, 1992), and countless others has begun to reshape the contours of scholarly research about communities of color. Perhaps even more important is the work of scholars of color who have taken on the task of turning a critical gaze on the dominant paradigms. Scholars such as Said (1979), Ani (1994), Morrison (1992), and Hwang (1994) use deciphering knowledge to change "consciousness and [develop] cognitive autonomy . . . [in an] 'archaeology of knowledge' (Foucault, 1972) to expose the belief structures of race . . . and other discursive practices" (King, 1995, p. 276).

For example, although Collins (1990) has developed a theoretical rubric for explicating a Black feminist standpoint, this rubric also represents a framework for critique of Euro-American paradigms. Collins argues for concrete experiences as a criterion of meaning, the use of dialogue in the assessment of knowledge claims, an ethic of caring, and an ethic of personal accountability. In the vernacular, Collins asks, What have you been through? What are you talkin' about? How do I know you care and, by the way, who *are* you? Scrutiny about subjectivities generally is absent in positivist paradigms that rely on a notion of objectivity, even when it cannot be attained.

The return of researchers of color to communities of color and the casting of a critical eye on the Euro-American paradigm are not calls to a romantic, "noble savage" notion of otherness. Rather, this work is about uncovering the complexities of difference—race, class, and gender. Work such as Gilroy's (1993) makes a compelling case for complex and multiple readings of race, ethnicity, and gender:

> The themes of nationality, exile, and cultural affiliation accentuate the inescapable fragmentation and differentiation of the [racialized] subject. This fragmentation has recently been compounded further by the questions of gender, sexuality, and male domination which have been made unavoidable by the struggles of [racial and ethnic minority] women. . . . As indices of differentiation, they are especially important because of the intracommunal antagonisms which appear between the local and immediate levels of our struggles and their hemispheric and global dynamics can only grow. (p. 35)

The point of working in racialized discourses and ethnic epistemologies is not merely to "color" the scholarship. It is to challenge the hegemonic structures (and symbols) that keep injustice and inequity in place. The work also is not about dismissing the work of European and Euro-American scholars. Rather, it is about defining the limits of such scholarship. The push from scholars of color is to raise the bar or up the ante of qualitative inquiry.

Perhaps a crude but relevant analogue for what racialized discourses and ethnic epistemologies can do for scholarship can be found in the world of sports. Prior to 1947, "America's favorite pastime"—professional baseball—was a game for White men. No players of color were considered "qualified" to play in the big leagues. Once a Black player

421

was selected to play in the league, there was talk of "lowered standards." However, no such downward slide happened in professional baseball. Inclusion of players of color—African Americans, Latinos, Asians—has made for a more competitive game and a game more widely played throughout the world.

Similarly, scholars of color remain woefully underrepresented in the academy. Too often, concern is voiced that scholars of color will not be able to meet certain standards and that hiring such scholars will lower the prestige and status of the institution. But how can the full range of scholarship be explored if whole groups of people are systematically excluded from participating in the process of knowledge production? Some might argue that scholars of color who subscribe to these racialized discourses and ethnic epistemologies are "biased" in their approach to scholarly inquiry. But the point of the multiple-consciousness perspective and the view from the liminal is that scholars of color who have experienced racism and ethnic discrimination (yet survived the rigors of the degree credentialing process) have a perspective advantage. As Delgado (1995c) argues: "Many members of minority groups speak two languages, grow up in two cultures. . . . And so, . . . who has the advantage in mastering and applying critical social thought? Who tends to think of everything in two or more ways at the same time? Who is a postmodernist virtually as a condition of his or her being?" (p. 8).

The paradigm shifts that are occurring in qualitative research are both about representation and beyond representation. They are about developing a "tolerance for ambiguity" (Anzaldúa, 1987). Indeed, Anzaldúa (1987) has uttered prophetically:

> [La mestiza] has discovered that she can't hold concepts or ideas in rigid boundaries. The borders and walls that are supposed to keep the undesirable ideas out are entrenched habits and patterns of behavior; these habits and patterns are the enemy within. Rigidity means death. Only by remaining flexible is she able to stretch the psyche horizontally and vertically. La mestiza constantly has to shift out of habitual formations; from convergent thinking, analytical reasoning that tends to use rationality to move toward a single goal, to divergent thinking, characterized by movement away from set patterns and goals and toward a more whole perspective, one that includes rather than excludes. The new mestiza copes by developing a tolerance for contradictions, a tolerance for ambiguity. (p. 79)

The "gift" of the new *mestiza* is a new vision of scholarship. To be able to accept that gift, scholars must shed the bonds of rigid paradigms and stand in new relationship to knowledge, the knower, and the known. The position of alterity—the liminal—is not a privileged position, but it is an advantaged one. It offers an opportunity to create a "public scholarship" (J. E. King, personal communication, April 1998) that prompts social action and transformation.

◆ What Difference Can CRT Make for the Critical Qualitative Researcher?

Collins (1998) points out that rather than allow her language to "masquerade as seeming objectivity and apolitical authority," she chooses language through "both an intellectual and a political decision" (p. xxi). She cites legal scholar Patricia Williams, who asks, "What is 'impersonal' writing but denial of self?" (p. xxi). Thus CRT asks the critical qualitative researcher to operate in a self-revelatory mode, to acknowledge the double (or multiple) consciousness in which she or he is operating. My *decision* to deploy a critical race theoretical framework in my scholarship is intimately linked to my understanding of the political and personal stake I have in the education of Black children. All of my "selves" are invested in this work—the self that is a researcher, the self that is a parent, the self that is a community member, the self that is a Black woman. No technical-rational approach to this work would yield the deeply textured, multifaceted work I attempt to do. Nor would a technical-rational approach allow for the "archaeology of knowledge" (Foucault, 1972) that is necessary to challenge the inequitable social, economic, and political positions that exist between the mainstream and the margins.

The "gift" of CRT is that it unapologetically challenges the scholarship that would dehumanize and depersonalize us. The question we confront is not merely one of the difference between "quantitative" and "qualitative" scholarship. More than two decades ago, Cronbach (1975) tried to put to rest the false dichotomy of quantity versus quality. The significant issues with which we grapple are paradigmatic and epistemological. Out of those paradigms grow particular methodologies. Frankenstein (1990), Nettles and Perna (1997), and Wilson (1987) have all used quantitative methods to turn a critical gaze on social inequity. The sheer volume and disparity of the numbers they present underscore the ways in which people are systematically subordinated and excluded from the society. Thus there is no magic in employing participant observation, narrative inquiry, or interviews. Indeed, the qualitative researcher must guard against the connotation that qualitative work represents some more "authentic" form of research. As we consider various examples of qualitative research we must be mindful of the ways "the research" may render the researcher invisible. The ethnographer stands as a kind of *deus ex machina* who tells a tightly organized and neatly contrived story. Unlike the television journalist who conducts an interview in plain sight of a huge audience, no critique of the questions, the format, or the tone of voice is offered to the researcher.[9]

In CRT the researcher makes a deliberate appearance in his or her work or, like Bell (1987, 1992, 1998) and Delgado (1992, 1993), may create an alter ego who can speak directly to power. For Bell, Geneva Crenshaw, a Black woman, served this purpose. Delgado created Rodrigo, Crenshaw's half brother, to argue against mainstream legal scholarship. The deeply personal rendering of social science that CRT scholars bring to their work helps break open the mythical hold that traditional work has on knowledge. When Williams (1991) presented the bill of sale of her enslaved great-great-grandmother in her law school contracts course, she destabilized the students' notions of contracts as documents devoid of human emotion and personal consequences.

CRT helps to raise some important questions about the control and production of knowledge—particularly knowledge about people and communities of color. Where is "race" in the discourse of critical qualitative researchers? To what degree have critical qualitative researchers reinscribed liberalism in their work? How has the quest to embrace the postmodern perspectives on human agency obscured the need for collective effort? In what ways will critical qualitative research be forced to "work the hyphens" or "probe how we are in relation with the contexts we study and with our informants, understanding that we are all multiple in those relations" (Fine, 1988, p. 135)?

◆ Epilogue

As I reflect back on what I have written in this chapter, I am reminded that the nagging questions about the "mixing" of race and ethnicity with "scholarship" persist. The claims of lack of objectivity and politicized inquiry nip at my heels. For me, Lucius Outlaw (1995) offers a fitting last word:

> Why race and ethnicity in relation to philosophy? In short because I am convinced that we are living through a period in which race and ethnicity are so challenging to the prospect of our enjoying a future in which we can and will flourish that we are compelled to undertake a fundamental revision of some of our basic convictions regarding who we are, what our lives should be about, and how we will achieve our goals, both individually and collectively. Since such concerns have provided the motivating core for much of Western philosophy (and its sibling fields of inquiry) for more than two thousand years. . . . Finally, there is the deeply personal dimension to . . . focusing on these issues, for they come together in a poignant way to constitute my very being and to inform my daily life, and thereby to condition the lives of all who interact with me: I am a philosopher; I teach portions of the history of the discipline; but I do so as a person of a racial/ethnic group whose existence in America . . . is marked by the holocaust of enslavement and other forms of oppression which have been rationalized by some of the "best" minds in the pantheon of Western philosophers. Thus, not only in practical living must I contend with constricting factors having to do with the politics of race and ethnicity, I must do battle as well, inside the very citadel of reason where enlightenment leading to enhanced living is supposed to have its wellspring. . . . I have committed myself to confronting this seedy aspect of its underside and to the clearing of intellectual and social spaces in which we might come together to work and dwell in peace and harmony with justice. (pp. 305-306)

◆ Notes

1. The heading on this section is a reversal of Deborah King's (1988) "Multiple Jeopardy, Multiple Consciousness."

2. Although I refer to African Americans, Latinas/os, Asian Americans, Native Americans, and Whites throughout this essay, it is important not to reify what Hollinger (1995) terms the "ethnic pentagon." The boundaries separating various racial, ethnic, and cultural groups have become much more permeable and have created more complex and multifaceted identities in the late years of the 20th century.

3. Members of my own family made their livings by working as domestics in the homes of wealthy White people. From their jobs they learned about middle-class notions of etiquette, fashion, and financial sense.

4. Portions of this section are adapted from Ladson-Billings (1998).

5. This statement was made by Henry Louis Gates, Jr., in 1997 at a conference presenting the *Norton Anthology of African American Literature* at the University of Wisconsin–Madison.

6. Sylvia Wynter (1992) has referred to the ethnic studies of the 1960s—African American, American Indian, Asian American, Chicano, Puerto Rican, and Latino studies—as "New Studies" to represent their break from old paradigms and orthodoxy.

7. At a professional meeting, one of my colleagues, an African American woman, suggested that African American communities had become "data plantations" where researchers reap benefits without contributing much of substance.

8. This stance is particularly interesting in light of current controversies over the life story of Rigoberta Menchú (1984), titled *I, Rigoberta Menchú*. A Dartmouth researcher who visited Menchú's Guatemalan village discovered "inconsistencies" and "fabrications" in her autobiography (Stoll, 1999).

9. I am completing this chapter just after the airing of television journalist Barbara Walters's interview with the infamous Monica Lewinsky. I am struck by how many people commented after the interview on the types of questions Walters asked, the way she asked them, and the kinds of questions she omitted.

◆ References

Acuña, R. (1972). *Occupied America: The Chicano struggle toward liberation.* New York: Canfield.

Alarcón, N. (1990). Chicana feminism: In the tracks of "the" native woman. *Cultural Studies, 4,* 248-256.

Almaguer, T. (1974). Historical notes on Chicano oppression: The dialectics of racial and class domination in North America. *Aztlan, 5*(1-2), 27-56.

Ani, M. (1994). *Yurugu: An African-centered critique of European cultural thought and behavior.* Trenton, NJ: Africa World Press.

Anzaldúa, G. (1987). *Borderlands/la frontera: The new mestiza.* San Francisco: Aunt Lute.

Appiah, K. A. (1992). *In my father's house: Africa in the philosophy of culture.* New York: Oxford University Press.

Appleby, J., Hunt, L., & Jacob, M. (1994). *Telling the truth about history.* New York: W. W. Norton.

Asante, M. K. (1987). *The Afrocentric idea.* Philadelphia: Temple University Press.

Asante, M. K. (1991). The Afrocentric idea in education. *Journal of Negro Education, 60,* 170-180.

Balderrama, F. E. (1982). *In defense of la raza: The Los Angeles Mexican consulate and the Mexican community, 1929-1936.* Tucson: University of Arizona Press.

Barnes, R. (1990). Race consciousness: The thematic content of racial distinctiveness in critical race legal scholarship. *Harvard Law Review, 103,* 1864-1871.

Bell, D. (1980). *Brown v. Board of Education* and the interest convergence dilemma. *Harvard Law Review, 93,* 518-533.

Bell, D. (1987). *And we are not saved: The elusive quest for racial justice.* New York: Basic Books.

Bell, D. (1992). *Faces at the bottom of the well.* New York: Basic Books.

Bell, D. (1998). *Afrolantic legacies.* Chicago: Third World Press.

Bettelheim, B. (1965). Teaching the disadvantaged. *National Education Association Journal, 54,* 8-12.

Bloom, B., Davis, A., & Hess, R. (1965). *Comprehensive education for cultural deprivations.* Troy, MO: Holt, Rinehart & Winston.

Calmore, J. O. (1992). Critical race theory, Archie Shepp and fire music: Securing an authentic intellectual life in a multicultural world. *Southern California Law Review, 65,* 2129-2230.

Castillo, A. (1995). *Massacre of the dreamers: Essays on Xicanisma.* New York: Plume.

Churchill, W. (1992). *Fantasies of the master race: Literature, cinema, and the colonization of American Indians.* Monroe, ME: Common Courage.

Churchill, W. (1993). I am indigenist. In W. Churchill, *Struggle for the land: A land rights reader.* Monroe, ME: Common Courage.

Code, L. (1991). *What can she know? Feminist theory and the construction of knowledge.* Ithaca, NY: Cornell University Press.

Collins, P. H. (1990). *Black feminist thought: Knowledge, consciousness, and the politics of empowerment.* New York: Routledge, Chapman & Hall.

Collins, P. H. (1998). *Fighting words: Black women and the search for justice.* Minneapolis: University of Minnesota Press.

Connelly, F. M., & Clandinin, D. J. (1990). Stories of experience and narrative inquiry. *Educational Researcher, 19*(5), 2-14.

Crenshaw, K. (1988). Race, reform and retrenchment: Transformation and legitimation in anti-discrimination law. *Harvard Law Review, 101,* 1331-1387.

Crenshaw, K., Gotanda, N., Peller, G., & Thomas, K. (1995). Introduction. In K. Crenshaw, N. Gotanda, G. Peller, & K. Thomas (Eds.), *Critical race theory: The key writings that formed the movement.* New York: Free Press.

Cronbach, L. (1975). Beyond the two disciplines of scientific psychology. *American Psychologist, 30,* 116-127.

de la Torre, A., & Pesquera, B. (Eds.). (1993). *Building with our hands: New directions in Chicano studies.* Berkeley: University of California Press.

Delgado, R. (1992). Rodrigo's chronicle. *Yale Law Journal, 101,* 1357-1383.

Delgado, R. (1993). Rodrigo's sixth chronicle: Intersections, essences, and the dilemma of social reform. *New York University Law Review, 68,* 639-674.

Delgado, R. (Ed.). (1995a). *Critical race theory: The cutting edge.* Philadelphia: Temple University Press.

Delgado, R. (1995b). Introduction. In R. Delgado (Ed.), *Critical race theory: The cutting edge*. Philadelphia: Temple University Press.

Delgado, R. (1995c). Racial realism—after we're gone: Prudent speculations on America in a post-racial epoch. In R. Delgado (Ed.), *Critical race theory: The cutting edge*. Philadelphia: Temple University Press.

Delgado Bernal, D. (1998). Using a Chicana feminist epistemology in educational research. *Harvard Educational Review, 68,* 555-582.

Delgado-Gaitan, C. (1993). Researching change and changing the researcher. *Harvard Educational Review, 63,* 389-411.

Du Bois, W. E. B. (1953). *The souls of Black folk.* New York: Fawcett. (Original work published 1903)

Ellison, R. (1986). What America would be like without Blacks. In R. Ellison, *Going to the territory* (pp. 104-112). New York: Random House.

Espiritu, Y. L. (1992). *Asian American panethnicity: Bridging institutions and identities.* Philadelphia: Temple University Press.

Fanon, F. (1968). *The wretched of the earth.* New York: Grove.

Fine, M. (1998). Working the hyphens: Reinventing self and other in qualitative research. In N. K. Denzin & Y. S. Lincoln (Eds.), *The landscape of qualitative research: Theories and issues* (pp. 130-155). Thousand Oaks, CA: Sage.

Foucault, M. (1972). *The archaeology of knowledge* (A. M. Sheridan Smith, Trans.). New York: Harper & Row.

Foucault, M. (1973). *The order of things: An archaeology of the human sciences.* New York: Random House.

Frankenstein, M. (1990). Incorporating race, gender, and class issues into a critical mathematics literacy curriculum. *Journal of Negro Education, 59,* 336-351.

Geertz, C. (1983). *Local knowledge: Further essays in interpretive anthropology.* New York: Basic Books.

Gilroy, P. (1993). *Black Atlantic: Modernity and double consciousness.* Cambridge, MA: Harvard University Press.

Gomez-Quinones, J. (1977). On culture. *Revista Chicano-Riqueña, 5*(2), 35-53.

Gordon, R. (1990). New developments in legal theory. In D. Kairys (Ed.), *The politics of law: A progressive critique* (pp. 413-325). New York: Pantheon.

Gramsci, A. (1971). *Selections from the prison notebooks* (Q. Hoare & G. N. Smith, Eds. & Trans.). New York: International.

Guinier, L. (1994). *The tyranny of the majority: Fundamental fairness in representative democracy.* New York: Free Press.

Guy-Sheftall, B. (1993, April). *Black feminist perspectives on the academy.* Paper presented at the annual meeting of the American Educational Research Association, Atlanta.

Gwaltney, J. L. (1980). *Drylongso: A self-portrait of Black America.* New York: Random House.

Haney López, I. F. (1995). The social construction of race. In R. Delgado (Ed.), *Critical race theory: The cutting edge* (pp. 191-203). Philadelphia: Temple University Press.

Hertzberg, H. W. (1971). *The search for an American Indian identity.* Syracuse, NY: Syracuse University Press.

Highwater, J. (1981). *The primal mind: Vision and reality in Indian America.* New York: Meridian.

Hirabayashi, L. R., & Alquizola, M. C. (1994). Asian American studies: Re-evaluating for the 1990s. In K. Aguilar-San Juan (Ed.), *The state of Asian America: Activism and resistance in the 1990s* (pp. 351-364). Boston: South End.

Hollinger, P. (1995). *Postethnic America: Beyond multiculturalism.* New York: Basic Books.

hooks, b. (1984). *Feminist theory: From margin to center.* Boston: South End.

hooks, b. (1989). *Talking back: Thinking feminist, thinking Black.* Boston: South End.

hooks, b. (1992). *Black looks: Race and representation.* Boston: South End.

Hwang, D. H. (1994). Foreword: Facing the mirror. In K. Aguilar-San Juan (Ed.), *The state of Asian America: Activism and resistance in the 1990s* (pp. ix-xii). Boston: South End.

Jefferson, T. (1954). *Notes on the state of Virginia.* New York: W. W. Norton. (Original work published 1784)

Kincheloe, J. L., & McLaren, P. L. (1998). Rethinking critical theory and qualitative research. In N. K. Denzin & Y. S. Lincoln (Eds.), *The landscape of qualitative research: Theories and issues* (pp. 260-299). Thousand Oaks, CA: Sage.

King, D. K. (1988). Multiple jeopardy, multiple consciousness: The context of a Black feminist ideology. *Signs, 14,* 42-72.

King, J. E. (1995). Culture centered knowledge: Black studies, curriculum transformation, and social action. In J. A. Banks & C. M. Banks (Eds.), *Handbook of research on multicultural education* (pp. 265-290). New York: Macmillan.

Ladson-Billings, G. (1993). Through a looking glass: Politics and the history curriculum. *Theory and Research in Social Education, 21,* 84-92.

Ladson-Billings, G. (1994). *The dreamkeepers: Successful teachers of African American children.* San Francisco: Jossey-Bass.

Ladson-Billings, G. (1997). For colored girls who have considered suicide when the academy isn't enough: Reflections of an African American woman scholar. In A. Neumann & P. Peterson (Eds.), *Learning from our lives: Women, research and autobiography in education* (pp. 52-70). New York: Teachers College Press.

Ladson-Billings, G. (1998). Just what is critical race theory and what is it doing in a "nice" field like education? *International Journal of Qualitative Studies in Education, 11,* 7-24.

Ladson-Billings, G., & Tate, W. F. (1995). Toward a critical race theory of education. *Teachers College Record, 97,* 47-68.

Lawrence, C. (1995). The word and the river: Pedagogy as scholarship and struggle. In K. Crenshaw, N. Gotanda, G. Peller, & K. Thomas (Eds.), *Critical race theory: The writings that formed the movement* (pp. 336-351). New York: Free Press.

Legesse, A. (1973). *Three approaches to the study of an African society.* New York: Free Press.

Lewis, D. L. (1993). *W. E. B. Du Bois: Biography of a race 1868-1919.* New York: Henry Holt.

Lewontin, R. C., Rose, S., & Kamin, L. (1984). *Not in our genes: Biology, ideology and human nature.* New York: Pantheon.

Lomawaima, K. T. (1995). Educating Native Americans. In J. A. Banks & C. M. Banks (Eds.), *Handbook of research on multicultural education* (pp. 331-347). New York: Macmillan.

Lorde, A. (1984). *Sister outsider: Essays and speeches.* New York: Crossing.

Lowe, L. (1996). *Immigrant acts: On Asian American cultural politics.* Durham, NC: Duke University Press.

Menchú, R. (1984). *I, Rigoberta Menchú: An Indian woman in Guatemala* (E. Burgos-Debray, Ed.; A. Wright, Trans.). London: Verso.

Mirande, A., & Enriquez, E. (1979). *La Chicana: The Mexican American woman.* Chicago: University of Chicago Press.

Mohanty, C. T. (1991). Under Western eyes: Feminist scholarship and colonial discourses. In C. T. Mohanty, A. Russo, & L. Torres (Eds.), *Third World women and the politics of feminism* (pp. 50-80). Bloomington: Indiana University Press.

Morrison, T. (1992). *Playing in the dark: Whiteness and the literary imagination.* Cambridge, MA: Harvard University Press.

Narayan, K. (1993). How native is a "native" anthropologist? *American Anthropologist, 95,* 671-686.

Nettles, M., & Perna, L. (1997). *The African American education data book.* Fairfax, VA: Frederick D. Patterson Research Institute.

Nieto, S. (1992). We have stories to tell: A case study of Puerto Ricans in children's books. In V. A. Harris (Ed.), *Teaching multicultural literature in grades K-8* (pp. 171-201). Northwood, MA: Christopher-Gordon.

Oboler, S. (1995). *Ethnic labels, Latino lives: Identity and the politics of (re)presentation in the United States.* Minneapolis: University of Minnesota Press.

Omi, M., & Winant, H. (1994). *Racial formation in the United States: 1960-1990* (2nd ed.). New York: Routledge.

Ornstein, A., & Vairo, P. (1968). *How to teach disadvantaged youth.* New York: McKay.

Outlaw, L. (1995). Philosophy, ethnicity, and race. In F. L. Hord & J. S. Lee (Eds.), *I am because we are: Readings in Black philosophy* (pp. 304-328). Amherst: University of Massachusetts Press.

Padilla, F. (1987). *Latino ethnic consciousness.* Notre Dame, IN: Notre Dame University Press.

Pandian, J. (1985). *Anthropology and the Western tradition: Towards an authentic anthropology.* Prospects Heights, IL: Waveland.

Paz, O. (1961). *The labyrinth of solitude: Life and thought in Mexico.* New York: Random House.

Pirsig, R. M. (1972). *Zen and the art of motorcycle maintenance.* New York: Bantam.

Riessman, F. (1962). *The culturally deprived child.* New York: Harper & Row.

Rist, R. (1990). On the relations among educational research paradigms: From disdain to detentes. In K. Dougherty & F. Hammack (Eds.), *Education and society: A reader* (pp. 81-95). New York: Harcourt Brace Jovanovich.

Rosaldo, R. (1989). *Culture and truth: The remaking of social analysis.* Boston: Beacon.

Rosaldo, R. (1993). After objectivism. In S. During (Ed.), *The cultural studies reader* (pp. 104-117). New York: Routledge.

Said, E. W. (1979). *Orientalism.* New York: Vintage.

Scheurich, J. J., & Young, M. (1997). Coloring epistemologies: Are our research epistemologies racially biased? *Educational Researcher, 26*(4), 4-16.

Shujaa, M. (1997, April). *Transformation of the researcher working toward liberation.* Paper presented at the annual meeting of the American Educational Research Association, San Diego, CA.

Siddle-Walker, V. (1996). *Their highest potential: An African American school community in the segregated South.* Chapel Hill: University of North Carolina Press.

Silko, L. M. (1977). *Ceremony.* New York: Viking.

Silko, L. M. (1981). *Storyteller.* New York: Seaver.

Snipp, C. M. (1995). American Indian studies. In J. A. Banks & C. M. Banks (Eds.). *Handbook of research on multicultural education* (pp. 245-258). New York: Macmillan.

Spivak, G. C. (1988). *In other worlds: Essays in cultural politics.* New York: Routledge.

Stoll, D. (1999). *Rigoberta Menchú and the story of all poor Guatemalans.* Boulder, CO: Westview.

Takaki, R. (1989). *Strangers from a different shore: A history of Asian Americans.* Boston: Little, Brown.

Takaki, R. (1993). *A different mirror: A multicultural history of America.* Boston: Little, Brown.

Tate, W. F. (1997). Critical race theory and education: History, theory, and implications. In M. W. Apple (Ed.), *Review of research in education* (Vol. 22, pp. 191-243). Washington, DC: American Educational Research Association.

Torres-Guzman, M. E. (1992). Stories of hope in the midst of despair: Culturally responsive education for Latino students in an alternative high school in New York City. In M. Saravia-Shore & S. F. Arvizu (Eds.), *Cross cultural literacy: Ethnographies of communication in multiethnic classrooms* (pp. 477-490). New York: Garland.

Trinh T. M. (1909). *Woman, native, other: Writing postcoloniality and feminism.* Bloomington: Indiana University Press.

Unger, R. M. (1983). The critical legal studies movement. *Harvard Law Review, 96,* 561-675.

Villenas, S. (1966). The colonizer/colonized Chicana ethnographer: Identity, marginalization, and co-optation in the field. *Harvard Educational Review, 66,* 711-731.

Warrior, R. A. (1995). *Tribal secrets: Recovering American Indian intellectual traditions.* Minneapolis: University of Minnesota Press.

West, C. (1990). The new cultural politics of difference. In R. Ferguson, M. Gever, T. M. Trinh, & C. West (Eds.), *Out there: Marginalization and contemporary cultures* (pp. 19-36). Cambridge: MIT Press.

West, C. (1993). *Keeping faith: Philosophy and race in America.* New York: Routledge.

Williams, G. W. (1882-1883). *History of the Negro race in America from 1619 to 1880: Negroes as slaves, as soldiers, as citizens* (2 vols.). New York: G. P. Putnam's Sons.

Williams, P. (1991). *The alchemy of race and rights: Diary of a law professor.* Cambridge, MA: Harvard University Press.

Williams, R. (1995). Foreword. In R. Delgado, *The Rodrigo chronicles: Conversations about America and race* (pp. xi-xv). New York: New York University Press.

Wilson, W. J. (1987). *The truly disadvantaged: The inner city, the underclass, and public policy.* Chicago: University of Chicago Press.

Woodson, C. G. (1933). *The miseducation of the Negro.* Washington, DC: Association Press.

Wynter, S. (1992). *Do not call us "Negroes": How "multicultural" textbooks perpetuate racism.* San Francisco: Aspire.

Zinn, H. (1980). *A people's history of the United States.* New York: HarperCollins.

10

Rethinking

Critical Theory and

Qualitative Research

Joe L. Kincheloe and Peter McLaren

◆ The Roots of Critical Research

Some 70 years after its development in Frankfurt, Germany, critical theory retains its ability to disrupt and challenge the status quo. In the process, it elicits highly charged emotions of all types—fierce loyalty from its proponents, vehement hostility from its detractors. Such vibrantly polar reactions indicate at the very least that critical theory still matters. We can be against critical theory or for it, but, especially at the present historical juncture, we cannot be without it. Indeed, qualitative research that frames its purpose in the context of critical theoretical concerns still produces, in our view, undeniably dangerous knowledge, the kind of information and insight that upsets institutions and threatens to overturn sovereign regimes of truth.

Critical theory is a term that is often evoked and frequently misunderstood. It usually refers to the theoretical tradition developed by the Frankfurt school, a group of writers connected to the Institute of Social Research at the University of Frankfurt. However, none of the Frankfurt school theorists ever claimed to have developed a unified approach to cultural criticism. In its beginnings, Max Horkheimer, Theodor Adorno, and

Herbert Marcuse initiated a conversation with the German tradition of philosophical and social thought, especially that of Marx, Kant, Hegel, and Weber. From the vantage point of these critical theorists, whose political sensibilities were influenced by the devastations of World War I, postwar Germany with its economic depression marked by inflation and unemployment, and the failed strikes and protests in Germany and Central Europe in this same period, the world was in urgent need of reinterpretation. From this perspective, they defied Marxist orthodoxy while deepening their belief that injustice and subjugation shape the lived world (Bottomore, 1984; Gibson, 1986; Held, 1980; Jay, 1973). Focusing their attention on the changing nature of capitalism, the early critical theorists analyzed the mutating forms of domination that accompanied this change (Agger, 1998; Gall, Gall, & Borg, 1999; Giroux, 1983, 1997; Kellner, 1989; Kincheloe & Pinar, 1991; McLaren, 1997).

Only a decade after the Frankfurt school was established, the Nazis controlled Germany. The danger posed by the exclusive Jewish membership of the Frankfurt school, and its association with Marxism, convinced Horkheimer, Adorno, and Marcuse to leave Germany. Eventually locating themselves in California, these critical theorists were shocked by American culture. Offended by the taken-for-granted empirical practices of American social science researchers, Horkheimer, Adorno, and Marcuse were challenged to respond to the social science establishment's belief that their research could describe and accurately measure any dimension of human behavior. Piqued by the contradictions between progressive American rhetoric of egalitarianism and the reality of racial and class discrimination, these theorists produced their major work while residing in the United States. In 1953, Horkheimer and Adorno returned to Germany and reestablished the Institute of Social Research. Significantly, Herbert Marcuse stayed in the United States, where he would find a new audience for his work in social theory. Much to his own surprise, Marcuse skyrocketed to fame as the philosopher of the student movements of the 1960s. Critical theory, especially the emotionally and sexually liberating work of Marcuse, provided the philosophical voice of the New Left. Concerned with the politics of psychological and cultural revolution, the New Left preached a Marcusian sermon of political emancipation (Gibson, 1986; Hinchey, 1998; Kincheloe & Steinberg, 1997; Surber, 1998; Wexler, 1991, 1996b).

Many academicians who had come of age in the politically charged atmosphere of the 1960s focused their scholarly attention on critical theory.

Frustrated by forms of domination emerging from a post-Enlightenment culture nurtured by capitalism, these scholars saw in critical theory a method of temporarily freeing academic work from these forms of power. Impressed by critical theory's dialectical concern with the social construction of experience, they came to view their disciplines as manifestations of the discourses and power relations of the social and historical contexts that produced them. The "discourse of possibility" implicit within the constructed nature of social experience suggested to these scholars that a reconstruction of the social sciences could eventually lead to a more egalitarian and democratic social order. New poststructuralist conceptualizations of human agency and their promise that men and women can at least partly determine their own existence offered new hope for emancipatory forms of social research when compared with orthodox Marxism's assertion of the iron laws of history, the irrevocable evil of capitalism, and the proletariat as the privileged subject and anticipated agent of social transformation. For example, when Henry Giroux and other critical educators criticized the argument made by Marxist scholars Samuel Bowles and Herbert Gintis—that schools are capitalist agencies of social, economic, cultural, and bureaucratic reproduction—they contrasted the deterministic perspectives of Bowles and Gintis with the idea that schools, as venues of hope, could become sites of resistance and democratic possibility through concerted efforts among teachers and students to work within a liberatory pedagogical framework. Giroux (1988), in particular, maintained that schools can become institutions where forms of knowledge, values, and social relations are taught for the purpose of educating young people for critical empowerment rather than subjugation.

◆ Critical Humility: Our Idiosyncratic Interpretation of Critical Theory and Critical Research

Over the past 20 years of our involvement in critical theory and critical research, we have been asked by hundreds of people to explain more precisely what critical theory is. We find that question difficult to answer because (a) there are many critical theories, not just one; (b) the critical tradition is always changing and evolving; and (c) critical theory attempts to avoid too much specificity, as there is room for disagreement among critical theorists. To lay out a set of fixed characteristics of the position is contrary to the desire of such theorists to avoid the production of blueprints of sociopolitical and epistemological beliefs. Given these disclaimers, we will now attempt to provide one idiosyncratic "take" on the nature of critical theory and critical research at the beginning of the millennium. Please note that this is merely our subjective analysis and there are many brilliant critical theorists who will find many problems with our pronouncements.

In this humble spirit we tender a description of a reconceptualized, end-of-century critical theory that has been critiqued and overhauled by the "post-discourses" of the last quarter of the 20th century (Bauman, 1995; Carlson & Apple, 1998; Collins, 1995; Giroux, 1997; Kellner, 1995; Roman & Eyre, 1997: Steinberg & Kincheloe, 1998). In this context a reconceptualized critical theory questions the assumption that societies such as the United States, Canada, Australia, New Zealand, and the nations in the European Union, for example, are unproblematically democratic and free. Over the 20th century, especially since the early 1960s, individuals in these societies have been acculturated to feel comfortable in relations of domination and subordination rather than equality and independence. Given the social and technological changes of the last half of the century that led to new forms of information production and access, critical theorists argued that questions of self-direction and democratic egalitarianism should be reassessed. In this context critical researchers informed by the "post-discourses" (e.g., postmodern, critical feminism, poststructuralism) understand that individual's view of themselves and the world even more influenced by social and historical forces than previously believed. Given the changing social and informational conditions of late-20th-century media-saturated Western culture, critical theorists needed new ways of researching and analyzing the construction of individuals (Agger, 1992; Flossner & Otto, 1998; Hinchey, 1998; Leistyna, Woodrum, & Sherblom, 1996; Quail, Razzano, & Skalli, 2000; Smith & Wexler, 1995; Sünker, 1998). The following points briefly delineate our interpretation of a critical theory for the new millennium.

◆ A Reconceptualized Critical Theory

In this context it is important to note that we understand a social theory as a map or a guide to the social sphere. In a research context it does not determine how we see the world but helps us devise questions and strategies for exploring it. A critical social theory is concerned in particular with issues of power and justice and the ways that the economy, matters of race, class, and gender, ideologies, discourses, education, religion and other social institutions, and cultural dynamics interact to construct a social system.

Critical enlightenment. In this context critical theory analyzes competing power interests between groups and individuals within a society— identifying who gains and who loses in specific situations. Privileged groups, criticalists argue, often have an interest in supporting the status quo to protect their advantages; the dynamics of such efforts often become a central focus of critical research. Such studies of privilege often revolve around issues of race, class, gender, and sexuality (Carter, 1998; Howell, 1998; Kincheloe & Steinberg, 1997; Kincheloe, Steinberg, Rodriguez, & Chennault, 1998; McLaren, 1997; Rodriguez & Villaverde, 1999; Sleeter & McLaren, 1995). In this context to seek critical enlightenment is to uncover the winners and losers in particular social arrangements and the processes by which such power plays operate (Cary, 1996; Fehr, 1993; King, 1996; Pruyn, 1994; Wexler, 1996a).

Critical emancipation. Those who seek emancipation attempt to gain the power to control their own lives in solidarity with a justice-oriented community. Here critical research attempts to expose the forces that prevent individuals and groups from shaping the decisions that crucially affect their lives. In this way greater degrees of autonomy and human agency can be achieved. At the beginning of the new millennium we are cautious in our use of the term *emancipation* because, as many critics have pointed out, no one is ever completely emancipated from the sociopolitical context that has produced him or her. Also, many have questioned the arrogance that may accompany efforts to emancipate "others." These are important criticisms and must be carefully taken into account by critical researchers. Thus, as critical inquirers who search for those forces that insidiously shape who we are, we respect those who reach different conclusions in their personal journeys (Butler, 1998; Cannella, 1997; Kellogg, 1998; Knobel, 1999; Steinberg & Kincheloe, 1998; Weil, 1998).

The rejection of economic determinism. A caveat of a reconceptualized critical theory involves the insistence that the tradition does not accept the orthodox Marxist notion that "base" determines "superstructure"— meaning that economic factors dictate the nature of all other aspects of human existence. Critical theorists understand at the beginning of the 21st century that there are multiple forms of power, including the aforementioned racial, gender, sexual axes of domination. In issuing this caveat, however, a reconceptualized critical theory in no way attempts to argue that economic factors are unimportant in the shaping of everyday life. Economic factors can never be separated from other axes of oppression (Aronowitz & DiFazio, 1994; Carlson, 1997; Gabbard, 1995; Gee, Hull, & Lankshear, 1996; Gibson, 1986; Haymes, 1995; Kincheloe, 1995, 1999; Kincheloe & Steinberg, 1999; Martin & Schumann, 1996; Rifkin, 1995).

The critique of instrumental or technical rationality. A reconceptualized critical theory sees instrumental/technology rationality as one of the most oppressive features of contemporary society. Such a form of "hyper-reason" involves an obsession with means in preference to ends. Critical theorists claim that instrumental/technical rationality is more interested in method and efficiency than in purpose. It delimits its questions to "how to" instead of "why should." In a research context, critical theorists claim that many rationalistic scholars become so obsessed with issues of technique, procedure, and correct method that they forget the humanistic purpose of the research act. Instrumental/technical rationality often separates fact from value in its obsession with "proper" method, losing in the process an understanding of the value choices always involved in the production of so-called facts (Alfino, Caputo, & Wynyard, 1998; Giroux, 1997; Hinchey, 1998; Kincheloe, 1993; McLaren, 1998; Ritzer, 1993; Stallabrass, 1996; Weinstein, 1998).

The impact of desire. A reconceptualized critical theory appreciates post-structuralist psychoanalysis as an important resource in pursuing an emancipatory research project. In this context critical researchers are empowered to dig more deeply into the complexity of the construction of the human psyche. Such a psychoanalysis helps critical researchers discern the unconscious processes that create resistance to progressive change and induce self-destructive behavior. A poststructural psychoanalysis, in its rejection of traditional psychoanalysis's tendency to view individuals as rational and autonomous beings, allows critical researchers new tools to rethink the interplay among the various axes of power, identity, libido, rationality, and emotion. In this configuration the psychic is no longer separated from the sociopolitical realm; indeed, desire can be socially constructed and used by power wielders for destructive and oppressive outcomes. On the other hand, critical theorists can help mobilize desire for progressive and emancipatory projects. Taking their lead from feminist theory, critical researchers are aware of the patriarchal inscriptions within traditional psychoanalysis and work to avoid its bourgeois, ethnocentric, and misogynist practices. Freed from these blinders, poststructural psychoanalysis helps researchers gain a new sensitivity to the role of fantasy and imagination and the structures of sociocultural and psychological meaning they reference (Alford, 1993; Atwell-Vasey, 1998; Barrows, 1995; Block, 1995; Britzman & Pitt, 1996; Elliot, 1994; Gresson, 2000; Kincheloe, Steinberg, & Villaverde, 1999; Pinar, 1998; Pinar, Reynolds, Slattery, & Taubman, 1995; Samuels, 1993).

A reconceptualized critical theory of power: hegemony. Our conception of a reconceptualized critical theory is intensely concerned with the need to understand the various and complex ways that power operates to dominate and shape consciousness. Power, critical theorists have learned, is an extremely ambiguous topic that demands detailed study and analysis. A consensus seems to be emerging among criticalists that power is a basic constituent of human existence that works to shape the oppressive and productive nature of the human tradition. Indeed, we are all empowered and we are all unempowered, in that we all possess abilities and we are all limited in the attempt to use our abilities. Because of limited space, we will focus here on critical theory's traditional concern with the oppressive aspects of power, although we understand that an important aspect of critical research focuses on the productive aspects of power—its ability to empower, to establish a critical democracy, to engage marginalized people in the rethinking of their sociopolitical role (Apple, 1996b; Fiske, 1993; Freire, 2000; Giroux, 1997; Macedo, 1994; Nicholson & Seidman, 1995).

In the context of oppressive power and its ability to produce inequalities and human suffering, Antonio Gramsci's notion of hegemony is central to critical research. Gramsci understood that dominant power in the 20th century is not always exercised simply by physical force but also through social psychological attempts to win people's consent to domination through cultural institutions such as the media, the schools, the family, and the church. Gramscian hegemony recognizes that the winning of popular consent is a very complex process and must be researched carefully on a case-by-case basis. Students and researchers of power, educators, sociologists, all of us are hegemonized as our field of knowledge and understanding is structured by a limited exposure to competing definitions of the sociopolitical world. The hegemonic field, with its bounded sociopsychological horizons, garners consent to an inequitable power matrix—a set of social relations that are legitimated by their depiction as natural and inevitable. In this context critical researchers note that hegemonic consent is never completely established, as it is always contested by various groups with different agendas (Grossberg, 1997; Lull, 1995; McLaren, 1995a, 1995b; McLaren, Hammer, Reilly, & Sholle, 1995; West, 1993).

A reconceptualized critical theory of power: ideology. Critical theorists understand that the formation of hegemony cannot be separated from the production of ideology. If hegemony is the larger effort of the powerful to win the consent of their "subordinates," then ideological hegemony involves the cultural forms, the meanings, the rituals, and the representations that produce consent to the status quo and individuals' particular places within it. Ideology vis-à-vis hegemony moves critical inquirers beyond simplistic explanations of domination that have used terms such as *propaganda* to describe the way media, political, educational, and other sociocultural productions coercively manipulate citizens to adopt oppressive meanings. A reconceptualized critical research endorses a much more subtle, ambiguous, and situationally specific form of domination that refuses the propaganda model's assumption that people are passive, easily manipulated victims. Researchers operating with an awareness of this hegemonic ideology understand that dominant ideological practices and discourses shape our vision of reality (Lemke, 1995, 1998). Thus our notion of hegemonic ideology is a critical form of epistemological constructivism buoyed by a nuanced understanding of power's complicity in the constructions people make of the world and their role in it (Kincheloe, 1998). Such an awareness corrects earlier delineations of ideology as a monolithic, unidirectional entity that was imposed on individuals by a secret cohort of ruling-class czars. Understanding domination in the context of concurrent struggles among different classes, racial and gender groups, and sectors of capital, critical researchers of ideology explore the ways such competition engages different visions, interests, and agendas in a variety of social locales—venues previously thought to be outside the domain of ideological struggle (Brosio, 1994; Steinberg, 2000).

A reconceptualized critical theory of power: linguistic/discursive power. Critical researchers have come to understand that language is not a mirror of society. It is an unstable social practice whose meaning shifts, depending upon the context in which it is used. Contrary to previous understandings, critical researchers appreciate the fact that language is not a neutral and objective conduit of description of the "real world." Rather, from a critical perspective, linguistic descriptions are not simply about the world but serve to construct it. With these linguistic notions in mind, criticalists begin to study the way language in the form of discourses serves as a form of regulation and domination. Discursive practices are defined as a set of tacit rules that regulate what can and cannot be said, who can speak with the blessings of authority and who must listen, whose social constructions are valid and whose are erroneous and unimportant. In an educational context, for example, legitimated discourses of power insidiously tell educators what books may be read by students, what instructional methods may be utilized, and what belief systems and views of success may be taught. In all forms of research discursive power validates particular research strategies, narrative formats, and modes of representation. In this context power discourses undermine the multiple meanings of language, establishing one correct reading that implants a particular hegemonic/ ideological message into the consciousness of the reader. This is a process often referred to as the attempt to impose discursive closure. Critical researchers interested in the construction of consciousness are very attentive to these power dynamics (Blades, 1997; Gee, 1996; Lemke, 1993; Morgan, 1996; McWilliam & Taylor, 1996; Steinberg, 1998).

Focusing on the relationships among culture, power, and domination. In the last decades of the 20th century, culture has taken on a new importance in the effort to understand power and domination. Critical researchers have argued that culture has to be viewed as a domain of struggle where the production and transmission of knowledge is always a contested process (Giroux, 1997; Kincheloe & Steinberg, 1997; McLaren, 1997; Steinberg & Kincheloe, 1997; Steinberg, 1998). Dominant and subordinate cultures deploy differing systems of meaning based on the forms of knowledge produced in their cultural domain. Popular culture, with its TV, movies, video games, computers, music, dance, and other productions, plays an increasingly important role in critical research on power and domination. Cultural studies, of course, occupies an ever-expanding role in this context, as it examines not only popular culture but the tacit rules that guide cultural production. Arguing that the development of mass media has changed the way the culture operates, cultural studies

441

researchers maintain that cultural epistemologies at the beginning of the new millennium are different from those of only a few decades ago. New forms of culture and cultural domination are produced as the distinction between the real and the simulated is blurred. This blurring effect of hyperreality constructs a social vertigo characterized by a loss of touch with traditional notions of time, community, self, and history. New structures of cultural space and time generated by bombarding electronic images from local, national, and international spaces shake our personal sense of place. This proliferation of signs and images functions as a mechanism of control in contemporary Western societies. The key to successful counterhegemonic cultural research involves (a) the ability to link the production of representations, images, and signs of hyperreality to power in the political economy; and (b) the capacity, once this linkage is exposed and described, to delineate the highly complex effects of the reception of these images and signs on individuals located at various race, class, gender, and sexual coordinates in the web of reality (Ferguson & Golding, 1997; Garnham, 1997; Grossberg, 1995; Joyrich, 1996; Thomas, 1997).

The role of cultural pedagogy in critical theory. Cultural production can often be thought of as a form of education, as it generates knowledge, shapes values, and constructs identity. From our perspective, such a framing can help critical researchers make sense of the world of domination and oppression as they work to bring about a more just, democratic, and egalitarian society. In recent years this educational dynamic has been referred to as cultural pedagogy (Berry, 1998; Giroux, 1997; Kincheloe, 1995; McLaren, 1997; Pailliotet, 1998; Semali, 1998; Soto, 1998). *Pedagogy* is a useful term that has traditionally been used to refer only to teaching and schooling. By using the term *cultural pedagogy,* we are specifically referring to the ways particular cultural agents produce particular hegemonic ways of seeing. In our critical interpretive context, our notion of cultural pedagogy asserts that the new "educators" in the electronically wired contemporary era are those who possess the financial resources to use mass media. This corporate-dominated pedagogical process has worked so well that few complain about it at the beginning of the new millennium—such informational politics doesn't make the evening news. Can we imagine another institution in contemporary society gaining the pedagogical power that corporations now assert over information and signification systems? What if the Church of Christ was sufficiently powerful to run pedagogical "commercials" every few minutes on TV and radio touting the necessity for everyone to accept that denomination's faith? Replayed scenes of Jews, Muslims, Hindus, Catholics, and Methodists being condemned to hell if they rejected the official pedagogy (the true doctrine) would greet North Americans and their children 7 days a week. There is little doubt that many people would be outraged and would organize for political action. Western societies have to some degree capitulated to this corporate pedagogical threat to democracy, passively watching an elite gain greater control over the political system and political consciousness via a sophisticated cultural pedagogy. Critical researchers are intent on exposing the specifics of this process (Deetz, 1993; Drummond, 1996; Molnar, 1996; Pfeil, 1995; Steinberg & Kincheloe, 1997).

◆ Critical Research and the Centrality of Interpretation: Critical Hermeneutics

One of the most important aspects of a critical theory-informed qualitative research involves the often-neglected domain of the interpretation of information. As we have taught and written about critical research in the 1990s, this interpretive or hermeneutical aspect has become increasingly important. Many students of qualitative research approach us in classes and presentations with little theoretical background involving the complex and multidimensional nature of data interpretation in their work. Although there are many moments within the process of researching when the *critical* dynamic of critical theory-informed research appears, there is none more important than the moment(s) of interpretation. In this context we begin our discussion of critical qualitative research, linking it as we go to questions of the relationship between critical hermeneutics and knowledge production (Madison, 1988; Slattery, 1995).

The critical hermeneutic tradition (Grondin, 1994; Gross & Keith, 1997; Rosen, 1987; Vattimo, 1994) holds that in qualitative research there is only interpretation, no matter how vociferously many researchers may argue that the facts speak for themselves. The hermeneutic act of interpretation involves in its most elemental articulation making sense of what has been observed in a way that communicates understanding. Not only is all research merely an act of interpretation, but, hermeneutics contends, perception itself is an act of interpretation. Thus the quest for understanding is a fundamental feature of human existence, as encounter with the unfamiliar always demands the attempt to make meaning, to make sense. The same, however, is also the case with the familiar. Indeed, as in the study of commonly known texts, we come to find that sometimes the familiar may be seen as the most strange. Thus it should not be surprising that even the so-called objective writings of qualitative research are interpretations, not value-free descriptions (Denzin, 1994; Gallagher, 1992; Jardine, 1998; Smith, 1999).

Learning from the hermeneutic tradition and the postmodern critique, critical researchers have begun to reexamine textual claims to authority. No pristine interpretation exists—indeed, no methodology, social or educational theory, or discursive form can claim a privileged position that enables the production of authoritative knowledge. Researchers must always speak/write about the world in terms of something else in the world, "in relation to . . . ." As creatures of the world, we are oriented to it in a way that prevents us from grounding our theories and perspectives outside of it. Thus, whether we like it or not, we are all destined as interpreters to analyze from within its boundaries and blinders. Within these limitations, however, the interpretations emerging from the hermeneutic process can still move us to new levels of understanding, appreciations that allow us to "live our way" into an experience described to us. Despite the impediments of context, hermeneutical researchers can transcend the inadequacies of thin descriptions of decontextualized facts and produce thick descriptions of social texts characterized by the contexts of their production, the intentions of their producers, and the meanings mobilized in the processes of their construction. The production of such thick descriptions/interpretations follows no step-by-step blueprint or mechanical formula. As with any art form, hermeneutical analysis can be learned only in the Deweyan sense—by doing it. Researchers in the context practice the art by grappling with the text to be understood, telling its story in relation to its contextual dynamics and other texts first to themselves and then to a public audience (Carson & Sumara, 1997; Denzin, 1994; Gallagher, 1992; Jardine, 1998; Madison, 1988).

Critical Hermeneutical Methods of Interpretation

These concerns with the nature of hermeneutical interpretation come under the category of philosophical hermeneutics. Working this domain, hermeneutical scholars attempt to think through and clarify the conditions under which interpretation and understanding take place. The critical hermeneutics that grounds critical qualitative research moves more in the direction of normative hermeneutics in that it raises questions about the purposes and procedures of interpretation. In its critical theory-driven context, the purpose of hermeneutical analysis is to develop a form of cultural criticism revealing power dynamics within social and cultural texts. Qualitative researchers familiar with critical hermeneutics build bridges between reader and text, text and its producer, historical context and present, and one particular social circumstance and another. Accomplishing such interpretive tasks is difficult, and researchers situated in normative hermeneutics push ethnographers, historians, semioticians, literary critics, and content analysts to trace the bridge-building processes employed by successful interpretations of knowledge production and culture (Gallagher, 1992; Kellner, 1995; Kogler, 1996; Rapko, 1998).

Grounded by the hermeneutical bridge building, critical researchers in a hermeneutical circle (a process of analysis in which interpreters seek the historical and social dynamics that shape textual interpretation) engage in the back-and-forth of studying parts in relation to the whole and the whole in relation to parts. No final interpretation is sought in this context, as the activity of the circle proceeds with no need for closure (Gallagher, 1992; Peters & Lankshear, 1994; Pinar et al., 1995). This movement of whole to parts is combined with an analytic flow between abstract and concrete. Such dynamics often tie interpretation to the interplay of larger social forces (the general) to the everyday lives of individuals (the particular). A critical hermeneutics brings the concrete, the parts, the particular into focus, but in a manner that grounds them contextually in a larger understanding of the social forces, the whole, the abstract (the general). Focus on the parts is the dynamic that brings the particular into focus, sharpening our understanding of the individual in light of the social and psychological forces that shape him or her. The parts and the unique places they occupy ground hermeneutical ways of seeing by providing the contextualization of the particular—a perspective often erased in traditional inquiry's search for abstract generalizations (Gallagher, 1992; Kellner, 1995; Miller & Hodge, 1998; Peters & Lankshear, 1994).

The give-and-take of the hermeneutical circle provokes analysts to review existing conceptual matrices in light of new understandings. Here the analysts reconsider and reconceptualize preconceptions so as to provide a new way of exploring a particular text. Making use of an author's insights hermeneutically does not mean replicating his or her response to his or her original question. In the hermeneutical process the author's answer is valuable only if it catalyzes the production of a new question for

445

our consideration in the effort to make sense of a particular textual phenomenon (Gallagher, 1992). In this context participants in the hermeneutical circle must be wary of techniques of textual defamiliarization that have become clichéd. For example, feminist criticisms of Barbie's figure and its construction of the image of ideal woman became such conventions in popular cultural analysis that other readings of Barbie were suppressed (Steinberg, 1997). Critical hermeneutical analysts in this and many other cases have to introduce new forms of analysis to the hermeneutical circle—to defamiliarize conventional defamiliarizations—in order to achieve deeper levels of understanding (Berger, 1995; Steinberg, 1998).

Within the hermeneutical circle we may develop new metaphors to shape our analysis in ways that break us out of familiar modes. For example, thinking of movies as mass-mediated dreams may help critical researchers of popular culture to reconceptualize the interpretive act as a psychoanalytic form of dream study. In this way, critical researchers could examine psychoanalytic work in the analysis of dream symbolization for insights into their cultural studies of the popular culture and the meanings it helps individuals make through its visual images and narratives. As researchers apply these new metaphors in the hermeneutical circle, they must be aware of the implicit metaphors researchers continuously bring to the interpretive process (Berger, 1995; Clough, 1998). Such metaphors are shaped by the sociohistorical era, the culture, and the linguistic context in which the interpreter operates. Such awarenesses are important features that must be introduced into the give-and-take of the critical hermeneutical circle. As John Dewey (1916) observed decades ago, individuals adopt the values and perspectives of their social groups in a manner that such factors come to shape their views of the world. Indeed, the values and perspectives of the group help determine what is deemed important and what is not, what is granted attention and what is ignored. Hermeneutical analysts are aware of such interpretational dynamics and make sure they are included in the search for understanding (Madison, 1988; Mullen, 1999).

Critical researchers with a hermeneutical insight take Dewey's insight to heart as they pursue their inquiry. They are aware that the consciousness, and the interpretive frames, they bring to their research are historically situated, ever changing, ever evolving in relationship to the cultural and ideological climate (Hinchey, 1998; Kincheloe, Steinberg, & Hinchey, 1999). Thus there is nothing simple about the social construction of interpretive lenses—consciousness construction is contradictory and the result of the collision of a variety of ideologically oppositional forces. Critical qualitative researchers who understand the relationship between identity formation and interpretive lenses are better equipped to understand the etymology of their own assertions—especially the way power operates to shape them. Linguistic, discursive, and many other factors typically hidden from awareness insidiously shape the meanings researchers garner from their work (Goodson, 1997). It was this dynamic that Antonio Gramsci had in mind when he argued that a critical philosophy should be viewed as a form of self-criticism. The starting point, he concluded, for any higher understanding of self involves consciousness of oneself as a product of power-driven sociohistorical forces. A critical perspective, he once wrote, involves the ability of its adherents to criticize the ideological frames that they use to make sense of the world (see Coben, 1998).

Analyzing Dewey's and Gramsci's notions of self-production in light of the aims of critical hermeneutics vis-à-vis critical qualitative research, we begin to gain insight into how the ambiguous and closeted interpretive process operates. This moves us in a critical direction, as we understand that the "facts" do not simply demand particular interpretations.

Hermeneutical Horizons: Situating Critical Research

Researchers who fail to take these points into account operate at the mercy of unexamined assumptions. Because all interpretation is historically and culturally situated, it is the lot of critical researchers to study the ways both interpreters (often the analysts themselves) and the objects of interpretation are constructed by their time and place. In this context the importance of social theory emerges. Operating in this manner, researchers inject critical social theory into the hermeneutical circle to facilitate an understanding of the hidden structures and tacit cultural dynamics that insidiously inscribe social meanings and values (Cary, 1996; Gallagher, 1992; Kellner, 1995). This social and historical situating of interpreter and text is an extremely complex enterprise that demands a nuanced analysis of the impact of hegemonic and ideological forces that connect the microdynamics of everyday life with the macrodynamics of structures such as white supremacy, patriarchy, and class elitism. The central hermeneutic of many critical qualitative works involves the interactions among research, subject(s), and these situating sociohistorical structures.

447

When these aspects of the interpretation process are taken into account, analysts begin to understand Hans-Georg Gadamer's (1989) contention that social frames of reference influence researchers' questions, which, in turn, shape the nature of interpretation itself. In light of this situating process, the modernist notion that a social text has one valid interpretation evaporates into thin air. Researchers, whether they admit it or not, always have points of view, disciplinary orientations, social or political groups with which they identify (Kincheloe, 1991; Lugg, 1996). Thus the point, critical hermeneuts argue, is not that researchers should shed all worldly affiliations but that they should identify those affiliations and understand their impacts on the ways the researchers approach social and educational phenomena. Gadamer labels these world affiliations of researchers their "horizons" and deems the hermeneutic act of interpretation the "fusion of horizons." When critical researchers participate in the fusion of horizons, they enter into the tradition of the text. Here they study the conditions of its production and the circle of previous interpretations. In this manner they begin to uncover the ways the text has attempted to over determine meaning (Berger, 1995; Ellis, 1998; Jardine, 1998; Miller & Hodge, 1998; Slattery, 1995).

The hermeneutical tradition puts the politics of interpretation at center stage. Like ordinary human beings, critical researchers make history and live their lives within structures of meaning they have not necessarily chosen for themselves. Understanding this, critical hermeneuts realize that a central aspect of their sociocultural analysis involves dissecting the ways people connect their everyday experiences to the cultural representations of such experiences. Such work involves the unraveling of the ideological codings embedded in these cultural representations. This unraveling is complicated by the taken-for-grantedness of the meanings promoted in these representations and the typically undetected ways these meanings are circulated into everyday life (Denzin, 1992; Kogler, 1996). The better the analyst, the better he or she can expose these meanings in the domain of the "what-goes-without-saying," that activity previously deemed noise unworthy of comment.

At this historical juncture, electronic modes of communication become extremely important to the production of meanings and representations that culturally situate human beings in general and textual interpretations in particular (Goldman & Papson, 1994; Hall, 1997). In many ways it can be argued that the postmodern condition produces a secondhand culture, filtered and preformed in the marketplace and constantly communicated

448

via popular and mass media. Critical analysts understand that the pedagogical effects of such a mediated culture can range from the political/
ideological to the cognitive/epistemological. For example, the situating
effects of print media tend to promote a form of linearity that encourages
certain forms of rationality, continuity, and uniformity; on the other hand,
electronic media promote a nonlinear immediacy that may encourage
more emotional responses that lead individuals in very different directions
(du Gay, Hall, Janes, MacKay, & Negus, 1997; Shelton & Kincheloe,
1999). Thus the situating influence and pedagogical impact of electronic
media of the postmodern condition must be assessed by those who study
cultural and political processes and, most important at the turn of the millennium, the research processes itself (Bell & Valentine, 1997; Berger,
1995; Bertman, 1998; Denzin, 1992; Kellner, 1995).

Critical Hermeneutics: Laying
the Groundwork of Critical Research

Critical hermeneutics is suspicious of any model of interpretation that
claims to reveal the final truth, the essence of a text or any form of experience (Goodson & Mangan, 1996). Critical hermeneutics is more comfortable with interpretive approaches that assume that the meaning of human
experience can never be fully disclosed—neither to the researcher nor
even to the human who experienced it. Because language is always slip-
pery, with its meanings ever "in process," critical hermeneutics understands that interpretations will never be linguistically unproblematic, will
never be direct representations. Critical hermeneutics seeks to understand
how textual practices such as scientific research and classical theory work
to maintain existing power relations and to support extant power structures (Denzin, 1992). As critical researchers we draw, of course, on the latter model of interpretation, with its treatment of the personal as political.
Critical hermeneutics grounds a critical research that attempts to connect
the everyday troubles individuals face to public issues of power, justice,
and democracy. Typically, within the realm of cultural studies and cultural
analysis in general critical hermeneutics has deconstructed sociocultural
texts that promote demeaning stereotypes of the disempowered (Denzin,
1992; Gross & Keith, 1997; Rapko, 1998). In this context critical hermeneutics is also being deployed in relation to cultural texts that reinforce
an ideology of privilege and entitlement for empowered members of the
society (Allison, 1998; Fine, Weis, Powell, & Wong, 1997; Frankenberg,

1993; Kincheloe et al., 1998; Rains, 1998; Rodriguez & Villaverde, 1999).

In its ability to render the personal political, critical hermeneutics provides a methodology for arousing a critical consciousness through the analysis of the generative themes of the present era. Such generative themes can often be used to examine the meaning-making power of the contemporary cultural realm (Peters & Lankshear, 1994). Within the qualitative research community there is still resistance to the idea that movies, television, and popular music are intricately involved in the most important political, economic, and cultural battles of the contemporary epoch. Critical hermeneutics recognizes this centrality of popular culture in the postmodern condition and seeks to uncover the ways it impedes and advances the struggle for a democratic society (Kellner, 1995). Appreciating the material effects of media culture, critical hermeneutics traces the ways cultural dynamics position audiences politically in ways that not only shape their political beliefs but formulate their identities (Steinberg & Kincheloe, 1997). In this context, Paulo Freire's (1985) contribution to the development of a critical hermeneutics is especially valuable. Understanding that the generative themes of a culture are central features in a critical social analysis, Freire assumes that the interpretive process is both an ontological (pertaining to being) and an epistemological (pertaining to knowledge) act. It is ontological on the level that our vocation as humans, the foundation of our being, is grounded on the hermeneutical task of interpreting the world so we can become more fully human. It is epistemological in the sense that critical hermeneutics offers us a method for investigating the conditions of our existence and the generative themes that shape it. In this context we gain the prowess to both live with a purpose and operate with the ability to perform evaluative acts in naming the culture around us. This ability takes on an even greater importance in the contemporary electronic society, where the sociopolitical effects of the cultural domain have often been left unnamed, allowing our exploration of the shaping of our own humanness to go unexplored in this strange new social context. Critical hermeneutics addresses this vacuum (Kincheloe & Steinberg, 1997; McLaren, 1997; Peters & Lankshear, 1994).

Critical hermeneutics names the world as a part of a larger effort to evaluate it and make it better. Knowing this, it is easy to understand why critical hermeneutics focuses on domination and its negation, emancipation. Domination limits self-direction and democratic community building, whereas emancipation enables them. Domination, legitimated as it is by ideology, is decoded by critical hermeneuts who help critical researchers discover the ways they and their subjects have been entangled in the ideological process. The exposé and critique of ideology is one of the main objectives of critical hermeneutics in its effort to make the world better. As long as our vision is obstructed by the various purveyors of ideology, our effort to live in democratic communities will be thwarted (Gallagher, 1992). Power wielders with race, class, and gender privilege (Kincheloe & Steinberg, 1997) have access to the resources that allow them to promote ideologies and representations in ways individuals without such privilege cannot (Bartolomé, 1998; Carlson & Apple, 1998; Denzin, 1992; Gresson, 1995; Hinchey, 1998; Jipson & Paley, 1997; Leistyna et al., 1996; Peters & Lankshear, 1994; Pinar, 1998).

◆ Partisan Research in a "Neutral" Academic Culture

In the space available here it is impossible to do justice to all of the critical traditions that have drawn inspiration from Marx, Kant, Hegel, Weber, the Frankfurt school theorists, Continental social theorists such as Foucault, Habermas, and Derrida, Latin American thinkers such as Paulo Freire, French feminists such as Irigaray, Kristeva, and Cixous, or Russian sociolinguists such as Bakhtin and Vygotsky—most of whom regularly find their way into the reference lists of contemporary critical researchers. Today there are criticalist schools in many fields, and even a superficial discussion of the most prominent of these schools would demand much more space than we have available.

The fact that numerous books have been written about the often-virulent disagreements among members of the Frankfurt school only heightens our concern with the "packaging" of the different criticalist schools. Critical theory should not be treated as a universal grammar of revolutionary thought objectified and reduced to discrete formulaic pronouncements or strategies. Obviously, in presenting our idiosyncratic version of a reconceptualized critical theory, we have defined the critical tradition very broadly for the purpose of generating understanding; as we asserted earlier, this will trouble many critical researchers. In this move we decided to focus on the underlying commonality among critical schools of thought, at the cost of focusing on differences. This, of course, is always risky business in terms of suggesting a false unity or consensus where none exists, but such concerns are unavoidable in a survey chapter such as this. We are defining a criticalist as a researcher or theorist who attempts to use her or his work as a form of social or cultural criticism and who accepts certain basic assumptions: that all thought is fundamentally mediated by power relations that are social and historically constituted; that facts can never be isolated from the domain of values or removed from some form of ideological inscription; that the relationship between concept and object and between signifier and signified is never stable or fixed and is often mediated by the social relations of capitalist production and consumption; that language is central to the formation of subjectivity (conscious and unconscious awareness); that certain groups in any society are privileged over others and, although the reasons for this privileging may vary widely, the oppression that characterizes contemporary societies is most forcefully reproduced when subordinates accept their social status as natural, necessary, or inevitable; that oppression has many faces and that focusing on only one at the expense of others (e.g., class oppression versus racism) often elides the interconnections among them; and, finally, that mainstream research practices are generally, although most often unwittingly, implicated in the reproduction of systems of class, race, and gender oppression (Kincheloe & Steinberg, 1997).

In today's climate of blurred disciplinary genres, it is not uncommon to find literary theorists doing anthropology and anthropologists writing about literary theory, or political scientists trying their hand at ethnomethodological analysis, or philosophers doing Lacanian film criticism. We offer this observation not as an excuse to be wantonly eclectic in our treatment of the critical tradition but to make the point that any attempts to delineate critical theory as discrete schools of analysis will fail to capture the hybridity endemic to contemporary critical analysis.

Readers familiar with the criticalist traditions will recognize essentially four different "emergent" schools of social inquiry in this chapter: the neo-Marxist tradition of critical theory associated most closely with the work of Horkheimer, Adorno, and Marcuse; the genealogical writings of Michel Foucault; the practices of poststructuralist deconstruction associated with Derrida; and postmodernist currents associated with Derrida, Foucault, Lyotard, Ebert, and others. In our view, critical ethnography has been influenced by all of these perspectives in different ways and to different degrees. From critical theory, researchers inherit a forceful criticism of the positivist conception of science and instrumental rationality, especially in Adorno's idea of negative dialectics, which posits an unstable relationship of contradiction between concepts and objects; from Derrida, researchers are given a means for deconstructing objective truth, or what is referred to as "the metaphysics of presence." For Derrida, the meaning of a word is constantly deferred because the word can have meaning only in relation to its difference from other words within a given system of language; Foucault invites researchers to explore the ways in which discourses are implicated in relations of power and how power and knowledge serve as dialectically reinitiating practices that regulate what is considered reasonable and true. We have characterized much of the work influenced by these writers as the "ludic" and "resistance" postmodernist theoretical perspectives.

Critical research can be best understood in the context of the empowerment of individuals. Inquiry that aspires to the name *critical* must be connected to an attempt to confront the injustice of a particular society or public sphere within the society. Research thus becomes a transformative endeavor unembarrassed by the label *political* and unafraid to consummate a relationship with emancipatory consciousness. Whereas traditional researchers cling to the guard rail of neutrality, critical researchers frequently announce their partisanship in the struggle for a better world. Traditional researchers see their task as the description, interpretation, or reanimation of a slice of reality, whereas critical researchers often regard their work as a first step toward forms of political action that can redress the injustices found in the field site or constructed in the very act of research itself. Horkheimer (1972) puts it succinctly when he argues that critical theory and research are never satisfied with merely increasing knowledge (see also Agger, 1998; Andersen, 1989; Britzman, 1991; Giroux, 1983, 1988, 1997; Kincheloe, 1991; Kincheloe & Steinberg, 1993; Quantz, 1992; Shor, 1996; Villaverde & Kincheloe, 1998).

Research in the critical tradition takes the form of self-conscious criticism—self-conscious in the sense that researchers try to become aware of the ideological imperatives and epistemological presuppositions that inform their research as well as their own subjective, intersubjective, and normative reference claims. Thus critical researchers enter into an investigation with their assumptions on the table, so no one is confused concerning the epistemological and political baggage they bring with them to the research site. Upon detailed analysis, these assumptions may change. Stimulus for change may come from the critical researchers' recognition that such assumptions are not leading to emancipatory actions. The source of this emancipatory action involves the researchers' ability to expose the contradictions of the world of appearances accepted by the dominant culture as natural and inviolable (Giroux, 1983, 1988, 1997; McLaren, 1992a, 1997; San Juan, 1992; Zizek, 1990). Such appearances may, critical researchers contend, conceal social relationships of inequality, injustice, and exploitation. For instance, if we view the violence we find in classrooms not as random or isolated incidents created by aberrant individuals willfully stepping out of line in accordance with a particular form of social pathology, but as narratives of transgression and resistance, then this could indicate that the "political unconscious" lurking beneath the surface of everyday classroom life is not unrelated to practices of race, class, and gender oppression but rather intimately connected to them.

◆ Babes in Toyland: Critical Theory in Hyperreality

Postmodern Culture

Over the last quarter of the 20th century, traditional notions of critical theory have had to come to terms with the rise of postmodernism. Our reconceptualized notion of critical theory is our way of denoting the conversation between traditional criticalism and postmodernism (Kincheloe, Steinberg, & Tippins, 1999). We will first analyze postmodernism and then address the relationship between it and our notion of critical theory.

In a contemporary era marked by the delegitimation of the grand narratives of Western civilization, a loss of faith in the power of reason, and a shattering of traditional religious orthodoxies, scholars continue to debate what the term *postmodernism* means, generally positing it as a periodizing concept following modernism. Indeed, scholars have not agreed if this epochal break with the "modern" era even constitutes a discrete period. In the midst of such confusion it seems somehow appropriate that scholars are fighting over the application of the term *postmodernism* to the contemporary condition. Accepting postmodernism as an apt moniker for the end of the 20th century, a major feature of critical academic work has involved the exploration of what happens when critical theory encounters the postmodern condition, or hyperreality. *Hyperreality* is a term used to describe an information society socially saturated with ever-increasing forms of representation: filmic, photographic, electronic, and so on. These have had profound effects on the construction of the cultural narratives that shape our identities. The drama of living has been portrayed so often on television that individuals, for the most part, are increasingly able to predict the outcomes and consider such outcomes to be the "natural" and "normal" course of social life (Fraser, 1995; Gergen, 1991; Heshusius & Ballard, 1996; Kellner, 1994; Morley & Chen, 1996; Nicholson & Seidman, 1995).

As many postmodern analysts have put it, we become pastiches, imitative conglomerations of one another. In such a condition we approach life with low affect, with a sense of postmodern ennui and irremissible anxiety. Our emotional bonds are diffused as television, computers, VCRs, and stereo headphones assault us with representations that have shaped our cognitive and affective facilities in ways that still remain insufficiently understood. In the political arena, traditionalists circle their cultural wagons and fight off imagined bogeymen such as secular humanists, "extreme liberals," and utopianists, not realizing the impact that postmodern hyperreality exerts on their hallowed institutions. The nuclear family, for example, has declined in importance not because of the assault of "radical feminists" but because the home has been redefined through the familiar presence of electronic communication systems. Particular modes of information put individual family members in constant contact with specific subcultures. While they are physically in the home, they exist emotionally outside of it through the mediating effects of various forms of communication (Gergen, 1991; McGuigan, 1996; McLaren, 1997; Poster, 1989; Steinberg & Kincheloe, 1997). We increasingly make sense of the social world and judge other cultures through conventional and culture-bound television genres. Hyperreality has presented us with new forms of literacy that do not simply refer to discrete skills but rather constitute social skills and relations of symbolic power. These new technologies cannot be seen apart from the social and institutional contexts in which they are used and the roles they play in the family, the community, and the workplace. They also need to be seen in terms of how "viewing competencies" are socially distributed and the diverse social and discursive practices in which these new media literacies are produced (Buckingham, 1989; Hall, 1997; Taylor & Saarinen, 1994).

Electronic transmissions generate new formations of cultural space and restructure experiences of time. We often are motivated to trade community membership for a sense of pseudobelonging to the mediascape. Residents of hyperreality are temporarily comforted by proclamations of community offered by "media personalities" on the 6 o'clock *Eyewitness News*. "Bringing news of your neighbors in the Tri-State community home to you," media marketers attempt to soften the edges of hyperreality, to soften the emotional effects of the social vertigo. The world is not brought into our homes by television as much as television brings its viewers to a quasi-fictional place—hyperreality (Luke, 1991).

Postmodern Social Theory

We believe that it is misleading to identify postmodernism with post-structuralism. Although there are certainly similarities involved, they cannot be considered discrete homologies. We also believe that it is a mistake to equate postmodernism with postmodernity or to assert that these terms can be contrasted in some simple equivalent way with modernism and modernity. As Michael Peters (1993) notes, "To do so is to frame up the debate in strictly (and naïvely) modernist terminology which employs exhaustive binary oppositions privileging one set of terms against the other" (p. 14). We are using the term *postmodernity* to refer to the post-modern condition that we have described as *hyperreality* and the term *postmodern theory* as an umbrella term that includes antifoundationalist writing in philosophy and the social sciences. Again, we are using this term in a very general sense that includes poststructuralist currents.

Postmodern theoretical trajectories take as their entry point a rejection of the deeply ingrained assumptions of Enlightenment rationality, traditional Western epistemology, or any supposedly "secure" representation of reality that exists outside of discourse itself. Doubt is cast on the myth of the autonomous, transcendental subject, and the concept of praxis is marginalized in favor of rhetorical undecidability and textual analysis of social practices. As a species of criticism, intended, in part, as a central requestioning of the humanism and anthropologism of the early 1970s, postmodernist social theory rejects Hegel's ahistorical state of absolute knowledge and resigns itself to the impossibility of an ahistorical, transcendental, or self-authenticating version of truth. The reigning conviction that knowledge is knowledge only if it reflects the world as it "really" exists has been annihilated in favor of a view in which reality is socially constructed or semiotically posited. Furthermore, normative agreement on what should constitute and guide scientific practice and argumentative consistency has become an intellectual target for epistemological uncertainty (Pinar et al., 1995; Shelton, 1996).

Postmodern criticism takes as its starting point the notion that meaning is constituted by the continual playfulness of the signifier, and the thrust of its critique is aimed at deconstructing Western metanarratives of truth and

456

the ethnocentrism implicit in the European view of history as the unilinear progress of universal reason. Postmodern theory is a site of both hope and fear, where there exists a strange convergence between critical theorists and political conservatives, a cynical complicity with status quo social and institutional relations and a fierce criticism of ideological manipulation and the reigning practices of subjectivity in which knowledge takes place.

◆ Ludic and Resistance Postmodernism

Postmodernist criticism is not monolithic, and for the purposes of this essay we would like to distinguish between two theoretical strands. The first has been astutely described by Teresa Ebert (1991) as "ludic postmodernism" (p. 115)—an approach to social theory that is decidedly limited in its ability to transform oppressive social and political regimes of power. Ludic postmodernism generally occupies itself with a reality that is constituted by the continual playfulness of the signifier and the heterogeneity of differences. As such, ludic postmodernism (see, e.g., Lyotard, Derrida, Baudrillard) constitutes a moment of self-reflexivity in the deconstruction of Western metanarratives, asserting that "meaning itself is self-divided and undecidable."

We want to argue that critical researchers should assume a cautionary stance toward ludic postmodernism critique because, as Ebert (1991) notes, it tends to reinscribe the status quo and reduce history to the supplementarity of signification or the free-floating trace of textuality. As a mode of critique, it rests its case on interrogating specific and local enunciations of oppression, but often fails to analyze such enunciations in relation to larger dominating structures of oppression (Aronowitz & Giroux, 1991; McLaren, 1995a; Sünker, 1998).

The kind of postmodern social theory we want to pose as a counterweight to skeptical and spectral postmodernism has been referred to as "oppositional postmodernism" (Foster, 1983), "radical critique-al theory" (Zavarzadeh & Morton, 1991), "postmodern education" (Aronowitz & Giroux, 1991), "resistance postmodernism" (Ebert, 1991), "affirmative postmodernism" (Slattery, 1995), "critical postmodernism" (Giroux, 1992; McLaren, 1992b, 1997; McLaren & Hammer, 1989), and "postformalism" (Kincheloe, 1993, 1995; Kincheloe & Steinberg, 1993; Kincheloe, Steinberg, & Hinchey, 1999; Kincheloe, Steinberg, & Villaverde, 1999). These forms of critique are not alternatives to ludic postmodernism but appropriations and extensions of this critique. Resistance postmodernism brings to ludic critique a form of materialist intervention because it is not based solely on a textual theory of difference but rather on one that is also social and historical. In this way, postmodern critique can serve as an interventionist and transformative critique of Western culture. Following Ebert (1991), resistance postmodernism attempts to show that "textualities (significations) are material practices, forms of conflicting social relations" (p. 115). The sign is always an arena of material conflict and competing social relations as well as ideas. From this perspective we can rethink a signifier as an ideological dynamic ever related to a contextually possible set of signifieds. In other words, difference is politicized by being situated in real social and historical conflicts.

The synergism of the conversation between resistance postmodernism and critical theory involves an interplay between the praxis of the critical and the radical uncertainty of the postmodern. As it invokes its strategies for the emancipation of meaning, critical theory provides the postmodern critique with a normative foundation (i.e., a basis for distinguishing between oppressive and liberatory social relations). Without such a foundation the postmodern critique is ever vulnerable to nihilism and inaction. Indeed, the normatively ungrounded postmodern critique is incapable of providing an ethically challenging and politically transformative program of action. Aronowitz, Giroux, Kincheloe, and McLaren argue that if the postmodern critique is to make a valuable contribution to the notion of schooling as an emancipatory form of cultural politics, it must make connections to those egalitarian impulses of modernism that contribute to an emancipatory democracy. In doing this, the postmodern critique can extend the project of an emancipatory democracy and the schooling that supports it by promoting new understandings of how power operates and by incorporating groups who had been excluded because of race, gender, or class (Aronowitz & Giroux, 1991; Codd, 1984; Godzich, 1992; Kincheloe, 1995, 1999; Lash, 1990; McLaren, 1997, 1999; Morrow, 1991; Pinar, 1994, 1998; Rosenau, 1992; Steinberg & Kincheloe, 1998; Surber, 1998; Welch, 1991; Wexler, 1996a, 1997; Yates, 1990).

◆ Critical Research and Cultural Studies

Cultural studies is an interdisciplinary, transdisciplinary, and sometimes counterdisciplinary field that functions within the dynamics of competing definitions of culture. Unlike traditional humanistic studies, cultural studies questions the equation of culture with high culture; instead, cultural studies asserts that myriad expressions of cultural production should be analyzed in relation to other cultural dynamics and social and historical structures. Such a position commits cultural studies to a potpourri of artistic, religious, political, economic, and communicative activities. In this context, it is important to note that although cultural studies is associated with the study of popular culture, it is not primarily about popular culture. The interests of cultural studies are much broader and generally tend to involve the production and nature of the rules of inclusivity and exclusivity that guide academic evaluation—in particular, the way these rules shape and are shaped by relations of power. The rules that guide academic evaluation are inseparable from the rules of knowledge production and research. Thus cultural studies provides a disciplinary critique that holds many implications (Abercrombie, 1994; Ferguson & Golding, 1997; Grossberg, 1995; Hall & du Gay, 1996; McLaren, 1995a; Woodward, 1997).

One of the most important sites of theoretical production in the history of critical research has been the Centre for Contemporary Cultural Studies (CCCS) at the University of Birmingham. Attempting to connect critical theory with the particularity of everyday experience, the CCCS researchers have argued that all experience is vulnerable to ideological inscription. At the same time, they have maintained that theorizing outside of everyday experience results in formal and deterministic theory. An excellent representative of the CCCS's perspectives is Paul Willis, whose *Learning to Labour: How Working Class Kids Get Working Class Jobs* was published in 1977, seven years after Colin Lacey's *Hightown Grammar* (1970). Redefining the nature of ethnographic research in a critical manner, *Learning to Labour* inspired a spate of critical studies: David Robins and Philip Cohen's *Knuckle Sandwich: Growing Up in the Working-Class City* in 1978, Paul Corrigan's *Schooling the Smash Street Kids* in 1979, and Dick Hebdige's *Subculture: The Meaning of Style* in 1979.

Also following Willis's work were critical feminist studies, including an anthology titled *Women Take Issue* (Women's Studies Group, 1978). In 1985, Christine Griffin published *Typical Girls?* the first extended feminist study produced by the CCCS. Conceived as a response to Willis's *Learning to Labour, Typical Girls?* analyzes adolescent female consciousness as it is constructed in a world of patriarchy. Through their recognition of patriarchy as a major disciplinary technology in the production of

459

subjectivity, Griffin and the members of the CCCS gender study group move critical research in a multicultural direction. In addition to the examination of class, gender and racial analyses are beginning to gain in importance (Quantz, 1992). Poststructuralism frames power not simply as one aspect of a society, but as the basis of society. Thus patriarchy is not simply one isolated force among many with which women must contend; patriarchy informs all aspects of the social and effectively shapes women's lives (see also Douglas, 1994; Finders, 1997; Fine et al., 1997; Frankenberg, 1993; Franz & Stewart, 1994; Shohat & Stam, 1994).

Cornel West (1993) pushes critical research even further into the multi-cultural domain as he focuses critical attention on women, the Third World, and race. Adopting theoretical advances in neo-Marxist post-colonialist criticism and cultural studies, he is able to shed greater light on the workings of power in everyday life. In this context, Ladislaus Semali and Joe Kincheloe, in *What Is Indigenous Knowledge? Voices from the Academy* (1999), explore the power of indigenous knowledge as a re-source for critical attempts to bring about social change. Critical research-ers, they argue, should analyze such knowledges in order to understand emotions, sensitivities, and epistemologies that move in ways unimagined by many Western knowledge producers. In this postcolonially informed context, Semali and Kincheloe employ concerns raised by indigenous knowledge to challenge the academy, its "normal science," and its accepted notions of certified information. Moving the conversation about critical research in new directions, these authors understand the concep-tual inseparability of valuing indigenous knowledge, developing post-colonial forms of resistance, academic reform, the reconceptualization of research and interpretation, and the struggle for social justice.

In *Schooling as a Ritual Performance*, Peter McLaren (1999) integrates poststructuralist, postcolonialist, and Marxist theory with the projects of cultural studies, critical pedagogy, and critical ethnography. He grounds his theoretical analysis in the poststructuralist claim that the connection of signifier and signified is arbitrary yet shaped by historical, cultural, and economic forces. The primary cultural narrative that defines school life is the resistance by students to the school's attempts to marginalize their street culture and street knowledge. McLaren analyzes the school as a cul-tural site where symbolic capital is struggled over in the form of ritual dramas. *Schooling as a Ritual Performance* adopts the position that re-searchers are unable to grasp themselves or others introspectively without social mediation through their positionalities with respect to race, class, gender, and other configurations. The visceral, bodily forms of knowledge, and the rhythms and gestures of the street culture of the students, are distinguished from the formal abstract knowledge of classroom instruction. The teachers regard knowledge as it is constructed informally outside of the culture of school instruction as threatening to the universalist and decidedly Eurocentric ideal of high culture that forms the basis of the school curriculum.

As critical researchers pursue the reconceptualization of critical theory pushed by its synergistic relationship with cultural studies, postmodernism, and poststructuralism, they are confronted with the post-discourses' redefinition of critical notions of democracy in terms of multiplicity and difference. Traditional notions of community often privilege unity over diversity in the name of Enlightenment values. Poststructuralists in general and poststructuralist feminists in particular see this communitarian dream as politically disabling because of the suppression of race, class, and gender differences and the exclusion of subaltern voices and marginalized groups whom community members are loath to engage. What begins to emerge in this instance is the movement of feminist theoretical concerns to the center of critical theory. Indeed, after the feminist critique, critical theory can never return to a paradigm of inquiry in which the concept of social class is antiseptically privileged and exalted as the master concept in the Holy Trinity of race, class, and gender. A critical theory reconceptualized by poststructuralism and feminism promotes a politics of difference that refuses to pathologize or exoticize the Other. In this context, communities are more prone to revitalization and revivification (Wexler, 1996b, 1997); peripheralized groups in the thrall of a condescending Eurocentric gaze are able to edge closer to the borders of respect, and "classified" objects of research potentially acquire the characteristics of subjecthood. Kathleen Weiler's *Women Teaching for Change: Gender, Class, and Power* (1988) serves as a good example of critical research framed by feminist theory. Weiler shows not only how feminist theory can extend critical research, but how the concept of emancipation can be reconceptualized in light of a feminist epistemology (Aronowitz & Giroux, 1991; Behar & Gordon, 1995; Bersani, 1995; Brents & Monson, 1998; Britzman, 1995; Christian-Smith & Keelor, 1999; Clatterbaugh, 1997; Clough, 1994; Cooper, 1994; Hammer, 1999; Hedley, 1994; Johnson, 1996; Kelly, 1996; King & Mitchell, 1995; Lugones, 1987; Maher & Tetreault, 1994; Morrow, 1991; Rand, 1995; Scott, 1992; Sedgwick, 1995; Steinberg, 1997; Young, 1990).

◆ Focusing on Critical Ethnography

As critical researchers attempt to get behind the curtain, to move beyond assimilated experience, to expose the way ideology constrains the desire for self-direction, and to confront the way power reproduces itself in the construction of human consciousness, they employ a plethora of research methodologies. In this context Patti Lather (1991, 1993) extends our position with her notion of catalytic validity. Catalytic validity points to the degree to which research moves those it studies to understand the world and the way it is shaped in order for them to transform it. Noncritical researchers who operate within an empiricist framework will perhaps find catalytic validity to be a strange concept. Research that possesses catalytic validity will not only display the reality-altering impact of the inquiry process, it will direct this impact so that those under study will gain self-understanding and self-direction.

Theory that falls under the rubric of *postcolonialism* (see McLaren, 1999; Semali & Kincheloe, 1999) involves important debates over the knowing subject and object of analysis. Such works have initiated important new modes of analysis, especially in relation to questions of imperialism, colonialism, and neocolonialism. Recent attempts by critical researchers to move beyond the objectifying and imperialist gaze associated with the Western anthropological tradition (which fixes the image of the so-called informant from the colonizing perspective of the knowing subject), although laudatory and well-intentioned, are not without their shortcomings (Bourdieu & Wacquaat, 1992). As Fuchs (1993) has so presciently observed, serious limitations plague recent efforts to develop a more reflective approach to ethnographic writing. The challenge here can be summarized in the following questions: How does the knowing subject come to know the Other? How can researchers respect the perspective of the Other and invite the Other to speak (Abdullah & Stringer, 1999; Ashcroft, Griffiths, & Tiffin, 1995; Brock-Utne, 1996; Goldie, 1995; Macedo, 1994; Myrsiades & Myrsiades, 1998; Pieterse & Parekh, 1995; Prakash & Esteva, 1998; Rains, 1998; Scheurich & Young, 1997; Semali & Kincheloe, 1999; Viergever, 1999)?

Although recent confessional modes of ethnographic writing attempt to treat so-called informants as "participants" in an attempt to avoid the objectification of the Other (usually referring to the relationship between Western anthropologists and non-Western culture), there is a risk that uncovering colonial and postcolonial structures of domination may, in fact, unintentionally validate and consolidate such structures as well as reassert liberal values through a type of covert ethnocentrism. Fuchs (1993) warns that the attempt to subject researchers to the same approach to which other societies are subjected could lead to an " 'othering' of one's own world" (p. 108). Such an attempt often fails to question existing ethnographic methodologies and therefore unwittingly extends their validity and applicability while further objectifying the world of the researcher.

Michel Foucault's approach to this dilemma is to "detach" social theory from the epistemology of his own culture by criticizing the traditional philosophy of reflection. However, Foucault falls into the trap of ontologizing his own methodological argumentation and erasing the notion of prior understanding that is linked to the idea of an "inside" view (Fuchs, 1993). Louis Dumont fares somewhat better by arguing that cultural texts need to be viewed simultaneously from the inside and from the outside. However, in trying to affirm a "reciprocal interpretation of various societies among themselves" (Fuchs, 1993, p. 113) through identifying both transindividual structures of consciousness and transsubjective social structures, Dumont aspires to a universal framework for the comparative analysis of societies. Whereas Foucault and Dumont attempt to "transcend the categorical foundations of their own world" (Fuchs, 1993, p. 118) by refusing to include themselves in the process of objectification, Pierre Bourdieu integrates himself as a social actor into the social field under analysis. Bourdieu achieves such integration by "epistemologizing the ethnological content of his own presuppositions" (Fuchs, 1993, p. 121). But the self-objectification of the observer (anthropologist) is not unproblematic. Fuchs (1993) notes, after Bourdieu, that the chief difficulty is "forgetting the difference between the theoretical and the practical relationship with the world and of imposing on the object the theoretical relationship one maintains with it" (p. 120). Bourdieu's approach to research does not fully escape becoming, to a certain extent, a "confirmation of objectivism," but at least there is an earnest attempt by the researcher to reflect on the preconditions of his own self-understanding—an attempt to engage in an "ethnography of ethnographers" (p. 122).

Postmodern ethnography often intersects—to varying degrees—with the concerns of postcolonialist researchers, but the degree to which it fully addresses issues of exploitation and the social relations of capitalist exploitation remains questionable. Postmodern ethnography—and we are thinking here of works such as Paul Rabinow's *Reflections on Fieldwork in*

Morocco (1977), James Boon's *Other Tribes, Other Scribes* (1982), and Michael Taussig's *Shamanism, Colonialism, and the Wild Man* (1987)—shares the conviction articulated by Marc Manganaro (1990) that "no anthropology is apolitical, removed from ideology and hence from the capacity to be affected by or, as crucially, to effect social formations. The question ought not to be if an anthropological text is political, but rather, what kind of sociopolitical affiliations are tied to particular anthropological texts" (p. 35).

Judith Newton and Judith Stacey (1992-1993) note that the current postmodern textual experimentation of ethnography credits the "post-colonial predicament of culture as the opportunity for anthropology to reinvent itself" (p. 56). Modernist ethnography, according to these authors, "constructed authoritative cultural accounts that served, however inadvertently, not only to establish the authority of the Western ethnographer over native others but also to sustain Western authority over colonial cultures" (p. 56). They argue (following James Clifford) that ethnographers can and should try to escape the recurrent allegorical genre of colonial ethnography—the pastoral, a nostalgic, redemptive text that preserves a primitive culture on the brink of extinction for the historical record of its Western conquerors. The narrative structure of this "salvage text" portrays the native culture as a coherent, authentic, and lamentably "evading past," whereas its complex, inauthentic, Western successors represent the future (p. 56).

Postmodern ethnographic writing faces the challenge of moving beyond simply the reanimation of local experience, an uncritical celebration of cultural difference (including figural differentiations within the ethnographer's own culture), and the employment of a framework that espouses universal values and a global role for interpretivist anthropology (Silverman, 1990). What we have described as resistance postmodernism can help qualitative researchers challenge dominant Western research practices that are underwritten by a foundational epistemology and a claim to universally valid knowledge at the expense of local, subjugated knowledges (Peters, 1993). The choice is not one between modernism and postmodernism, but one of whether or not to challenge the presuppositions that inform the normalizing judgments one makes as a researcher. Vincent Crapanzano (1990) warns that "the anthropologist can assume neither the Orphic lyre nor the crown of thorns, although I confess to hear salvationist echoes in his desire to protect his people" (p. 301).

Connor (1992) describes the work of James Clifford, which shares an affinity with ethnographic work associated with Georges Bataille, Michel Lerris, and the College de Sociologie, as not simply the "writing of culture" but rather "the interior disruption of categories of art and culture correspond[ing] to a radically dialogic form of ethnographic writing, which takes place across and between cultures" (p. 251). Clifford (1992) describes his own work as an attempt "to multiply the hands and discourses involved in 'writing culture' . . . not to assert a naïve democracy of plural authorship, but to loosen at least somewhat the monological control of the executive writer/anthropologist and to open for discussion ethnography's hierarchy and negotiation of discourses in power-charged, unequal situations" (p. 100). Citing the work of Marcus and Fischer (1986), Clifford warns against modernist ethnographic practices of "representational essentializing" and "metonymic freezing" in which one aspect of a group's life is taken to represent the group as a whole; instead, Clifford urges forms of multilocale ethnography to reflect the "transnational political, economic and cultural forces that traverse and constitute local or regional worlds" (p. 102). Rather than fixing culture into reified textual portraits, culture needs to be better understood as displacement, transplantation, disruption, positionality, and difference.

Although critical ethnography allows, in a way conventional ethnography does not, for the relationship of liberation and history, and although its hermeneutical task is to call into question the social and cultural conditioning of human activity and the prevailing sociopolitical structures, we do not claim that this is enough to restructure the social system. But it is certainly, in our view, a necessary beginning. We follow Patricia Ticineto Clough (1992) in arguing that "realist narrativity has allowed empirical social science to be the platform and horizon of social criticism" (p. 135). Ethnography needs to be analyzed critically not only in terms of its field methods but also as reading and writing practices. Data collection must give way to "rereadings of representations in every form" (p. 137). In the narrative construction of its authority as empirical science, ethnography needs to face the unconscious processes upon which it justifies its canonical formulations, processes that often involve the disavowal of oedipal or authorial desire and the reduction of differences to binary oppositions. Within these processes of binary reduction, the male ethnographer is most often privileged as the guardian of "the factual representation of empirical positivities" (p. 9).

◆ New Questions Concerning Validity in Critical Ethnography

Critical research traditions have arrived at the point where they recognize that claims to truth are always discursively situated and implicated in relations of power. Yet, unlike some claims made within "ludic" strands of postmodernist research, we do not suggest that because we cannot know truth absolutely that truth can simply be equated with an effect of power. We say this because truth involves regulative rules that must be met for some statements to be more meaningful than others. Otherwise, truth becomes meaningless and, if that is the case, liberatory praxis has no purpose other than to win for the sake of winning. As Phil Carspecken (1993, 1999) remarks, every time we act, in every instance of our behavior, we presuppose some normative or universal relation to truth. Truth is internally related to meaning in a pragmatic way through normative referenced claims, intersubjective referenced claims, subjective referenced claims, and the way we deictically ground or anchor meaning in our daily lives.

Carspecken explains that researchers are able to articulate the normative evaluative claims of others when they begin to see them in the same way as their participants by living inside the cultural and discursive positionalities that inform such claims. Claims to universality must be recognized in each particular normative claim, and questions must be raised about whether such norms represent the entire group. When the limited claim of universality is seen to be contradictory to the practices under observation, power relations become visible. What is crucial here, according to Carspecken, is that researchers recognize where they are ideologically located in the normative and identity claims of others and at the same time be honest about their own subjective referenced claims and not let normative evaluative claims interfere with what they observe. Critical research continues to problematize normative and universal claims in a way that does not permit them to be analyzed outside of a politics of representation, divorced from the material conditions in which they are produced, or outside of a concern with the constitution of the subject in the very acts of reading and writing.

In his book, *Critical Ethnography in Educational Research* (1996), Carspecken addresses the issue of critical epistemology, an understanding of the relationship between power and thought, and power and truth claims. In a short exposition of what is "critical" to critical epistemology, he debunks facile forms of social constructivism and offers a deft criticism of mainstream epistemologies by way of Continental phenomenology, poststructuralism, and postmodernist social theory, mainly the work of Edmund Husserl and Jacques Derrida. Carspecken makes short work of facile forms of constructivist thought purporting that what we see is strongly influenced by what we already value and that criticalist research simply indulges itself in the "correct" political values. For instance, some constructivists argue that all that criticalists need to do is to "bias" their work in the direction of social justice. This form of constructivist thought is not viable, according to Carspecken, because it is plainly ocular-centric; that is, it depends upon visual perception to form the basis of its theory. Rather than rely on perceptual metaphors found in mainstream ethnographic accounts, critical ethnography, in contrast, should emphasize communicative experiences and structures as well as cultural typifications.

Carspecken argues that critical ethnography needs to differentiate among ontological categories (i.e., subjective, objective, normative-evaluative) rather than adopt the position of "multiple realities" defended by many constructivists. He adopts a principled position that research value orientations should not determine research findings, as much as this is possible. Rather, critical ethnographers should employ a critical epistemology; that is, they should uphold epistemological principles that apply to all researchers. In fecundating this claim, Carspecken rehabilitates critical ethnography from many of the misperceptions of its critics who believe that it ignores questions of validity.

To construct a socially critical epistemology, critical ethnographers need to understand holistic modes of human experience and their relationship to communicative structures. Preliminary stages of this process that Carspecken articulates include examining researcher bias and discovering researcher value orientations. Following stages include compiling the primary record through the collection of monological data, preliminary reconstructive analysis, dialogical data generation, discovering social systems relations, and using systems relations to explain findings. Anthony Giddens's work forms the basis of Carspecken's approach to systems analysis. Accompanying discussions of each of the complex stages Carspecken develops are brilliantly articulated approaches to horizontal and vertical validity reconstructions and pragmatic horizons of analysis. In order to help link theory to practice, Carspecken uses data from his study of an inner-city Houston elementary school program that is charged with helping students learn conflict management skills.

Another impressive feature is Carspecken's exposition and analysis of communicative acts, especially his discussion of meaning as embodiment and understanding as intersubjective, not objective or subjective. Carspecken works from a view of intersubjectivity that combines Hegel, Mead, Habermas, and Taylor. He recommends that critical ethnographers record body language carefully because the meaning of an action is not in the language, it is rather in the action and the actor's bodily states. In Carspecken's view, subjectivity is derivative from intersubjectivity (as is objectivity), and intersubjectivity involves the dialogical constitution of the "feeling body." Finally, Carspecken stresses the importance of macro-level social theories, environmental conditions, socially structured ways of meeting needs and desires, effects of cultural commodities on students, economic exploitation, and political and cultural conditions of action.

Much of Carspecken's inspiration for his approach to validity claims is taken from Habermas's theory of communicative action. Carspecken reads Habermas as grasping the prelinguistic foundations of language and intersubjectivity, making language secondary to the concept of intersubjectivity. Yet Carspecken departs from a strict Habermasian view of action by bringing in an expressive/praxis model roughly consistent with Charles Taylor's work. Although Habermas and Taylor frequently argue against each other's positions, Carspecken puts them together in a convincing manner. Taylor's emphasis on holistic modes of understanding and the act constitution that Carspecken employs make it possible to link the theory of communicative rationality to work on embodied meaning and the metaphoric basis of meaningful action. It also provides a means for synthesizing Giddens's ideas on part/whole relations, virtual structure, and act constitution with communicative rationality. This is another way in which Carspecken's work differs from Habermas and yet remains consistent with his theory and the internal link between meaning and validity.

◆ Recent Innovations in Critical Ethnography

In addition to Carspecken's brilliant insights into critically grounded ethnography, the late 1990s have witnessed a proliferation of deconstructive approaches as well as reflexive approaches (this discussion is based on Trueba & McLaren, in press). In her important book *Fictions of Feminist Ethnography* (1994), Kamala Visweswaran maintains that reflexive ethnography, like normative ethnography, rests on the "declarative mode" of imparting knowledge to a reader whose identity is anchored in a shared discourse. Deconstructive ethnography, in contrast, enacts the "interrogative mode" through a constant deferral or a refusal to explain or interpret. Within deconstructive ethnography, the identity of the reader with a unified subject of enunciation is discouraged. Whereas reflexive ethnography maintains that the ethnographer is not separate from the object of investigation, the ethnographer is still viewed as a unified subject of knowledge that can make hermeneutic efforts to establish identification between the observer and the observed (as in modernist interpretive traditions). Deconstructive ethnography, in contrast, often disrupts such identification in favor of articulating a fractured, destabilized, multiply positioned subjectivity (as in postmodernist interpretive traditions). Whereas reflexive ethnography questions its own authority, deconstructive ethnography forfeits its authority. Both approaches to critical ethnography can be used to uncover the clinging Eurocentric authority employed by ethnographers in the study of Latino/a populations. The goal of both these approaches is criticalist in nature: that is, to free the object of analysis from the tyranny of fixed, unassailable categories and to rethink subjectivity itself as a permanently unclosed, always partial, narrative engagement with text and context. Such an approach can help the ethnographer to caution against the damaging depictions propagated by Anglo observers about Mexican immigrants. As Ruth Behar (1993) notes, in classical sociological and ethnographic accounts of the Mexican and Mexican American family,

> stereotypes similar to those surrounding the black family perpetuated images of the authoritarian, oversexed, and macho husband and the meek and submissive wife surrounded by children who adore their good and suffering mother. These stereotypes have come under strong critique in the last few years, particularly by Chicana critics, who have sought to go beyond the various "deficiency theories" that continue to mark the discussion of African-American and Latina/Latino family life. (p. 276)

The conception of culture advanced by critical ethnographers generally unpacks culture as a complex circuit of production that includes myriad dialectically reinitiating and mutually informing sets of activities such as routines, rituals, action conditions, systems of intelligibility and meaning making, conventions of interpretation, systems relations, and conditions both external and internal to the social actor (Carspecken, 1996). In her recent ethnographic study *A Space on the Side of the Road* (1996), Kathleen Stewart cogently illustrates the ambivalent character of culture, as well as its fluidity and ungraspable multilayeredness, when she remarks:

> Culture, as it is seen through its productive forms and means of mediation, is not, then, reducible to a fixed body of social value and belief or a direct precipitant of lived experience in the world but grows into a space on the side of the road where stories weighted with sociality take on a life of their own. We "see" it . . . only by building up multilayered narratives of the poetic in the everyday life of things. We represent it only by roaming from one texted genre to another—romantic, realist, historical, fantastic, socio-logical, surreal. There is no final textual solution, no way of resolving the dialogic of the interpreter/interpreted or subject/object through efforts to "place" ourselves in the text, or to represent "the fieldwork experience," or to gather up the voices of the other as if they could speak for themselves. (p. 210)

According to E. San Juan (1996), a renewed understanding of culture—as both discursive and material—becomes the linchpin for any emanci-patory politics. San Juan writes that the idea of culture as social processes and practices that are thoroughly grounded in material social relations—in the systems of maintenance (economics), decision (politics), learning and communication (culture), and generation and nurture (the domain of social reproduction)—must be the grounding principle, or paradigm if you like, of any progressive and emancipatory approach (p. 177; Gresson, 1995).

Rejecting the characterization of anthropologists as either "adaptation-alists" (e.g., Marvin Harris) or "ideationalists" (e.g., cognitivists, Lévi-Straussian structuralists, Schneiderian symbolists, Geertzian interpre-tivists), E. Valentine Daniel remarks in his recent ethnography *Charred Lullabies: Chapters in an Anthropology of Violence* (1996) that culture is "no longer something out there to be discovered, described, and ex-plained, but rather something into which the ethnographer, as interpreter, enter[s]" (p. 198). Culture, in other words, is cocreated by the anthropolo-gist and informant through conversation. Yet even this semeiosic concep-tualization of culture is not without its problems. As Daniel himself notes, even if one considers oneself to be a "culture-comaking processualist," in contrast to a "culture-finding essentialist," one still has to recognize that one is working within a logocentric tradition that, to a greater or lesser extent, privileges words over actions.

Critical ethnography has benefited from this new understanding of culture and from the new hybridic possibilities for cultural critique that have been opened up by the current blurring and mixing of disciplinary genres—those that emphasize experience, subjectivity, reflexivity, and dialogical understanding. The advantage that follows such perspectives is that social life is not viewed as preontologically available for the researcher to study. It also follows that there is no perspective unspoiled by ideology from which to study social life in an antiseptically objective way. What is important to note here is the stress placed on the ideological situatedness of any descriptive or socioanalytic account of social life. Critical ethnographers such as John and Jean Comaroff (1992) have made significant contributions to our understanding of the ways in which power is entailed in culture, leading to practices of domination and exploitation that have become naturalized in everyday social life. According to Comaroff and Comaroff, hegemony refers to "that order of signs and practices, relations and distinctions, images and epistemologies—drawn from a historically situated cultural field—that come to be taken-for-granted as the natural and received shape of the world and everything that inhabits it" (p. 23). These axiomatic and yet ineffable discourses and practices that are presumptively shared become "ideological" precisely when their internal contradictions are revealed, uncovered, and viewed as arbitrary and negotiable. Ideology, then, refers to a highly articulated worldview, master narrative, discursive regime, or organizing scheme for collective symbolic production. The dominant ideology is the expression of the dominant social group.

Following this line of argument, hegemony "is nonnegotiable and therefore beyond direct argument," whereas ideology "is more susceptible to being perceived as a matter of inimical opinion and interest and therefore is open to contestation" (Comaroff & Comaroff, 1992, p. 24). Ideologies become the expressions of specific groups, whereas hegemony refers to conventions and constructs that are shared and naturalized throughout a political community. Hegemony works both through silences and repetition in naturalizing the dominant worldview. There also may exist oppositional ideologies among subordinate or subaltern groups—whether well formed or loosely articulated—that break free of hegemony. In this way hegemony is never total or complete; it is always porous.

◆ Conclusion: Critical Research in a Globalized, Privatized World

A critical postmodern research requires researchers to construct their perception of the world anew, not just in random ways but in a manner that undermines what appears natural, that opens to question what appears obvious (Slaughter, 1989). Oppositional and insurgent researchers as maieutic agents must not confuse their research efforts with the textual suavities of an avant-garde academic posturing in which they are awarded the sinecure of representation for the oppressed without actually having to return to those working-class communities where their studies took place. Rather, they need to locate their work in a transformative praxis that leads to the alleviation of suffering and the overcoming of oppression. Rejecting the arrogant reading of metropolitan critics and their imperial mandates governing research, insurgent researchers ask questions about how what is has come to be, whose interests are served by particular institutional arrangements, and where our own frames of reference come from. Facts are no longer simply "what is"; the truth of beliefs is not simply testable by their correspondence to these facts. To engage in critical postmodern research is to take part in a process of critical world making, guided by the shadowed outline of a dream of a world less conditioned by misery, suffering, and the politics of deceit. It is, in short, a pragmatics of hope in an age of cynical reason. The obstacles that critical postmodern research has yet to overcome in terms of a frontal assault against the ravages of global capitalism and its devastation of the global working class has led McLaren to a more sustained and sympathetic engagement with Marx and the Marxist tradition.

The educational left in the United States has not been able to provide a counterforce to resist the ferocious orbit of capital and what we believe is the creation of a transnational global society in which the nation-state as the principal form of social organization has been superseded. We see as already under way an integration of all national markets into a single international market and division of labor and the erosion of national affiliations of capital (Robinson, 1998). The transnationalism of labor and capital has brought about material shifts in cultural practices and the proliferation of new contradictions between capitalism and labor. The deepening instability following in the wake of global capitalism has been driven by overaccumulation, overinvestment, overcapacity, overproduction, and new developments in the theater of global finance. The bottom line is the production of goods must return a profit by selling at market prices. Despite efforts of working classes throughout the globe to resist capital's drive to exploit their labor, capitalism is able dynamically and continuously to reorganize and reengineer itself such that its drive to accumulate is unhampered. Efforts at regulating markets are not effective at overcoming capital's reign of global terror. What is called for is the overturning of the basic laws of capitalism and the defeat of the dominion of capital itself. Capitalism's concentration, centralization, and transnationalism have reterritorialized the laws of motion of capital. We need to view the phenomena of globalized capitalism not merely in terms of market competition but rather from the perspective of production. Given that the logic of privatization and free trade—where social labor is the means and measure of value, and surplus social labor lies at the heart of profit—now odiously shapes archetypes of citizenship, manages our perceptions of what should constitute the "good society," and creates ideological formations that produce necessary functions for capital in relation to labor, it stands to reason that new ethnographic research approaches must take global capitalism not as an end point of analysis, but as a starting point. As schools are financed more by corporations that function as service industries for transnational capitalism, and as neoliberalism continues to guide educational policy and practice, the U.S. population faces a challenging educational reality (Kincheloe, 1999). It is a reality that is witnessing the progressive merging of cultural pedagogy and the productive processes within advanced capitalism (Giroux & Searles, 1996; McLaren, 1997). Although, as researchers, we may not be interested in global capitalism, we can be sure that it is interested in us.

Critical ethnography faces a daunting challenge in the years to come, especially because capitalism has been naturalized as commonsense reality—even as a part of nature itself—and the term *social class* has been replaced by the less antagonistic term *socioeconomic status*. The focus of much recent postmodern ethnography is on asymmetrical gender and ethnic relations, and although this focus is important, class struggle has become an outdated issue (Kincheloe & Steinberg, 1999). When social class is discussed, it is usually viewed as relational, not as oppositional. In the context of discussions of "social status" rather than "class struggle," postmodern ethnography has secured a privileged position that is functionally advantageous to the socially reproductive logic of entrepreneurial capitalism, private ownership, and the personal appropriation of social production (McLaren, 1995b). More than ever before, critical research needs to address the objective, material conditions of the workplace and labor relations in order to prevent the further resecuring of the ideological hegemony of the neoliberal corporatist state.

In many ways the globalization process, and the strengthening of the free market capitalism that accompanies it, takes us back to the roots of critical research. As we have gained profound insights into the impact of the inscriptions of patriarchy, white supremacy, and class elitism on the consciousness of researchers operating under the banner of humanistic values, we also appreciate—mainly because it has profound implications for defeating the exploitation of human labor and the consolidation of a global ruling elite—critical insights into the domination of capital. In this context we envision important new developments of Marxist ethnographic practices that both complement and extend many of the exciting new approaches that we are witnessing within the precincts of postmodern and postcolonial ethnography. Future practitioners of critical research must take all of these crucial dynamics into account if their work is to help create a more just, democratic, and egalitarian world. The realm of the critical has yet to reach the potential it envisions. We hope that this essay challenges its readers to engage in the hard work and research necessary to move critical praxis closer to its realization.

◆ References

Abdullah, J., & Stringer, E. (1999). Indigenous knowledge, indigenous learning, indigenous research. In L. Semali & J. L. Kincheloe (Eds.), *What is indigenous knowledge? Voices from the academy.* Bristol, PA: Falmer.

Abercrombie, N. (1994). Authority and consumer society. In R. Keat, N. Whiteley, & N. Abercrombie (Eds.), *The authority of the consumer.* New York: Routledge.

Agger, B. (1992). *The discourse of domination: From the Frankfurt school to postmodernism.* Evanston, IL: Northwestern University Press.

Agger, B. (1998). *Critical social theories: An introduction.* Boulder, CO: Westview.

Alfino, M., Caputo, J., & Wynyard, R. (Eds.). (1998). *McDonaldization revisited: Critical essays on consumer and culture.* Westport, CT: Praeger.

Alford, C. (1993). Introduction to the special issue on political psychology and political theory. *Political Psychology, 14,* 199-208.

Allison, C. (1998). Okie narratives: Agency and whiteness. In J. L. Kincheloe, S. R. Steinberg, N. M. Rodriguez, & R. E. Chennault (Eds.), *White reign: Deploying whiteness in America.* New York: St. Martin's.

Anderson, G. (1989). Critical ethnography in education: Origins, current status, and new directions. *Review of Educational Research, 59,* 249-270.

Apple, M. (1996a). Dominance and dependency: Situating *The bell curve* within the conservative restoration. In J. L. Kincheloe, S. R. Steinberg, & A. D. Gresson III (Eds.), *Measured lies: The bell curve examined.* New York: St. Martin's.

Apple, M. (1966b). *Cultural politics and education.* New York: Teachers College Press.

Aronowitz, S., & DiFazio, W. (1994). *The jobless future.* Minneapolis: University of Minnesota Press.

Aronowitz, S., & Giroux, H. (1991). *Postmodern education: Politics, culture, and social criticism.* Minneapolis: University of Minnesota Press.

Ashcroft, B., Griffiths, G., & Tiffin, H. (Eds.). (1995). *The post-colonial studies reader.* New York: Routledge.

Atwell-Vasey, W. (1998). Psychoanalytic feminism and the powerful teacher. In W. F. Pinar (Ed.), *Curriculum: Toward new identities.* New York: Garland.

Barrows, A. (1995). The ecopsychology of child development. In T. Roszak, M. Gomes, & A. Kanner (Eds.), *Ecopsychology:* Restoring the earth, healing the mind. San Francisco: Sierra Club Books.

Bartolomé, L. I. (1998). *The misteaching of academic discourses: The politics of language in the classroom.* Boulder, CO: Westview.

Bauman, Z. (1995). *Life in fragments: Essays in postmodern morality.* Cambridge, MA: Blackwell.

Behar, R. (1993). *Translated woman: Crossing the border with Esperanza's story.* Boston: Beacon.

Behar, R., & Gordon, D. A. (Eds.). (1995). *Women writing culture.* Berkeley: University of California Press.

Bell, D., & Valentine, G. (1997). *Consuming geographics: We are where we eat.* New York: Routledge.

Berger, A. A. (1995). *Cultural criticism: A primer of key concepts.* Thousand Oaks, CA: Sage.

Berry, K. (1998). Nurturing the imagination of resistance: Young adults as creators of knowledge. In J. L. Kincheloe & S. R. Steinberg (Eds.), *Unauthorized methods: Strategies for critical teaching.* New York: Routledge.

Bersani, L. (1995). Loving men. In M. Berger, B. Wallis, & S. Watson (Eds.), *Constructing masculinity.* New York: Routledge.

Bertman, S. (1998). *Hyperculture: The human cost of speed.* Westport, CT: Praeger.

Blades, D. (1997). *Procedures of power and curriculum change: Foucault and the quest for possibilities in science education.* New York: Peter Lang.

Block, A. (1995). *Occupied reading: Critical foundations for an ecological theory.* New York: Garland.

Boon, J. A. (1982). *Other tribes, other scribes: Symbolic anthropology in the comparative study of cultures, histories, religions, and texts.* Cambridge: Cambridge University Press.

Bottomore, T. (1984). *The Frankfurt school.* London: Tavistock.

Bourdieu, P., & Wacquaat, L. (1992). *An invitation to reflexive sociology.* Chicago: University of Chicago Press.

Brents, B., & Monson, M. (1998). Whitewashing the strip: The construction of whiteness in Las Vegas. In J. L. Kincheloe, S. R. Steinberg, N. M. Rodriguez, & R. E. Chennault (Eds.), *White reign: Deploying whiteness in America.* New York: St. Martin's.

Britzman, D. (1991). *Practice makes practice: A critical study of learning to teach.* Albany: State University of New York Press.

Britzman, D. (1995). What is this thing called love? *Taboo: The Journal of Culture and Education, 1,* 65-93.

Britzman, D., & Pitt, A. (1996). On refusing one's place: The ditchdigger's dream. In J. L. Kincheloe, S. R. Steinberg, & A. D. Gresson III (Eds.), *Measured lies: The bell curve examined.* New York: St. Martin's.

Brock-Utne, B. (1996). Reliability and validity in qualitative research within Africa. *International Review of Education, 42,* 605-621.

Brosio, R. (1994). *The radical democratic critique of capitalist education.* New York: Peter Lang.

Buckingham, D. (1989). Television literacy: A critique. *Radical Philosophy, 51,* 12-25.

Butler, M. (1998). Negotiating place: The importance of children's realities. In S. R. Steinberg & J. L. Kincheloe (Eds.), *Students as researchers: Creating classrooms that matter* (pp. 94-112). London: Taylor & Francis.

Cannella, G. (1997). *Deconstructing early childhood education: Social justice and revolution.* New York: Peter Lang.

Carlson, D. (1997). *Teachers in crisis.* New York: Routledge.

Carlson, D., & Apple, M. (Eds.). (1998). *Power/knowledge/pedagogy: The meaning of democratic education in unsettling times.* Boulder, CO: Westview.

Carson, T. R., & Sumara, D. (Eds.). (1997). *Action research as a living practice.* New York: Peter Lang.

Carspecken, P. F. (1993). *Power, truth, and method: Outline for a critical methodology.* Unpublished manuscript.

Carspecken, P. F. (1996). *Critical ethnography in educational research: A theoretical and practical guide.* New York: Routledge.

Carspecken, P. F. (1999). *Four scenes for posing the question of meaning and other essays in critical philosophy and critical methodology.* New York: Peter Lang.

Carter, V. (1998). Computer-assisted racism: Toward an understanding of cyberwhiteness. In J. L. Kincheloe, S. R. Steinberg, N. M. Rodriguez, & R. E.

Chennault (Eds.), *White reign: Deploying whiteness in America.* New York: St. Martin's.

Cary, R. (1996). I.Q. as commodity: The "new" economics of intelligence. In J. L. Kincheloe, S. R. Steinberg, & A. D. Gresson III (Eds.), *Measured lies: The bell curve examined.* New York: St. Martin's.

Christian-Smith, L., & Keelor, K. S. (1999). *Everyday knowledge and women of the academy: Uncommon Truths.* Boulder, CO: Westview.

Clatterbaugh, K. (1997). *Contemporary perspectives on masculinity: Men, women, and politics in modern society.* Boulder, CO: Westview.

Clifford, J. (1992). Traveling cultures. In L. Grossberg, C. Nelson, & P. A. Treichler (Eds.). *Cultural studies* (pp. 96-116). New York: Routledge.

Clough, P. T. (1994). *Feminist thought: Desire, power and academic discourse.* Cambridge, MA: Blackwell.

Clough, P. T. (1992). *The end(s) of ethnography: From realism to social criticism.* Newbury Park, CA: Sage.

Clough, P. T. (1998). *The end(s) of ethnography: From realism to social criticism* (2nd ed.). New York: Peter Lang.

Coben, D. (1998). *Radical heroes: Gramsci, Freire and the politics of adult education.* New York: Garland.

Codd, J. (1984). Introduction. In J. Codd (Ed.), *Philosophy, common sense, and action in educational administration* (pp. 8-28). Geelong, Victoria, Australia: Deakin University Press.

Collins, J. (1995). *Architectures of excess: Cultural life in the information age.* New York: Routledge.

Comaroff, J., & Comaroff, J. (1992). *Ethnography and the historical imagination.* Boulder, CO: Westview.

Connor, S. (1992). *Theory and cultural value.* Cambridge, MA: Blackwell.

Cooper, D. (1994). Productive, relational, and everywhere? Conceptualizing power and resistance within Foucauldian feminism. *Sociology, 28,* 435-454.

Corrigan, P. (1979). *Schooling the Smash Street kids.* London: Macmillan.

Crapanzano, V. (1990). Afterword. In M. Manganaro (Ed.). *Modernist anthropology: From fieldwork to text* (pp. 300-308). Princeton, NJ: Princeton University Press.

Daniel, E. V. (1996). *Charred lullabies: Chapters in an anthropology of violence.* Princeton, NJ: Princeton University Press.

Deetz, S. A. (1993, May). *Corporations, the media, industry, and society: Ethical imperatives and responsibilities.* Paper presented at the annual meeting of the International Communication Association, Washington, DC.

Denzin, N. K. (1992). *Symbolic interactionism and cultural studies.* Newbury Park, CA: Sage.

Denzin, N. K. (1994). The art and politics of interpretation. In N. K. Denzin & Y. S. Lincoln (Eds.), *Handbook of qualitative research* (pp. 500-515). Thousand Oaks, CA: Sage.

Dewey, J. (1916). *Democracy and education.* New York: Free Press.

Douglas, S. (1994). *Where the girls are: Growing up female in the mass media.* New York: Times Books.

Drummond, L. (1996). *American dreamtime: A cultural analysis of popular movies, and their implications for a science of humanity.* Lanham, MD: Littlefield Adams.

du Gay, P., Hall, S., Janes, L., MacKay, H., & Negus, K. (1997). *Doing cultural studies: The story of the Sony Walkman.* London: Sage.

Ebert, T. (1991). Political semiosis in/or American cultural studies. *American Journal of Semiotics, 8,* 113-135.

Elliot, A. (1994). *Psychoanalytic theory: An introduction.* Cambridge, MA: Blackwell.

Ellis, J. (1998). Interpretive inquiry as student research. In S. R. Steinberg & J. L. Kincheloe (Eds.), *Students as researchers: Creating classrooms that matter* (pp. 49-63). London: Taylor & Francis.

Fehr, D. (1993). *Dogs playing cards: Powerbrokers of prejudice in education, art, and culture.* New York: Peter Lang.

Ferguson, M., & Golding, P. (Eds.). (1997). *Cultural studies in question.* London: Sage.

Finders, M. (1997). *Just girls: Hidden literacies and life in junior high.* New York: Teachers College Press.

Fine, M., Powell, L. C., Weis, L., & Wong, L. M. (Eds.). (1997). *Off white: Readings on race, power and society.* New York: Routledge.

Fiske, J. (1993). *Power works, power plays.* New York: Verso.

Flossner, G., & Otto, H. (Eds.). (1998). *Towards more democracy in social services: Models of culture and welfare.* New York: de Gruyter.

Foster, H. (Ed.). (1983). *The anti-aesthetic: Essays on postmodern culture.* Port Townsend, WA: Bay.

Frankenberg, R. (1993). *White women, race matters: The social construction of whiteness.* Minneapolis: University of Minnesota Press.

Franz, C., & Stewart, A. (Eds.). (1994). *Women creating lives.* Boulder, CO: Westview.

Fraser, N. (1995). Politics, culture, and the public sphere: Toward a postmodern conception. In L. J. Nicholson & S. Seidman (Eds.), *Social postmodernism: Beyond identity politics.* New York: Cambridge University Press.

Freire, A. M. A. (2000). Foreword by Ana Maria Araujo Freire. In P. McLaren, *Che Guevara, Paulo Freire, and the Pedagogy of Revolution.* Boulder, CO: Rowman and Littlefield.

Freire, P. (1985). *The politics of education: Culture, power, and liberation.* South Hadley, MA: Bergin & Garvey.

Fuchs, M. (1993). The reversal of the ethnological perspective: Attempts at objectifying one's own cultural horizon. Dumont, Foucault, Bourdieu? *Thesis Eleven, 34,* 104-125.

Gabbard, D. (1995). NAFTA, GATT, and Goals 2000: Reading the political culture of post-industrial America. *Taboo: The Journal of Culture and Education, 2,* 184-199.

Gadamer, H.-G. (1989). *Truth and method* (2nd rev. ed.; J. Weinsheimer & D. G. Marshall, Eds. & Trans.). New York: Crossroad.

Gall, J., Gall, M., & Borg, W. (1999). *Applying educational research: A practical guide.* New York: Longman.

Gallagher, S. (1992). *Hermeneutics and education.* Albany: State University of New York Press.

Garnham, N. (1997). Political economy and the practice of cultural studies. In M. Ferguson & P. Golding (Eds.), *Cultural studies in question.* London: Sage.

Gee, J. (1996). *Social linguistics and literacies: Ideology in discourses* (2nd ed.). London: Taylor & Francis.

Gee, J., Hull, G., & Lankshear, C. (1996). *The new work order: Behind the language of the new capitalism.* Boulder, CO: Westview.

Gergen, K. J. (1991). *The saturated self: Dilemmas of identity in contemporary life.* New York: Basic Books.

Gibson, R. (1986). *Critical theory and education.* London: Hodder & Stroughton.

Giroux, H. (1983). *Theory and resistance in education: A pedagogy for the opposition.* South Hadley, MA: Bergin & Garvey.

Giroux, H. (1988). Critical theory and the politics of culture and voice: Rethinking the discourse of educational research. In R. Sherman & R. Webb (Eds.), *Qualitative research in education: Focus and methods* (pp. 190-210). New York: Falmer.

Giroux, H. (1992). *Border crossings: Cultural workers and the politics of education.* New York: Routledge.

Giroux, H. (1997). *Pedagogy and the politics of hope: Theory, culture, and schooling.* Boulder, CO: Westview.

Giroux, H., & Searles, S. (1996). The bell curve debate and the crisis of public intellectuals. In J. L. Kincheloe, S. R. Steinberg, & A. D. Gresson III (Eds.), *Measured lies: The bell curve examined.* New York: St. Martin's.

Godzich, W. (1992). Afterword: Reading against literacy. In J.-F. Lyotard, *The postmodern explained.* Minneapolis: University of Minnesota Press.

Goldie, T. (1995). The representation of the indigene. In B. Ashcroft, G. Griffiths, & H. Tiffin (Eds.), *The post-colonial studies reader.* New York: Routledge.

Goldman, R., & Papson, S. (1994). The postmodernism that failed. In D. Dickens & A. Fontana (Eds.), *Postmodernism and social inquiry.* New York: Guilford Press.

Goodson, I. (1997). *The changing curriculum: Studies in social construction.* New York: Peter Lang.

Goodson, I., & Mangan, J. (1996). Exploring alternative perspectives in educational research. *Interchange, 27*(1), 41-59.

Gresson, A. (1995). *The recovery of race in America.* Minneapolis: University of Minnesota Press.

Gresson, A. (2000). *America's atonement: Racial pain, recovery discourse and the psychology of healing.* New York: Peter Lang.

Griffin, C. (1985). *Typical girls? Young women from school to the job market.* London: Routledge & Kegan Paul.

Grondin, J. (1994). *Introduction to philosophical hermeneutics* (J. Weinsheimer, Trans.). New Haven, CT: Yale University Press.

Gross, A., & Keith, W. (Eds.). (1997). *Rhetorical hermeneutics: Invention and interpretation in the age of science.* Albany: State University of New York Press.

Grossberg, L. (1995). What's in a name (one more time)? *Taboo: The Journal of Culture and Education, 1,* 1-37.

Grossberg, L. (1997). *Bringing it all back home: Essays on cultural studies.* Durham, NC: Duke University Press.

Hall, S. (Ed.). (1997). *Representation: Cultural representations and signifying practices.* London: Sage.

Hall, S., & du Gay, P. (Eds.). (1996). *Questions of cultural identity.* London: Sage.

Hebdige, D. (1979). *Subculture: The meaning of style.* London: Methuen.

Hedley, M. (1994). The presentation of gendered conflict in popular movies: Affective stereotypes, cultural sentiments, and men's motivation. *Sex Roles, 31,* 721-740.

Held, D. (1980). *Introduction to critical theory: Horkheimer to Habermas.* Berkeley: University of California Press.

Heshusius, L., & Ballard, K. (Eds.). (1996). *From positivism to interpretivism and beyond: Tales of transformation in educational and social research.* New York: Teachers College Press.

Hicks, D. E. (1999). *Ninety-five languages and seven forms of intelligence.* New York: Peter Lang.

Hinchey, P. (1998). *Finding freedom in the classroom: A practical introduction to critical theory.* New York: Peter Lang.

Horkheimer, M. (1972). *Critical theory.* New York: Seabury.

Howell, S. (1998). The learning organization: Reproduction of whiteness. In J. L. Kincheloe, S. R. Steinberg, N. M. Rodriguez, & R. E. Chennault (Eds.), *White reign: Deploying whiteness in America.* New York: St. Martin's.

Jardine, D. (1998). *To dwell with a boundless heart: Essays in curriculum theory, hermeneutics, and the ecological imagination.* New York: Peter Lang.

Jay, M. (1973). *The dialectical imagination: A history of the Frankfurt school and the Institute of Social Research 1923-1950.* Boston: Little, Brown.

Jipson, J., & Paley, N. (1997). *Daredevil research: Recreating analytic practice.* New York: Peter Lang.

Johnson, C. (1996). Does capitalism really need patriarchy? Some old issues reconsidered. *Women's Studies International Forum, 19,* 193-202.

Joyrich, L. (1996). *Reviewing reception: Television, gender, and postmodern culture.* Bloomington: Indiana University Press.

Kellner, D. (1989). *Critical theory, Marxism, and modernity.* Baltimore: Johns Hopkins University Press.

Kellner, D. (Ed.). (1994). *Baudrillard: A critical reader.* Cambridge, MA: Blackwell.

Kellner, D. (1995). *Media culture: Cultural studies, identity and politics between the modern and the postmodern.* New York: Routledge.

Kellogg, D. (1998). Exploring critical distance in science education: Students researching the implications of technological embeddedness. In S. R. Steinberg & J. L. Kincheloe (Eds.), *Students as researchers: Creating classrooms that matter* (pp. 212-227). London: Falmer.

Kelly, L. (1996). When does the speaking profit us? Reflection on the challenges of developing feminist perspectives on abuse and violence by women. In M. Hester, L. Kelly, & J. Radford (Eds.), *Women, violence, and male power.* Bristol, PA: Open University Press.

Kincheloe, J. L. (1991). *Teachers as researchers: Qualitative paths to empowerment.* London: Falmer.

Kincheloe, J. L. (1993). *Toward a critical politics of teacher thinking: Mapping the postmodern.* Granby, MA: Bergin & Garvey.

Kincheloe, J. L. (1995). *Toil and trouble: Good work, smart workers, and the integration of academic and vocational education.* New York: Peter Lang.

Kincheloe, J. L. (1998). Critical research in science education. In B. Fraser & K. Tobin (Eds.), *International handbook of science education* (Pt. 2). Boston: Kluwer.

Kincheloe, J. L. (1999). *How do we tell the workers? The socioeconomic foundations of work and vocational education.* Boulder, CO: Westview.

Kincheloe, J. L., & Pinar, W. F. (1991). Introduction. In J. L. Kincheloe & W. F. Pinar, *Curriculum as social psychoanalysis: Essays on the significance of place* (pp. 1-23). Albany: State University of New York Press.

Kincheloe, J. L., & Steinberg, S. R. (1993). A tentative description of post-formal thinking: The critical confrontation with cognitive theory. *Harvard Educational Review, 63,* 296-320.

Kincheloe, J. L., & Steinberg, S. R. (1997). *Changing multiculturalism: New times, new curriculum.* London: Open University Press.

481

Kincheloe, J. L., Steinberg, S. R., & Hinchey, P. (Eds.). (1999). *The post-formal reader: Cognition and education.* New York: Falmer.

Kincheloe, J. L., Steinberg, S. R., Rodriguez, N. M., & Chennault, R. E. (Eds.). (1998). *White reign: Deploying whiteness in America.* New York: St. Martin's.

Kincheloe, J. L., Steinberg, S. R., & Tippins, D. (1999). *The stigma of genius: Einstein, consciousness and Education.* New York: Peter Lang.

Kincheloe, J. L., Steinberg, S. R., & Villaverde, L. (Eds.). (1999). *Rethinking intelligence: Confronting psychological assumptions about teaching and learning.* New York: Routledge.

King, J. (1996). Bad luck, bad blood, bad faith: Ideological hegemony and the oppressive language of hoodoo social science. In J. L. Kincheloe, S. R. Steinberg, & A. D. Gresson III (Eds.), *Measured lies: The bell curve examined.* New York: St. Martin's.

King, J., & Mitchell, C. (1995). *Black mothers to sons.* New York: Peter Lang.

Knobel, M. *Everyday literacies: Students, discourse, and social practice.* New York: Peter Lang.

Kogler, H. (1996). *The power of dialogue: Critical hermeneutics after Gadamer and Foucault.* Cambridge: MIT Press.

Lacey, C. (1970). *Hightown Grammar: The school as a social system.* London: Routledge & Kegan Paul.

Lash, S. (1990). Learning from Leipzig . . . or politics in the semiotic society. *Theory, Culture & Society, 7*(4), 145-158.

Lather, P. (1991). *Getting smart: Feminist research and pedagogy with/in the postmodern.* New York: Routledge.

Lather, P. (1993). Fertile obsession: Validity after poststructuralism. *Sociological Quarterly, 34,* 673-693.

Leistyna, P., Woodrum, A., & Sherblom, S. (1996). *Breaking free: The transformative power of critical pedagogy.* Cambridge, MA: Harvard Educational Review.

Lemke, J. (1993). Discourse, dynamics, and social change. *Cultural Dynamics, 6,* 243-275.

Lemke, J. (1995). *Textual politics: Discourse and social dynamics.* London: Taylor & Francis.

Lemke, J. (1998). Analyzing verbal data: Principles, methods, and problems. In B. Fraser & K. Tobin (Eds.), *International handbook of science education* (Pt. 2). Boston: Kluwer.

Lugg, C. (1996). Attacking affirmative action: Social Darwinism as public policy. In J. L. Kincheloe, S. R. Steinberg, & A. D. Gresson III (Eds.), *Measured lies: The bell curve examined.* New York: St. Martin's.

Lugones, M. (1987). Playfulness, "world"-traveling, and loving perception. *Hypatia, 2*(2), 3-19.

Luke, T. (1991). Touring hyperreality: Critical theory confronts informational society. In P. Wexler (Ed.), *Critical theory now* (pp. 1-26). New York: Falmer.

Lull, J. (1995). *Media, communication, culture: A global approach.* New York: Columbia University Press.

Macedo, D. (1994). *Literacies of power: What Americans are not allowed to know.* Boulder, CO: Westview.

Madison, G. B. (1988). *The hermeneutics of postmodernity: Figures and themes.* Bloomington: Indiana University Press.

Maher, F., & Tetreault, M. (1994). *The feminist classroom: An inside look at how professors and students are transforming higher education for a diverse society.* New York: Basic Books.

Manganaro, M. (1990). Textual play, power, and cultural critique: An orientation to modernist anthropology. In M. Manganaro (Ed.), *Modernist anthropology: From fieldwork to text* (pp. 3-47). Princeton, NJ: Princeton University Press.

Marcus, G. E., & Fischer, M. M. J. (1986). *Anthropology as cultural critique: An experimental moment in the human sciences.* Chicago: University of Chicago Press.

Martin, H., & Schuman, H. (1996). *The global trap: Globalization and the assault on democracy and prosperity.* New York: Zed Books

McGuigan, J. (1996). *Culture and the public sphere.* New York: Routledge.

McLaren, P. (1992a). Collisions with otherness: "Traveling" theory, post-colonial criticism, and the politics of ethnographic practice—the mission of the wounded ethnographer. *International Journal of Qualitative Studies in Education, 5,* 77-92.

McLaren, P. (1992b). Literacy research and the postmodern turn: Cautions from the margins. In R. Beach, J. Green, M. Kamil, & T. Shanahan (Eds.), *Multidisciplinary perspectives on research.* Urbana, IL: National Council of Teachers of English.

McLaren, P. (1995a). *Critical pedagogy and predatory culture: Oppositional politics in a postmodern era.* New York: Routledge.

McLaren, P. (1995b). *Life in schools* (3rd ed.). New York: Longman.

McLaren, P. (1997). *Revolutionary multiculturalism: Pedagogies of dissent for the new millennium.* New York: Routledge.

McLaren, P. (1998). Revolutionary pedagogy in post-revolutionary times: Rethinking the political economy of critical education. *Educational Theory, 48,* 431-462.

McLaren, P. (1999). *Schooling as a ritual performance: Toward a political economy of educational symbols and gestures* (3rd ed.). Boulder, CO: Rowman & Littlefield.

McLaren, P. (2000). *Che Guevara, Paulo Freire, and the pedagogy of revolution.* Boulder, CO: Rowman & Littlefield.

McLaren, P., & Hammer, R. (1989). Critical pedagogy and the postmodern challenge. *Educational Foundations, 3*(3), 29-69.

McLaren, P., Hammer, R., Reilly, S., & Sholle, D. (1995). *Rethinking media literacy: A critical pedagogy of representation.* New York: Peter Lang.

McWilliam, E., & Taylor, P. (Eds.). (1996). *Pedagogy, technology, and the body.* New York: Peter Lang.

Miller, S., & Hodge, J. (1998). *Phenomenology, hermeneutics, and narrative analysis: Some unfinished methodological business.* Unpublished manuscript.

Molnar, A. (1996). *Giving kids the business: The commercialization of America's schools.* Boulder, CO: Westview.

Morgan, W. (1996). Personal training: Discourses of (self) fashioning. In E. McWilliam & P. Taylor (Eds.), *Pedagogy, technology, and the body.* New York: Peter Lang.

Morley, D., & Chen, K.-H. (Eds.). (1996). *Stuart Hall: Critical dialogues in cultural studies.* New York: Routledge.

Morrow, R. (1991). Critical theory, Gramsci and cultural studies: From structuralism to post-structuralism. In P. Wexler (Ed.), *Critical theory now* (pp. 27-69). New York: Falmer.

Mullen, C. (1999). Whiteness, cracks and ink-stains: Making cultural identity with Euroamerican preservice teachers. In P. Diamond & C. Mullen (Eds.), *The postmodern educator: Arts-based inquiries and teacher development.* New York: Peter Lang.

Myrsiades, K., & Myrsiades, L. (Eds.). (1998). *Race-ing representation: Voice, history, and sexuality.* Lanham, MD: Rowman & Littlefield.

Newton, J., & Stacey, J. (1992-1993). Learning not to curse, or, feminist predicaments in cultural criticism by men: Our movie date with James Clifford and Stephen Greenblatt. *Cultural Critique, 23,* 51-82.

Nicholson, L. J., & Seidman, S. (Eds.). (1995). *Social postmodernism: Beyond identity politics.* New York: Cambridge University Press.

Pailliotet, A. (1998). Deep viewing: A critical look at visual texts. In J. L. Kincheloe & S. R. Steinberg (Eds.), *Unauthorized methods: Strategies for critical teaching.* New York: Routledge.

Peters, M. (1993). *Against Finkielkraut's la defaite de la pensee: Culture, postmodernism and education.* Unpublished manuscript.

Peters, M., & Lankshear, C. (1994). Education and hermeneutics: A Freirean interpretation. In P. McLaren & C. Lankshear (Eds.), *Politics of liberation: Paths from Freire.* New York: Routledge.

Pfeil, F. (1995). *White guys: Studies in postmodern domination and difference.* New York: Verso.

Pieterse, J., & Parekh, B. (1995). Shifting imaginaries: Decolonization, internal decolonization, and postcoloniality. In J. Pieterse & B. Parekh (Eds.), *The *decolonialization of imagination: Culture, knowledge, and power.* Atlantic Highlands, NJ: Zed.

Pinar, W. F. (1994). *Autobiography, politics, and sexuality: Essays in curriculum theory, 1972-1992.* New York: Peter Lang.

Pinar, W. F. (Ed.). (1998). *Curriculum: Toward new identities.* New York: Garland.

Pinar, W. F., Reynolds, W., Slattery, P., & Taubman, P. (1995). *Understanding curriculum.* New York: Peter Lang.

Poster, M. (1989). *Critical theory and poststructuralism: In search of a context.* Ithaca, NY: Cornell University Press.

Prakash, M., & Esteva, G. (1998). *Escaping education: Living as learning within grassroots cultures.* New York: Peter Lang.

Pruyn, M. (1994). Becoming subjects through critical practice: How students in an elementary classroom critically read and wrote their world. *International Journal of Educational Reform, 3*(1), 37-50.

Pruyn, M. (1999). *Discourse wars in Gotham-West: A Latino immigrant urban tale of resistance and agency.* Boulder, CO: Westview.

Quantz, R. A. (1992). On critical ethnography (with some postmodern considerations). In M. D. LeCompte, W. L. Millroy, & J. Preissle (Eds.), *The handbook of qualitative research in education* (pp. 447-505). New York: Academic Press.

Quail, C. B., Razzano, K. A., & Skalli, L. H. (2000). *Tell me more: Rethinking daytime talk shows.* New York: Peter Lang.

Rabinow, P. (1977). *Reflections on fieldwork in Morocco.* Berkeley: University of California Press.

Rains, F. (1998). Is the benign really harmless? Deconstructing some "benign" manifestations of operationalized white privilege. In J. L. Kincheloe, S. R. Steinberg, N. M. Rodriguez, & R. E. Chennault (Eds.), *White reign: Deploying whiteness in America.* New York: St. Martin's.

Rand, E. (1995). *Barbie's queer accessories.* Durham, NC: Duke University Press.

Rapko, J. (1998). Review of *The power of dialogue*: Critical hermeneutics after Gadamer and Foucault. *Criticism, 40*(1), 133-138.

Ritzer, G. (1993). *The McDonaldization of society.* Thousand Oaks, CA: Pine Forge.

Robins, D., & Cohen, P. (1978). *Knuckle sandwich: Growing up in the working-class city.* Harmondsworth: Penguin.

Robinson, W. (1998). Beyond nation-state paradigms: Globalization, sociology, and the challenge of transnational studies. *Sociological Forum, 13,* 561-594.

Rodriguez, N. M., & Villaverde, L. (2000). *Dismantling whiteness.* New York: Peter Lang.

Roman, L., & Eyre, L. (Eds.). (1997). *Dangerous territories: Struggles for difference and equality in education.* New York: Routledge.

Rosen, S. (1987). *Hermeneutics as politics.* New York: Oxford University Press.

Rosenau, P. M. (1992). *Post-modernism and the social sciences: Insights, inroads, and intrusion.* Princeton, NJ: Princeton University Press.

Samuels, A. (1993). *The political psyche.* New York: Routledge.

San Juan, E., Jr. (1992). *Articulations of power in ethnic and racial studies in the United States.* Atlantic Highlands, NJ: Humanities Press.

San Juan, E., Jr. (1996). *Mediations: From a Filipino perspective.* Pasig City, Philippines: Anvil.

Scheurich, J. J., & Young, M. (1997). Coloring epistemologies: Are our research epistemologies racially biased? *Educational Researcher, 26*(4), 4-16.

Scott, J. W. (1992). Experience. In J. Butler & J. W. Scott (Eds.), *Feminists theorize the political* (pp. 22-40). New York: Routledge.

Sedgwick, E. (1995). Gosh, Boy George, you must be awfully secure in your masculinity? In M. Berger, B. Wallis, & S. Watson (Eds.), *Constructing masculinity.* New York: Routledge.

Semali, L. (1998). Still crazy after all these years: Teaching critical media literacy. In J. L. Kincheloe & S. R. Steinberg (Eds.), *Unauthorized methods: Strategies for critical teaching.* New York: Routledge.

Semali, L., & Kincheloe, J. L. (1999). *What is indigenous knowledge? Voices from the academy.* New York: Falmer.

Shelton, A. (1996). The ape's I.Q. In J. L. Kincheloe, S. R. Steinberg, & A. D. Gresson III (Eds.), *Measured lies: The bell curve examined.* New York: St. Martin's.

Shohat, E., & Stam, R. (1994). *Unthinking Eurocentrism: Multiculturalism and the media.* New York: Routledge.

Shor, I. (1996). *When students have power: Negotiating authority in a critical pedagogy.* Chicago: University of Chicago Press.

Silverman, E. K. (1990). Clifford Geertz: Towards a more "thick" understanding? In C. Tilley (Ed.), *Reading material culture* (pp. 121-159). Cambridge, MA: Blackwell.

Slattery, P. (1995). *Curriculum development in the postmodern era.* New York: Garland.

Slaughter, R. (1989). Cultural reconstruction in the post-modern world. *Journal of Curriculum Studies, 3,* 255-270.

Sleeter, C., & McLaren, P. (Eds.). (1995). *Multicultural education, critical pedagogy, and the politics of difference.* Albany: State University of New York Press.

Smith, D. G. (1999). *Interdisciplinary essays in the Pedagon: Human sciences, pedagogy and culture.* New York: Peter Lang.

Smith, R., & Wexler, P. (Eds.). (1995). *After post-modernism: Education, politics, and identity.* London: Falmer.

Smyth, J. (1989). A critical pedagogy of classroom practice. *Journal of Curriculum Studies, 21*(6), 483-401.

Soto, L. (1998). Bilingual education in America: In search of equity and justice. In J. L. Kincheloe & S. R. Steinberg (Eds.), *Unauthorized methods: Strategies for critical teaching.* New York: Routledge.

Stallabrass, J. (1996). *Gargantua: Manufactured mass culture.* London: Verso.

Steinberg, S. (1997). Kinderculture: The cultural studies of childhood. In N. Denzin (Ed.), *Cultural studies: A research volume* (Vol. 2, pp. 17-44). Greenwich, CN: JAI.

Steinberg, S. (Ed.). (2000). *Multi/intercultural conversations.* New York: Peter Lang.

Steinberg, S. R. (1997). The bitch who has everything. In S. R. Steinberg & J. L. Kincheloe (Eds.), *Kinderculture: The corporate construction of childhood.* Boulder, CO: Westview.

Steinberg, S. R., & Kincheloe, J. L. (Eds.). (1997). *Kinderculture: Corporate constructions of childhood.* Boulder, CO: Westview.

Steinberg, S. R., & Kincheloe, J. L. (Eds.). (1998). *Students as researchers: Creating classrooms that matter.* London: Taylor & Francis.

Stewart, K. (1996). *A space on the side of the road: Cultural poetics in an "other" America.* Princeton, NJ: Princeton University Press.

Sünker, H. (1998). Welfare, democracy, and social work. In G. Flosser & H. Otto (Eds.), *Towards more democracy in social services: Models of culture and welfare.* New York: de Gruyter.

Surber, J. (1998). *Culture and critique: An introduction to the critical discourses of cultural studies.* Boulder, CO: Westview.

Taussig, M. (1987). *Shamanism, colonialism, and the wild man: A study in terror and healing.* Chicago: University of Chicago Press.

Taylor, M., & Saarinen, E. (1994). *Imagologies: Media philosophy.* New York: Routledge.

Thomas, S. (1997). Dominance and ideology in cultural studies. In M. Ferguson & P. Golding (Eds.), *Cultural studies in question.* London: Sage.

Trueba, E. T., & McLaren, P. (in press). Critical ethnography for the study of immigrants. In E. T. Trueba & L. I. Bartolomé (Eds.), *Immigrant voices: In search of educational equity.* Boulder, CO: Rowman & Littlefield.

Vattimo, G. (1994). *Beyond interpretation: The meaning of hermeneutics for philosophy.* Stanford, CA: Stanford University Press.

Viergever, M. (1999). Indigenous knowledge: An interpretation of views from indigenous peoples. In L. Semali & J. L. Kincheloe (Eds.), *What is indigenous knowledge? Voices* from the academy. Bristol, PA: Falmer.

Villaverde, L., & Kincheloe, J. L. (1998). Engaging students as researchers: Researching and teaching Thanksgiving in the elementary classroom. In S. R. Steinberg & J. L. Kincheloe (Eds.), *Students as researchers: Creating classrooms that matter* (pp. 149-166). London: Falmer.

Visweswaran, K. (1994). *Fictions of feminist ethnography.* Minneapolis: University of Minnesota Press.

Weil, D. (1998). *Towards a critical multi-cultural literacy: Theory and practice for education for liberation.* New York: Peter Lang.

Weiler, K. (1988). *Women teaching for change: Gender, class, and power.* South Hadley, MA: Bergin & Garvey.

Weinstein, M. (1998). *Robot world: Education, popular culture, and science.* New York: Peter Lang

Welch, S. (1991). An ethic of solidarity and difference. In H. Giroux (Ed.), *Postmodernism, feminism, and cultural politics: Redrawing educational boundaries* (pp. 83-99). Albany: State University of New York Press.

West, C. (1993). *Race matters.* Boston: Beacon.

Wexler, P. (1991). Preface. In P. Wexler (Ed.), *Critical theory now.* New York: Falmer.

Wexler, P. (1996a). *Critical social psychology.* New York: Peter Lang.

Wexler, P. (1996b). *Holy sparks: Social theory, education, and religion.* New York: St. Martin's.

Wexler, P. (1997). *Social research in education: Ethnography of being.* Paper presented at the International Conference on the Culture of Schooling, Halle, Germany.

Willis, P. E. (1977). *Learning to labour: How working class kids get working class jobs.* Farnborough, UK: Saxon House.

Women's Studies Group, Centre for Contemporary Cultural Studies. (1978). *Women take issue: Aspects of women's subordination.* London: Hutchinson, with Centre for Contemporary Cultural Studies, University of Birmingham.

Woodward, K. (Ed.). (1997). *Identity and difference.* London: Sage.

Yates, T. (1990). Jacques Derrida: "There is nothing outside of the text." In C. Tilley (Ed.), *Reading material culture* (pp. 206-280). Cambridge, MA: Blackwell.

Young, I. (1990). The ideal of community and the politics of difference. In L. J. Nicholson (Ed.), *Feminism/postmodernism* (pp. 300-323). New York: Routledge.

Zavarzadeh, M., & Morton, D. (1991). *Theory, (post)modernity, opposition.* Washington, DC: Maison-neuve.

Zizek, S. (1990). *The sublime object of ideology.* London: Verso.

11

Cultural Studies

John Frow and Meaghan Morris

◆ During the 1980s, as academics debated "postmodernism" and policy battles began to be waged about "globalization," the word *culture* came to be used by the media in a sense that seemed far removed from anything to do with artistic and literary texts. When an Australian politician declared that "resetting industrial policy is really a matter of reshaping cultural attitudes" (quoted in Loosley, 1991), he was not defining culture as a domain of aesthetic pleasure, as a set of masterpieces, or as an expression of national identity. Nor was he speaking in economic terms of culture as a major export industry, although he might have done so ("Culture Fills," 1990). Rather, he was referring to a complex of social customs, values, and expectations that affect our ways of working. So, too, was the media magnate Rupert Murdoch in a television interview aired in Australia in 1990. Just as the worst company crashes in Australian history ended an era of financial mismanagement and entrepreneurial crime, the Melbourne host of ABC-TV's *The 7.30 Report* asked Murdoch what "we" should do to save our economy. Murdoch replied perfunctorily, "Oh, you know: Change the culture."

AUTHORS' NOTE: For their assistance with the reference list, we would like to thank Chua Beng-Huat, Larry Grossberg, Gay Hawkins, Vivien Johnson, Allan Luke, Brian Massumi, Tony Mitchell, Elspeth Probyn, David Rowe, Darren Tofts, Keyan Tomaselli, Graeme Turner, and Rob Wilson.

Murdoch expected us to "know" that he was quoting a formula of the neoliberal rhetoric now broadly shared in Australia, as elsewhere, by bureaucrats, politicians, economists, journalists, and financiers as well as union and corporate leaders: Economic problems need "cultural" solutions. Culture in this sense is not just a topic for specialized debate by an esoteric caste of interpreters ("critics"). On the contrary, "changing the culture" is a way of challenging the conduct of other people's everyday working lives, whether within the framework of a single company ("Changing the culture is not a quick process in something as old and as large as ARC," says a chief executive of Australia's main producer of concrete reinforcing steel), of an industry (a marketing expert offers a paper titled "Changing Culture for Service: How to Effect a Change to the Service Culture in Shopping Centres"), or an entire national economy ("Professor Hughes said Australians 'have got to cultivate an export culture' ").[1]

In other words, culture itself is imagined as a plastic medium that politically powerful social elites may rework and remold at will. For these economic critics of everyday life, changing the culture primarily means that "fewer workers must produce more for less"; globalization is widely invoked as the inexorable force that makes this imperative rational. But this program has social implications, and these may vary from place to place. It means changing the minutiae of behavior ("work practices") at the workplace, and thus the texture and organization of home and family life. It can mean inducing workers to invest more actively in the corporate ethos. In some contexts, it can also mean improving race and gender relations in the interests of achieving an "international outlook." It can sharpen class consciousness by making "inequality of outcomes" and, therefore, poverty more acceptable to people—at lest to those who have work. *Aesthetic* implications follow. In an Australian context, where the "ideology of the collective" (Knight, 1990, p. 5) has been strong, accepting these changes has meant questioning the value of canonical myths of our modern history—egalitarianism, "mateship" (solidarity), upward mobility, and a "fair go" for all—along with the associated ethical images of pleasure, personal development, and social worth that still circulate in our society (Morris, 1998a; Turner, 1994).

Despite appearances, then, the neoliberal critique of culture cannot be neatly disentangled from "artistic and literary" concerns. By the end of the 1980s it had prompted a media debate about the *worth* of various aspects of Australia's traditional national identity (hedonism and "welfarism" were popular topics for criticism; see Robinson, 1989), and over the next

490

10 years the economic and social arrangements that for a century had sustained social democracy in Australia were dismantled or undermined. However, this debate was only a fraction of the coverage devoted to the "cultural" dimensions of East Asia's economic boom (Garnaut, 1989). Commentators promoted "Confucian capitalism" as a new model of development with cultural lessons to teach the West, and civilizational theories of history came back into mainstream fashion after decades in disrepute (Huntington, 1996; see also Chen, 1998a). After the Asian financial meltdown of 1997-1998, "crony capitalism" became for the very same commentators an object lesson in the need for "cultural reform" as prescribed by the International Monetary Fund (immiserating millions of people; see Arndt & Hill, 1999).

Shorn of its subordination of all other goals to that of economic productivity, and without the *moralism* (and determinism) of neoliberal rhetoric, this usage turns out to be strikingly close to one dimension of the way the word *culture* is used in contemporary cultural studies. In this context, too, culture is thought of as directly bound up with work and its organization; with relations of power and gender in the workplace, the home, the neighborhood, and the street; with the pleasures and the pressures of consumption; with the complex relations of class and kith and kin through which a sense of self and belonging is formed; and with the fantasies and desires through which social relations are carried and actively shaped. In short, *culture* is a term that can designate, in Raymond Williams's (1958/1961) phrase, the "whole way of life" (p. 16) of a social group as it is structured by representation and by power. It is not a detached domain for playing games of social distinction (Bourdieu, 1984) and "good" taste. It is a network of embedded practices and representations (texts, images, talk, codes of behavior, and the narrative structures organizing these) that shapes every aspect of social life.

◆ Identity and Community

The notion that culture is all-pervasive is often called anthropological, and, as Renato Rosaldo (1997) points out, one way of understanding cultural studies is as the product of a "rapid diffusion" of this notion "from anthropology to literary studies, law, social history, communication, business, media studies, and more" (p. 29). But to say that the concept of culture refers to the existence of social groups—their formation, their maintenance, their definition against other groups, the constant process of their re-formation—is to raise difficult questions about the kinds of unity that groups lay claim to. If for anthropologists "it no longer seems possible to study culture as an objectified thing or as a self-enclosed, coherent, patterned field of meaning" (Rosaldo, 1997, p. 29), we have all the more reason to ask at what level the concept of culture operates for cultural studies—that of the nation-state and/or of a "national" culture? That of class, gender, race, sexuality, age, ethnicity, community? The answer is that it may operate at any of these levels, and that they do not slot neatly into each other.

Much the same answer is given today right across the humanities and social sciences. With their colleagues in many other fields of qualitative research, practitioners of cultural studies have shared in decades of debate about cultural identity and difference, social location and movement, historical experience and change; any comprehensive cultural studies bibliography would overlap with many chapters in this *Handbook*. However, it is fair to say that for cultural studies these debates have not transformed an existing disciplinary formation but rather have directly constituted the field. As the most cursory survey of key publications will suggest, the very substance of cultural studies has been shaped in *encounters between* diverse feminisms (Butler, 1990; de Lauretis, 1986; Grewal & Kaplan, 1994; hooks, 1981; Hull, Scott, & Smith, 1982; Mohanty, Russo, & Torres, 1991; Probyn, 1993; Sheridan, 1988; Shiach, 1999; Wallace, 1978) interacting with class-conscious ethnic and critical race studies (Anzaldúa, 1987; Frankenberg, 1993; hooks, 1990; Jordan & Weedon, 1995; Matsuda, 1996; Moraga & Anzaldúa, 1981; Roediger, 1991; Ware, 1992), with gay, lesbian, and queer studies (Butler, 1993; Chang, 1998; Crimp, 1987; de Lauretis, 1991; Fuss, 1991; Sedgwick, 1993; Warner, 1993; Watney, 1987), with postcolonial and diasporic research (Ang, 1999; Bhabha, 1994; Chambers & Curti, 1996; Chow, 1991, 1993; Clifford, 1997; Gilroy, 1993; Hargreaves & McKinney, 1997; Morley & Chen, 1996; Prakash, 1995; Spivak, 1988, 1990), and with indigenous peoples' scholarship (Bennett & Blundell, 1995; Bennett, Turner, & Volkerling, 1994; Langton, 1993; Valaskakis, 1988, in press).

Given this history of interaction and often heated debate, most work in cultural studies has been acutely aware of the danger of positing imaginary social unities as the *explanatory* basis for its accounts of cultural texts. Its constant impetus is to think of cultures as being processes that divide as much as they bring together (see, e.g., Carby, 1982/1996; Chambers &

Curti, 1996; Gilroy, 1987, 1996; hooks, 1992b; McRobbie, 1981; Steedman, 1986; Williams, 1985; Women's Studies Group, 1978), to stress the diversity and the contestation always involved in "defining" social groups (Frankenberg, 1997; Hall, 1996; Hall & du Gay, 1996; Lowe, 1996; Sedgwick, 1990), and to question those totalizing notions of culture that assume that at the end of cultural processes there lies the achievement of a whole and coherent "society" or "community" (Hunter, 1988b). At the same time, this very impetus pushes cultural studies to ask how groups "get to know themselves *as groups* (as a particular organization of individual and social interests, of sameness and difference) through cultural activity" (Frith, 1996a, p. 111); to investigate "the deep ambivalence of identification and desire" (Hall, 1996, p. 444) that can reach across and complicate the most rigid, historically deep-seated divisions and inequalities structuring *relationships* between groups (hooks, 1992a; Mercer, Ugwu, & Bailey, 1996; Muecke, 1997); and to seek a politics of connection and translation across prevailing boundaries rather than one of "unity" within or between radically separate groups (Benterrak, Muecke, & Roe, 1996; Clifford, 1997; Grossberg, 1992; Haraway, 1991; Hayward, 1998; McRobbie, 1994).

This double movement of critique and affirmation tends to put cultural studies at odds not only with an "evasive cosmopolitanism" (Willemen, 1994, p. 210) that denies the efficacy and the *burden* of actual boundaries between groups, treating difference as a consumable good and identity purely as fiction, but also with those militant cultural nationalisms, essentialisms, and particularisms that some critics fear will always arise with "the fateful question of culture" (Hartman, 1997). For example, Paul Gilroy (1992, 1993) rejects both a "notional pluralist" and an "exceptionalist" approach to black popular culture and outlines a third perspective, an "anti-antiessentialism" for which black identity is neither a freely disposable category nor an immutable racial essence but "the outcome of practical activity: language, gesture, bodily significations, desires," including the activities and impacts of racism. "Racialized subjectivity," Gilroy (1993) writes, is "the product of the social practices that supposedly derive from it" (p. 102). In a different context, Naoki Sakai (1997) makes a comparable argument about "the subject of 'Japan.'" Analyzing the complicity binding "universalism" to "particularism" in modern imperial nationalism, both in the West and in Japan, he shows that a rivalrous capacity to affirm the unity of a single language, *ethnos,* and nation is the outcome of a specific regime of translation installed in the 18th century (see Sakai, 1991), and not a precondition *for* translation.

Addressing debates in distinct academic areas, these arguments share with Willemen's work in cinema studies a disposition to see "the kinds of unity that groups lay claim to" not only as mobile and provisional (as the postmodern truism has it) but *also* as the real and consequential products of definite practices that it is the analyst's task to specify. Cultural studies has generally been less concerned with debating the pros and cons of essentialism as a philosophical stance (Fuss, 1989; see also Grossberg, 1997a, pp. 18-19; McRobbie, 1997b) than with examining the *political* conflicts at stake, in concrete contexts and for particular groups of people, between differing stories of community or nation (Baker, Diawara, & Lindeborg, 1996; D. Bennett, 1998; Chen, 1998b; Parker, Russo, Sommer, & Yaeger, 1992; Teer-Tomaselli & Roome, 1997) and with articulating the *historical* struggles occurring in the gaps between competing narrative programs (of "identity," for example) and the complex social experiences that these aspire to organize (Abbas, 1997; Berlant, 1997; Bhabha, 1990; Chakrabarty, in press; Chow, 1998a; Lilley, 1998; Morris, 1998a). Thus when Greg Noble, Scott Poynting, and Ken Tabar (1999) borrow from Gayatri Spivak (1990) the idea of a "strategic" essentialism, extending it to the study of cultural hybridity, they do so to investigate how young Arabic-speaking men in southwestern Sydney handle different contexts of everyday living by variably fashioning selves as migrants, as "Lebanese" (some are in fact from Syrian backgrounds), and as Australians inhabiting a socially particular place; for these young men, "the interplay of identity and context produces curiously practical amalgams" (Noble et al., 1999, p. 39).

Given this emphasis on material *contexts* (see Grossberg, 1993, 1998a)[2] of constraint and empowerment in everyday life, research in cultural studies in fact draws as deeply on geographic and historical ways of understanding culture as it does on anthropology in its recurring struggle with aesthetic concepts of culture (Clifford, 1988). Spatial and temporal framings of experience are equally important to contextual analysis, which seeks to grasp the complexity of the mundane processes, events, and *occasions* in which "identities" are formed and transformed; as Martin Allor (1997) puts it in an essay on "the Main" (Boulevard Saint-Laurent) in Montreal, a cultural studies aiming to render visible the politics of location "must focus precisely on [the] *coming into being* of forms of life" (p. 52).

◆ Situating Cultural Studies

One reason for this broadly skeptical approach to "culture" as the field's own unifying category lies in the complex international context in which cultural studies has developed since the 1970s. A smooth professional consensus about the limits and potentials of culture does not easily emerge when new struggles, conversations, and alliances are forming across once-formidable geopolitical and even linguistic boundaries while old colonial hierarchies, spacings, and "structures of feeling" (Williams, 1961b, p. 64; 1979) continue to shape the social meanings of events in landscapes newly produced or remade by economic globalization (Appadurai, 1996; Jacobs, 1996; Jameson & Miyoshi, 1998; Said, 1993; Wilson & Dissanayake, 1996; Wood, in press). For many scholars now, questions of identity and community are framed not only by issues of race, class, and gender but by a deeply political concern with place, cultural memory, and the variable terms of these scholars' access to an "international" space of debate dominated not only by Western preoccupations (Chen, 1992; Tomaselli, 1998b) but by the English language (Cho, 1996). In these conditions, as Jody Berland (1997a) observes, "culture and place demand our attention not because our concepts of them are definite or authoritative, but because they are fragile and fraught with dispute" (p. 9).

In cultural studies, as in other disciplines, globalization is contested both as *fact* and as *problematic,* to adapt a useful distinction from Allen Chun (1994; see also Chua, 1998; Grossberg, 1997b, 1999; King, 1991; Massey, 1997). Whatever value we accord this term, it is at least clear that large-scale economic, geopolitical, and technological changes have helped to transform both higher education and academic publishing over the past 30 years (Cohen, 1993; Morris, 1998b; Readings, 1996) and that these changes have not only shaped topics for work *in* cultural studies but have provided the conditions *for* its emergence as a transnational movement in scholarship. Those conditions include new opportunities and incentives for scholars to travel, talk, and publish, compare, and translate their work far more widely and diversely than before. However, they also include the corporatization of university life and its rationalization across national borders toward an increasing similarity at the level of institutional values and procedures. In some countries, conditions further include higher enrollments combined with a decline in state funding for public universities, thus making cultural studies attractive as a "cheap" form of pedagogy (Steedman, 1992b), and the reduction of formerly distinct faculties of "humanities" and "social sciences" into a single uneasy compound. It is not surprising, then, that an ambivalence about the "success" of cultural studies is one of its recurring themes (Ferguson & Golding, 1997; Grossberg, 1993; Kraniauskas, 1998; Morris, 1997a).

However, like English as a global language, cultural studies differs greatly according to the contexts in which it is practiced. The well-known difficulty of providing a "map" or an "overview" of the field is not simply a matter of epistemological squeamishness (disavowing the claim "to know"), but results from a practical limitation: There is always more going on than one is aware of from a particular situation *in* the field. For example, when James Carey (1997) regrets the passing of the "parochialism" of early British cultural studies, complaining as an American that cultural studies today is "pretty much a nowhere college," he reads the new internationalism of the field as just "a pattern of cross-reference and mutual citation spanning a couple of continents but hardly intellectually dominating on any campus" (p. 2; see also Carey, 1995). From our own situation on a third continent, Australia—where it is difficult to ignore work going on across parts of a fourth (East and Southeast Asia), and where cultural studies paradigms effectively dominate faculties at several "somewhere" colleges—Carey's account of the present seems not only parochial but wrong.

Yet it also has a certain plausibility. A general impression of cultural studies as a U.K./U.S. affair (give or take a few imported authors) is created by major anthologies (During, 1999; Grossberg, Nelson, & Treichler, 1992; Storey, 1996) as well as by some histories and thematic collections in wide distribution (Brantlinger, 1990; Ferguson & Golding, 1997; Hall & du Gay, 1996; Harris, 1992; McGuigan, 1997; McRobbie, 1997a; Nelson & Gaonkar, 1996). Read from elsewhere, however, these books do not appear from "nowhere"; on the contrary, they come from a strongly self-centralizing somewhere that is sometimes mistaken for everywhere. The problem, then, is how to situate, say, Carey's geography of "cultural studies" in relation to other ways of mapping the field, such as Kuan-Hsing Chen's (1998a) organization of an "inter-Asia cultural studies" around "the decolonization question," Peter Gibian's (1997) genealogy of a "North American" cultural studies based on the lively critiques of "mass culture" published by the journal *Tabloid,* or Keyan Tomaselli's (1998b) insistence that diverse African cultural studies will "derive from 'historicisation'; the recovery of African scholarship from all periods and societies within the frames of reference provided by various approaches within the field as a whole" (p. 395).

A bigger map won't do, although it's a start. What is striking about the geographically situated work easily available in our own vicinity is the flexibility of the categories in use; scanning the field, one can see nations begin to form regions, regions break up into areas, and areas form around communities within nations as well as between them. Thus there are collections of Australian cultural studies (Frow & Morris, 1993; Turner, 1993), of Australian-Asian "transactions" (Dever, 1997), and of "Asian and Pacific inscriptions" crossing Australia (Perera, 1995); others connect Australia with South Africa (Darien-Smith, Gunner, & Nuttall, 1996) and several countries historically linked by British colonialism (D. Bennett, 1998). There are collections of, and essays in, Asia-Pacific cultural studies (Birch, 1994; Wilson & Dirlik, 1995), Pacific cultural studies (Hereniko & Wilson, in press; Wilson, in press), Latin American cultural studies (García Canclini, 1995; Moreiras, 1999; Yudice, Franco, & Flores, 1992), Mexican cultural studies (García Canclini, 1993), and "Chicana/o" cultural studies (Chabram-Dernersesian, 1999; Fregoso & Chabram, 1990). Along with British cultural studies (Turner, 1996), we find Irish cultural studies (Gibbons, 1996; Sharkey, 1997; Waters, 1996) and "nationally" organized collections on French (Forbes & Kelly, 1996), German (Burns, 1995), Russian (Kelly & Shepherd, 1998), Spanish (Graham & Labanyi, 1996), and Italian cultural studies (Forgacs & Lumley, 1996). We find "Nordic" cultural studies (Vainikkala & Eskola, 1994) and the continental frame of African cultural studies (Diawara, 1998; Tomaselli, 1998a; Wright, 1998). The diverse "inscriptions" situating projects in black cultural studies exemplify best the geopolitical fluidity of the field as well as the importance within it of precise contextualizations: Alongside transnational work on black popular culture (Dent, 1992) and black cultural studies (Mercer, 1994), there is an internationally edited collection of black British cultural studies (Baker et al., 1996); other essays consider black experience as regionalized within Britain (Owusu, 1999) and the United States (Lubiana, 1997), as well as diasporic between them (Gilroy, 1993).

Far from being produced in a nowhere college, then, these projects are actively developing a sense of the *situated* nature of intellectual work in its historical as well as social and geopolitical commitments—a point made in passing by Anthony Appiah (1992) when he describes as a "legacy" his father's capacity to make use of his many identities "as Asante, as a Ghanian, as an African, and as a Christian and a Methodist" (p. ix). If this sense of situatedness distances cultural studies from the context-free disciplinarity espoused by many social scientists, the understanding it entails of "situation" as an open, multiply directed, and relational *process* also contests the traditional claim of "language and literature" studies to read culture as expressive of a bounded nation or a civilization. National formations, after all, include the disciplines that define their ideal forms of unity. Aesthetics (sometimes conflated with "textualism" by scholars trained in the social sciences) has powerfully shaped modern Western thinking about culture not only through "self-shaping" pedagogies of reading (Hunter, 1988a, 1992) and writing (Clifford & Marcus, 1986; Steedman, 1997) but through the "national language" programs that linked it to history in the arts and humanities curriculum. Cultural studies refuses to privilege "the literary" and rejects any equation between "a language" and "a culture"; with its suspicion of homogenizing narratives, its affinity with "studies" areas generated by social movements, and its remapping of European universals as imperially powered provincialisms (Chakrabarty, 2000), cultural studies has been welcomed as a "challenge" by scholars "coming out of English" (Bennett, 1993), Chinese studies (Chow, 1991, 1998b), French (Chambers, 1996), and German (Bathrick, 1992), to mention only a few examples.

At a methodological level, whatever the geographies and histories at stake, cultural studies sets great store on "situating" particular objects for analysis (Hebdige, 1988). However, the notion of particularity is prized away from the values of opacity and untranslatability associated with it by modernist social theory (Harvey, 1989; Morris, 1992); it is not conceptualized in opposition to another register deemed "general" or "universal." Thus Alec McHoul (1997) argues that a *general* model for "finding the local specifics of cultural objects" becomes possible precisely when we shift our attention toward "the determination of particular cultural objects by their pragmatic and empirical (that is, their accidental) situatedness" (p. 15). Recently, cultural theorists drawing on the work of Michel de Certeau (1984), Gilles Deleuze and Félix Guattari (1987), and Giorgio Agamben (1993) have used the term *singularity* to designate a "mode of existence which is neither universal (i.e. conceptual) nor particular (i.e. individual)" (Grossberg, 1996, p. 103; see also Shaviro, 1997); as Brian Massumi (1992) explains, its singularity is precisely what "prevents a body from coinciding entirely with its identity category" (pp. 123-124), where identity is understood as a common property that differentiates a group.[3]

Taken up in cultural studies, these rather difficult arguments have practical implications for any work concerned with cultural identity and difference. Most immediately, they challenge the terms in which much debate about these issues is conducted, whether in social or geopolitical frames. For Grossberg (1996), they suggest a "concept of a belonging without identity," enabling new ways of thinking about collective agency and *political* identities and alliances. Citing the U.S. civil rights movement as a successful example from the past, a "politics of singularity," he writes, "would need to define places people can belong to or, even more fundamentally, places people can find their way to" (pp. 103-104). In her aptly titled *Outside Belongings* (1996), Elspeth Probyn calls for a greater attention to the *movement* carried by the "wish to belong"; her descriptively rich, empirically alert studies of "interstitial moments" in the everyday politics of national, feminist, and queer belonging in the city of Montreal use the concept of singularity to "capture some of the ways in which we continually move in between categories of specificity" (p. 9).

◆ Culture, Cultural Studies, and the Media

The importance of the media in debates about identity, place, and community highlights the second contextual feature of cultural studies that we want to emphasize. If the widespread idea that the field is interested only in popular media culture is mistaken, cultural studies has nevertheless been shaped as a response to the *social uptake* of communications technologies in the second half of the 20th century (see Meyrowitz, 1985), and it is deeply concerned with the transformations wrought by this uptake in "whole ways of life" around the world.

Most work on modern popular culture discusses the media to varying degrees (see Dent, 1992; Grossberg, 1997c; McRobbie, 1994; Storey, 1994), and the sheer size of the literature on the interface between "popular" and "media" cultural studies makes any effort to sustain a hard distinction a matter of local convenience; cultural studies broadly thrives on the connection and overlap between them. However, this does not mean that studies of media are "typical" of cultural studies or interchangeable with it; a redefinition of the relations between the latter and the various branches of media studies has been a feature or even the focus in recent years of work on cinema (Diawara, 1993; Friedberg, 1993; Naficy & Gabriel, 1993; O'Regan & Miller, 1994; Willemen, 1994), journalism

(Hartley, 1992a, 1996), music (Frith, 1996b; Keil & Feld, 1994; Lipsitz, 1994; Mitchell, 1996; Rose, 1994), music video (Frith, Goodwin, & Grossberg, 1993), radio (Johnson, 1988; Miller, 1992), and, perhaps most significant, television (Allen, 1987; Ang, 1996; Geraghty & Lusted, 1998; Hartley, 1992b; Mellencamp, 1990; Morley, 1992; Silverstone, 1994).

Television has been important to the development of cultural studies in part because of the obstacles it presents to any effort to divide the study of aesthetic forms from the study of their economics and their social uptake. As a primarily "domestic" object amenable to a multiplicity of public, communal, familial, and personal uses, television can be defined with equal plausibility as an art, as an industry, as a social force, as a pedagogical regime, as a sales medium, as a space-shaping feature of home and interior design, as a site of negotiation between markets and government, as a relay point in a "lifestyle" circuit or network of consumption (Kowinski, 1985), and, more recently, as potentially a terminal for home-based work as well as entertainment and education. John Hartley (1998) explains the implications for critical method: "TV is one of those many arts where form follows function, and thus 'textual analysis' is required of the semiotic environment surrounding the medium, not simply of individual shows or segments" (p. 42). Because the "semiotic" environment here includes practical political and economic activities as well as social relations (see Tomaselli, 1996), a rigorous reading of televisual textuality involves an analytic move to the "outside" of whatever boundaries may operate as given at the outset of a study (see Probyn, 1999b).

If this understanding of form as open-ended and "in process" distinguishes most work in cultural studies from the "close reading" techniques sometimes applied to films or TV shows but modeled on the kind of literary criticism that treats a poem as a self-contained artifact, it has also opened up new areas of study in which the media are positioned in wider networks of social and cultural activity that they create, transform, or enable but do not subsume. Alongside a continuing tradition of "subcultures" research (Gelder & Thornton, 1997; Hall & Jefferson, 1976; Hebdige, 1979; McRobbie, 1981, 1994), sports studies is rapidly developing as an interdisciplinary field in its own right (Martin & Miller, 1999; Morse, 1983; Rowe, 1995; Whannel, 1992), as is the study of scientific culture (Haraway, 1989, 1991; Ross, 1996) and of cyberspace and "technoculture" (Aronowitz, Martinsons, Menser, & Rich, 1996; Benedikt, 1991; Penley & Ross, 1991; Turkle, 1984); a growing literature on political culture is forming yet another area of study (Berlant, 1997; Chua, 1995; Clarke, 1991; Feuer, 1995; Grossberg, 1992; Hall, 1988; Massumi, 1996; Morris, 1998a; Street, 1997).

At the same time, the "close" (i.e., detailed and careful) study of aesthetic form is not abandoned; rather, it is extended and enriched by the inclusion of the semiotic "environment" in the object of study. For example, Patricia Mellencamp (1992) stretches fine-grained readings of films, media events, and TV situation comedies to grasp the nexus of "catastrophe, scandal, age, and comedy" that is organized *socioeconomically* around women in U.S. media culture; Barbara Browning (1995) uses her dancer's knowledge of bodily forms of eloquence to write a social history of Brazilian dance cultures as well as their political and religious stakes; and Jim Collins (1995) spills his case studies across several visual and performance media to show how the very stuff of art and cultural history is transformed in the richly localized uses of information technology that proliferate rather than vanish in an economy of media "excess."

In short, instead of isolating for study a single text, "author," industry, technology, or program format, cultural studies tends to emphasize questions or problems in circulation *between* various media and other spaces and times of social life. The fact that some studies do this by examining from multiple perspectives a widely distributed media event (Dayan & Katz, 1992; Wark, 1994) or a well-known media icon has prompted a caricature of the field as "Madonna studies" (see Benson & Metz, 1999). Well, there are also Barbie studies (Rand, 1995), Diana studies (Re:Public, 1997) and Elvis studies (Rodman, 1996), not to mention "Gulf War" studies (Kellner, 1992) and "mad cow disease" studies (McCalman, 1998). However, as Toni Morrison's (1992) collection of "Anita Hill" studies amply demonstrates, most of this work is not a coy celebration of this or that pop item but a critical investigation of media as a *force* that not only acts upon existing social conflicts, desires, and power relations, but continuously helps to produce them and sometimes to change them. This concern links the serious study of so-called pop ephemera to the significant work produced in recent years on the politics of the HIV/AIDS pandemic (Crimp, 1987, 1990; Erni, 1994; Patton, 1992, 1994) and indeed to "cultural studies" of ecological crisis and struggle (Berland, 1994; Jagtenberg & McKie, 1997; Langton, 1998; Ross, 1991, 1994; Slack & White, 1992).

Cultural studies itself has sometimes occasioned media events, creating controversy that travels well beyond the academy and across national borders. Following a fuss about "political correctness" in the U.S. academy in the early 1990s, the scandal over a "science wars" issue of the journal *Social Text* (Ross, 1996; see Michael, 1996; Nakayama, 1997; Slack & Semati, 1997) is the best-known recent example. These occasions usefully prompt academics to clarify their work for nonacademic audiences (see Berube, 1994; Gates, 1992; Lumby, 1997; Morris, 1997b; Wark, 1999). However, beyond inspiring self-defense, the media circulation of contending "images of cultural studies" is of interest because of the wider context of "representation wars" (Perera, 1993) in which it occurs. In her analysis of a major diplomatic wrangle between Australia and Malaysia in 1991 over an Australian TV drama series called *Embassy* (set in a fictitious "Asian" country apparently resembling Malaysia), Suvendrini Perera (1993) suggests that the show itself functioned "at once as agent and object" of dispute; relating this incident to others in which the media played an active role, she points out that such crises raise "questions about cultural status and authority that need to be rearticulated within a number of global discursive fields" (in this instance, the Gulf War, the Rushdie affair, and postmodernism) but must also be understood in "*worldly*, historical frames" of conflict (pp. 19-21).

"Representation wars" are occurring with increasing frequency between and across societies, in part because new communications technologies are enabling more people to receive and compare differing local, regional, national, and "global" representations of their own and others' lives—and sometimes to take issue with what they see. However, this does not entail a more or less even progression toward a universal plenitude of "global culture." On the contrary, the impact of technological change (and the distributions of its costs and benefits) varies greatly according to the context in which it occurs. In some countries, for example, having access to a *national* space or network of representation may be more novel and consequential than saturation by "international" (i.e., American) media product; Tom O'Regan (1993) argues that in Australia it was not until satellite networking was introduced in the 1980s, together with changes in federal broadcasting regulations as well as in media markets, that a "space-binding," nationalizing emphasis could fully emerge in our once strongly regionalized media system. Paradoxically, he suggests, this emphasis has actually favored "decontextualized" ways of thinking about self, politics, and identity while simultaneously fostering a more national *and* international mind-set; it confirms as well as disconfirms state boundaries and regional autonomies while encouraging the further development of "corridors of information" (on these concepts see also Berland, 1992; Carey, 1989).

The pressure of these contradictory movements helps to explain the intensification of public debates about power, propriety, and representation; who has, and who should have, the power to represent whom, how, and under which conditions? If new national frames of reference are, in fact, emerging just as local, regional, and global flows of information are redrawing cultural and political boundaries, then the complex issue of *control* over image production, circulation, and consumption becomes enmeshed in a whole range of political, economic, legal, and diplomatic concerns in ways that vary between societies and from polity to polity (see Birch, 1994; Chua, 1995; Gaines, 1992; Im, 1998; Kang, 1999; Ma, 1999; Wark, 1994). At the same time, the technological and geoeconomic conditions forcing the question of "what is involved in the representation of another culture, especially when that representation is seen by members of that culture" (Chow, 1991, p. 19) to circulate among government, academic, and media agendas are precisely those that make it impossible for control to be fully assured from any point in a given system. Historically dense anxieties about "modern youth" and "the child" as victims and carriers of media uncontrollability are acquiring a new intensity in this context (see Davis, 1997; Grossberg, 1992; Jenkins, 1998; Johnson, 1993; Kim, 1998; Stratton, 1992).

Two major strands of cultural studies have been shaped by these developments. One of these is primarily historical, researching "representation wars" in the past as these have variously worked to install, legitimate, complicate, and sometimes challenge colonial regimes, nation-building programs, and/or the "domestic," everyday race, class, and gender divisions of particular social formations (Chun, 1994; Dyer, 1997; Lott, 1993; McClintock, 1995; Spigel, 1992; Stam, 1997; Tomaselli & Mpofu, 1997); a closely related body of work examines what Healy (1997) calls the "memory-work" of the museum as a powerful form of modern public cultural pedagogy (Bennett, 1995; Crimp, 1995; Dibley, 1997; Marrie, 1989). The second major strand focuses on the pluralized and networked "public cultures" of the media present and future, exploring the new practices of subjectivity, citizenship, democracy, and community that are emerging across and between them (Gilbert, Glover, Kapal, Taylor, & Wheeler, 1999; Hartley, 1996; Hawkins, 1999; Lumby, 1999; McGuigan, 1996; Miller, 1998; Moon & Davidson, 1995; Morris & McCalman, 1999; Robbins, 1993a; Wallace, 1990). In practice, these two strands are more closely entangled than a sharp distinction between "cultural history" and "media studies" might lead us to expect: John Hartley's (1996) study of journalism in modernity is a scholarly history of "popular reality" as well as a vivid manifesto for a "postmodern public sphere"; Darren Tofts writes a prehistory of cyberculture that explores its continuity with older forms of "memory trade" (Tofts & McKeitch, 1998); and Emily Apter (1999) analyzes historically the implications of "virtual" citizenship for people living across the territories formed as "nations" by French colonialism.

Studies of tourism perhaps best illustrate the complex intertwining of ethical and "image" concerns with political and economic struggles that interests practitioners of cultural studies. As tourism has vastly expanded in scale and in importance to many local and regional economies, so conflict has intensified about its social costs and environmental effects (Craik, 1991; Lanfant, Allcock, & Bruner, 1995). An important influence in this context has come from indigenous peoples directly *confronting* those costs and effects on an international scale (Chiu, 1995; Palmer, 1998; Teaiwa, 1999). Historically used in Australia as targets for the technological practices, "nationing" experiments, and ethnocidal image campaigns of settler society (Mickler, 1998), Aboriginal groups have used the media to wage a representation "war" of their own to protect their languages and ways of life (Michaels, 1986, 1994), to increase their economic independence by developing their own artistic and tourist ventures (Healy, 1999; Johnson, 1994), to bring pressure to bear on governments sensitive to embarrassment and reactive to "credibility," to educate the public and demand more control over Aboriginal images (Johnson, 1996), and, by these means, to further their political struggle for self-determination in international as well as local and national contexts (see Bennett & Blundell, 1995; Fourmile, 1989; Langton, 1993; Meadows, 1996).

Although there is always controversy about the practical results of this kind of "symbolic" politics, Aboriginal media practices have, at the very least, challenged (and, we would argue, altered) the terms on which issues of race, colonialism, cultural value, national identity and history, land-ownership, and environmental ethics are publicly discussed in Australia—which is to say, they have powerfully affected our political and intellectual life (Muecke, 1992). So have feminist campaigns around images of women, and so, too, have the efforts of migrant groups to change the representational "norm" of an Anglo/Celtic Australia. In this context, it is not simply a conceit of cultural studies to claim that people can contest and transform the meanings circulated by the culture industries of a media society, perhaps the most famous claim associated with the field (Ang, 1985; Chambers, 1986; Hall & Jefferson, 1976; Hebdige, 1979; Fiske, 1989a, 1989b; Jenkins, 1992). On the contrary—the fact that people actually *do* this is a given of contemporary politics, and one determinant of the social context in which cultural studies is practiced.

◆ Concepts and Methods

At the beginning of his essay on the gift, Marcel Mauss (1970) writes:

> In these "early" societies, social phenomena are not discrete; each phenomenon contains all the threads of which the social fabric is composed. In these total social phenomena, as we propose to call them, all kinds of institutions find simultaneous expression: religious, legal, moral, and economic. In addition, the phenomena have their aesthetic aspect and they reveal morphological types. (p. 1)

For cultural studies, we suggest, a similar concentration of social relations is thought to occur in the pressure points of complex modern societies, but without the microcosmic expressiveness that Mauss finds in "archaic" social structures; rather, social relations are dispersed through these points, composing their complexity but permitting no read-off of a social totality. Instead of the "total social phenomenon," the corresponding concept for cultural studies is perhaps that of the "site" (the point of intersection and of negotiation of radically different kinds of determination and semiosis), whereas "expression" is displaced by the concept of "event" (a moment of practice that crystallizes diverse temporal and social trajectories).

Thus a shopping mall—to take a banal but central example—offers no quintessential insight into the organization of an epoch or a culture (it is not an emblem or an essence of the postmodern condition or of consumer capitalism); it is a place where many different things happen and where many different kinds of social relations are played out. It is, of course, the end point of numerous chains of production and transportation of goods, as well as of the marketing systems that channel them to consumers (and of the financial structures that underlie all this); these chains belong to regional and national as well as to global circuits (the "gourmet" aisle in the supermarket or the shelves of a delicatessen make visible the global nature of the capitalist marketplace, and may evoke something of the history of its formation, whereas the produce section may or may not be quite local in its reach; in each case the forms of packaging and presentation—"exotic" or "fresh," for example—will carry particular ideologies and particular aesthetic strategies). In another of its dimensions, the mall is an architectural construct, designed in accordance with an international format (anchored strategically by one or two large stores, with a particular disposition of parking and pedestrian traffic, a particular mix of boutiques, of services, of facilities, and so on); it constructs (or perhaps fails to construct) a particular existence and image of community and works in calculated ways to display the rewards and pleasures that follow upon work (or, again, that fail to). It sets up a normative distinction between men's and women's interactions with this space, as well as distinctions among the uses of the space by adults, children, and teenagers; it distinguishes sharply, of course, between its affluent clientele (the proper subjects of its community) and those who are less welcome (some of them, such as schoolkids, it may tolerate; others, such as vagrants and drunks, it will not). The aesthetic organization of the mall has to do with the gratification of desire and the organization of bodies in space; it is a sensual, subtly coercive kind of space.

But it is also a space that is put to use, that is diverted to ends other than those foreseen by its architects and its managers and its guards. This is perhaps the most familiar lesson of cultural studies: that structures are always structures-in-use, and that uses cannot be contained in advance. The semiotic space of the shopping mall is a conflictual space, where meanings are negotiated and projected through quite different formations of fantasy and need. This is to suggest a certain freedom, a function perhaps merely of the complexity of these interactions; but, knowing how readily the appearance of freedom can itself be a ruse of power, a cultural studies critic is likely to be wary of positing any transcendental value for this ability to use public space.

In order to get at these disparate structures that meet in and flow through a complex site like a shopping mall, the theorist (because this is never simply a *descriptive* activity) will, of necessity, have to draw upon, and to cross, the discourses of a number of different disciplines—and again, this cross-disciplinary or "multiperspectival" (Kellner, 1997) approach is characteristic of the working methods of cultural studies. These might include the following:

♦ Several rather different forms of economic discourse; some relatively technical ways of discussing mall management, commodity supply and demand, and regional patterns of employment; and a more theoretical discourse about commodity production and circulation;

♦ An aesthetic discourse, relating particularly to architecture, but also to advertising and display; a discourse of musicology, or sociomusicology, to talk about the workings of Muzak or of live performance; and a higher-level discourse to deal with the interrelation between aesthetics and economics;

♦ A discourse of politics, both of the "mundane" kind that refers to zoning permits and struggles over property values and a micrological discourse concerned with the politics of bodies in space; the first of these might draw in turn upon the discourses of the law and of town planning, and the latter upon a Foucauldian account of corporeal discipline, or upon symbolic interactionism or ethnomethodology, or upon urban geography;

♦ A discourse about gender (itself necessarily a mixed discourse) to analyze the organization of gender relations by a mythologized spatial structure, by the gender-specific targeting of consumer desire, by the structure of employment, by child-care provision or its absence, and so on;

♦ An ethnographic discourse, to get at the particularity of responses to and uses of the mall, to understand it as lived experience;

♦ A discourse of history, capable of talking about changes in the organization of consumption, perhaps in terms of the "postmodern" or "post-Fordist" centrality of consumption to a reorganized capitalist system, and of theorizing the changing modes of organization of community and of the public sphere;

♦ A discourse, one perhaps more specific to cultural studies, that would understand the mall as an intricate textual construct and understand shopping as a form of popular culture directly interrelated with other cultural forms and with an economy of representations and practices that make up a "way of life."

Governing the use of some of the discourses listed above might be a policy discourse, serving either the managers of and investors in shopping malls or local government, or perhaps community groups with an interest in reshaping the forms of community structured by the mall. And finally, one might draw upon some mix of sociology, semiotics, and philosophy to talk about the position(s) from which such an analysis can be enunciated—to come to terms with the odd duality that splits the critic into participant and observer, practitioner and reflexive intellectual, on the basis of the privilege given by the possession of cultural capital and a relation of some kind to the institutions of knowledge that make such reflexivity possible.

It is perhaps this "self-situating" and *limiting* moment of analysis that most clearly distinguishes work in cultural studies from some other modes of analysis on which its practitioners may draw. Unlike much positivist work in social science, cultural studies tends to incorporate in its object of study a critical account of its own motivating questions—and thus of the institutional frameworks and the disciplinary rules by which its research imperatives are formed. At the same time, cultural studies is not a form of that "multidisciplinarity" that dreams of producing an exhaustive knowledge map, and it does not posit (unlike some totalizing forms of Marxism) a transcendental space from which knowledges could be synthesized and a "general" theory achieved (see Deutsche, 1996; Morris, 1992).

On the contrary, work in cultural studies accepts its partiality (in both senses of the term); it is openly incomplete, and it is partisan in its insistence on the political dimensions of knowledge. For this reason, the "splitting" of critical practice among diverse and often conflicting social functions does not give rise, in cultural studies, to a discourse of intellectual *alienation*. Although there is no consensus about the politics of intellectual work shared by cultural studies imagined "as a whole," the intellectual project of cultural studies is always at some level marked, we would argue, by a discourse of social *involvement* (T. Bennett, 1998b; Frow, 1995; hooks, 1990; Robbins, 1993b; Ross, 1989).

The point of this discussion of an imaginary object (the shopping mall) is to give a sense not only of the working methods of cultural studies but of their rationale. Cultural studies often tends to operate in what looks like an eccentric way, starting with the particular, the detail, the scrap of ordinary or banal existence, and then working to unpack the density of relations and of intersecting social domains that inform it. To say that the shopping mall is organized by a range of diverse and overlapping systems (economic, aesthetic, demographic, regulatory, spatial, and so on) and can be the object of very different discourses, none of which has a privileged relation to its object, is to say that it is subject to very different kinds of *readings,* and that there is no principle of totality that can bring these readings into a coherent complementarity. To cast it in terms of readings is then to suggest a relation between the specialized readings of the various disciplines of knowledge and the "folk" readings performed by the users of the site (readings that are bound up with the "things to do" in shopping centers rather than being detached analytic exercises—but that are also themselves, however, pleasurable and interesting "things to do"). This, too, is a characteristic move in cultural studies: a relativizing and democratizing move that seeks to ensure that talk about an object is not closed off on the assumption that we know everything there is to know about it and to ensure that the relationality of any discourse to the full range of others is kept constantly in view.

Another way of talking about all this might be to say that it has to do with the way we understand the concept of *genre*. The mixing of discourses and genres in much work in cultural studies has to do with methodological impurity, perhaps with a certain fruitful insecurity about the legitimacy of cultural studies as a discipline, but perhaps too with the way cultural studies conceives its object as being relational (a network of connections) rather than substantial. Anne Freadman (1992) puts it this way:

> With the professionalisation of the social sciences and of the humanities, we put ourselves at risk of writing and reading with carefully administered "methods" that can only be called monogeneric. . . . if I am right, that the conditions of sociality are best described as the occupation of, and enablement by, heterogeneous ranges of generic practices, then monogeneric strategies of interpretation will always miss the mark. (p. 280)

The concept of "sociality" here carries that active, processual sense that cultural studies gives to the concept of culture, and the two are directly related: Both have to do with the practice (rather than the implementation) of structures of meaning—genres or codes, for example—and with the construction of social space out of the weaving together, the crisscrossing, of such practices (there are clear analogies here with the way ethnomethodology understands the construction and maintenance of the social).

There is a precise sense in which cultural studies uses the concept of *text* as a fundamental model. However, the concept of text undergoes a mutation so that, rather than designating a place where meanings are constructed in a single level of inscription (writing, speech, film, dress, and so on), still less a single artifact ("a" text), it works as an interleaving of levels. If a shopping mall is conceived on the model of textuality, then this "text" involves practices, institutional structures and the complex forms of agency they entail, legal, political, and financial conditions of existence, and particular flows of power and knowledge, as well as a particular multilayered semantic organization. At the same time, this "text" exists only within a network of *intertextual* relations (the textual networks of commodity culture, let's say, of architecture, of formations of community, of postmodern spatiality); it is an ontologically mixed entity, and one for which there can be no privileged or "correct" form of reading. It is this, more than anything else, that forces the attention of cultural studies to the diversity of audiences or users of the structures of textuality it analyzes—that is, to the open-ended social life of texts—and that forces it, thereby, to question the authority or finality of its own readings (Ang, 1991, 1996; Hay, Grossberg, & Wartella, 1996; hooks, 1992a; Morley, 1992; Morris, 1990; Stacey, 1994).

◆ Cultural Studies and Disciplinarity

The conception of culture that, we argue, informs the discipline of cultural studies—that is, culture as a contested and conflictual set of practices of representation bound up with the processes of formation and re-formation of social groups—depends upon a theoretical paradox, because it presupposes an opposition (between culture and society, between representations and reality) that is the condition of its existence but that it must constantly work to undo. Both the undoing of these oppositions and the failure ever to resolve completely the tension between them are constitutive of work in cultural studies. If representations are dissolved into the real (if they are thought only to reflect or to re-present, in a secondary way and either more or less accurately, a reality that has an autonomous existence and against which the representation can thus be measured), then the sense of the ways in which the real is textually constructed (as story, as desire, as repetition) gets lost. Conversely, if the real is nothing more than the sum of its representations ("nothing but texts," as the caricature goes), then the sense of *urgency* to the cultural studies project gets lost.

The concerns of this project are not, however, primarily epistemological; rather, they have to do with the social processes by which the categories of the real and of group existence are formed. The word *social* here means at once semiotic and political, in the sense of involving relations of power. Foucault's concept of power/knowledge has provided one influential way of thinking this intertwining of meaning and social relationality (Burchell, Gordon, & Miller, 1991; Foucault, 1980; Frow, 1988; Morris & Patton, 1979). Another develops the Gramscian notion of "articulation" (Grossberg, 1992; Hanczor, 1997; Laclau, 1977; Morley & Chen, 1996; Tomaselli & Mpofu, 1997), and another derives from the linguistic

510

concept of enunciation (Chambers, 1998, 1999; Morse, 1998; O'Regan, 1992; Probyn, 1993).

The concept of culture is an important one for many other disciplines, most notably perhaps for cultural anthropology and the sociology of culture. What, we might ask, is special or different about its use in cultural studies? One answer may be nothing; and it may be, too, that cultural studies should not be described as a "discipline." It is perhaps too young and unformed to have the strong sense of boundaries required of a discipline; it is also shaped—although this is a different issue—by its rebellion against disciplinarity itself (see T. Bennett, 1998a, 1998b; Nelson & Gaonkar, 1996; Striphas, 1998). Nevertheless, those who work in cultural studies tend to have strong opinions about what distinguishes their work from other fields of inquiry—"It does matter whether cultural studies is this or that" (S. Hall, 1992, p. 278)—and it might be useful to explore briefly both the differences and the overlap with these other fields.

The most obvious difference is in the object of study. Whereas anthropology is defined by its relation to an "allochronic" other (Fabian, 1983)—an other defined as such by its sociocultural difference within a quite different structure of time, and especially by what is understood as a qualitative difference in social organization—cultural studies takes as its object the ordinary culture (two very loaded words, but let them stand for the moment) of its own society. Certainly there are movements toward such an orientation in contemporary anthropology (see Augé, 1995), but often—for example, in ethnographic studies of rural or working-class communities or of the homeless—this continues to reproduce the same structure of otherness, an exoticism now caught within the home society. Cultural studies is sometimes caught in this trap, too, treating subcultures, for example, as an exotic or subversive other within the dominant culture, but its *impulse* is toward studying the diverse forms of cultural organization without recourse to such exoticization.

There are also, however, differences in methodological orientation. Although cultural studies has adopted many of the techniques of fieldwork observation and description developed by ethnography (Ang, 1985; Brunsdon & Morley, 1978; Radway, 1991; Skeggs, 1997; Thomas, 1999; Willis, 1977), its focus on complex industrialized societies means that other methodologies may also be appropriate. Information about cultural codes and practices can be obtained in many ways other than through discussion with informants and participant observation (vast archives of written and electronic texts are available in many instances), and sometimes the writer is a member of the culture that is being studied. Cultural studies tends, as a consequence, to make greater use of techniques of textual analysis, to make use of a greater diversity of sources, to make more eclectic use of methodologies, and, once again, to work with a perhaps more complex problematic of the relation between the writer and the culture being studied—that is, with an *intensification* of the anthropological problem of the tension between personal and political distance and personal and political involvement (Byrne, 1995; Field, 1991; Jackson, 1998; M. Z. Rosaldo, 1984; R. Rosaldo, 1989; Stewart, 1996; Taussig, 1997).

In relation to the sociology of culture, cultural studies has certainly learned from its use of statistical survey techniques (Bennett, Emmison, & Frow, 1999). The interest of cultural studies, however, tends to lie much more in the lived effects and formations of culture, and questions of the distribution of competence, preference, and access are usually made secondary to this concern. But the difference between the two disciplines is perhaps increasingly one of focus rather than of kind (see Alasuutari, 1995; Chaney, 1994; Denzin, 1992, 1997; Long, 1997), and the same holds true of the overlapping relationships between cultural studies and social as well as cultural history (Davis, 1983; Denning, 1996; C. Hall, 1992; Johnson, 1993; Pickering, 1997; Steedman, 1986, 1992a, 1992b; Steinberg, 1996) and between cultural studies and critical geography (Duncan & Ley, 1993; Fincher & Jacobs, 1998; Jacobs, 1996; Keith & Pile, 1993; Massey, 1994). One can observe, finally, an overlap with literary studies to the extent that the latter has retheorized its object in recent years to cover the analysis and history of social relations of textuality rather than texts or textual systems in themselves (Armstrong, 1987; Barrell, 1991; Brown, 1996; Chambers, 1999; Grewal, 1996; Guillory, 1993; Mignolo, 1995; Radway, 1997; Suleri, 1992; Viswanathan, 1989). It is worth noting that cultural studies is not restricted to the study of popular culture, and certainly has little in common with folkloric studies, including the "folkloric" orientation to mass-media studies. Rather, as Nelson, Treichler, and Grossberg (1992) write:

> Cultural studies does not require us to repudiate elite cultural forms—or simply to acknowledge, with Bourdieu, that distinctions between elite and popular cultural forms are themselves the products of relations of power. Rather, cultural studies requires us to identify the operation of specific prac-

tices, of how they continuously reinscribe the line between legitimate and popular culture, and of what they accomplish in specific contexts. (p. 13)

The concern of cultural studies is with the constitution and working of systems of relations rather than with the domains formed by these processes. Hence a further characteristic concern of cultural studies (one it shares with much poststructuralist thought): a concern with boundaries and limits, and especially with the fuzziness of such edges and the consequent impurity of genres and disciplines. For example, John Hartley (1992b) suggests that it is possible "to see in impurities not a problem but a fundamental criterion for cultural studies" (p. 102), and he defends an international television criticism on the grounds that neither television nor nations can be understood except in relational terms. Tom O'Regan (1992) reformulates the vexed question of the relationship between cultural criticism and cultural policy by considering both as "porous systems," and Helen Grace (1993) examines the increasingly fluid relations between value and utility, art and commerce, aesthetics and logic, "play" and "war" now being produced in the "serious business" of management culture.

The effect of this concern is not to dissolve analysis into an all-encompassing description ("cultural studies" as "studying culture"), but rather to foreground the question of the relation *between* the description of textual/cultural networks and the position of enunciation from which that description is possible (Hartley, 1999). This question is, again, at once *semiotic* (it has to do with the organization and enablement of textuality by structures of genre) and *political* (it has to do with the social relations of textuality—that is, with the relative positioning of speakers and their discursive construction as the carriers of a certain social identity and authority). It follows that an interest in the concrete conditions and particular instances in which conflicts of authority and problems of authorship are negotiated (or not negotiated) and settled (or unsettled) is not confined to studies that are explicitly concerned with cross-cultural conflict and postcolonial struggle: McKenzie Wark's (1993) essay on the band Midnight Oil, for example, considers the politics of authority in popular media culture, and Ross Chambers (1998) reads three AIDS diaries (written in France, the United States, and Australia) to come to terms with "the problematics of survivorhood" shared among authors whose subject is their own dying and death and readers for whom the act of reading becomes a form of mourning. The self-situating impulse of cultural studies also foregrounds issues of *intellectual* authority and authorship as they arise in the course of particular projects; much work in cultural studies shares with other forms of qualitative inquiry a strong interest in the use of dialogic, collaborative, and composite modes of writing and research to foster more open and responsive relations between academics and the communities with whom they work (see, e.g., Frankenberg, 1993; Johnson, 1990; Langton, 1993; McRobbie, 1999; Muecke, 1997; Owusu, 1999; Ross, 1997).

◆ Genealogies and Potentials

In recent years a number of critical accounts have begun to take stock of the achievements and difficulties of cultural studies, many of them offering a "genealogy" of the emergence of cultural studies as a serious academic field (T. Bennett, 1998b; Brantlinger, 1990; Clarke, 1991; Crimp, 1999; Ferguson & Golding, 1997; Gilroy, 1987; Grossberg, 1997a; S. Hall, 1992; Harris, 1992; Rodman, 1997; Williams, 1989). In one sense, genealogies are as misleading for intellectual work as they are for studying personal behavior: They can tell us nothing about where we are going, or should go, or might want to go. However, if the best-known genealogy for cultural studies is British, this is so not least because it continues to provide a useful model against which other projects can define their own precedents and concerns (McNeil, 1998; Tomaselli, 1998b; Wright, 1998). The influential enterprise of "British cultural studies" took shape in the 1950s as a challenge to hierarchical distinctions between the public and the private, the major and the minor, the "great" and the "everyday," as these regulated the field of culture (and the discipline of English; Bennett, 1993) in Britain at the time.[4] Emerging as a program with the work of the Birmingham Centre for Contemporary Cultural Studies, founded in 1964 (where the study of subcultures and the politics of race and gender came to the foreground in the 1970s and early 1980s), British cultural studies developed an insistence on notions of agency in cultural theory. This means studying not how people *are* in a passively inherited culture but what we *do* with the cultural commodities that we encounter and use in daily life ("practice") and thus what we *make* as "culture." Inflected by post-structuralist theories of reading as well as by empirical audience research, this shift enabled a redefinition of popular culture not as a stratum (the "low" one) of aesthetic practice but as a social "zone of contestation," in Stuart Hall's (1981) famous phrase—the ground in and over which different interests struggle for hegemony (Hall, Critcher, Jefferson, Clarke, & Roberts, 1979).

This emphasis on agency and contestation is shared by cultural studies in most parts of the world today. However, other genealogies and other kinds of intellectual practice, we suggest, have been at least as important to the field's development. The pioneering work of the Canadian thinker Harold Innis on technology, imperialism, and space (Berland, 1997a, 1997b; Kroker, 1984) and of James Carey (1989) in the United States on space and communication (see also Munson & Warren, 1997) has been influential in linking the study of place and cultural history to work on media and cultural policy (Bennett, 1992, 1998b; Meadows, 1996; O'Regan, 1993). Two texts by Foucault have been particularly influential: *The Archaeology of Knowledge* (1972) opened the way to a more extended and institutionally anchored model of discursivity than was available in other, language- and text-centered, notions of discourse; and the first volume of *The History of Sexuality* (1978) offered a complex micro-sociological mapping of social power as well as new ways of conceptualizing sexuality. The writings of Henri Lefebvre (1971/1984) and Michel de Certeau (1984) have also fed into the way cultural studies theorizes the structure and practice of everyday life; and Bourdieu's sociology of culture provides a strong countertradition to the culture-and-society line that descends from Raymond Williams.

The list of inputs into this emerging discipline could be extended almost indefinitely; it is perhaps the mark of the newness of a discipline that, lacking an established methodology and even a well-defined object, cultural studies draws eclectically and energetically upon a variety of theoretical sources as it seeks to define its own specificity. The influence of phenomenology and ethnomethodology can certainly be traced in its refusal to privilege the interpretations of "expert" readers and its concern with the experiential dimension of everyday life. The Gramscian understanding of culture as a site of contestation has been more recently inflected by postcolonial theory, as it variously draws on the works of, for example, Franz Fanon (Alessandrini, 1999), Ashish Nandy (1983; Chen, 1998a), C. L. R. James (Buhle, 1986; Grimshaw, 1992), and Ranajit Guha (1997) to give a more ambivalent and complex account of both the flow of power and the projective identifications and identities of actors in situations of cultural struggle.

515

As fundamental and lasting as any single intellectual influence, however, has been the feminist understanding of the politics of the everyday and of "personal" life. A critique of culture (and of theories of culture) was crucial to the "second wave" of the women's liberation movement in the early 1970s, and although it would be difficult to characterize the "effects" on cultural studies of such a complex and diverse social movement, we can point to two of the consequences that have followed from the influence of particular currents in feminism. One is a tendency to think of "the self" as a site of *social* creativity, rather than simply as a medium of individual expression. Many feminists, for example, have always taken the slogan "The personal is political" to mean that the resources of the state must be captured and used in the interests of transforming women's lives by increasing their access to social equity and power; work on cultural policy is able to refer for a precedent (although it does not always do so) to a record of significant feminist achievement. The other consequence is a tendency to assume that a politics of the everyday involves confronting not only the workings of class, racism, and colonialism as well as sex and gender, but their impact in intellectual life and in education. Ann Curthoys (1988) argued in 1970 that we "must analyse why public life has been considered to be the focus of history, and why public life has been so thoroughly occupied by men" (p. 4); cultural studies continues this line of questioning in an expanded framework today, as it develops both as a critique of education and as a pedagogical experiment (Giroux & Shannon, 1997; Luke, 1996; McCarthy & Crichlow, 1993; Striphas, 1998).

The point here is that cultural studies has not only been a response to the political and social movements of the past three decades but has also derived many of its themes, its research priorities, its polemics, and, in some ways, its theoretical emphases and privileged working methods from an *engagement* with those movements. For this reason, the most innovative work, in our view, continues to be more interested in developing the implications of particular forms of symbolic action and the consequences of particular moments of cultural practice—implications and consequences that experimental "genealogies" of the field may sometimes help us to see—than in proving the case for doing so against older theories of culture. It is not that cultural studies (as we see it) is in any way hostile to "theory"; theoretical work can also be considered a form of cultural practice. It is merely that the doctrinal disputes that have marked the emergence of the field—disputes between humanism and formalism, for-malism and Marxism, Marxism and poststructuralism, deconstruction and new historicism—are often resolved in practice by a kind of rigorous *mixing* (see Deutsche, 1996; Grace, 1993; Nightingale, 1996; O'Regan, 1996).

A similar tendency is at work, we would argue, in the "disciplinary" dis-putes that have intensified in recent years between proponents of "textual-ism" and ethnography (Ang, 1996; Hartley, 1992a, 1998; Morley, 1998; Murdock, 1995, 1997) and between political economy and "interpre-tive" cultural studies (Garnham, 1995a, 1995b; Gibson-Graham, 1996; Grossberg, 1995). However useful and necessary these debates continue to be for consolidating the field, its future directions are perhaps being shaped more directly by the experimental empiricism of, for example, Elspeth Probyn's (1998, 1999a) work on food, fashion, and agricultural economics; Kuan-Hsing Chen's (in press) political-historical mapping of the emergence of "KTV" (karaoke-TV) across the city of Taipei; or Julia Emberley's (1998) study of the cultural politics of the fur trade. Such empirical projects, far from being "antitheoretical," have to reflect on complex issues of disciplinary difference and convergence in order to articulate their aims.

In this they share a commitment to learning and thinking *from* prac-tice with recent "theoretical" critiques of the pervasive concept of cul-ture (Grossberg, 1998b; Massumi 1996, 1997; Readings, 1996; Spivak, 1993). Addressing the effects in academic as well as broader social and economic life of the neoliberalism we discussed at the beginning of this chapter, these critiques have begun to challenge, once again, the founding categories and the institutional formation of cultural studies itself—a necessary condition, perhaps, of its practice. Whatever the future of "cul-ture," it is clear that both a commitment to empirical research and a constant questioning of the social and political frames in which that "research" is formulated and practiced will continue to be indispensable to a field so vitally concerned with the uncertain boundaries of "art" and "everyday life" in mediated societies; with the multiple ways in which "popular culture" informs the practices, and shapes the dreams, of mod-ern citizenship; with the impact of institutional knowledges, and desires, on their objects of study; and the intricate, charged relations between stories and spaces, events and sites, "making history" and "taking place" in contemporary cultural economies.

517

◆ Notes

1. These citations are taken from, respectively, the following newspaper items: "Swan Steels" (1989); an advertisement for a Shopping Centres Conference, published in *Australian Financial Review* (August 13, 1992); and "Poor Performance" (1989).

2. The concept of "context" does a lot of work in cultural studies, where it never refers (as it can in some sociologies of culture) to a background of influences and determinants detachable from a "text" or other object of study. In a number of essays on the problem of distinguishing cultural studies from other ways of "studying culture" (see Rodman, 1997), Lawrence Grossberg (1997a) argues that its "radical contextualism" is a feature "unique to cultural studies" (p. 253; see also Grossberg, 1997b, 1998a). In this usage, a "context" is not an environment but, on the contrary, a "specific bit of everyday life" positioned *between* culture, understood as "a specific body of practices," and "particular social forces, institutions and relations of power" (Grossberg, 1993, p. 9). The analyst's task is to specify this positioning, case by case: "The context of a particular research is not empirically given beforehand; it has to be defined by the project, by the political question that is at stake. The context can be as narrow as a neighbourhood at a particular moment, or an urban region, or perhaps even some local high school that is having race problems, or it can be as broad as global capitalism after the cold war. To put it succinctly, for cultural studies context is everything and everything is contextual" (Grossberg, 1997a, p. 255). In this view, cultural studies is primarily the study of contexts rather than "culture," insofar as contexts (including those of research, theorization, and conceptual definition) are produced *in* social practice. From this it follows that although anything can become an object of investigation in cultural studies, cultural studies does not, in fact, claim that *culture* is "everything" or that everything is cultural; construed as a specific body of practices, culture does not subsume the social and economic forces, institutions, and relations of power that both enable and *limit* those practices.

3. De Certeau (1984), for example, projected in his influential study of the practice of everyday life a "*science of singularity*; that is to say, a science of the relationship that links everyday pursuits to particular circumstances" (p. ix), whereas Agamben (1993) describes his philosophy as seeking a way past "the false dilemma that obliges knowledge to choose between the ineffability of the individual and the intelligibility of the universal" (p. 1).

4. According to the usual narrative, this challenge emerged from the "scholarship" generation of scholars formed, as Turner (1996) explains, by "the expansion of educational opportunities within Britain after the war, and the spread of adult education as a means of postwar reconstruction as well as an arm of the welfare state" (p. 44; see also Steele, 1997). Children of the working class, such as Richard Hoggart (1957) and Raymond Williams, saw their task as one of validating the culture of the common people over and against the canonical values of British high-cultural elitism; where the latter fostered a nostalgia for pre-industrial English *folk* culture, the new intellectuals examined and affirmed the *popular* culture of the industrial working class. But, as Turner points out, this phase of educational modernization also corresponded to the postwar expansion of "industrial" *mass* culture—often American in source or inspiration. Early critical responses to this "inauthentic" development were ambiguous or negative; wedged between the "folk" and the "mass," the "popular" became an unstable and contested object of study (see Frow, 1995; Grossberg, 1997c; Hall, 1981; Miller & McHoul, 1999).

◆ References

Abbas, A. (1997). *Hong Kong: Culture and the politics of disappearance*. Minneapolis: University of Minnesota Press.

Agamben, G. (1993). *The coming community* (M. Hardt, Trans.). Minneapolis: University of Minnesota Press.

Alasuutari, P. (1995). *Researching culture: Qualitative method and cultural studies*. London: Sage.

Alessandrini, A. C. (Ed.). (1999). *Frantz Fanon: Critical perspectives*. New York: Routledge.

Allen, R. C. (Ed.). (1987). *Channels of discourse: Television and contemporary criticism*. Chapel Hill: University of North Carolina Press.

Allor, M. (1997). Locating cultural activity: The "Main" as chronotope and heterotopia. *Topia, 1,* 42-54.

Ang, I. (1985). *Watching Dallas: Soap opera and the melodramatic imagination*. London: Methuen.

Ang, I. (1991). *Desperately seeking the audience*. London: Routledge.

Ang, I. (1996). *Living room wars: Rethinking media audiences for a postmodern world*. London: Routledge.

Ang, I. (1999). On not speaking Chinese: Postmodern ethnicity and the politics of diaspora. In M. Shiach (Ed.), *Feminism and cultural studies* (pp. 540-564). Oxford: Oxford University Press.

Anzaldúa, G. (1987). *Borderlands/la frontera: The new mestiza*. San Francisco: Aunt Lute.

Appadurai, A. (1996). *Modernity at large: Cultural dimensions of globalization*. Minneapolis: University of Minnesota Press.

Appiah, K. A. (1992). *In my father's house: Africa in the philosophy of culture*. Oxford: Oxford University Press.

Apter, E. (1999). *Continental drift: From national characters to virtual subjects*. Chicago: University of Chicago Press.

Armstrong, N. (1987). *Desire and domestic fiction: A political history of the novel*. New York: Oxford University Press.

Arndt, H. W., & Hill, H. (Eds.). (1999). *Southeast Asia's economic crisis: Origins, lessons and the way forward*. Sydney: Allen & Unwin.

Aronowitz, S., Martinsons, B., Menser, M., & Rich, J. (Eds.). (1996). *Technoscience and cyberculture*. London: Routledge.

Augé, M. (1995). *Non-places: Introduction to an anthropology of supermodernity* (J. Howe, Trans.). London: Verso.

Baker, H. A., Jr., Diawara, M., & Lindeborg, R. H. (Eds.). (1996). *Black British cultural studies: A reader*. Chicago: University of Chicago Press.

Barrell, J. (1991). *The infection of Thomas de Quincey: A psychopathology of imperialism*. New Haven, CT: Yale University Press.

Bathrick, D. (1992). Cultural studies. In J. Gibaldi (Ed.), *Introduction to scholarship in modern languages and literatures* (pp. 320-340). New York: Modern Language Association of America.

Benedikt, M. (Ed.). (1991). *Cyberspace: First steps.* Cambridge: MIT Press.

Bennett, D. (Ed.). (1998). *Multicultural states: Rethinking difference and identity.* London: Routledge.

Bennett, T. (1992). Putting policy into cultural studies. In L. Grossberg, C. Nelson, & P. A. Treichler (Eds.), *Cultural studies* (pp. 23-37). New York: Routledge.

Bennett, T. (1993). Coming out of English: A policy calculus for cultural studies. In K. K. Ruthven (Ed.), *Beyond the disciplines: The new humanities* (pp. 33-44). Canberra: Australian Academy of the Humanities.

Bennett, T. (1995). *The birth of the museum: History, theory, politics.* London: Routledge.

Bennett, T. (1998a). Cultural studies: A reluctant discipline. *Cultural Studies, 12,* 528-545.

Bennett, T. (1998b). *Culture: A reformer's science.* London/Sydney: Sage/Allen & Unwin.

Bennett, T., & Blundell, V. (Eds.). (1995). First peoples: Cultures, policies, politics [Special issue]. *Cultural Studies, 9*(1).

Bennett, T., Emmison, M., & Frow, J. (1999). *Accounting for tastes: Australian everyday cultures.* Cambridge: Cambridge University Press.

Bennett, T., Turner, G., & Volkerling, M. (Eds.). (1994). Post-colonial formations [Special issue]. *Culture and Policy, 6*(1).

Benson, C., & Metz, A. (Eds.). (1999). *The Madonna companion: Two decades of commentary.* New York: Schirmer.

Benterrak, K., Muecke, S., & Roe, P. (1996). *Reading the country* (Rev. ed.). Fremantle, Western Australia: Fremantle Arts Centre Press.

Berland, J. (1992). Angels dancing: Cultural technologies and the production of space. In L. Grossberg, C. Nelson, & P. A. Treichler (Eds.), *Cultural studies* (pp. 38-55). New York: Routledge.

Berland, J. (1994). On reading "the weather." *Cultural Studies, 8,* 99-114.

Berland, J. (1997a). Nationalism and the modernist legacy: Dialogues with Innis. *Culture and Policy, 8*(3), 9-39.

Berland, J. (1997b). Space at the margins: Colonial spatiality and critical theory after Innis. *Topia, 1,* 55-82.

Berlant, L. (1997). *The queen of America goes to Washington City: Essays on sex and citizenship.* Durham, NC: Duke University Press.

Berube, M. (1994). *Public access: Literary theory and American cultural politics.* London: Verso.

Bhabha, H. K. (Ed.). (1990). *Nation and narration.* London: Routledge.

Bhabha, H. K. (1994). *The location of culture.* London: Routledge.

Birch, D. (Ed.). (1994). Cultural studies in the Asia Pacific [Special issue]. *Southeast Asian Journal of Social Science, 22*(1-2).

Bourdieu, P. (1984). *Distinction: A social critique of the judgement of taste* (R. Nice, Trans.). Cambridge. MA: Harvard University Press.

Brantlinger, P. (1990). *Crusoe's footprints: Cultural studies in Britain and America.* New York: Routledge.

Brown, B. (1996). *The material unconscious: American amusement, Stephen Crane, and the economics of play.* Cambridge, MA: Harvard University Press.

Browning, B. (1995). *Samba: Resistance in motion.* Bloomington: Indiana University Press.

Brunsdon, C., & Morley, D. (1978). *Everyday television: "Nationwide."* London: British Film Institute.

Buhle, P. (Ed.). (1986). *C. L. R. James: His life and work.* London: Allison & Busby.

Burchell, G., Gordon, C., & Miller, P. (1991). *The Foucault effect: Studies in governmentality.* London: Harvester Wheatsheaf.

Burns, R. (Ed.). (1995). *German cultural studies: An introduction.* Oxford: Oxford University Press.

Butler, J. (1990). *Gender trouble: Feminism and the subversion of identity.* New York: Routledge.

Butler, J. (1993). *Bodies that matter: On the discursive limits of "sex."* New York: Routledge.

Byrne, D. (1995). Intramuros' return. *UTS Review, 1*(2), 2-29.

Carby, H. (1996). White woman listen! In H. A. Baker, Jr., M. Diawara, & R. H. Lindeborg (Eds.), *Black British cultural studies: A reader* (pp. 223-239). Chicago: University of Chicago Press. (Reprinted from *The empire strikes back: Race and racism in seventies Britain,* pp. 212-235, by Centre for Contemporary Cultural Studies, Ed., 1982, London: Hutchinson)

Carey, J. W. (1989). *Communication as culture: Essays on media and society.* Boston: Unwin Hyman.

Carey, J. W. (1995). Abolishing the old spirit world. *Critical Studies in Mass Communication, 12*(1), 82-88.

Carey, J. W. (1997). Reflections on the project of (American) cultural studies. In M. Ferguson & P. Golding (Eds.), *Cultural studies in question* (pp. 1-24). London: Sage.

Chabram-Dernersesian, A. (Ed.). (1999). Chicana/o Latina/o cultural studies: Transnational and transdisciplinary movements [Special issue]. *Cultural Studies, 13*(2).

Chakrabarty, D. (in press). *Provincializing Europe: Postcolonial thought and historical difference.* Princeton, NJ: Princeton University Press.

Chambers, I. (1986). *Popular culture: The metropolitan experience.* London: Methuen.

Chambers, I., & Curti, L. (Eds.). (1996). *The post-colonial question: Common skies, divided horizons.* London: Routledge.

Chambers, R. (1996). Cultural studies as a challenge to French studies. *Australian Journal of French Studies, 33*(2), 137-156.

Chambers, R. (1998). *Facing it: AIDS diaries and the death of the author.* Ann Arbor: University of Michigan Press.

Chambers, R. (1999). *Loiterature.* Lincoln: University of Nebraska Press.

Chaney, D. (1994). *The cultural turn: Scene-setting essays on contemporary cultural history.* London: Routledge.

Chang, H.-H. (1998). Taiwan queer valentines. In K.-H. Chen (Ed.), *Trajectories: Inter-Asia cultural studies* (pp. 283-298). London: Routledge.

Chen, K.-H. (1992). Voices from the outside: Towards a new internationalist localism. *Cultural Studies, 6,* 476-484.

Chen, K.-H. (1998a). Introduction: The decolonization question. In K.-H. Chen (Ed.), *Trajectories: Inter-Asia cultural studies* (pp. 1-53). London: Routledge.

Chen, K.-H. (Ed.). (1998b). *Trajectories: Inter-Asia cultural studies.* London: Routledge.

Chen, K.-H. (in press). The formation and consumption of KTV in Taiwan. In B.-H. Chua (Ed.), *Consumption in Asia: Lifestyle and identity.* London: Routledge.

Chiu, Y.-L. (1995). From the politics of identity to an alternative cultural politics: On Taiwan primordial inhabitants' a-systemic movement. In R. Wilson & A. Dirlik (Eds.), *Asia/Pacific as space of cultural production* (pp. 120-144). Durham, NC: Duke University Press.

Cho, H. (1996). Feminist intervention in the rise of "Asian" discourse. In Asian Centre for Women's Studies, *The rise of feminist consciousness against the patriarchy* (pp. 144-170). Seoul: Ewha Woman's University.

Chow, R. (1991). *Woman and Chinese modernity: The politics of reading between West and East.* Minneapolis: University of Minnesota Press.

Chow, R. (1993). *Writing diaspora: Tactics of intervention in contemporary cultural studies.* Bloomington: Indiana University Press.

Chow, R. (1998a). *Ethics after idealism: Theory-culture-ethnicity-reading.* Bloomington: Indiana University Press.

Chow, R. (Ed.). (1998b). Modern Chinese literary and cultural studies in the age of theory: Reimagining a field [Special issue]. *Boundary 2, 25*(3).

Chua, B.-H. (1995). *Communitarian ideology and democracy in Singapore.* London: Routledge.

Chua, B.-H. (1998). Globalisation: Finding the appropriate words and levels. *Communal Plural, 6*(1), 117-124.

Chun, A. (1994). The culture industry as national enterprise: The politics of heritage in contemporary Taiwan. *Culture and Policy, 6*(1), 69-89.

Clarke, J. (1991). *New times and old enemies: Essays on cultural studies and America.* London: HarperCollins.

Clifford, J. (1988). *The predicament of culture: Twentieth-century ethnography, literature, and art.* Cambridge, MA: Harvard University Press.

Clifford, J. (1997). *Routes: Travel and translation in the late twentieth century.* Cambridge, MA: Harvard University Press.

Clifford, J., & Marcus, G. E. (Eds.). (1986). *Writing culture: The poetics and politics of ethnography.* Berkeley: University of California Press.

Cohen, S. (1993). *Academia and the luster of capital.* Minneapolis: University of Minnesota Press.

Collins, J. (1995). *Architectures of excess: Cultural life in the information age.* New York: Routledge.

Craik, J. (1991). *Resorting to tourism: Cultural policies for tourist development in Australia.* Sydney: Allen & Unwin.

Crimp, D. (Ed.). (1987). AIDS: Cultural analysis, cultural activism [Special issue]. *October, 43.*

Crimp, D. (with Rolston, A.). (1990). *AIDS demo graphics.* Seattle: Bay.

Crimp, D. (1995). *On the museum's ruins* (L. Lawler, Photog.). Cambridge: MIT Press.

Crimp, D. (1999). Getting the Warhol we deserve. *Social Text, 59,* 49-66.

Culture fills Aussie tills. (1990, October 11). *Daily Telegraph Mirror.*

Curthoys, A. (1988). *For and against feminism.* Sydney: Allen & Unwin.

Darien-Smith, K., Gunner, L., & Nuttall, S. (Eds.). (1996). *Text, theory, space: Land, literature and history in South Africa and Australia.* London: Routledge.

Davis, M. (1997). *Gangland: Cultural elites and the new generationalism.* Sydney: Allen & Unwin.

Davis, N. Z. (1983). *The return of Martin Guerre.* Cambridge, MA: Harvard University Press.

Dayan, D., & Katz, E. (1992). *Media events: The live broadcasting of history.* Cambridge, MA: Harvard University Press.

de Certeau, M. (1984). *The practice of everyday life* (S. F. Rendall, Trans.). Berkeley: University of California Press.

de Lauretis, T. (Ed.). (1986). *Feminist studies/critical studies.* Bloomington: Indiana University Press.

de Lauretis, T. (Ed.). (1991). Queer theory: Lesbian and gay sexualities [Special issue]. *Differences, 3*(1).

Deleuze, G., & Guattari, F. (1987). *A thousand plateaus: Capitalism and schizophrenia* (B. Massumi, Trans.). Minneapolis: University of Minnesota Press.

Denning, M. (1996). *The cultural front: The laboring of American culture in the twentieth century.* London: Verso.

Dent, G. (Ed.). (1992). *Black popular culture.* Seattle: Bay.

Denzin, N. K. (1992). *Symbolic interactionism and cultural studies.* Newbury Park, CA: Sage.

Denzin, N. K. (1997). *Interpretive ethnography: Ethnographic practices for the 21st century*. Thousand Oaks, CA: Sage.

Deutsche, R. (1996). *Evictions: Art and spatial politics*. Cambridge: MIT Press.

Dever, M. (Ed.). (1997). *Australia and Asia: Cultural transactions*. Richmond, UK: Curzon.

Diawara, M. (Ed.). (1993). *Black American cinema*. New York: Routledge.

Diawara, M. (1998). *In search of Africa*. Cambridge, MA: Harvard University Press.

Dibley, B. (1997). Museum, nation, narration: The Museum of New Zealand— Te Papa Tongarewa "telling New Zealand's story." *Culture and Policy, 8*(3), 97-118.

Duncan, J., & Ley, D. (Eds.). (1993). *Place/culture/representation*. London: Routledge.

During, S. (Ed.). (1999). *The cultural studies reader* (2nd ed.). London: Routledge.

Dyer, R. (1997). *White*. London: Routledge.

Emberley, J. V. (1998). *The cultural politics of fur*. Ithaca, NY: Cornell University Press.

Erni, J. N. (1994). *Unstable frontiers: Technomedicine and the cultural politics of "curing" AIDS*. Minneapolis: University of Minnesota Press.

Fabian, J. (1983). *Time and the other: How anthropology makes its object*. New York: Columbia University Press.

Ferguson, M., & Golding, P. (Eds.). (1997). *Cultural studies in question*. London: Sage.

Feuer, J. (1995). *Seeing through the eighties: Television and Reaganism*. Durham, NC: Duke University Press.

Field, N. (1991). *In the realm of a dying emperor*. New York: Pantheon.

Fincher, R., & Jacobs, J. M. (Eds.). (1998). *Cities of difference*. New York: Guilford.

Fiske, J. (1989a). *Reading the popular*. Boston: Unwin Hyman.

Fiske, J. (1989b). *Understanding popular culture*. Boston: Unwin Hyman.

Forbes, J., & Kelly, M. (Eds.). (1996). *French cultural studies: An introduction*. Oxford: Oxford University Press.

Forgacs, D., & Lumley, R. (Eds.). (1996). *Italian cultural studies: An introduction*. Oxford: Oxford University Press.

Foucault, M. (1972). *The archaeology of knowledge* (A. M. Sheridan Smith, Trans.). London: Tavistock.

Foucault, M. (1978). *The history of sexuality: Vol. 1. An introduction* (R. Hurley, Trans.). New York: Random House.

Foucault, M. (1980). *Power/knowledge: Selected interviews and other writings, 1972-1977* (C. Gordon, Ed.; L. Marshall, J. Mepham, & K. Soper, Trans.). New York: Pantheon.

Fourmile, H. (1989). Aboriginal heritage legislation and self-determination. *Australian-Canadian Studies, 7*(1-2), 45-61.

Frankenberg, R. (1993). *White women, race matters: The social construction of whiteness.* Minneapolis: University of Minnesota Press.

Frankenberg, R. (Ed.). (1997). *Displacing whiteness: Essays in social and cultural criticism.* Durham, NC: Duke University Press.

Freadman, A. (1992). The vagabond arts. In *In the place of French: Essays in and around French studies in honour of Michael Spencer* (pp. 257-291). Mt. Nebo: University of Queensland/Boombana.

Fregoso, R. L., & Chabram, A. (Eds.). (1990). Chicana/o cultural representations [Special issue]. *Cultural Studies, 4*(3).

Friedberg, A. (1993). *Window shopping: Cinema and the postmodern.* Berkeley: University of California Press.

Frith, S. (1996a). Music and identity. In S. Hall & P. du Gay (Eds.), *Questions of cultural identity* (pp. 108-127). London: Sage.

Frith, S. (1996b). *Performing rites: The value of popular music.* Oxford: Oxford University Press.

Frith, S., Goodwin, A., & Grossberg, L. (Eds.). (1993). *Sound and vision: The music video reader.* London: Routledge.

Frow, J. (1988). Some versions of Foucault. *Meanjin, 47*(1-2), 144-156, 353-365.

Frow, J. (1995). *Cultural studies and cultural value.* Oxford: Oxford University Press.

Frow, J., & Morris, M. (Eds.). (1993). *Australian cultural studies: A reader.* Sydney/ Chicago: Allen & Unwin/University of Illinois Press.

Fuss, D. (1989). *Essentially speaking: Feminism, nature, and difference.* New York: Routledge.

Fuss, D. (Ed.). (1991). *Inside/out: Lesbian theories, gay theories.* New York: Routledge.

Gaines, J. (1992). *Contested culture: The image, the voice and the law.* London: British Film Institute.

García Canclini, N. (1993). *Transforming modernity: Popular culture in Mexico.* Austin: University of Texas Press.

García Canclini, N. (1995). *Hybrid cultures: Strategies for entering and leaving modernity.* Minneapolis: University of Minnesota Press.

Garnaut, R. (1989). *Australia and the Northeast Asian ascendancy.* Canberra: Australian Government Publishing Service.

Garnham, N. (1995a). Political economy and cultural studies: Reconciliation or divorce? *Critical Studies in Mass Communication, 12*(1), 62-71.

Garnham, N. (1995b). Reply to Grossberg & Carey. *Critical Studies in Mass Communication, 12*(1), 95-100.

Gates, H. L., Jr. (1992). *Loose canons: Notes on the culture wars.* New York: Oxford University Press.

Gelder, K., & Thornton, S. (Eds.). (1997). *The subcultures reader.* London: Routledge.

Geraghty, C., & Lusted, D. (Eds.). (1998). *The television studies book.* London: Edward Arnold.

Gibbons, L. (1996). *Transformations in Irish culture.* Cork: Cork University Press.

Gibian, P. (Ed.). (1997). *Mass culture and everyday life.* New York: Routledge.

Gibson-Graham, J.-K. (1996). *The end of capitalism (as we knew it): A feminist critique of political economy.* Cambridge, MA: Blackwell.

Gilbert, J., Glover, D., Kapal, C., Taylor, J. B., & Wheeler, W. (Eds.). (1999). Diana and democracy [Special issue]. *New Formations, 36.*

Gilroy, P. (1987). *There ain't no black in the Union Jack: The cultural politics of race and nation.* London: Hutchinson.

Gilroy, P. (1992). Cultural studies and ethnic absolutism. In L. Grossberg, C. Nelson, & P. A. Treichler (Eds.), *Cultural studies* (pp. 187-198). New York: Routledge.

Gilroy, P. (1993). *The Black Atlantic: Modernity and double consciousness.* Cambridge, MA: Harvard University Press.

Gilroy, P. (1996). British cultural studies and the pitfalls of identity. In H. A. Baker, Jr., M. Diawara, & R. H. Lindeborg (Eds.), *Black British cultural studies: A reader* (pp. 223-239). Chicago: University of Chicago Press.

Giroux, H., & Shannon, P. (Eds.). (1997). *Education and cultural studies: Toward a performative practice.* London: Routledge.

Grace, H. (1993). A house of games: Serious business and the aesthetics of logic. In J. Frow & M. Morris (Eds.), *Australian cultural studies: A reader* (pp. 69-85). Sydney/Chicago: Allen & Unwin/University of Illinois Press.

Graham, H., & Labanyi, J. (Eds.). (1996). *Spanish cultural studies: An introduction.* Oxford: Oxford University Press.

Grewal, I. (1996). *Home and harem: Nation, gender, empire, and the cultures of travel.* Durham, NC: Duke University Press.

Grewal, I., & Kaplan, C. (Eds.). (1994). *Scattered hegemonies: Postmodernity and transnational feminist practices.* Minneapolis: University of Minnesota Press.

Grimshaw, A. (Ed.). (1992). *The C. L. R. James reader.* Oxford: Blackwell.

Grossberg, L. (1992). *We gotta get out of this place: Popular conservatism and postmodern culture.* New York: Routledge.

Grossberg, L. (1993). *Cultural studies: What's in a name?* [B. Aubrey Fisher Memorial Lecture]. Salt Lake City: University of Utah, Department of Communication.

Grossberg, L. (1995). Cultural studies vs. political economy: Is anyone else bored with this debate? *Critical Studies in Mass Communication, 12*(1), 72-81.

Grossberg, L. (1996). Identity and cultural studies: Is that all there is? In S. Hall & P. du Gay (Eds.), *Questions of cultural identity* (pp. 87-107). London: Sage.

Grossberg, L. (1997a). *Bringing it all back home: Essays on cultural studies.* Durham, NC: Duke University Press.

Grossberg, L. (1997b). Cultural studies, modern logics, and theories of globalisation. In A. McRobbie (Ed.), *Back to reality? Social experience and cultural studies* (pp. 7-35). Manchester: Manchester University Press.

Grossberg, L. (1997c). *Dancing in spite of myself: Essays on popular culture.* Durham, NC: Duke University Press.

Grossberg, L. (1998a). The cultural studies' crossroads blues. *European Journal of Cultural Studies, 1,* 64-82.

Grossberg, L. (1998b). The victory of culture: Part 1. Against the logic of mediation. *Angelaki, 3*(3), 3-29.

Grossberg, L. (1999). Speculations and articulations of globalization. *Polygraph, 11,* 11-48.

Grossberg, L., Nelson, C., & Treichler, P. A. (Eds.). (1992).*Cultural studies.* New York: Routledge.

Guha, R. (1997). *Dominance without hegemony: History and power in colonial India.* Cambridge, MA: Harvard University Press.

Guillory, J. (1993). *Cultural capital: The problem of literary canon formation.* Chicago: University of Chicago Press.

Hall, C. (1992). *White, male and middle-class: Explorations in feminism and history.* New York: Routledge.

Hall, S. (1981). Notes on deconstructing "the popular." In R. Samuel (Ed.), *People's history and socialist theory* (pp. 227-240). London: Routledge & Kegan Paul.

Hall, S. (1988). *The hard road to renewal: Thatcherism and the crisis of the left.* London: Verso.

Hall, S. (1992). Cultural studies and its theoretical legacies. In L. Grossberg, C. Nelson, & P. A. Treichler (Eds.), *Cultural studies* (pp. 277-294). New York: Routledge.

Hall, S. (1996). New ethnicities. In D. Morley & K.-H. Chen (Eds.), *Stuart Hall: Critical dialogues in cultural studies* (pp. 441-449). New York: Routledge.

Hall, S., Critcher, C., Jefferson, T., Clarke, J., & Roberts, B. (1979). *Policing the crisis: Mugging, the state, and law and order.* London: Macmillan.

Hall, S., & du Gay, P. (Eds.). (1996). *Questions of cultural identity.* London: Sage.

Hall, S., & Jefferson, T. (1976). *Resistance through rituals: Youth subcultures in post-war Britain.* London: Hutchinson.

Hanczor, R. S. (1997). Articulation theory and public controversy: Taking sides over *NYPD blue. Critical Studies in Mass Communication, 14*(1), 1-30.

Haraway, D. J. (1989). *Primate visions: Gender, race, and nature in the world of modern science.* New York: Routledge.

Haraway, D. J. (1991). *Simians, cyborgs, and women: The reinvention of nature.* New York: Routledge.

Hargreaves, A. G., & McKinney, M. (Eds.). (1997). *Post-colonial cultures in France.* London: Routledge.

Harris, D. (1992). *From class struggle to the politics of pleasure: The effects of Gramscianism on cultural studies.* London: Routledge.

Hartley, J. (1992a). *The politics of pictures: The creation of the public in the age of popular media.* London: Routledge.

Hartley, J. (1992b). *Tele-ology: Studies in television.* London: Routledge.

Hartley, J. (1996). *Popular reality: Journalism, modernity, popular culture.* London: Edward Arnold.

Hartley, J. (1998). Housing television: Textual traditions in TV and cultural studies. In C. Geraghty & D. Lusted (Eds.), *The television studies book* (pp. 33-50). London: Edward Arnold.

Hartley, J. (1999). "Text" and "audience": One and the same? Methodological tensions in media research. *Textual Practice, 13,* 491-512.

Hartman, G. H. (1997). *The fateful question of culture.* New York: Columbia University Press.

Harvey, D. (1989). *The condition of postmodernity: An enquiry into the origins of cultural change.* Oxford: Blackwell.

Hawkins, G. (1999). Public service broadcasting in Australia: Value and difference. In A. Calabrese & J. Burgelman (Eds.), *Communication, citizenship and social policy: Rethinking the welfare state* (pp. 173-187). Boulder, CO: Rowman & Littlefield.

Hay, J., Grossberg, L., & Wartella, E. (Eds.). (1996). *The audience and its landscape.* Boulder, CO: Westview.

Hayward, P. (Ed.). (1998). *Sound alliances: Indigenous peoples, cultural politics and popular music in the Pacific.* London: Cassell.

Healy, C. (1997). *From the ruins of colonialism: History as social memory.* Cambridge: Cambridge University Press.

Healy, C. (1999). White feet and black trails: Travelling cultures at the Lurujarri Trail. *Postcolonial Studies, 2*(1), 55-73.

Hebdige, D. (1979). *Subculture: The meaning of style.* London: Methuen.

Hebdige, D. (1988). *Hiding in the light: On images and things.* London: Routledge.

Hereniko, V., & Wilson, R. (Eds.). (in press). *Inside out: Literature, cultural politics, and identity in the new Pacific.* Boulder, CO: Rowman & Littlefield.

Hoggart, R. (1957). *The uses of literacy.* London: Chatto & Windus.

hooks, b. (1981). *Ain't I a woman: Black women and feminism.* Boston: South End.

hooks, b. (1990). *Yearning: Race, gender, and cultural politics.* Boston: South End.

hooks, b. (1992a). *Black looks: Race and representation.* Boston: South End.

hooks, b. (1992b). Representing whiteness in the black imagination. In L. Grossberg, C. Nelson, & P. A. Treichler (Eds.), *Cultural studies* (pp. 338-346). New York: Routledge.

Hull, G. T., Scott, P. B., & Smith, B. (Eds.). (1982). *All the women are white, all the blacks are men, but some of us are brave: Black women's studies.* Old Westbury, NY: Feminist Press.

Hunter, I. (1988a). *Culture and government: The emergence of literary education.* London: Macmillan.

Hunter, I. (1988b). Setting limits to culture. *New Formations, 4,* 103-124.

Hunter, I. (1992). Aesthetics and cultural studies. In L. Grossberg, C. Nelson, & P. A. Treichler (Eds.), *Cultural studies* (pp. 347-372). New York: Routledge.

Huntington, S. P. (1996). *The clash of civilizations and the remaking of world order.* New York: Simon & Schuster.

Im, Y.-H. (1998). The media, civil society and new social movements in Korea, 1985-93. In K.-H. Chen (Ed.), *Trajectories: Inter-Asia cultural studies* (pp. 330-345). London: Routledge.

Jackson, M. (1998). *Minima ethnographica: Intersubjectivity and the anthropological project.* Chicago: University of Chicago Press.

Jacobs, J. M. (1996). *Edge of empire: Postcolonialism and the city.* London: Routledge.

Jagtenberg, T., & McKie, D. (1997). *Eco-impacts and the greening of postmodernity.* London: Sage.

Jameson, F., & Miyoshi, M. (Eds.). (1998). *The cultures of globalization.* Durham, NC: Duke University Press.

Jenkins, H. (1992). *Textual poachers: Television fans and participatory cultures.* New York: Routledge.

Jenkins, H. (Ed.). (1998). *The children's culture reader.* New York: New York University Press.

Johnson, L. (1988). *The unseen voice: A cultural study of early Australian radio.* London: Routledge.

Johnson, L. (1993). *The modern girl: Childhood and growing up.* Sydney/Milton Keynes, UK: Allen & Unwin/Open University Press.

Johnson, V. (1990). *Radio birdman.* Sydney: Sheldon Booth.

Johnson, V. (1994). *Western desert artists: A biographical dictionary.* Sydney: Craftsman House.

Johnson, V. (1996). *"Copyrites": Aboriginal art in the age of reproductive technologies.* Sydney: Macquarie University/National Indigenous Arts Advocacy Association.

Jordan, G., & Weedon, C. (1995). *Cultural politics: Class, gender, race and the postmodern world.* Oxford: Blackwell.

Kang, M. K. (1999). Postmodern consumer culture without postmodernity: Copying the crisis of signification. *Cultural Studies, 13,* 18-33.

Keil, C., & Feld, S. (1994). *Music grooves.* Chicago: University of Chicago Press.

Keith, M., & Pile, S. (Eds.). (1993). *Place and the politics of identity.* London: Routledge.

Kellner, D. (1992). *The Persian Gulf TV war.* Boulder, CO: Westview.

Kellner, D. (1997). Critical theory and cultural studies: The missed articulation. In J. McGuigan (Ed.), *Cultural methodologies* (pp. 12-41). London: Sage.

Kelly, C., & Shepherd, D. (Eds.). (1998). *Russian cultural studies: An introduction.* Oxford: Oxford University Press.

Kim, S. (1998). "Cine-mania" or cinephilia: Film festivals and the identity question. *UTS Review, 4*(2), 174-187.

King, A. D. (Ed.). (1991). *Culture, globalization and the world system.* London: Macmillan.

Knight, S. (1990). *The selling of the Australian mind: From first fleet to third Mercedes.* Port Melbourne: Heinemann Australia.

Kowinski, W. S. (1985). *The malling of America: An inside look at the great consumer paradise.* New York: William Morrow.

Kraniauskas, J. (1998). Globalization is ordinary: The transnationalization of cultural studies. *Radical Philosophy, 90,* 9-19.

Kroker, A. (1984). *Technology and the Canadian mind: Innis, McLuhan, Grant.* Montreal: New World Perspectives.

Laclau, E. (1977). *Politics and ideology in Marxist theory.* London: Verso.

Lanfant, M.-F., Allcock, J. B., & Bruner, E. M. (Eds.). (1995). *International tourism: Identity and change.* London: Sage.

Langton, M. (1993). *"Well, I heard it on the radio and I saw it on the television . . . : An essay for the Australian Film Commission on the politics and aesthetics of filmmaking by and about Aboriginal people and things.* North Sydney: Australian Film Commission.

Langton, M. (1998). *Burning questions: Emerging* environmental issues for indigenous peoples in Northern Australia. Darwin: Northern Territory University, Centre for Indigenous Natural and Cultural Resource Management.

Lefebvre, H. (1984). *Everyday life in the modern world* (S. Rabinovitch, Trans.). New Brunswick, NJ: Transaction. (Original work published 1971)

Lilley, R. (1998). *Staging Hong Kong: Gender and performance in transition.* Richmond, UK: Curzon.

Lipsitz, G. (1994). *Dangerous crossroads.* London: Verso.

Long, E. (Ed.). (1997). *From sociology to cultural studies.* Oxford: Blackwell.

Loosley, S. (1991, March 17). Step towards real changes. *Sunday Telegraph.*

Lott, E. (1993). *Love and theft: Blackface minstrelsy and the American working class.* New York: Oxford University Press.

Lowe, L. (1996). *Immigrant acts: On Asian American cultural politics.* Durham, NC: Duke University Press.

Lubiana, W. (Ed.). (1997). *The house that race built.* New York: Pantheon.

Luke, C. (Ed.). (1996). *Feminisms and pedagogies of everyday life.* Albany: State University of New York Press.

Lumby, C. (1997). *Bad girls: The media, sex and feminism in the 90s.* Sydney: Allen & Unwin.

Lumby, C. (1999). *Gotcha: Life in a tabloid world.* Sydney: Allen & Unwin.

Ma, E. K.-W. (1999). *Culture, politics and television in Hong Kong.* London: Routledge.

Marrie, A. (1989). Museums and Aborigines: A case study in internal colonialism. *Australian-Canadian Studies, 7*(1-2), 63-80.

Martin, R., & Miller, T. (Eds.). (1999). *SportCult.* Minneapolis: University of Minnesota Press.

Massey, D. (1994). *Space, place and gender.* Cambridge: Polity.

Massey, D. (1997). Problems with globalisation. *Soundings, 7,* 7-12.

Massumi, B. (1992). *A user's guide to capitalism and schizophrenia: Deviations from Deleuze and Guattari.* Cambridge: MIT Press.

Massumi, B. (1996). The autonomy of affect. In P. Patton (Ed.), *Deleuze: A critical reader* (pp. 217-239). Oxford: Blackwell.

Massumi, B. (1997). The political economy of belonging and the logic of relation. In C. Davidson (Ed.), *Anybody* (pp. 174-189). Cambridge: MIT Press.

Matsuda, M. (1996). *Where is your body? And other essays on race, gender, and the law.* Boston: Beacon.

Mauss, M. (1970). *The gift: Forms and functions of exchange in archaic societies* (I. Cunnison, Trans.). London: Cohen & West.

McCalman, I. (Ed.). (1998). *Mad cows and modernity: Cross-disciplinary reflections on the crisis of Creutzfeldt-Jakob disease.* Canberra: Humanities Research Centre/National Academies Forum.

McCarthy, C., & Crichlow, W. (Eds.). (1993). *Race, identity and representation in education.* New York: Routledge.

McClintock, A. (1995). *Imperial leather: Race, gender and sexuality in the colonial contest.* New York: Routledge.

McGuigan, J. (1996). *Culture and the public sphere.* London: Routledge.

McGuigan, J. (Ed.). (1997). *Cultural methodologies.* London: Sage.

McHoul, A. (1997). Ordinary heterodoxies: Towards a theory of cultural objects. *UTS Review, 3*(2), 7-22.

McNeil, M. (1998). De-centring or re-focusing cultural studies: A response to Handel K. Wright. *European Journal of Cultural Studies, 1,* 57-64.

McRobbie, A. (1981). Settling accounts with subcultures: A feminist critique. In T. Bennett, G. Martin, C. Mercer, & J. Woollacott (Eds.), *Culture, ideology and social process: A reader* (pp. 113-123). London: Batsford Academic & Education.

McRobbie, A. (1994). *Postmodernism and popular culture.* London: Routledge.

McRobbie, A. (Ed.). (1997a). *Back to reality? Social experience and cultural studies.* Manchester: Manchester University Press.

McRobbie, A. (1997b). The Es and the anti-Es: New questions for feminism and cultural studies. In M. Ferguson & P. Golding (Eds.), *Cultural studies in question* (pp. 170-186). London: Sage.

McRobbie, A. (1999). *British fashion design: Rag trade or image industry?* London: Routledge.

Meadows, M. (1996). Indigenous cultural diversity: Television northern Canada. *Culture and Policy, 7*(1), 25-44.

Mellencamp, P. (Ed.). (1990). *Logics of television.* Bloomington: Indiana University Press.

Mellencamp, P. (1992). *High anxiety: Catastrophe, scandal, age, and comedy.* Bloomington: Indiana University Press.

Mercer, K. (1994). *Welcome to the jungle: New positions in black cultural studies.* London: Routledge.

Mercer, K., Ugwu, C., & Bailey, D. A. (Eds.). (1996). *Mirage: Enigmas of race, difference and desire.* London: ICA Editions.

Meyrowitz, J. (1985). *No sense of place: The impact of electronic media on social behavior.* New York: Oxford University Press.

Michael, J. (1996). Science friction and cultural studies: Intellectuals, interdisciplinarity, and the profession of truth. *Camera Obscura, 37,* 125-154.

Michaels, E. (1986). *The Aboriginal invention of television in central Australia 1982-1986.* Canberra: Australian Institute of Aboriginal Studies.

Michaels, E. (1994). *Bad Aboriginal art: Tradition, media, and technological horizons.* Minneapolis: University of Minnesota Press.

Mickler, S. (1998). *The myth of privilege: Aboriginal status, media visions, public ideas.* Fremantle, Western Australia: Fremantle Arts Centre Press.

Mignolo, W. D. (1995). *The darker side of the Renaissance: Literacy, territoriality and colonization.* Ann Arbor: University of Michigan Press.

Miller, T. (Ed.). (1992). Radio-sound [Special issue]. *Continuum, 6*(1).

Miller, T. (1998). *Technologies of truth: Cultural citizenship and the popular media.* Minneapolis: University of Minnesota Press.

Miller, T., & McHoul, A. (1999). *Popular culture and everyday life.* London: Sage.

Mitchell, T. (1996). *Popular music and local identity: Rock, pop and rap in Europe and Oceania.* Leicester: University of Leicester Press.

Mohanty, C. T., Russo, A., & Torres, L. (Eds.). (1991). *Third World women and the politics of feminism.* Bloomington: Indiana University Press.

Moon, M., & Davidson, C. N. (Eds.). (1995). *Subjects and citizens: Nation, race and gender from Oroonoko to Anita Hill.* Durham, NC: Duke University Press.

Moraga, C., & Anzaldúa, G. (Eds.). (1981). *This bridge called my back: Writings by radical women of color.* New York: Kitchen Table/Women of Color Press.

Moreiras, A. (1999). The order of order: On the reluctant culturalism of anti-subalternist critiques. *Journal of Latin American Cultural Studies, 8*(1), 125-145.

Morley, D. (1992). *Television, audiences and cultural studies.* London: Routledge.

Morley, D. (1998). So-called cultural studies: Dead ends and reinvented wheels. *Cultural Studies, 12,* 476-497.

Morley, D., & Chen, K.-H. (Eds.). (1996). *Stuart Hall: Critical dialogues in cultural studies.* New York: Routledge.

Morris, M. (1990). Banality in cultural studies. In P. Mellencamp (Ed.), *Logics of television* (pp. 14-43). Bloomington: Indiana University Press.

Morris, M. (1992). The man in the mirror: David Harvey's "condition" of postmodernity. In M. Featherstone (Ed.), *Cultural theory and cultural change* (pp. 253-279). London: Sage.

Morris, M. (1997a). A question of cultural studies. In A. McRobbie (Ed.), *Back to reality? Social experience and cultural studies* (pp. 36-57). Manchester: Manchester University Press.

Morris, M. (1997b). The truth is out there. *Cultural Studies, 11,* 367-375.

Morris, M. (1998a). *Too soon, too late: History in popular culture.* Bloomington: Indiana University Press.

Morris, M. (1998b). Truth and beauty in our times. In J. Bigelow (Ed.), *Our cultural heritage* (pp. 75-87). Canberra: Australian Academy of the Humanities.

Morris, M., & McCalman, I. (1999). "Public culture" and humanities research in Australia: A report. *Public Culture, 11*(2), 319-345.

Morris, M., & Patton, P. (Eds.). (1979). *Michel Foucault: Power, truth, strategy.* Sydney: Feral.

Morrison, T. (Ed.). (1992). *Race-ing justice, en-gendering power: Essays on Anita Hill, Clarence Thomas, and the construction of social reality.* New York: Pantheon.

Morse, M. (1983). Sport on television: Replay and display. In E. A. Kaplan (Ed.), *Regarding television* (pp. 44-66). Los Angeles: American Film Institute.

Morse, M. (1998). *Virtualities: Television, media art, and cyberculture.* Bloomington: Indiana University Press.

Muecke, S. (1992). *Textual spaces: Aboriginality and cultural studies.* Kensington: New South Wales University Press.

Muecke, S. (1997). *No road (bitumen all the way).* Fremantle, Western Australia: Fremantle Arts Centre Press.

Munson, E. S., & Warren, C. A. (Eds.). (1997). *James Carey: A critical reader.* Minneapolis: University of Minnesota Press.

Murdock, G. (1995). Across the great divide: Cultural analysis and the condition of democracy. *Critical Studies in Mass Communication, 12*(1), 89-95.

Murdock, G. (1997). Cultural studies at the crossroads. In A. McRobbie (Ed.), *Back to reality? Social experience and cultural studies* (pp. 58-73). Manchester: Manchester University Press.

Naficy, H., & Gabriel, T. H. (Eds.). (1993). *Otherness and the media: The ethnography of the imagined and the imaged.* Newark, NJ: Harwood.

Nakayama, T. K. (1997). The empire strikes back: The Sokal controversy and the vilification of cultural studies. *Journal of Communication Inquiry, 21*(2), 45-55.

Nandy, A. (1983). *The intimate enemy: Loss and recovery of self under colonialism.* Bombay: Oxford University Press.

Nelson, C., & Gaonkar, D. P. (Eds.). (1996). *Disciplinarity and dissent in cultural studies.* New York: Routledge.

Nelson, C., Treichler, P. A., & Grossberg, L. (1992). Cultural studies: An introduction. In L. Grossberg, C. Nelson, & P. A. Treichler (Eds.), *Cultural studies* (pp. 1-16). New York: Routledge.

Nightingale, V. (1996). *Studying audiences: The shock of the real.* London: Routledge.

Noble, G., Poynting, S., & Tabar, P. (1999). Youth, ethnicity and the mapping of identities: Strategic essentialism and strategic hybridity among male Arabic-speaking youth in south-western Sydney. *Communal Plural, 7*(1), 29-45.

O'Regan, T. (1992). Some reflections on the "policy moment." *Meanjin, 51,* 517-532.

O'Regan, T. (1993). *Australian television culture.* Sydney: Allen & Unwin.

O'Regan, T. (1996). *Australian national cinema.* London: Routledge.

O'Regan, T., & Miller, T. (Eds.). (1994). Screening cultural studies [Special issue]. *Continuum, 7*(2).

Owusu, K. (Ed.). (1999). *Black British culture and society.* London: Routledge.

Palmer, L. (1998). On or off the beaten track? Tourist trails in Thailand. *UTS Review, 4*(1), 67-91.

Parker, A., Russo, M., Sommer, D., & Yaeger, P. (Eds.). (1992). *Nationalisms and sexualities.* New York: Routledge.

Patton, C. (1992). From nation to family: Containing African AIDS. In A. Parker, M. Russo, D. Sommer, & P. Yaeger (Eds.), *Nationalisms and sexualities* (pp. 218-234). New York: Routledge.

Patton, C. (1994). *Last served? Gendering the HIV pandemic.* London: Falmer.

Penley, C., & Ross, A. (Eds.). (1991). *Technoculture.* Minneapolis: University of Minnesota Press.

Perera, S. (1993). Representation wars: Malaysia, *Embassy,* and Australia's *Corps Diplomatique.* In J. Frow & M. Morris (Eds.), *Australian cultural studies: A reader* (pp. 15-29). Sydney/Chicago: Allen & Unwin/University of Illinois Press.

Perera, S. (Ed.). (1995). *Asian and Pacific inscriptions: Identities, ethnicities, nationalities.* Bundoora, Victoria, Australia: Meridian.

Pickering, M. (1997). *History, experience and cultural studies.* London: Macmillan.

Poor performance "shooting Aust in the head." (1989, October 26). *Australian Financial Review.*

Prakash, G. (Ed.). (1995). *After colonialism: Imperial histories and postcolonial displacements*. Princeton, NJ: Princeton University Press.

Probyn, E. (1993). *Sexing the self: Gendered positions in cultural studies*. London: Routledge.

Probyn, E. (1996). *Outside belongings*. New York: Routledge.

Probyn, E. (1998). McIdentities: Food and the familial citizen. *Theory, Culture & Society, 15*(2), 155-173.

Probyn, E. (1999a). Beyond food/sex: Eating and an ethics of existence. *Theory, Culture & Society, 16*(2), 215-228.

Probyn, E. (1999b). Disciplinary desires: The outside of queer feminist cultural studies. In M. Shiach (Ed.), *Feminism and cultural studies* (pp. 431-458). Oxford: Oxford University Press.

Radway, J. A. (1991). *Reading the romance: Women, patriarchy and popular literature* (2nd ed.). Chapel Hill: University of North Carolina Press.

Radway, J. A. (1997). *Feeling for books: The Book-of-the-Month Club, literary taste, and middle-class desire*. Chapel Hill: University of North Carolina Press.

Rand, E. (1995). *Barbie's queer accessories*. Durham, NC: Duke University Press.

Readings, B. (1996). *The university in ruins*. Cambridge, MA: Harvard University Press.

Re:Public. (Ed.). (1997). *Planet Diana: Cultural studies and global mourning*. Nepean: University of Western Sydney, Research Centre in Intercommunal Studies.

Robbins, B. (Ed.). (1993a). *The phantom public sphere*. Minneapolis: University of Minnesota Press.

Robbins, B. (1993b). *Secular vocations: Intellectuals, professionalism, culture*. London: Verso.

Robinson, P. (1989, June 18). Fair go, we're all bludgers. *Sun Herald*.

Rodman, G. (1996). *Elvis after Elvis: The posthumous career of a living legend*. New York: Routledge.

Rodman, G. (1997). Subject to debate: (Mis)reading cultural studies. *Journal of Communication Inquiry, 21*(2), 56-69.

Roediger, D. R. (1991). *The wages of whiteness: Race and the making of the American working class*. London: Verso.

Rosaldo, M. Z. (1984). Toward an anthropology of self and feeling. In R. A. Shweder & R. A. Levine (Eds.), *Culture theory: Essays on mind, self and emotion* (pp. 137-157). Cambridge: Cambridge University Press.

Rosaldo, R. (1989). *Culture and truth: The remaking of social analysis*. Boston: Beacon.

Rosaldo, R. (1997). Whose cultural studies? Cultural studies and the disciplines. In P. Gibian (Ed.), *Mass culture and everyday life* (pp. 26-33). New York: Routledge.

Rose, T. (1994). *Black noise: Rap music and black culture in contemporary America.* Boston: Wesleyan University Press.

Ross, A. (1989). *No respect: Intellectuals and popular culture.* New York: Routledge.

Ross, A. (1991). *Strange weather: Culture, science and technology in the age of limits.* London: Verso.

Ross, A. (1994). *The Chicago gangster theory of life: Nature's debt to society.* London: Verso.

Ross, A. (Ed.). (1996). *Science wars.* London: Duke University Press.

Ross, A. (Ed.). (1997). *No sweat: Fashion, free trade and the rights of garment workers.* London: Verso.

Rowe, D. (1995). *Popular cultures: Rock music, sport and the politics of pleasure.* London: Sage.

Said, E. W. (1993). *Culture and imperialism.* London: Chatto & Windus.

Sakai, N. (1991). *Voices of the past: The status of language in eighteenth-century Japanese discourse.* Ithaca, NY: Cornell University Press.

Sakai, N. (1997). *Translation and subjectivity: On "Japan" and cultural nationalism.* Minneapolis: University of Minnesota Press.

Sedgwick, E. K. (1990). *Epistemology of the closet.* Berkeley: University of California Press.

Sedgwick, E. K. (1993). *Tendencies.* Durham, NC: Duke University Press.

Sharkey, S. (1997). Irish cultural studies and the politics of Irish studies. In J. McGuigan (Ed.), *Cultural methodologies* (pp. 155-177). London: Sage.

Shaviro, S. (1997). Beauty lies in the eye. *Canadian Review of Comparative Literature, 25,* 461-471.

Sheridan, S. (Ed.). (1988). *Grafts: Feminist cultural criticism.* London: Verso.

Shiach, M. (Ed.). (1999). *Feminism and cultural studies.* Oxford: Oxford University Press.

Silverstone, R. (1994). *Television and everyday life.* London: Routledge.

Skeggs, B. (1997). *Formations of class and gender.* London: Sage.

Slack, J. D., & Semati, M. M. (1997). Intellectual and political hygiene: The "Sokal affair." *Critical Studies in Mass Communication, 14*(3), 201-227.

Slack, J. D., & White, L. A. (1992). Ethics and cultural studies. In L. Grossberg, C. Nelson, & P. A. Treichler (Eds.), *Cultural studies* (pp. 571-592). New York: Routledge.

Spigel, L. (1992). *Make room for TV: Television and the family ideal in postwar America.* Chicago: University of Chicago Press.

Spivak, G. C. (1988). *In other worlds: Essays in cultural politics.* London: Routledge.

Spivak, G. C. (1990). *The post-colonial critic: Interviews, strategies, dialogues.* New York: Routledge.

Spivak, G. C. (1993). *Outside in the teaching machine.* New York: Routledge.

Stacey, J. (1994). *Star gazing: Hollywood cinema and female spectatorship*. London: Routledge.

Stam, R. (1997). *Tropical multiculturalism: A comparative history of race in Brazilian cinema and culture*. Durham, NC: Duke University Press.

Steedman, C. (1986). *Landscape for a good woman: A story of two lives*. London: Virago.

Steedman, C. (1992a). Culture, cultural studies, and the historians. In L. Grossberg, C. Nelson, & P. A. Treichler (Eds.), *Cultural studies* (pp. 613-622). New York: Routledge.

Steedman, C. (1992b). *Past tenses: Essays on writing, autobiography and history*. London: Rivers Oram.

Steedman, C. (1997). Writing the self: The end of the scholarship girl. In J. McGuigan (Ed.), *Cultural methodologies* (pp. 106-125). London: Sage.

Steele, T. (1997). *The emergence of cultural studies 1945-65: Cultural politics, adult education and the English question*. London: Lawrence & Wishart.

Steinberg, M. P. (1996). Cultural history and cultural studies. In C. Nelson & D. P. Gaonkar (Eds.), *Disciplinarity and dissent in cultural studies* (pp. 103-129). New York: Routledge.

Stewart, K. (1996). *A space on the side of the road: Cultural poetics in an "other" America*. Princeton, NJ: Princeton University Press.

Storey, J. (Ed.). (1994). *Cultural theory and popular culture*. Hertfordshire: Harvester Wheatsheaf.

Storey, J. (Ed.). (1996). *What is cultural studies? A reader*. London: Edward Arnold.

Stratton, J. (1992). *The young ones: Working-class culture, consumption and the category of youth*. Perth, Western Australia: Black Swan.

Street, J. (1997). *Politics and popular culture*. Cambridge: Polity.

Striphas, T. (Ed.). (1998). The institutionalization of cultural studies [Special issue]. *Cultural Studies, 12*(4).

Suleri, S. (1992). *The rhetoric of English India*. Chicago: University of Chicago Press.

Swan steels ARC for competition. (1989, November 26). *Sunday Telegraph*.

Taussig, M. (1997). *The magic of the state*. New York: Routledge.

Teaiwa, T. (1999). Reading Gauguin's *Noa Noa* with Hau'ofa's Nederends: "Militourism," feminism and the "Polynesian" body. *UTS Review, 5*(1), 53-69.

Teer-Tomaselli, R. E., & Roome, D. (Eds.). (1997). Popular culture and identity [Special issue]. *Critical Arts, 11*(1-2).

Thomas, M. (1999). *Dreams in the shadows: Australian-Vietnamese lives in transition*. Sydney: Allen & Unwin.

Tofts, D., & McKeitch, M. (1998). *Memory trade: A prehistory of cyberculture*. Sydney: 21C/Interface.

Tomaselli, K. G. (1996). *Appropriating images: The semiotics of visual representation*. Durban/Hojbjerg: Smyrna/Intervention.

Tomaselli, K. G. (1998a). African cultural studies: Excavating for the future. *International Journal of Cultural Studies, 1*(1), 143-153.

Tomaselli, K. G. (1998b). Recovering praxis: Cultural studies in Africa. *European Journal of Cultural Studies, 1*, 387-402.

Tomaselli, K. G., & Mpofu, A. (1997). The rearticulation of meaning of national monuments: Beyond apartheid. *Culture and Policy, 8*(3), 57-76.

Turkle, S. (1984). *The second self: Computers and the human spirit.* New York: Simon & Schuster.

Turner, G. (Ed.). (1993). *Nation, culture, text: Australian cultural and media studies.* London: Routledge.

Turner, G. (1994). *Making it national: Nationalism and Australian popular culture.* Sydney: Allen & Unwin.

Turner, G. (1996). *British cultural studies: An introduction* (Rev. ed.). Boston: Unwin Hyman.

Vainikkala, E., & Eskola, K. (Eds.). (1994). Nordic cultural studies [Special issue]. *Cultural Studies, 8*(2).

Valaskakis, G. (1988). The Chippewa and the other: Living the heritage of Lac du Flambeau. *Cultural Studies, 2*, 267-293.

Valaskakis, G. (in press). *Being native in North America.* Boulder, CO: Westview.

Viswanathan, G. (1989). *Masks of conquest: Literary study and British rule in India.* New York: Columbia University Press.

Wallace, M. (1978). *Black macho and the myth of the superwoman.* New York: Dial.

Wallace, M. (1990). *Invisibility blues: From pop to theory.* London: Verso.

Ware, V. (1992). *Beyond the pale: White women, racism and history.* London: Verso.

Wark, M. (1993). Homage to catatonia: Culture, politics and Midnight Oil. In J. Frow & M. Morris (Eds.), *Australian cultural studies: A reader* (pp. 105-116). Sydney/Chicago: Allen & Unwin/University of Illinois Press.

Wark, M. (1994). *Virtual geography: Living with global media events.* Bloomington: Indiana University Press.

Wark, M. (1999). *Celebrities, culture and cyberspace.* St. Leonards: Allen & Unwin.

Warner, M. (Ed.). (1993). *Fear of a queer planet: Queer politics and social theory.* Minneapolis: University of Minnesota Press.

Waters, J. P. (1996). Ireland and Irish cultural studies [Special issue]. *South Atlantic Quarterly, 95*(1).

Watney, S. (1987). *Policing desire: Pornography, AIDS, and the media.* Minneapolis: University of Minnesota Press.

Whannel, G. (1992). *Fields in vision: Television sport and cultural transformation.* London: Routledge.

Willemen, P. (1994). *Looks and frictions: Essays in cultural studies and film theory.* London/Bloomington: British Film Institute/Indiana University Press.

Williams, R. (1961a). *Culture and society 1780-1950*. Harmondsworth: Penguin. (Original work published 1958)

Williams, R. (1961b). *The long revolution*. London: Chatto & Windus.

Williams, R. (1979). *Politics and letters*. London: New Left.

Williams, R. (1985). *The country and the city*. London: Hogarth.

Williams, R. (1989). The future of cultural studies. In R. Williams, *The politics of modernism* (pp. 151-162). London: Verso.

Willis, P. E. (1977). *Learning to labour: How working class kids get working class jobs*. Farnborough, UK: Saxon House.

Wilson, R. (in press). *Reimagining the American Pacific: From "South Pacific" to Bamboo Ridge and beyond*. London: Duke University Press.

Wilson, R., & Dissanayake, W. (Eds.). (1996). *Global/local: Cultural production and the transnational imaginary*. Durham, NC: Duke University Press.

Wilson, R., & Dirlik, A. (Eds.). (1995). *Asia/Pacific as space of cultural production*. Durham, NC: Duke University Press.

Women's Studies Group, Centre for Contemporary Cultural Studies. (1978). *Women take issue: Aspects of women's subordination*. London: Hutchinson, with Centre for Contemporary Cultural Studies, University of Birmingham.

Wood, H. (in press). *Displacing native: The rhetorical production of Hawai'i*. Boulder, CO: Rowman & Littlefield.

Wright, H. K. (1998). Dare we de-centre Birmingham? Troubling the "origin" and trajectories of cultural studies. *European Journal of Cultural Studies, 1*, 33-56.

Yudice, G., Franco, J., & Flores, J. (Eds.). (1992). *On edge: The crisis of contemporary Latin American culture*. Minneapolis: University of Minnesota Press.

12
Sexualities,
Queer Theory, and
Qualitative Research

Joshua Gamson

◆ When social researchers began discovering and investigating homosexual lives in the early part of this century, they faced obvious pragmatic obstacles to finding research participants. At a time when homosexuality was subject to severe social stigmatization and onerous penalties,
when people with same-sex desires and practices were the keepers of great
secrets and the livers of fragile "double lives," finding homosexuals to
study was not an easy task. Some half a century later, when movements for
lesbian and gay rights and liberation have altered the terrain considerably,
one would think that willing subjects would be easy enough to track down.

Indeed, on one level, this is the case. Despite the ongoing strength of
stigma, penalty, and secrecy, lesbians and gay men living lesbian and gay
lives openly and unapologetically, often as members of organized communities, are no longer tough to find and study. The history of social research
on sexualities has elements familiar from the histories of women's studies,
ethnic studies, and the like: It is a history intertwined with the politics of

AUTHOR'S NOTE: This chapter benefited enormously from the insightful comments of
Patricia Clough, Norman Denzin, Rosanna Hertz, Yvonna Lincoln, and William Tierney.

social movements, wary of the ways "science" has been used against the marginalized, and particularly comfortable with the strategies of qualitative research—which at least appear to be less objectifying of their subjects, to be more concerned with cultural and political meaning creation, and to make more room for voices and experiences that have been suppressed. Thus, on the one hand, the coming-of-age of the field is a coming-to-voice of new sexual subjects on the terrains of both politics and academia. It is about invisible people becoming visible.

Yet as soon as the subject began to appear, she began to disappear. Over the past decade, in particular, the research subject has become problematic and elusive in striking new ways. With the growth of "queer theory," which took social constructionist insights and forcefully added a poststructuralist critique of the unified, autonomous self, the lesbian and gay subject has become, in a different way, increasingly hard to recognize, let alone research. Like many other recent intellectual developments, queer studies is largely a deconstructive enterprise, taking apart the view of a self defined by something at its core, be it sexual desire, race, gender, nation, or class. This is the central piece of the story I want to tell: of how we have gone from unreflective confidence in the existence of sexual subjects— who only needed to be found and documented—to a boom in lesbian and gay studies filled with subjects speaking and writing about their own lives, to a suspicion that sexual subjects do not exactly exist to be studied, an ongoing deconstruction of sexual subjectivity. This is a story, moreover, that runs parallel to, meets up with, and contributes to a similar history in the nature and meaning of qualitative research; as Norman Denzin and Yvonna Lincoln (1994) argue, the early traditional enterprise of "objective" study of stable subjects has, over time, in large part given way to a postmodern questioning of objectivity and embrace of "an always shifting center" (Lincoln & Denzin, 1994, p. 575).

As I trace these linked histories, I want to point to several key tensions built into the field that are ultimately productive for qualitative research on sexualities: over what it really means for researchers to include in their study people calling themselves lesbian, gay, bisexual, or transgender; over what it means to do qualitative research that is at most skeptical about the stability and literal reality of the social categories gay, bisexual, transgender, and lesbian; over the place of "lived experience" in such research and representation; and over what it means to research the discursive and the institutional simultaneously, especially in a field where research and politics are so closely tied.

◆ The Politics of Sexuality Studies: The Qualitative Push

The study of sexualities in general, and homosexualities in particular, has long been closely intertwined with qualitative research—by which, as a general starting point that I will quickly complicate, I mean a loose set of research practices (ethnography and participant observation, in-depth interviewing, textual analysis, historical research, and the like) distinct from quantitative methods and often suspicious of the epistemological assumptions of positivism, and a correspondingly loose but distinct set of research foci (cultural meaning creation and interpretive processes, collective and personal identities, social interaction, the practices of everyday life, and so on).

The qualitative push has come largely from the political context in which sexualities research has taken shape. Although there has been a long-standing stream of social science research on sexuality, there has been an even stronger, well-founded suspicion that positivist sciences, and some scientific professions, have been at odds with the interests of self-defining homosexuals—pathologizing, stigmatizing, seeking the "cause" of deviant sexualities and, by implication, their cure. This suspicion has given qualitative research an inside track. Further, qualitative methods, with their focus on meaning creation and the experiences of everyday life, fit especially well with movement goals of visibility, cultural challenge, and self-determination. Finally, as lesbian and gay studies gave rise to its own new theoretical developments—in particular, a critical focus on the social construction of sexual categories and identities, and then a "queer" focus on the broad role of the homo/heterosexual binary in contemporary life—it put the spotlight on interpretive issues especially suited to qualitative research.

At the same time, qualitative research, in part pushed by the entry of previously silent voices into its activities, has undergone a series of twists and turns that have affected, and been affected by, sexualities study. Denzin and Lincoln (1994) have identified five key "moments" in the history of qualitative research, and sexualities study has taken its place within this complex chronology: from traditional "colonializing accounts of field experiences," concerned with "valid, reliable, and objective interpretations" (1900-1950); to modernist attempts at formalized qualitative research presenting causal narratives (1950-1970); to a period in which

542

boundaries between social sciences and humanities became blurred, and in which the observer came to have "no privileged voice in the interpretations that were written" (1970-1986); to a subsequent "crisis of representation," in which research and writing became more reflexive and the assumption that "qualitative researchers can directly capture lived experience" was undercut (1986-1990); to the current "postmodern moment," in which both "grand theories" and the "concept of the aloof researcher" have been abandoned (pp. 7, 9, 11).

Qualitative research, clearly, has meant and been different things in its different moments. In fact, none of the terms in the story I'm telling stays still for long—which is actually the central story line. I use the broad term *sexualities* here to underline the point that, although the fields to which I refer are largely focused on nonheterosexual, nonconforming sexual statuses, identities, and practices, how those objects of analysis are conceived has changed in important ways: Studying homosexuality or homosexualities is not necessarily the same as studying gays and lesbians or gayness, which is not necessarily the same as studying queers or queerness, which is not necessarily the same as studying society from a queer perspective. *Gay and lesbian studies* and even the more recent *queer studies* have changed meaning, largely through the various political struggles to which these terms have been attached. *Lesbian, bisexual, gay, homosexual,* and *transgender* have all been typically used to capture sexual and gender identities, senses of self that are either inherently stable or stabilized through various social processes; the term *lesbian and gay studies* (and, more recently, *lesbian, gay, bisexual, and transgender studies*) has typically been used to capture the study of these populations. *Queer* has been a more vexed, conflict-ridden and confusing term, both as identity and disciplinary marker (Gamson, 1995). Although it has sometimes been used as a "people of color"-like shorthand for *gay, lesbian, bisexual, and transgender,* a politically volatile expansion of the identity category to include all sorts of sex and gender outsiders, I use it here in its more distinctive sense, as a marker of the instability of identity. *Queer* marks an identity that, defined as it is by a deviation from sex and gender norms either by the self inside or by specific behaviors, is always in flux; *queer theory* and *queer studies* propose a focus not so much on specific populations as on sexual categorization processes and their deconstruction. Each term, that is, comes with its own set of politics.

543

The Ambivalent Relationship to Positivism

Especially after the growth of the feminist and lesbian and gay movements in the 1960s and 1970s, sexuality studies have been, to begin with,
closely allied with a political project of redressing the pathologized and
stigmatized status of homosexuals (Adam, 1995). Because, historically,
positivist natural and social sciences had been heavily involved in bolster-
ing the notion of homosexuality as illness or deviance or both, much post-
Stonewall sexuality study has tended to be ambivalent about, if not openly
hostile to, "scientific" approaches to sexuality. The relationship to positivist social research has therefore often been an adversarial one.

The earliest approaches to homosexuality, for instance, conducted primarily by sex researchers trained in medicine and natural sciences, worked
from a positivist model, searching for the objective truths of nature that
moralizing about sexuality had apparently obscured. Although they often
began with a liberalizing intent—to rescue sexuality from the clutches of
religion—these studies often began and ended with the assumption that
homosexuality is a deviation from the normal; their aim was more often
than not to decipher the roots of the pathology (Weeks, 1985). To put it
simply, researchers, however liberal, tended to share the taken-for-
granted picture of homosexuals as sick, dangerous, or criminal.[1] That
homosexuality officially remained a psychiatric disorder until 1973, when
it was removed from the American Psychiatric Association's *Diagnostic
and Statistical Manual of Mental Disorders* after much struggle, captures
the political link between "scientific" study of homosexuality and the stigmatized, pathologized social status of homosexuals (Bayer, 1981).[2] It is no
wonder, then, that qualitative approaches—especially those that search
for and interpret meaning rather than "facts"—have often seemed more
attractive to scholars politically aligned with lesbian and gay movements,
because they put some distance between the researcher and the "master's
tools."

There has, of course, been a long, effective, and significant tradition of
quantitatively oriented scientific research on sexual practices and opinions, much of it focused on same-sex practices, much of which has gone far
toward demonstrating the normality and respectability of nonnormative
sexualities: from Kinsey in the 1940s and 1950s (Kinsey, Pomeroy, &
Martin, 1948; Kinsey, Pomeroy, Martin, & Gebhard, 1953) to Masters
and Johnson (1966) in the 1960s and 1970s to the 1990s' massive survey-
based *Social Organization of Sexuality* (Laumann, Gagnon, Michael, &

Michaels, 1994). The strategy of the Kinsey reports, according to one biographer, for example, "was to shout 'Science!' through an exhaustive accumulation of technical jargon and massed statistics" (Jones, 1997, p. 107). Kinsey's contributions—the notion of a sexual continuum, the revelation of how widespread and typical so-called deviant practices are—revolutionized popular discourse on sexuality by offering "scientific evidence conducive to a reevaluation of conventional moral attitudes" (D'Emilio, 1983, p. 33), with the result that "the extent of premarital sex, adultery, and homosexuality became acceptable topics of polite conversation" (Jones, 1997, p. 100). Similarly, Evelyn Hooker's (1958) studies comparing the psychological profiles of a sample of homosexual men to their nonhomosexual counterparts helped to "demonstrate empirically the 'normality' of the homosexual" (Nardi & Schneider, 1998, p. 3).

Such myth-bashing studies continue to this day—although now typically conducted by those identifying personally, or aligning politically, with the sexually marginalized. Indeed, especially in the discipline of psychology, and to a lesser degree in political science and economics, social researchers have often attempted to beat heterosexist science at its own game, using the tools and logic of science to bash myths about gay people: studies demonstrating that the children of lesbians and gay men differ very little from those of heterosexuals (e.g., Patterson, 1992, 1995), documenting the extent of antigay or homophobic public opinion in various populations and the prevalence and nature of hate crimes (e.g., Herek, 1989, 1997), or analyzing the economic circumstances of lesbians and gay men (e.g., Badgett, 1995). Tellingly, this is often essentially defensive social research, testing and disconfirming the hypotheses of a homophobic society with "facts."[3] As the mission statement of the Institute for Gay and Lesbian Strategic Studies, an organization "designed to conduct impartial and independent academic research and analysis on public policy issues of critical concern to the gay, lesbian, bisexual and transgender communities," puts it, "It is vital that we produce the unbiased, independent research which will counter [right-wing] lies" (Institute for Gay and Lesbian Strategic Studies, 1998). Even when the natural science model has been taken up by sexuality researchers, that is, it has been informed by the historically problematic relationship between science and lesbian and gay lives.

Another early response to the problematic relationship between sexuality and science was to investigate the "deviants" themselves, in their own space and time, in methodological (and sometimes political) departures. Research on sexualities partook of the tendencies of the "traditional" and "modernist" periods' qualitative work: "Reflective of the positivist scientist paradigm," fieldwork studied "alien, foreign, and strange" others, in "a social science version of literary naturalism" that often "romanticized the subject" (Denzin & Lincoln, 1994, pp. 7, 8). Although moving the researcher much closer to the subjective experience of the participants, such research did not of course suddenly jump from its political environment. Qualitative sociological work on male homosexuality through the early 1970s, for instance, focused largely on stigma management (e.g., Humphreys, 1970; Leznoff & Westley, 1956; Reiss, 1961), studying the homosexual as "part of a deviant sexual underworld of hustlers, prostitutes, prisons, tearooms, baths, and bars" (Seidman, 1996, p. 7). Yet, as Steven Seidman (1996) points out, although "much of this sociology aimed to figure the homosexual as a victim of unjust discrimination," such work "contributed to the public perception of the homosexual as a strange, exotic human type in contrast to the normal, respectable heterosexual" (p. 7). As gay and lesbian movements grew in strength, however, the strange, exotic humans started doing their own research, researching and reporting on themselves, triggering along the way new complications for both sexualities study and qualitative research.

Movements, Minority Research, and Narratives of the Self

In the 1970s and 1980s, taking their cues from feminist-inspired women's studies and civil rights-inspired African American and ethnic studies, scholars developing the new field of lesbian and gay studies (themselves mostly identifying as gay and lesbian) began the still-ongoing task of "uncovering" the "hidden" history of gay and lesbian people, both "reclaiming the gay and lesbian past" (Duberman, Vicinus, & Chauncey, 1989; see also Faderman, 1981; Katz, 1976) and recording the experiential present (e.g., Krieger, 1983; Levine, 1979; Newton, 1972). Much of this took place through conventional historical and ethnographic study, but it was also joined by, and shared assumptions with, a sort of qualitative reporting that emerged outside of the academy, in which personal narratives and experiential truths were used to reclaim a gay or lesbian subjectivity that had been historically denied (Jay & Young, 1972). The further one went from the white, heterosexual male center, the more one found, in fact, autobiographical work written from the personal standpoint of the marginalized, in classic collections such as *This Bridge Called My Back: Writings by Radical Women of Color* (Moraga & Anzaldúa, 1981).[4]

This politically charged enterprise of "telling our own stories" not only gave qualitative research an extra edge, it came with an implicit epistemological critique of objective scientific research. Like feminist and Afrocentric standpoint theories, which makes the everyday experiences of marginality a ground for theory building (Collins, 1990; Harding, 1987; Smith, 1974), built into the strategies of personal narratives, and the reclaiming of gay and lesbian lives both past and present, was an implication that the experience of the outsider provides a unique outlook on social and political life, that what have been presented as the objective facts of sexuality are instead the subjective view from a heterosexual male standpoint—indeed, ultimately, that all knowledge is socially situated. The drama of such a change cannot be overstated: Lesbians studying lesbians was not only a great political challenge in an environment that had stigmatized lesbians as invisible or ill, but also a more general challenge to qualitative research in which the objectivity of an "outsider" was thought to lend validity, and in which the nonnative researcher retained "the power to represent the subject's story" (Denzin & Lincoln, 1994, p. 8). The lesbian or gay self, given voice through interviews, ethnographies, autobiography, and historical re-creation, while plainly resting on claims of authenticity, gave the lie to objectivity.

These various strands of research and representation also tended to share "essentialist" assumptions about the self, and the collections of selves gathering strength in neighborhoods and institutions after Stonewall, with the relatively new "sexual minority" movement to which they were tied: that whatever their roots, sexual differences are natural variations; that sexual categories are congruent with those natural variations; and that homosexuals therefore constitute a minority much like racial and ethnic minorities. When scholars in the early 1980s, for instance, began uncovering and describing the ins and outs of lesbian and gay life both past and present, *gay* and *lesbian* were typically assumed to describe similar types of individuals and a stable chunk of a population across time and space. As Steven Epstein (1987) has argued, and as John D'Emilio (1983) has documented, models of sexuality as "essence" and of sexual communities as "minorities" were critical political mobilization tools. The ethnic self-characterization running through both the politics and the research of the 1970s and 1980s, Epstein (1987) suggests, "has a clear political utility, for it has permitted a form of group organizing that is particularly suited to the American experience, with its history of civil-rights struggles and ethnic-based, interest-group competition" (p. 20). Research in sexualities developed, that is, not only in the midst of an ambivalent stance toward positivist science, but also in response to the American political tradition of minority group organizing; qualitative research would bring the shared, lived experience of sexual minorities into the spotlight. With an emphasis on the shared characteristics of the authentic lesbian or gay self, this was minority group research.

The Constructionist Turn

Effective and legitimating as these various approaches have been—especially in a political environment filled with myths and stereotypes about nonnormative sexuality and sensitive to the claims of minorities—they have also set pathways for profound challenges to their own assumptions, challenges that have given qualitative research a further significance and centrality. "Assuming the specificity of gay identity and gay experience," as Patricia Clough (1994) puts it, "only opened both to further specification and to the elaboration of their specific historical and cultural constructions, eventually undermining any sense of a uniform gay experience or a unified gay identity" (p. 143). As the scattershot, multidisciplinary field of sexualities study began to congeal and consolidate, its major "essentialist" premises came quickly under fire. The notion that sexual subjects share a sexual core (an orientation or a preference), that underneath the skin they have the same kind of self, was questioned; shaken along with it was the claim that, being the same sorts of beings, they therefore share a minority status. The related, more general view that there is a "truth" of sexuality provided by nature, and therefore to be investigated along the lines of other natural subjects, a truth beyond the meanings attached socially to sex, bodies, and desire, also began to break apart (on critiques of sexual "essentialism," see Stein, 1992).

Indeed, over time the positivist tradition of sexuality studies has been very much overshadowed by a strategy that rejects the notion that the tools and assumptions of natural science are appropriate for the study of sexuality. Like feminism, from which many activists and some researchers took their cues—and which, in lesbian feminism, was directly tied to lesbian (and gay) politics (Phelan, 1989; Whittier, 1995)—lesbian and gay scholars criticized positivist approaches for mistaking the social order of sexuality for a natural one. These objections had early roots in the work of social researchers within distinctly qualitative fields (symbolic interactionists, phenomenologists, and labeling theorists) who argued for the need to distinguish the social and interactional processes by which bodies and desires are given meaning, are transformed into social categories with political significance and into bases for the sorts of collective action taking strong shape at the time.

Tied to a more general rebellion against positivist social research, the loose field of sexuality studies began to fix itself, from the 1970s onward, in "denaturalizing" gear: Sexuality was not a stable phenomenon of nature to be studied like plants or cells, but a set of meanings attached to bodies and desires by individuals, groups, and societies (Gagnon & Simon, 1973). "Against naturalized conceptions of sexuality as a biological given, against Freudian models of the sexual drive, and against the Kinseyan obsession with the tabulation of behavior," as Steven Epstein (1996) summarizes it, "sociologists asserted that sexual meanings, identities, and categories were intersubjectively negotiated social and historical products—that sexuality was, in a word, constructed" (p. 145). Historians and anthropologists documented the variability of cultural and historical systems of sexual meaning (e.g., Greenberg, 1988; Ortner & Whitehead, 1981) as focus shifted from research about "the homosexual" as a universal entity and oddity to "homosexual" (and later "heterosexual") as a social category and identity that "should itself be analyzed and its relative historical, economic, and political base be scrutinized" (Nardi & Schneider, 1998, p. 4; see also McIntosh, 1968; Plummer, 1981, 1992).

Although often theoretical in orientation, the constructionist approach focused attention on questions particularly suited to qualitative research, with its attempts "to make sense of, or interpret, phenomena in terms of the meanings people bring to them" (Denzin & Lincoln, 1994, p. 2): How do sexual categories get created and challenged, and with what effects? How do same-sex practices relate to identities that are built, or not built, around them? Whereas positivist approaches took sexual categories for granted and investigated those assumed to belong to them (how homosexuals live, the etiology of homosexuality, and so on), students of sexualities began to investigate the politics, history, and sociology of the *categories and identities* themselves; the various "sex/gender systems" (Rubin, 1975) giving meaning to bodies and pleasures became a focal point. In one early study, Barbara Ponse (1978), for instance, used ethnographic methods to explicate "the social construction of identity and its meanings within the lesbian subculture," and many subsequent studies used similar methods for similar purposes. Given the profoundly interpretive nature of the questions asked by a constructionist framework, moreover, qualitative research methods—ethnographic, sociohistorical, and so on—began to establish themselves as the cutting edge.[5] And given the growing antipathy to the "essentialist" assumptions about sexuality rooted largely in sexual science, the gap between quantitative and qualitative studies of sexuality widened even more.[6]

At the same time, within the political movements to which many scholars were tied, related category challenges were being raised by those who found themselves defined *out* of the collective identity (working-class people, people of color, sex radicals, and so on). These critiques added to the focus on the problematic construction of sexual identities, to the ongoing critical deconstruction of the homosexual "minority," and to the relationships among race, gender, and sexual identity (e.g., Clarke, 1981; Hemphill, 1991; Seidman, 1993). Who "we" are, these conflicts suggested, is never a given, and is much more complex and multiple than gay minority studies was assuming. In an important precursor to the queer critique, those marginalized *within* the gay scene argued that asserting the primacy of sexuality forced false choices (between an identity as lesbian and as black, for instance) and obscured the important connections among race, gender, ethnicity, sexuality, physical ability, and class.

These movement-driven concerns with exclusion and diversity made their way, gradually, into qualitative research: Tomás Almaguer, for instance, reviewed ethnographic and autobiographical writings to map the ways Chicano male homosexuals negotiated their ways through two distinct sexual systems, a European American one emphasizing the gay-straight axis, and a Mexican/Latin American one organized along the passive-active axis (Almaguer, 1991). Coinciding with a period in which the "boundaries between the social sciences and the humanities had become blurred" (Denzin & Lincoln, 1994, p. 9), moreover, much of the retheorizing of sexual-identities-as-multiple came through the interpretive voices of gay men and lesbians of color working in fields such as film and literary studies, or from outside of the academy (e.g., Harper, 1991; Hemphill, 1991; Trujillo, 1991).

The sociological roots of constructionism and the political roots of multiple-identity arguments met up, of course, with the highly influential work of Michel Foucault (1978), and those influenced by him, from historical studies (e.g., Greenberg, 1988). The forceful entry of Foucault's work both solidified the tie between qualitative research and the study of sexualities and began a new phase in the theorizing of sexual identities. The homosexual was distinguished as a contemporary historical and cultural "invention" made possible by a conflation of acts with identities: In Foucault's (1978) famous statement, whereas sodomy had been a "category of forbidden acts" and temporary aberration, over the course of the "discursive explosion" of the 19th century the homosexual became "a species," "a personage, a past, a case history, a life form" (p. 43).

Foucault's *History of Sexuality* (1978) focused attention more than ever on the social construction of sexual "discourse," reinforced a skepticism about scientific knowledge as progress, and encouraged a renewed questioning of the categories of sexuality still taken for granted by many working within the field. While institutional analyses became somewhat sidelined, the *discourses* through which sexuality became, and continues to be, the "truth of our being"—including the "counterdiscourses" such as minority identity, and especially scientific sex research—now became subject to analysis and deconstruction. With category construction, discourse, meaning creation, and identity work becoming firmly entrenched subjects for investigation, qualitative approaches to sexualities study moved even more to the center of the stage.

Yet that stage was also beginning to be guided by a sort of methodological and epistemological turmoil. The crises of authority and legitimation for qualitative researchers that came to fruition in the late 1980s (see, e.g., Clifford & Marcus, 1986) were also given, in the field of sexualities and elsewhere, a firm push by Foucault, whose critique of methodological practices such as the psychoanalytic case study forcefully suggested that all methods take their place in particular "regimes of truth," and that no knowledge creation is divorced from political relations. Queer theory and queer studies emerged out of this methodologically critical, epistemologically skeptical mix.

♦ "Queer Theory" and the Critique of Identity

As quantitative study of sexuality continued on its own path, albeit increasingly divorced from and eclipsed by qualitative approaches in lesbian and gay studies,[7] research on sexuality entered a new phase in the early 1990s with the emergence of "queer theory." Heavily influenced by post-structuralist theory, emerging primarily from humanities-based cultural studies, and tied somewhat loosely to a confrontational, antinormative "queer" politics, queer theory first began to take shape in a series of late 1980s academic conferences (Epstein, 1996; Gamson, 1995; Stein &

Plummer, 1996). Queer theory built on the insights of constructionism and Foucault, but moved poststructuralist and postmodernist concerns to the forefront—critiques of identity and identity politics, an emphasis on discourse and its deconstruction, a suspicion of "grand narratives" (Kellner, 1988; Seidman & Wagner, 1991). With queer theory, the postmodern moment in qualitative inquiry—with its elusive center that "shifts and moves as new, previously oppressed or silenced voices enter the discourse" (Lincoln & Denzin, 1994, p. 575)—arrived full force in sexualities study. Not only the foci of inquiry but also what *counts* as qualitative research were, through a process that continues to be contested, starting to shape-shift.

Queer theory put forth several core changes and challenges, dramatically altering the terrain of qualitative research for those taking the challenges to heart. For one thing, the substantive territory of analysis was broadened: It was not so much the lives or identities of gays and lesbians, or the construction of homosexual identities or minority status, that required attention, but the ways the very homo/hetero distinction underpinned all aspects of contemporary life. "An understanding of virtually any aspect of modern Western culture," wrote Eve Kosovsky Sedgwick, for example, in *Epistemology of the Closet* (1990), generally considered the founding text of queer theory, "must be, not merely incomplete, but damaged in its central substance to the degree that it does not incorporate a critical analysis of modern homo/heterosexual definition" (p. 1).

This was quite a departure from the theory and research that preceded queer theory and made it possible, moving the aim from "explaining the modern homosexual to questions of the operation of the hetero/homosexual binary, from an exclusive preoccupation with homosexuality to a focus on heterosexuality as a social and political organizing principle, and from a politics of minority interest to a politics of knowledge and difference" (Seidman, 1996, p. 9). The deconstruction and criticism of "heteronormativity" in its various forms and guises, of the notion that "humanity and heterosexuality are synonymous" (Warner, 1993, p. xxiii), became a key goal and rallying cry of queer studies.

Queer theory, moreover, often called for theoretical interventions that paralleled the antiassimilationist, in-your-face, antinormative, deconstructive spirit of queer politics (Berlant & Freeman, 1993; Cohen, 1997; Duggan, 1992). As Alexander Doty (1993) puts it, "Queerness should challenge and confuse our understanding and uses of sexual and gender categories" (p. xvii). Just as bisexual and transgender people were being included in the "queer" political category, sharing the status of sex and gender dissidents (Gamson, 1995), for instance, bisexuality and transgenderism became much more central subjects for theory and research, celebrated in queer studies for their capacity to confound sex and gender categories (e.g., Epstein & Straub, 1991; Garber, 1995; Stryker, 1998a). Built into these substantive shifts were epistemological and methodological perspectives that have shaken the ground for qualitative research on sexualities.

Discourse, Language, and Identity

One dynamic set in motion by these changes, not surprisingly, has been a methodological one: Field study of lesbians, gay men, transsexuals, bisexuals, and so on has consistently been edged out in queer studies by discourse analysis, with literary criticism at the head. Like much qualitative inquiry of the early 1990s more generally, queer theory questions the assumption that lived experience can be captured and directly represented by researchers, and looks instead at the textual and linguistic practices (including the discourse of "social research") through which sexual subjectivity takes shape. As Steven Seidman (1996) explains:

> Queer theorists view heterosexuality and homosexuality not simply as identities or social statuses but as categories of knowledge, a language that frames what we know as bodies, desires, sexualities, identities. This is a normative language as it shapes moral boundaries and political hierarchies. . . . Queer theory is suggesting that the study of homosexuality should not be a study of a minority—the making of the lesbian/gay/bisexual subject—but a study of those knowledges and social practices that organize "society" as a whole by sexualizing—heterosexualizing or homosexualizing—bodies, desires, acts, identities, social relations, knowledges, culture, and social institutions. (pp. 12-13)

It is this study of knowledges, language, and discourse that makes the tools of literary analysis so key for queer theorists. Indeed, as Patricia Clough (1994) points out, for queer theorists, "gender [or sexuality] is not a literal reality, not even a socially constructed reality, but rather a literary reality," and thus theorists such as Judith Butler propose "a new mode of reading the social that collapses the distinction between fantasy and reality, fiction and history, polemic and academic discourse, social science and literary criticism—all figured in the opposition of homosexuality and heterosexuality" (p. 155).

Seen through a "queer" lens, qualitative researchers investigating the "reality" of, say, lesbian and gay experiences of the closet, or of major heterosexist institutions such as the military or schools, tend to appear naïve in their assumptions about "social reality" and their methods for getting at it. Indeed, the poststructuralist collapsing of the social into the literary, and the practice of "reading" the social as text, has often meant an edging out of field research on social behavior, be it individual, collective, or institutional. "To the extent that poststructuralists reduce cultural codes to textual practice," Seidman (1993) argues effectively, "and to the extent that these practices are abstracted from institutional contexts, we come up against the limits of poststructuralism as social critique" (p. 135). Queer theoretical perspectives have begun to redefine what "counts" as qualitative research, with literary techniques taking up territory—although not without strenuous objections (e.g., Plummer, 1998)—previously claimed by empirical social researchers.

Yet if the focus with queer theory moves from the lived experiences of sexuality to "the grammar of culture," the "relationship of language and discourse to power and the production, organization, and circulation of diverse texts and institutions" (Tierney, 1997, pp. 9-10), this is only partially due to the intellectual imperialism of cultural studies. Central to the poststructuralist turn in sexuality studies is a profound and well-articulated skepticism about the existence of social subjects who preexist their discursive constitution, whose "experience" can simply be studied and represented. Underlying the focus on knowledge, language, sexualizing, and so on is a core objection by queer theory to "the dominant foundational concept of both homophobic and affirmative homosexual theory: the assumption of a unified homosexual identity" (Seidman, 1996, p. 11).

The critique of identity runs throughout queer theoretical writings: Identities are multiple, contradictory, fragmented, incoherent, disciplinary, disunified, unstable, fluid—hardly the stuff that allows a researcher to confidently run out and study sexual subjects as if they are coherent and available social types. "I'm permanently troubled by identity categories," says Judith Butler (1991), for instance, "consider them to be invariable stumbling-blocks, and understand them, even promote them, as sites of necessary trouble" (p. 14). Identity is, she argues, a "necessary error" (Butler, 1993, p. 21). Queer theorists, Shane Phelan (1993) suggests, "while retaining *lesbian* as a meaningful category," have "worked against reification of lesbians, toward views of lesbianism as a *critical site of gender deconstruction* rather than as a unitary experience with a singular political meaning" (p. 766). Michael Warner (1993) notes:

> A lesbian and gay population is defined by multiple boundaries that make the question of who is and is not "one of them" not merely ambiguous but rather a perpetually and necessarily contested issue. Identity as a lesbian or gay is ambiguously given and chosen, in some ways the product of the performative act of coming out. . . . "Queer" therefore also suggests the difficulty in defining the population whose interests are at stake in queer politics. (pp. xxv-xxvi)

Identity, that is, cannot be taken as a starting point for social research, can never be assumed by a researcher to be standing still, ready for its close-up.

In fact, according to the poststructuralist queer critique, the subject does not precede his or her recognition as a subject, but is created through discursive processes—such as social research—and the continual bodily repetition, or "performance," of gender and sexuality. Butler (1993) writes:

> The discursive condition of social recognition *precedes and conditions* the formation of the subject: recognition is not conferred on a subject, but forms that subject. Further, the impossibility of a full recognition, that is, of ever fully inhabiting the name by which one's social identity is inaugurated and mobilized, implies the instability and incompleteness of subject-formation. (p. 18)

Thus, as Ken Plummer (1992) puts it a bit more simply, "there is no essential object of study . . . gay and lesbian studies 'construct' an object for analysis that is itself much more diffuse, fragmented, overlapping, and multiple: it forces a unity that does not exist" (p. 11).[8] The forms of agency and subjectivity that had been assumed by earlier sexualities research, then, are shot full of holes by the queer theoretical "refusal to name a subject" (Seidman, 1993, p. 132). This is not, of course, unique to the study of sexuality—feminist scholars and activists, for instance, have been working through such issues for years (Nicholson, 1990; Spelman, 1989)—but it is acutely present in queer studies.

The rise of queer studies has been, not surprisingly, filled with conflict, much of it focused on what Ken Plummer (1998) has called "the overtextualization of lesbian and gay experiences," in which "analyses of discourse overtake the analysis of real world events." As he writes:

> There are important studies to be done in the empirical world, and an obsession with texts is dangerous indeed. It is time to move beyond the text—and rapidly. Whilst lesbian and gay studies "plays" more and more fancifully with a wide array of poems, novels, and films, relatively little research actually exists on what is going on in lesbian and gay worlds right now. (p. 611)

Plummer may overstate the case. In fact, plenty of research continues on gay and lesbian lives that is not "queer" in the sense I have been using the term, work that is untouched by or simply rejects the poststructuralist identity critique: studies on the experiences of gay men in corporations (Woods & Lucas, 1994), on sexual diversity in Native American cultures (Williams, 1992), on media coverage of lesbians and gays (Alwood, 1996), on the experiences of lesbian and gay youth (Herdt & Boxer, 1993), to name just a few. That such work continues testifies not simply to disciplinary division, but to an important and ongoing struggle over what qualitative inquiry into sexualities can and should look like, especially given the undeniable experience of political and social marginalization, institutionalized heterosexism, and antigay mobilizations to which lesbian and gay people are subject. Whatever the complexities of identity this work points up, the societies and institutions in which gay, lesbian, bisexual, and transgender subjects live their lives seem to have no difficulty recognizing and targeting them.

Yet while the direction of the qualitative sexualities study is far from settled, the issues raised by queer approaches, and the turmoil they provoke over the study of "lived experience," have become increasingly difficult to shake. Just as sexuality studies was establishing itself, it began to take itself apart. The qualitative focus especially, given its own twist by queer theory, has wound up twisting and turning on the wrenches thrown into it. The queer theoretical challenge to the unified subject creates epistemological difficulties that translate into methodological ones. If lived experiences of "the social" are always constituted by systems of discourse, then to study such experiences as *experiences* rather than narratives, or to report on them autobiographically as though reporting were a direct translation of reality, is hopelessly distorted. If the idea of an autonomous, gendered self is a "literary reality" produced by "heteronormativity," a fiction of sorts that exists only in a series of ongoing bodily performances, taking such a self as a basis for research naïvely reproduces rather than interrupts the workings of heteronormativity. If "gay" and "lesbian" are provisional, discursively produced, unstable, performative, and decidedly partial identities—if they are forever in quotation marks—how does one go about studying sexuality and sexually identified populations? Even taking normative discourse as the object of analysis, how does one study its operation when one is, by definition, not "outside" of it? On what grounds does a researcher or author, herself a discursively created subject, himself available for textual deconstruction, wage a critique of normatively constructed sexuality? What's a researcher to do?

◆ Shared Challenges for Qualitative Inquiry

The strands of research and theory I have recounted—lesbian and gay minority studies, constructionist sexualities research, queer theory—coexist in considerable tension within sexualities study, with their differently constituted objects of study, their different disciplinary roots, their different rules of evidence, and their different assumptions about the intellectual and political utility of identity categories. Although they often share a profoundly qualitative focus on meaning construction and a concern for the relationship between research and the politics of sexuality, each has had somewhat different implications for the sort of research that can and should be done. Taken together, however, they both intentionally and inadvertently pose significant theoretical and substantive challenges to researchers.

The Substantive Challenge of Queer Inclusion in Qualitative Research

Like other fields with origins in identity-based movements, lesbian and gay studies, and especially queer theory, have waged systematic challenges to the research agendas of more traditional fields of scholarship. If "the closet" is indeed a central organizing feature of Western thought and practices, all investigations, as Sedgwick has suggested, must arguably consider it. Thus a primary substantive challenge currently issuing to and from the field of sexuality studies is not simply to "include" gay and lesbian subjects in research areas that have rendered them invisible, but even more fundamentally to uncover the ways *any* social arena (including, of course, the production of social scientific knowledge) is structured in part by the homo/hetero dichotomy. There is great productive promise for new topics of qualitative research as this charge is asserted and absorbed.

Thus far, the action has rarely taken place through empirical work; it is happening instead through a tracing out of the reconceptualizations that queer thinking implies, but such rethinking has also begun to trigger new research directions. Lisa Duggan (1998), for instance, has argued for "queering the state" through strategies that "work to destabilize hetero-normativity rather than to naturalize gay identities" (p. 570), and legal scholars, political scientists, and sociologists have begun to investigate the ways the state in fact depends on intersecting racial, sexual, and gender codes (Alexander, 1991; Eaton, 1994), revealing the state's hetero-normativity through detailed deconstruction of its legal discourse (e.g., Duggan & Hunter, 1995, pt. II). Similar substantive directions can be expected as other social processes and institutions are subjected to an analysis that asks not just how gay men, lesbians, bisexuals, and transgendered people fit into this picture but how particular institution's work to hetero-sexualize and gender, and with what material effects.[9] This remains a question for which qualitative research and analysis are particularly suited.

The Deconstruction of Unified Subjects

Queer theory undercuts earlier notions of an autonomous, coherent self (and collection of selves) defined by gender and desire, raising, as we have seen, epistemological and methodological questions that make trouble for research and writing on sexualities. Although many of these questions will remain, perhaps healthfully, in the air for a good long time, re-searchers have begun to take these complexities of identity into account as they go about their work. One strategy is to build on the long-standing tra-dition of making identity itself the focus of research while integrating the instability, multiplicity, and partiality of identities into the research pro-gram and analysis. Sociologist Arlene Stein, for instance, based her *Sex and Sensibility* (1997) on "self stories"—that is, interviews in which women told stories "of and about the self in relation to an experience, in this case the development of a lesbian identity, that positions the self of the teller centrally in the narrative" (p. 7). The queer influence is embedded in this formulation of the research project: Stein's is not a study of the ways a "true self" gets revealed, but of the ever-changing stories that get told as people conduct "identity work." It takes into account "the permanently unsettled nature of identities and group boundaries," as Stein puts it, "a decentered model of identity [that] mirrors the decentering of lesbian culture and communities" (p. 201). Indeed, the booming interest in bisexual and transgender lives and identities is driven by a similar agenda, the analysis of confounding identities—in the words of Susan Stryker (1998b), their promise of "a profound destabilization of naturalized heteronormative configurations of gender, embodiment, and identity" (p. 145).

In another related vein, researchers on sexuality-based social movements have been among those at the forefront of making "collective identity" the subject of empirical and theoretical revision. Rather than assuming a group "we-ness" that preexists social movement action, researchers have investigated the ways group boundaries, interests, and consciousness are established and negotiated (Phelan, 1989; Taylor & Whittier, 1992). Queerness here becomes both a topic and a resource for investigating logics of collective action. In an article on debates over "queerness," for instance, I myself have argued:

> Queerness spotlights a dilemma shared by other identity movements (racial, ethnic, and gender movements, for example): Fixed identity categories are both the basis for oppression and the basis for political power. . . . If identities are indeed much more unstable, fluid, and constructed than movements have tended to assume—if one takes the queer challenge seriously, that is— what happens to identity-based social movements such as gay and lesbian rights? . . . The case of queerness . . . calls for a more developed theory of collective identity formation and its relationship to both institutions and meanings, an understanding that *includes the impulse to take apart the identity from within*. (Gamson, 1995, p. 391)

Taking queer critiques of identity seriously pushed forward for me a different set of investigations—necessarily qualitative ones, because they involve everyday identity work: how, when and why collective identity gets deconstructed as well as solidified, how collective identity is shaped by specific organizational exigencies and communication environments (Gamson, 1996, 1997).

Although these studies remain relatively conventional in their data collection and representational strategies, social researchers have begun to take queer problematizing of representation to heart as well. Although the older tradition of autobiographical writing as both political act and representation of an authentic sexual self continues, in queer qualitative texts the researcher's authoritative voice is increasingly positioned as one among many competing, partial voices—none and all of them "authentic." The notion that a gay ethnography is "one in which the identity of the ethnographer as a lesbian or as a gay man is an explicit and integral part of the text" (Wafer, 1996, p. 261) does not sit easily with poststructuralist notions that such an identity is neither unitary nor stable; in its place, increasingly, is "a growing focus in lesbian [and gay] ethnography on the permeability of both communities and identities and on our Hexpanding awareness of the instability of identity, particularly in complex cultural settings" (Lewin, 1995, p. 327). Ethnographic research, rather than being a site for the revelation of identity, is redefined as "yet another context for defining identity" with and against the various others (however they are defining themselves) in the field (Lewin, 1995, p. 332).

Kath Weston's *Render Me, Gender Me* (1996), for instance, uses a mix of personal narratives to represent what could be called a queer take on the gendering process. "Anything and anybody can be gendered in a variety of ways," Weston writes; the point of placing same-sex relationships at the center is not to make lesbians more visible, as it was in earlier studies, but to make "the modes of gendering more obvious" (pp. 2-3). Importantly, doing so also involves a more experimental strategy of representation, in which the author's voice and the author's version of lesbian identity are not privileged. Thus Weston brings together long passages from interviews with a variety of lesbian-identified women—teachers, writers, factory workers, nurses, artists, strippers, women from all sorts of racial, class, and religious backgrounds—with her own analytic observations. This is a textual strategy informed by queer thinking. "Representations," Weston asserts, "do not do a very good job of depicting the specific people assigned to cultural categories" (p. 4). Her book is designed to make that explicit, and accordingly to invite a different reading strategy:

I have deliberately edited and organized [the] interviews to call into question the concept of identity. Lesbians who consistently named themselves "androgynous" or "butch" or "femme" appear alongside lesbians who used these terms sparingly or not at all. This strategic juxtaposition shifts oral history away from chronology toward montage in order to disrupt cultural assumptions about what makes women women, lesbians women, and gay women gay. The back-and-forth movement between interview and commentary . . . opens a space for you, the reader, to gender yourself alternately

560

as storyteller, anthropologist, traveling companion, theorist, voyeur . . . [and] to walk the fine line that weaves difference together with desire. (p. 5)

Although such a representational strategy remains rare, it makes very plain the potential impact on qualitative research reporting that serious considerations of queer identity critiques can provoke.

Researching and Theorizing the Institutions-Discourse Relationship

The final and perhaps most productive challenge comes not from queer theory and gay and lesbian studies themselves, but from the differences between them and the growing attempts to reconcile them. "In both defenders of identity politics and its poststructural critics," Steven Seidman (1993) has argued, "there is a preoccupation with the self and the politics of representation. Institutional and historical analysis and an integrative political vision seems to have dropped out." He urges "a shift away from the preoccupation with self and representations characteristic of identity politics and poststructuralism to an analysis that embeds the self in institutional and cultural practices" (pp. 136-137). Or, put somewhat differently: Whereas lesbian and gay studies, including its more sophisticated constructionist versions rooted in sociology, has underplayed the *discursive,* queer theory, with its heavy, humanities-driven analysis on social-life-as-text, has underplayed the *institutional.* The *relationship* between the institutional and the discursive (a strong tension within political activism as well; see Gamson, 1995) is therefore itself undertheorized and underresearched. This predicament has been exacerbated by a disciplinary divide between social researchers (often more attuned to institutional forces) and humanities scholars (often more attuned to the dynamics of discourse), and between empirical work and theoretical work—divisions that are only beginning to be bridged in the field.

The complex tension between institutionally oriented qualitative analysis of lesbian and gay studies and the discursively oriented queer theory, however, can and should itself be a resource for important new directions in qualitative research. There is much at stake here, not just for research and theory but for everyday politics: Collective action, be it organizing for protection against discrimination (or for benefits) on the base of existing social categories of "gay" and "lesbian" and "bisexual" and "transsexual" or challenging the boundaries and utility of those categories through cultural interventions, requires sophisticated inquiry into the simulta-neous, and linked, processes by which the experiences of sexual desire are given institutional, textual, and experiential shape. In the coming years, qualitative social researchers have a critical role to play in closing the angst-ridden, politically volatile gaps between different qualitative pur-suits, not by choosing between text and experience, or between discourse and institution, not by settling the necessary competition between queer fluidity and gay solidity, but by transforming the tensions on which sexual-ity studies has been built into new sources of productivity.

◆ Notes

1. This is actually an important way in which the terms of oppression for homosexuals differed from those of other marginalized groups: Although women, for instance, were stereotyped in various ways (for example, as having a propensity for hysteria), the status of female was not itself seen as an illness or as abnormal; although racist research treated Afri-can Americans as inferior in a variety of ways (including a propensity for criminality), the status of black was not itself seen as criminal or in need of a cure.

2. This association, Jeffrey Weeks (1985) argues, has been a constant in sexual science: "In the rush to protect themselves, many sexologists have become little more than propa-gandists of the sexual norm, whatever it is at any particular time. The call upon science then becomes little more than a gesture to legitimize interventions governed largely by specific relations of power. The production of a body of knowledge that is apparently scientifically neutral (about women, about sexual variants, delinquents or offenders) can become a resource for utilization in the production of normative definitions that limit and demarcate erotic behavior" (p. 79).

3. These studies have been especially good at directing attention toward institutional-ized heterosexism and homophobia, providing an institutional focus that, as we will see, has gotten somewhat lost as qualitative research has become more prominent.

4. It is interesting to note that as the budding bisexual movement took shape in the 1980s, much of the writing by bisexuals and about bisexuality used the same strategy of per-sonal narrative. See, for example, Hutchins and Ka'ahumanu (1990).

5. Constructionist thought and work, despite its challenges to the assumptions of "essentialism," also partook of the minority building of the 1980s; while historicizing the process by which "the homosexual" was created, for instance, and rejecting the notion of a universal homosexual subject, the study of "the social factors that produced a homosexual identity which functioned as the foundation for homosexuals as a new ethnic minority" also "legitimated a model of lesbian and gay subcultures as ethnic-like minorities" (Seidman, 1996, p. 9).

6. Much has been written on the "essentialist-constructionist" debate (Stein, 1992), and I will not belabor it here. It is worth noting, however, that although essentialism and constructionism do not line up neatly with quantitative and qualitative methods,

constructionist conceptualizations of sexuality do tend to favor qualitative approaches, and essentialist conceptualizations are often more closely aligned with positivist science, as in the search for the biological roots of homosexuality (Burr, 1996).

7. The divorce is at times quite extreme, so much so that a 1995 Social Science Research Council report on sexuality research in the social and behavioral sciences could call for a "much-needed framework" of "sexual behaviors in the context of society and culture" and for recognizing that "sexuality is not a series of individual, episodic behaviors linked to specific acts and the physical body, but represents a range of sexual activities and norms, whose meaning and significance for both the individual and society change over time" (di Mauro, 1995, pp. 4-5)—that is, could treat as novel the very assumptions of most qualitative research on sexuality of the past two decades.

8. As Plummer (1992) notes, the elusiveness of the object of analysis is embedded in the constructionist arguments that preceded and fed into queer theory; also, queer theory makes explicit and problematizes the role of lesbian and gay studies itself, among other practices, in the construction of a false unity of "lesbian and gay" subjects.

9. For an example of this approach applied to entertainment media, see *Freaks Talk Back: Tabloid Talk Shows and Sexual Nonconformity* (Gamson, 1998).

◆ References

Adam, B. (1995). *The growth of a gay and lesbian movement* (2nd ed.). Boston: Twayne.

Alexander, J. (1991). Redrafting morality: The postcolonial state and the Sexual Offences Bill of Trinidad and Tobago. In C. T. Mohanty, A. Russo, & L. Torres (Eds.), *Third World women and the politics of feminism* (pp. 133-152). Bloomington: Indiana University Press.

Almaguer, T. (1991). Chicano men: A cartography of homosexual identity and behavior. *differences, 3*, 75-100.

Alwood, E. (1996). *Straight news: Gays, lesbians, and the news media*. New York: Columbia University Press.

Badgett, M. V. L. (1995). The wage effects of sexual orientation discrimination. *Industrial and Labor Relations Review, 48*(4).

Bayer, R. (1981). *Homosexuality and American psychiatry*. New York: Basic Books.

Berlant, L., & Freeman, E. (1993). Queer nationality. In M. Warner (Ed.), *Fear of a queer planet: Queer politics and social theory* (pp. 193-229). Minneapolis: University of Minnesota Press.

Burr, C. (1996). *A separate creation: The search for the biological origins of sexual orientation*. New York: Hyperion.

Butler, J. (1991). Imitation and gender insubordination. In D. Fuss (Ed.), *Inside/out: Lesbian theories, gay theories* (pp. 13-31). New York: Routledge.

Butler, J. (1993). Critically queer. *GLQ, 1*, 17-32.

Clarke, C. (1981). Lesbianism: An act of resistance. In C. Moraga & G. Anzaldúa (Eds.), *This bridge called my back: Writings by radical women of color* (pp. 128-137). New York: Kitchen Table/Women of Color Press.

Clifford, J., & Marcus, G. E. (Eds.). (1986). *Writing culture: The poetics and politics of ethnography*. Berkeley: University of California Press.

Clough, P. T. (1994). *Feminist thought: Desire, power and academic discourse.* Cambridge, MA: Blackwell.

Cohen, C. (1997). Punks, bulldaggers, and welfare queens: The radical potential of queer politics? *GLQ, 3,* 437-465.

Collins, P. H. (1990). *Black feminist thought: Knowledge, consciousness, and the politics of empowerment.* New York: Routledge, Chapman & Hall.

D'Emilio, J. (1983). *Sexual politics, sexual communities.* Chicago: University of Chicago Press.

Denzin, N. K., & Lincoln, Y. S. (1994). Introduction: Entering the field of qualitative research. In N. K. Denzin & Y. S. Lincoln (Eds.), *Handbook of qualitative research* (pp. 1-22). Thousand Oaks, CA: Sage.

di Mauro, D. (1995). *Sexuality research in the United States: An assessment of the social and behavioral sciences* (Executive summary). New York: Social Science Research Council.

Doty, A. (1993). *Making things perfectly queer: Interpreting mass culture.* Minneapolis: University of Minnesota Press.

Duberman, M., Vicinus, M., & Chauncey, G. (Eds.). (1989). *Hidden from history: Reclaiming the gay and lesbian past.* New York: Penguin.

Duggan, L. (1992). Making it perfectly queer. *Socialist Review, 22,* 11-32.

Duggan, L. (1998). Queering the state. In P. M. Nardi & B. E. Schneider (Eds.), *Social perspectives in lesbian and gay studies* (pp. 564-572). London: Routledge.

Duggan, L., & Hunter, N. D. (1995). *Sex wars: Sexual dissent and political culture.* New York: Routledge.

Eaton, M. (1994). Homosexual unmodified: Speculations on law's discourse, race, and the construction of sexual identity. In D. Herman & C. Stychin (Eds.), *Legal inversions: Lesbians, gay men, and the politics of law* (pp. 46-73). Philadelphia: Temple University Press.

Epstein, J., & Straub, K. (Eds.). (1991). *Body guards: The cultural politics of gender ambiguity.* New York: Routledge.

Epstein, S. (1987). Gay politics, ethnic identity: The limits of social constructionism. *Socialist Review, 93/94,* 9-54.

Epstein, S. (1996). A queer encounter: Sociology and the study of sexuality. In S. Seidman (Ed.), *Queer theory/sociology* (pp. 145-167). Cambridge, MA: Blackwell.

Faderman, L. (1981). *Surpassing the love of men: Romantic friendship and love between women from the Renaissance to the present.* New York: William Morrow.

Foucault, M. (1978). *The history of sexuality: Vol. 1. An introduction* (R. Hurley, Trans.). New York: Vintage.

Gagnon, J., & Simon, W. (1973). *Sexual conduct.* Chicago: University of Chicago Press.

Gamson, J. (1995). Must identity movements self-destruct? A queer dilemma. *Social Problems, 42,* 390-407.

Gamson, J. (1996). The organizational shaping of collective identity: The case of lesbian and gay film festivals in New York. *Sociological Forum, 11,* 231-262.

Gamson, J. (1997). Messages of exclusion: Gender, movements, and symbolic boundaries. *Gender & Society, 11,* 178-199.

Gamson, J. (1998). *Freaks talk back: Tabloid talk shows and sexual nonconformity.* Chicago: University of Chicago Press.

Garber, M. (1995). *Vice versa: Bisexuality and the eroticism of everyday life.* New York: Simon & Schuster.

Greenberg, D. (1988). *The construction of homosexuality.* Chicago: University of Chicago Press.

Harding, S. (1987). Conclusion: Epistemological questions. In S. Harding (Ed.), *Feminism and methodology: Social science issues* (pp. 181-190). Bloomington: Indiana University Press.

Harper, P. B. (1991). Eloquence and epitaph: Black nationalism and the homophobic impulse in responses to the death of Max Robinson. *Social Text, 28*(9), 68-86.

Hemphill, E. (Ed.). (1991). *Brother to brother: New writings by black gay men.* Boston: Alyson.

Herdt, G. H., & Boxer, A. M. (1993). *Children of Horizons: How gay and lesbian teens are leading a new way out of the closet.* Boston: Beacon.

Herek, G. M. (1989). Hate crimes against lesbians and gay men. *American Psychologist, 44,* 948-955.

Herek, G. M. (1997). Heterosexuals' attitudes towards lesbians and gay men. In M. Duberman (Ed.), *A queer world: The Center for Lesbian and Gay Studies reader* (pp. 331-344). New York: New York University Press.

Hooker, E. (1958). Male homosexuality in the Rorschach. *Journal of Projective Techniques, 22,* 33-54.

Humphreys, L. (1970). *Tearoom trade: Impersonal sex in public places.* Chicago: Aldine.

Hutchins, L., & Ka'ahumanu, L. (Eds.). (1990). *Bi any other name: Bisexual people speak out.* Boston: Alyson.

Institute for Gay and Lesbian Strategic Studies. (1998). Mission statement [Online]. Available Internet: http://www.iglss.org

Jay, K., & Young, A. (Eds.). (1972). *Out of the closets: Voices of gay liberation*. New York: Harcourt Brace Jovanovich.

Jones, J. H. (1997, August 25-September 1). Dr. Yes. *New Yorker*, pp. 98-113.

Katz, J. N. (1976). *Gay American history*. New York: Thomas Y. Crowell.

Kellner, D. (1988). Postmodernism as social theory: Some challenges and problems. *Theory, Culture & Society, 5*, 239-269.

Kinsey, A. C., Pomeroy, W. B., & Martin, C. E. (1948). *Sexual behavior in the human male*. Philadelphia: W. B. Saunders.

Kinsey, A. C., Pomeroy, W. B., Martin, C. E., & Gebhard, P. (1953). *Sexual behavior in the human female*. Philadelphia: W. B. Saunders.

Krieger, S. (1983). *The mirror dance: Identity in a women's community*. Philadelphia: Temple University Press.

Laumann, E. O., Gagnon, J. H., Michael, R. T., & Michaels, S. (1994). *The social organization of sexuality: Sexual practices in the United States*. Chicago: University of Chicago Press.

Levine, M. (1979). Gay ghetto. *Journal of Homosexuality, 4*, 363-377.

Lewin, E. (1995). Writing lesbian ethnography. In R. Behar & D. A. Gordon (Eds.), *Women writing culture* (pp. 322-335). Berkeley: University of California Press.

Leznoff, M., & Westley, W. A. (1956). The homosexual community. *Social Problems, 3*, 257-263.

Lincoln, Y. S., & Denzin, N. K. (1994). The fifth moment. In N. K. Denzin & Y. S. Lincoln (Eds.), *Handbook of qualitative research* (pp. 575-586). Thousand Oaks, CA: Sage.

Masters, W., & Johnson, V. (1966). *Human sexual response*. Boston: Little, Brown.

McIntosh, M. (1968). The homosexual role. *Social Problems, 16*, 182-192.

Moraga, C., & Anzaldúa, G. (Eds.). (1981). *This bridge called my back: Writings by radical women of color*. New York: Kitchen Table/Women of Color Press.

Nardi, P. M., & Schneider, B. E. (1998). Looking: The sociological baselines [Part introduction]. In P. M. Nardi & B. E. Schneider (Eds.), *Social perspectives in lesbian and gay studies* (pp. 3-4). London: Routledge.

Newton, E. (1972). *Mother camp*. Chicago: University of Chicago Press.

Nicholson, L. (Ed.). (1990). *Feminism/postmodernism*. New York: Routledge.

Ortner, S., & Whitehead, H. (Eds.). (1981). *Sexual meanings: The cultural construction of gender and sexuality*. Cambridge: Cambridge University Press.

Patterson, C. (1992). Children of lesbian and gay parents. *Child Development, 63*, 1025-1043.

Patterson, C. (1995). Families of the lesbian baby boom: Parents' division of labor and children's adjustment. *Developmental Psychology, 31*, 115-124.

Phelan, S. (1989). *Identity politics: Lesbian feminism and the limits of community*. Philadelphia: Temple University Press.

Phelan, S. (1993). (Be)coming out: Lesbian identity and politics. *Signs, 18,* 765-790.

Plummer, K. (1981). Homosexual categories: Some research problems in the labelling perspective of homosexuality. In K. Plummer (Ed.), *The making of the modern homosexual* (pp. 53-75). London: Hutchinson.

Plummer, K. (1992). Speaking its name: Inventing a lesbian and gay studies. In K. Plummer (Ed.), *Modern homosexualities: Fragments of a lesbian and gay experience* (pp. 3-25). London: Routledge.

Plummer, K. (1998). Afterword: The past, present, and futures of the sociology of same-sex relations. In P. M. Nardi & B. E. Schneider (Eds.), *Social perspectives in lesbian and gay studies* (pp. 605-614). London: Routledge.

Ponse, B. (1978). *Identities in the lesbian world: The social construction of self.* Westport, CT: Greenwood.

Reiss, A. J. (1961). The social integration of queers and peers. *Social Problems, 9,* 102-120.

Rubin, G. (1975). The traffic in women. In R. Reiter (Ed.), *Toward an anthropology of women* (pp. 157-210). New York: Monthly Review Press.

Sedgwick, E. K. (1990). *Epistemology of the closet.* Berkeley: University of California Press.

Seidman, S. (1993). Identity and politics in a "postmodern" gay culture: Some historical and conceptual notes. In M. Warner (Ed.), *Fear of a queer planet: Queer politics and social theory* (pp. 105-142). Minneapolis: University of Minnesota Press.

Seidman, S. (1996). Introduction. In S. Seidman (Ed.), *Queer theory/sociology* (pp. 1-29). Cambridge, MA: Blackwell.

Seidman, S., & Wagner, D. (Eds.). (1991). *Postmodernism and social theory.* New York: Blackwell.

Smith, D. E. (1974). Women's perspective as a radical critique of sociology. *Sociological Inquiry, 4,* 1-13.

Spelman, E. V. (1989). *Inessential woman: Problems of exclusion in feminist thought.* Boston: Beacon.

Stein, A. (1997). *Sex and sensibility: Stories of a lesbian generation.* Berkeley: University of California Press.

Stein, A., & Plummer, K. (1996). "I can't even think straight": "Queer" theory and the missing sexual revolution in sociology. In S. Seidman (Ed.), *Queer theory/sociology* (pp. 129-144). Cambridge, MA: Blackwell.

Stein, E. (Ed.). (1992). *Forms of desire: Sexual orientation and the social constructionist controversy.* New York: Routledge.

Stryker, S. (Ed.). (1998a). The transgender issue [Special issue]. *GLQ, 4*(2).

Stryker, S. (1998b). The transgender issue: An introduction. *GLQ, 4,* 145-158.

Taylor, V., & Whittier, N. (1992). Collective identity in social movement communities: Lesbian feminist mobilization. In A. Morris & C. Mueller (Eds.),

, *Frontiers in social movement theory* (pp. 104-129). New Haven, CT: Yale University Press.

Tierney, W. G. (1997). *Academic outlaws: Queer theory and cultural studies in the academy.* Thousand Oaks, CA: Sage.

Trujillo, C. (Ed.). (1991). *Chicana lesbians: The girls our mothers warned us about.* Berkeley, CA: Third Woman.

Wafer, J. (1996). Out of the closet and into print: Sexual identity in the textual field. In E. Lewin & W. L. Leap (Eds.), *Out in the field: Reflections of lesbian and gay anthropologists* (pp. 261-273). Urbana: University of Illinois Press.

Warner, M. (1993). Introduction. In M. Warner (Ed.), *Fear of a queer planet: Queer politics and social theory* (pp. vii-xxxi). Minneapolis: University of Minnesota Press.

Weeks, J. (1985). *Sexuality and its discontents.* New York: Routledge.

Weston, K. (1996). *Render me, gender me: Lesbians talk sex, class, color, nation, studmuffins . . . .* New York: Columbia University Press.

Whittier, N. (1995). *Feminist generations: The persistence of the radical women's movement.* Philadelphia: Temple University Press.

Williams, W. (1992). *The spirit and the flesh: Sexual diversity in American Indian culture.* Boston: Beacon.

Woods, J. D., & Lucas, J. H. (1994). *The corporate closet: The professional lives of gay men in America.* New York: Free Press.

PART III

The Future of
Qualitative Research

And so we come to the end, which is only the starting point for a new beginning. Several observations have structured our arguments to this point. The field of qualitative research continues to transform itself. The changes that took shape in the early 1990s are gaining momentum. The gendered, narrative turn has been taken. Foundational epistemologies, what Schwandt (1997, p. 40) calls epistemologies with a big *E*, have been replaced by constructivist, hermeneutic, feminist, poststructural, pragmatist, critical race, and queer theory approaches to social inquiry. Epistemology with a small *e* has become normative, displaced by discourses on ethics and values, conversations on and about the good, and about the just and moral society.

The chapters in this volume collectively speak to the great need for a compassionate, critical, interpretive civic social science. This is an interpretive social science that blurs both boundaries and genres. Its participants are committed to politically informed action research, inquiry directed to praxis and social change. Hence as the reformist movement called qualitative research gains momentum, its places in the discourses of a free democratic society become ever more clear. With the action researchers, we seek a set of disciplined interpretive practices that will produce radical democratizing transformations in the public and private spheres of the global postcapitalist world. Qualitative research is the means to these ends. It is the bridge that joins multiple interpretive communities. It stretches across many different landscapes and horizons, moving back and forth between the public and the private, the sacred and the secular.

Paradigm shifts and dialogues have become a constant presence within and across the theoretical frameworks that organize both qualitative inquiry and the social and human sciences. The move to standpoint epistemologies has accelerated. No one any longer believes in the concept of a unified sexual subject or, indeed, any unified subject. Epistemology has come out of the closet. The desire for critical, multivoiced, postcolonial ethnographies increases as capitalism extends its global reach.

We now understand that the civic-minded qualitative researcher uses a set of material practices that bring the world into play. These practices are not neutral tools. This researcher thinks historically and interactionally, always mindful of the structural processes that make race, gender, and class potentially repressive presences in daily life. The material practices of qualitative inquiry turn the researcher into a methodological (and epistemological) *bricoleur*. This person is an artist, a quilt maker, a skilled craftsperson, a maker of montages and collages. The interpretive *bricoleur* can interview, observe, study material culture, think within and beyond visual methods; write poetry, fiction, and autoethnography; construct narratives that tell explanatory stories; use qualitative computer software; do text-based inquiries; construct *testimonios* using focus group interviews; even engage in applied ethnography and policy formulation.

It is apparent that the constantly changing field of qualitative research is defined by a series of tensions and contradictions as well as emergent understandings. These tensions and understandings have been felt in every chapter in this volume. Here, as in the *Handbook*, we list many of them for purposes of summary only. They take the form of questions and assertions:

1. How will the emphasis on multiple standpoint epistemologies and moral philosophies crystallize around a set of shared understandings concerning the contributions of qualitative inquiry to civil society, civic discourse, and critical race theory?

2. How will studies of ourselves as research subjects lead to greater understandings of the other?

3. If the meanings of experience are given only in representations, then will the performance turn in ethnography produce a shift away from attempts to represent the stream of consciousness and the world of internal meanings of the conscious subject?

4. How will feminist, communitarian, and race-based ethical codes change institutional review boards?

5. Will a new interpretive paradigm, with new methods and strategies of inquiry, emerge out of the interactions that exist among the many paradigms and perspectives presented in this volume?

6. How will ethnic, queer, postcolonial, and feminist paradigms be fitted to this new synthesis, if it comes?

7. How will the next generation of cultural studies scholars, with their critical focus on textual (narrative) and contextual (ethnographic) models of analysis, shape qualitative inquiry?

8. How will the next generation of qualitative researchers react to computer-assisted models of analysis, especially as these models continue to redefine (and erode) issues surrounding privacy and personal, sacred space?

9. Will the postmodern, antifoundational sensibility begin to form its own foundational criteria for evaluating the written and performed text?

10. What place will postpositivism and its successors have in research endeavors that favor local interpretation, question the existence of a guiding "truth," and emphasize subjectivity in the research process?

11. What part can "sixth and seventh moments" qualitative research, including program evaluation and analysis, play in the understanding and improvement of programs and policy?

12. When all universals are gone, including the postmodern worldview, in favor of local interpretations, how can we continue to talk and learn from one another?

There are no definitive answers to any of these questions. Here we can only suggest, in the barest of detail, our responses to them. In our concluding chapter we elaborate these responses, grouping them around several basic themes, or issues: text and voice; the existential, sacred text; reflexivity and being in the text; working the hyphen; ethics and critical moral consciousness; and the textual subject, including our presence in the text. Examined from another angle, the questions listed above focus on the social text, history, politics, ethics, the other, and interpretive paradigms more broadly.

◆ Into the Future

Chapter 13, by Mary Gergen and Kenneth Gergen, reflexively moves qualitative inquiry into the next century. Gergen and Gergen validate our argument that this field is filled with creativity, enthusiasm, intellectual ferment, cross-fertilizations, catalytic dialogues, and a prevailing sense of participation in a living revolution. They analyze these fractious crosscurrents, focusing explicitly on the crisis in validity, the rights of representation, and the place of the political in qualitative inquiry.

The collapse of foundational epistemologies has led to emerging innovations in methodology that have reframed what is meant by *validity*. They have shaped the call for increased textual reflexivity, greater textual self-exposure, multiple voicing, stylized forms of literary representation, and performance texts. These innovations shade into the next, issues surrounding representation.

Representational issues involve how the other will be presented in the text. Gergen and Gergen discuss several different types of representation: empowerment, conjoint, distributed, and multivoiced. These representational strategies converge with a concern over the place of politics in the text. We can no longer separate ideology and politics from methodology. Gergen and Gergen are quite forceful on this point. Methods always acquire their meaning within broader systems of meaning, from epistemology to ontology. These systems are themselves embedded in ethical and ideological frameworks as well as in particular interpretive communities. In a parallel vein, as Gergen and Gergen note, studies of individual consciousness support the ideology of individualism. Our methods are always grafted onto our politics.

To repeat: Scientific practice does not stand outside ideology. As we argued in the *Handbook,* a poststructural social science project seeks its external grounding not in science, but rather in a commitment to post-Marxism and an emancipatory feminism. A good text is one that invokes these commitments. A good text exposes how race, class, and gender work their ways into the concrete lives of interacting individuals.

Gergen and Gergen foresee a future where research becomes more relational, where working the hyphen becomes easier, and more difficult, for researchers are always on both sides of the hyphen. They also see a massive spawning of populist technology. This technology will serve to undermine qualitative inquiry as we know it, including disrupting what we mean by a "stable" subject (where is the cyberself located?). The new information technologies also increase the possibilities of dialogue and communication across time and space. We may be, as Gergen and Gergen observe, participating in the reconstruction of the social sciences. If so, qualitative inquiry is taking the lead in this reconstruction.

Finally, we predict that there will be no dominant form of qualitative textuality in the sixth and seventh moments; rather, several different hybrid textual forms will circulate alongside one another. The first form will be the classic, realist ethnographic text, redefined in poststructural terms. We will hear more from first-person voices in these texts. The second hybrid textual form will blend and combine poetic, fictional, and performance texts into critical interventionist presentations. The third textual form will include *testimonios* and first-person (autoethnographic) texts. The fourth form will be narrative evaluation texts, which work back and forth between first-person voices and the *testimonio*. These forms will be evaluated in terms of an increasingly sophisticated set of local, antifoundational, moral, and ethical criteria.

Variations on these textual forms will rest on a critical rethinking of the notion of the reflexive, self-aware subject. Lived experience cannot be studied directly. We study representations of experience: stories, narratives, performances, dramas. We have no direct access to the inner psychology and inner world of meanings of the reflexive subject. The subject in performance ethnographies becomes a performer. We study performers and performances, persons making meaning together, the how of culture as it connects persons in moments of cocreation and coperformance.

◆ History, Paradigms, Politics, Ethics, and the Other

Many things are changing as we write our way out of writing culture and move into the seventh moment of qualitative research. Multiple histories and theoretical frameworks, where before there were just a few, now circulate in this field. Today foundationalism and postpositivism are challenged and supplemented by a host of competing paradigms and perspectives. Many different applied action and participatory research agendas inform program evaluation and analysis.

We now understand that we study the other to learn about ourselves, and many of the lessons we have learned have not been pleasant. We seek a new body of ethical directives fitted to postmodernism. The old ethical codes failed to examine research as a morally engaged project. They never seriously located the researcher within the ruling apparatuses of society. A feminist, communitarian ethical system will continue to evolve, informed at every step by critical race, postcolonial, and queer theory sensibilities. Blatant voyeurism in the name of science or the state will continue to be challenged.

Performance-based cultural studies and critical theory perspectives, with their emphases on moral criticism, will alter the traditional empiricist foundations of qualitative research. The dividing line between science and morality will continue to be erased. A postmodern, feminist, post-structural, communitarian science will move closer to a sacred science of the moral universe.

As we edge our way into the 21st century, looking back, and borrowing Max Weber's metaphor, we see more clearly how we were trapped by the 20th century and its iron cage of reason and rationality. Like a bird in a cage, for too long we were unable to see the pattern in which we were caught. Coparticipants in a secular science of the social world, we became part of the problem. Entangled in the ruling apparatuses we wished to undo, we perpetuated systems of knowledge and power that we found, underneath, to be all too oppressive. It's not too late for us to get out of that cage—today we leave the cage behind.

And so we enter, or leave, the sixth moment. In our concluding chapter we elaborate our thoughts about the next generation of qualitative research.

◆ Reference

Schwandt, T. A. (1997). *Qualitative inquiry: A dictionary of terms.* Thousand Oaks, CA: Sage.

13

Qualitative Inquiry

Tensions and Transformations

Mary M. Gergen and Kenneth J. Gergen

◆ The domain of qualitative inquiry offers some of the richest and
most rewarding explorations available in contemporary social science. This bounty is the outcome of a host of historical convergences. The
area has welcomed scores of scholars who have found their disciplinary
traditions narrow and constraining. Other denizens have found outlets for
expressing particular commitments or skills; here there is space for societal critique and political activism, just as there are clearings for literary,
artistic, and dramatic expressions. Further, scholars from diverse arenas—
AIDS researchers, market analysts, ethnographers, and more—have entered in search of ways to bring vitality to their customary pursuits.
Perhaps most significant, the tidal wave of theoretical and metatheoretical
debates dashing across the intellectual world—variably indexed as post-
foundational, poststructural, post-Enlightenment, and postmodern—has
swept into the qualitative harbor. Here these turbulent interchanges have
produced profound challenges to the ways in which the social sciences are
understood and practiced.

As a result of these convergences, the field of qualitative inquiry is
replete with enthusiasm, creativity, intellectual ferment, and action. As
one researcher, Virginia Olesen, has described it, "I don't think there's

ever been a more exciting moment in terms of careful thought about the epistemologies of the methods, relations with participants, new modes and the growing strength of qualitative methods in important substantive fields such as education and nursing" (e-mail, November 25, 1998). There are cross-fertilizations, catalytic dialogues, and a prevailing sense of participation in a living revolution. Contrasting beliefs, skeptical challenges, and resistance are also in evidence. In the present chapter we turn our attention to some of these fractious crosscurrents in order to highlight some of the more salient differences and to deliberate on possible futures. We do so, however, not with the aim of settling the disputes or of moving the field toward coherence or univocality. We do not view the doubts and disagreements as the birth pangs of a new methodological foundation, but rather as opportunities for new conversations and new evolutions in practice. Approaching the issues from a social constructionist standpoint, we treat these tumultuous dialogues as harboring the generative potential that will sustain the vitality of the qualitative domain in the new century. We also explore what we feel to be some of the more promising vistas of inquiry, emerging challenges that may significantly shape the future of the field.

We do not embark on this enterprise alone. To sharpen and expand our deliberations, we surveyed distinguished colleagues who are contributors to the present volume and members of the *Handbook*'s International Advisory Board. We asked them where they see themselves moving in the qualitative domain during the next 5 years, what kinds of projects they have under way, what particular turns of methodology seem especially inviting and exciting to them, and what modes of inquiry seem most appealing to their graduate students. The replies were most generous, enlightening, and provocative; we wish to thank all who gave of their views for the enrichment of this chapter.

In what follows we attend specifically to three sites of controversy in qualitative inquiry: the crisis of validity, the rights of representation, and the place of the political in qualitative investigations. In each case we review the principal lines of development, exploring the ways in which controversy has sparked development. And in each case we point to what we believe to be the most useful lines of emerging argument and practice. Following this discussion, we address specific agendas for the new century. As we see it, developments within the major sites of controversy position the field for new and significant transformations. We pay special attention to research as relational process, transformations through technology, and the reconstruction of the self.

◆ The Crisis of Validity

One of the most catalytic influences on the qualitative domain within the past 10 years has been the lively dialogue on the nature of language, and particularly the relationship of language to the world it purports to describe. Developments in poststructural semiotics, literary theory, and rhetorical theory all challenge the pivotal assumption that scientific accounts can accurately and objectively represent the world as it is. At a minimum, such work makes clear the impossibility of linguistic mimesis; there is no means of privileging any particular account on the grounds of its unique match to the world. The intelligibility of our accounts of the world derive not from the world itself, but from our immersion within a tradition of cultural practices we inherit from previous generations. It is only as our accounts approximate these conventions that we make sense at all. Thus it is from our relationships within interpretive communities that our constructions of the world derive.[1]

Deteriorating Foundations of Methodology

This view of language has led to substantial skepticism concerning the epistemological foundations of scientific practices. The pursuit of universal or general laws, the capacity of science to produce accurate portrayals of its subject matter, the possibility of scientific progression toward objective truth, and the right to claims of scientific expertise are all undermined. We confront, then, what Denzin and Lincoln (1994) have called a crisis of validity. If there is no means of correctly matching word to world, then the warrant for scientific validity is lost, and researchers are left to question the role of methodology and criteria of evaluation. As Denzin and Lincoln cogently ask, "How are qualitative studies to be evaluated in the poststructural moment?" (p. 11).

Within the qualitative arena these developments have simultaneously stimulated heated debate and bursts of creative energy. For many qualitative researchers, critiques of validity resonate with other long-standing misgivings about nomothetic methodologies for their inability to reflect the complexities of human experience and action. Indeed, such researchers turn to qualitative methods in the hope of generating richer and more finely nuanced accounts of human action. Within these circles, many argue that the empiricist emphasis on quantifiable behavior left out the crucial ingredient of human understanding, namely, the private experiences of the agent. Both of these views—that qualitative methods are more faithful to the social world than quantitative ones and that individual human experiences are important—remain robust in today's qualitative community, with diverse proponents of grounded theory research (Strauss & Corbin, 1990, 1994), phenomenology (Georgi, 1994; Moustakas, 1994), and feminist standpoint researchers (Belenky, Clinchy, Goldberger, & Tarule, 1986; Brown & Gilligan, 1992; Harding, 1986, 1991; Komesaroff, Rothfield, & Daly, 1997; Miller & Stiver, 1997) among them.

Yet, as the validity critiques have played out, they bite the hand of the qualitative enthusiasts who feed them. If the idea of language as a picture or map of the real is rejected, then there is no rationale by which qualitative researchers can claim that their methods are superior to quantitative ones in terms of accuracy or sensitivity to what exists. A thousand-word description is no more valid a "picture of the person" than a single score on a standardized test. By the same token, the validity critiques challenge the presumption that language can adequately map individual experience (Bohan, 1993; Butler, 1990). In what sense, it is asked, can words map or picture an inner world? Accounts of "experience" seem more adequately understood as the outcome of a particular textual/cultural history in which people learn to tell stories of their lives to themselves and others. Such narratives are embedded within the sense-making processes of historically and culturally situated communities (see Bruner, 1986, 1990; Gergen, 1992, in press; Morawski, 1994; Sarbin, 1986).

Emerging Innovations in Methodology

Although sometimes accused of no-exit nihilism, such skepticism has had enormous catalytic effects in the qualitative arena. An effulgent range of methodological innovation has resulted from efforts to replace the traditional effort to discover and record the truth. We consider here four of these innovations: reflexivity, multiple voicing, literary representation, and performance. Their particular importance derives in part from the way in which they challenge the traditional binary between research and representation, that is, between acts of observing or "gathering data" and subsequent reports on this process. There is increasing recognition that because observation is inevitably saturated with interpretation, and research reports are essentially exercises in interpretation, research and representation are inextricably entwined (Behar & Gordon, 1995; Gergen, Chrisler, & LoCicero, 1999; Visweswaran, 1994). Let us explore.

Reflexivity

Among the primary innovations have been those emphasizing reflexivity. Here investigators seek ways of demonstrating to their audiences their historical and geographic situatedness, their personal investments in the research, various biases they bring to the work, their surprises and "undoings" in the process of the research endeavor, the ways in which their choices of literary tropes lend rhetorical force to the research report, and/or the ways in which they have avoided or suppressed certain points of view (see Behar, 1996; Kiesinger, 1998). Rosanna Hertz elaborates on these implications for her work:

> After delving into issues of voice and reflexivity, I find myself freer to think about how to incorporate my own voice into a piece of work where I have no personal experience. I want a reader to understand that . . . I bring to the topic my own history and perspective. I still believe that my primary obligation as a social scientist is to tell the stories of the people I have studied. But I also find that the accounts they tell have been constructed through the dialogue that my respondents created in conjunction with me. (e-mail, April 9, 1998)

Such forms of self-exposure have more recently led to the flourishing of autoethnography (Ellis & Bochner, 1996). Here investigators explore in depth the ways in which their personal histories saturate the ethnographic inquiry. However, rather than giving the reader pause to consider the biases, here the juxtaposition of self and subject matter is used to enrich the ethnographic report. The reader finds the subject/object binary deteriorating and is informed of ways in which confronting the world from moment to moment is also confronting the self. In all these reflexive moves, the investigator relinquishes the "God's-eye view" and reveals his or her work as historically, culturally, and personally situated. In the case of autoethnography, the distinction between the research and the report or representation is also fully challenged. Personal investments in the observational act are not only recognized but become a subject of the research. Although a valuable addition to the vocabulary of inquiry, reflexive moves are not entirely successful in subverting the concept of validity. Ultimately, the act of reflexivity asks the reader to accept itself as authentic, that is, as a conscientious effort to "tell the truth" about the making of the account. We are thus poised at the threshold of an infinite regress of reflections on reflection.

Multiple Voicing

A second significant means of disclaiming validity is to remove the single voice of omniscience and to relativize it by including multiple voices within the research report. There are many variations on this theme. For example, research subjects or clients may be invited to speak on their own behalf—to describe, express, or interpret within the research report itself (Anderson, 1997; Lather & Smithies, 1997; Reinharz, 1992). In other cases researchers may seek out respondents with wide-ranging perspectives on a given matter and include the varying views without pressing them into coherence (Fox, 1996). Or researchers may reflexively locate a range of conflicting interpretations that they find plausible and thereby avoid reaching a single, integrative conclusion (Ellis, Kiesinger, & Tillmann-Healy, 1997). Some researchers also work collectively with their subjects so that their conclusions do not eradicate minority views. Multiple voicing is especially promising in its capacity to recognize the problems of validity while simultaneously providing a potentially rich array of interpretations or perspectives (Hertz, 1997). Doubt gives way to the positive potentials of multiplicity.

Yet multiple voicing is not without its complexities. One of the most difficult questions is how the author/researcher should treat his or her own voice. Should it simply be one among many, or should it have special privileges by virtue of professional training? There is also the question of identifying who the author and the participants truly are; once we realize the possibility of multiple voicing, it also becomes evident that each individual participant is polyvocal (Franklin, 1997). Which of these voices is speaking in the research and why? What is, at the same time, suppressed? The way in which Shulamit Reinharz raises this question has significant implications for deliberating on this issue:

Using detailed field notes from a project I completed quite a while ago, . . . I trace the way I referred to myself during the course of the year, and saw how different parts of my self became relevant over time. I discuss these "selves" as emergent through the process of immersion in the field. At first, the most obvious "difference" with the [other group] members is what defines myself there. After that, more layers are unpeeled. As these different layers are uncovered, people get to know me in different ways, which leads to their telling me different things. This in turn allows me to know them in different ways over time. . . . Different lengths of time in the field therefore yield different types of knowledge. At first glance this seems self-evident because clearly a one-day visit is different from a one-year stay (for example). But this difference has not been explained or demonstrated. I think my notes demonstrate the process. (e-mail, April 18, 1998)

Finally, moves toward multiplicity are not always successful in giving all sides their due. Typically, the investigator functions as the ultimate author of the work (or the coordinator of the voices) and thus serves as the ultimate arbiter of inclusion, emphasis, and integration. The author's arts of literary rendering are often invisible to the reader.

Literary Styling

A third important reaction to validity critiques is the deployment of stylized representation, and particularly the replacement of traditional realist discourse with forms of writing cast in opposition to "truth telling." For example, the investigator's descriptions may take the form of fiction, poetry, or autobiographical invention. The use of literary styling signals to the reader that the account does not function as a map of the world (and, indeed, that the mapping metaphor is flawed), but as an interpretive activity addressed to a community of interlocutors. For many qualitative researchers, such writing is especially appealing because it offers a greater expressive range and an opportunity to reach audiences outside the academy (Communication Studies 298, 1999; Diversi, 1998; S. H. Jones, 1998, 1999; Richardson, 1997, 1998; Rinehart, 1998) and to do significant political work (Behar & Gordon, 1995). While generating significant openings for creative expression, such writing is vulnerable to the criticism of singularity of voice. The lone author commands the discursive domain in full rhetorical regalia. Again, however, critique gives way to innovation: Literary styling may be combined with other methodologies to offset the criticism. For example, in her dissertation on relationships among African Americans after the Million Man March, Deborah Austin (1996) co-constructed a narrative poem with one of the participants. This is a small excerpt:

> Africans are the same
> wherever we are, she says to me
> matter-of-factly
> I look at her and smile
> and ask
> like a good researcher should
> How so?
> I can't explain, she says
> with that voice that sounds
> like the rush of many rivers. (pp. 207-208)

Many of the issues brought forth about reflexivity and multiple voicings can also be directed at forms of nontraditional writing. Although certain pitfalls of traditional literary forms are avoided in these innovations, claims that they are not appropriate for scientific representations are prevalent. These critiques are even more pronounced with regard to performance.

Performance

Finally, to remove the thrall of objectivity while sustaining voice, an increasing number of scholars are moving toward *performance* as a mode of research/representation. This move is justified by the notion that if the distinction between fact and fiction is largely a matter of textual tradition, as the validity critiques suggest, then forms of scientific writing are not the only mode of expression that might be employed. Although visual aids such as film and photography have also been accepted as a means of "capturing reality," they have generally been viewed as auxiliary modes within written traditions. However, when we realize that the communicative medium itself has a formative effect on what we take to be the object of research, the distinction between film as recording device as opposed to performance (e.g. "a film for an audience") is blurred (Gergen & Gergen, 1991). And with this blurring, investigators are invited into considering the entire range of communicative expression in the arts and entertainment world—graphic arts, video, drama, dance, magic, multimedia, and so on—as forms of research and presentation. Again, in moving toward performance the investigator avoids the mystifying claims of truth and simultaneously expands the range of communities in which the work can stimulate dialogue.

Significant contributions to this developing form of research/representation include Carlson's *Performance: A Critical Introduction* (1996) and Case, Brett, and Foster's edited volume *Cruising the Performative* (1995), as well as work by Blumenfeld-Jones (1995), Case (1997), Clark (1996), Denzin (1997), Donmoyer and Yennie-Donmoyer (1995), Jipson and Paley (in press), Mienczakowski (1996), Morris (1995), and Van Maanen (1995). An example specifically relevant to the qualitative domain is a performance piece concerning the lives of Mexican American migrants by Jim Scheurich, Gerardo Lopez, and Miguel Lopez. The performance includes music, video, and a slide show—all operating simultaneously. In addition, there is a script that requires the participation of a cast along with members of the audience. Apropos the issue of validity, Scheurich notes, "The originators make no assumptions about the nature of these experiences or their relationship to Mexican American migrant life" (e-mail, April 19, 1998). In effect, the performance provides the audience with possibilities for a rich engagement with the issues, but leaves them free to interpret as they wish. In another format, Glenda Russell and Janis Bohan (1999) responded performatively to the passage of Amendment 2 to the Colorado State Constitution (which removed legal recourse from those who encounter discrimination based on sexual orientation). Using themes and statements taken from the transcripts of interviews with persons opposed to the legislation, the researchers helped to create two highly sophisticated and complex artistic projects: one a five-part oratorio, *Fire,* written by a professional composer and sung by a highly skilled choir at a national competition; and the other a professionally produced television documentary aired on PBS. In their work one senses the blurring of many boundaries, between professional and amateur, insider and outsider, researcher and researched, and performer and audience.

Enrichment or Erosion?

Judging from the reactions of our correspondents, investments in these groundbreaking explorations are likely to increase considerably. As John Frow put it, "Where do I go from here? I suspect into ever greater levels of suspicion of the protocols of intellectual discourse, and into exploration of the limits of the genre of 'academic' knowledge.... the use of nonlinear and recursive textual structures, seems to me increasingly unavoidable as I try to work my way out of the constraints and certainties of routine academic argument" (e-mail, April 5, 1998). And as Kathy Charmaz wrote, "One top priority for me is finishing a handbook about writing research. My approach combines methods of qualitative analysis with writing techniques ... that professional writers use" (e-mail, May 30, 1998). Similarly, Jim Scheurich commented, "I have turned to video in search of a ... more multidimensional medium. I like adding visual and sound to written words. I also like the storying aspect though I don't want to tell conventional stories. I see this medium as supportive of more levels of meaning" (e-mail, April 19, 1998).

Yet, in spite of the bold and creative zest accompanying many of these ventures, there is also a growing unease among some qualitative researchers with the drift from conventional scientific standards. Epithets of excess—narcissistic, navel gazing, exhibitionistic—are familiar reframes. In this vein, George Marcus suggested that "new thinking ... and to some degree discursive practice in the things we write about reflexivity, subjectivity, power in intersubjectivity has run its course, nearly so, and that conditions of research—especially of fieldwork—need attention now" (e-mail, April 4, 1998). Marcus argues that anthropologists must continue to engage in the long, hard work required to produce "thick descriptions," and not let other intellectual pursuits distract from that duty (Marcus, 1998). Patricia Clough (1997) takes emotionally charged autoethnographic writing to task for its symbiotic relationship with television drama and for "keeping theoretically motivated critical interventions at a distance" (p. 101). In a similar vein, William Tierney worries that too often "adventurous texts are little more than experiments with words. Those of us who are critics are increasingly skeptical of literary wordsmithing without any concern for change" (e-mail, April 10, 1998). The harshest words among those we surveyed came from David Silverman, who wrote: "The last two decades have been obsessed with fashions that will quickly be forgotten or integrated into other ways of working. The best of Post-Modernism (Foucault, Latour) will be incorporated into sober studies of institutional practices. The 'fun and games' (wordplays, experimental writing etc.) will be dismissed. [The] endless open-ended interviews will be understood as the Oprah Winfrey cop-out it really is" (e-mail, April 3, 1998).

Vistas of Validity

One might view such critiques as numbing in consequence, possibly functioning as an enervating backlash, a return to the conventional, and the end to methodological experiments. It could also fragment the field, as researchers may simply terminate dialogue and go their separate ways. However, such outcomes would be both unfortunate and unwarranted. At the outset, it would be intellectually irresponsible simply to return to business as usual—as if the validity critiques had never occurred. At the same time, those engaged in the new endeavors can scarcely declare that the validity critiques are fully justified. By their own account, there are no foundational rationalities from which such warrants could be derived. Further, few of any persuasion would welcome a unified field of inquiry—guided by a coherent, conceptually rigid framework—in which all methods are prescribed in advance. Thus, rather than a domain of noncommunicating, nomadic tribes, we may properly reinvoke the metaphor of generative tension. Placing these innovations and their critiques into an appreciative dialogue, which is where we think they should be, what new avenues are now encouraged? What futures could be opened? Drawing from disparate dialogues, the following would appear prominent.

Reframing Validity

In the conventional terms by which it has been formulated, the debate on validity has reached an impasse. On the one hand, those pursuing their work as if their descriptions and explanations were transparent reflections of their subject matter lack any rationale for this posture. They are vulnerable to host of deconstructive logics. Yet those who find fault with this tradition are, in the end, without means of justifying their critique. In the very process of deprivileging they are relying on the selfsame assumptions of language as correspondent with its object. Thus, rather than either reinstantiating the modernist tradition of objective truth or opening the throttle on anything goes, discussion is invited into ways of reconceptualizing the issue. At a minimum, we might profitably revisit the issue of linguistic reference. If research or critique is "about" something, and this relationship is not one of mimesis, how can it be otherwise envisioned? Even those employing fictional genres or performance in their work do not treat their work as mere entertainment; the underlying presumption is that in some fashion it is a contribution to understanding. Frow's communiqué offers an attractive beginning to the task of rethinking reference:

> The concept of "text" or "discourse" refers to a matter which is ontologically heterogeneous: that is, which is not reducible either to *language* or to a reality which is external to the symbolic, but is rather a heterogeneous mix of language and other (e.g. iconic) symbolizations, of social relations, of built environments, of consolidated institutional structure, of roles and hierarchies of authority, of bodies, etc. It's only on this basis, I believe, that the metaphor of textuality or discursivity can work without being reductive either to language or to social relations. (e-mail, April 5, 1998)

Here we begin to consider the achievement of reference in far richer terms than heretofore. If reference is born of such heterogeneity, then we are positioned to reconsider the means by which validity is achieved, by whom, for whom, and under what conditions.

We might also abandon concern with validity, an option favored by not a few, including several reviewers of this chapter, who cautioned us to avoid the term, given its embattled history and predicted demise. However, a more promising direction for us seemed to be toward reconceptualizing the concept. Here Patti Lather's (1991, 1993) work on validity is particularly catalytic. Lather proposes a "transgressive-list" of ways in which validity might be reconceptualized: Ironic validity foregrounds the insufficiencies of language in picturing the world; paralogical validity is concerned with undecidables, limits, paradoxes, discontinuities, and complexities in language; rhizomatic validity, symbolized by the taproot metaphor, expresses how conventional research procedures are undermined and new locally determined norms of understanding are generated; and voluptuous validity—"excessive," "leaky," "risky," and "unbounded"—brings issues of ethics and epistemology together. Robin McTaggart (1997b) has also raised the interesting question of validity in relation to participatory action research. He suggests that the concept might be reconceptualized in terms of the efficacy of research in changing relevant social practices. "Our thinking about validity must engage much more than mere knowledge claims. . . . [It must be] comprehensive enough to reflect [what] the social action researchers . . . are committed to, by the trenchant and withering critiques of other more inert and detached forms of social enquiry" (pp. 17-18). Conversations around such viewpoints are rich in potential for reconfiguring the concept of validity.

Situated Knowledge

Closely related to the revisioning of validity, but raising questions of its own, are explorations into situated knowledge. As Donna Haraway (1988) as well as other theorists have suggested, the concept typically serves an ameliorating function, reconciling constructionist and realist positions. Because few traditionalists wish to argue that their interpretations are uniquely articulated with the subject matter they wish to portray, and few constructionists would maintain that there is "nothing outside of text," a space is opened for situated truth, that is, "truth" located within particular communities at particular times and used indexically to represent their condition (see Landrine, 1995). In this way we can commonly speak as if the term *sunset* maps the sinking sun in the evening sky and astronomers can simultaneously agree that "the sun does not set." Descriptions and explanations can be valid so long as one does not mistake local conventions for universal truth. It is in this vein that Jim Holstein wrote positively of research that "tries to be mindful of the constructed, the ephemeral, the hyperreal, while not giving up on empirical analysis of lived experience in a world that still seems quite real and solid to its inhabitants (even if it doesn't seem as solid as it might once have felt)" (e-mail, April 23, 1998).

Yet, although a useful beginning, further dialogues on the conceptual possibilities of situated knowledge are needed. It borders on the banal to suggest that everything can be valid for someone, sometime, somewhere. Such a conclusion both closes off dialogue among diverse group and leads to the result that no one can speak about another. Such an outcome would spell the end of social science inquiry. Dialogue is invited, then, into how situated validity is achieved, maintained, and subverted. Further, how do various qualitative methods function in this regard, and for whom? By what means do they variously achieve a sense of validity?

One important option is for the qualitative community to develop methods by which situated knowledges can be brought into productive (as opposed to conflicting) relationships with each other. Frequently our methods of inquiry support (or "empower") particular groups. This outcome contributes to the situated knowledge of these groups, but also tends to diminish or erase alternative realities. The challenge, then, is to develop methods of inquiry that can generate productive exchanges at the border of competing or clashing "situations." Here we found the words of Yen Espiritu provocative:

I am trying to think about how scholars of color can expand upon the premise of studying "our own" by studying other "others." For example, as a Vietnam-born woman who studies Filipino Americans, I come to the research project not as an "objective" outsider but as a fellow Asian immigrant who shares some of the life experiences of my respondents. I do not claim that these shared struggles grant me "insider status" into the Filipino American community. But I do claim that these shared experiences enable me to bring to the work a comparative perspective that is implicit, intuitive, and informed by my own identities and positionalities. These implicitly comparative aspects are important because they permit us to highlight the different and differentiating functional forces of racialization. (e-mail, April 12, 1998)

More broadly, however, the need is for transversing conversations, dialogues that crisscross the moguled terrains of discourse and practice (see Cooperrider & Dutton, 1999). We return to this issue later in the chapter.

Rhetorical/Political Deliberation

Finally, our contemporary debates would be enriched by an extension of the process of rhetorical/political deliberation. That is, we might usefully bracket the question of validity in favor of a range of alternative queries into the ways various methods/representations function within the culture. Given the impact of social science pursuits on cultural life, how do we estimate the comparative value of various methodological/ representational forms? There is already an extensive sociopolitical critique of the patriarchal, colonialist, individualist, and hegemonic aspects of realism/objectivism (Braidotti, 1995; hooks, 1990; Penley & Ross, 1985; Said, 1978; Smith, in press). Although such work represents an important opening, there has been little exploration of what many would consider to be the positive functions of the realist orientation—both politically and in terms of rhetorical potential. For example, the language of statistics is but one form of rhetoric; however, it is a rhetoric that, for certain audiences and in certain circumstances, can be more compelling and more functional than a case study, poem, or autoethnographic report. More significant is that we have yet to explore the various sociopolitical and rhetorical implications of the new developments discussed above. For example, do ventures into multivoicing or fictional styling diminish or enhance audience interest or engagement? As Jay Gubrium, after expressing reservations about the work, declared, "The stuff can be riveting and, to me, that's important enough in its own right" (e-mail, April 2, 1998). Yet in a society where clear, no-nonsense answers to serious issues are often demanded, such offerings may seem too impractical, irrelevant, or playful. As Linda Smircich wrote: "I am located in a business school . . . and the dominant mode of thinking and researching is still positivist/ quantitative/functionalist and directed toward managerial interests. . . . I rarely get a daring student" who will challenge these barriers of tradition (e-mail, April 23, 1998). Either way, we must continue the inquiry into societal functions and repercussions of diverse modes of communicating.

In a different dimension, we might ask whether self-reflexivity and autoethnographic reportage function in such a way that individual experience is privileged over social or communal renditions. Can these orientations be faulted for their contribution to an ideology of self-contained individualism? In sum, broadscale comparative analyses are needed of the various rhetorical/political assets and liabilities of the many emerging methodologies. Lincoln's (1995, 1998) analyses of the criteria for qualitative research furnish a significant background to this conversation (see also Garratt & Hodkinson, 1998). However, a closer analysis of the relational repercussions of alternative forms of discourse is much to be welcomed.

◆ Rights of Representation

Critical reflection on the empiricist program has provoked a second roiling of the qualitative waters, in this case over issues of representation, its control, responsibilities, and ramifications (Tierney & Lincoln, 1997). It is perhaps Foucault's (1979, 1980) disquisitions on power/knowledge that have figured most centrally in these critiques. For Foucault, knowledge-generating disciplines—including the social sciences—function as sources of authority, and as their descriptions, explanations, and diagnoses are disseminated through education and other practices they enlarge the potential realm of subjugation. For example, as the concept of mental disorders and the diagnostic categories of the psychiatric profession are recognized by all professionals and laypersons involved with such issues, so does the culture capitulate to the disciplining power of psychiatry. The implications of such arguments are sobering to the research community. Increasingly painful questions are confronted: To what extent does research convert the

589

commonsense, unscrutinized realities of the culture to disciplinary discourse? In what ways does research empower the discipline as opposed to those under study? When is the researcher exploiting his or her subjects for purposes of personal or institutional prestige? Does research serve agencies of surveillance, increasing their capacities of control over the research subject?

Confrontation with such issues has been intensified by increasing resistance among those subjected to social science inquiry. Feminists were among the first to issue complaints, regarding both omissions and commissions in characterizations of women in the research literature (Bohan, 1992). Minority group members have become increasingly aware that the long-standing critiques of the public media's distortion or misrepresentation of their lives apply no less to human science research. The psychiatric establishment was among the first of the professional groups to be targeted when it was forced by 1960s gay activists to withdraw homosexuality from the nosology of mental illness. It has also been the message delivered by African Americans angered by a social science literature depicting them as unintelligent or criminal. Similarly, the elderly, AIDS victims, "psychiatric survivors," and many others now join to question the rights of scientists to represent (appropriate) their experience, actions, and/or traditions. Given the problems of validity discussed above, these various critiques have troubling implications for future research.

Yet such contentions are not without their limitations. When extended to their extreme, they are as problematic as what they challenge. In reply to Foucauldian critiques, human science research often functions in counterhegemonic ways, bringing into critical focus the institutions of governance, economic control, educational institutions, the media, and so on. In this sense, such research can function as a force of resistance and social justice. Further, to suspend all knowledge claims would be to terminate virtually all traditions—ethnic, religious, and otherwise—that depend on the capacity to "name the world." In addition, there are limits to the claims and critiques of interest groups as well. For one, claims to rights of self-representation exist alongside a host of competing claims made by human scientists—including rights to freedom of speech, to speak the truth from one's own perspective, to contribute to science, and to pursue one's own moral ends. Self-representation may be a good, but it is not the only good. Further, the concept of self-representation is not unproblematic. If it were pressed to its conclusion, no one would have the right to speak for or describe anyone else. One might even question the possibility of individuals' representing themselves, for to do so would require that they appropriate the language of other persons. The solitary individual would have no private voice, no language of private experience. Without depending on the language of others, we cannot achieve intelligibility.

Expanding the Methodological Arena

With these crosscurrents of opinion in motion, what is again required is a more tolerant and mutually reflective orientation to the research process. Consistent with the central theme of this chapter, we see these various tensions as generative in potential. They have already stimulated a range of significant developments and currently set agendas for a creative future. Let us consider three such developments garnered from the qualitative domain.

Empowerment Research

Perhaps the most obvious response to the critical concerns with representation, and one already well developed within the qualitative community, is empowerment research. Here the researcher offers his or her skills and resources in order to assist groups in developing projects of mutual interest. Participatory action research is the most well developed genre of this kind (Lykes, 1996; McTaggart, 1997a; Reason, 1994; Smyth, 1991). In one variation on the empowerment theme, Elijah Anderson (1978, 1990) has mounted research aimed at fostering connection among members of otherwise hostile communities. Anderson essentially "hung out" for many years in the public housing projects and on the streets of Philadelphia, creating focus groups and collecting extensive narratives from clusters of people frequenting street corners and other public places. His recent book, *Code of the Street* (1999), is designed to speak to sociologists but also to public policy planners, neighborhood groups, educators, and others involved with diverse client populations. While not abandoning an explanatory goal of making sense of the "code" of the street and its functions, Anderson develops an interpretive framework that has meaning for both marginalized and mainstream society and thus functions as a bridge between them. The attempt is to reduce the mutual disrespect and sense of alienated difference that otherwise prevail.

591

Conjoint Representations

The use of conjoint representations to deal with issues of validity, as mentioned above, also has ramifications for issues of representation. As researchers join participants in inquiry and writing, the line between researcher and subject is blurred, and control over representation is increasingly shared. In early attempts of this sort, research participants were given a broader space in which to "tell their own stories." Often, however, the researcher's hand subtly, but strongly, shaped the voice through editing and interpretation. To compensate, some researchers now ask participants to join in writing the research accounts themselves. One of the most innovative and far-reaching examples of the genre is Lather and Smithies's volume *Troubling the Angels* (1997). Here the investigators worked in a support group composed of women with the AIDS virus. The report includes the women's firsthand accounts of their lives and what they want to share with the world about their conditions. Rather than obscuring their own positions, the investigators devote special sections of the book to their own experiences and understandings. To compensate for the ways in which these various accounts are cut away from the discourses of medicine, economics, and media, Lather and Smithies supplement with more formal academic and scientific materials. Before publication, the entire volume was submitted to the participants for their comments.

Distributed Representation

Representational critiques are also countered with emerging explorations into distributed representation, that is, attempts by the investigator to set in motion an array of different voices in dialogical relationship. A fascinating example is provided by Karen Fox (1996), who combines her own views, as researcher, with the related experiences of a survivor of child sexual abuse, along with the rarely available views of the abuser himself. The account is based on extensive open-ended interviews and participant observation in which Fox attended a therapy session with the convicted sex offender. The piece is arranged in a three-column format, with the columns representing the three voices. The flow of the text encourages the reader to consider the three different perspectives—separately and in relationship. All of the words are those of the speakers. Although the selection and arrangement are Fox's, each of the participants had the opportunity to read and comment on all of the materials. Ultimately, the arrangement facilitates a full expression of emotion—ambivalence, sorrow, rage, and affection. Fox also includes her own abuse story within the frame, thus breaking with the tradition of author insularity.

Another variation of distributed representation is offered by a group of three researchers who are also the objects of their mutual study (Ellis et al., 1997). For 5 months, the trio met in various configurations in diverse settings to discuss the topic of bulimia. Two of the researchers have long histories of eating disorders. The culmination of their research is a jointly written and edited account in which they describe a dinner at an elegant restaurant. This setting is very provocative for their particular involvements with food and permits the authors to treat complex relations as they write of ordering and eating food among others who are aware of their "problems." The text of their combined efforts reveals the private reflections and active engagement of each within a single narrative. Unlike the presentation by Fox discussed above, in which quotations are separated by blank spaces and individual perspectives are clearly delineated, this presentation is seamless. One achieves a form of "God's-eye view" by discovering almost simultaneously the private reactions of each author. For example, the reader discovers how ordering dessert takes on momentous significance for each woman, and how each resolves her interpersonal dilemmas concerning this challenge. Such experiments in representation open new and exciting vistas.

◆ The Place of the Political

A third site of controversy is closely related to issues of validity and representation but raises issues of a distinct nature. The focal point in this case concerns the political or valuational investments of the researcher. Thirty years ago, it was commonly argued that rigorous methods of research are politically or valuationally neutral. Ideological interests might, or might not, determine the topic of research or the ways in which the results are used, but the methods should themselves be ideologically free. However, as the postmodern critiques of validity have become more sophisticated, it has become increasingly clear that there is no simple means of separating method from ideology. For one, methods acquire their meaning and significance within broader networks of meaning—metaphysical, epistemological, ontological—which are themselves wedded to ideological and ethical traditions. For example, to conduct psychological experiments on individuals is to presume the centrality of individual mental functioning in the production of human affairs. Much the same privilege is granted by qualitative methods attempting to tap individual experience. In this way, both methods implicitly support an ideology of individualism. In the same way, methods that presume a separation of the researcher from the object of study (a subject/object binary) favor an instrumentalist attitude toward the world and a fundamental condition of alienation between the researcher and the researched.

This expanding realization of the political has had a significant impact on the posture of research. If inquiry is inevitably ideological, the major challenge is to pursue the research that most deeply expresses one's political and valuational investments (Smith, 1999). To paraphrase: If science is politics by other means, then we should pursue the inquiry that most effectively achieves our ends. It is also within the qualitative domain, with its lack of a fixed metaphysics, ontology, or epistemology, that the politically invested are most at liberty to generate methods uniquely crafted to their political or valuational commitments (Crawford & Kimmel, 1999).

It is this realization of the political potentials of methodology that now leads to significant tension within the qualitative sphere. We confront a range of highly partisan but quite separate commitments—to feminism, Marxism, lesbian and gay activism, ethnic consciousness-raising, and anti-colonialism, among others.[2] Each group champions a particular vision of the good, and, by implication, those not participating in the effort are less than good and possibly obstructionist. Many also wish to see qualitative research become fully identified with a particular political position. For example, as Lincoln and Denzin (1994) propose: "A poststructural social science project seeks its external grounding not in science . . . but rather in a commitment to a post-Marxism and a feminism. . . . A good text is one that invokes these commitments. A good text exposes how race, class, and gender work their ways in the concrete lives of interacting individuals" (p. 579). For others, however, such cementing of the political agenda threatens to remove them from the dialogue. There are many whose humane concerns turn toward other groups—the aged, abused, ill, handicapped, and so on—and still others who find much to value in the long-standing traditions and use of their research to enlighten policy makers, organizational leaders, and so on.

It is here, however, that the same logic inviting unabashed ideological commitment begins to turn reflexively and critically upon these very commitments. If the postmodern turn undermines validity claims, it simultaneously opens a space for political or valuational investments; however, all reality posits serving to ground ideologically based research are simultaneously thrown into question. If one cannot legitimately claim truth through observational method, then accounts of poverty, marginality, oppression, and the like are similarly rendered rhetorical. Remove the rational and evidential foundations from empirical science and you simultaneously remove them from the sphere of value critique. And, as this form of critique has become progressively articulated, so has it produced a new range of tensions. The politically partisan turn on the postmodern arguments once favoring their causes to condemn them variously as "relativist," "conservative," and "irrelevant" (see, e.g., Reason, 1994).

From Partisanship to Polyvocality

Given such conflicts over matters of political partisanship, we again find opportunity for expanding the potential of qualitative methodology. Perhaps the most promising development in this domain is in conceptual and methodological explorations of polyvocality. There is a pervasive tendency for scholars—at least in their public writings—to presume coherence of self. Informed by Enlightenment conceptions of the rational and morally informed mind, they place a premium on coherence, integration, and clarity of purpose. The ideal scholar should know where he or she stands and should be responsible to his or her conception of the good. It is in this same sense that one may lay claim, for example, to being "a Marxist," "a masculinist," or a "Gray Panther." Yet, as the postmodern literatures on "the death of self," social construction, dialogism, and the like have made increasingly clear, the conception of the singular or unified self is both intellectually and politically problematic. There is much to be gained by suspending such an orientation in favor of polyvocality. Specifically, we are encouraged in this case to recognize both within ourselves as scholars and within those who join our research as participants the multiplicity of competing and often contradictory values, political impulses, conceptions of the good, notions of desire, and senses of our "selves" as persons (Banister, 1999). We may each carry impulses toward Marxism, liberalism, anarchism, and so on, along with potentials for those ideologies most antagonistic to them.

This view of polyvocal subjects offers a significant means of going beyond the animosities pervading the qualitative arena. Rosie Braidotti (1995), a feminist theorist, avails this end with her conception of "nomadic subjectivity." A nomadic consciousness "entails a total dissolution of the notion of a center and consequently of originary sites of authentic identities of any kind" (p. 5). Chantal Mouffe (1993), a political theorist, suggests that a liberal socialist conception of citizenship "allows for the multiplicity of identities that constitute an individual" (p. 84). As we see it, the presumption of polyvocality opens the door to new forms of research methodology. We have already touched on methods in which multiple voices are given entry into the interpretive arena—voices of the research participants, the scientific literature, the private views of the investigators, the media, and so on (Ribbens & Edwards, 1998). However, the challenge of polyvocality is more radical in that we are sensitized to the possibility that all parties to the research may "contain multitudes." The question is whether researchers enable participating parties (and themselves) to give expression to their multiplicity—to the full complexity and range of contradictions that are typical of life in postindustrial society. There is movement in this direction (see, e.g., Jacobs, Munor, & Adams, 1995; Richardson, 1998; Travisano, 1998), but we have scarcely crossed the threshold. Two pieces that work toward this end involve the practice of overwriting, in which the author allows each overlay of description to erase, revise, and change her identities and activities. Among those under reconstruction are all of the principal actors—herself as stripper, dancer, wrestler, researcher, and professor (Ronai, 1998, 1999). Performance pieces that cut between character expositions and reflexive commentary also serve to undermine univocal subject positions (Gergen, in press).

◆ New-Century Agendas

Thus far, our discussion has remained closely interwoven with debates currently circulating within the qualitative arena, along with a focus on propitious opportunities for further development. In this final section we wish to explore three domains of future exploration that are congenially related to the preceding but considerably expand the domain of possibility. In our view, to follow these paths could potentially transform the conception of methodology, along with our understanding of social science and its subject matter. More important, we glimpse the potential of the social sciences to enter more actively into cultural life, transforming both common conceptions and forms of action. These are bracing challenges, but in our view the dialogues on qualitative methodology now deposit us on the threshold of just such reformations. We outline, then, the potentials of research as relational process, the vistas of technology, and the refiguring of the Western conception of self.

Research as Relational Process

As we find, the qualitative field has become a major source of creative innovation in modes of representation. Experiments in reflexivity, literary form, and multiple voicing, for example, have injected new vitality into the research endeavor. Yet there is good reason to press farther in such pursuits. Earlier, we stressed the inextricable relationship between research and representation: Any form of recording or describing is simultaneously a form of representation. At the same time, however, representation is inevitably "for an audience." To write, for example, is to invite an audience into a particular form of relationship. At a minimum, the act of writing serves to position both self and reader, to give each an identity and a role within a relationship. In this sense every form of representation—like a move in a dance—favors certain forms of relationship while discouraging others. Thus the various genres of social science writing—ranging from the mystical and the democratic to the ludic—all favor differing forms of relationship (Gergen, 1997). More broadly, we may say that our forms of representation in social sciences are themselves invitations to particular forms of cultural life.

In this context, we are enjoined to pay critical attention to our existing forms of representation and to consider future developments in methodology in terms of the kinds of relationships they favor. For example, much traditional writing tends to sustain structures of privilege: We write from the position of "knowing" to an audience positioned as "not knowing." The form tends toward the monological, inasmuch as the audience has no opportunity to participate and the choice of vocabulary and sentence structure tends to insulate the writing from examination by the broader public. We have also seen how various literary experiments within the qualitative domain open new forms of relationship. New forms of writing enable the author to abdicate the position of authority, for example, and invite the reader into a more egalitarian relationship. The immediate challenge for the future is that of expanding forms of representation to achieve specific relational ends. How can we set in motion particular processes of relationship, and more specifically processes with positive potentials for the culture at large?

It is here that we might ask, with Michelle Fine, "What elements of qualitative research are productively engaging toward democratic/ revolutionary practices; toward community organizing; toward progressive social policy; toward democratizing public engagement with social critique?" (personal communication, 1998). To illustrate, in her work attempting to enhance the understanding of medical practitioners working with aging populations, Arlene Katz and her colleagues have established a panel of the elderly who serve as dialogical resources for students at the Harvard Medical School (see Katz & Shotter, 1996). The traditional "subjects of research" are positioned here as "cultural insiders" in matters of living with illness or its threat. In the same vein, researchers who provide ghetto inhabitants with cameras or video cameras and enable them to generate visual materials of their own choosing re-create the "research subject" as both learner and teacher/informer/performer. Further, the Public Conversations Project has generated methods for bringing together bitter antagonists (for example, prolife and prochoice advocates) for productive conversation (Becker, Chasin, Chasin, Herzig, & Roth, 1995; Chasin et al., 1996); David Cooperrider and his colleagues have developed a method of exchange, called "appreciative inquiry," that wholly transforms relationships among otherwise hostile members of an organization or community (see Cooperrider, 1990; Hammond, 1996; Hammond & Royal, 1998). In all these cases, new forms of relationship are forged.

There is a latent potential in these moves that, if allowed full expression, would wholly reconstitute the conception and practice of research. If we first abandon the long-standing scopic metaphor of re/search and replace it with the relational metaphor of re/present, then those formerly serving as the subjects of research and the readers of research outcomes become relational participants. And if we abandon the traditional goal of research as the accumulation of products—static or frozen findings—and replace it with the generation of communicative process, then a chief aim of research becomes that of establishing productive forms of relationship. The researcher ceases to be a passive bystander who generates representational products communicating to a minuscule audience of researchers. Rather, he or she becomes an active participant in forging generative, communicative relationships, in building ongoing dialogues and expanding the domain of civic deliberation. For example, much has been said about the value of global forums of exchange, national dialogues on prejudice, and the revitalization of communities (the "civil society"). Yet efforts to achieve these ends have been scattered and have infrequently included social science researchers. At present, our skills in creating social forms are meager; with this challenging reconceptualization of research we can and should become progenitors of relational practices. We shall return to this issue shortly.

The Challenge of the Technorevolution

The massive spawning of populist technology—including the telephone, radio, television, the automobile, mass-transit systems, jet travel, television, mass publication, and computer communication—may well constitute the most significant cultural transformation of the 20th century. To be sure, there is a rapidly growing corpus of work treating the myriad dimensions of this transformation. However, as yet there has been little exploration of the implications of such changes for research methodology. As William G. Tierney wrote to us, "I keep getting this sense that the way we do qualitative research over the next generation will change incredibly because of technology" (e-mail, April 10, 1998). We wholly concur. It is not simply that new sites for research are opened (e.g., Internet communication, MUDs), nor is it that as researchers we can now reach many populations more effectively and efficiently than heretofore. Rather, the technological watershed invites new ways of conceptualizing research methods, along with a refiguring of the very idea of research, including the identities of the researcher, researched, and audience. Let us speak to the conceptual issues first, and then turn to methodological implications.

Of preeminent significance for the researcher is the challenge of a *vanishing subject matter*. Traditional research methodologies are wedded to a conception of a relatively fixed object of study. One may spend several years in studying a topic within a given population or subculture; several years later the work may be published, with the hope that it will remain informative for the foreseeable future. The underlying presumption is that the subject matter will remain relatively stable and the research will retain relevance. Yet, with the global proliferation of communication technologies in particular, processes of meaning making are also accelerated. Values, attitudes, and opinions are all subject to rapid fluctuation, and with them patterns of related action. In effect, the temporal relevance of a research study is increasingly circumscribed, and the half-life of cultural analysis increasingly shortened. The question, then, is whether our traditional methods of research/representation are rapidly becoming irrelevant to contemporary conditions. How are we to justify studying various cultures or subcultures, for example, when the very conception of culture as a group of people who share an enduring pattern of meaning and action is being eroded (Hermans & Kempen, 1993)? Cultures, like those who make them up, are everywhere in motion (S. G. Jones, 1998).

At the outset the condition of vanishing subject matter invites researchers to envision themselves more as journalists than as traditional scientists—commentators on the contemporary as opposed to stonemasons at the edifice of progressive knowledge. Our mission should be that of contributing to the cultural dialogues on the here and now as opposed to the there and then. However, there are limits to this conclusion as well. In particular, as communication linkages are extended in all directions, we move into a condition of broadscale *interdependency of meaning*. The traditional conception of research methods in the social sciences was developed under conditions of relatively low technological saturation. In this circumstance, research subjects could make themselves available to scrutiny with little concern for repercussions. Not only were their identities typically shielded, but accounts of their activities (invariably value laden) were subject to great temporal delay and shared with only a small community of scientists. As we move into conditions of sophisticated communication technology, the situation changes dramatically. Traces of an individual's identity as research participant accumulate (consider the challenge of Internet privacy), and the information a person conveys to a researcher may be immediately transmitted to an extended population. Further, these very technologies have also enhanced consciousness of the political and moral uses to which research is put (Ceglowski, in press). Thus the very fact of being invited to participate in a research project may generate defensive caution or may be seen as an opportunity to proselytize. As telephone researchers are well aware, there is now broad sensitivity to such questions as, What group is sponsoring this research, and how will it use the results? In a metaphoric sense, we approach a condition not unlike that of contemporary physics. No longer are we studying independent individuals (social atoms); instead, we are entering a field of relationships in which we as researchers are integers. And, as with the Heisenberg effect, as we embark on our research we alter the composition of the field. To act as a researcher is inherently to perturb the system of relationships, and, much like the butterfly wing in China, the effects of research itself may give rise to multiple unanticipated events at a distance.

Further deliberation on these issues is essential, and we see three significant research vistas opening to the social scientist. The first grows from our preceding proposal for *establishing communities of dialogue*. If the subject matter of social research is in continuous motion, and our research inevitably alters the flow, then there is further reason to generate research sites of active dialogue. The Internet serves as a significant context for such inquiry. Consider, for example, the political configuration of the World Wide Web. Thousands of political, religious, ethnic, and value-centered groups now offer sites informing and inviting participation. One can join with neo-Nazis, the KKK, or Druids as easily as one can participate in the Democratic, Republican, or Reform Party. Yet, while each of these groups is essentially centripetal in form, inviting others into a relatively closed circle of reiterative meanings, there are virtually no efforts to generate dialogue across sites of meaning making. Particularly in the case of antagonistic groups, there is a vital need for productive dialogue. In our view, research undertakings that would foster on-line interchange across lines of difference would be salutary. Further, for many persons who cannot physically be in contact with others with whom they share vital interests, computer-mediated interchanges would be highly desirable. Again, the research community could actively generate such resources.

The development of *conduit methods*—that is, technological efforts bringing into public visibility the voices, opinions, needs, and aspirations of various marginalized or suppressed groups of the world—would also be favored. Such efforts are already evident in print media. Social researchers have been highly effective over the years in representing the voices and conditions of numerous subaltern groups in writing. Yet these contributions are typically written for a professional audience with circumscribed circulation. With the availability of the Internet, the potentials for rendering visibility and effective communication are exponentially increased. An ample illustration of these potentials is provided by the revolutionary grassroots movement in the Mexican state of Chiapas. This group could have been eradicated by the government militia, but their ability to take their case before a global audience through the Internet radically altered their political circumstances. Numerous groups throughout the world came to their aid, intense communication was directed toward Mexican government officials, and government policies were significantly restrained. It is precisely such efforts that current social sciences curricula should facilitate.

Finally, and most challengingly, the technological transformation currently taking place invites the creation of what may be viewed as *living laboratories*. That is, the technological conditions allow social experimentation on an unprecedented scale—the creation of new conditions of interchange that could provide a sense of possible futures or, indeed, achieve those futures in fact. Just as in the case of politics in Chiapas, the grassroots culture points the way. Internet technologies have now spawned the development of myriad cybercommunities (see, e.g., S. G. Jones, 1998; Markham, 1998; Porter, 1997) and sites where individuals may experiment with multiple identities or participate in new and imaginary ones (Rochlin, 1997; Turkle, 1995). As a research community, then, we are confronted with the possibility of moving from theoretical and political abstractions into the construction of virtual worlds that could shape the future. These virtual worlds could enable us to experiment with relational processes—such as forms of dialogue for reducing conflict, depression, or anomie—or, indeed, provide participants with new and growth-inviting experiences. In one relevant line of inquiry, the Dutch public administration scholar Paul Frissen and his colleagues work with policy makers concerned with how and whether the government should develop and enforce laws regarding Internet communication. Recognizing the rapid transformation taking place in the Internet world, Frissen and his colleagues have established a virtual community existing beyond the law of any particular nation. Without any public mandate, this community generates its own "laws" of Internet communication. Government officials are then invited into this world to speak with participants, sample the powers of the network, and explore its potentials as they unfold. It is through this immersion in this world—virtual yet potentially palpable in consequence—that both participants and policy makers enrich their perspectives (Gergen, 2000). In our view, the possibilities for creating experimental worlds are enormous.

Qualitative Methods and the Reconstruction of Self

Most qualitative methodologies are deeply infused with individualist conceptions and ideologies. To focus research on the individual's experience, feelings, identity, suffering, or life story, for example, is to presume the primacy of the individual mind. To employ methodology that attempts to give voice to "the other" is already to favor a metaphysics of self/other difference. Similarly, forms of representation that favor hierarchy and monologue tend toward reifying the "knowing one." Even the recognition of authorship on the research report constructs a world of separate, self-contained individuals. By and large, qualitative methods sustain a posture of methodological and ideological individualism. At the same time, as we have outlined above, with the influx of postmodern, constructionist, and dialogical formulations, we have become increasingly aware of the limitations—both conceptual and ideological—of the individualist tradition. Further, as many of the qualitative innovations begin to suggest, there are alternatives to this tradition. In our view, the most important of these alternatives may be termed *relational*. As our methodologies become increasingly sensitive to the relationship of researchers to their subjects as dialogical and co-constructive, the relationship of researchers to their audiences as interdependent, and the negotiation of meaning within any relationship as potentially ramifying outward into the society, individual agency ceases to be our major concern. We effectively create the reality of relational process.

It is thus that innovations in co-constructed narratives, multivoiced methods, participatory performance, conjoint and distributed representation, and participatory action research, for example, do far more than expand the methodological arena. Rather, in subverting methodological individualism they begin to generate a new form of consciousness. It is not the private mind that is celebrated, but integral connectivity. Dialogical methodologies nicely illustrate the point. For example, Mary Gergen (in press) introduced the topic of menopause to a discussion group of eight women as a means of counteracting the medical model of menopause and opening new spaces of meaning making. Through extended dialogue, the group generated new and more positive visions of the aging process. In a similar vein, Frigga Haug and her students (1987; Crawford, Kippax, Onyx, Gault, & Benton, 1992) arranged situations in which women shared their stories of their emotional development. Through their mutual dialogues and interpretive sessions, they were able to reconstruct their past and to generate a sense of how the culture creates femininity. In these cases the dialogue was circumscribed to the researcher/participants. To extend the preceding concern with research as relationship, one can see the potential for using research to generate dialogue that expands as it moves outward from the originary site. The goal of the research becomes one of inciting dialogue that may undergo continuous change as it moves through an extended network.

In our view, these are but beginning moves in what should become a new vocabulary of research methodology and ultimately a relational re-conceptualization of self. Such methodologies will become more integral to emerging concepts of communal memory, distributed cognition, and relational emotion. Invited will be concepts specifically illuminating the relational process out of which the very concept of individual mind emerges. With both practices and theory set in motion, the qualitative community may come to play a vital role in cultural transformation.

◆ Conclusion

In their introduction to the 1994 edition of the *Handbook of Qualitative Research,* Denzin and Lincoln aver that "we are in a new age where messy, uncertain, multivoiced texts, cultural criticisms, and new experimental works will become more common" (p. 15). At the same time, they suggest that "the field of qualitative research is defined by a series of tensions, con-tradictions, and hesitations" (p. 15). This analysis lends strong support to their prognoses. Along with the critique and experimentation, the ten-sions, contradictions, and hesitations they mention are present, but in our view, they are scarcely signs of deterioration. Rather, it is from within this matrix of uncertainty, where we are unceasingly crossing the boundaries of established enclaves—appropriating, reflecting, creating—that the vitality of qualitative inquiry is drawn. It is here that we locate the innovative power that is transforming the face of the social sciences. If we can avoid impulses toward elimination, the rage to order, and the desire for unity and singularity, we can anticipate the continued flourishing of qualitative inquiry, full of serendipitous incidents and generative expansions. In par-ticular, if we bear out the implications of the increasing centrality of rela-tionship over individuals—and realize these implications practically within the emerging spheres of technology—we may effectively participate in the reconstruction of the social sciences and alteration of the trajectories of the cultures in which we participate.

◆ Notes

1. For further discussion of these arguments and their implications for the social sci-ences, see Gergen (1994, 1999).

2. Michelle Fine (personal communication, 1998) questioned this line: "Are only feminism, Marxism, lesbian, gays . . . political? What happened to good old right-wing, mainstream, run-of-the-mill psychology—isn't that deeply political? Are the rules different with explicitly political (or left) work?"

◆ References

Anderson, E. (1978). *A place on the corner.* Chicago: University of Chicago Press.

Anderson, E. (1990). *Streetwise: Race, class, and change in an urban community.* Chicago: University of Chicago Press.

Anderson, E. (1999). *Code of the street.* New York: W. W. Norton.

Anderson, H. (1997). *Conversation, language, and possibilities: A postmodern approach to therapy.* New York: HarperCollins.

Austin, D. (1996). Kaleidoscope: The same and different. In C. Ellis & A. P. Bochner (Eds.), *Composing ethnography: Alternative forms of qualitative writing* (pp. 206-230). Walnut Creek, CA: AltaMira.

Banister, E. M. (1999). Evolving reflexivity: Negotiating meaning of women's midlife experience. *Qualitative Inquiry, 5,* 3-23.

Becker, C., Chasin, L., Chasin, R., Herzig, M., & Roth, S. (1995). From stuck debate to new conversation on controversial issues: A report from the Public Conversations Project. *Journal of Feminist Family Therapy, 7,* 143-163.

Behar, R. (1996). *The vulnerable observer: Anthropology that breaks your heart.* Boston: Beacon.

Behar, R., & Gordon, D. A. (Eds.). (1995). *Women writing culture.* Berkeley: University of California Press.

Belenky, M. F., Clinchy, B. M., Goldberger, N. R., & Tarule, J. M. (1986). *Women's ways of knowing: The development of self, voice, and mind.* New York: Basic Books.

Blumenfeld-Jones, D. S. (1995). Dance as a mode of research representation. *Qualitative Inquiry, 1,* 391-401.

Bohan, J. (Ed.). (1992). *Seldom seen, rarely heard: Women's place in psychology.* Boulder, CO: Westview.

Bohan, J. (1993). Regarding gender: Essentialism, constructionism, and feminist psychology. *Psychology of Women Quarterly, 17,* 5-21.

Braidotti, R. (1995). *Nomadic subjects: Embodiment and sexual difference in contemporary feminist theory.* New York: Columbia University Press.

Brown, L. M., & Gilligan, C. (1992). *Meeting at the crossroads: Women's psychology and girls' development.* Cambridge, MA: Harvard University Press.

Bruner, J. (1986). *Actual minds: Possible worlds.* Cambridge, MA: Harvard University Press.

Bruner, J. (1990). *Acts of meaning.* Cambridge, MA: Harvard University Press.

Butler, J. (1990). *Gender trouble: Feminism and the subversion of identity*. New York: Routledge.

Carlson, M. (1996). *Performance: A critical introduction*. New York: Routledge.

Case, S.-E. (1997). *The domain-matrix; Performing lesbian at the end of print culture*. Bloomington: Indiana University Press.

Case, S.-E., Brett, P., & Foster, S. L. (Eds.). (1995). *Cruising the performative: Interventions into the representation of ethnicity, nationality, and sexuality*. Bloomington: Indiana University Press.

Ceglowski, D. (in press). *Research as relationship*. New York: Teachers College Press.

Chasin, R., Herzig, M., Roth, S., Chasin, L., Becher, C., & Stains, R., Jr. (1996). From diatribe to dialogue on divisive public issues: Approaches drawn from family therapy. *Mediation Quarterly, 13*, 4.

Clark, C. D. (1996). Interviewing children in qualitative research: A show and tell. *Canadian Journal of Marketing Research, 15*, 74-78.

Clough, P. T. (1997). Autotelecommunication and autoethnography: A reading of Carolyn Ellis's *Final negotiations*. *Sociological Quarterly, 38*, 95-110.

Communication Studies 298. (1999). Shopping for family. *Qualitative Inquiry, 5*, 147-180.

Cooperrider, D. L. (1990). Positive image, positive action: The affirmative basis of organizing. In S. Srivastva & D. L. Cooperrider (Eds.), *Appreciative management and leadership: The power of positive thought and action in organizations*. San Francisco: Jossey-Bass.

Cooperrider, D. L., & Dutton, J. E. (Eds.). (1999). *Organizational dimensions of global change: No limits to cooperation*. Thousand Oaks, CA: Sage.

Crawford, J., Kippax, S., Onyx, J., Gault, U., & Benton, P. (1992). *Emotion and gender: Constructing meaning from memory*. London: Sage.

Crawford, M., & Kimmel, E. (Eds.). (1999). Innovative methods in feminist psychology [Special issue]. *Psychology of Women Quarterly, 23*(4).

Denzin, N. K. (1997). *Interpretive ethnography: Ethnographic practices for the 21st century*. Thousand Oaks, CA: Sage.

Denzin, N. K., & Lincoln, Y. S. (1994). Introduction: Entering the field of qualitative research. In N. K. Denzin & Y. S. Lincoln (Eds.), *Handbook of qualitative research* (pp. 1-17). Thousand Oaks, CA: Sage.

Diversi, M. (1998). Glimpses of street life: Representing lived experience through short stories. *Qualitative Inquiry, 4*, 131-147.

Donmoyer, R., & Yennie-Donmoyer, J. (1995). Data as drama: Reflections on the use of readers theater as a mode of qualitative data display. *Qualitative Inquiry, 1*, 402-428.

Ellis, C., & Bochner, A. P. (Eds.). (1996). *Composing ethnography: Alternative forms of qualitative writing*. Walnut Creek, CA: AltaMira.

Ellis, C., Kiesinger, C. E., & Tillmann-Healy, L. (1997). Interactive interviewing: Talking about emotional experience. In R. Hertz (Ed.), *Reflexivity and voice* (pp. 119-149). Thousand Oaks, CA: Sage.

Foucault, M. (1979). *Discipline and punish: The birth of the prison* (A. Sheridan, Trans.). New York: Vintage.

Foucault, M. (1980). *Power/knowledge: Selected interviews and other writings, 1972-1977* (C. Gordon, Ed.; L. Marshall, J. Mepham, & K. Soper, Trans.). New York: Pantheon.

Fox, K. V. (1996). Silent voices: A subversive reading of child sexual abuse. In C. Ellis & A. P. Bochner (Eds.), *Composing ethnography: Alternative forms of qualitative writing* (pp. 330-356). Walnut Creek, CA: AltaMira.

Franklin, M. B. (1997). Making sense: Interviewing and narrative representation. In M. Gergen & S. N. Davis (Eds.), *Toward a new psychology of gender* (pp. 99-116). New York: Routledge.

Garratt, D., & Hodkinson, P. (1998). Can there be criteria for selecting research criteria? A hermeneutical analysis of an inescapable dilemma. *Qualitative Inquiry, 4,* 515-539.

Georgi, A. (1994). *Phenomenology and psychological research.* Pittsburgh, PA: Duquesne University Press.

Gergen, K. J. (1994). *Realities and relationships: Soundings in social construction.* Cambridge, MA: Harvard University Press.

Gergen, K. J. (1997). Who speaks and who responds in the human sciences? *History of the Human Sciences, 10,* 151-173.

Gergen, K. J. (1999). *An invitation to social construction.* Thousand Oaks, CA: Sage.

Gergen, K. J. (2000). *The saturated self* (2nd ed.). New York: Perseus.

Gergen, K. J., & Gergen, M. M. (1991). From theory to reflexivity in research practice. In F. Steier (Ed.), *Method and reflexivity: Knowing as systemic social construction* (pp. 76-95). London: Sage.

Gergen, M. M. (1992). Life stories: Pieces of a dream. In G. Rosenwald & R. Ochberg (Eds.), *Storied lives* (pp. 127-144). New Haven, CT: Yale University Press.

Gergen, M. M. (in press). *Impious improvisations: Feminist reconstructions in psychology.* Thousand Oaks, CA: Sage.

Gergen, M. M., Chrisler, J. C., & LoCicero, A. (1999). Innovative methods: Resources for research, teaching and publishing. *Psychology of Women Quarterly, 23*(4).

Hammond, S. A. (1996). *The thin book of appreciative inquiry.* Plano, TX: CSS.

Hammond, S. A., & Royal, C. (Eds.). (1998). *Lessons from the field: Applying appreciative inquiry.* Plano, TX: Practical Press.

Haraway, D. J. (1988). Situated knowledges: The science question in feminism and the privilege of partial perspective. *Feminist Studies, 14,* 575-599.

Harding, S. (1986). *The science question in feminism.* Ithaca, NY: Cornell University Press.

Harding, S. (1991). *Whose science? Whose knowledge? Thinking from women's lives.* Ithaca, NY: Cornell University Press.

Haug, F., et al. (1987). *Female sexualization: A collective work of memory* (E. Carter, Trans.). New York: Verso.

Hermans, H. J. M., & Kempen, H. J. G. (1993). *The dialogical self: Meaning as movement.* New York: Academic Press.

Hertz, R. (Ed.). (1997). *Reflexivity and voice.* Thousand Oaks, CA: Sage.

hooks, b. (1990). *Yearning: Race, gender, and cultural politics.* Boston: South End.

Jacobs, M.-E., Munor, P., & Adams, N. (1995). Palimpsest: (Re)reading women's lives. *Qualitative Inquiry, 1,* 327-345.

Jipson, J., & Paley, N. (Eds.). (in press). *Daredevil research.* New York: Peter Lang.

Jones, S. G. (Ed.). (1998). *Cybersociety 2.0.* Thousand Oaks, CA: Sage.

Jones, S. H. (1998). Kaleidoscope notes: Writing women's music and organizational culture. *Qualitative Inquiry, 4,* 148-177.

Jones, S. H. (1999). Torch. *Qualitative Inquiry, 5,* 235-250.

Katz, A. M., & Shotter, J. (1996). Hearing the patient's "voice": Toward a social poetics in diagnostic interviews. *Social Science and Medicine, 43,* 919-931.

Kiesinger, C. E. (1998). From interview to story: Writing Abbie's life. *Qualitative Inquiry, 4,* 71-95.

Komesaroff, P., Rothfield, P., & Daly, J. (1997). *Reinterpreting menopause: Cultural and philosophical issues.* New York: Routledge.

Landrine, H. (Ed.). (1995). *Bringing cultural diversity to feminist psychology: Theory, research, and practice.* Washington, DC: American Psychological Association.

Lather, P. (1991). *Getting smart: Feminist research and pedagogy with/in the postmodern.* New York: Routledge.

Lather, P. (1993). Fertile obsession: Validity after poststructuralism. *Sociological Quarterly, 34,* 673-693.

Lather, P., & Smithies, C. (1997). *Troubling the angels: Women living with HIV/AIDS.* Boulder, CO: Westview.

Lincoln, Y. S. (1995). Emerging criteria for quality in qualitative and interpretive inquiry. *Qualitative Inquiry, 1,* 275-289.

Lincoln, Y. S. (1998). From understanding to action: New imperatives, new criteria, new methods for interpretive researchers. *Theory and Research in Social Education, 26,* 12-29.

Lincoln, Y. S., & Denzin, N. K. (1994). The fifth moment. In N. K. Denzin & Y. S. Lincoln (Eds.), *Handbook of qualitative research* (pp. 575-586). Thousand Oaks, CA: Sage.

Lykes, M. B. (1996). Meaning making in a context of genocide and silencing. In M. B. Lykes, A. Bánuazizi, R. Liem, & M. Morris (Eds.), *Myths about the powerless: Contesting social inequalities* (pp. 159-178). Philadelphia: Temple University Press.

Marcus, G. E. (1998). *Ethnography through thick and thin: A new research imaginary for anthropology's changing professional culture.* Princeton, NJ: Princeton University Press.

Markham, A. (1998). *Life online: Researching real experience in virtual space.* Thousand Oaks, CA: Sage.

McTaggart, R. (Ed.). (1997a). *Participatory action research: International contexts and consequences.* Albany: State University of New York Press.

McTaggart, R. (1997b). Reading the collection. In R. McTaggart (Ed.), *Participatory action research: International contexts and consequences* (pp. 1-24). Albany: State University of New York Press.

Mienczakowski, J. (1996). An ethnographic act: The construction of consensual theater. In C. Ellis & A. P. Bochner (Eds.), *Composing ethnography: Alternative forms of qualitative writing* (pp. 244-266). Walnut Creek, CA: AltaMira.

Miller, J. B., & Stiver, I. P. (1997). *The healing connection: How women form relationships in therapy and in life.* Boston: Beacon.

Morawski, J. G. (1994). *Practicing feminisms, reconstructing psychology: Notes on a liminal science.* Ann Arbor: University of Michigan Press.

Morris, R. C. (1995). All made up: Performance theory and the new anthropology of sex and gender. *Annual Review of Anthropology, 24,* 567-592.

Mouffe, C. (1993). Liberal socialism and pluralism: Which citizenship? In J. Squires (Ed.), *Principled positions: Postmodernism and the rediscovery of value.* London: Lawrence & Wishart.

Moustakas, C. (1994). *Phenomenological research methods.* Thousand Oaks, CA: Sage.

Penley, C., & Ross, A. (1985). Interview with Trinh T. Minh-ha. *Camera Obscura, 13-14,* 87-103.

Porter, D. (Ed.). (1997). *Internet culture.* New York: Routledge.

Reason, P. (1994). Three approaches to participative inquiry. In N. K. Denzin & Y. S. Lincoln (Eds.), *Handbook of qualitative research* (pp. 324-339). Thousand Oaks, CA: Sage.

Reinharz, S. (1992). *Feminist methods in social research.* New York: Oxford University Press.

Ribbens, J., & Edwards, R. (Eds.). (1998). *Feminist dilemmas in qualitative research: Public knowledge and private lives.* Thousand Oaks, CA: Sage.

Richardson, L. (1997). *Fields of play: Constructing an academic life.* New Brunswick, NJ: Rutgers University Press.

Richardson, L. (1998). Meta-jeopardy. *Qualitative Inquiry, 4,* 464-468.

Rinehart, R. (1998). Fictional methods in ethnography: Believability, specks of glass, and Chekhov. *Qualitative Inquiry, 4,* 200-224.

Rochlin, G. I. (1997). *Trapped in the Net: The unanticipated consequences of computerization.* Princeton, NJ: Princeton University Press.

Ronai, C. R. (1998). Sketching with Derrida: An ethnography of a researcher/erotic dancer. Qualitative Inquiry, 4, 405-420.

Ronai, C. R. (1999). The next night *sou rature:* Wrestling with Derrida's mimesis. *Qualitative Inquiry, 5,* 114-129.

Russell, G. M., & Bohan, J. S. (1999). Hearing voices: The use of research and the politics of change. *Psychology of Women Quarterly, 23*(4).

Said, E. W. (1978). *Orientalism.* New York: Pantheon.

Sarbin, T. (Ed.). (1986). *Narrative psychology: The storied nature of human conduct.* New York: Praeger.

Smith, L. T. (in press). *De-colonizing methodology: Research and indigenous peoples.* London: Zed.

Smith, P. (1999). Food truck's party hat. *Qualitative Inquiry, 5,* 244-262.

Smyth, A. (1991). The floozie in the jacuzzi: The problematics of culture and identity for an Irish woman. *Feminist Studies, 17,* 7-28.

Strauss, A. L., & Corbin, J. (1990). *Basics of qualitative research: Grounded theory procedures and techniques.* Newbury Park, CA: Sage.

Strauss, A. L., & Corbin, J. (1994). Grounded theory methodology: An overview. In N. K. Denzin & Y. S. Lincoln (Eds.), *Handbook of qualitative research* (pp. 273-285). Thousand Oaks, CA: Sage.

Tierney, W. G., & Lincoln, Y. S. (Eds.). (1997). *Representation and the text: Reframing the narrative voice.* Albany: State University of New York Press.

Travisano, R. V. (1998). On becoming Italian American: An autobiography of an ethnic identity. *Qualitative Inquiry, 4,* 540-563.

Turkle, S. (1995). *Life on the screen: Identity in the age of the Internet.* New York: Simon & Schuster.

Van Maanen, J. (Ed.). (1995). *Representation in ethnography.* Thousand Oaks, CA: Sage.

Visweswaran, K. (1994). *Fictions of feminist ethnography.* Minneapolis: University of Minnesota Press.

14

The Seventh Moment

Out of the Past

Yvonna S. Lincoln and Norman K. Denzin

◆ As we have argued in our conclusion to the first edition of the
Handbook of Qualitative Research, writing the present is always
dangerous, a biased project conditioned by distorted readings of the past
and utopian hopes for the future. In what follows we once again sketch our
hopeful vision of the future of qualitative research. This vision is based on
our reading of the seventh moment. We begin by delineating the central
characteristics of this moment and the problems that define it. We conclude with predictions about the seventh moment based on our readings of
the present.[1]

Four theses organize our discussion. First, as we have repeatedly observed, the history of qualitative research is defined more by breaks and
ruptures than by a clear, evolutionary, progressive movement from one
stage to the next. These breaks and ruptures move in cycles and phases, so
that what is passé today may be in vogue a decade from now, and vice
versa. Just as the postmodern, for example, reacts to the modern, some-
day there may well be a retro-postmodern phase that extols Boas, Mead,
Benedict, Strauss, Becker, Goffman, and the Chicago school and finds the
current postexperimental, "messy" moment flawed and unacceptable.

Our second assumption builds on the tensions that now define qualitative research. There is an elusive center emerging in this contradictory, tension-riddled enterprise. We seem to be moving farther and farther away from grand narratives and single, overarching ontological, epistemological, and methodological paradigms. The center lies in the humanistic commitment of the qualitative researcher to study the world always from the perspective of the gendered, historically situated, interacting individual. From this complex commitment flows the liberal and radical politics of qualitative research. Action, feminist, clinical, constructionist, cultural studies, queer, and critical race theory researchers are all united on this point. They all share the belief that a politics of liberation must always begin with the perspective, desires, and dreams of those individuals and groups who have been oppressed by the larger ideological, economic, and political forces of a society or a historical moment.

This commitment defines an ever-present, but shifting, center in the discourses of qualitative research. The center shifts as new, previously oppressed or silenced voices enter the discourse. Thus, for example, feminists and critical race researchers have articulated their own relationship to the postpositivist, poststructuralist, and critical paradigms. These new articulations then refocus and redefine previous ontologies, epistemologies, and methodologies, including empiricism, postpositivism, and postmodernism.

Third, we anticipate a continued performance turn in qualitative inquiry, with more and more writers performing their texts for others. As ethnographic stagings, performances are always "enmeshed in moral matters" (Conquergood, 1985, p. 2). Such performances ask audiences to take a stand on the performances and their meanings and, indeed, to join the performances and the creation of meaning. In these productions, performers and the audience members become cultural critics. If culture is an ongoing performance, then performers bring the spaces, meanings, ambiguities, and contradictions of culture critically alive in their performances (Conquergood, 1985). The performed text is one of qualitative research's last frontiers. It is a version of Victor Turner's (1986, p. 25) "liminal space," an old, but new, border to be crossed. When fully embraced, this crossing will forever transform qualitative research methodology. It will serve, at the same time, to redefine the meanings of this project in its other moments and formations.

Fourth, the future, the seventh moment, is concerned with moral discourse, and with the development of sacred textualities. The seventh moment asks that the social sciences and the humanities become sites for critical conversations about democracy, race, gender, class, nation, freedom, and community.

These four theses suggest that only the broad outlines of the future, the seventh moment, can be predicted. Returning to our opening metaphor of the bridge, we seek to outline a project that connects the past with the present and the future. In charting this future, we group our discussion around the following themes, or issues: text and voice; the existential, sacred performance text; the return to narrative as a political act; text, reflexivity, and being vulnerable in the text; and inquiry as a moral act, ethics, and critical moral consciousness. These are the hallmarks of the sixth and seventh moments.

◆ Defining the Present

Recall our definition of this sprawling field. Slightly rephrased, it reads:

> Qualitative research is an interdisciplinary, transdisciplinary, and sometimes counterdisciplinary field. It crosscuts the humanities, the social sciences, and the physical sciences. Qualitative research is many things at the same time. It is multiparadigmatic in focus. Its practitioners are sensitive to the value of the multimethod approach. They are committed to the naturalistic perspective and to the interpretive understanding of human experience. At the same time, the field is inherently political and shaped by multiple ethical and political allegiances.
>
> Qualitative research embraces two tensions at the same time. On the one hand, it is drawn to a broad, interpretive, postexperimental, postmodern, feminist, and critical sensibility. On the other hand, it is shaped to more narrowly defined positivist, postpositivist, humanistic, and naturalistic conceptions of human experience and its analysis.

In the seventh moment all of these tensions will continue to operate as the field confronts and continues to define itself in the face of six fundamental issues that are embedded in these tensions.

The first issue involves the collapse of foundationalism. The present moment is characterized, in part, by a continuing critique of postpositivism and by poststructuralism and postmodernism. This critique is coupled with ongoing self-criticism and self-appraisal. Every contributor to this volume has reflectively wrestled with the location of his or her topic in the present moment, discussing its relationship to postpositivist and anti-foundational formulations.

On this, Smith and Deemer (Volume 3, Chapter 12) remind us that the "demise of empiricism" created a new space for human interpretation and, in turn, for new criteria for judging and honoring human knowledge in all its forms. As Smith and Deemer make clear, relativism is not about paradigm choice; it is about the way we are in the world, about living contingent lives, about having to find new rationales for the judgments we make, because absolutes and foundationalist principles are little more than smoke and mirrors.

The second and third issues are what we have called the crises of representation and legitimation. These two crises speak, respectively, to the Other and the representation of the Other in our texts and to the authority we claim for our texts. Although these crises have circulated widely for two decades, their critiques have only recently reached full flower. Fourth, there is the continued emergence of a cacophony of voices speaking with varying agendas from specific gender, race, class, ethnic, and Third World perspectives.

Fifth, throughout its history, qualitative research has been defined in terms of shifting scientific, moral, sacred, and religious discourses. Vidich and Lyman clearly establish this fact in the history of colonial ethnography that they present in Chapter 2 of this volume. Since the Enlightenment, science and religion have been separated, but only at the ideological level, for in practice, as Vidich and Lyman argue, religion has constantly informed science and the scientific project. The divisions between these two systems of meaning are becoming more and more blurred. Critics increasingly see science from within a magical, interpretive framework (Rosaldo, 1989, p. 219), whereas others imagine a sacred epistemology (Bateson, 1979). Others are moving science away from its empiricist foundations and closer to a critical, interpretivist project that stresses ethics and moral standards of evaluation (Clough, 1992, pp. 136-137; see also Clough, 1998). Sixth, conceptualizing inquiry as a moral act returns our dialogue to the topics of ethics, vulnerability, and truth.

To summarize: The tensions that surround these six issues and the strategies that are developed to address them will continue to define the center and the margins of qualitative research well into the first decade of the 21st century. We begin with a discussion of the present.

◆ Coping With the Present

Of the following, we continue to be certain:

◆ The qualitative researcher is not an objective, authoritative, politically neutral observer standing outside and above the text.

◆ The qualitative researcher is "historically positioned and locally situated [as] an all-too-human [observer] of the human condition" (Bruner, 1993, p. 1).

◆ Meaning is "radically plural, always open, and . . . there is politics in every account" (Bruner, 1993, p. 1).

◆ Qualitative inquiry is properly conceptualized as a civic, participatory, collaborative project. This joins the researcher and the researched in an ongoing moral dialogue.

These certainties shape the questions we have listed in our introduction to Part III.

Correcting Excesses and Revisiting the Past

This moment addresses these certainties in three ways. First, it continues to sharpen the above critique while, second, it attempts to correct its excesses. Qualitative research, like other scholarly domains, displays a tendency to move from one intellectual fashion to another, from critical race theory to queer theory, from semiotics to poststructuralism, from postmodernism to posthumanism, and so on. In such moves there is often a tendency to reject wholesale entire theoretical perspectives, or paradigms, as if postpositivism were passé, for example. It should not work this way. There is a real need to return, as Bruner (1993) argues, to "the originals of out-of-fashion texts" (p. 24). Such a return is necessary for two reasons: First, we need to relearn these texts and see if standard criticisms of them still hold today; second, we need to study the best works from these traditions so as to understand how the masters in a given "passé" perspective in fact did their work.

It must be noted that revisiting works from earlier historical moments operates at different levels of abstraction. Although colonialist, positivist ethnography may be passé, the basic strategies and techniques of case studies, ethnographies, observation, interviewing, and textual analysis still form the basis for sixth- and seventh-moment research. In a parallel vein,

615

although certain of the assumptions of the grounded theory approach may be criticized, the generic method of building interpretations up out of observations and interactions with the world will not change.

Third, as we have argued in the first edition of this *Handbook*, it is time to get on with the multidisciplinary project called qualitative research. Too much critique will stifle this project. This critique, it must be noted, assumes two forms, and both can be counterproductive. Endless self-referential criticisms by the poststructuralist can produce mountains of texts, with few referents to concrete human experience. Such are not needed. The same conclusion holds for positivist and postpositivist criticisms of poststructuralism (and the responses to these criticisms). These criticisms and exchanges can operate at a level of abstraction, with opposing sides preaching to the already converted. No dialogue occurs, and the discourse does little to help the people who seek to engage the world empirically.

The basic issue is simple: How best to describe and interpret the experiences of other peoples and cultures? The problems of representation and legitimation flow from this commitment.

The Crisis of Representation

As indicated above, this crisis asks the questions, Who is the Other? Can we ever hope to speak authentically of the experience of the Other, or an Other? And if not, how do we create a social science that includes the Other? The short answer to these questions is that we move to including the Other in the larger research processes that we have developed. For some, this means participatory, or collaborative, research and evaluation efforts (see in this volume Greenwood & Levin, Chapter 3; Ladson-Billings, Chapter 9; in Volume 2, Kemmis & McTaggart, Chapter 11; Miller & Crabtree, Chapter 12; and in Volume 3, Greene, Chapter 16; Rist, Chapter 17). These activities can occur in a variety of institutional sites, including clinical, educational, corporate, and social welfare settings.

For others, it means a form of liberatory investigation wherein Others are trained to engage in their own social and historical interrogative efforts and then are assisted in devising answers to questions of historical and contemporary oppression that are rooted in the values and cultural artifacts that characterize their communities. In Volume 2, Kemmis and McTaggart (Chapter 11) and in Volume 3, Greene (Chapter 16) discuss various strategies for undertaking such inquiries, including the major different forms of participatory action and evaluation research.

For yet other social scientists, including the Other means becoming coauthors in narrative adventures. And for still others, it means constructing what are called "experimental," or "messy," texts where multiple voices speak (see in Volume 3 Ellis & Bochner, Chapter 6; Richardson, Chapter 14), often in conflict, and where readers are left to sort out which experiences speak to their personal lives. For still others, it means presenting to the inquiry and policy community a series of autohistories, personal narratives, lived experiences, poetic representations, and sometimes fictive and/or fictional texts (see in Volume 2 Tierney, Chapter 9; Beverley, Chapter 10; Richardson, Volume 3, Chapter 14) that allow the Other to speak for her- or himself. The inquirer or evaluator becomes merely the connection joining the field text, the research text, and the consuming community in making certain that such voices are heard. Sometimes, increasingly, it is the Institutionalized Other who speaks, especially as the Other gains access to the knowledge-producing corridors of power and achieves *entrée* into the particular group of elites known as intellectuals and academics or faculty. In Chapter 9 of this volume, Gloria Ladson-Billings elaborates the issues that are involved when this happens.

The point is that both the Other and more mainstream social scientists recognize that there is no such thing as unadulterated truth; that speaking from a faculty, an institution of higher education, or a corporate perspective automatically means speaking from a privileged and powerful vantage point; and that this vantage point is one to which many do not have access, through either social station or education.

Virginia Olesen (Chapter 8) speaks of the difficulties involved in representing the experiences of the Other about whom texts are written. Writing from a critical feminist perspective, she argues that a major contradiction exists in this project, despite the qualitative researcher's desire to engage in egalitarian research characterized by authenticity, reciprocity, and trust. This is so because actual differences of power, knowledge, and structural mobility still exist in the researcher-subject relationship. The subject is always at grave risk of manipulation and betrayal by the ethnographer. In addition, there is the crucial fact that the final product is too often controlled by the researcher, no matter how much it has been modified or influenced by the subject. Thus even when research is written from the perspective of the Other—for example, women writing about women—the women doing the writing may perpetuate the very power relations they most oppose. A proper feminist solution requires a merger of politics with collaborative, participatory scholarship.

The Author's Place in the Text

The feminist solution clarifies the issue of the author's place in the interpretations that are written. This problem is directly connected to the problem of representation. It is often phrased in terms of a false dichotomy—that is, "the extent to which the personal self should have a place in the scientific scholarly text" (Bruner, 1993, p. 2). This false division between the personal and the ethnographic self rests on the assumption that it is possible for an author to write a text that does not bear the traces of its author. Of course, this is impossible. As Geertz (1988) has demonstrated, all texts are personal statements.

The correct phrasing of this issue turns on the amount of the personal, subjective, poetic self that is openly given in the text. As Ellis and Bochner (Volume 3, Chapter 6) and Richardson (Volume 3, Chapter 14) observe, there are many ways to return the author openly to the qualitative research text. Fictional narratives of the self may be written. Performance texts can be produced. Dramatic readings can be given. Field interviews can be transformed into poetic texts and poetry; short stories and plays can be written as well (McCall, Volume 2, Chapter 4). The author can engage in a dialogue with those studied. The author may write through a narrator, "directly as a character . . . or through multiple characters, or one character may speak in many voices, or the writer may come in and then go out of the [text]" (Bruner, 1993, p. 6).

The Crisis of Legitimation

It is clear that critical race theory, queer theory, and feminist arguments are moving farther and farther away from postpositivist models of validity and textual authority. This is the crisis of legitimation that follows the collapse of foundational epistemologies. This so-called crisis arose when anthropologists and other social scientists addressed the authority of the text. By *the authority of the text* we reference the claim any text makes to being accurate, true, and complete—a "God's-eye view." Is a text, that is, faithful to the context and the individuals it is supposed to represent? Does the text have the right to assert that it is a report to the larger world that addresses not only the researcher's interests, but also the interests of those studied?

This is not an illegitimate set of questions, and it affects all of us and the work that we do. Although social scientists might enter the question from many different angles, all of them confront these twin crises.

◆ A Bridge Into the Future: Toward a Sacred Discourse

We imagine a form of qualitative inquiry in the 21st century that is simultaneously minimal, existential, autoethnographic, vulnerable, performative, and critical. This form of inquiry erases traditional distinctions among epistemology, ethics, and aesthetics; nothing is value-free. It seeks to ground the self in a sense of the sacred, to connect the ethical, respectful self dialogically to nature and the worldly environment (Christians, 1995, p. 129). It seeks to embed this self in deeply storied histories of sacred spaces and local places, to illuminate the unity of the self in its relationship to the reconstructed, moral, and sacred natural world (see Abram, 1996, p. 269; Christians, 1998, p. 3; Kittredge, 1996, p. 4; Macnaghten & Urry, 1998, p. 7). This model of inquiry seeks a sacred epistemology that recognizes the essential ethical unity of mind and nature (Bateson, 1972, pp. 336-337; Bateson, 1979, p. 213; Bateson & Bateson, 1987, pp. 8-9, 11; Christians, 1998, p. 3). A sacred, existential epistemology places us in a noncompetitive, nonhierarchical relationship to the earth, to nature, and to the larger world (Bateson, 1972, p. 335; Reason, 1993). This sacred epistemology is political, presuming a feminist, communitarian moral ethic stressing the values of empowerment, shared governance, care, solidarity, love, community, covenant, morally involved observers, and civic transformation (Denzin, 1997, p. 275; Lincoln, 1995, p. 287).

This epistemology recovers the moral values that were excluded by the Enlightenment science project (Christians, 1997, p. 6). This sacred epistemology, as we have argued in our introduction to Part I, is based on a philosophical anthropology that declares, "All humans are worthy of dignity and sacred status without exception for class or ethnicity" (Christians, 1995, p. 129; see also Christians, 1997, p. 13; 1998, p. 6). A universal human ethic emphasizing the sacredness of life, human dignity, truth telling, and nonviolence (Christians, 1997, pp. 12-15) derives from this position. This sacred epistemology interrogates the ways in which race, class, and gender operate as important systems of oppression in the world today (Collins, 1990, p. 227; West, 1989).

After Behar (1996) and Jackson (1998), this project works outward from those moments of existential crisis in the culture, from those moments that affirm the truth that says humans must have "some say in the world into which they are thrown, that they must in some measure choose their own lives and feel that they have a right to be here, to be free to make a difference" (Jackson, 1998, p. 3). This is an ethnography that interrogates and illuminates those interactional moments when humans come together in their struggles over love, loss, pain, joy, shame, violence, betrayal, dignity; those instances "when self and other are constituted in mutuality and acceptance rather than violence and contempt" (Jackson, 1998, p. 208).

This is interpretive scholarship that refuses to retreat to abstractions and high theory. It is a way of being in the world that avoids jargon and incomprehensible discourse. It celebrates the local, the sacred, the act of constructing meaning. Viewing culture as a complex process of improvisation, it seeks to understand how people enact and construct meaning in their daily lives. It celebrates autoethnography, the personal account, "mystories," myth, and folklore.

This is a return to narrative as a political act (Jackson, 1998, p. 35), a minimal ethnography with political teeth. It asks how power is exercised in concrete human relationships, understanding that power means empowerment, the give-and-take of scarce material resources. The play of power in daily lives is best revealed in performance texts, in narrative accounts that tell stories about how humans experience moral community.

Here is an example from one of the stories ("An Island in the Stream") Michael Jackson (1998) tells in his recent book. It is about a man named Desmond, a "wiry, weather-beaten man in bare feet . . . part aboriginal" (p. 196), who lives on an island in the middle of a river. One Sunday, Jackson, his wife (Francine), and his two children (Heidi and Joshua) call on Desmond. As Jackson relates, they are sitting in the middle of the buffalo grass near Desmond's hut. Desmond is rolling a cigarette. Heidi asks him if he would prefer a tailor-made, and she tosses him her pack of Winfields and cigarette lighter. Desmond has to lean forward to pick up the cigarettes and lighter. As he does so, he snaps, "Don't throw things at me! Don't treat me like a dog! Don't make me take them. If you meant to give them to me you should have got up and put them in my hand. Then I would have received them gladly. . . . Do you know what I say to people at the mission? I say to them, 'Name me one white person who has ever done anything for you?' "

Jackson replies, "We're whites."

Desmond retorts, "Well, you might be okay. I don't know. You might have an ulterior motive here, I don't know" (pp. 198-199).

It can be argued that Desmond believed that Jackson and Heidi (as whites) were denying him some degree of control and dignity in his life. Clearly, he felt that whites routinely did this to Aboriginals.

With Jackson (1998, p. 204), West (1989, p. 233), Collins (1990, pp. 226-227), and Du Bois (1903/1989, p. 9), we seek a redemptive, pragmatically prophetic, existential ethnography, a vulnerable scholarship that shows us how to act morally, in solidarity, with passion, with dignity; to engage the world and its dispossessed in complementary, not competitive or destructive, ways. Such an ethnography moves from the researcher's biography to the biographies of others, to those rare moments when our lives connect, as when Jackson's daughter gives Desmond her cigarettes.

This project asks that we make ourselves visible in our texts. Each of us is a universal singular, universalizing in our singularity the crises and experiences of our historical epoch (Sartre, 1981, p. ix). In this way, this version of the social sciences attempts to inscribe and represent the human crises of a specific culture. It endeavors to connect those crises to the public sphere, to the media, and to the apparatuses of the culture that commodify the personal, turning it into political, public spectacle: a movie of the week about this or that personal trouble.

In so doing, this ethnography attempts to understand more fully the conditions of oppression and commodification that operate in the culture, seeking to make these ways of the world more visible to others. The moral ethnographer searches for those moments when humans resist these structures of oppression and representation and attempt, in the process, to take control over their lives and the stories about them. Consider Ralph Ellison's (1964, pp. 307-308) interrogations of the image of the American Negro as given in the work of Robert E. Park. Park (1918/1950) states:

> The Negro has always been interested rather in expression than in action; interested in life itself rather than in its reconstruction or reformation. The Negro is by natural disposition, neither an intellectual nor an idealist, like the Jew; nor a brooding introspective, like the East Indian; nor a pioneer and frontiersman, like the Anglo-Saxon. He is primarily an artist, loving life

for its own sake. His metier is expression rather than action. He is, so to speak, the lady among the races. (p. 280)

Ellison (1964) responds:

Park's metaphor is so pregnant with mixed motives as to birth a thousand compromises and indecisions. Imagine the effect such teachings have had upon Negro students alone! Thus what started as part of a democratic attitude, ends not only uncomfortably close to the preachings of Sumner, but to those of Dr. Goebbels as well. (p. 308)

An existential, interpretive form of qualitative inquiry offers a blueprint for cultural criticism. This criticism is grounded in the specific worlds made visible in the ethnography. It understands that all ethnography is theory and value laden. There can be no value-free ethnography, no objective, dispassionate, value-neutral account of a culture and its ways (see Volume 3, Smith & Deemer, Chapter 12). Taking a lead from mid-century African American cultural critics (Du Bois, Hurston, Ellison, Wright, Baldwin, Hines), it is presumed that the ethnographic, the aesthetic, and the political can never be neatly separated. Ethnography, like art, is always political. It speaks to and for its historical moment as a political reflection.

Accordingly, after Ford (1950/1998), a critical, literary ethnography is one that must meet four criteria. It must evidence a mastery of literary craft, the art of good writing. It should present a well-plotted, compelling, but minimalist narrative, based on realistic, natural conversation, with a focus on memorable, recognizable characters. These characters should be located in well-described, "unforgettable scenes" (Ford, 1950/1998, p. 1112). Second, the work should articulate clearly identifiable cultural and political issues, including injustices based on the structures and meanings of race, class, gender, and sexual orientation. Third, the work should articulate a politics of hope. It should criticize how things are and imagine how they could be different. Finally, it should do all this through direct and indirect symbolic and rhetorical means. Writers who do these things are fully immersed in the oppressions and injustices of their time. They direct their ethnographic energies to higher, utopian, morally sacred goals.

Such work is vulnerable precisely at that moment when it makes its values and criticisms public, when it risks taking sides, aligning itself with one political and moral position and not another. This is a political vulnerability that goes beyond Behar's (1996, p. 177) call for an anthropology that breaks your heart. It is more than writing that inserts the personal into the ethnographic. It is more than stories that move others to tears, more than first-person narratives that turn the self and its experiences into the site of inquiry (Behar, 1996, pp. 19, 167). It is more than autoethnography born of regret, fear, self-loathing, and anger.

This is writing that angers and sorrows the reader, writing that challenges the reader to take action in the world, to reconsider the conditions under which the moral terms of the self and community are constituted. This critical vulnerability dares to use the particular and the personal as vehicles for criticizing the status quo. Thus Ellison moves from his own experiences to criticize Park's theory of race relations in America. In the same way, Jackson presents Desmond's refusal of Heidi's cigarettes as an instance of perceived cultural prejudice toward Aboriginals.

Behar's vulnerability, on the other hand, is a modernist emotion. It is a product of an age that insists on maintaining a division between private troubles and public issues. Behar's self becomes vulnerable when its private experiences, fears, and doubts are made public. Her vulnerability presumes a gendered, multilayered self hiding behind many masks; it is a self with much to lose if it displays too much emotion. But it is not clear what Behar's term, *vulnerability,* means in an age when little is hidden, or invisible, as in the postmodern moment. How does vulnerability operate when freedom means only that there is "nothing left to lose," as Kris Kristofferson argues in his famous road song "Me and Bobbie McGee"? The existentially vulnerable researcher no longer has anywhere left to hide. The insertion of personal tales into the ethnographic text becomes a moot issue. The writing self is now called to a higher purpose, to use its experiences for social criticism, for imagining new configurations of the morally sacred self.

A vulnerable, performative ethnography moves in three directions at the same time. On the one hand, it represents *a call to action and morally informed social criticism.* Second, in so doing, it *asks the ethnographer always to connect good and bad stories to the circumstances of the media (and media representations), to history, culture, and political economy.* This structural move introduces another layer into the account. In connecting the personal to the historical, the political, and the representational, the writer contextualizes the story being told. This pinpoints local conditions that require change, and thereby provides the grounds for moving from the particular (the singular) to the universal.

In this move, the writer produces "mystory" accounts—multimedia, personal texts grafted onto scholarly, scientific, media, and popular culture discourses (Denzin, 1997, p. 116; Ulmer, 1989; White, Mogilka, & Slack, 1998). These mystory texts function as personal mythologies, improvised (and rehearsed) public performance stories. These narratives begin with the sting of personal memory, epiphanies, and existential crises in the person's biography. The writer moves from these moments into critical readings of those personal, community, popular, and expert systems of discourse that offer interpretations of such experiences. From these critical rereadings, the author fashions a mystory. In these tellings the writer claims ownership over a story previously interpreted from within other systems of discourse. These interpretations are, accordingly, replaced by empowerment narratives suited to personal, political, and community purposes.

The truth of these new texts is determined pragmatically, by their truth effects; by the critical, moral discourse they produce; by the "empathy they generate, the exchange of experience they enable, and the social bonds they mediate" (Jackson, 1998, p. 180). The power of these texts is not a question of whether "they mirror the world as it 'really' is" (Jackson, 1998, p. 180). The world is always already constructed through narrative texts. Rorty (1979) is firm on this point. There is no mirror of nature. The world as it is known is constructed through acts of representation and interpretation.

Third, this performative ethnography *searches for new ways to locate and represent the gendered, sacred self in its ethical relationships to nature.* It seeks an exploration of other forms of writing, including personal diaries, nature writing, and performance texts anchored in the natural world (Berry, 1981; Hasselstrom, Collier, & Curtis, 1997, p. xv; Rawlins, 1994; Stegner, 1980; Turner, 1986). These texts, written in the first-person voice, from the point of view of the ethnographer, focus on performance and experience as the sites of meaning. (As the emphasis on performance implies, there is little attempt to enter the minds of other people, to argue about what a performance means for the other person.)

A sacred ethnography celebrates the small performance rituals that bring us together in the natural world. This project understands that in these moments we become something more than our everyday lives allow. Thus an interpretive ethnography for the next century endeavors to ennoble this all-too-human project called making culture together. These moments display the sacredness of the organization of the natural and cultural world (Bateson & Bateson, 1987, p. 9). They show us how to enact the sacred, existential epistemology discussed above.

And so we must learn how to enact an enabling, interpretive ethnography, an ethnography that aspires to higher, sacred goals. We can scarcely afford to do otherwise. We are at a critical crossroads in the histories of our disciplines and our nation (Lincoln, 1998). Cornel West (1994) reminds us that "we simply cannot enter the twenty-first century at each other's throats" (p. 159). But with West we must ask, "Do we have the intelligence, humor, imagination, courage, tolerance, love, respect, and will to meet the challenge?" (p. 159).

◆ The Crisis of Vocality: New and Old Voices Coping With the Present

A variety of new and old voices—those of critical theory, feminist, ethnic, and other scholars—have also entered the present situation, offering solutions to the crises and problems we have identified above. The move is toward pluralism, and many social scientists now recognize that no picture is ever complete—that we need to employ many perspectives, hear many voices, before we can achieve deep understandings of social phenomena and before we can assert that a narrative is complete.

The modernist dream of a grand or master narrative is now a dead project. The recognition of the futility and oppression of such a project is the postmodern condition. The postmodern project challenges the modernist belief in (and desire to develop) a progressive program for incorporating all the cultures of the world under a single umbrella. The postmodern era is defined, in part, by the belief that there has been no single umbrella in the history of the world that might incorporate and represent fairly the dreams, aspirations, and experiences of all peoples.

Critical Theorists

The critical theorists, from the Frankfurt to the Annales, world-system, and participatory action research schools, continue to be a major presence in qualitative research, as Kincheloe and McLaren observe in Chapter 10 of this volume. The critique and concern of the critical theorists has been

an effort to design a pedagogy of resistance within communities of difference. The pedagogy of resistance, of taking back "voice," of reclaiming
narrative for one's own rather than adapting to the narratives of a dominant majority, was most explicitly laid out by Paolo Freire in his work with
adults in Brazil. His work is echoed most faithfully by a group of activist
priests and scholars who are exploring "liberation theology"—the joining
of the Catholic Church to egalitarian ends for the purposes of overturning
oppression and achieving social justice through empowerment of the
marginalized, the poor, the nameless, the voiceless. Their program is nothing less than the radical restructuring of society toward the ends of
reclaiming historic cultural legacies, social justice, the redistribution of
power, and the achievement of truly democratic societies.

Feminist Researchers

The feminists have argued that there is a missing voice, and a missing
picture, in the history of the sciences, religion, and the arts. Three different groups—feminist philosophers, scientists, and theologians—are represented in this discourse. Each has had an unsettling—if not unnerving—
effect on arguments about how we "do" qualitative research.

The first two groups—the philosophers and the scientists—have
mounted two separate, but related, arguments. The first argument is that
traditional science has acted to maintain the Enlightenment dualism, with
its major premise that there is a separate and distinct "social reality," "out
there" somewhere, separated from those who experience it, and that it is
the scientist's job to uncover this separate reality and report on it, for that
is the essence of "Truth."

Poststructural feminists urge the abandonment of any distinction between empirical science and social criticism. That is, they seek a morally
informed social criticism that is not committed to the traditional concerns
or criteria of empirical science. This traditional science, they argue, rests a
considerable amount of its authority on the ability to make public what has
traditionally been understood to be private (Clough, 1992, p. 137). Feminists dispute this distinction. They urge a social criticism that takes back
from science the traditional authority to inscribe and create subjects
within the boundaries and frameworks of an objective social science. This
social criticism "gives up on data collection and instead offers rereadings
of representations in every form of information processing, empirical

science, literature, film, television, and computer simulation" (Clough, 1992, p. 137).

A second set of feminist philosophers notes distinct problems with several of the scientific method's most basic premises: the idea that scientific objectivity is possible, the effect that the mandate for objectivity has on the subjects of research, and the possibility of conducting unbiased science at all. Olesen reviews these arguments, which explicate the disastrous consequences of objectifying the targets, subjects, and participants of our research, in Chapter 8 of this volume.

Liberation and feminist theologians are central to this new discourse. They ask hard questions, including, Where and what are the places of women, persons of color, the poor, the homeless, and the hungry, in the church, in science, in art, and literature?

Critical Race and Queer Theory Scholars

There is yet another group of concerned scholars determining the course of qualitative research; these are the critical race and queer theory scholars, who examine the question of whether history has deliberately silenced and/or misrepresented them and their cultures. The members of this new generation of scholars, many of them persons of color, challenge both historical and contemporary social scientists on the accuracy, veracity, and authenticity of the latter's work, contending that no picture can be considered final when the perspectives and narratives of so many are missing or distorted to serve dominant majority interests. The results of such challenges have been twofold: First has been the reconsideration of the Western canon, and second has been an increase in the number of historical and scientific works that recognize and reconstruct the perspectives of those whose perspectives and constructions have been for so long missing. Gloria Ladson-Billings outlines this literature and its major moments, figures, and arguments in Chapter 9 of this volume. She offers a scathing criticism of traditional science and its inability to speak to these questions.

Thus have we written the present, the sixth moment. It is a messy moment, full of multiple voices, experimental texts, breaks, ruptures, crises of legitimation and representation, self-critique, new moral discourses, and technologies. We venture now into the future, attempting to inscribe and describe the possibilities of the seventh moment. Several themes emerge, or will not go away: the voice and presence of the other, historically called "the native"; the social text; and the sacred, the humanistic, and the technological.

◆ Back to the Future

We cannot foretell the future, but we can speculate about it, because the future never represents a clean break with the past. Indeed, many moments overlap. It is up to the reader to choose from among the voices in the contest of moments and to choose the future.

The Other's Voice

Throughout its 20th-century history, up to a scant quarter century ago, qualitative research was still seriously concerned about the problem of researchers' "going native"—*native* being the word that then inscribed the Other in qualitative discourse. Who today can even use that term? In after-hours tales, over drinks, mostly white, male, middle-class North American ethnographic researchers whispered of those of their colleagues who had engaged that final perdition, overidentification with those they had studied. Today, no one takes seriously talk of "going native." In fact, its disappearance as a category of concern among sociologists and anthropologists is scarcely remarked, but, like the silences between lovers, it is all the more significant for its absence. In its place looms the "Other," whose voice researchers now struggle to hear.

The disappearance of the word *native* is significant. Its silence is deafening. In the postmodern world we are executing as our own heirs, in the legacy we have left ourselves and the students who come after us, "going native" is a category that speaks volumes to both our distorted sense of scientific objectivity and our colonial past. We struggle to find ways to make our texts meaningful beyond the artificial structures of conventional objectivity. We try to come to terms with our own "critical subjectivities." All the while, we have also admitted our guilt and complicity in the colonizing aspects of our work, pointedly subsumed by the term *native* itself. Even using the term is offensive.

But worse than politically incorrect, it stands as witness to our conceits as field-workers. How could we have considered ourselves civilized and objective alongside another class of individuals clearly not "civilized," or well below us on a presumed continuum of becoming civilized? Vidich and

628

Lyman, in Chapter 2 of this volume, trace the history of those ideas that undergirded and supported the very concepts that gave rise to the professional tragedy of "going native." Key to this was the Enlightenment legacy that led us to believe we could, indeed, prepare texts that purported to be whole and truthful accounts, objective accounts, of those "native-Others."

So we are not likely to hear much about "going native" again. That world has passed, and few mourn its passing. Quite the opposite—today we are trying to live ever closer to the lives about which we write. Many examples are discussed in this volume, and others are forthcoming. We are today trying to show not that we can live those lives, but that we have lived close enough to them to begin to understand how the people who live those lives have constructed their worlds.

The Social Text: Telling Stories From the Field

This brings us to our second theme: We are become extremely conscious of how our "tales of the field" can be categorized. We now understand at least the flaws that accompany "realist" and "confessional" tales, if not other kinds (Van Maanen, 1988). And many researchers are trying to move toward extended understandings, extended vicariousness, in their texts. Many now are experimenting with form, format, voice, shape, and style. Laurel Richardson, in her excellent and moving chapter in this volume, shares with us some of the more powerful literary narrative styles contemporary ethnographers are using.

This experimentation with text grows from several sources: our concern with representation of the Other; our willingness to all but abandon, or at least drastically modify, the realist text; and our growing sophistication surrounding the problems of situatedness in texts. We know that our texts have specific locations. We know that they represent—whether in some hidden way or openly—our baggage as individual social scientists. We care less about our "objectivity" as scientists than we do about providing our readers with some powerful propositional, tacit, intuitive, emotional, historical, poetic, and empathic experience of the Other via the texts we write.

The problem of representation will not go away. Indeed, at its heart lies an inner tension, an ongoing dialectic, a contradiction that will never be resolved. On the one hand, there is the concern for validity, or certainty in the text as a form of isomorphism and authenticity. On the other hand,

there is the sure and certain knowledge that all texts are socially, historically, politically, and culturally located. We, like the texts we write, can
never be transcendent.

So the experiments will continue, proliferate, grow both more "ironic"
and simultaneously less self-mocking. There will also be an expansion of
the genres of literature from which they borrow. The tension of this dialectic will continue to be felt throughout the ethnographic community, but it
will be resolved publicly and privately in many more ways than we have
yet seen.

Vulnerability and Truth, Vulnerability Versus Truth

Rigoberta Menchú (1984), the book and the woman, has created a firestorm. On the one hand are readers who are sympathetic to the message of
the book, which captures some sense of the suffering of the Guatemalan
indigenous peoples at the hands of the *ladinos,* the primarily European-
descent, landowning class in Guatemala. The *ladinos,* as one might expect,
also control the national army, a group comprising European-descent officers and regulars as well as *mestizo* and indigenous soldiers.

On the other side of the argument are both scholars (Gugelberger,
1996; Stoll, 1999) and assorted others who study thoughtfully, laud,
reject, and sometimes revile *I, Rigoberta Menchú* because it is a chronicle
proven patently false in some (or all) of its facts and therefore suspect.
The radical right wing of the culture war militia has accused the "liberal
left" of using the book to propagandize on behalf of some unspecified
liberal agenda, primarily Latin American revolution. The evidence that
Rigoberta Menchú, the person, provided so-called facts that are not true,
that have no basis in her experience or witness, is not complete, but it is
strong and nearly overwhelming (Lincoln, 2000, in press).

What do we do with a text like *I, Rigoberta Menchú?* John Beverley provides some answers in his thoughtful chapter here on the *testimonio* form.
Instead of treating such works as subject to Eurocentric validity criteria,
we need to look at them through another lens. They are, in fact, a bridge
into subalternity, an avenue for us to use in crossing into the world of the
subaltern, the border dweller, the margin-definer previously without
voice. They represent power turned on its head in several directions. They
signal a capture of authority by colonized voices, a reestablishment of the
authority of indigenous peoples to speak for themselves, in their own
terms. They also portend a refusal of the colonized to have their stories

told solely by outsiders, by those with little political stake, or by those whose major interests are not historically perceived to be with indigenous others.

They signify, too, that although Stoll (1999) and others may argue on epistemological grounds, their arguments are all too often political (Beverley, 1996; see also Volume 2, Beverley, Chapter 10; Tierney, Chapter 9). Just as researchers, particularly feminist theorists, recognize that the personal is the political, subaltern voices recognize that the epistemological is also the political. *How* we know is intimately bound up with *what* we know, where we learned it, and what we have experienced. Enlisting the storytelling tradition to make statements that are epistemologically political narratives leaves the traditions of Western ethnography unsettled, threatened, vulnerable, and adrift from their moorings. The firestorm surrounding *I, Rigoberta Menchú* is the precise consequence of the meeting of majority criteria with subaltern purposes. Thus we are left with a new form of truth: the "truth" as civic sociology shaped by the experiences of alterity.

Just as we argued earlier that we will need to revisit the old texts to see, criticism aside, just what they taught us and what their purposes and uses might be for a postmodern era, we will have to consider carefully the issues of the civic social science for which we as editors call in light of what a civic social science means for, and from, subaltern voices. Clearly, a subaltern social science, a call for action from alterity, is shaped differently from a civic social science envisioned by Eurocentric and mainstream voices. Taking *I, Rigoberta* and Menchú on their own terms radically remakes what constitutes an entire genre of ethnographic work. This refashioning might ultimately include life histories, autoethnographies, "mystories," autobiographies, critical journals, and other narrative forms in this genre. The debut of *testimonio* as a form of critical ethnography has literally sent life history spinning out of control into another lane on the bridge.

Getting on With It

We confront another problematic in the sixth moment. Arguments around paradigms previously have centered on whether "competitor" paradigms are worthwhile (Guba & Lincoln, 1981, 1989; Lincoln & Guba, 1985) and whether students and others entering the fray might usefully select to operate in nonconventional scientific modes. Smith and Deemer (Volume 3, Chapter 12) show that this was a foolish argument (although perhaps a useful place to start the conversation). Ensuring that students and new practitioners did have choices in the paradigms they applied to their work at least kept us from "closing down the conversation" prematurely. But as Smith and Deemer make clear, it is not really about paradigm choices now. Rather, it is about taking account of the world that we have inherited. Recent understandings in the social sciences now convince us that there *is* no "God's-eye view"; there is no "voice from nowhere," no "voice from everywhere." It is not that we might elect to engage in work that is postmodern. Rather, it is that we have inherited a postmodern world, and there is no going back. We do not "choose" to be postmodern. The historical moment has chosen us.

The implications of this understanding, of this resituating of the argument, are enormous. We have come and gone in the "great paradigm wars." The wars are over. While we were fighting, the boundaries and borders over which we were fighting were redrawn until they were meaningless. We are not free to "choose" postmodernism. It is the historical moment when the modernist epoch ends: contingent, pluralistic, ambiguous, freed (or jettisoned) from the certainties of yesterday, decentered, noisy with previously unheard voices. We may still hear, for some years to come, echoes of modernism. Assuredly, our more conservative intellectual and political organizations (such as universities) will long cling to modernist forms and structures, even as the mind-set of a new era takes shape.

Whose Self? What/Which Self?

We confront, too, the issue of self: Whose self? What self? Which self? The decentering of the Eurocentric grand narrative, the centering of polyvocality, the ragged race between margin and center, the deconstruction of the "authentic self"—all signal that the time of the fiction of a single, true, authentic self has come and gone. It is hard to know whether, in fact, it will even be missed, except as a psychoanalytic figment of the imagination. Instead, we confront multiple identities: identities formed in and around our social locations, identities evoked in the field, identities created as a result of the interaction between our data and our selves, in and out of the field, experience-near and time-distant. Bridges to the self seem to be as many as bridges to our respondents, each of them eliciting new glimpses, new images of what our own possibilities might be, of how we might become, of how and in what ways we might come to know.

The flowering of multiple paradigms and methods has been accompanied, to some extent, by a flowering of possibilities for the human spirit. Just as the Enlightenment opened possibilities for lives of choice not dictated by theological doctrine, so this abandonment of a rigid Eurocentrism in our social sciences leaves open the potential for a new flowering of the human spirit, a new sense of the sacredness of the human spirit, human community, and human flourishing. Rather than viewing multiple identities as a mark of psychic disorder, we see in them possibilities and potential. The reflexive self is a self freed to choose, to enact, to perform new roles, new relationships. The multiple selves summoned by a more complex and committed social science possess richness beyond our ability to understand or tell at the moment.

Mary Gergen and Ken Gergen (Chapter 13) argue that we are already in the "post"-post period—post-poststructuralism, post-postmodernism— an age of reconstruction. What this means for interpretive, ethnographic practices is still not clear. But it is certain that things will never again be the same. We are in a new age where multivoiced texts, cultural criticism, and postexperimental works will become more common, as will more reflexive forms of fieldwork, analysis, and intertextual representation.

Another way, then, of describing this moment in time and space is to paraphrase Thomas Berry, who has commented that we are between stories. The Old Story will no longer do, and we know that it is inadequate. But the New Story is not yet in place. And so we look for the pieces of the Story, the ways of telling it, and the elements that will make it whole, but it hasn't come to us yet. So we are now the ultimate *bricoleurs*, trying to cobble together a story that we are beginning to suspect will never enjoy the unity, the smoothness, the wholeness that the Old Story had. As we assemble different pieces of the Story, our *bricolage* begins to take not one, but many shapes.

Slowly it dawns on us that there may not be one future, one "moment," but rather many; not one "voice," but polyvocality; not one story, but many tales, dramas, pieces of fiction, fables, memories, histories, autobiographies, poems, and other texts to inform our sense of lifeways, to extend our understandings of the Other, to provide us with the material for "cultural critique" (Marcus & Fischer, 1986). The modernist project has bent and is breaking under the weight of postmodern resistance to its narratives, to what Berry calls "the Old Story."

◆ Conclusion: The Seventh Moment

It is hard to know whether it is easier to live in a time of certainty or a time of great uncertainty. John Naisbitt (1982), author of *Megatrends*, has observed:

> We are living in the *time of the parenthesis*, the time between eras. Those who are willing to handle the ambiguity of this in-between period and to anticipate the new era will be a quantum leap ahead of those who hold on to the past. The time of the parenthesis is a time of change and questioning.
>
> Although the time between eras is uncertain, it is a great and yeasty time, filled with opportunity. If we can learn to make uncertainty our friend, we can achieve much more than in stable eras. In stable eras, everything has a name, and everything knows its place, and we can leverage very little.
>
> But in the time of the parenthesis, we have extraordinary leverage and influence—individually, professionally and institutionally—if we can only get a clear sense, a clear conception, a clear vision, of the road ahead. (pp. 249-252)

We believe that Naisbitt is suggesting that while we are letting go of the certainties and absolutes of the past, we also have enormous opportunity to make of the future what we wish it to be.

◆ Coda

The answer to the question, Where have we come to? is unclear, as is the answer to the question, What are the many futures that lie ahead for qualitative research? We are not wandering, for that implies that we have no direction. But likewise, as is plain from the several ontologies and many epistemologies that inform and contradict each other, we are not necessarily marching in a column toward a common future. Like the *bricoleurs* of Lévi-Strauss, we are creating solutions to our problems with makeshift equipment, spare parts, and assemblage.

But interpretive *bricoleurs* are more than simply jacks-of-all-trades; they are also inventors, in the best sense of the word. *Bricoleurs* know that they have few tools, and little by way of appropriate parts, and so becomes inventors. They invent ways of repairing; they recycle fabric and cloth into beautiful quilts; they, like Pirsig's hero in *Zen and the Art of Motorcycle Maintenance*, know that for a particular repair, nothing is better than a strip of Coors beer aluminum can; having no art lessons, they become Grandma Moses. In the interpretive *bricoleur's world, invention is not only the child of necessity, it is the demand of restless art.* The methods of qualitative research thereby become the "invention," and the telling of the tales—the representation—becomes the art, even though, as *bricoleurs,* we all know we are not working with standard-issue parts, and we have come to suspect that there are no longer any "standard-issue parts" made (if ever there were). And so we cobble. We cobble together stories that we may tell each other, some to share our profoundest links with those whom we studied; some to help us see how we can right a wrong or relieve oppression; some to help us and others to understand how and why we did what we did, and how it all went very wrong; and some simply to sing of difference.

And perhaps it is the case that this *Handbook* itself is the sixth moment. Perhaps it is the particular time in our history to take stock of where we are, to think about where we are going, to try to imagine a new future. Perhaps what we have asked our authors to do is to define this sixth moment and to speculate about what the seventh moment might be like—whether it will be a time when the Story is once again in place, or whether it will continue to be a time when fields and disciplines appear to be in disarray. This book, this effort, might well become, to historians long after us, a moment unto itself, a chapter in an evolution that we ourselves are not able to bound, to frame, or to capture for its essence.

We believe we are poised to cross the bridge into the seventh moment. We cannot see that landscape clearly yet, but we can discern some of its contours. First, we are not the only scholars calling for a social science that is more responsive—not to the policy community, which has often used research for its own ends, but to the communities in which we do our work. The press for a civic sociology (see in this volume Christians, Chapter 5; Denzin, Volume 3, Chapter 13) is not without its dangers. We may find that as we work more often with communities to answer their questions, we have less funding available with which we can do such work. We may also find that this work takes us away from campuses far more than our home institutions would like. Certainly, such work is far more labor-intensive and time-devouring than our traditional ethnographies dictated (Lincoln, in press). The calls for a civic sociology—by which we mean fieldwork located not only in sociology, but in an extended, enriched, cultivated social science embracing all the disciplines—nevertheless characterize a whole new generation of qualitative researchers: educationists, sociologists, political scientists, clinical practitioners in psychology and medicine, nurses, communications and media specialists, cultural studies workers, and a score of other assorted disciplines.

The moral imperatives of such work cannot be ignored. There have been several generations of social science that not only has not solved serious human problems, but many times has only worsened the plight of the persons studied (see Fine, Weis, Weseen, & Wong, Chapter 4, this volume). Beyond morality is something equally important—the mandates for such work come from our own sense of the human community. A detached social science frequently serves only those with the means, the social designations, and the intellectual capital to keep themselves detached. We face a choice, in the seventh moment, of declaring ourselves committed to detachment or in solidarity with the human community. We come to know, and we come to exist meaningfully, only in community. We have the opportunity to rejoin that community as its resident intellectuals and change agents.

An interesting, and significant, concomitant to expressions of interest in a civic social science is the implied end of the commitment to the Enlightenment dualism of means and ends. We are emerging from many moments in social science where ends and means have been carefully, objectively, separated. The implications of a civic social science go far beyond human solidarity. Such a social science also signals the dying of means-ends dualism. In a civic social science, the ends of ethnography—strong, just, egalitarian communities—are reconciled with the means for achieving those ends. In the seventh moment, the means (methods) of social science are developed, refined, and cherished for their contributions to communities characterized by respectful and loving difference, social justices and equal access to material, social, educational, and cultural capital (the ends of ethnography). Methods vie among themselves not for experimental robustness, but for vitality and vigor in illuminating the ways to achieve profound understanding of how we can create human flourishing.

We are also seeing an emerging dialogue around what paradigms mean and how we learn to trust their results (Lincoln, in press). The vast array of methods, paradigms, and proposals for trustworthiness has the power to blind us to the fact that many individuals and paradigm adherents, working from very different embarkation points, have arrived at quite similar destinations. The feminists, for example, with their critical emphasis on women's ways of knowing, share many understandings with the race and ethnic theorists, who likewise argue that nondominant, subaltern ways of knowing, while different from majority, academic, or conventional scientific epistemologies, have much to offer to our understanding of the vast array and variety of human social life. Critical theorists and those who work with life history and *testimonio* forms intuitively understand that the epistemological is the political, and both have similar proposals for how we might view validity and therefore the "truth" of any account.

As a consequence, we have before us the possibility of entering into more meaningful dialogue with each other, not about how we can create a new metaparadigm, but about the similarities we are uncovering in our work. We see many affinities and parallels emerging from methodological reflections on fieldwork under way. If a seventh moment is yet to be charted, such dialogues among paradigm and methodological adherents might well be undertaken.

One final characteristic that marks this moment is the activity and ferment between margins and center. What was center is now decentered; what was margin and border is now taking center stage. The staggering array of new materials, new resources, new stories, new critiques, new methods, new epistemological proposals, new forms of validity, new textual improvisations, new performed interpretations—all demonstrate an undeniably new, if shifting, center to this work. What was marked formerly by the firm and rigid shapes of a Eurocentric geometry is now the fluid, shape-shifting image of chemical flux and transformation, as margins move to the center, the center moves to the margins, and the whole is reconstituted again in some new form. The whole concept of center and margins is being transfigured by methods, methodologies, research practices, and epistemologies scarcely dreamed of a generation ago—or even when the first edition of the *Handbook* was published.

For whatever the moment, we hope that this volume is a prompt for new tales, improvisations, experiments, interpolations, dialogues, and additional interpretations. The Story is by no means in place yet, although we await the visit of yet another blind Homer to piece together not only what we know of this fabulous land, but a new set of chapters for us. And as we wait, we remember that our most powerful effects as storytellers come when we expose the cultural plots and the cultural practices that guide our writing hands. These practices and plots lead us to see coherence where there is none, or to create meaning without an understanding of the broader structures that tell us to tell things in a particular way. Erasing the boundaries separating self, other, and history, we seek to learn how to tell

637

new stories, stories no longer contained within or confined to the tales of the past. And so we embark together on a new project, a project with its own as yet not fully understood cultural plots and cultural practices. And what remains, throughout, will be the steady but always changing commitment of all qualitative researchers—the commitment, that is, to study human experience from the ground up, from the point of interacting individuals who, together and alone, make and live histories that have been handed down to them from the ghosts of the past.

◆ Note

1. The moments once more: traditional (1900-1950); modernist (1950-1970); blurred genres (1970-1986); crisis of representation (1986-1990); postmodern, a period of experimental and new ethnographies (1990-1995); postexperimental inquiry (1995-2000); and the future, which is now (2000-).

◆ References

Abram, D. (1996). *The spell of the sensuous.* New York: Vintage.

Bateson, G. (1972). *Steps to an ecology of mind.* New York: Ballantine.

Bateson, G. (1979). *Mind and nature: A necessary unity.* New York: E. P. Dutton.

Bateson, G. P., & Bateson, M. C. (1987). *Anger's fear: Towards an epistemology of the sacred.* New York: Macmillan.

Behar, R. (1996). *The vulnerable observer: Anthropology that breaks your heart.* Boston: Beacon.

Berry, W. (1981). *Recollected essays: 1965-1980.* New York: Farrar, Strauss & Giroux.

Beverley, J. (1996). The real thing. In G. M. Gugelberger (Ed.), *The real thing: Testimonial discourse and Latin America* (pp. 266-286). Durham, NC: Duke University Press.

Bruner, E. M. (1993). Introduction: The ethnographic self and the personal self. In P. Benson (Ed.), *Anthropology and literature* (pp. 1-26). Urbana: University of Illinois Press.

Christians, C. G. (1995). The naturalistic fallacy in contemporary interactionist-interpretive research. In N. K. Denzin (Ed.), *Studies in symbolic interaction: A research annual* (Vol. 19, pp. 125-130). Greenwich, CT: JAI.

Christians, C. G. (1997). The ethics of being. In C. G. Christians & M. Traber (Eds.), *Communication ethics and universal values* (pp. 3-23). Thousand Oaks, CA: Sage.

Christians, C. G. (1998). The sacredness of life. *Media Development, 45*(2), 3-7.

Clough, P. T. (1992). *The end(s) of ethnography: From realism to social criticism.* Newbury Park, CA: Sage.

Clough, P. T. (1998). *The end(s) of ethnography: From realism to social criticism* (2nd ed.). New York: Peter Lang.

Collins, P. H. (1990). *Black feminist thought: Knowledge, consciousness, and the politics of empowerment.* New York: Routledge, Chapman & Hall.

Conquergood, D. (1985). Performing as a moral act: Ethical dimensions of the ethnography of performance. *Literature in Performance, 5,* 1-13.

Denzin, N. K. (1997). *Interpretive ethnography: Ethnographic practices for the 21st century.* Thousand Oaks, CA: Sage.

Du Bois, W. E. B. (1989). *The souls of black folk.* New York: Bantam. (Original work published 1903)

Ellison, R. (1964). *Shadow and act.* New York: Random House.

Ford, N. A. (1998). A blueprint for Negro authors. In P. L. Hill (Ed.), *Call and response: The Riverside anthology of the African American literary tradition* (pp. 1112-1114). Boston: Houghton Mifflin. (Original work published 1950)

Geertz, C. (1988). *Works and lives: The anthropologist as author.* Stanford, CA: Stanford University Press.

Guba, E. G., & Lincoln, Y. S. (1981). *Effective evaluation: Improving the usefulness of evaluation results through responsive and naturalistic approaches.* San Francisco: Jossey-Bass.

Guba, E. G., & Lincoln, Y. S. (1989). *Fourth generation evaluation.* Newbury Park, CA: Sage.

Gugelberger, G. M. (Ed.). (1996). *The real thing: Testimonial discourse and Latin America.* Durham, NC: Duke University Press.

Hasselstrom, L., Collier, G., & Curtis, N. (1997). Introduction: Grass widows and wrinklebelly women. In L. Hasselstrom, G. Collier, & N. Curtis (Eds.), *Leaning into the wind: Women write from the heart of the West* (pp. xiii-xxi). Boston: Houghton Mifflin.

Jackson, M. (1998). *Minima ethnographica: Intersubjectivity and the anthropological project.* Chicago: University of Chicago Press.

Kittredge, W. (1996). *Who owns the West?* San Francisco: Murray House.

Lincoln, Y. S. (1995). Emerging criteria for quality in qualitative and interpretive inquiry. *Qualitative Inquiry, 1,* 275-289.

Lincoln, Y. S. (1998, November). *When research is not enough: Community, care, and love.* Presidential Address delivered at the annual meeting of the Association for the Study of Higher Education, Miami, FL.

Lincoln, Y. S. (1999, June). *Courage, vulnerability and truth.* Keynote address delivered at the conference "Reclaiming Voice II: Ethnographic Inquiry and Qualitative Research in a Postmodern Age," University of California, Irvine.

Lincoln, Y. S. (in press). Varieties of validities. In J. S. Smart (Ed.), *Higher education: Handbook of theory and research* (Vol. 14). Lexington, MA: Agathon.

Lincoln, Y. S., & Guba, E. G. (1985). *Naturalistic inquiry*. Beverly Hills, CA: Sage.

Macnaghten, P., & Urry, J. (1998). *Contested natures*. London: Sage.

Marcus, G. E., & Fischer, M. M. J. (1986). *Anthropology as cultural critique: An experimental moment in the human sciences*. Chicago: University of Chicago Press.

Menchú, R. (1984). *I, Rigoberta Menchú: An Indian woman in Guatemala* (E. Burgos-Debray, Ed.; A. Wright, Trans.). London: Verso.

Naisbitt, J. (1982). *Megatrends: Ten new directions transforming our lives*. New York: Time Warner.

Park, R. E. (1950). Education in its relation to the conflict and fusion of cultures. In R. E. Park, *Race and culture* (pp. 261-283). Glencoe, IL: Free Press. (Reprinted from *Publications of the American Sociological Society, 13*, 1918, 38-63)

Rawlins, C. L. (1994). The meadow at the corner of your eye. In D. Clow & D. Snow (Eds.), *Northern lights: A selection of new writing from the American West* (pp. 389-395). New York: Vantage.

Reason, P. (1993). Sacred experience and sacred science. *Journal of Management Inquiry, 2*, 10-27.

Rorty, R. (1979). *Philosophy and the mirror of nature*. Princeton, NJ: Princeton University Press.

Rosaldo, R. (1989). *Culture and truth: The remaking of social analysis*. Boston: Beacon.

Sartre, J.-P. (1981). *The family idiot: Gustave Flaubert, 1821-1857* (Vol. 1). Chicago: University of Chicago Press.

Stegner, W. (1980). *The sound of mountain water: The changing American West*. Garden City, NY: Doubleday.

Stoll, D. (1999). *Rigoberta Menchú and the story of all poor Guatemalans*. Boulder, CO: Westview.

Turner, V. (1986). *The anthropology of performance*. New York: Performing Arts Journal Publications.

Ulmer, G. (1989). *Teletheory*. New York: Routledge.

Van Maanen, J. (1988). *Tales of the field: On writing ethnography*. Chicago: University of Chicago Press.

West, C. (1989). *The American evasion of philosophy: A genealogy of pragmatism*. Madison: University of Wisconsin Press.

West, C. (1994). *Race matters*. New York: Vantage.

White, C. J., Mogilka, J., & Slack, P. J. F. (1998). Disturbing the colonial frames of ethnographic representation: Releasing feminist imagination on the academy. *Cultural Studies: A Research Annual, 3*, 3-27.

Suggested Readings

♦ **Chapter 2**

Appiah, K. A., & Gutman, A. (1996). *Color conscious: The political morality of race.* Princeton, NJ: Princeton University Press.

Bensman, J., & Lilienfeld, R. (1991). *Craft and consciousness: Occupational technique and the development of world images* (2nd ed.). New York: Aldine de Gruyter.

Denzin, N. K. (1997). *Interpretive ethnography: Ethnographic practices for the 21st century.* Thousand Oaks, CA: Sage.

Fine, M., Powell, L. C., Weis, L., & Wong, L. M. (Eds.). (1997). *Off white: Readings on race, power and society.* New York: Routledge.

Goldberg, D. T. (1997). *Racial subjects: Writing on race in America.* New York: Routledge.

Habermas, J. (1996). *Between facts and norms: Contributions to a discourse theory of law and democracy* (W. Rehg, Trans.). Cambridge: MIT Press.

Haraway, D. J. (1991). *Simians, cyborgs, and women: The reinvention of nature.* New York: Routledge.

Hutchinson, J., & Smith, A. D. (Eds.). (1996). *Ethnicity.* New York: Oxford University Press.

Lopez, I. F. H. (1996). *White by law: The legal construction of race.* New York: New York University Press.

Lyman, S. M. (1997). *Postmodernism and a sociology of the absurd and other essays on the "nouvelle vague" in American social science.* Fayetteville: University of Arkansas Press.

Min, P. G. (1996). *Caught in the middle: Korean communities in New York and Los Angeles.* Berkeley: University of California Press.

Oakes, G., & Vidich, A. J. (1999). *Collaboration, reputation, and ethics in American academic life: Hans H. Genth and C. Wright Mills.* Urbana: University of Illinois Press.

Radin, P. (1987). *The method and theory of ethnology.* South Hadley, MA: Bergin & Garvey. (Original work published 1933)

Salomon, A. (1963). Symbols and images in the constitution of society. In A. Salomon, *In praise of enlightenment* (pp. 237–260). Cleveland, OH: World. ·

Schutz, A. (1967). On multiple realities. In A. Schutz, *Collected papers* (M. Natanson, Ed. & Trans.; pp. 207–259). The Hague: Martinus Nijhoff.

Soja, E. W. (1990). *Postmodern geographies: The reassertion of space in critical social theory.* London: Verso.

Vidich, A. J., Bensman, J., & Stein, M. R. (Eds.). (1964). *Reflections on community studies.* New York: John Wiley.

Waldinger, R. (1996). *Still the promised city? African-Americans and new immigrants in postindustrial New York.* Cambridge, MA: Harvard University Press.

Weber, M. (1949). *The methodology of the social sciences* (E. Shils & H. Finch, Ed. & Trans.). Glencoe, IL: Free Press. (See especially "The Meaning of Ethical Neutrality in Sociology and Economics," pp. 1–49; and "Objectivity in Social Science and Social Policy," pp. 50–112.)

◆ Chapter 3

Abbott, A. (1988). *The system of professions: An essay on the division of expert labor.* Chicago: University of Chicago Press.

Birnbaum, R. (2000). *Management fads in higher education: Where they come from, what they do, why they fail.* San Francisco: Jossey-Bass.

Elliott, K. (1996). *Death of the guilds: Professions, states, and the advance of capitalism, 1930 to the present.* New Haven: Yale University Press.

Ehrenberg, R. (2000). *Tuition rising: Why college costs so much.* Cambridge, MA: Harvard University Press.

Fuller, S. (2002). *Knowledge management foundations.* Boston: Butterworth/ Heinemann.

Gibbons, M., Limoges, C., Nowotny, H., Schwartzman, S., Scott, P., & Trow, M. (1994). *The new production of knowledge.* London: Sage.

Greenwood, D. J, & Levin, M. (1998). *Introduction to action research.* Thousand Oaks, CA: Sage.

McDermott, J. J. (1981). *The philosophy of John Dewey.* Chicago: Univeristy of Chicago Press.

Reason, P., & Bradbury, H. (2001). *Handbook of action research.* London: Sage.

Ross, D. (1991). *The origins of American social science*. Cambridge, UK: Cambridge University Press.

◆ Chapter 4

Austin, R. (1995). Sapphire bound! In K. Crenshaw, N. Gotanda, D. Peller, & K. Thomas (Eds.), *Critical race theory: The key writings that formed the movement*. New York: New Press.

Farmer, P. (1999). *Infections and inequalities: The modern plagues*. Berkeley: University of California Press.

Fine, M., Torre, M. E., Boudin, K., Bowen, I., Clark, J., Hylton, D., Martinez, M. M., Roberts, R. A., Smart, P., & Upegui, D. (2001). *Changing minds: The impact of college in prison*.

Fine, M., & Weis, L. (1998). *The unknown city: The lives of poor and working class young adults*. Boston: Beacon.

Frank, G. (2000). *Venus on wheels: Two decades of dialogue on disability, biography, and being female in America*. Berkeley: University of California Press.

Harris, A., & Fine, M. (2001). "Under the Covers: Theorising the Politics of Counter Stories." Edited volume of the *International Journal of Critical Psychology, 4*. (See especially Apfelbaum, E., "The Dread: An Essay on Communication Across Cultural Boundaries," pp. 19-34; and Torre, M. E. et al., "A Space for Co-Constructing Counter Stories Under Surveillance," pp. 149-166.)

Kelley, R.D.G. (1997). *Yo' mama's disfunktional! Fighting the culture wars in urban America*. Boston: Beacon.

Lutz, C. A., & Collins, J. L. (1993). *Reading* National Geographic. Chicago: University of Chicago Press.

Smith, L. T. (1999). *Decolonizing methodologies: Research and indigenous peoples*. London: Zed Books.

Tolman, D., & Brydon-Miller, M. (2001). *From subjects to subjectivities: A handbook of interpretive and participatory methods*. New York: New York University Press.

Twine, F. W., & Warren, J. (Eds.). *Racing research, researching race*. New York: New York University Press.

Weis, L., & Fine, M. (2001). *Speedbumps: A student friendly guide to qualitative research*. New York: Teachers College Press.

◆ Chapter 5

Bracci, S. L., & Christians, C. G. (Eds.). (2002). Moral engagement for public life: Theorists for contemporary ethics. New York: Peter Lang.

◆ Chapter 6

Cohen, M. Z. Kahn, D. L., & Steeves, R. H. (2000). *Hermeneutic phenomeno-logical research: A practical guide for nurse researchers.* Thousand Oaks, CA: Sage.

Stronach, I., & MacLure, M. (1997). *Educational research undone: The post-modern embrace.* Buckingham, UK: Open University Press.

◆ Chapter 7

Bernstein, R. J. (1988). *Beyond objectivism and relativism: Science, hermeneutics, and praxis.* Philadelphia: University of Pennsylvania Press.

Crotty, M. (1998). *The foundations of social research.* London: Sage.

Fay, B. (1996). *Contemporary philosophy of social science.* Oxford: Blackwell.

Flyvbjerg, B. (2001). *Making social science matter.* Cambridge: Cambridge University Press.

Gallagher, S. (1992). *Hermeneutics and education.* Albany, NY: State University of New York Press.

Gergen, K. J. (1999). *An invitation to social construction.* London: Sage.

Hacking, I. (1999). *The social construction of what?* Cambridge, MA: Harvard University Press.

Hiley, D. R., Bohman, J. F., and Shusterman, R. (Eds.). *The interpretive turn: Philos-ophy, science, culture.* Ithaca, NY: Cornell University Press.

Schwandt, T. A. (2001). *Dictionary of qualitative inquiry* (2nd ed.) Thousand Oaks, CA: Sage.

Warnke, G. (1987). *Gadamer: Hermeneutics, tradition and reason.* Stanford, CA; Stanford University Press.

◆ Chapter 8

St. Pierre, E. A., & Pillow, W. S. (Eds.). (2000). Working the ruins: Feminist poststructural theory and methods in education. New York: Routledge.

◆ Chapter 9

Qualitative Inquiry, 8(1). (2002). M. Lynn, T. J. Yosso, D. Solorzano, & L. Parker (Eds.). *Special issue: Critical race theory and qualitative research.*

Qualitative Studies in Education, 13(4). (2000). 4: F. V. Rains, J. A. Archibald, & D. Deyhle (Eds.). Special issue: Through our eyes and in our own words— The voicecs of indigenous scholars.

◆ Chapter 10

McLaren, P. (2001). Che Guevara, Paulo Freire, and the politics of hope: Reclaiming critical pedagogy. *Cultural Studies—Critical Methodologies,* 1:108-131.

◆ Chapter 11

Giroux, H. (2000). *Impure acts: The practical politics of cultural studies.* New York: Routledge.

◆ Chapter 12

Lewin, E., & Leap, W. (Eds.). (1996). *Out in the field: Reflections of lesbian and gay anthropologists.* Urbana, IL: University of Illinois Press.

Nardi, P. M., & Schneider, B. E. (Eds.). (1998). *Social perspectives in lesbian and gay studies.* London: Routledge.

Seidman, S. (Ed.). (1996). *Queer theory/sociology.* Cambridge, MA: Blackwell.

Williams, C. L., and Stein, A. (Eds.). (2002). *Sexuality and gender.* Malden, MA: Blackwell.

◆ Chapter 13

Bochner, A. P., & Ellis, C. (Eds.). (2001). *Ethnographically speaking.* Walnut Creek, CA: AltaMira.

Counsell, C., & Wolf, L. (Eds.). (2001). *Performance analysis: An introductory coursebook.* New York: Routledge.

Ellis, C., & Bocher, A. P. (Eds.). (1996). *Composing ethnography.* Walnut Creek, CA: AltaMira.

Gergen, K. J. (1999). *An invitation to social construction.* Thousand Oaks, CA: Sage.

Gergen, M. M. (2001). *Feminist reconstructions in psychology: Narrative, gender, and performance.* Thousand Oaks, CA: Sage.

Reason, P., & Bradbury, H. (Eds.). (2000). *Handbook of participatory action research.* Thousand Oaks, CA: Sage.

Wetherell, M., Taylor, S., & Yates, S. J. (2001). *Discourse theory and practice: A reader.* London: Sage.

◆ Chapter 14

Smith, L. T. (1999). *Decolonizing methodologies: Research and indigenous peoples.*
Dunedin: University of Otago Press.

Author Index

Subject Index

Academic practice. *See* Universities
Acculturation, 63
Accurate data, 219, 220
Action research, 29, 48-49, 131-132, 267-269
  autopoesis vs. participatory evaluation, 160-161
  case examples of, 153-160
  cogenerative inquiry, 149-150
  context-bound knowledge and, 150, 152
  co-optation and, 161-162
  credibility/reliability/validity and, 150
  democratizing research, 161
  enterprise modeling case, 153-157
  generalization and, 151-152
  local-professional knowledge, 149-150
  pragmatic philosophy and, 147-148
  science, theory of, 148
  social research praxis and, 145-147
  social responsibility and, 133, 268
  theory/praxis, integration of, 148-149
  university-industry cooperation, 153-157
  university organization, transformation of, 157-160
  university research practice and, 160-162
  See also Universities
Amerindian ethnography, 68-71
Analytic induction, 87-89, 91
Anthropology, 56, 60

civilized/primitive dichotomy,
  American Indian culture and, 69-70
  classification framework, 65
  colonialist ethnography and, 62-63
  cultural/social evolution, 64-65
  decolonization movements, cultural pluralism and, 65-68
  postmodernism and, 89-90, 91, 92-93
  See also Ethnography; Sociology
Assimilation, 81
  pluralistic paradigm and, 83-86
  race relations cycles and, 82-83
  unmeltable ethnics, 81-82
Authenticity criteria, 277-279
Authority claims, 28, 444, 618-619
Autoethnography, 579-580
Autonomy doctrine, 208-210, 215, 218, 222
Axiology, 265-266

Belmont Report, 219-220
Bias, 12, 15
  cultural/social evolution, Eurocentric framework of, 64-65, 86
  feminist qualitative research and, 355-356
  interpretive activity and, 301-302
  subjectivity and, 278-279
Black communities, 71-72, 77
  black women's experience, 344
  See also Representation

About the Authors

Clifford G. Christians is a Research Professor of Communications at the University of Illinois, Urbana-Champaign, where he is Director of the Institute of Communications Research. He has been a visiting scholar in philosophical ethics at Princeton University, in social ethics at the University of Chicago, and a PEW Fellow in Ethics at Oxford University. He completed the third edition of Rivers and Schramm's Responsibility in Mass Communication, has coauthored *Jacques Ellul: Interpretive Essays* with Jay Van Hook, and has written *Teaching Ethics in Journalism Education* with Catherine Covert. He is also the coauthor, with John Ferre and Mark Fackler, of *Good News: Social Ethics and the Press* (1993). His *Media Ethics: Cases and Moral Reasoning*, with Kim Rotzoll and Mark Fackler, is now in its fifth edition (1983, 1987, 1991, 1995, 1998). *Communication Ethics and Universal Values*, which he coauthored with Michael Traber, was published in 1997. He has lectured or given academic papers on ethics in Norway, Russia, Finland, France, Belgium, Italy, Netherlands, Switzerland, England, Singapore, Korea, Scotland, Philippines, Slovenia, Canada, Brazil, Mexico, Puerto Rico, Spain, and Sweden.

Norman K. Denzin is Distinguished Professor of Communications, College of Communications Scholar, and Research Professor of Communications, Sociology and Humanities at the University of Illinois, Urbana-Champaign. He is the author of numerous books, including *Interpretive Ethnography: Ethnographic Practices for the 21st Century, The Cinematic Society: The Voyeur's Gaze, Images of Postmodern Society, The Research Act: A Theoretical Introduction to Sociological Methods, Interpretive*

Interactionism, Hollywood Shot by Shot, The Recovering Alcoholic, and *The Alcoholic Self,* which won the Charles Cooley Award from the Society for the Study of Symbolic Interaction in 1988. In 1997 he was awarded the George Herbert Award from the Study of Symbolic Interaction. He is the editor of *the Sociological Quarterly,* coeditor of *Qualitative Inquiry,* and editor of the book series *Cultural Studies: A Research Annual and Studies in Symbolic Interaction.*

Michelle Fine is Professor of Social/Personality Psychology at the Graduate School and University Center at the City University of New York. She has authored and coauthored numerous books, including, most recently, *The Unknown City: The Lives of Poor and Working-Class Young Adults* (with Lois Weis; 1998), *Becoming Gentlemen: Women, Law School and Institutional Change* (with Lani Guinier and Jane Balin; 1997), and *Off White: Readings on Race, Power and Society* (with Linda Powell, Lois Weis, and Loonmun Wong, 1997). An activist in urban school reform, she is now working closely with a prison-based college program in New York State.

John Frow is Regius Professor of Rhetoric and English Literature at the University of Edinburgh. He is the author of *Marxism and Literary History* (1986), *Cultural Studies and Cultural Value* (1995), *Time and Commodity Culture* (1997), and, with Tony Bennett and Michael Emmison, *Accounting for Tastes: Australian Everyday Cultures* (1999). With Meaghan Morris he edited *Australian Cultural Studies: A Reader* (1993). He is currently working on a book on cultural memory and on another on the moral economy of everyday life, and he and Meaghan Morris are editing a reader in cultural theory.

Joshua Gamson is Associate Professor of Sociology at Yale University. In addition to numerous academic and nonacademic articles, he is the author of *Freaks Talk Back: Tabloid Television and Sexual Nonconformity* (1998) and *Claims to Fame: Celebrity in Contemporary America* (1994), and a participating author of *Ethnography Unbound: Power and Resistance in the Modern Metropolis* (1991). His research, teaching, and writing focus on the sociology of culture, with an emphasis on contemporary Western commercial culture and mass media; social movements, especially on cultural aspects of contemporary movements; on participant observation methodology and techniques, particularly as applied in urban settings; and on the history, theory, and sociology of sexuality.

Kenneth J. Gergen is Mustin Professor of Psychology at Swarthmore College and founder of the Swarthmore College Program in Interpretation Theory. He is a joint editor of the Sage Ltd series *Inquiry in Social Construction* and associate editor of *Theory and Psychology* and the *American Psychologist*. He is a cofounder of the Taos Institute, a nonprofit organization dedicated to the cross-fertilization of social constructionist theory and societal practice. His edited works include *Historical Social Psychology* (with Mary Gergen) and *Psychological Discourse in Historical Perspective* (with Carl Graumann). His authored volumes include *The Saturated Self* (1991), *Toward Transformation in Social Knowledge* (1993), *Realities and Relationships* (1994), and *An Invitation to Social Construction* (1999).

Mary M. Gergen is Professor of Psychology and Women's Studies at Pennsylvania State University, Delaware County. She works at the crossroads of social constructionism and feminist psychology. She is coeditor, with Sara N. Davis, of *Toward a New Psychology of Gender* (1997). Her most recent work is *Feminist reconstructions in psychology: Narrative, gender & performanc* (2001), a collection of innovative experiences in the quantitative realm. She recently published, with Joan C. Chrisler and Alice LoCicero, "Innovative Methods: Resources for Research, Teaching and Publishing" (in *Psychology of Women Quarterly*), which endeavors to expand the range of methods available to academic psychologists. She is a cofounder of the Taos Institute, a nonprofit organization dedicated to the cross-fertilization of social constructionist theory and societal practice. She also writes and acts in performative psychology pieces.

Davydd J. Greenwood is Goldwin Smith Professor of Anthropology at Cornell University and a Corresponding Member of the Spanish Royal Academy of Moral and Political Sciences. His work centers on action research, political economy, and the Spanish Basque country. His action research work includes work in the health care system, industrial cooperatives, community development, industrial work reorganization, and higher-education reform. He serves on the editorial boards *of Dialogues on Work and Innovation, Concepts and Transformation, Systemic Practice and Action Research, Action Research International,* and *Revista de Antropología Aplicada.* Four of his books deal with action research, including two collaborative volumes written with the members of the Mondragón industrial cooperatives and one book coauthored with Morten Levin, *Introduction to Action Research: Social Research for Social Change* (1998).

Egon G. Guba is Professor Emeritus of Education, Indiana University. He received his Ph.D. degree from the University of Chicago in quantitative inquiry (education) in 1952, and thereafter served on the faculties of the University of Chicago, the University of Kansas City, the Ohio State University, and Indiana University. For the past 20 years, he has studied paradigms alternative to the received view and has espoused a personal commitment to one of these: constructivism. He is the coauthor of *Effective Evaluation* (1981), *Naturalistic Inquiry* (1985), and *Fourth Generation Evaluation* (1989), all with Yvonna S. Lincoln, and he is editor of *The Paradigm Dialog* (1990), which explores the implications of alternative paradigms for social and educational inquiry. He is the author of more than 150 journal articles and more than 100 conference presentations, many of them concerned with elements of new-paradigm inquiry and methods.

Joe L. Kincheloe is Belle Zeller Chair of Public Policy and Administration at City University of New York, Brooklyn College, and Professor of Cultural Studies and Pedagogy at Pennsylvania State University. He has written articles and books in the area of research and interpretation as well as culture, politics, cognition, and teaching. His latest books include *The Sign of the Burger: McDonald's and the Culture of Control*; *How Do We Tell the Workers? The Socio-Economic Foundations of Work and Vocational Education*; *The Post-Formal Reader: Cognition and Education* (with Shirley Steinberg and Patricia Hinchey); *The Stigma of Genius: Einstein, Consciousness, and Education* (with Shirley Steinberg and Deborah Tippins); *Rethinking Intelligence: Confronting Psychological Assumptions About Teaching and Learning* (with Shirley Steinberg and Leila Villaverde); and *What is Indigenous Knowledge? Voices From the Academy* (with Ladislaus Semali).

Gloria Ladson-Billings is Professor in the Department of Curriculum and Instruction at the University of Wisconsin–Madison and a Senior Fellow in Urban Education at the Annenberg Institute for School Reform at Brown University. The focus of her work is on examining new notions of pedagogical expertise for African American students and critical race theory applications to education.

Morten Levin is Professor in the Department for Sociology and Political Science at the Norwegian University of Science and Technology in Trondheim. He holds graduate degrees in engineering and sociology. Throughout his professional life, he has worked as an action researcher, with a particular focus on processes and structures of social change in the relationships between technology and organization. This action research has taken place in industrial contexts, in local communities, and in university teaching, where he has developed and been in charge of Ph.D. programs in action research. The author of a number of books and articles, he serves on the editorial boards of *Systems Practice and Action Research, Action Research International, The Handbook of Qualitative Inquiry,* and *The Handbook of Action Research.*

Yvonna S. Lincoln is Professor of Higher Education, Texas A&M University, and coeditor of this volume and the first edition of the *Handbook of Qualitative Research* (1994). She is also coeditor of the journal *Qualitative Inquiry,* with Norman K. Denzin. She is, with her husband Egon G. Guba, coauthor of *Effective Evaluation* (1981), *Naturalistic Inquiry* (1985), *and Fourth Generation Evaluation* (1989); she is also the editor of *Organizational Theory and Inquiry* (1985) and coeditor of *Representation and the Text* (1997). She has been the recipient of numerous awards for research, including the AERA-Division J Research Achievement Award, the AIR Sidney Suslow Award for Research Contributions to Institutional Research, and the American Evaluation Association's Paul Lazarsfeld Award for Contributions to Evaluation Theory. She is the author of numerous journal articles, chapters, and conference presentations on constructivist and interpretive inquiry, and also on higher education.

Stanford M. Lyman is Robert J. Morrow Eminent Scholar and Professor of Social Science, Florida Atlantic University. In addition to holding posts at major universities in the United States, he has served as Fulbright Lecturer in Japan (1981), Visiting Foreign Expert at Beijing Foreign Studies University, China (1986), and U.S. Information Agency Lecturer in Singapore, Taiwan, Hong Kong, Ghana, Liberia, Nigeria, and former Yugoslavia. In 1976, he was elected to a lifetime honorary appointment as Senior Lecturer, Linacre College, Oxford. He is author or coauthor of 18 books, including *Civilization: Contents, Discontents, Malcontents, and Other Essays in Social Theory* (1990), *The Seven Deadly Sins: Society and Evil* (revised and expanded edition, 1989), *A Sociology of the Absurd* (with

Marvin B. Scott; second edition, 1989), *Social Order and the Public Philosophy: An Analysis and Interpretation of the Work of Herbert Blumer* (with Arthur J. Vidich; 1988), and *Color, Culture, Civilization: Race and Minority Issues in American Society* (1994).

Peter McLaren is Professor in the Division of Urban Schooling, Graduate School of Education and Information Studies at the University of California, Los Angeles. He has authored or edited more than 30 books on topics that include the sociology of education, critical ethnography, ritual and resistance, critical social theory, critical literacy, critical pedagogy, Marxist theory, and the politics of multiculturalism. A social activist, he travels worldwide. His works have been published in 12 languages. His most recent books include *Critical Pedagogy and Predatory Culture* (1995), *Revolutionary Multiculturalism* (1997), *Schooling as a Ritual Performance* (third edition, 1999), and *Che Guevara and Paulo Freire: An Introduction to the Pedagogy of Revolution* (1999).

Meaghan Morris is Chair Professor of Cultural Studies at Lingnan University, Hong Kong, and Adjunct Professor to the Faculty of Humanities and Social Sciences, University of Technology, Sydney. Her books include *Too Soon, Too Late: History in Popular Culture* (1998), *Australian Cultural Studies: A Reader* (coedited with John Frow, 1993), and *The Pirate's Fiancee: Feminism, Reading, Postmodernism* (1988).

Virginia L. Olesen, Professor Emerita of Sociology at the University of California, San Francisco, teaches seminars on feminisms and qualitative research and on the sociology of the body and emotions. She is coeditor, with Sheryl Ruzek and Adele Clarke, of *Women's Health: Complexities and Diversities* (1997) and, with Adele Clarke, of *Revisioning Women, Health and Healing: Feminist, Cultural and Technoscience Perspectives* (1999). She is currently working on issues of skepticism in qualitative research and the problems of "the third voice" constituted between and among participants and researchers.

Thomas A. Schwandt is Professor of Education and Associate Dean for Graduate Studies at Indiana University. His research and teaching focus on interpretive methodologies, social science epistemology, and theory of evaluation. His most recent publications include *Qualitative Inquiry: A Dictionary of Terms* and, with Luise McCarty, "Seductive Illusions:

Von Glasersfeld and Gergen on Epistemology and Education," to appear in *Constructivism and Education: Opinions and Second Opinions on Controversial Issues*, edited by D. C. Phillips. He is at work on a book of essays tentatively titled *Evaluation Practice Reconsidered*.

Arthur J. Vidich is Emeritus Professor of Sociology and Anthropology at the Graduate Faculty of the New School for Social Research. He has conducted research on the United States, the Western Caroline Island of Palau, Colombia, Puerto Rico, and Slovenia. His books include *The Political Impact of Colonial Administration, Small Town in Mass Society* (coauthored), *American Society: The Welfare State and Beyond* (coauthored), *American Sociology: Religious Rejections of the World and Their Directions* (coauthored), *The New Middle Classes: Lifestyles, Status Claims and Political Orientations*, and *Collaboration, Reputation and Ethics in American Academic Life: Haus H. Gerth and C. Wright Mills* (with Guy Oakes). His sociological analyses of the United States are published in *Arthur J. Vidich: Cultura, Economia e classi sociali mella politica degli stati Uniti damerica*. He is coeditor, with Robert Jackall, of a 12-volume series titled *Main Trends in the Modern World*.

Lois Weis is Professor of Sociology of Education at the State University of New York at Buffalo. She is the author and/or editor of numerous books and articles on the subject of social class, race, gender, and schooling. Her most recent publications include *The Unknown City: The Lives of Poor and Working-Class Young Adults* (with Michelle Fine; 1998), *Working Class Without Work: High School Students in a De-Industrializing Economy* (1990), *Beyond Silenced Voices* (with Michelle Fine, 1994), *Beyond Black and White* (with Maxine Seller, 1997), and *Off White: Readings on Race, Power and Society* (with Michelle Fine, Linda Powell, and Loonmun Wong, 1997). She is the recipient of two Spencer Foundation grants and a Carnegie Foundation grant. She sits on numerous editorial boards and is a former editor of *Education Policy*.

Susan Weseen is an advanced doctoral student in social-personality psychology who has previously published on issues related to qualitative research. She is currently researching the ways in which first-time mothers negotiate cultural constructions of motherhood.

Loonmun Wong, Ph.D., is a social psychologist and works for a non-governmental organization dealing with issues of aging in Singapore. His work focuses on care management and caregiving in relation to the elderly. In addition, he is collaborating with a local hospice on the psychosocial aspects of cancer. He is one of the editors of *Off White: Readings on Race, Power and Society* (1997).